LONGMAN

Basic

ENGLISH

DICTIONARY

Pearson Education Limited
Edinburgh Gate, Harlow, Essex CM20 2JE, England
and Associated Companies throughout the world

Visit our website at: http://www.longman.com/dictionaries

First published 2002

Thirteenth impression 2006

ISBN-10: 0-582-43850-0 ISBN-13:978-0-582-43850-7

British Library Cataloguing-in-Publication Data
A catalogue record for this book is available from the British Library.

Set in Helvetica Condensed, Light and Medium,
with NeuzeitS Book and BookHeavy

Printed in India at Nutech Photolithographers

Acknowledgements

Director
Della Summers

Editorial Director
Adam Gadsby

Publisher
Laurence Delacroix

Managing Editor
Stephen Bullon

Senior Production Editor
Michael Brooks

Lexicographers
Penny Stock
Jenny Watson

Pronunciation Editor
Dinah Jackson

Production
Clive McKeough

Design
Jonathan Barnard
Alex Ingr

Illustrators
Dave Bowyer
Robin Edmonds

Exercises
Michael Brooks

Administrative Assistant
Denise Denney

Proofreader
Gerard Delaney

The Publishers wish to acknowledge Gillian Lazar, Sinda Lopez,
Carole Owen and Valerie Smith for their contribution to the
Longman New Junior Dictionary on which this dictionary is based.

Contents

Quick Guide to the Dictionary

different meanings of the word

set·tle /'setl/ *verb* (*present participle* **settling**, *past* **settled**)
1 to decide something, especially after an argument or talk: *We finally settled who should pay for the accident.*
2 to move into a comfortable position: *He settled back and turned on the TV.*

definition

3 to go and live in a place where you plan to stay: *My son has settled happily in France.*
4 **settle a bill** to pay a bill

phrasal verbs

5 **settle down** to become calmer and more comfortable: *It took the children a while to settle down.*
6 **settle in** to get used to a new place or job: *How are you settling in?*

example

set·tle·ment /'setlmənt/ *noun*
a formal decision or agreement at the end of an argument or talk: *After hours of talks, they finally **reached** a settlement.*

spelling

part of speech

fish[1] /fɪʃ/ *noun* (*plural* **fish** or **fishes**)
a creature that lives in water and can swim, and which people eat as food

fish[2] *verb*

fish¹ and fish² are separate even though they have the same spelling because one is a noun and the other is a verb. Look at *Which word?* on page 10

1 to try to catch fish: *Dad's fishing **for** salmon.*

pictures with labels for clarity

fish
scales
tail
fin
gills

freeze /friːz/ *verb* (*present participle* **freezing**, *past* **froze** /frəʊz/, *past participle* **frozen** /'frəʊzn/)
1 to become very cold and change from a liquid into a solid: *When water freezes it becomes ice.*
2 to feel very cold: *If you don't put a coat on, you'll freeze.*

difficult past tenses

This is shown when a verb does not add -ed to form the past tense

difficult comparatives and superlatives

good[1] /gʊd/ *adjective* (**better**, **best**)
1 of a high standard or quality: *It's a very good school.*
2 pleasant: *Have a good time! I a good party*
3 successful: *She's good **at** languages. I He's good **with** babies.*

difficult plurals

wom·an /'wʊmən/ *noun* (*plural* **women** /'wɪmɪn/)
a fully grown female human ⇨ compare
MAN

nouns with no plural

traf·fic /'træfɪk/ *noun* (**no plural**)
the movement of cars and people in the streets, or of ships or planes: *The city streets are full of traffic.*

This is shown when a noun does not add -s to form the plural

The meaning of the word is explained using simple words. Any difficult words are written in SMALL CAPITAL LETTERS and you will always find them in the dictionary. The examples show you how to use the word

prepositions

a·muse·ment /ə'mju:zmənt/ *noun* (*no plural*)
the feeling that you have when you think something is funny: *She listened to his stories* **with** *amusement.*

hap·pen /'hæpən/ *verb*
1 if an event or situation happens, it starts to exist and continues for a period of time: *The accident happened outside my house.*
2 **happen to do something** to do something by chance: *If you happen to see her will you give her a message?*

notes

NOTE: If an event **occurs** or **happens**, it is not planned: *The explosion happened on Friday evening.* If an event **takes place** it is the result of a plan or arrangement: *The wedding will take place on June 6th.*

pronunciation

hap·pen·ing /'hæpənɪŋ/ *noun*
an event: *a strange happening*

hap·pi·ly /'hæpɪli/ *adverb*
feeling happy: *They were laughing happily.* ⬦ opposite UNHAPPILY

hap·pi·ness /'hæpɪnəs/ *noun* (*no plural*)
pleasure: *They've had years of happiness together.*

information about other words

hap·py /'hæpi/ *adjective* (**happier, happiest**)
1 very pleased: *I am happy to see you again.*
2 full of happiness: *It was a very happy time.* | *Happy Birthday!* ⬦ opposite UNHAPPY

bed /bed/ *noun*
1 a piece of furniture you sleep on: *I lay in bed reading.*
2 **go to bed** to go to your bed to sleep: *What time did you go to bed last night?*
3 **make the bed** to tidy a bed and make it ready for sleeping in
4 the ground at the bottom of a river or the sea: *the sea bed*

pictures

You can find information about which prepositions to use with a word

There are notes to help you to use a word without making mistakes

Sometimes it is useful or interesting to know about another word that is like the word you are looking at, or to know what the opposite of a word is. You can find this information in your dictionary

There are pictures to help you understand the meanings of words

Remember, there are also 16 colour pictures in your dictionary that help you understand lots of words

beds

bunk beds

cot

double bed   single bed

Exercises

How to find the word you need in your dictionary

Alphabetical order

This is the English alphabet:

a b c d e f g h i j k l m n o p q r s t u v w x y z
A B C D E F G H I J K L M N O P Q R S T U V W X Y Z

A is the first letter in the alphabet and **Z** is the last.

Exercise 1

Look at the letters below and put them in the correct order:

n t k a s l d i c o

a

Now look at the alphabet above to see if you have the right answer.

Exercise 2

In a dictionary the words are in the same order as the letters of the alphabet (this is called **alphabetical order**), so that words that start with **a** are at the beginning of the dictionary and words that start with **z** are at the end.

Look at these words and put them in alphabetical order, beginning with letter **a** and ending in letter **m**.

chair	flag	lake
elephant	brush	house
inside	difference	grandson
kangaroo	monument	
journalist	arrow	

Now look at the main part of the dictionary to see if you have the right answers.

Exercise 3

The word **alphabet** comes before the word **asleep** in the dictionary. These words both begin with the letter **a**, so you must look at the second letters (**l** and **s**) to see which one comes first. When the first two letters are the same you look at the third letter. When the first three letters are the same you look at the fourth letter, and so on.

Look at these words and put them in alphabetical order:

think	thirsty	thermometer
through	thunder	thumb
throw	theory	throat
therefore	thirteen	

Exercise 4

The following words all begin with the same letters. Put them in alphabetical order and then look to see if your answers are correct.

goodbye	good-looking
goodness	good
good afternoon	goodnight
good morning	

In this dictionary **good-looking** and **good afternoon** are in alphabetical order in the same way as if they were one word instead of two, so that **good a̲fternoon** comes before **good-l̲ooking** because a comes before l in the alphabet.

Phrasal verbs

A phrasal verb is a group of words that acts like a verb and consists usually of a verb with an adverb and/or a preposition and has a particular meaning. You can find phrasal verbs such as **take off** and **put on** by looking at the verb (**take off** is at **take**, **put on** is at **put**).

get up	get off	get back
get away	get on	

Exercise 5

Complete the following sentences with the correct phrasal verb in its correct tense from the list above:

1 When did you _____ from Spain?

2 He _____ his motorbike and rode home.

3 He _____ the bus and opened his umbrella.

4 Sam normally _____ at quarter past seven.

5 They tried to catch him but he _____ .

Phrases and expressions

Phrases and expressions are groups of words that together have a particular meaning, especially when they express the meaning well in a few words. If you want to find a phrase or an expression in this dictionary, look at the most important word. For example, to find the phrase **out of date**, look at **date**.

Exercise 6

Where would you look to find these expressions?

1 **drive someone mad**

2 **cover something up**

3 **make someone sick**

4 **for the time being**

5 **keep a secret**

What do these phrases and expressions mean? Look them up in the dictionary to find out.

Exercise 7

Now look at these phrases and expressions and write down what you think they might mean:

1 be **crazy** about someone

2 get on someone's **nerves**

3 **pick** someone's pocket

4 be **short** of something

5 play a **trick** on someone

6 **shake** your head

7 behind **bars**

8 catch **sight** of something

Now look up the words in bold in the dictionary to see if you were right.

Plural forms

The plural form of most nouns is formed by adding **-s** or **-es**. In this dictionary, the plural form is only given when it is formed in a way that is unusual or difficult to remember. For example:

> **wife** /waɪf/ *noun* (*plural* **wives** /waɪvz/)
> the woman who a man is married to
> ⇨ compare HUSBAND

Exercise **8**

Look at these words and write the plural forms next to them:

1 lorry

2 goose

3 mouse

4 leaf

5 echo

6 tornado

7 sheep

8 shelf

Now check your answers in the dictionary.

Opposites

Some of the words in the dictionary show their opposites with an arrow at the end of the entry for that word. For example:

> **far**[2] *adjective*
> **1** a long way away from something else: *We can walk if it's not far.*
> ⇨ opposite NEAR, CLOSE

Exercise **9**

Look up these words in the dictionary and write down their opposites:

1 interesting

2 fast

3 open

4 generous

5 polite

6 weak

7 noisy

8 relaxed

Exercise **10**

Use the opposites in the exercise above to complete these sentences:

1 The students were all very _____ before taking the exam.

2 This is such a peaceful, _____ place to have a picnic.

3 Athletes are often very _____.

4 Share the cake. Don't be so _____.

5 Hurry up. Don't be so _____.

6 _____ the door, please – it's very cold.

7 It was very _____ not to write and thank them.

8 The film was _____, so we left before the end.

Cross-references

Words that are similar in meaning are also indicated by an arrow but with the word **compare** next to it. These are called cross-references. They tell you to look at another word in the dictionary and will help you understand other words related to the words you are looking up. For example:

> **com·e·dy** /ˈkɒmədɪ/ *noun* (*plural* **comedies**)
> a funny play, film, book, etc: *The film is a comedy and it's very funny.* ✧ compare TRAGEDY

Exercise 11

Look up these words in your dictionary and write down their cross-references:

1 seaside

2 flesh

3 dinner

4 crisp

5 vowel

6 moustache

7 heaven

8 moon

Illustrations

Look at this group of pictures under the entry **containers**. The dictionary illustrates different types of containers, and the illustrations will help you understand better the meanings when you look these words up.

containers

a tube of toothpaste

a can of cat food

a carton of milk

a jar of honey

a box of chocolates

a bottle of orange juice

a packet of pasta

Exercise 12

Fill in the blanks with the correct types of containers:

1 A soft narrow container

2 A container made of metal

3 A tall round glass or plastic container, with a narrow neck

4 A round glass container with a lid, used for storing food

5 A small box in which goods are packed

6 A plastic or stiff paper box for holding food or drink

7 A container with straight sides

Exercise **13**

Now look at the colour picture on page 193 which shows a countryside scene, then fill in the blanks with the words that match these descriptions of some geographical features in the picture:

1 An area where a lot of trees grow together

2 A very high hill

3 The pointed top of a hill or mountain

4 A place where water falls over rocks from a high place to a lower place

5 An area of high, steep rock, often close to the sea

6 A small river

7 A piece of ground higher than usual, or a small mountain

8 A small forest

Which word?

Parts of speech

Sometimes you will find that there are two or more words with the same spelling (look at **hand**, for example).

---

hand[1] /hænd/ *noun*
1 the part of your body at the end of your arm, with which you hold things: *She held out her hand and I gave her some of my sweets.* | *She ran her hand through her hair.*
2 by hand not by machine: *This toy was made by hand.*
3 give someone a hand to help someone: *Will you give me a hand **with** the cleaning?*
4 hand in hand holding each other by the hand: *They were walking hand in hand.*
5 the part of a clock that moves to show the time: *When the minute hand points to twelve and the hour hand points to three, it's three o'clock.*

hand[2] *verb*
1 to give something to someone using your hands: *Hand me that plate, please.* | *She handed the letter **to** John.*
2 hand something in to give something to someone, usually a teacher: *Please hand in your books at the end of the lesson.*
3 hand things out to give one thing to each person: *Hand out the pencils.*

---

hand[1] and **hand**[2] are separate because they are different types of words. **hand**[1] is a noun and **hand**[2] is a verb. If you are using the dictionary to find information about a new word, you need to know what type of word it is.

Exercise **14**

The sentences below have a space where a word is missing. Look at the list of words and decide which words you can put in the first sentence, for example

beautiful (their house is beautiful). Choose suitable words for these three sentences. Remember that there is more than one word for each sentence.

1 Their house is ▓▓▓▓▓▓ .

2 We ▓▓▓▓▓▓ every day.

3 I've got a new ▓▓▓▓▓▓ .

computer	**read**	**eat**
hat	**old**	**beautiful**
sleep	**bicycle**	**big**

The words that can be used in the first sentence are all **adjectives**. An **adjective** is a word that describes someone or something. The words that can be used in the second sentence are all **verbs**. A **verb** is a word that tells you what someone or something does. The words that can be used in the third sentence are all **nouns**. A **noun** is a word that is the name of a person, place, animal or thing.

▓▓▓▓ Exercise **15** ▓▓▓▓

Look at the sentences below and write **v** (verb), **n** (noun), or **a** (adjective) for the words you see in bold. The first one has already been done.

1 After leaving home, he became a very good **cook**. *n*

I'll **cook** tonight, because you've been working all day. *v*

2 We **waved** goodbye to our friends.

▓▓▓▓

The **waves** are too big and dangerous to go swimming today. ▓▓▓▓

3 I went for a long **walk** after lunch.

▓▓▓▓

The children **walk** to school every day. ▓▓▓▓

4 You'll find some glasses on the **top** shelf. ▓▓▓▓

They climbed to the **top** of the mountain. ▓▓▓▓

5 He can perform some amazing magic **tricks**. ▓▓▓▓

I was **tricked** into giving him a lot of money. ▓▓▓▓

6 I can't drink this coffee; it's far too **sweet**. ▓▓▓▓

I'm so full I don't think I could eat any **sweet**. ▓▓▓▓

7 This is one of the most beautiful **flats** I've ever seen. ▓▓▓▓

Our house has a **flat** roof. ▓▓▓▓

8 The boys **ducked** behind a wall when they saw the teacher approach. ▓▓▓▓

The dog chased the **ducks** into the lake. ▓▓▓▓

Adjectives

▓▓▓▓ Exercise **16** ▓▓▓▓

Choose the correct adjective to complete each of the following sentences. Be careful because the two words you must choose from are often confused by students of English.

1 (bored/boring)

The weather is so ▓▓▓▓ at this time of year. Wind and rain every day.

2 (sensible/sensitive)

Paul made a ▓▓▓▓ decision. He decided to study law at university.

3 (interested/interesting)

Are you ▓▓▓▓ in coming camping with us this weekend?

4 (pleased/pleasant)

We were so   to see our
grandchildren after such a long time.

5 (rare/unusual)

In Barcelona I saw some
architecture.

6 (satisfied/satisfactory)

My exam results were not
            , so I will have to take
them all again.

7 (tall/high)

It's a beautiful apartment with large
windows and   ceilings.

8 (valuable/expensive)

I can't afford this car – it's too
            .

Now check your answers in the
dictionary.

Nouns

Exercise **17**

Choose the correct noun to complete
each of the following sentences. Again,
be careful because the two words you
must choose from are often confused by
students of English.

1 (costs/prices)

I never go to that shop because the
            are too high.

2 (discussion/argument)

We had a serious
and I went home alone.

3 (dishes/courses)

We made a fantastic meal for our
friends consisting of five
            .

4 (travel/journey)

The   from here by car
takes about 7 hours.

5 (camping/campsite)

This is the most impressive
            I have ever visited in
France.

6 (choice/decision)

Leaving America to work in Europe
was the most important
of my life.

7 (relation/relationship)

The   between
teachers and students in this school
is excellent.

8 (roof/ceiling)

I decided to paint the   in
my kitchen.

Now check your answers in the
dictionary.

Verbs

Exercise **18**

Choose the correct verb to complete
each of the following sentences. Don't
forget that the two words you must
choose from are often confused by
students of English.

1 (avoid/prevent)

His injury will possibly
him from playing in the big game
tomorrow.

2 (convince/persuade)

Can you   him to play.
He's an excellent pianist.

3 (do/make)

Don't worry if you   a
mistake.

4 (pass/spend)

Every year we   our holidays by the sea.

5 (propose/suggest)

I   you speak to your father about that.

6 (rent/hire)

When we go skating we always   the skates.

7 (invent/discover)

Did Alexander Graham Bell   the telephone in 1876 or 1886?

8 (increase/improve)

I'm taking classes because I want to   my level in English.

Now check your answers in the dictionary.

A word with several meanings

A word often has more than one meaning with exactly the same spelling. Look at the entry for **trunk** which has 5 different meanings or uses. The definition for the word **trunk** tells you that it has 5 separate meanings, the main part of a tree, the main part of the human body, a large box, the nose of an elephant, and the word **trunks** which are a piece of clothing men wear for swimming.

> **trunk** /trʌŋk/ *noun*
> **1** the thick main stem of a tree ⇨ see picture at TREE
> **2** the main part of your body, not including your head, arms, or legs
> **3** a large box that you carry clothes, books, etc in when you travel
> **4** the long nose of an ELEPHANT
> **5 trunks** (*plural noun*) a piece of clothing that men wear for swimming: *He was wearing a pair of black trunks.*

Exercise **19**

From the dictionary find out which meaning explains the use of the words in **bold** in these 10 sentences, and write the number of the dictionary entry in the blanks. The first one has already been done.

1 He's just bought a new **bow** for his cello. *2*

2 This water is from a famous **spring** in Spain.

3 The floor is covered in broken **glass**.

4 Press this **key** if you want to switch the computer off.

5 Do you want **chips** for dinner tonight?

6 Most people write with their **right** hands not their left.

7 There's a footpath that **runs** along the canal bank.

8 Could you tell me the **way** to the nearest post office please?

Words that sound the same

A lot of words in English look and/or sound very similar with almost the same spelling but have very different meanings. They are called homophones and often cause some confusion for learners. Look at the entries for piece and peace for example.

> **piece** /piːs/ *noun*
> a part of something that is separated or broken off from a larger thing: *He took a piece of the cake.* | *I need a piece of paper.* | *The plate was in pieces* (=broken into pieces) *on the floor.*

peace /piːs/ *noun* (*no plural*)
  1 quiet and calm: *I love the peace of this village.* I *Go away and leave me in peace.*
  2 a time when there is no war or fighting: *There has been peace in the area for six years now.*

Exercise 20

The dictionary shows you how to use the word with an example showing clearly which meaning you want. Look at the entries for these words in **bold** and then complete the sentence with the correct word.

1 We didn't **(know/no)**   the way, or **(where/wear)**   we were going.

2 They washed **(there/their)**   hands before coming to the table.

3 The Nile is one of the **(principle/ principal)**   rivers in Africa.

4 I had such a long **(wait/weight)**   at the post office this morning.

5 We couldn't decide **(whether/weather)**   to go to the seaside or to the countryside.

6 The post office is about 100 metres **(past/passed)**   the library.

7 The motorbike was **(stationery/ stationary)**   when the car hit it from behind.

8 She decided to **(dye/die)**   her hair black.

Exercise 21

Now write the correct word to complete these sentences:

1 **(flour/flower)**

Her boyfriend gave her a beautiful   .

You need eggs, sugar and   to bake a cake.

2 **(fair/fare)**

The taxi   to the airport is about five pounds.

Come on, let's go to the   .

3 **(missed/mist)**

I   the train by about five minutes.

The   was so thick it was impossible to see.

4 **(bear/bare)**

My grandfather saw a   in the forest this morning.

We played football in   feet.

5 **(meat/meet)**

I'll   you this afternoon at 4 o'clock.

I don't eat   because I'm vegetarian.

6 **(here/hear)**

Come   , please!

I can't   you. Please speak louder.

7 **(weak/week)**

I go swimming at least two or three times a   .

Babies are very   when they are first born.

8 **(sale/sail)**

There's a great   at the department store at the moment.

We raised the   on the boat to catch the wind.

Definitions

The definitions in this dictionary often tell you more than just what a word means. For example, look at the definition for **bread** and the question and answer below.

bread = a food made by mixing flour and water and then baking it

Question: What are the ingredients you would use for baking bread?

Answer: Flour and water

Exercise 22

Now answer the following questions. Look up the definition of the word in **bold** to help you.

1 Write down four facts about a **badger**.

2 What would you do with a **surfboard**?

3 What does a **guitar** look like?

4 What is the weather like when it is **mild**?

5 Describe a situation when you might be **proud**.

6 Where does **wood** come from?

7 When is the beginning of the day, **sunrise** or **sunset**?

8 What types of food can you **grill**?

Exercise 23

The definitions also provide useful extra information and vocabulary. Fill in the gaps in the sentences below. Then check your answers by looking up the word in **bold**.

Example: a **cyclist** is a *person* who rides a bicycle.

1 A **butterfly** is an ▓▓▓ that has delicate wings with bright colours on them.

2 A **cactus** is a ▓▓▓ with sharp points and a thick stem that grows in hot places.

3 **Rubber** is a soft ▓▓▓ that is made from chemicals or the juice of a tree and is used for making things such as car tyres.

4 A **cooker** is a piece of ▓▓▓ for cooking food.

5 A **dalmation** is a white ▓▓▓ with black spots.

6 A **pyramid** is a solid ▓▓▓ that is square at the base and pointed at the top.

7 **Football** is a ▓▓▓ played by two teams who each try to kick a ball into a net.

8 **Autumn** is the ▓▓▓ before winter, when the leaves fall off the trees.

Exercise 24

Read the definitions and fill in the gaps for the words below:

1 l▓▓nade: a sweet drink made from lemons

2 t▓▓pet: a musical instrument made of brass that you play by blowing through it

3 c▓▓lar: a room under the ground in a house, used especially for storing things

4 as▓▓aut: a person who travels in space

5 st▓▓ue: a figure of a person, animal, etc made of stone, metal, or wood

6 **vi___o**: a tape of a film, television programme, or real event

7 **py___as**: a loose shirt and trousers that you wear in bed

8 **sc___r**: a light small motorcycle

How to say the word

Exercise 25

Look at the phonetic symbols on the inside front cover of this dictionary. Now look at the words below and put the right word with the right sound.

cat law shop father often
hand more car door got narrow

1 æ *cat*

2 ɔː

3 ɒ

4 ɑː

Notice that different spellings may have the same sound.

Exercise 26

Now look at these words beginning with **th-** and see if you can match the pronunciation for each word.

1 this   θɔːt
2 though   'θɪətə'
3 these   ðəʊ
4 theatre   ðɪs
5 thought   ðeər
6 their   ðiːz

If you look again at the pronunciation for theatre 'θɪətə' you can see that there is a small mark like this ['] in front of it. This is to tell you that you must say the first part of **theatre** a little bit louder and with

a little more force than the rest of the word *(THEatre)*. Making one part of a word more important when you say it is called **stress**, and stress does not always come at the beginning of a word.

A syllable is either a whole word or one of the parts into which a word is separated when it is spoken. For example, the word **police** has two syllables *(po-lice)* and the word **hospital** has three syllables *(hos-pi-tal)*.

Exercise 27

Where should the stress be in the following words? Put a stress mark ' in front of the part of the word where the stress should be, then check by looking at the entry for the word.

**explain   explanation   dictionary
village   fire engine**

Exercise 28

In the following list of 10 words, 5 words should be pronounced with the stress on the first syllable and 5 words should be pronounced with the stress on the second syllable.

**abandon   peanut   tomato   lemon
piano   extinguish   exit   jewellery
laboratory   hovercraft**

First syllable   1
Second syllable   1

First syllable   2
Second syllable   2

First syllable   3
Second syllable   3

First syllable   4
Second syllable   4

First syllable   5
Second syllable   5

In the following list of 10 words, 5 words should be pronounced with the stress on the third syllable.

consideration satisfaction pyjamas pilgrimage grasshopper seventeenth handwriting competition introduction submarine

Third syllable **1**

Third syllable **2**

Third syllable **3**

Third syllable **4**

Third syllable **5**

Sometimes nouns and verbs that look the same have different stress. Stressing the wrong syllable can therefore change the whole meaning of a word and sometimes also the pronunciation. For example:

'**record** which is a noun meaning information that is written down and kept *(medical records)* and **re** '**cord** which is a verb meaning to copy electronic sounds or television programmes *(to record a piece of music on a cassette).*

Another example is '**progress** which is a noun meaning movement in a particular direction *(to make good progress)* and **pro** '**gress** which is a verb meaning to go on or continue *(I progressed from a low level in English to quite a high one).*

Look at these examples and say whether the stress is the same or different.

1 There has been an **increase** in the number of students at the school.

The number of students at the school will **increase** next year.

2 Our country **exports** oil.

What are Britain's main **exports**?

Check your answers by looking at the entries in the dictionary at **export** and **increase**.

Crossword

All the words in this crossword are included as labels in the 16-page colour section and all the clues are definitions from the dictionary. The number in brackets at the end of every clue shows you how many letters there are in each word.

Across

1 Trousers with a piece of material at the top that covers your chest (9)

4 To stop something that is moving in the air and hold it (5)

7 A long orange root that is eaten as a vegetable (6)

9 To move very quickly, moving your legs faster than when you walk (3)

10 A large printed notice or picture (6)

13 In a position on the other side of an area or road (8)

15 Up to and further than something (4)

16 A round container, especially one with a handle, that is used for cooking (3)

17 A vehicle that travels along a railway (5)

19 A type of thick coloured pen (4,3)

21 A strong vehicle with large wheels, used for pulling farm equipment (7)

23 A person or company whose job is to print books, magazines, etc (7)

24 A green fruit with a sour taste (4)

25 A frame used to hold a picture that is being painted (5)

26 A large vehicle that takes people from one place to another (3)

Down

1 A person who looks after people's health (6)

2 A person, often a woman, who is trained to help doctors and look after people who are ill or old (5)

3 A green fruit the same shape as a pear with a very large hard seed in the middle (7)

4 A person whose job is to make things out of wood (9)

5 A shelter made of thick cloth spread over poles (4)

6 A piece of ground higher than usual, or a small mountain (4)

8 A large animal with a long body, a hard skin, and sharp teeth, that lives in or near rivers in hot countries (9)

11 A large wild animal with hard skin and one or two horns on its nose, that lives in Africa and Asia (10)

12 A long thin green plant that is eaten as a vegetable (9)

14 A long narrow object that is filled with ink and is used to write or draw with (3)

15 A round white vegetable that grows under the ground and is cooked before eating (6)

18 A dangerous wild animal like a big cat, that lives in Africa (4)

19 Starting at or coming from a place (4)

20 To make something fly through the air by letting it go from your hand with a quick movement of your arm (5)

22 Higher than other people or other things (4)

A, a /eɪ/
the first letter of the English alphabet

a /ə; *strong* eɪ/
1 one or any: *I gave him a pencil. | She was wearing a red skirt.*
2 each or every: *A square has four sides. | She phones me three times a week.*

NOTE: **An** is used instead of **a** before a word that starts with the sound of a, e, i, o, or u ⇨ LOOK AT: **an**

a·ban·don /əˈbændən/ *verb*
to leave someone or something without intending to go back to them: *She abandoned her baby outside a hospital. | We abandoned our holiday because we had no money.*

ab·bre·vi·a·tion /əˌbriːviˈeɪʃn/ *noun*
a shorter way of writing a word or name. For example 'Dr' is the abbreviation for 'Doctor'

ABC /ˌeɪ biː ˈsiː/ *noun*
the letters of the English alphabet: *She's learning her ABC.*

ab·do·men /ˈæbdəmən/ *noun*
the part of your body between your chest and legs that contains your stomach: *He has a cough and pain in his abdomen.*

a·bil·i·ty /əˈbɪləti/ *noun (no plural)*
when someone can do something successfully: *A teacher must have the ability **to** keep students interested.*

a·ble /ˈeɪbl/ *adjective*
if someone is able to do something, they can do it: *Is he able to swim? | I won't be able to come.* ⇨ opposite UNABLE

a·board /əˈbɔːd/ *adverb, preposition*
on or onto a ship or plane: *Are all the passengers aboard?*

a·bol·ish /əˈbɒlɪʃ/ *verb*
to make a law to end something: *The new government abolished the tax on wine.*

a·bol·i·tion /ˌæbəˈlɪʃn/ *noun (no plural)*
when a law is made to end something or to make it illegal: *the abolition of slavery in America in the nineteenth century*

a·bout /əˈbaʊt/
1 if something is about something else, it describes it or deals with it: *What are you talking about? | a book about birds*
2 slightly more or less than a particular number, time, or amount: *Come at about six o'clock. | I live about 2 miles from here.*
3 in different directions or in different parts of a place: *The children were kicking a ball about. | The children have left their toys about the place.*
4 be about to do something to be going to do something very soon: *I was about to come and see you.*
5 how about/what about used when you are suggesting ideas for an activity: *What about some lunch? | How about going to the cinema?*

a·bove /əˈbʌv/ *adverb, preposition*
1 if something is above something else, it is higher than it or over it: *The picture is on the wall above my desk. | The noise came from the room above.* ⇨ see picture on page 208
2 more than a particular number or amount or older than a particular age: *children above the age of five | The temperature is above 35 degrees.*
3 above all more than anything else: *I want you to remember this above all.*

a·broad /əˈbrɔːd/ *adverb*
in or to another country: *My brother is studying abroad. | Have you ever been abroad?*

a·brupt /əˈbrʌpt/ *adjective*
1 sudden: *There was an abrupt knock at the door.*
2 if someone is abrupt, they are not polite because they do not want to take the time to be friendly: *She gave an abrupt answer to his question.*

ab·sence /ˈæbsəns/ *noun (no plural)*
when someone or something is not in a place: *Her absence was noticed by her friends.* ⇨ opposite PRESENCE

ab·sent /ˈæbsənt/ *adjective*
not in a place: *He was absent **from** school last Tuesday.*

absent-mind·ed /ˌæbsənt ˈmaɪndɪd/
adjective
not noticing things that are happening around you, and often forgetting things

ab·so·lute /ˈæbsəluːt/ adjective
complete or exact: *Are you telling me the absolute truth?* | *The party was an absolute disaster – everything went wrong.*

ab·so·lute·ly /ˌæbsəˈluːtlɪ/ adverb
1 very or completely: *It's absolutely beautiful.* | *You must keep it absolutely secret.*
2 used to say that you completely agree with someone: *"Do you think I'm right?" "Absolutely!"*

ab·sorb /əbˈsɔːb/ verb
1 to take in liquid slowly: *This cloth will absorb the spilled water.*
2 to hear, read, or learn information and understand it: *I haven't absorbed all the instructions yet.*

ab·sor·bent /əbˈsɔːbənt/ adjective
able to take in liquid: *We need a thick piece of absorbent material.*

ab·sorb·ing /əbˈsɔːbɪŋ/ adjective
very interesting and getting your full attention: *an absorbing book about space travel*

ab·surd /əbˈsɜːd/ adjective
very silly: *The story was so absurd that no one believed it.*

a·buse¹ /əˈbjuːz/ verb (present participle **abusing**, past **abused**)
1 to do cruel or violent things to someone
2 to use something in a wrong or harmful way: *He abuses drugs.*

a·buse² /əˈbjuːs/ noun (no plural)
1 when someone uses something in a wrong or harmful way: *the problem of drug abuse*
2 when someone treats another person in a cruel or violent way: *child abuse*
3 rude things said to someone: *He shouted abuse at me.*

ac·a·dem·ic /ˌækəˈdemɪk/ adjective
relating to the work done in schools, colleges, or universities: *students' academic achievements*

ac·cent /ˈæksənt/ noun
a way of speaking that shows that a person comes from a particular place:

Maria speaks English with an Italian accent.

ac·cept /əkˈsept/ verb
1 to receive or take something that is offered to you: *I accepted another piece of cake.* | *He would not accept any money from us.*
2 to agree that something is true or right, or should be done: *The school accepted that there had been some mistakes.*

ac·cept·a·ble /əkˈseptəbl/ adjective
of good enough quality: *Your work is not acceptable.*

ac·cept·ance /əkˈseptəns/ noun (no plural)
when you agree to take something that is offered to you or agree that something is true or right: *You must sign to show your acceptance of the contract's terms.*

ac·cess /ˈækses/ noun (no plural)
1 a way to get to a place: *There is no access **to** the street through that door.*
2 when you are able to use or do something: *Students need access **to** computers.*

accident

ac·ci·dent /ˈæksɪdənt/ noun
1 when something happens, especially something bad, by chance: *I'm sorry I broke the cup; it was an accident.*
2 when a vehicle such as a car or plane hits something: *The number of accidents on the roads is rising every year.*
3 by accident if something happens by accident, no one plans it, but it happens by chance: *I discovered by accident that he lied.*

ac·ci·den·tal /ˌæksɪˈdentl/ adjective
not planned but happening by chance: *an accidental meeting*

ac·ci·den·tal·ly /ˌæksɪˈdentlɪ/ *adverb*
if you do something accidentally, you do it without intending to: *I accidentally broke a glass.*

ac·com·mo·date /əˈkɒmədeɪt/ *verb* (*present participle* **accommodating**, *past* **accommodated**)
1 to give someone a place to live or stay in
2 to have space for something: *You could accommodate another four children in your class.*

ac·com·mo·da·tion /əˌkɒməˈdeɪʃn/ *noun* (*no plural*)
somewhere to live or stay: *I must find some accommodation.*

NOTE: Remember that in British English the noun **accommodation** has no plural: *Accommodation will be provided for the students.* I *Do you have any accommodation?*

ac·com·pa·ny /əˈkʌmpənɪ/ *verb* (*present participle* **accompanying**, *past* **accompanied**)
1 to go somewhere with someone: *He accompanied me to the doctor's.*
2 to play music while someone else is singing or playing another instrument: *Maria sang and I accompanied her on the piano.*

ac·com·plish /əˈkʌmplɪʃ/ *verb*
to do or finish something successfully: *We accomplished a lot during the day.*

ac·com·plish·ment /əˈkʌmplɪʃmənt/ *noun*
something that you achieve or are able to do well: *Passing the exam was quite an accomplishment.*

ac·cord /əˈkɔːd/ *noun* (*no plural*)
of your own accord if you do something of your own accord, you do it without being told or asked to: *No one forced her to go. She left of her own accord.*

ac·cord·ing to /əˈkɔːdɪŋ tuː/
using information that is written or that someone has told you: *She's a great teacher, according to Angela.* I *According to the map we're very close to the sea.*

ac·count[1] /əˈkaʊnt/ *noun*
1 a story or description: *He gave us an exciting account of the match.*

2 an amount of money kept in a bank: *She paid the money into her bank account.*
3 **take something into account** to think about something before making a decision: *You must take the price into account when choosing which one to buy.*
4 **on account of something** because of something: *We stayed at home on account of the bad weather.*
5 **accounts** (*plural noun*) a record that shows the money that a person or company spends and earns: *You can look at the company's accounts for last year.*

account[2] *verb*
account for something to give the reason for something: *I can't account for her strange behaviour.*

ac·coun·tant /əˈkaʊntənt/ *noun*
a person whose job is to keep records of the money spent and earned by a person or company

ac·cu·ra·cy /ˈækjʊrəsɪ/ *noun*
the quality of being exactly right or correct

ac·cu·rate /ˈækjʊrət/ *adjective*
exactly correct: *Is this watch accurate?* ⇨ opposite INACCURATE

ac·cu·sa·tion /ˌækjʊˈzeɪʃn/ *noun*
a statement saying that someone has done something wrong: *Serious accusations have been made **against** him.*

ac·cuse /əˈkjuːz/ *verb* (*present participle* **accusing**, *past* **accused**)
to say that someone has done something wrong: *Sally accused Paul **of** cheating.*

ac·cus·tomed /əˈkʌstəmd/ *adjective*
be accustomed to something to have done or experienced something so often that it seems normal or usual: *I'm not accustomed to getting out of bed this early.*

ache[1] /eɪk/ *verb* (*present participle* **aching**, *past* **ached**)
to hurt with a continuous pain: *Her head ached.*

ache[2] *noun*
a continuous pain: *I've got stomach ache.*

a·chieve /əˈtʃiːv/ verb (present participle **achieving**, past **achieved**)
to succeed in doing something by working hard: *He achieved top marks in the examination.*

a·chieve·ment /əˈtʃiːvmənt/ noun
something that you have worked hard for and done well: *Beating Dad at chess was quite an achievement.*

ac·id /ˈæsɪd/ noun
a chemical liquid that can burn things

acid rain /ˌæsɪd ˈreɪn/ noun (no plural)
rain that damages trees and plants because it contains substances put into the air by factory smoke

ac·knowl·edge /əkˈnɒlɪdʒ/ verb (present participle **acknowledging**, past **acknowledged**)
1 to agree that something is true: *Do you acknowledge that you've been wrong?*
2 to write to someone who has sent you something to say that you have received it: *Please acknowledge my letter.*

a·corn /ˈeɪkɔːn/ noun
a small nut that grows on OAK trees

ac·quaint·ance /əˈkweɪntəns/ noun
a person you know slightly because you have met them before ⇨ compare FRIEND

ac·quaint·ed /əˈkweɪntɪd/
be acquainted with someone to know someone: *Are you acquainted with Mr Smith?*

a·cre /ˈeɪkəʳ/ noun
a measure of land that is equal to 4,047 square metres

ac·ro·bat
/ˈækrəbæt/ noun
a person who performs in a CIRCUS and does difficult tricks with their body

acrobat

a·cross /əˈkrɒs/ adverb, preposition
1 from one side of a place to the other: *They swam across the river.* ⇨ see picture on page 208
2 on the other side of something: *She lives across the street from me.*

act¹ /ækt/ verb
1 to do something or behave in a particular way: *I had to act fast because I thought she was going to fall.* | *You're acting like a fool.*
2 to pretend to be someone else, in a play or film: *He's got a job acting in a new television play.* ⇨ see picture at THEATRE
3 **act as** to do something instead of someone else, or to be used instead of something else: *This room acts as her office.*

act² noun
1 something that you do: *an act of bravery* | *That was a kind act.*
2 something you pretend to feel or think: *She seems happy but it's just an act.*
3 a part of a play

act·ing /ˈæktɪŋ/ noun (no plural)
the work done by an ACTOR or ACTRESS

ac·tion /ˈækʃən/ noun
1 something that you do: *His quick action saved her life.* | *The government must take action to help the poor.*
2 **out of action** injured or broken and not able to work or be used: *My car is out of action.* | *His accident means that Jim will be out of action for two weeks.*

ac·tive /ˈæktɪv/ adjective
1 doing something or always ready or able to do things: *He is an active member of the club.* | *She's 80 years old but she's still active.*
2 an active verb is one used to say that a person or thing is doing something. In the sentence 'John kicked the ball', 'kicked' is an active verb ⇨ compare PASSIVE

ac·tiv·i·ty /ækˈtɪvətɪ/ noun
1 (plural **activities**) something that you do, especially to enjoy yourself: *Dancing is her favourite activity.*
2 (no plural) when people are moving around and doing lots of things: *The classroom was full of activity, with every child busy.*

ac·tor /ˈæktəʳ/ noun
a person who performs in plays or films

ac·tress /ˈæktrɪs/ noun (plural **actresses**)
a woman who performs in plays or films ⇨ see picture on page 200

ac·tu·al /ˈæktʃʊəl/ *adjective*
real and clear: *We think he stole the money, but we have no actual proof.* | *The actual cost is much higher than we thought.*

ac·tu·al·ly /ˈæktʃʊəlɪ/ *adverb*
1 really or as a true fact: *Do you actually believe that?* | *I've spoken to him on the telephone but I've never actually met him.*
2 used when you want to say in a polite way that someone has a wrong idea: *Actually, the film starts at 3 o'clock, not 4.* | *"You're Jane, aren't you?" "No, I'm Jo, actually."*

A.D. /ˌeɪ ˈdiː/
after the birth of Christ, used in dates: *He was born in 1471 AD.*

ad /æd/ *noun*
an advertisement

a·dapt /əˈdæpt/ *verb*
1 to change your behaviour or ideas because of a new situation you are in: *The children have adapted to their new school.*
2 to change something so that it is suitable for a new situation: *The kitchen is adapted for blind people to use.*

a·dapt·a·ble /əˈdæptəbl/ *adjective*
able to change and be successful in a new situation: *Young children are very adaptable.*

add /æd/ *verb*
1 to put something together with something else: *To make the cake, mix butter and sugar and then add flour.*
2 also **add up** to put numbers or amounts together to find a total: *If you add 2 and 7 you get 9.* | *Add up 47 and 52.*
3 to say something more: *He added that everything he had just said must be kept secret.*

ad·dict /ˈædɪkt/ *noun*
someone who is not able to stop taking harmful drugs

ad·dic·tion /əˈdɪkʃən/ *noun*
when someone cannot stop taking harmful drugs

ad·di·tion /əˈdɪʃn/ *noun*
1 *(no plural)* when numbers or amounts are added together
2 someone or something added: *She was a welcome addition to the group.*
3 in addition to something adding

another thing to something already done or known: *In addition to English, the children also learn German and Spanish.*

ad·dress[1] /əˈdres/ *noun (plural addresses)*
the name of the place where you live: *Please write your name and address.*

address[2] *verb*
1 to speak to someone: *The captain addressed his team.*
2 to write a name and address on something: *She addressed the letter to Mrs Wilson.*

ad·e·quate /ˈædɪkwət/ *adjective*
enough: *an adequate amount of food*
⇨ opposite INADEQUATE

ad·jec·tive /ˈædʒɪktɪv/ *noun*
a word that describes someone or something. In the phrase 'a beautiful song', 'beautiful' is an adjective

ad·just /əˈdʒʌst/ *verb*
to make a small change in something to make it better: *If you're going to drive you need to adjust the car seat.*

ad·min·is·tra·tion /ədˌmɪnɪˈstreɪʃn/ *noun (no plural)*
when someone manages or organizes a business, government, etc

ad·mi·ral /ˈædmərəl/ *noun*
the most important officer in the navy

ad·mi·ra·tion /ˌædməˈreɪʃn/ *noun (no plural)*
the feeling that you have towards a person who is very good, beautiful, clever, etc

ad·mire /ədˈmaɪər/ *verb (present participle admiring, past admired)*
1 to respect and approve of someone or something: *I always admired his work.*
2 to look at something thinking how beautiful or impressive it is: *I was just admiring your new car.*

ad·mis·sion /ədˈmɪʃn/ *noun*
1 when you say that you have done something wrong or bad: *an admission of guilt*
2 *(no plural)* permission to go into a place: *Admission was free for children.*

ad·mit /ədˈmɪt/ *verb*
1 to agree that something unpleasant about yourself is true: *She admitted she was lazy.* ⇨ opposite DENY
2 to allow someone to enter a place:

*This ticket admits two people **to** the football match.*

ad·o·les·cent /ˌædəˈlesənt/ *noun*
a boy or girl between about 13 and 18 years old ⇨ same meaning TEENAGER

a·dopt /əˈdɒpt/ *verb*
to take a child into your family and treat him or her as your own child

a·dore /əˈdɔːr/ *verb (present participle* **adoring,** *past* **adored)**
to love someone or something very much: *She adored her son.* I *I adore chocolate.*

ad·ult /ˈædʌlt, əˈdʌlt/ *noun*
a fully grown person who is no longer a child: *a group of three adults and four children*

ad·vance[1] /ədˈvɑːns/ *verb (present participle* **advancing,** *past* **advanced)**
to move forward: *The army advanced towards the town.* ⇨ compare RETREAT

advance[2] *noun*
in advance before something happens or before you do something: *You must pay in advance.*

ad·vanced /ədˈvɑːnst/ *adjective*
1 at a high or difficult level: *advanced English classes*
2 using the most modern ideas or equipment: *the most advanced mobile phone the company has developed*

ad·van·tage /ədˈvɑːntɪdʒ/ *noun*
something that helps a person: *It is an advantage to speak several languages.* ⇨ opposite DISADVANTAGE

ad·ven·ture /ədˈventʃər/ *noun*
something exciting that happens to someone: *She wrote a book about her adventures in Europe.*

ad·ven·tur·ous /ədˈventʃərəs/ *adjective*
liking new and exciting experiences

ad·verb /ˈædvɜːb/ *noun*
a word that tells you how, when, or where something is done. In the sentence 'She spoke loudly', 'loudly' is an adverb

ad·vert /ˈædvɜːt/ *noun*
(*British*) an advertisement

ad·ver·tise /ˈædvətaɪz/ *verb (present participle* **advertising,** *past* **advertised)**
to use to persuade people a public notice, a photograph, a short film, etc to try to persuade people to buy, do, or use something: *The*

company has spent a lot of money advertising its new shampoo.

ad·ver·tise·ment /ədˈvɜːtɪsmənt/ *noun*
a notice, a photograph, a short film, etc that tries to persuade people to buy, do, or use something: *a newspaper advertisement* I *an advertisement for jeans*

ad·vice /ədˈvaɪs/ *noun (no plural)*
a suggestion about what someone should do: *Can I ask your advice about what classes to take?* I *She **gave** me some good advice.*

ad·vise /ədˈvaɪz/ *verb (present participle* **advising,** *past* **advised)**
to tell someone what you think they should do: *The doctor advised me **to** rest for a few days.*

aer·i·al /ˈeəriəl/ *noun*
a wire on top of a building or a piece of equipment that sends out or receives radio or television signals

aer·o·bics /eəˈrəubɪks/ *noun (no plural)*
a form of very active exercise done to music

aer·o·plane /ˈeərəpleɪn/ *noun*
(*British*) a large vehicle that flies, in which people can travel (*American* **airplane**) ⇨ see picture on page 206

aer·o·sol /ˈeərəsɒl/ *noun*
a container from which a liquid can be SPRAYED

af·fair /əˈfeər/ *noun*
1 an event or set of related events: *The party was a noisy affair.*
2 a sexual relationship between two people, especially one that is secret: *Her husband was having an affair.*
3 affairs (*plural noun*) situations or subjects that a person, organization, or government must deal with: *government affairs*

af·fect /əˈfekt/ *verb*
to produce a change in someone or something: *The disease affected his breathing.*

af·fec·tion /əˈfekʃən/ *noun (no plural)*
the feeling of liking and caring for another person: *Barry felt great affection for her.*

af·fec·tion·ate /əˈfekʃənət/ *adjective*
feeling or showing that you like or love someone: *an affectionate child*

af·ford /əˈfɔːd/ *verb*
to have enough money to pay for something: *We can't afford a holiday.*

a·fraid /əˈfreɪd/ *adjective*
feeling fear: *Are you afraid of the dark?*
⇨ same meaning SCARED

af·ter /ˈɑːftər/ *preposition*
1 later than something in time: *Tomorrow is the day after today.* | *My new computer broke down three days after I bought it.*
2 moving towards or behind someone or something else: *The child ran after her dog.*
3 **after all** used for showing that what you did or thought before was wrong: *Don't worry about it. It's not your fault after all.*
4 **be after something** to be trying to get something: *I think he's after more money.*

af·ter·noon /ˌɑːftəˈnuːn/ *noun*
the time between the middle of the day and evening: *I saw Jim yesterday afternoon.* ⇨ compare MORNING

af·ter·wards /ˈɑːftəwədz/ *adverb*
later, after something else has happened: *We saw the film and afterwards we walked home together.*

a·gain /əˈgen/ *adverb*
1 one more time: *Come and see us again soon.*
2 **again and again** many times: *Repeat it again and again until you have learned it.*
3 **now and again** sometimes but not very often: *My aunt visits us now and again.*

a·gainst /əˈgenst, əˈgeɪnst/ *preposition*
1 not agreeing with someone or something: *I'm against killing animals for their fur.*
2 on the other side in a game or match: *We're playing against the village team.*
3 touching a surface: *Put the ladder against the wall.* ⇨ see picture on page 208
4 **against the law, against the rules** not allowed by the law or by the rules: *It's against the law to drive too fast.*

age /eɪdʒ/ *noun*
1 the number of years someone has lived or something has existed: *games for children of all ages* | *He won his first race at the age of 19.*

NOTE: When you want to know someone's age, do not say "What age is he?"; say "How **old** is he?"

2 *(no plural)* when something is old: *The wine improves with age.*
3 **old age** when someone is old: *Who will take care of me in my old age?*
4 a period of time in history
5 **ages** a long time: *We talked for ages.*

ag·gres·sive /əˈgresɪv/ *adjective*
behaving as if you want to fight or attack someone

a·go /əˈgəʊ/ *adverb*
in the past: *We came to live here six years ago.* | *It happened just a few minutes ago.*

NOTE: Compare **ago, for,** and **since.** Use the simple past tense of a verb with **ago** to say when something happened in the past. You can say: *She left an hour ago.* Do not say: *She has left an hour ago.* Use **have** with the past participle of the verb followed by **for** to say that something started to happen in the past and is still happening now: *I've lived here for six months* (I still live here). Use the past tense of the verb with **for** to say that something happened for a period of time and then stopped: *I studied English for three years* (I stopped after that). Use **have been** or **has been** with the present participle of the verb with **since** when you are talking about the time in the past when something began: *I have been learning English since I was ten* (=I started learning English when I was ten and I am still learning it). ⇨ LOOK AT: **before**

ag·o·ny /ˈægəni/ *noun (no plural)*
extremely bad pain

a·gree /əˈgriː/ *verb (present participle* **agreeing,** *past* **agreed)**
1 to have the same opinion as someone else: *I agree with you.* | *We all agreed.* ⇨ opposite DISAGREE
2 **agree to something** to say that you will do something or you approve of something: *He agreed to the plan.*

3 agree with something to believe that something is right: *I do not agree with hitting children.*

a·gree·ment /ə'gri:mənt/ *noun*
1 an arrangement or promise between people or countries: *Mum and Dad have an agreement. Mum cooks and Dad washes up the dishes.*
2 (*no plural*) having the same opinion as someone else: *They finally reached agreement on the price.*
3 in agreement having the same opinion: *We are all in agreement.*

ag·ri·cul·tu·ral /ˌægrɪ'kʌltʃərəl/ *adjective*
used or grown on a farm, or about farming: *agricultural machinery*

ag·ri·cul·ture /'ægrɪkʌltʃər/ *noun (no plural)*
the activity of growing crops and raising animals for food ⇨ same meaning FARMING

a·head /ə'hed/ *adverb*
1 at a distance in front of someone or something: *I saw her ahead of me. | Joe ran ahead to see what was happening.*
2 into the future: *We need to plan ahead if we are to succeed.*
3 arriving, waiting, finishing, etc before you: *There were four people ahead of me at the doctor's.*

aid[1] /eɪd/ *noun (no plural)*
help, especially in the form of money, food, equipment, etc: *The UN is sending aid to the area after the earthquake.*

aid[2] *verb*
to help someone ⇨ same meaning ASSIST

AIDS /eɪdz/ *noun (no plural)*
a very serious illness which destroys the body's ability to fight other illnesses ⇨ compare HIV

aim[1] /eɪm/ *verb*
1 to plan or want to do something: *We aim to win.*

2 to point a weapon at someone or something: *She aimed the gun at his head.*

aim[2] *noun*
1 something you want to do or get: *Their aim is to provide better schools for everyone.*
2 take aim to point a weapon at someone or something: *He took aim at the bird and fired.*

air[1] /eər/ *noun (no plural)*
1 the gas surrounding the Earth, which people breathe
2 the air the space above you: *He threw his hat into the air.*
3 by air in a plane: *We travelled by air.*

air[2] *verb*
to make a room fresh by letting air from outdoors flow into it

air·con·di·tion·ing /'eə kən‚dɪʃnɪŋ/ *noun (no plural)*
a system for making the air in a building colder when the air outside is very hot

air·craft /'eəkrɑːft/ *noun (plural aircraft)*
a vehicle that flies

air·force /'eəfɔːs/ *noun*
the part of a country's military organization that uses planes for fighting ⇨ compare ARMY, NAVY

air·line /'eəlaɪn/ *noun*
a company that carries people or goods by plane

air·mail /'eəmeɪl/ *noun (no plural)*
letters and parcels sent by plane

air·plane /'eəpleɪn/ *noun*
(*American*) a large vehicle that flies, in which people can travel (*British* **aeroplane**)

air·port /'eəpɔːt/ *noun*
a place that planes arrive at and leave from and where you can get on and off them

air raid /'eə reɪd/ *noun*
an attack by planes that drop bombs

air·y /'eəri/ *adjective*
with fresh air inside: *an airy room*

aisle /aɪl/ *noun*
a narrow area between rows of seats or shelves

aim

taking aim

open   ajar   closed

a·jar /əˈdʒɑːʳ/ *adjective*
a door or window that is ajar is not completely closed

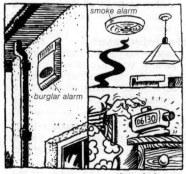

smoke alarm

burglar alarm

alarm clock

a·larm [1] /əˈlɑːm/ *noun*
   1 (*no plural*) a feeling of fear or danger
   2 a noise such as a bell that wakes someone up or warns people of danger: *a fire alarm*

alarm [2] *verb*
   to worry someone or make them afraid: *I don't want to alarm you but your car is on fire.*

alarm clock /əˈlɑːm ˌklɒk/ *noun*
   a clock that makes a noise at the time you want to wake up ⟡ see picture at ALARM[1]

al·bum /ˈælbəm/ *noun*
   1 a group of songs recorded by a performer or group on a record, CD, or TAPE: *Do you have the first Spice Girls album?*
   2 a book with empty pages where you can put photographs, stamps, etc

al·co·hol /ˈælkəhɒl/ *noun* (*no plural*)
   drinks such as beer or wine that can make you feel drunk: *We do not sell alcohol to anyone under 18.*

al·co·hol·ic /ˌælkəˈhɒlɪk/ *adjective*
   alcoholic drinks contain alcohol

a·lert /əˈlɜːt/ *adjective*
   quick to notice things

al·ge·bra /ˈældʒɪbrə/ *noun* (*no plural*)
   a kind of MATHEMATICS in which you use letters to represent numbers

a·li·en /ˈeɪliən/ *noun*
   1 someone who lives and works in a country that is not their own country
   2 a creature from another world: *a spaceship full of aliens*

a·like /əˈlaɪk/ *adjective, adverb*
   the same in some way: *They were all dressed alike in white dresses.* ⟡ compare SIMILAR

a·live /əˈlaɪv/ *adjective*
   living, not dead: *Is his grandfather still alive?*

all /ɔːl/ *adjective, adverb*
   1 the whole of something: *Don't eat all that bread!* | *I've been waiting for her to call all day.*
   2 every person or thing in a group of people or things: *Answer all twenty questions.* | *We all wanted to go home.*
   3 completely: *He was dressed all in black.*
   4 **not at all** not in any way: *I'm not at all hungry.* | *She didn't understand it at all.*

al·ler·gic /əˈlɜːdʒɪk/ *adjective*
   becoming ill when you eat, breathe, or touch a particular thing: *I'm allergic to cats.*

al·ler·gy /ˈælədʒɪ/ *noun* (*plural* **allergies**)
   a condition that makes you ill when you eat, touch, or breathe a particular thing: *an allergy to peanuts*

al·ley /ˈælɪ/ *noun*
   a very narrow street between buildings or walls

al·li·ance /əˈlaɪəns/ *noun*
   an agreement between countries or groups to work together

al·li·ga·tor /ˈælɪɡeɪtəʳ/ *noun*
   a large animal with a long body, short legs, and sharp teeth which lives in hot wet areas

A
B
C
D
E
F
G
H
I
J
K
L
M
N
O
P
Q
R
S
T
U
V
W
X
Y
Z

alligator

al·low /ə'laʊ/ *verb*
to let someone do something: *You're not allowed to go in there.* ⇨ opposite FORBID

all right /,ɔːl 'raɪt/ *adjective, adverb*
1 good enough but not very good: *The film was all right but I've seen better ones.*
2 not hurt or ill: *Do you feel all right?*
3 used to say "yes, I agree": *"Shall we go to town?" "All right, let's go now."*

al·ly /'ælaɪ/ *noun* (*plural* **allies**)
someone who helps you or supports you in a fight, argument, war, etc

al·most /'ɔːlməʊst/ *adverb*
nearly: *It's almost 9 o'clock.* | *We're almost there.*

a·lone /ə'ləʊn/ *adjective, adverb*
1 not with other people: *He lives alone.* ⇨ compare LONELY
2 only: *She alone knows the truth.*
3 **leave someone alone** to stop annoying someone: *Leave me alone. I'm busy.*
4 **leave something alone** to stop touching or changing something: *Leave that clock alone or you'll break it.*

a·long /ə'lɒŋ/ *adverb, preposition*
1 following the length of something or from end to end of something long and thin: *We walked along the road.* | *the houses along the street*
2 forward: *He was driving along, listening to the radio.*
3 **bring someone along** to bring someone somewhere with you: *Can I bring my friend along?*
4 **come along, go along** to go somewhere with someone: *I decided to go along too.*

a·long·side /ə,lɒŋ'saɪd/ *adverb, preposition*
by the side of something: *a boat tied up alongside the dock*

a·loud /ə'laʊd/ *adverb*
in a voice that is easy to hear: *She read the story aloud.*

al·pha·bet /'ælfəbet/ *noun*
the letters of a language in a special order. In English, the alphabet begins with A and ends with Z

al·pha·bet·i·cal /,ælfə'betɪkl/ *adjective*
in the same order as the letters of the alphabet: *The words in this dictionary are in alphabetical order.*

al·read·y /ɔːl'redi/ *adverb*
1 before now: *He has seen that film twice already.*
2 by this or that time: *It was already raining when we started our journey.*

al·right /ɔːl'raɪt/ *adjective, adverb*
another spelling of **all right**. The spelling 'alright' is often considered to be incorrect

al·so /'ɔːlsəʊ/ *adverb*
used when you are adding something to what you have already said: *The shop sells mostly shoes but they also sell some bags.* | *We can also go to the museum if there's time.*

NOTE: When there is only one verb, put **also** before the verb, unless it is the verb **be** which must have **also** after it: *He enjoys football and cricket, and he also likes tennis.* | *She likes music and she is also interested in sport.* When there is a verb like **would, should, can**, etc followed by another verb, put **also** between the two verbs: *James would also like to come.* | *It is an expensive sport which can also be dangerous.*

al·tar /'ɔːltər/ *noun*
a raised table in a religious place

al·ter /'ɔːltər/ *verb*
to change something: *She altered her plans.*

al·ter·a·tion /,ɔːltə'reɪʃn/ *noun*
a change: *We can make alterations to your trousers.*

al·ter·nate¹ /ɔːl'tɜːnət/ *adjective*
repeating first one thing, then another thing, then the first one, etc: *alternate sunshine and rain*

al·ter·nate² /'ɔːltəneɪt/ *verb*
to do first one thing, then another thing,

then the first thing again, etc: *We try to alternate the difficult work with tasks that are easier.*

al·ter·na·tive[1] /ɔːlˈtɜːnətɪv/ *noun*
something you can do or use instead of something else: *Many farmers are growing maize as an alternative to wheat.*

alternative[2] *adjective*
different from something else: *an alternative plan*

al·though /ɔːlˈðəʊ/
in spite of the fact that something is true: *Although they are poor, they are happy.*

al·to·geth·er /ˌɔːltəˈɡeðəʳ/ *adverb*
1 completely: *He's not altogether sure what to do.*
2 including everyone or everything: *There were 12 people in the bus altogether.*

al·ways /ˈɔːlweɪz/ *adverb*
1 at all times: *He always arrives late.*
2 for a very long time: *I shall always remember you.*

NOTE: When there is only one verb, put **always** before the verb, unless it is the verb **be** which must have **always** after it: *We always enjoy our holidays.* | *It is always nice to see you.* When there is a verb like **would**, **should**, **can**, etc followed by another verb, put **always** between the two verbs: *You must always be careful when you cross the road.* | *He said he would always love her.*

---

am /əm; *strong* æm/ *verb*
the part of the verb **be** that we use with **I**: *I am very sorry.* | *Am I late for dinner?*

a.m. /ˌeɪ ˈem/
in the morning: *I got up at 8 a.m.* ⇨ compare P.M.

a·maze /əˈmeɪz/ *verb (present participle* **amazing**, *past* **amazed***)*
to surprise someone very much: *She was amazed to see so many people there.*

a·maze·ment /əˈmeɪzmənt/ *noun (no plural)*
very great surprise: *His mouth opened in amazement.*

a·maz·ing /əˈmeɪzɪŋ/ *adjective*
very surprising and exciting: *What amazing news!*

am·bas·sa·dor /æmˈbæsədəʳ/ *noun*
an important person who represents his or her government in another country

am·bi·tion /æmˈbɪʃn/ *noun*
1 (*no plural*) a strong wish to be successful or powerful
2 something you very much want to do: *Her ambition was to be a famous singer.*

am·bi·tious /æmˈbɪʃəs/ *adjective*
determined to be successful or powerful: *a young, ambitious business-man*

am·bu·lance /ˈæmbjʊləns/ *noun*
a special vehicle for carrying people who are ill or wounded to hospital ⇨ see picture on page 206

A·mer·i·can /əˈmerɪkən/ *noun*
someone from the United States of America

am·mu·ni·tion /ˌæmjʊˈnɪʃn/ *noun (no plural)*
something that you can shoot from a weapon

a·mong /əˈmʌŋ/ (also **amongst** /əˈmʌŋst/) *preposition*
1 in a particular group of people: *It's nice to be among friends.*
2 in the middle of a lot of people or things: *We looked for the ball among the bushes.*
3 between three or more people: *The money was shared among the children* ⇨ compare BETWEEN

a·mount /əˈmaʊnt/ *noun*
how much of something there is: *It cost a large amount of money.*

amp /æmp/ *noun*
a measure of electricity

am·ple /ˈæmpl/ *adjective*
as much as you need and more: *The car has ample room for five people.* ⇨ compare ENOUGH

a·muse /əˈmjuːz/ *verb (present participle* **amusing**, *past* **amused***)*
to make someone laugh or smile: *Harry's jokes always amuse me.*

a·muse·ment /əˈmjuːzmənt/ *noun (no plural)*
the feeling that you have when you think something is funny: *She listened to his stories with amusement.*

amusement park /əˈmjuːzmənt ˌpɑːk/ *noun*
a large park where people can have fun

A B C D E F G H I J K L M N O P Q R S T U V W X Y Z

riding on exciting machines and playing games for small prizes

a·mus·ing /ə'mju:zɪŋ/ adjective
making you laugh or smile: an amusing story ⇨ compare FUNNY

an /ən; *strong* æn/
used instead of **a** before a word that starts with the sound of a, e, i, o, or u: an apple | an orange | half an hour ⇨ look at A

NOTE: You use **an** instead of **a** before words beginning with a vowel sound, e.g. a dog, a girl, a house but an umbrella, an elephant, an object. Remember that there is sometimes a difference in the way a word is spelled and the way it sounds. Use **an** before words that begin with a vowel sound but are not spelled with a, e, i, o, or u at the beginning, e.g. an hour (auə^r), an honest ('ɒnɪst) person, an X-ray ('eks reɪ). In the same way use **a**, not **an**, with words that are spelled with a vowel at the beginning but do not begin with a vowel sound, e.g. a European (juərə'pi:ən) country.

an·aes·thet·ic /ˌænəs'θetɪk/ noun
a drug that stops you feeling pain, especially during a medical operation

an·a·lyse /'ænəlaɪz/ verb (present participle **analysing**, past **analysed**)
to look at something very carefully to find out what it is made of or to understand it: We need to analyse this problem carefully before deciding what to do.

a·nal·y·sis /ə'næləsɪs/ noun (plural **analyses** /ə'næləsi:z/)
a careful examination of something: They are carrying out a detailed analysis of the test results.

an·ces·tor /'ænsestə^r/ noun
a person in your family who lived a long time before you were born

an·chor /'æŋkə^r/ noun
a heavy weight dropped down from a ship to the bottom of the water to stop the ship from moving

an·cient /'eɪnʃənt/ adjective
very old: ancient history | an ancient building

and /ən, ənd; *strong* ænd/
used to join two words, expressions, or parts of a sentence: a burger and chips | I had a drink and a piece of cake. | I went to the station and bought my ticket.

an·gel /'eɪndʒəl/ noun
a spirit who lives with God, usually shown in pictures as a person with wings

an·ger /'æŋgə^r/ noun (no plural)
a strong violent feeling that you can have when someone has behaved badly or been unkind to you

angle /'æŋgl/ noun
the shape made when two straight lines meet each other

an·gri·ly /'æŋgrɪli/ adverb
in a way that shows anger: "Go away!" she shouted angrily.

an·gry /'æŋgri/ adjective
feeling anger: I'm very angry with them. ⇨ same meaning CROSS

an·i·mal /'ænɪml/ noun
something alive that is not a person or a plant. Dogs, goats, and lions are animals: the animals in the zoo

an·kle /'æŋkl/ noun
the bottom part of your leg just above your foot ⇨ see picture at FOOT

an·ni·ver·sa·ry /ˌænɪ'vɜːsəri/ noun (plural **anniversaries**)
the same date each year that something important happened on in the past: the 50th anniversary of India's independence

NOTE: Compare **anniversary** and **birthday**. An **anniversary** is a day when you remember something special or important that happened on the same date in an earlier year: Their wedding anniversary is June 12th (=they got married on June 12th). | That year was the 50th anniversary of the end of the war (=the war ended exactly 50 years earlier). A person's **birthday** is the date on which they were born: My birthday is on October 20th and I will be twenty (=I was born on October 20th twenty years earlier).

an·nounce /ə'naʊns/ verb (present participle **announcing**, past **announced**)
to tell people about something so that everyone knows: The captain announced that the plane was going to land.

an·nounce·ment /ə'naʊnsmənt/ *noun*
something written or spoken to tell people important news: *Listen everyone, I have an important announcement to make.*

an·nounc·er /ə'naʊnsə^r/ *noun*
a person who gives information on the radio or television

an·noy /ə'nɔɪ/ *verb*
to make someone feel rather angry: *Jane was really annoying me.*

an·noyed /ə'nɔɪd/ *adjective*
rather angry: *I was annoyed because I missed the bus and was late for school.*

an·nu·al /'ænjʊəl/ *adjective*
happening every year: *The flower show is an annual event.*

an·oth·er /ə'nʌðə^r/
1 one more: *Would you like another cup of tea?*
2 a different one: *This plate is broken – can you get me another?*

an·swer[1] /'ɑːnsə^r/ *verb*
1 to say or write something after you have been asked a question: *"Did you do it?" "No, I didn't," she answered.* | *Try to answer all the questions in the test.*
2 answer the door to open the door when someone knocks on it
3 answer the telephone to pick up the telephone when it rings

answer[2] *noun*
1 something that you say or write after you have been asked a question: *He e-mailed me yesterday but is still waiting for an answer.* ⇨ same meaning REPLY
2 the correct result of a sum or the correct name or fact asked for in a question: *Do you know the answer?* | *That's the wrong answer.*

an·swer·ing ma·chine /'ɑːnsərɪŋ mə,ʃiːn/ *noun*
a machine that answers your telephone and records messages when you are out

ant /ænt/ *noun*

ant

a small red or black insect that lives in large groups

An·tarc·tic
/æn'tɑːktɪk/ *noun*
the Antarctic the very cold, most southern part of the world

an·te·lope /'æntɪləʊp/ *noun*
a wild animal that runs very fast and has horns on its head

an·ti·bi·ot·ic /,æntɪbaɪ'ɒtɪk/ *noun*
a type of drug used to fight illness in a person's body: *The doctor gave me some antibiotics for my sore throat.*

an·tic·i·pate /æn'tɪsɪpeɪt/ *verb* (*present participle* **anticipating**, *past* **anticipated**)
to expect something to happen: *The police are anticipating trouble at the match.* | *We anticipate **that** there will be a few problems.*

an·ti·clock·wise /,æntɪ'klɒkwaɪz/ *adjective, adverb*
in the opposite direction to the way the hands of a clock move round ⇨ opposite CLOCKWISE

an·tique /æn'tiːk/ *noun*
an object that is old and worth a lot of money: *This table is an antique.*

anx·i·e·ty /æŋ'zaɪəti/ *noun* (*no plural*)
a feeling of worry

anx·ious /'æŋkʃəs/ *adjective*
worried: *She always feels anxious when she has to travel by plane.*

an·y[1] /'eni/
used to say that it is not important which one something is: *You can buy them in any big shop.*

NOTE: Use **any**, not **some**, in questions and in negative sentences: *Is there any coffee?* | *There isn't any coffee.* But in questions when you are asking for something or offering something you use **some**: *Would you like some coffee?* | *Can I have some coffee please?*

any[2] *adverb*
used in negative questions and sentences to mean much, more, or a small amount: *Please do not drive any faster.* | *Are you feeling any better?*

an·y·bod·y /'eni,bɒdi/
any person: *Has anybody seen my pen?* | *Anybody can learn to swim.*

NOTE: Use **anybody** or **anyone** in questions and negative sentences: *Is there anybody there?* | *There wasn't anyone there.* Use **somebody** or **someone** in positive sentences: *There's someone waiting for you by the door.*

an·y·how /'enɪhaʊ/ *adverb*
another word for **anyway**

an·y·one /'enɪwʌn/
another word for **anybody** ⇨ look at ANYBODY

an·y·thing /'enɪθɪŋ/
1 used in questions and negative sentences to mean 'something': *Do you need anything from the shops?* | *Her father didn't know anything about it.*
2 used when it is not important which thing is done, chosen, etc: *My dog will eat anything.* | *I could have told her anything and she would have believed me.*

NOTE: Use **anything**, in questions and negative sentences: *Do you want anything to drink?* | *I don't want anything to drink.* Use **something** in positive sentences: *I want something to drink.*

an·y·way /'enɪweɪ/ *adverb*
1 in spite of something else: *The dress cost a lot of money, but I bought it anyway.*
2 used when you are saying something that supports what you have just said: *He decided to sell his bike – he never used it anyway.*
3 used when you are continuing what you are saying or changing the subject of what you are saying: *Anyway, where do you want to go for lunch?*

an·y·where /'enɪweəʳ/ *adverb*
in, at, or to any place: *I can't find my key anywhere.* | *You can use this ticket to fly anywhere in Europe.*

a·part /ə'pɑːt/ *adverb*
1 separated by distance or time: *The two villages are six miles apart.* | *Our birthdays are only two days apart.*
2 separated into many pieces: *I had to take the camera apart to fix it.*
3 apart from someone or something not including someone or some-

thing: *All the children like music apart from Joseph.*

a·part·ment /ə'pɑːtmənt/ *noun*
(*American*) a part of a building, on one floor, where someone lives (*British* **flat**)

ape /eɪp/ *noun*
a large animal like a monkey, but with a very short tail or no tail

a·pol·o·gize /ə'pɒlədʒaɪz/ *verb* (*present participle* **apologizing**, *past* **apologized**)
to say that you are sorry about something you have done: *Billy apologized for telling a lie.*

a·pol·o·gy /ə'pɒlədʒɪ/ *noun* (*plural* **apologies**)
something that you say or write to show that you are sorry about something you have done: *I hope you will accept my apology.*

a·pos·tro·phe /ə'pɒstrəfɪ/ *noun*
the sign ('), used to show that letters have been left out, for example 'don't' instead of 'do not', or used with 's' to show that someone owns something, as in 'Sarah's book'

ap·pal·ling /ə'pɔːlɪŋ/ *adjective*
extremely bad: *an appalling accident* | *an appalling film* ⇨ same meaning DREADFUL

ap·pa·ra·tus /ˌæpə'reɪtəs/ *noun* (*no plural*)
tools or other equipment needed for a special purpose: *The firemen were wearing breathing apparatus.*

ap·par·ent /ə'pærənt/ *adjective*
clearly able to be seen or understood: *It was apparent that he knew nothing about how to repair cars.* ⇨ same meaning OBVIOUS

ap·par·ent·ly /ə'pærəntlɪ/ *adverb*
used to say that something seems to be true but you cannot be sure: *They've been married for 20 years, and apparently they're very happy.*

ap·peal[1] /ə'piːl/ *verb*
1 to ask for something such as money, information, or help: *The police appealed to the public for information.*
2 appeal to someone to be attractive or interesting to someone: *That type of holiday doesn't appeal to me.*

appeal[2] *noun*
when someone asks for something such as money, information, etc: *The*

Red Cross is making an appeal **for** *medicine and blankets.*

ap·pear /ə'pɪər/ *verb*
1 to seem: *He appears upset.* | *The situation appears to be calm.*
2 to start to be seen: *Her head appeared round the door.*

ap·pear·ance /ə'pɪərəns/ *noun*
1 the way a person looks to other people: *ways to improve your personal appearance*
2 when someone or something arrives: *The children's shouting suddenly stopped with the appearance of Peter's father.*

ap·pe·tite /'æpɪtaɪt/ *noun*
1 the feeling that you want to eat: *I lost my appetite when I was ill.*
2 lose your apetite to stop feeling that you want to eat something

ap·plaud /ə'plɔːd/ *verb*
to hit your hands together many times to show that you enjoyed a play, speaker, etc: *Everyone applauded when the music ended.* ⇨ same meaning CLAP

ap·plause /ə'plɔːz/ *noun (no plural)*
when people hit their hands together many times to show that they enjoyed a play, speaker, etc: *the sound of applause*

ap·ple /'æpl/ *noun*
a round hard juicy fruit that is usually red or green ⇨ see picture on page 199

ap·pli·ance /ə'plaɪəns/ *noun*
a machine or piece of equipment used in someone's home: *kitchen appliances such as washing machines*

ap·pli·ca·tion /ˌæplɪ'keɪʃn/ *noun*
a document in which you ask for something such as a job, or the process of asking for something such as a job: *an application for a job*

ap·ply /ə'plaɪ/ *verb (present participle* **applying**, *past* **applied)**
1 to ask for a job, place at college, etc, especially by writing a letter showing why you should get it: *Kevin has applied* **for** *a computing job.*
2 to affect or be intended for someone or something: *The rules apply* **to** *everyone.*
3 to spread something such as paint on a surface: *Apply the glue along the edge of the wood.*

ap·point /ə'pɔɪnt/ *verb*
to choose someone for a job: *They are appointing Mr Jones as the new head teacher.*

ap·point·ment /ə'pɔɪntmənt/ *noun*
a time arranged for seeing someone: *I made an appointment to see the doctor.*

ap·pre·ci·ate /ə'priːʃieɪt/ *verb (present participle* **appreciating**, *past* **appreciated)**
to be grateful for something: *I appreciate your help.*

ap·pre·ci·a·tion / əˌpriːʃ'eɪʃn/ *noun*
when you are grateful for something: *John showed his appreciation* **for** *her help by giving her flowers.*

ap·pren·tice /ə'prentɪs/ *noun*
someone who is learning a new job

ap·proach[1] /ə'prəʊtʃ/ *verb*
to come near: *We watched as the car approached.*

approach[2] *noun*
a way of doing something or dealing with a problem: *Mr James had an exciting approach to teaching science.*

ap·pro·pri·ate /ə'prəʊpriət/ *adjective*
suitable for a particular time, situation, or purpose: *You have to wear appropriate clothes when you go to school.* ⇨ opposite INAPPROPRIATE

ap·prov·al /ə'pruːvəl/ *noun (no plural)*
someone's judgement or opinion that someone or something is good: *She works hard to get her parents' approval.* ⇨ opposite DISAPPROVAL

ap·prove /ə'pruːv/ *verb (present participle* **approving**, *past* **approved)**
to think that something is good: *I don't approve* **of** *smoking.* ⇨ opposite DISAPPROVE

ap·prox·i·mate /ə'prɒksɪmət/ *adjective*
slightly more or less than an exact amount, number, time, etc: *Our approximate time of arrival is two o'clock.*

ap·prox·i·mate·ly /ə'prɒksɪmətlɪ/ *adverb*
a little more or less than an exact amount, number, time, etc: *Approximately a quarter of the students are from Japan.*

a·pri·cot /'eɪprɪkɒt/ *noun*
a round soft yellow fruit

A·pril /'eɪprəl/ noun
the fourth month of the year

a·pron /'eɪprən/ noun
a large piece of cloth that you put on top of your clothes, to keep your clothes clean when you cook

a·quar·i·um /ə'kweərɪəm/ noun
a large glass box in which fish are kept alive in water ⇨ see picture on page 197

arch /ɑːtʃ/ noun (plural **arches**)
a curved shape at the top of a door, window etc: The old church had large arches supporting the weight of the roof.

ar·chae·ol·o·gist /ˌɑːkɪ'ɒlədʒɪst/ noun
a person who studies very old things made by people who lived a long time ago

ar·chae·o·l·o·gy /ˌɑːkɪ'ɒlədʒɪ/ noun (no plural)
the study of very old things made by people who lived a long time ago

ar·chi·tect /'ɑːkɪtekt/ noun
a person whose job is to plan and draw buildings ⇨ compare BUILDER

ar·chi·tec·ture /'ɑːkɪtektʃər/ noun (no plural)
1 the shape and style of buildings: modern architecture
2 the job of planning and drawing buildings: He studies architecture.

Arc·tic /'ɑːktɪk/ noun
the Arctic the very cold land and countries in the most northern part of the world

are /ər; strong ɑːr/ verb
the part of the verb **be** that is used with **we**, **you**, and **they**: Who are you? | They are all very tall in your family.

ar·e·a /'eərɪə/ noun
1 a part of a place, city, or country: We used to live in this area.
2 the size of a surface: The area is 2 kilometres long and half a kilometre wide.

a·re·na /ə'riːnə/ noun
a building with a large central area surrounded by seats, used for sports and performances

aren't /ɑːnt/
1 are not: Bob and Sue aren't coming to the party. | Things aren't the same since you left.

2 used in questions instead of 'am not': I'm your best friend, aren't I?

ar·gue /'ɑːgjuː/ verb (present participle **arguing**, past **argued**)
to not agree, often speaking loudly and angrily: Mum and Dad often argue **about** money.

ar·gu·ment /'ɑːgjʊmənt/ noun
when you argue, especially if you are angry: They **had** an argument.

a·rise /ə'raɪz/ verb (present participle **arising**, past **arose** /ə'rəʊz/, past participle **arisen** /ə'rɪzn/)
to happen or appear: Several problems arose when I lost my job.

a·rith·me·tic /ə'rɪθmətɪk/ noun (no plural)
sums done with numbers, including adding, dividing, MULTIPLYING etc

arm[1] /ɑːm/ noun
1 the part of your body between your shoulder and your hand
2 weapons such as guns and bombs

arm[2] verb
to give someone weapons

arm·chair /'ɑːmtʃeər/ noun
a comfortable chair with sides to rest your arms on ⇨ see pictures at CHAIR and on page 204

armed /ɑːmd/ adjective
carrying a weapon, especially a gun: an armed robber ⇨ opposite UNARMED

armed for·ces /ˌɑːmd 'fɔːsɪz/
all the people in a country's military organizations who fight on land, at sea, or in planes

ar·mour /'ɑːmər/ noun (no plural)
a covering of metal worn as protection by soldiers in the past

arm·pit /'ɑːmpɪt/ noun
the place under your arm where your arm joins your body

ar·my /'ɑːmɪ/ noun (plural **armies**)
the soldiers of a country who fight on land ⇨ compare AIR FORCE, NAVY

a·rose /ə'rəʊz/
the past tense of the verb **arise**

a·round /ə'raʊnd/ adverb, preposition
1 on all sides of something: We built a wall around the garden. ⇨ see picture on page 208
2 with a movement or shape like a circle: The Earth moves around the sun.
3 in or to different places: They walked around the town.

4 in or near a particular place: *Is there a restaurant around here?*

5 close to but not exactly an amount, number, time, etc: *Come at around 10 o'clock.*

6 in a position that is facing another way: *Let me turn the car around.*

ar·range /əˈreɪndʒ/ *verb (present participle* **arranging**, *past* **arranged**)
1 to make plans for something: *I have arranged a meeting for tomorrow.*
2 to put things in a particular order or position: *She arranged the flowers in a vase.*

ar·range·ment /əˈreɪndʒmənt/ *noun*
a plan or agreement that something will happen: *They're making arrangements for the wedding.*

ar·rest[1] /əˈrest/ *verb*
if a police officer arrests someone, he or she takes them away, believing them to be guilty of a crime: *Police arrested several people for fighting in the street.*

arrest[2] *noun*
when a police officer arrests someone: *The police made three arrests yesterday.*

ar·riv·al /əˈraɪvl/ *noun (no plural)*
when a person, plane, etc gets to a place: *We are sorry for the late arrival of your train.* ⇨ opposite DEPARTURE

ar·rive /əˈraɪv/ *verb (present participle* **arriving**, *past* **arrived**)
to get to a place: *Your letter arrived yesterday.* I *We arrived in London on Tuesday.* ⇨ opposite LEAVE

ar·row /ˈærəʊ/ *noun*
1 a thin straight weapon like a sharp stick that you shoot from a BOW
2 a sign that shows direction or points to where something is

art /ɑːt/ *noun*
1 (*no plural*) the skill of drawing and painting: *Steve's studying art at college.*
2 an activity that you need skill to do: *the art of cooking*
3 **the arts** music, books, painting, films, etc

ar·te·ry /ˈɑːtəri/ *noun (plural* **arteries**)
one of the tubes in your body that carry blood from your heart to the rest of your body

ar·thri·tis /ɑːˈθraɪtɪs/ *noun (no plural)*
an illness that makes the joints in your hands, legs, etc painful and difficult to move

ar·ti·cle /ˈɑːtɪkl/ *noun*
1 a piece of writing in a newspaper: *Did you read that article about the floods?*
2 a thing: *articles of clothing*
3 the words **a** or **an** (=indefinite article) or **the** (=definite article)

ar·ti·choke /ˈɑːtɪtʃəʊk/ *noun*
a green vegetable that looks like a flower ⇨ see picture on page 199

ar·ti·fi·cial /ˌɑːtɪˈfɪʃl/ *adjective*
not natural but made by people: *artificial flowers* I *an artificial leg*

artist

painting | model | easel | paints

art·ist /ˈɑːtɪst/ *noun*
a person who has skill in an art such as painting, music, etc

ar·tis·tic /ɑːˈtɪstɪk/ *adjective*
having skill in an art such as painting, music, etc

as /əz; *strong* æz/
1 used to say what someone's job is or what something is used for: *She's working as a teacher for a few months.* I *We can use this box as a table.*
2 **as ... as** used when comparing things: *I'm not as old as you.* I *It's just as good as the other one.*
3 while something is happening: *We sang as we worked.*
4 because: *I can't come as I'm too busy.*
5 **as well** also: *Can I have some cake as well?*

ash /æʃ/ *noun (plural* **ashes**)
the grey powder that is left after something has burned

a·shamed /əˈʃeɪmd/ *adjective*
feeling bad about something you have done wrong: *She was very ashamed that she had stolen the money.* ⇨ compare EMBARRASSED

a·shore /ə'ʃɔːʳ/ adverb
onto the land: Brian pulled the boat ashore.

ash·tray /'æʃtreɪ/ noun
a small dish that is used for the ash from cigarettes

a·side /ə'saɪd/ adverb
to or towards one side: I moved aside to let her go past.

ask /ɑːsk/ verb
1 to say something that is a question: "Who are you?" she asked.
2 to try to get help, information, etc from someone: They asked me the time. I She asked me for some money.
3 to invite someone to a place or event: John asked me to go to the dance with him.

a·sleep /ə'sliːp/ adjective
1 sleeping: The baby is asleep.
2 **fall asleep** to begin to sleep: I fell asleep in front of the TV.

as·par·a·gus /ə'spærəgəs/ noun (no plural)
a long thin green plant that is eaten as a vegetable ⇨ see picture on page 199

as·pect /'æspekt/ noun
one of the parts of a situation, idea, problem, etc: We need to discuss several aspects of your plan.

as·pirin /'æsprɪn/ noun
a medicine that makes pain in your body go away ⇨ see picture at FIRST AID

as·sas·sin /ə'sæsɪn/ noun
someone who kills an important person, especially for political reasons

as·sas·si·nate /ə'sæsɪneɪt/ verb (present participle **assassinating**, past **assassinated**)
to kill an important person, especially for political reasons ⇨ compare MURDER

as·sas·si·na·tion /ə,sæsɪ'neɪʃn/ noun
when someone kills an important person, especially for political reasons: the assassination of President Kennedy ⇨ compare MURDER

as·sault¹ /ə'sɔːlt/ verb
to attack or hit someone: He was arrested for assaulting a neighbour.

assault² noun
a violent attack on someone: an assault on a woman

as·sem·ble /ə'sembl/ verb (present participle **assembling**, past **assembled**)
1 to bring people or things together in a group: She assembled the children beside the bus. ⇨ same meaning GATHER
2 to put the parts of something together: furniture that you can assemble yourself at home

as·sem·bly /ə'semblɪ/ noun (plural **assemblies**)
a group of people who have come together for a special purpose or meeting: the United Nations General Assembly

as·sign·ment /ə'saɪnmənt/ noun
a job or piece of work that you must do: a homework assignment

as·sist /ə'sɪst/ verb
to help someone: Two nurses assisted the doctor during the operation.

as·sist·ance /ə'sɪstəns/ noun (no plural)
help or support

as·sis·tant /ə'sɪstənt/ noun
a person who helps someone in their job

as·so·ci·ate /ə'səʊʃɪeɪt/ verb (present participle **associating**, past **associated**)
to connect two things or ideas in your mind: She associated Florida **with** sunshine and sandy beaches.

as·so·ci·a·tion /ə,səʊsɪ'eɪʃn/ noun
an organization of people with a particular purpose or interest: the Association of University Teachers

as·sume /ə'sjuːm/ verb (present participle **assuming**, past **assumed**)
to think that something is true when you do not know that it is true: I assumed she was his mother, but in fact she's his aunt.

as·sure /ə'ʃɔːʳ/ verb (present participle **assuring**, past **assured**)
to tell someone that something is true so that they can feel less worried: I assure you that we are not closing the hospital.

as·te·risk /'æstərɪsk/ noun
the sign (*)

as·ton·ish /ə'stɒnɪʃ/ verb
to surprise someone very much: The fact that I could run faster than her astonished me.

as·ton·ish·ment /əˈstɒnɪʃmənt/ noun
(no plural)
when you are very surprised: He showed astonishment when his sister came top in the exam.

as·trol·o·ger /əˈstrɒlədʒəʳ/ noun
a person who studies astrology

as·trol·o·gy /əˈstrɒlədʒɪ/ noun (no plural)
the study of the planets and stars in the belief that they influence people's lives

as·tro·naut
/ˈæstrənɔːt/ noun
a person who travels in space

astronaut

as·tro·no·mer
/əˈstrɒnəməʳ/
a scientist who studies astronomy

as·tron·o·my
/əˈstrɒnəmɪ/ noun
(no plural)
the scientific study of the stars and planets

at /ət; strong æt/
1 in a particular place: Meet me at my place around six. | She is at work
2 when something happens: It gets cold at night. | The film starts at seven o'clock.
3 towards someone or something: Look at me! | Stop shouting at the children.
4 because of something: None of the kids laughed at his joke. | Jenny, I'm surprised at you.
5 used to say what the price, speed, level, etc of something is: He was driving at ninety miles an hour. | The toy is in the shops now at £9.50.
6 **good at something, bad at something** able or not able to do something well: Debbie's always been good at learning languages.

ate /et, eɪt/
the past tense of the verb **eat**

ath·lete /ˈæθliːt/ noun
someone who is good at sports especially someone who takes part in sports competitions

ath·let·ics /æθˈletɪks/ noun (no plural)
sports in which people run, jump, or throw things to see who is the best
⇨ see picture on page 196

at·las /ˈætləs/ noun (plural **atlases**)
a book of maps

at·mo·sphere /ˈætməsfɪəʳ/ noun (no plural)
1 a feeling that a place or group of people give you: I enjoyed the exciting atmosphere of the game.
2 **the atmosphere** the air that surrounds the Earth
3 the air in a room, building, etc: a smoky atmosphere

at·om /ˈætəm/ noun
the smallest part that a SUBSTANCE can be divided into

a·tom·ic en·er·gy /əˌtɒmɪk ˈenədʒɪ/ noun (no plural)
power produced by dividing an atom, used for making electricity

at·tach /əˈtætʃ/ verb
1 to fasten or join something to something else: There's a health club attached **to** the hotel.
2 **be attached to someone** to like someone very much: Mary was very attached to her brother.

at·tack[1] /əˈtæk/ verb
1 to use violence against a person or place: The rebels attacked the camp at dawn.
2 to criticize someone or something strongly: Several newspapers attacked the President for not doing enough.

attack[2] noun
to try to hurt someone or damage something: an attack **on** an army base

at·tempt[1] /əˈtempt/ verb
to try to do something difficult: The second question was so complicated I didn't even attempt it.

attempt[2] noun
when you try to do something difficult: She made an attempt **to** speak their language.

at·tend /əˈtend/ verb
to go to an event or be present at an event: Will you attend the meeting?

at·tend·ance /əˈtendəns/ noun (no plural)
when someone goes somewhere such as school or church regularly: His attendance **at** school is bad (=he does not go often enough).

at·tend·ant /əˈtendənt/ noun
a person whose job is to take care of a public place

A B C D E F G H I J K L M N O P Q R S T U V W X Y Z

at·ten·tion /əˈtenʃn/ *noun (no plural)*
1 when you are looking at and listening to someone or something: *May I have your attention?* (=will you listen to me?)
2 special care or interest that you give to someone or something: *Old cars need more attention than new ones.*
3 pay attention to someone to listen to someone very carefully

at·tic /ˈætɪk/ *noun*
the area at the top of a house under the roof, often used for storing things ⇨ see picture on page 204

at·ti·tude /ˈætɪtjuːd/ *noun*
the way you think or feel about something: *Her attitude **towards** her job is very positive.*

at·tract /əˈtrækt/ *verb*
1 to make someone interested in something: *What was it that attracted you to our company?*
2 if something attracts people or animals, they go there because they think it will be good: *Disneyland attracts many visitors every year.*
3 be attracted to someone to like someone and want to be with them

at·trac·tion /əˈtrækʃən/ *noun (no plural)*
when you like someone or something very much

at·trac·tive /əˈtræktɪv/ *adjective*
pretty, beautiful, or pleasant to look at: *an attractive girl* ⇨ opposite UNATTRACTIVE

au·ber·gine /ˈəʊbəʒiːn/ *noun*
a large vegetable with a dark purple skin ⇨ see picture on page 199

auc·tion /ˈɔːkʃən/ *noun*
a public sale where things are sold to the people who offer the most money

au·di·ence /ˈɔːdɪəns/ *noun*
all the people watching a play, listening to music, etc

au·di·o /ˈɔːdɪəʊ/ *adjective*
for recording and broadcasting sounds: *an audio tape* | *an audio signal*

au·di·o·vis·u·al /ˌɔːdɪəʊ ˈvɪʒʊəl/ *adjective*
using recorded pictures and sound: *audiovisual equipment for language teaching*

Au·gust /ˈɔːɡəst/ *noun*
the eighth month of the year

aunt /ɑːnt/ *noun*
the sister of one of your parents, or the wife of the brother of one of your parents

au·thor /ˈɔːθəʳ/ *noun*
a person who has written a book, play, poem, etc

au·thor·i·ty /ɔːˈθɒrətɪ/ *noun*
1 *(no plural)* the power to control people and make them do what you want: *The police have **the** authority **to** stop the march.*
2 the authorities the people who control a place or system

au·to·bi·og·ra·phy /ˌɔːtəbaɪˈɒɡrəfɪ/ *noun (plural* **autobiographies***)*
a book that someone has written about their own life ⇨ compare BIOGRAPHY

au·to·graph /ˈɔːtəɡrɑːf/ *noun*
a famous person's name, written by them ⇨ compare SIGNATURE

au·to·mat·ic /ˌɔːtəˈmætɪk/ *adjective*
1 intended to work without much human control: *a train with automatic doors*
2 done without thinking: *an automatic reaction*

au·tumn /ˈɔːtəm/ *noun, adjective*
the season between summer and winter, when the leaves fall off the trees ⇨ see picture on page 194

a·vai·la·ble /əˈveɪləbl/ *adjective*
able to be seen, used, etc: *Is the doctor available?*

avalanche

av·a·lanche /ˈævəlɑːntʃ/ *noun*
a large amount of snow that falls down a mountain

av·e·nue /ˈævənjuː/ *noun*
a road in a town or city, especially one with trees on both sides ⇨ compare STREET

ave·rage /ˈævrɪdʒ/ adjective
1 usual or ordinary: The average child enjoys listening to stories.
2 calculated by adding several amounts together, and then dividing the total by the number of amounts: | The average rainfall in July is two centimetres.

average noun
the amount you get by adding several numbers together and dividing the total by the number of amounts. For example: the average of 3, 5, and 7 is 5

av·o·ca·do /ˌævəˈkɑːdəʊ/ noun
a green fruit the same shape as a PEAR with a very large hard seed in the middle ⇨ see picture on page 199

a·void /əˈvɔɪd/ verb
to stay away from a person, place, or thing: Are you trying to avoid me?

a·wait /əˈweɪt/ verb
to wait for someone or something

a·wake /əˈweɪk/ adjective
not sleeping: The baby is awake. ⇨ opposite ASLEEP

a·ward[1] /əˈwɔːd/ noun
a prize given to someone for doing something well: He won the award **for** best actor.

award[2] verb
to give someone an award

a·ware /əˈweəʳ/ adjective
if you are aware of something, you know it is happening: I was not aware **of** the problem.

a·way /əˈweɪ/ adverb
1 to another place: Go away! | He turned round and walked away. ⇨ see picture on page 208
2 distant from a place: Do you live far away? | The nearest town is 3 miles away.
3 not at home or at work: I'll be away for a few days.
4 **put something away** to put something in a safe place: The children put their toys away.

aw·ful /ˈɔːfəl/ adjective
1 very bad or unpleasant: The food tastes awful.
2 **look awful, feel awful** to look or feel ill

aw·ful·ly /ˈɔːflɪ/ adverb
very: That poor little girl looks awfully scared. ⇨ same meaning TERRIBLY

awk·ward /ˈɔːkwəd/ adjective
1 making you feel uncomfortable and difficult to deal with: There was an awkward silence, when no one knew what to say. | She asked several awkward questions.
2 moving in a way that does not seem relaxed, comfortable, or attractive: He's very awkward; he keeps dropping things.
3 not easy to hold or use: This camera is awkward to use.

axe /æks/ noun
a tool with a blade fixed to a handle, used for cutting wood

A B C D E F G H I J K L M N O P Q R S T U V W X Y Z

Bb

B, b /biː/
the second letter of the English alphabet

ba·by /'beɪbi/ noun (plural **babies**)
1 a very young child: *A baby was crying upstairs.*
2 **have a baby** if a woman has a baby, the baby is born

ba·by·sit /'beɪbɪsɪt/ verb (present participle **babysitting**, past **babysat**)
to care for a child while his or her parents are away: *I babysit for my aunt's children some evenings.*

ba·by·sit·ter /'beɪbɪsɪtəʳ/ noun
a person who is paid to care for a child when the child's parents are away

bach·e·lor /'bætʃələʳ/ noun
a man who is not married and has never been married ⇨ compare SPINSTER

back¹ /bæk/ noun
1 the part of your body that is behind you and goes from your neck to your bottom: *I lay on my back on the grass looking at the sky.* | *Jo says that her back aches.*
2 the part of something that is furthest from the front: *Write this exercise at the back of your book.* | *We got into the back of the car.* ⇨ opposite FRONT
3 **back to front** with the back where the front should be: *You're wearing your sweater back to front.*
4 **talk about someone behind their back** to say unkind things about someone when they do not know what you are saying: *You shouldn't talk about Helen behind her back.*
5 **turn your back on someone** to refuse to help or be friendly with someone: *Now that he's famous he's turned his back on his friends.*

back² adverb
1 where something or someone was before: *Put the book back on the shelf when you've finished it.* | *When do you come back from your holiday?*
2 in or into the condition that something was in before: *I woke up very early and couldn't get back to sleep.*
3 in the direction that is behind you: *She looked back to see if Tom was still there.*
4 in reply: *Call me back when you can.* | *Gina smiled at the boy and he smiled back.*

back³ verb
1 to make a vehicle move in the direction behind you: *She backed the car into the street.* ⇨ same meaning REVERSE
2 **back down** to accept that you were wrong about something
3 **back someone up** to support someone by agreeing that what they are saying is true

back⁴ adjective
at the back or behind something: *the back door* | *The children were playing in the back garden.* ⇨ opposite FRONT

back·bone /'bækbəʊn/ noun
the line of bones going from your neck to your bottom ⇨ same meaning SPINE

back·ground /'bækɡraʊnd/ noun
1 the type of education, experience, or family that someone has: *He has a background in computer science.*
2 the area that is behind the main objects or people in a picture: *This is a photo of Mary, with our house in the background.*

back·pack /'bækpæk/ noun
a bag that you carry on your back ⇨ same meaning RUCKSACK ⇨ see picture at BAG

back·ward /'bækwəd/ adjective
in the direction that is behind you: *After a backward glance, she stopped and waited for him.*

back·wards /'bækwədz/ adverb
1 in the direction that is behind you: *He took two steps backwards.*
2 in the opposite way to the usual way. For example, if you count backwards from 5, you say 5, 4, 3, 2, 1
3 **backwards and forwards** moving many times first in one direction and then in the opposite direction: *He travels backwards and forwards between London and New York.*

back·up /'bækʌp/ noun
a copy of something that you can use if the first one is lost or damaged: *Always make a backup of your files.*

back·yard /ˌbæk'jɑːd/ noun
a small area of land behind a house

ba·con /'beɪkən/ noun (no plural)
meat from a pig, that is prepared in salt, cooked, and eaten hot ⇨ compare HAM

bac·te·ri·a /bæk'tɪərɪə/ plural noun
living substances that are so small that you cannot see them, some of which can make people ill

bad /bæd/ adjective (**worse, worst**)
1 not good or not nice: I'm afraid I have some bad news. | The weather is bad for June.
2 not able to do something well: I'm bad **at** maths and singing. | He is a bad driver.
3 serious or severe: He's got a very bad cold.
4 too old to be good to eat: The milk has gone bad.
5 **be bad for someone** to cause harm to someone: Smoking is bad for you.
6 **not bad** good enough, but not extremely good: The film wasn't bad.

badge /bædʒ/ noun
a small piece of metal, plastic, or cloth with a picture or words on, that you fix to your clothes ⇨ compare BROOCH

bad·ger /'bædʒə/ noun
a wild animal with black and white fur that lives in a hole and comes out at night ⇨ see picture on page 195

bad·ly /'bædlɪ/ adverb
1 not well or nicely: She sang very badly. | a badly written essay
2 very much: He wanted very badly to be a success. | They badly needed help.

bad-tem·pered /,bæd 'tempəd/ adjective
becoming angry very easily: You're very bad-tempered today. | a bad-tempered man

bag /bæg/ noun
a container made of cloth, paper, plastic, or leather that opens at the top and that you use for carrying things: a shopping bag | a bag **of** old clothes

ba·gel /'beɪgl/ noun
a type of bread in the shape of a ring

bag·gage /'bægɪdʒ/ noun (no plural)
all the bags that you take with you when you travel ⇨ same meaning LUGGAGE

NOTE: Remember that the noun **baggage** has no plural: You haven't got much baggage with you. | We've got our passports and our baggage and we're ready to go.

bag·gy /'bægɪ/ adjective (**baggier, baggiest**)
baggy clothes are very loose: baggy trousers

bait /beɪt/ noun (no plural)
food that you use to catch fish or animals with

bake /beɪk/ verb (present participle **baking**, past **baked**)
to cook food in an OVEN, using dry heat: She's baking a cake. ⇨ compare ROAST

baked beans /,beɪkt 'biːnz/ plural noun
white beans cooked with TOMATOes, sold in tins

bak·er /'beɪkə/ noun
1 a person whose job is making bread and cakes ⇨ see picture on page 200
2 **baker's** British a shop that sells bread and cakes: I'm going to the baker's to get some bread.

bak·er·y /'beɪkərɪ/ noun (plural **bakeries**)
a building where bread and cakes are baked for selling ⇨ see picture on page 201

bal·ance[1] /'bæləns/ noun (no plural)
1 the ability to stay steady and not fall to one side or the other
2 **keep your balance** to stay steady and not fall
3 **lose your balance** to fall, although you tried to stay steady

bags

handbag
sports bag
backpack
rucksack

4 when two things have the same importance: *Children need the balance between being protected and being able to explore.*

balance[2] *verb (present participle* **balancing,** *past* **balanced)**
1 to keep yourself or something else steady, instead of falling to one side or the other: *You have to learn to balance to ride a bicycle.*
2 to give the right amount of importance to two different things: *I need to balance time doing homework with time playing sports.*

bal·co·ny /'bælkənɪ/ *noun (plural* **balconies)**
1 a place above the ground on the outside of a building where people can sit: *Our flat has a large balcony.*
2 the upper level in a theatre: *We were sitting in the balcony.*

bald /bɔːld/ *adjective*
with no hair on the head: *a bald old man*

ball /bɔːl/ *noun*
1 a round object that you throw, hit, or kick in some games: *Throw me the ball.*
2 an object with a round shape: *a ball of wool*
3 a large important party at which people dance: *The queen attended a ball.*

bal·let /'bæleɪ/ *noun*
a performance in which a story is told by dancing to music

bal·loon /bə'luːn/ *noun*
balloon
a thing made of rubber that you fill with air and use as a decoration or as a toy: *Each child was given a toy and a balloon.*

ball·point
/'bɔːlpɔɪnt/ *noun*
a pen full of ink with a very small metal ball at the end that rolls ink onto the paper as you write ⇨ same meaning BIRO

bam·boo /bæm'buː/ *noun (no plural)*
a tall hard grass that is like wood and is sometimes used for making furniture

ban[1] /bæn/ *verb (present participle* **banning,** *past* **banned)**
to make a rule or law saying that something is not allowed: *Smoking is banned in school.* ⇨ compare FORBID

ban[2] *noun*
an order that says you must not do a particular thing: *Our country has signed the ban on nuclear testing.*

ba·na·na /bə'nɑːnə/ *noun*
a long fruit with a yellow skin ⇨ see picture on page 199

band /bænd/ *noun*
1 a group of people who play music together: *She plays the drums in a band.*
2 a group of people who are together for some purpose: *A small band of people come to every match whatever the weather.*
3 a narrow piece of material used for holding things together: *Put a rubber band around these books.*

ban·dage[1] /'bændɪdʒ/ *noun*
a long piece of cloth that is tied on to your body when you have hurt yourself ⇨ compare PLASTER ⇨ see picture at FIRST AID

bandage[2] *verb (present participle* **bandaging,** *past* **bandaged)**
to tie a bandage on a part of someone's body: *If you bandage my ankle tightly I should be able to walk.*

ban·dit /'bændɪt/ *noun*
a thief who attacks people travelling in quiet country areas

bang[1] /bæŋ/ *noun*
1 a loud noise like the noise made by a gun: *The door slammed shut with a bang.*
2 when part of your body hits something: *a bang on the head*

bang[2] *verb*
1 to hit something hard against something else: *He banged his fist on the table.* | *She banged the phone down.*
2 to hit part of your body against something: *Joe banged his head on the door.*

ban·ish /'bænɪʃ/ *verb*
to send someone away from a place, country etc: *The children were banished from the house while their mother was cleaning the floors.*

ban·is·ter /'bænɪstə^r/ *noun*
a type of fence along the outer edge of STAIRS to stop people from falling

bank¹ /bæŋk/ *noun*
1 a business that keeps your money and lets you borrow money, or the building this business is in: *I need to go to the bank at lunchtime to pay in a cheque.* ⇨ see picture on page 201
2 the raised land along the side of a lake or river

bank² *verb*
1 to put or keep money in a bank: *Where do you bank?*
2 bank on someone or something to depend on someone or something: *We're banking on you to help us.*

bank ac·count /'bæŋk ə,kaʊnt/ *noun*
an agreement you make to leave your money in a bank until you need it: *He wanted to open a bank account.*

bank·er /'bæŋkə^r/ *noun*
a person who has an important job in a bank

bank hol·i·day /,bæŋk 'hɒlɪdeɪ, -dɪ/ *noun*
an official holiday when all the banks and some of the shops are closed

bank·ing /'bæŋkɪŋ/ *noun (no plural)*
the business done by a bank

bank note /'bæŋk nəʊt/ *noun*
British a piece of paper money (*American* **bill**)

bank·rupt /'bæŋkrʌpt/ *adjective*
not able to pay the money that you owe people

ban·ner /'bænə/ *noun*
a long piece of cloth with writing on it: *Crowds waved banners which said "Welcome Home".*

ban·quet /'bæŋkwɪt/ *noun*
a formal meal for a lot of people on a special occasion

bap·tis·m /'bæptɪzəm/ *noun*
a religious ceremony in which someone is touched or covered with water and becomes a member of the church

bap·tize /bæp'taɪz/ *verb (present participle* **baptizing***, past* **baptized***)*
to make someone a member of the church by performing a special ceremony in which they are touched or covered with water

bar¹ /bɑː^r/ *noun*
1 a place where people go to buy and drink alcohol: *He worked in a bar.*
2 a solid piece of something, longer than it is wide: *a bar of chocolate* | *a bar of soap*
3 a long piece of wood or metal across a door or window to stop people from going in or out: *Some of the houses had bars on the windows.*
4 behind bars in prison

bar² *verb (present participle* **barring***, past* **barred***)*
1 to put a bar across a door to stop people from going in or out: *She barred the door.*
2 to officially stop someone from doing something: *He was barred* **from** *playing baseball for six months.*

bar·be·cue /'bɑːbɪkjuː/ *noun*
1 a meal that is cooked outside over a fire, on a metal frame: *They invited their friends around for a barbecue.*
2 a metal frame for cooking food outside over a fire ⇨ see picture at GRILL

barbed wire /,bɑːbd 'waɪə^r/ *noun (no plural)*
wire with short sharp points in it: *a barbed wire fence*

bar·ber /'bɑːbə^r/ *noun*
1 a person whose job is to cut men's hair
2 barber's *British* a shop where men can go to have their hair cut

bar code /'bɑː kəʊd/ *noun*
a row of black lines on products for sale that a computer reads when you buy the products

bare /beə^r/ *adjective*
1 not covered by anything: *His bare feet made no sound in the soft sand.*
2 empty: *It was a bare room with no furniture*

bare·foot /,beə'fʊt/ *adjective, adverb*
not wearing any shoes or socks: *The children went barefoot all summer.*

bare·ly /'beəlɪ/ *adverb*
almost not: *He had barely enough money to buy food.* | *I could barely stay awake.* ⇨ same meaning HARDLY

bar·gain¹ /'bɑːgɪn/ *noun*
1 something that you buy for less than it usually costs: *These shoes are a bargain at only £25.*

barefoot

playing football barefoot

2 an agreement in which two people or groups each promise to do something: *We've made a bargain. Paul does the shopping and I cook.*

bargain [2] *verb*
to talk or argue about the price of something that you are buying or selling: *She bargained for jewellery in the market.*

barge /bɑːdʒ/ *noun*
a large boat with a flat bottom used for carrying goods

bark [1] /bɑːk/ *verb*
if a dog barks, it makes short loud sounds

bark [2] *noun*
1 (*no plural*) the strong hard part that covers the outside of the wood of a tree
2 the sound that a dog makes

bar·ley /ˈbɑːli/ *noun* (*no plural*)
a type of grass that is used for making food, beer, and other drinks

barn /bɑːn/ *noun*
a large building on a farm, used as a place for keeping animals and crops

bar·racks /ˈbærəks/ *plural noun*
a group of buildings that soldiers live in: *They went back to the barracks after work.*

bar·rel /ˈbærəl/ *noun*
1 a large round container with flat ends, used for keeping liquids such as oil and beer: *barrels of beer*
2 the part of a gun that is a metal tube

bar·ri·er /ˈbæriər/ *noun*
1 a fence or wall that stops people going somewhere: *The police put a barrier across the road.*
2 something such as a rule or problem that stops you doing something: *She didn't speak English, which was a barrier to her career.*

base [1] /beɪs/ *noun*
1 the bottom of something or the part something stands on: *the base of a triangle | We walked to the base of the cliff.*
2 the main place where an organization is controlled: *The company has offices all over the world, but their base is in London.*

base [2] *verb* (*present participle* **basing**, *past* **based**)
1 **base something on something** to use information or facts as a point for developing an idea, plan, etc: *She wrote a book based on her experiences during the war.*
2 **be based somewhere** to have your main home, office, etc in a place: *We're based in the city but we spend a lot of time in the country.*

base·ball /ˈbeɪsbɔːl/ *noun* (*no plural*)
a game in which two teams try to hit a ball with a round stick and then run round a field: *a baseball game*

base·ment /ˈbeɪsmənt/ *noun*
a part of a house, shop, or building that is below the level of the street: *They live in the basement.* ⇨ compare CELLAR

bas·es [1] /ˈbeɪsɪz/ *noun*
the plural of the noun **base**

ba·ses [2] /ˈbeɪsiːz/ *noun*
the plural of the noun **basis**

ba·sic /ˈbeɪsɪk/ *adjective*
simple and more important than anything else: *People need basic skills such as reading and writing.*

ba·sin /ˈbeɪsn/ *noun*
1 *British* a round bowl: *Pour the hot water into a basin.*
2 *British* a large bowl fixed to the wall in a bathroom for washing your hands

ba·sis /ˈbeɪsɪs/ *noun* (*plural* **bases** /ˈbeɪsiːz/)
the part of something from which something else develops: *The video will provide a basis for class discussion. | These ideas formed the basis of the plan.*

bas·ket /ˈbɑːskɪt/ *noun*
a container made of thin pieces of wood, wire, etc that you use for carrying things: *a shopping basket*

bas·ket·ball /ˈbɑːskɪtbɔːl/ *noun*
a game in which two teams try to throw

a ball through a round net that is high above the ground ➪ see picture on page 196

bat¹ /bæt/ noun

1 a piece of wood used for hitting the ball in some games: a baseball bat | a cricket bat ➪ see picture on page 196

2 a small animal with wings that flies at night and hangs upside-down when it sleeps

bat² verb (present participle **batting**, past **batted**)

to hit a ball with a bat

batch /bætʃ/ noun (plural **batches**)

a number of people or things arriving or being dealt with together: She cooked a fresh batch of cakes. | This is the last batch.

bath¹ /bɑːθ/ noun

1 British a large container that you fill with water and then sit in to wash yourself

2 **have a bath, take a bath** to wash yourself in a bath: I have a bath every day.

NOTE: Do not confuse the verb **bath** (=to wash in a bath) with the verb **bathe** (=to swim). People do not usually use the verb **bath**. In British English people usually say **have a bath** and in American English people usually say **take a bath**: I think I'll have a bath (British). | I think I'll take a bath (American).

bath² verb

1 British to wash someone in a bath: I love bathing the baby.

2 British to wash yourself in a bath: She baths every morning.

bathe /beɪð/ verb (present participle **bathing** /ˈbeɪðɪŋ/, past **bathed**)

1 if you bathe a wound, you wash it

2 to swim for pleasure in a river or the sea

bath·ing suit /ˈbeɪðɪŋ ˌsuːt/ noun

a piece of clothing that you wear when you swim

bath·robe /ˈbɑːθrəʊb/ noun

a type of loose soft coat that you put on after you have had a bath

bath·room /ˈbɑːθruːm/ noun

a room in a house where people wash themselves ➪ see picture on page 204

bat·ter /ˈbætər/ verb

to hit someone or something hard, again and again: The waves battered against the cliffs.

bat·ter·y /ˈbætəri/ noun (plural **batteries**)

an object that provides electricity for a car, radio, electronic toy, etc: I need new batteries for my radio.

bat·tle /ˈbætl/ noun

a fight between soldiers, ships, or planes: It was one of the most important battles of the war. ➪ compare WAR

bay /beɪ/ noun

a part of the sea that curves inwards, so that there is land at the sides: a beautiful sandy bay

B.C. /ˌbiː ˈsiː/

used after a date to show how many years before the birth of Christ something happened: The Great Pyramid was built about 2600 B.C.

be /bɪ; strong biː/

1 used to describe people or things or give information about them: His name is Peter. | My mother is a teacher. | The milk is on the table. | I'm (=I am) very happy. | "How old are you?" "I am 16." | "What's (=what is) your name?" "It's (=it is) Emma." | It was my birthday yesterday.

2 used with the -ing form of other verbs to show that something is happening now: "What are you doing?" "I am painting a picture." | He is cleaning his room. | Don't disturb me while I'm (=I am) working.

3 used with other verbs to show that something happens to a person or thing: He was attacked by a dog. | The house was built 50 years ago.

4 used with other verbs to show what you expect to happen or what must happen: I will be leaving tomorrow. | The children are to be in bed when I get home.

5 **there is/there are/there were, etc** used to say that someone or something exists: Look, there's (=there is) Sue! | There are too many people in here. | How many children are there in your class? | There was a loud noise.

present tense

singular	plural
I **am** (I'**m**)	We **are** (We'**re**)
You **are** (You'**re**)	You **are** (You'**re**)
He/She/It **is**	They **are**
(He'**s**/She'**s**/It'**s**)	(They'**re**)

past tense

singular	plural
I **was**	We **were**
You **were**	You **were**
He/She/It **was**	They **were**

present participle **being**
past participle **been**
negative short **aren't, isn't,**
  forms **wasn't, weren't**
(you can find each of these words in its own place in the dictionary)

beach /biːtʃ/ noun (plural **beaches**)
an area covered in sand or small stones by the sea: Children were playing **on** the beach.

bead /biːd/ noun
a small ball of glass, wood, or plastic with a hole for string or wire to pass through: She wore a string of beads round her neck.

beak /biːk/ noun
the hard pointed mouth of a bird ⇨ see picture at EAGLE

beam¹ /biːm/ noun
1 a large long heavy piece of wood used to support the roof of a building
2 a line of light shining from a bright object: A beam of light shone through the window. | She could see the path in the beam from her torch.

beam² verb
to smile in a very happy way: She beamed with pleasure.

bean /biːn/ noun
1 a seed, or the part of a plant that contains seeds, eaten as a vegetable: green beans ⇨ see picture on page 199
2 a seed that is used for making food or drink: coffee beans

bear¹ /beər/ verb (past **bore** /bɔːr/, past participle **borne** /bɔːn/)
1 **can't bear someone or something** to definitely not like someone or something: He can't bear loud music. | I can't bear people who complain all the time.
2 **bear in mind** to not forget an important fact: You need to bear in mind **that** not everyone will win a prize. | He did very well, bearing in mind he's only ten.
3 to carry or support the weight of something: That chair won't bear your weight.
4 to accept something bad without complaining: The pain was too much for me to bear.

bear² /beər/ noun
a large wild animal with a thick coat

beard /bɪəd/ noun
hair on a man's face below his mouth
⇨ compare MOUSTACHE ⇨ see picture on page 202

beast /biːst/ noun
1 a wild and dangerous animal
2 an unkind or cruel person: You beast – I hate you!

beat¹ /biːt/ verb (past **beat**, past participle **beaten** /ˈbiːtn/)
1 if you beat someone in a battle or competition, you win: Spain beat Italy 3–1. | I beat my Dad at chess.
2 to hit someone or something again and again: He was beating his drums.
3 when your heart beats, it moves regularly to push blood round your body: Her heart was beating fast.
4 **to beat someone up** to hit someone until they are hurt: There was a fight and the bad guy beat up the hero of the film.

beat² noun
one of a series of regular sounds or movements: the beat of your heart | I heard the slow beat of the drum.

beau·ti·cian /bjuːˈtɪʃn/ noun
a person who treats your face and body, to make you look and feel good

beau·ti·ful /ˈbjuːtɪfəl/ adjective
1 very attractive and nice to look at: a beautiful woman | a beautiful view
2 very pleasant or nice: What a beautiful day! | beautiful music

NOTE: The adjectives **beautiful** and **pretty** can be used to describe women, children, and things, but you should never use them to describe a man. If you want to say a man looks very nice, you can describe him as **handsome**.

beau·ti·ful·ly /'bjuːtɪflɪ/ adverb
in a way that looks or sounds good: *She speaks French beautifully.*

beau·ty /'bjuːtɪ/ noun
1 (no plural) when someone or something is beautiful: *a woman of great beauty* | *the beauty **of** the mountains*

be·came /bɪ'keɪm/
the past tense of the verb **become**

be·cause /bɪ'kɒz/
1 used when you are giving a reason for something: *I missed the train because I was late.* | *She sings because she enjoys it.*
2 **because of something** for this reason: *We stayed at home because of the bad weather.*

beck·on /'bekən/ verb
to make a sign with your finger asking someone to come to you

be·come /bɪ'kʌm/ verb (present participle **becoming** /bɪ'kʌmɪŋ/, past **became** /bɪ'keɪm/, past participle **become**)
1 to begin to be something: *The prince became king when his father died.* | *The actor became famous.*
2 **What has become of someone?** a question you ask when you want to know what has happened to a person, or where someone is: *What has become of that friend of yours who went to live in Australia?*

bed /bed/ noun
1 a piece of furniture you sleep on: *I lay in bed reading.*
2 **go to bed** to go to your bed to sleep: *What time did you go to bed last night?*
3 **make the bed** to tidy a bed and make it ready for sleeping in
4 the ground at the bottom of a river or the sea: *the sea bed*

bed and break·fast /ˌbed ən 'brekfəst/ noun
a family house or small hotel where you can pay to sleep and have breakfast: *We stayed in a bed and breakfast.*

bed·clothes /'bedkləʊðz/ plural noun
another word for **bedding**

bed·ding /'bedɪŋ/ noun
all the covers put on a bed

bed·room /'bedruːm/ noun
a room for sleeping in ⇨ see picture on page 204

bed·sit /bed'sɪt/ noun
a room used for both living and sleeping in: *Many students live in bedsits.*

bed·spread /'bedspred/ noun
a cloth cover for a bed, used to keep you warm or to make the bed look attractive ⇨ compare DUVET

bed·time /'bed,taɪm/ noun
the time when you usually go to bed to sleep

bee /biː/ noun
a flying insect that can sting and that makes HONEY

bee

beef /biːf/ noun
(no plural)
the meat from cattle

bee·hive /'biːhaɪv/ noun
(also **hive**) a box or structure that BEES live in ⇨ see picture at BEE

beehive

beds

bunk beds

cot

double bed   single bed

been /biːn, bɪn/
1 the past participle of the verb **be**: *It has been very cold this week.*
2 **have been somewhere** to have visited a place and come back from it: *She's been away on holiday.* | *Have you ever been to Scotland?*

beep·er /'biːpər/ *noun*
a small machine that you can carry that makes a sound when someone telephones you

beer /bɪər/ *noun*
1 (*no plural*) an alcoholic drink made from grain
2 a glass or bottle of this drink: *Can I have two beers, please?*

bee·tle /'biːtl/ *noun*
an insect whose outside wings make a hard cover for its body

beet·root /'biːtruːt/ *noun*
a round red vegetable that grows under the ground

be·fore[1] /bɪˈfɔːr/ *preposition*
earlier than something: *You must leave before 8 o'clock.* | *Finish your work before you go.* | *the day before yesterday* ⇨ opposite AFTER

NOTE: **Before** means 'earlier than something else', e.g. *She left before I arrived.* | *Clean your teeth before you go to bed.* **Ago** means 'in the past'. Look at these sentences: *We went to Scotland three years ago.* | *Our second visit to America was in 1993, and our first visit was three years before (=in 1990).* | *It happened many years ago, before the war.*

before[2] *adverb*
at an earlier time: *We have met before, at one of Sally's parties.* | *I have never seen you before.*

be·fore·hand /bɪˈfɔːhænd/ *adverb*
before something else happens: *She knew I was coming because I telephoned her beforehand.* | *When you are taking an exam, it's natural to feel nervous beforehand.*

beg /beg/ *verb* (*present participle* **begging**, *past* **begged**)
1 to ask someone very strongly to do something: *I begged her not to go.* | *She begged him for help.*

2 to ask people in the street for money or food: *He was trying to make some money by begging.*
3 **I beg your pardon** used as a very polite way of telling someone that you did not hear what they said and you want them to say it again: *I beg your pardon, could you repeat that?* | *"It's 7 o'clock." "I beg your pardon." "I said it's 7 o'clock."*

be·gan /bɪˈgæn/
the past tense of the verb **begin**

beg·gar /'begər/ *noun*
a person who asks people in the street for money or food

be·gin /bɪˈgɪn/ *verb* (*present participle* **beginning**, *past tense* **began** /bɪˈgæn/, *past participle* **begun** /bɪˈgʌn/)
1 to start, or start something: *The film begins at 2 o'clock.* | *When do you begin your new job?* | *It's beginning to rain.* ⇨ opposite END
2 **to begin with** at the start of something or from the beginning: *To begin with I didn't like school, but now I enjoy it.* | *I didn't break it. It was like that to begin with.*

be·gin·ner /bɪˈgɪnər/ *noun*
a person who is starting to do or learn something: *a swimming class for beginners*

be·gin·ning /bɪˈgɪnɪŋ/ *noun*
the start: *They were married at the beginning of the year.* | *The beginning of the film is very exciting.* ⇨ opposite END

be·gun /bɪˈgʌn/
the past participle of the verb **begin**

be·half /bɪˈhɑːf/ *noun*
on behalf of someone, on someone's behalf instead of someone or for someone: *I have come on behalf of my brother who is ill.* | *I paid the money on your behalf.*

be·have /bɪˈheɪv/ *noun*
1 to do or say things in a particular way: *The children behaved very badly.*
2 **behave yourself** to do things in a way that will not make other people angry or upset: *If you behave yourself you can have an ice cream.* ⇨ opposite MISBEHAVE

be·hav·iour /bɪˈheɪvjər/ *noun* (*no plural*)
the way a person acts: *The teacher will*

not allow bad behaviour in class. | *Can violence on TV affect people's behaviour?*

be·hind /bɪˈhaɪnd/ *adverb, preposition*

1 at the back of something: *He hung his coat on the nail behind the door.* | *My brother went in front and I walked behind.* ⟳ see picture on page 208

2 not as successful as someone or something else: *We were three points behind at half time.* | *Mark's always behind the rest of his class in mathematics.*

3 in the place where someone or something was before: *Oh no! I left my money behind.*

beige /beɪʒ/ *adjective*
a very light brown colour: *a beige dress*

be·ing ¹ /ˈbiːɪŋ/
the present participle of the verb **be**

being ² *noun*
a person: *Men, women, and children are human beings.*

be·lief /bɪˈliːf/ *noun*

1 (*no plural*) the feeling that something is true or exists: *She has a strong belief in God.* | *There's a growing belief that young children learn best through play.*

2 an opinion or idea that you think is true: *His father will never change his political beliefs.*

be·liev·a·ble /bɪˈliːvəbl/ *adjective*
able to be believed: *The story in the book is very believable.* ⟳ opposite UNBELIEVABLE

be·lieve /bɪˈliːv/ *verb* (*present participle* **believing**, *past* **believed**)

1 to think that something is true: *I don't believe the things you say.* | *It's hard to believe she's over 70.*

2 to think that someone is telling the truth: *Don't you believe me?*

3 to have an opinion, although you cannot be sure: *I believe she will be back on Monday.*

4 believe in something to be sure that something exists: *Do you believe in God?* | *I don't believe in ghosts.*

5 believe in someone to trust someone and be sure they will succeed: *The whole team believed in their coach.*

be·liev·er /bɪˈliːvəʳ/ *noun*
someone who believes that a particular idea or thing is good: *He's a believer in eating lots of fruit and vegetables.*

bell /bel/ *noun*
a round hollow metal object that makes a musical sound when it is hit: *church bells* ⟳ see pictures at TOWER and on page 205

be·long /bɪˈlɒŋ/ *verb*

1 belong to someone if something belongs to you, you own it: *The grey coat belongs to Jamie and the green one belongs to John.*

2 belong to something to be a member of a group or club: *She belongs to a health club.*

be·long·ings /bɪˈlɒŋɪŋz/ *plural noun*
your own property: *Please take all your belongings with you when you leave the plane.*

be·low /bɪˈləʊ/ *adverb, preposition*

1 in a lower place or position or on a lower level: *The children threw sticks from the bridge into the river below.* | *My brother is in the class below me.* ⟳ see picture on page 208

2 less than a particular number or amount: *children below the age of five* | *It's ten degrees below zero outside!*

belt /belt/ *noun*
a piece of cloth or leather that you wear around the middle of your body ⟳ see pictures at FASTENER and on page 203

bench /bentʃ/ *noun* (*plural* **benches**)
a long seat for more than one person: *a bench in the park*

bend

bend   snap

bend ¹ /bend/ *verb* (*past* **bent** /bent/)

1 also **bend down**, **bend over** to move the top part of your body down towards the ground: *She bent down to pick up a book from the floor.* ⟳ see picture on page 207

2 to move something so that it is not straight: *Bend your knees slightly.*

bend ² *noun*
a curve: *There's a bend in the road just after the bridge.*

A B C D E F G H I J K L M N O P Q R S T U V W X Y Z

be·neath /bɪ'niːθ/ preposition
below or under something: *Shall we sit beneath these trees?* | *I felt the warm sand beneath my feet.*

ben·e·fi·cial /ˌbenɪ'fɪʃl/ adjective
good or useful

ben·e·fit[1] /'benɪfɪt/ noun
1 an advantage: *the benefits **of** a good education*
2 for someone's benefit to help someone: *I did it for your benefit.*

benefit[2] verb
to be useful or helpful to someone: *The new books bought for the school will benefit all the pupils.*

bent /bent/
the past tense and past participle of the verb **bend**

be·ret /'bereɪ/ noun
a flat round hat made of woollen cloth

ber·ry /'berɪ/ noun (plural **berries**)
a small soft fruit that grows on a bush or tree

be·side /bɪ'saɪd/ preposition
next to someone or something: *Come and sit beside me.* | *They had a house beside the lake.* ⇨ see picture on page 208

be·sides /bɪ'saɪdz/ adverb
used when you are giving another reason or fact to support what you are saying: *I'm too tired to go to the film tonight – besides, I haven't got any money.* ⇨ same meaning ANYWAY

best[1] /best/ adjective
1 the superlative of **good**: *It was the best film I've ever seen.* | *He is the best player on the team.* ⇨ opposite WORST
2 best wishes used at the end of a letter when the person you are writing to is not a close friend: *Have a happy Christmas, with best wishes from Mrs Jones and family.*

best[2] adverb
the superlative of **well**: *Jane is the best dressed person in the room.* | *The blue dress suits you best.* | *Which one do you like best?*

best[3] noun (no plural)
1 the best someone or something that is better than any other: *You're the best!* | *Which computer game is the best?*
2 do your best to try as hard as you can to succeed in something: *It doesn't matter if you didn't win – you did your best.*

best man /ˌbest 'mæn/ singular noun
a male friend who is chosen to help and support a man who is getting married: *Will you be best man at my wedding?* ⇨ compare BRIDESMAID

bet[1] /bet/ verb (present participle **betting**, past **bet**)
to risk money on the result of a future event: *He bet me $10 that his team would win.*

bet[2] noun
an agreement to risk money on the result of a future event: *Why not have a bet on one of the horses in the race?*

be·tray /bɪ'treɪ/ verb
to harm someone who trusts you: *I asked you not to tell anyone, but you betrayed me.*

bet·ter[1] /'betər/ adjective
1 the comparative of **good**: *This book is better than the other one.* | *He's trying to get better marks for his essays.*
2 not as ill as before: *I hope you're feeling better.*

better[2] adverb
1 the comparative of **well**: *He can sing better than me.* | *I like him better **than** his brother.*
2 better off with more money, or in a better position or job: *I'm better off now than I've ever been.*
3 had better used to tell someone that they should or should not do something: *You'd (=you had) better go home.* | *I'd (=I had) better not miss my train.*

be·tween /bɪ'twiːn/ adverb, preposition
1 (also **in between**) in the space in the middle of two people or things: *There is a fence between his garden and our garden.* ⇨ see picture on page 208
2 in the period before one time and after another: *The shop is open between 9 o'clock and 5 o'clock.* | *You shouldn't eat between meals.*
3 more than one number or amount but less than another number or amount: *The children are aged between five and ten.* | *The project will cost between 8 and 10 million dollars.*
4 joining two places: *The train goes between Cambridge and London.* | *flights between Paris and Geneva*

5 used when saying how things are shared or divided: *You and I can share the cost between us.* | *Between the three of them they managed to lift him into the ambulance.*

NOTE: Use **between** when you are talking about something that is done or shared by two people or things. Use **among** when you are talking about something that is done or shared by more than two people or things: *She divided the cake between the two children.* | *The money was divided among his brothers and sisters.*

be·ware /bɪˈweər/ *verb*
used to tell someone to be careful of something because it is dangerous: *Beware of the dog!* | *Please beware of signing anything without reading it carefully.*

be·yond /bɪˈjɒnd/ *adverb, preposition*
on or to the other side of something: *From here you can see beyond the mountains.*

bib /bɪb/ *noun*
a piece of material that is tied under a child's chin to keep its clothes clean when it is eating

Bi·ble /ˈbaɪbl/ *noun*
the religious book of Christianity

bib·li·cal /ˈbɪblɪkl/ *adjective*
from or in the Bible

bicycle

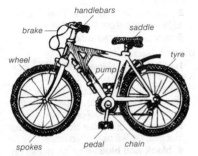

handlebars
brake
saddle
wheel
tyre
pump
spokes   pedal   chain

bi·cy·cle /ˈbaɪsɪkl/ *noun*
a vehicle with two wheels. You sit on it and move your legs to make it go forward: *I got a new bicycle for my birthday.* ⇨ same meaning BIKE, CYCLE ⇨ see picture on page 206

bid [1] /bɪd/ *verb* (*present participle* **bidding,** *past* **bid**)
to make an offer of money in order to buy something: *He bid £10,000 **for** the painting.*

bid [2] *noun*
an offer of an amount of money to buy something: *She made a bid of £700 **for** an antique table.*

big /bɪg/ *adjective*
1 large in size: *They live in a big house.* | *He is a big man.* ⇨ opposite LITTLE, SMALL
2 important, serious, or successful: *The song was a big hit.*

bike /baɪk/ *noun*
a vehicle with two wheels. You sit on it and move your legs to make it go forward: *Some kids were riding their bikes in the street.* ⇨ same meaning BICYCLE, CYCLE

bi·ki·ni /bɪˈkiːni/ *noun*
a piece of clothing in two parts which women and girls wear when they swim

bi·lin·gual /baɪˈlɪŋgwəl/ *adjective*
1 able to speak two languages equally well: *He's bilingual in French and German.*
2 spoken or written in two languages: *a bilingual dictionary*

bill /bɪl/ *noun*
1 a piece of paper showing the amount you must pay for something: *How much is the electricity bill?*
2 a plan for a new law: *The government is considering the new education bill.*
3 *American* a piece of paper money (*British* **note** or **bank note**)

bil·lion /ˈbɪljən/
the number 1,000,000,000,000 (=a million million), or, especially in America, 1,000,000,000 (=a thousand million)

bin /bɪn/ *noun*
a large container for storing things or putting waste in ⇨ compare DUSTBIN ⇨ see picture on page 205

bind /baɪnd/ *verb* (*past* **bound** /baʊnd/)
to tie someone or something with rope or string: *He bound her legs with rope.*

bin·go /ˈbɪŋgəʊ/ *noun* (*no plural*)
a game played with numbers in order to win prizes

A **B** C D E F G H I J K L M N O P Q R S T U V W X Y Z

bi·noc·u·lars binoculars
/bɪˈnɒkjʊləz/
plural noun
a pair of special
glasses that
make distant
things look
bigger: *He was
watching the
birds through
binoculars.*
⇨ compare
TELESCOPE

bi·og·ra·phy /baɪˈɒɡrəfɪ/ *noun (plural*
biographies)
the story of a person's life written by
someone else ⇨ compare AUTOBIOGRAPHY

bi·o·lo·gi·cal /ˌbaɪəˈlɒdʒɪkl/ *adjective*
related to biology

bi·ol·o·gist /baɪˈɒlədʒɪst/ *noun*
a person who studies biology

bi·ol·o·gy /baɪˈɒlədʒɪ/ *noun (no plural)*
the scientific study of living things

bird /bɜːd/ *noun*
an animal with wings and feathers that
produces eggs: *Most birds can fly.*

Bi·ro /ˈbaɪrəʊ/ *noun*
trademark a pen with a very small metal
ball at the end that rolls ink onto the
paper as you write ⇨ same meaning
BALLPOINT

birth /bɜːθ/ *noun*
1 give birth to have a baby: *She gave
birth **to** a baby boy last night.*
2 when a baby is born: *He wanted to
be there for the birth of his baby.* | *We
record the number of births and deaths
each year.*

birth con·trol /ˈbɜːθ kənˌtrəʊl/ *noun (no
plural)*
ways of limiting the number of children
you have

birth·day /ˈbɜːθdeɪ/ *noun*
the day of the year on which a person
was born: *My birthday is on January
6th.* ⇨ look at ANNIVERSARY

bis·cuit /ˈbɪskɪt/ *noun*
British a dry thin cake that is usually
sweet (*American* **cookie**): *a packet of
biscuits*

bish·op /ˈbɪʃəp/ *noun*
a priest who looks after the churches
and the people in a large area
⇨ compare VICAR

bit¹ /bɪt/
the past tense of the verb **bite**

bit² *noun*
1 a bit slightly: *I'm sorry I'm a bit late.* |
It's a bit too cold to go outside.
2 quite a bit a large amount: *He's
willing to pay quite a bit for the car.*
3 a small piece or amount: *Would you
like another bit **of** cake?* | *There were
tiny bits of glass on the floor.*
4 for a bit for a short time: *Why don't
you lie down for a bit?* | *Could you look
after the baby for a bit?*
5 bit by bit slowly: *Bit by bit they
discovered the truth.*

bite¹ /baɪt/ *verb (present participle*
biting /ˈbaɪtɪŋ/, *past* **bit** /bɪt/, *past
participle* **bitten** /ˈbɪtn/)
1 to cut something or wound someone, using the teeth: *I bit **into** the
apple.* | *Does your dog bite?*
2 if an insect bites you, it hurts you by
making a hole in your skin

bite² *noun*
1 when you bite something: *Do you
want a bite of my apple?*
2 a wound made when an animal or
insect bites you: *She was covered in
insect bites.*

bit·ten /ˈbɪtn/
the past participle of the verb **bite**

bit·ter /ˈbɪtəʳ/ *adjective*
1 angry: *We had a bitter argument.* |
*She's very bitter about the way she lost
her job.*
2 with a sharp sour taste: *I need some
sugar in my coffee; it's too bitter.*
3 very cold: *a bitter wind*

black¹ /blæk/ *adjective*
1 of the colour of the sky at night: *black
shoes* | *She had short black hair.*
2 belonging to a race of people with
dark-coloured skin: *Most of the
students in the school are black.*
3 black tea or coffee does not have
milk in it: *I'd like my coffee black.*
4 black and blue with dark marks on
your skin as a result of being hurt: *Her
arm was black and blue after the
accident.*
5 black and white containing only the
colours black, white, and grey: *an old
black and white film*

6 a black eye an eye surrounded by dark marks as a result of being hit: *He gave the other boy a black eye.*

black² *noun*
1 (*no plural*) the colour of the sky at night: *He was dressed in black.*
2 someone who belongs to a race of people with dark-coloured skin

black·ber·ry /'blækbərɪ/ *noun* (*plural* **blackberries**)
a small dark fruit that grows on bushes ⇨ see picture on page 199

black·bird /'blækbɜːd/ *noun*
a bird that is very common in Europe and America. The male is black and has a yellow beak

black·board /'blækbɔːd/ *noun*
a dark board on the wall at the front of a class that the teacher writes on: *She wrote the sums on the blackboard for all the children to see.* ⇨ see picture on page 205

black·cur·rant /'blæk-kʌrənt/ *noun*
a small round dark fruit that grows on bushes

black·smith /'blæk,smɪθ/ *noun*
someone who makes things out of iron, or who puts HORSESHOES on horses' feet

blade /bleɪd/ *noun*
1 the flat sharp part of anything that is used for cutting: *The blade of the knife needs to be sharp.*
2 a long flat leaf of grass

blame¹ /bleɪm/ *verb* (*present participle* **blaming**, *past* **blamed**)
1 to say that someone is the cause of something bad: *The policeman blamed the lorry for causing the accident.* I *Don't try to blame that on me.*

blame² *noun* (*no plural*)
when people say that you are responsible for something bad: *John always gets the blame for his brother's behaviour.*

blank /blæŋk/ *adjective*
1 a blank piece of paper, CASSETTE, etc has nothing written or recorded on it: *You will need a blank piece of paper for this.* I *Do you have a blank tape?*
2 not showing any expression: *She looked at him with a blank face.*

blank·et /'blæŋkɪt/ *noun*
a thick woollen cloth, used as a cover

on a bed to keep you warm ⇨ compare DUVET

blare /bleə^r/ *verb* (*present participle* **blaring**, *past* **blared**)
also **blare out** to make a loud and unpleasant noise: *The radio was blaring.* I *Music was blaring out of her car.*

blast¹ /blɑːst/ *noun*
1 an explosion: *Ten people were killed in the blast.*
2 a sudden strong movement of wind or air: *a blast of icy air*
3 a sudden very loud noise: *The driver gave a blast on his horn.*
4 full blast as loud as possible: *The television was on full blast.*

blast² *verb*
1 to break something by using an explosion: *They blasted away the rock.*
2 blast out to make a lot of loud noise: *I can't hear anything with that music blasting.*

blast-off /'blɑːst ɒf/ *noun*
the moment when a spaceship, etc leaves the ground: *Ten seconds to blast-off!*

blaze¹ /bleɪz/ *noun*
1 a very large strong fire: *The fire burned slowly at first, but soon became a blaze.* I *Fire fighters were looking for the cause of the blaze.*
2 a blaze of something a blaze of light, colour, etc is a very bright light or colour: *The flowers were a blaze of colour.*

blaze² *verb* (*present participle* **blazing**, *past* **blazed**)
to burn or shine strongly or brightly: *The fire was blazing through the house.* I *The house still blazed with lights though it was late at night.*

blaz·er /'bleɪzə^r/ *noun*
a short coat: *She was wearing her school blazer.*

bleach¹ /bliːtʃ/ *verb*
to make something white or lighter in colour: *Did you bleach this tablecloth?* I *Her hair was bleached by the sun.*

bleach² *noun* (*no plural*)
a liquid or powder used to make things clean or lighter in colour

bleak /bliːk/ *adjective*
1 a bleak situation seems very bad and

not likely to improve: *Without a job, Jim's future looks bleak.*
2 unpleasantly cold: *a bleak winter's day*

bleat¹ /bliːt/ *verb*
to make the sound made by a sheep or goat

bleat² *noun*
the sound made by a sheep or goat

bled /bled/
the past tense and past participle of the verb **bleed**

bleed /bliːd/ *verb (past **bled** /bled/)*
to lose blood: *The cut on his arm was bleeding again.*

blend¹ /blend/ *verb*
1 to mix things together: *Blend the sugar and eggs together.*
2 to look attractive or pleasant together: *The colours in the room blend nicely.*

blend² *noun*
a mixture of two or more things: *a blend of Brazilian and Columbian coffee*

blend·er /ˈblendəʳ/ *noun*
a small machine used for mixing foods or liquids together

bless /bles/ *verb*
1 to ask for God's protection for someone or something: *The priest blessed the new ship.*
2 Bless you! something you say to someone when they SNEEZE

blew /bluː/
the past tense of the verb **blow**

blind¹ /blaɪnd/ *adjective*
not able to see: *She was born blind. I He went blind when he was 74.*

blind² *noun*
a piece of material that you can pull down to cover a window ⇨ compare CURTAIN

blind·fold¹ /ˈblaɪndfəʊld/ *verb*
to cover someone's eyes with material so that they cannot see: *We must blindfold you before we take you to our leader.*

blindfold² *noun*
a piece of material used to cover someone's eyes so they cannot see

blink /blɪŋk/ *verb*
to shut and open your eyes quickly: *He blinked as he stepped out into the sunlight.* ⇨ compare WINK

blis·ter /ˈblɪstəʳ/ *noun*
a swelling under your skin, filled with liquid, usually caused by rubbing or burning: *My new shoes have given me blisters.*

blizzard

bliz·zard /ˈblɪzəd/ *noun*
a very bad storm with snow and strong winds ⇨ compare HURRICANE

blob /blɒb/ *noun*
a drop of thick liquid: *He left blobs of paint on the floor. I There was a blob of honey on the plate.*

block¹ /blɒk/ *noun*
1 a solid piece of wood, stone, etc: *The path was made from blocks of stone.*
2 a large building divided into separate homes or offices: *a block of flats I She worked in a big office block.*

block² *verb*
also **block up** to stop someone or something from moving through a place: *A truck was blocking the road. I Something is blocking the drain.*

blond /blɒnd/ *adjective*
another spelling of **blonde**

blonde¹ /blɒnd/ *noun*
blonde hair is light yellow

blonde² *noun*
a woman with light-coloured hair: *Jenny is a blonde.*

blood /blʌd/ *noun (no plural)*
the red liquid that flows through your body: *There was blood flowing from the wound on his leg.*

blood·y /ˈblʌdɪ/ (**bloodier, bloodiest**)
covered in blood or with blood flowing: *a bloody nose*

bloom¹ /bluːm/ *noun*
1 a flower
2 in full bloom having a lot of open flowers: *The roses are in full bloom.*

bloom² *verb*
to produce flowers or to open as flowers: *These trees bloom in the spring.*

blos·som /'blɒsəm/ noun (no plural)
the flowers on a tree: apple blossom

blot[1] /blɒt/
a dirty mark made by a drop of liquid: an ink blot

blot[2] verb (present participle **blotting**, past **blotted**)
to press paper or cloth onto a wet part to dry it: She blotted the drops of water with a tissue.

blouse /blaʊz/ noun
a shirt for women or girls

blow[1] /bləʊ/ verb
(past **blew** /bluː/, past participle **blown** /bləʊn/)
1 when the wind blows, it moves: The wind was blowing all night.
2 if the wind blows something, it moves it: The wind blew his hat off.

blow

blowing bubbles

3 to send out air through your mouth: She blew on her soup to cool it.
4 to send air into a musical instrument or whistle so that it makes a sound: The guard blew his whistle to call for help.
5 blow something out to stop a flame burning using a movement of air: Blow out the candles on your birthday cake!
6 blow something up (a) to fill something with air: Can you help me blow up the balloons? **(b)** to destroy something by making it explode: The bridge was blown up in the war.
7 blow your nose to push air out through your nose to clear it

blow[2] noun
1 a hard hit made with your hand, a tool, or a weapon: He received a blow on the head. I He hit the nail with three blows of the hammer.
2 an event that makes you unhappy or shocks you: The news of her death was a terrible blow to us all.

blown /bləʊn/
the past participle of the verb **blow**

blue /bluː/ adjective, noun
the colour of the sky when there are no clouds: a blue dress I She has blue eyes.

bluff /blʌf/ verb
to pretend that you know more about something than you really do: He says that he knows all about computers but I think he is bluffing.

blunt /blʌnt/ adjective
not sharp or not having a sharp enough point: This knife is too blunt to cut anything. I The pencils are all blunt and need sharpening. ⟡ see picture at SHARP

blush /blʌʃ/ verb
to become red in the face, usually because something embarrasses you: She blushes whenever he speaks to her.

board[1] /bɔːd/ noun
1 a flat surface used for a special purpose: Put this notice up on the board. I You play chess on a chess board. ⟡ see picture at CHESS
2 a group of people who run a company or organization: The school's board of governors are meeting today.
3 a long thin flat piece of wood
4 on board on a ship, plane, train, etc: Is everyone on board yet?

board[2] verb
1 to get on a ship, plane, train, bus, etc: Passengers should board the train now.
2 board something up to cover a window or door with boards

board·er /'bɔːdəʳ/ noun
a child who lives at school and goes home in the holidays

board·ing school /'bɔːdɪŋ ˌskuːl/ noun
a school where children live as well as study

boast /bəʊst/ verb
to talk too proudly about yourself: He boasted that he could run very fast.

boast·ful /'bəʊstfəl/ adjective
speaking too proudly about yourself: He's very boastful about his new car.

boat /bəʊt/ noun
a small open ship: He owns a fishing boat. I We're going to the island **by** boat.

bob /bɒb/ verb (present participle **bobbing**, past **bobbed**)
to move up and down on the surface of water: The small boat bobbed up and down on the lake.

bod·y /'bɒdɪ/ noun (plural **bodies**)

1 the whole of a person or animal: *He wants to have a strong healthy body.*

2 the central part of a person or animal, not the head, arms, or legs: *She has a short body and long legs.*

3 a dead person or animal: *The body was found in the woods.*

boil /bɔɪl/ verb

1 to make water or another liquid so hot that it produces steam: *Boil some water to make a cup of tea.*

2 to become very hot and produce steam: *The water began to boil.* | *Put the pasta into boiling water.*

3 to cook food in boiling water: *Boil the eggs for five minutes.*

bold /bəʊld/ adjective

not afraid to take risks: *He made a bold attempt to stop the thief.*

bolt[1] /bəʊlt/ noun

1 a piece of metal or wood used for keeping a door closed

2 a screw with no point that fastens into a NUT and holds two things together

bolt[2] verb

1 to fasten something with a bolt: *Bolt the door, please.*

2 to run away suddenly: *The horse bolted and threw its rider to the ground.*

bomb[1] /bɒm/ noun

a container full of a substance that will explode, used as a weapon: *They placed a bomb in the town's main railway station.* | *a nuclear bomb*

bomb[2] verb

to drop or leave bombs somewhere: *The airforce bombed the capital city.*

bone /bəʊn/ noun

one of the hard white parts inside a person's or an animal's body: *He fell and broke a bone in his leg.* ➪ see picture at SKELETON

bon·fire /'bɒnfaɪə^r/ noun

a fire made outdoors for burning waste or for fun

bon·net /'bɒnɪt/ noun

1 a soft hat that you tie under your chin

2 British the part of a car's body that covers the engine (American **hood**)

bon·y /'bəʊnɪ/ adjective

very thin so that you can see where a person's bones are: *bony fingers*

boo[1] /buː/ verb

to shout "boo" at someone, especially in a theatre, to show that you did not like their performance: *Some of the audience started booing.*

boo[2]

something you say loudly when you want to surprise someone who does not know you are there

book[1] /bʊk/ noun

1 a set of printed pages fastened together so that you can read them: *What book are you reading?* | *I'm reading a book by Charles Dickens.* ➪ see picture on page 197

2 a set of sheets of paper fastened together for writing on: *an address book* | *I have a book that I write poems in.*

book[2] verb

to arrange to have something that you want to use later: *I've booked tickets for tomorrow night's show.* | *She's booked us three nights in a hotel.*

book·case /'bʊk-keɪs/ noun

a piece of furniture with shelves for books

book·shop /'bʊkʃɒp/ noun

a shop that sells books ➪ see picture on page 201

book to·ken /'bʊk ˌtəʊkən/ noun

a card that is given to you as a present so that you can buy books with it: *My uncle gave me a £10 book token for my birthday.*

boom /buːm/ noun

a loud deep sound: *We could hear the boom of the guns.*

boot /buːt/ noun

1 a shoe that covers your foot and the bottom of your leg ➪ see picture on page 203

2 British the back part of a car's body where bags, boxes, etc can be carried (American **trunk**)

booth /buːð/ noun

a small place where one person can do something: *a phone booth*

bord·er /'bɔːdə^r/ noun

1 the dividing line between two countries: *the border between India and Pakistan*

2 an edge: *white plates with a blue border*

bore[1] /bɔː^r/ verb (present participle **boring** past **bored**)

1 to make someone feel bored: *He*

bored me all evening with his holiday photos.

2 to make a deep round hole in something, especially rock or stone: *This machine can bore **through** solid rock.*

bore² *noun*

someone who is boring: *He's such a bore!*

bore³

the past tense of the verb **bear**

bored /bɔːd/ *adjective*

not interested: *She was bored **with** her job.* ⇨ compare FED UP ⇨ look at BORING

bor·ing /'bɔːrɪŋ/ *adjective*

not interesting in any way: *a boring film | This book's so boring, I don't think I'll ever get to the end of it.*

NOTE: Do not confuse the adjectives **boring** and **bored**. If something is **boring**, it is not interesting, e.g. *a boring lesson.* **Bored** is used to describe the way you feel when something is boring: *The children were bored with the game and did not want to play any more.*

born /bɔːn/ *adjective*

be born to come into the world as a baby: *Her baby was born yesterday.*

borne /bɔːn/

the past participle of the verb **bear**

bor·row /'bɒrəʊ/ *verb*

to use something that belongs to someone else, usually after asking permission: *Can I borrow your bicycle until Saturday?*

NOTE: Compare the verbs **borrow** and **lend**. If you lend something to a person you let them use it for a while. If you borrow something from someone you take it from them, knowing that you will give it back to them later. *Can you lend me some money? | Can I borrow some money? | I lent that book to Jane. | Jane borrowed that book from me.*

boss¹ /bɒs/ *noun* (*plural* **bosses**)

a person who is responsible for other people at work and tells them what to do: *She asked her boss if she could have two days away from work.*

boss² *verb*

boss someone about to tell someone what to do, usually giving them too many orders: *My brother's always bossing me about.*

boss·y /'bɒsɪ/ *adjective*

liking to give orders to other people: *My older sister's really bossy.*

bot·a·ny /'bɒtənɪ/ *noun* (*no plural*)

the scientific study of plants

both /bəʊθ/

used to talk about two people or things together: *Hold the dish with both hands. | We both like dancing. | Both **of** my grandfathers were farmers.*

both·er¹ /'bɒðəʳ/ *verb*

1 to interrupt someone and annoy them: *I'm sorry to bother you but I need some help. | Don't bother your father now; he's very busy.*

2 to worry someone: *I always know when something is bothering him. | Mandy hates walking home alone at night, but it doesn't bother me.*

3 **not bother** not to make the effort to do something: *Don't bother to dry the plates. | He didn't even bother to say goodbye.*

4 **can't be bothered** to not want to do something because it is too much effort: *I can't be bothered to go out tonight.*

both·er² *noun* (*no plural*)

something that causes difficulty: *It's an old car but it's never caused me any bother.*

bot·tle¹ /'bɒtl/ *noun*

a tall round glass or plastic container, with a narrow neck: *a bottle **of** wine* ⇨ compare JAR ⇨ see picture at CONTAINER

bot·tle² *verb*

to put something into bottles: *This is where they bottle the water.*

bottle banks

bottle bank /'bɒtl bæŋk/ *noun*

a place where old glass bottles are

taken so that the glass can be used again

bot·tom /'bɒtəm/ *noun*

1 the lowest part of something: *Look at the diagram at the bottom **of** the page.* | *Go downstairs and wait for me at the bottom.*

2 the base of something: *The price is on the bottom **of** the box.* | *What's that on the bottom of your shoe?*

3 the lowest position in something, for example, a class: *He's not very good at maths – he's always at the bottom **of** the class.* | *The team is at the bottom of the league.* ⟡ opposite TOP

4 the part of your body that you sit on: *He fell on his bottom.*

bought /bɔːt/

the past tense and past participle of the verb **buy**

boul·der /'bəʊldər/ *noun*

a large rock

The ball bounced straight into the hole.

bounce /baʊns/ *verb* (*present participle* **bouncing**, *past* **bounced**)

1 to hit a surface and then move away from it, or to make an object do this: *The ball bounced twice.* | *He bounced the ball against the wall.*

2 to jump up and down on a soft surface: *The baby was bouncing on the bed.*

bound¹ /baʊnd/ *verb*

be bound to do something to be definitely going to do something: *You are bound to pass the exams – you've worked very hard.* | *Madeleine is such a nice girl, she's bound to make friends.*

bound² *verb*

to jump with a lot of energy: *The children came bounding down the stairs.*

bound³ *noun*

a big jump

bound⁴

the past tense and past participle of the verb **bind**

bound·a·ry /'baʊndəri/ *noun* (*plural* **boundaries**)

the dividing line between two places: *A wall marks the boundary **between** the two gardens.* ⟡ compare BORDER

bow¹ /baʊ/ *verb*

to bend the top part of your body forward to show respect: *Everyone bowed to the Queen.*

bow² *noun*

the action of bowing to someone

bows

bow³ /bəʊ/ *noun*

1 a piece of wood held in a curve by a string, used for shooting arrows

2 a long thin piece of wood with tight strings fastened along it, used for playing musical instruments like the VIOLIN

3 a knot used for tying shoelaces or a RIBBON: *She tied the ribbon in a bow.*

bowl /bəʊl/ *noun*

a deep round dish or container: *Fill the bowl with water.* | *I ate a bowl **of** ice cream.*

box¹ /bɒks/ *noun*

a container with straight sides: *He gave me a box **of** chocolates.* | *a cardboard box* ⟡ see picture at CONTAINER

box² *verb*

to fight someone by hitting them, as a sport

box·er /'bɒksər/ *noun*

someone who boxes for sport

box·ing /'bɒksɪŋ/ noun (no plural)
the sport of fighting by hitting someone

box of·fice /'bɒks ˌɒfɪs/ noun
a place in a theatre or cinema where you can buy tickets

boy /bɔɪ/ noun
a male child: *They have five children: three boys and two girls.* | *The boys all wanted to play football.*

boy·friend /'bɔɪfrend/ noun
a boy or man that you have a romantic relationship with: *Can my boyfriend come to the party?*

bra /brɑː/ noun
a piece of clothing that a woman wears under other clothes to support her BREASTS

brace /breɪs/ noun
a wire that some children wear inside their mouths to make their teeth straight

brace·let /'breɪslɪt/ noun
a piece of jewellery that you wear around your wrist ⇨ see picture at JEWELLERY

brac·es /'breɪsɪz/ plural noun
cloth bands that you wear over your shoulders to hold up your trousers

brack·et /'brækɪt/ noun
one of the signs ( ) put around words to show that the rest of the writing can be understood without these words: *Last year's figures are given in brackets.*

brag /bræg/ verb (present participle **bragging**, past **bragged**)
to talk too proudly about things you own or have done: *He bragged that he had passed the exam easily.* | *He was bragging about his new bicycle.* ⇨ same meaning BOAST

brain /breɪn/ noun
the part inside your head that controls how you think, feel, and move

brain·y /'breɪnɪ/ adjective (**brainier**, **brainiest**)
clever and quick at doing school work: *She's the brainiest girl in the class.* ⇨ same meaning BRIGHT

brake[1] /breɪk/ noun
the part of a bicycle, car, train, etc that you use to stop it: *Test your brakes regularly to make sure they are working.* ⇨ see picture at BICYCLE

brake[2] verb (present participle **braking**, past **braked**)
to make a bicycle, car, train, etc stop or go more slowly by using the brake: *The driver braked quickly to avoid an accident.*

branch /brɑːntʃ/ noun
1 a part of a tree that grows out from the TRUNK ⇨ compare TWIG ⇨ see picture at TREE
2 one part of an organization, a subject of study, or a family group: *The bank has branches all over the country.* | *Which branch of science are you studying?*

brand /brænd/ noun
the name of a particular kind of goods made by one company: *What brand of soap do you use?*

brand-new /ˌbrænd 'njuː/ adjective
new and not used before: *He won a brand-new car in the competition.*

bran·dy /'brændɪ/ noun (no plural)
a strong alcoholic drink made from wine

brass /brɑːs/ noun (no plural)
a very hard yellow metal that shines brightly, made by mixing COPPER and ZINC: *a wooden chest with brass handles*

brave /breɪv/ (**braver**, **bravest**) adjective
not afraid or not showing fear: *The soldiers were brave during the fighting.*

brav·e·ry /'breɪvərɪ/ noun (no plural)
willingness to do dangerous things without feeling afraid: *The fireman was praised for his bravery.* ⇨ same meaning COURAGE

brave·ly /'breɪvlɪ/ adverb
in a brave way: *They fought bravely.*

bread /bred/ noun (no plural)
a food made by mixing flour and water and then baking it: *a loaf of bread* | *a slice of bread*

breadth /bredθ/ noun (no plural)
the distance from one side of something to the other: *What's the breadth of this river?* | *The ship measured 20 metres in breadth.*

A B C D E F G H I J K L M N O P Q R S T U V W X Y Z

bread

loaf

roll

break[1] /breɪk/ *verb* (*past* **broke** /brəʊk/, *past participle* **broken** /'brəʊkən/)

1 to make something into separate pieces: *He broke the window with his football. I She broke the piece of bread in two and handed one piece to me.*

2 to separate into pieces: *The plate fell on the floor and broke. I Be careful with that bowl – it'll break if you drop it.*

3 to damage something so that it does not work: *Don't play with the radio – you'll break it! I We don't buy him expensive toys because he breaks them.*

4 **break down** if a large machine breaks down, it stops working: *My car broke down on the way to work.*

5 **break in** to get inside a place using force: *Someone broke in through the window and took the TV and the video.*

6 **break into something** to get inside a place or object that is locked, by using force: *Someone broke into my drawer and stole my money.*

7 **break the law** to do something that the law says you must not do

8 **break out** if something such as a fire or war breaks out, it starts suddenly: *The fire broke out at two o'clock in the morning.*

9 **break a promise** if you break a promise, you do not do something that you promised you would do

10 **break up (a)** to finish a romantic relationship with someone: *John and Sarah broke up last week. I Did you hear that Hilary had broken up* **with** *Simon?* **(b)** to stop going to school because the holidays are starting: *We break up next week.*

break[2] *noun*

1 a short period when you stop working: *I'm tired. Let's have a break.*

2 a space in the middle of something: *a break in the clouds*

break·down /'breɪkdaʊn/ *noun*

1 when a relationship or system fails: *Gail blames me for the breakdown of our marriage.*

2 an occasion when a car stops working

break·fast /'brekfəst/ *noun*
the first meal of the day

breast /brest/ *noun*

1 one of the two parts on the front of a woman's body that can give milk

2 the front of a bird's body or the meat from that part

breast·stroke /'brest,strəʊk/ *noun* (*no plural*)
a way of swimming by pulling the water back with your arms

breath /breθ/ *noun*

1 the air that you take in and let out through your nose and mouth: *He took a deep breath and jumped into the water.*

2 **be out of breath** to have difficulty breathing for a while because you have been running or exercising

3 **hold your breath** to deliberately stop breathing for a short time: *How long can you hold your breath?*

4 **a breath of fresh air** some clean air outside: *Let's go to the park for a breath of fresh air.*

breathe /briːð/ *verb* (*present participle* **breathing**, *past* **breathed**)
to take air into your body and let it out through your nose and mouth: *Is he still breathing?*

breath·less /'breθləs/ *adjective*
having difficulty breathing, especially after exercise: *After the long climb, Jan felt breathless.*

bred /bred/
the past tense and past participle of the verb **breed**

breed[1] /briːd/ *verb* (*past* **bred** /bred/)

1 if animals breed, they have babies: *Rats can breed every six weeks.*

2 to keep animals so that they will have babies: *He breeds cattle and horses.*

breed [2] *noun*
a type of animal: *What breed is your dog?*

breeze /briːz/ *noun*
a light wind: *There was a cool breeze.*

brew /bruː/ *verb*
1 be brewing if something bad is brewing, it will happen soon: *I think a storm is brewing.* | *There's trouble brewing.*
2 to make beer: *The new company is brewing excellent beer.*
3 to make a drink of tea or coffee

bribe [1] /braɪb/ *verb (present participle* **bribing**, *past* **bribed**)
to give someone money or a present, as a way of persuading them to do something: *He bribed another boy to lie about what had happened.*

bribe [2] *noun*
money or a present that you give to someone to bribe them: *He was accused of accepting bribes.*

brick /brɪk/ *noun*
a block of baked clay, used for building: *a brick wall*

bride /braɪd/ *noun*
a woman who is getting married ⇨ compare GROOM

bride·groom /ˈbraɪdgruːm/ *noun*
a man who is getting married ⇨ same meaning GROOM

brides·maid /ˈbraɪdzˌmeɪd/ *noun*
a girl or woman who helps a BRIDE at her wedding ⇨ compare BEST MAN

bridge

bridge /brɪdʒ/ *noun*
a road or railway line built over something: *A new bridge is being built across the river.*

bri·dle /ˈbraɪdl/ *noun*
bands of leather put on a horse's head to control its movements

brief /briːf/ *adjective*
1 continuing only for a short time: *The meeting was brief.* | *a brief visit*
2 using only a few words: *He gave a brief description of the man.*

brief·case /ˈbriːfkeɪs/ *noun*
a thin flat case for carrying documents or books ⇨ compare SUITCASE

bright /braɪt/ *adjective*
1 sending out a strong shining light: *bright sunlight* | *bright lights*
2 with a strong clear colour: *a bright yellow dress*
3 very clever: *Susan is a very bright child.*

bright·en /ˈbraɪtn/ *verb*
also **brighten up** to become brighter or more pleasant: *The weather should brighten up later.*

bril·liant /ˈbrɪljənt/ *adjective*
1 very clever: *What a brilliant idea!* | *He is a brilliant scientist.*
2 brilliant light or colour is very bright and strong: *Mary had brilliant green eyes.*
3 used to say that you like or enjoy something very much: *"Did you like the film?" "It was brilliant."*

brim /brɪm/ *noun*
1 the bottom part of a hat, that sticks out
2 full to the brim as full as possible: *The glass was full to the brim.*

bring /brɪŋ/ *verb (past* **brought** /brɔːt/*)*
1 to take something or someone with you to a place: *I brought these pictures to show you.* | *You can take that book home, but bring it back to school tomorrow.* | *Can I bring my friend to the party?* ⇨ look at FETCH
2 to cause something to happen: *Tourism brings a lot of money to the area.*
3 bring someone up to care for a child and teach him or her good behaviour: *She brought up three children by herself.*

brisk /brɪsk/ *adjective*
quick and active: *I went for a brisk walk this morning.* ⇨ opposite SLOW

Brit·ish [1] /ˈbrɪtɪʃ/ *adjective*
relating to or coming from Great Britain

British [2] *noun*
the British the people of Great Britain

brit·tle /ˈbrɪtl/ *adjective*
hard, but easily broken: *brittle glass*

broad /brɔːd/ *adjective*
wide: *He was six feet tall with broad shoulders.* | *The track was six metres broad.* ⇨ opposite NARROW

broad·cast¹ /'brɔːdkɑːst/ *verb (past broadcast)*
to send out a radio or television programme: *BBC1 will broadcast the game at seven o'clock.*

broadcast² *noun*
a radio or television programme: *a news broadcast*

broke /brəʊk/
the past tense of the verb **break**

bro·ken¹ /'brəʊkən/
the past participle of the verb **break**

broken

chipped   cracked

broken

broken² *adjective*
1 in pieces: *Can you glue together this broken plate?*
2 not working: *My watch is broken.*

bronze /brɒnz/ *noun (no plural)*
a hard metal, made by mixing COPPER and TIN

brooch /brəʊtʃ/ *noun (plural brooches)*
a piece of jewellery that a woman can put on her clothes ⇨ compare BADGE

broom /bruːm/ *noun*
a brush with a long handle

broth·er /'brʌðər/ *noun*
someone's brother is a boy or man with the same parents as them: *Peter is my brother.* ⇨ compare SISTER

brother-in-law /'brʌðər ɪn lɔː/ *noun (plural brothers-in-law)*
1 the brother of your wife or husband
2 the husband of your sister

brought /brɔːt/
the past tense and past participle of the verb **bring**

brown /braʊn/ *adjective, noun*
a dark colour like coffee, wood, or earth: *brown shoes* | *She had brown eyes.*

bruise¹ /bruːz/ *noun*
a mark left on your skin after something has hit you or you have fallen down: *He had a nasty bruise on his arm.*

bruise² *verb (present participle bruising, past bruised)*
to cause a bruise on someone's skin: *She fell and bruised her knee.*

brushes

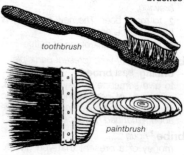

toothbrush

paintbrush

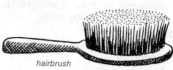

hairbrush

brush¹ /brʌʃ/ *noun (plural brushes)*
an object with strong hairs on the end of a handle that can be used for cleaning, painting, tidying your hair, etc ⇨ see picture on page 204

brush² *verb*
to clean or tidy something with a brush: *Have you brushed your hair?* | *He's brushing his teeth.*

bub·ble¹ /'bʌbl/ *noun*
a ball of air in a liquid: *soap bubbles* ⇨ see picture at BLOW¹

bubble² *verb*
to make bubbles: *The water was bubbling gently in the pan.*

buck /bʌk/ *noun*
a male DEER or rabbit

buck·et /'bʌkɪt/ *noun*
a container made of metal or plastic, with a handle, for holding or carrying water: *a bucket of water*

buck·le /'bʌkl/ *noun*
a metal object used to fasten a belt or shoe ⇨ see picture at FASTENER

bud /bʌd/ noun
a young flower or leaf before it opens
⇨ see picture at ROSE

Bud·dhis·m /'bʊdɪzəm/ noun (no plural)
the religion based on the teachings of Buddha

Bud·dhist /'bʊdɪst/ noun
a person who follows the teachings of Buddha

budge /bʌdʒ/ verb (present participle **budging**, past **budged**)
to move or make something move from one place to another: Mark hasn't budged from his room all morning.

bud·get [1] /'bʌdʒɪt/ noun
to plan how much money you can spend on different things: We have a budget of $1.5 million for the building.

budget [2] verb
to plan how much money you have to spend on certain things: The school has budgeted **for** more books.

bug /bʌg/ noun
1 a small insect
2 an illness that you can catch from other people but is not usually very serious: I can't go to school this week because I've got a bug.
3 a fault in a computer program

bu·gle /'bjuːgl/ noun
a musical instrument that is played by blowing and is used especially by the army

build /bɪld/ verb (past **built** /bɪlt/)
to make a building or large structure, for example a house, bridge, or ship: They're building a lot of new houses in the area.

build·er /'bɪldər/ noun
a person whose job it is to make houses and other buildings ⇨ see picture on page 200

build·ing /'bɪldɪŋ/ noun
something with a roof and walls such as a house or an office: The park is surrounded by tall buildings.

built /bɪlt/
the past tense and past participle of the verb **build**

bulb /bʌlb/ noun
also **light bulb** the glass part of an electric light, which the light shines from

bulge [1] /bʌldʒ/ verb (present participle **bulging**, past **bulged**)
to stick out or to look very full: His pocket was bulging with sweets.

bulge [2] noun
a place where something is bulging

bulk /bʌlk/ noun
the bulk of something the main or largest part of something: The bulk of the work has already been done.

bulk·y /'bʌlki/ adjective (**bulkier**, **bulkiest**)
big and difficult to move: The box was too bulky to carry.

bull /bʊl/ noun
the male of the cow family

bull·dog /'bʊldɒg/ noun
a strong dog with a thick neck and short legs

bull·doz·er /'bʊldəʊzər/ noun
a powerful machine that moves earth and rocks

bul·let /'bʊlɪt/ noun
a piece of metal that is fired from a gun: He fired three bullets.

bul·ly [1] /'bʊli/ noun (plural **bullies**)
a person who hurts weaker people or makes them afraid

bully [2] verb
to hurt weaker people or make them afraid: My little sister is being bullied at school.

bump [1] /bʌmp/ verb
1 to hit or knock something by accident: I bumped my knee on the chair. I He bumped **into** a tree and hit his head.
2 **bump into someone** to meet someone by chance: I bumped into John in town.

bump [2] noun
a round swelling on your body where you have hit it on something: He had a bump on his head.

bump·er /'bʌmpər/ noun
a bar at the front and back of a car that protects the car if it hits anything

bump·y /'bʌmpi/ adjective
rough, not smooth: a bumpy road

bun /bʌn/ noun
a small round sweet cake

bunch /bʌntʃ/ noun
several things of the same kind fastened, held, or growing together: a bunch **of** flowers I I bought a bunch of grapes.

bun·dle /'bʌndl/ *noun*
a number of things held together so that you can carry them or put them somewhere: *a bundle of newspapers*

bun·ga·low /'bʌŋgələʊ/ *noun*
a house that is all on the same level as the ground

bunk /bʌŋk/ *noun*
a narrow bed that is fixed to the wall on a ship or train

bunk bed /'bʌŋk bed/ *noun*
one of two beds that are put one on top of another and used especially for children to sleep in ⇨ see picture at BED

buoy /bɔɪ/ *noun*
a floating object used to show ships where there are rocks

bur·den /'bɜːdn/ *noun*
something difficult or worrying that you are responsible for: *She doesn't want to be a burden on her children when she's old.*

burg·er /'bɜːgə^r/ *noun*
meat that has been cut into very small pieces and then made into a round flat shape before being cooked: *We'll both have burgers and chips please.*

bur·glar /'bɜːglə^r/ *noun*
a person who enters buildings, usually by force, to steal things ⇨ compare ROBBER, THIEF ⇨ see pictures at ALARM and BURGLARY

bur·glar·y
/'bɜːglərɪ/
noun (plural
burglaries)
the crime of
entering a building
by force and
stealing things

bur·i·al /'berɪəl/
noun
a ceremony at
which a dead
person is put into
the ground ⇨ compare FUNERAL

burglary

burglar

burn[1] /bɜːn/ *verb (past* **burned** /bɜːnd/
or **burnt** /bɜːnt/)
1 to damage something or hurt someone with fire or heat: *We cut down the old tree and burned it.* | *I've burnt my fingers.*
2 to produce heat and flames: *Is the fire still burning?*

3 **burn down** if a building burns down, it is completely destroyed by fire: *The cinema burnt down last year.*

burn[2] *noun*
a wound or mark on your body caused by fire or by touching something very hot: *He has a burn on his arm.* | *People caught in the flames had severe burns.*

burnt /bɜːnt/
a past tense and past participle of the verb **burn**

bur·row /'bʌrəʊ/ *noun*
a hole in the ground made as a home by a small animal such as a rabbit

burst /bɜːst/ *verb (past* **burst**)
1 to break open because of too much pressure inside: *The bag will burst if you put any more things in it.* | *She accidentally burst one of the balloons.*
2 **be bursting** to be very full or too full of something: *In the summer the town's always bursting* **with** *tourists.*
3 **burst into tears** to start crying suddenly
4 **burst out laughing** to start laughing loudly and suddenly: *The joke was so funny she burst out laughing.*

bur·y /'berɪ/ *verb (present participle*
burying, *past* **buried**)
1 to put a dead person into the ground
2 to cover something with earth or with other things so that it is hidden: *The dog buried the bone.* | *Dad's glasses were buried under a pile of newspapers.*

bus /bʌs/ *noun (plural* **buses**)
a large vehicle that takes people from one place to another: *Let's go* **on** *the bus.* | *You can go* **by** *bus.* ⇨ see picture on page 206

bush /bʊʃ/ *noun*
a plant like a small tree

bus·i·ly /'bɪzɪlɪ/ *adverb*
done with a lot of activity and interest: *The children ran about busily.*

busi·ness /'bɪznɪs/ *noun*
1 *(plural* **businesses**) a company that provides a service or sells things to earn money: *He has a furniture business in the town.*
2 *(no plural)* making, buying, and selling things: *Business is good this year* (=we are earning a lot of money). | *We do a lot of business with companies in Rome.*

3 mind your own business a rude way of telling someone that you are not going to answer their questions: *"Who are you going to the party with?" "Mind your own business."*

4 none of your business a rude way of telling someone that something is private and not for them to know: *It's none of your business how she spends her money.*

busi·ness·man /'bɪznɪsmən/ *noun* (*plural* **businessmen** /-mən/)
a man who works in business, especially one who owns a company or helps to run it

busi·ness·wom·an /'bɪznɪswʊmən/ *noun* (*plural* **businesswomen** /-wɪmɪn/)
a woman who works in business, especially one who owns a company or helps to run it

bus stop /'bʌs stɒp/ *noun*
a place where buses stop for people to get off and on

bus·y /'bɪzɪ/ *adjective*
1 working or doing something so you cannot do other things: *He is busy now but he could see you this afternoon.* I *She's busy writing letters.*
2 full of people, vehicles, etc: *a busy airport* I *The roads were very busy this morning.*

but /bət; *strong* bʌt/
a word you use when you are saying that although one thing is true, another thing is opposite to it is also true: *They are poor, but happy.* I *I'd like to come but I can't.* I *Mum likes apricots but Dad hates them.*

butch·er /'bʊtʃər/ *noun*
1 a person who sells meat
2 **butcher's** *British* a shop that sells meat

but·ter /'bʌtər/ *noun* (*no plural*)
yellow fat made from milk: *a piece of bread and butter* I *Cook the onions in some butter.*

but·ter·fly /'bʌtəflaɪ/ *noun* (*plural* **butterflies**)
an insect that has delicate wings with bright colours on them ⇨ compare MOTH

but·tock /'bʌtək/ *noun*
one of the two soft round parts of your bottom

but·ton /'bʌtn/ *noun*
1 a small round object that you push through a hole to fasten clothes: *I lost a button from my shirt.* ⇨ see picture at FASTENER
2 a round object that you push to start or stop a machine: *Press the 'on' button to make it work.*

but·ton·hole /'bʌtnhəʊl/ *noun*
the hole that a button goes through

buy /baɪ/ *verb* (*past* **bought** /bɔːt/)
to get something by paying money for it: *I bought a new radio.* I *Have you bought Bobby a birthday present yet?* ⇨ compare SELL

buzz /bʌz/ *verb*
1 to make a low steady noise like the sound that a BEE makes: *The machine made a loud buzzing noise.*
2 **buzz off** a rude way of telling someone to go away: *Buzz off and leave me alone!*

by[1] /baɪ/ *preposition*
1 used to show who or what does something: *The house was damaged by fire.* I *A story by a famous writer*
2 near or beside something: *He was standing by the window.* I *Jane went and sat by Patrick.* ⇨ see picture on page 208
3 up to and past someone or something: *He walked by me without saying hello.* ⇨ same meaning PAST
4 holding, using, or doing a particular thing: *He held the hammer by the handle.* I *I earned some money by delivering newspapers.* I *Are you going by car?*
5 no later than a particular time: *Can you do it by tomorrow?*

by[2] *adverb*
up to and beyond someone or something: *I sat and watched people go by.* I *Many cars drove by.* ⇨ same meaning PAST

bye /baɪ/
also **bye-bye** a word you say when you leave someone or when they leave you ⇨ same meaning GOODBYE

butterfly

Cc

C, c /siː/
the third letter of the English alphabet

cab /kæb/ *noun*
a car with a driver who will take you somewhere if you pay ⇨ same meaning TAXI

cab·bage /ˈkæbɪdʒ/ *noun*
a large round vegetable with thick green leaves ⇨ see picture on page 199

cab·in /ˈkæbɪn/ *noun*
1 a room on a ship or plane
2 a small house made of wood ⇨ see picture on page 193

cab·i·net /ˈkæbɪnət/ *noun*
1 a piece of furniture with shelves or drawers: *a medicine cabinet*
2 **the Cabinet** a small group of people in a government who make decisions and give advice to the leader

ca·ble /ˈkeɪbl/ *noun*
1 a thick rope, usually made of metal
2 a tube containing wires that carry electricity, telephone calls, or television programmes
3 (*no plural*) a system of broadcasting television through cables

cac·tus /ˈkæktəs/ *noun* (*plural* **cacti** /ˈkæktaɪ/ or **cactuses**)
a plant with sharp points and a thick stem that grows in hot dry places

caf·e /ˈkæfeɪ/ *noun*
a place where you can buy drinks and simple meals ⇨ compare RESTAURANT

cage /keɪdʒ/ *noun*
a box with metal bars in which birds or animals can be kept

cake /keɪk/ *noun*
a sweet cooked food made of flour, sugar, fat, and eggs: *Mum baked me a cake for my birthday.* ⇨ see picture at PIECE

cal·cu·late /ˈkælkjʊleɪt/ *verb* (*present participle* **calculating**, *past* **calculated**)
to use numbers to find the answer to a sum: *Have you calculated the cost of the journey?* | *I'm trying to calculate how much paint we will need to decorate the kitchen.*

cal·cu·la·tion /ˌkælkjʊˈleɪʃn/ *noun*
when you add numbers, divide numbers, etc to find the answer to a sum

cal·cu·la·tor /ˈkælkjʊleɪtər/ *noun*
a small machine that you use to add numbers, divide numbers, etc ⇨ see picture on page 205

cal·en·dar /ˈkæləndər/ *noun*
a series of pages that show the days, weeks, and months of the year

calf /kɑːf/ *noun* (*plural* **calves** /kɑːvz/)
1 a young cow
2 the back of your leg between your knee and your foot

call¹ /kɔːl/ *verb*
1 to give someone a name: *They called their baby John.* | *Her name is Elizabeth but we call her Liz.*
2 to telephone someone: *I called my sister today.* | *He said he'd call me tomorrow.*
3 to ask someone to come to you: *Mother called the doctor.* | *The teacher called me into her room.*
4 also **call out** to shout: *"I'm coming!" Paula called down the stairs.* | *I heard his voice calling out my name.*
5 **call someone back** to telephone someone who tried to telephone you earlier: *John phoned and asked if you could call him back.*
6 **call on someone** to visit someone: *He called on me last Tuesday.*

call² *noun*
1 when you talk to someone on the telephone: *There's a call for you, Mr Brown.*
2 a shout: *I heard a call for help.*
3 a short visit: *She had a call from the doctor.*

calm /kɑːm/ *adjective*
quiet and peaceful: *The sea was calm after the storm.* | *He was calm when I told him the bad news.*

calm·ly /ˈkɑːmlɪ/ *adverb*
in a quiet and peaceful way: *He sat down calmly.*

calves /kɑːvz/
the plural of **calf**

cam·cor·der camcorder
/'kæmkɔːdəʳ/
noun
a machine that
you use to record
VIDEO films

came /keɪm/
the past tense of
the verb **come**

cam·el /'kæml/
noun
a large animal
with one or two HUMPS on its back, used
to carry things and people in deserts
⇨ see picture on page 195

cam·era camera
/'kæmrə/ *noun*
a piece of
equipment for
taking
photographs

camp[1] /kæmp/
noun
a place with tents
where people live
for a short time

camp[2] *verb*
to live in a tent for a short time

cam·paign /kæm'peɪn/ *noun*
a series of planned actions done to get
a result, especially in business or
politics: *There is a new campaign to
stop people smoking.* I *an election
campaign*

camp·ing /'kæmpɪŋ/ *noun (no plural)*
living in a tent for a short time, especially
when you are on holiday: *Do you want
to **go** camping this weekend?*

camp·site /'kæmpsaɪt/ *noun*
a large field where people can stay in
tents to have a holiday

can[1] /kən; *strong* kæn/ *verb*
to be able to do something: *"Can she
swim?" "Yes she can."* I *Jesse can
speak French fluently.* I *You can go
out when you have finished your
homework.*

can[2] /kæn/ *noun*
a container made of metal: *a can of
soup* ⇨ compare BOX ⇨ see picture at
CONTAINER

ca·nal /kə'næl/ *noun*
a long narrow channel that was built for
ships to travel along

ca·nar·y /kə'neərɪ/ *noun (plural
canaries)*
a small yellow bird that sings

can·cel /'kænsəl/ *verb (present
participle* **cancelling**, *past* **cancelled**)
to stop an event from happening: *We
had to cancel the match, because so
many people were ill.*

can·cer /'kænsəʳ/ *noun*
a serious illness in which bad CELLS
grow in the body

can·di·date /'kændɪdət/ *noun*
1 a person who hopes to be picked for
a job or position: *Sarah would be a
good candidate **for** the job.*
2 a person who takes an examination

can·dle /'kændl/ *noun*
an object with string in the middle, that
you burn to give light

can·dy /'kændɪ/ *noun (plural* **candies**)
American a sweet food made of sugar
or chocolate, or a piece of this (*British*
sweet)

cane /keɪn/ *noun*
a long thin stick that someone uses to
help them walk

can·non /'kænən/ *noun*
a large gun, usually on wheels

can·not /'kænət, 'kænɒt/
to be unable to do something: *I cannot
understand why she is so angry.* I *I
cannot accept your offer.*

ca·noe /kə'nuː/ *noun*
a narrow light boat for one or two people
⇨ see pictures on pages 193 and 206

can't /kɑːnt/
cannot: *I'm sorry I can't come to your
house tomorrow.* I *He can't understand
your question.*

can·teen /kæn'tiːn/ *noun*
a place where people in a factory,
school, or office can eat meals

can·vas /'kænvəs/ *noun (no plural)*
strong cloth used to make tents, bags,
etc

cap /kæp/ *noun*
1 a soft hat ⇨ see pictures at HAT and
on page 203
2 a cover for the end of a bottle or tube

ca·pa·ble /'keɪpəbl/ *adjective*
1 **capable of something** able to do
something: *I know he isn't capable of
murder.*

A
B
C
D
E
F
G
H
I
J
K
L
M
N
O
P
Q
R
S
T
U
V
W
X
Y
Z

2 good at something: *She's a very capable lawyer.*

ca·pac·i·ty /kə'pæsətɪ/ *noun*
1 the amount that something can contain: *The bowl has a capacity of two litres.*
2 an ability to do something: *Paul has a great capacity for hard work.*

cap·i·tal /'kæpɪtl/ *noun*
1 the city where the main government of a country is
2 also **capital letter** a large letter that you use at the beginning of a sentence. A, D, P are capital letters; a, d, p are small letters: *Write your name in capitals.*

cap·tain /'kæptɪn/ *noun*
1 the person who controls a ship or plane
2 an officer in the army or the navy
3 the leader of a team or group: *Stephen is the school tennis captain.*

cap·tive /'kæptɪv/ *noun*
a prisoner, especially in a war

cap·tiv·i·ty /kæp'tɪvətɪ/ *noun (no plural)*
being kept as a prisoner or in a small space: *Some animals can become ill in captivity.*

cap·ture /'kæptʃər/ *verb (present participle* **capturing**, *past* **captured**)
to take someone as a prisoner: *They captured four enemy soldiers.*

car /kɑːr/ *noun*
a small vehicle with four wheels and an engine ⇨ see picture on page 206

car·a·van /'kærəvæn/ *noun*
a vehicle that you can live in on holiday, that can be pulled by your car ⇨ see picture on page 206

card /kɑːd/ *noun*
1 a small piece of plastic or stiff paper that shows information about someone or something: *an identity card* | *a credit card*
2 a piece of stiff thick paper with a picture on the front and a message inside: *a birthday card*
3 one of a set of 52 small pieces of stiff paper with pictures and numbers that are used to play games
4 **play cards** to play a game using a set of 52 cards

card·board /'kɑːdbɔːd/ *noun (no plural)*
stiff thick paper used for making boxes

car·di·gan /'kɑːdɪgən/ *noun*
a piece of clothing, usually made of wool, that covers the top part of your body and opens with buttons down the front ⇨ see picture on page 203

care¹ /keər/ *verb (present participle* **caring**, *past* **cared**)
1 to feel interest in or worry about someone or something: *He doesn't care about anything but himself.* | *I don't care what you do!*
2 **care for someone** to look after someone: *His daughter cared for him when he was ill.*

care² *noun*
1 *(no plural)* the process of looking after a person or thing: *Take care of your brother while I'm away.* | *With proper care, a washing machine should last for many years.*
2 **take care** to be careful: *Take care when you are crossing the road.*

car·eer /kə'rɪər/ *noun*
the jobs that you do in your life: *Jim would like to have a career in banking.*

care·ful /'keəfəl/ *adjective*
thinking seriously as you do something, so that you do not make a mistake: *Be careful with that hot pan!*
carefully *adverb*: *Drive carefully.*

care·less /'keələs/ *adjective*
not giving enough attention to what you are doing: *It was careless of her to drop that glass.*
carelessly *adverb*: *She carelessly left the door unlocked.*

car·go /'kɑːgəʊ/ *noun (plural* **cargoes**)
something carried on a ship or in a plane: *The ship carries a cargo of oil.*

car·ol /'kærəl/ *noun*
a Christmas song

car park /'kɑː pɑːk/ *noun*
a building or a piece of land where cars can be parked

car·pen·ter /'kɑːpəntər/ *noun*
a person whose job is to make things out of wood ⇨ see picture on page 200

car·pen·try /'kɑːpəntrɪ/ *noun (no plural)*
the activity or job of making things out of wood

car·pet /'kɑːpɪt/ *noun*
a heavy material for covering floors and stairs ⇨ compare RUG ⇨ see picture at RUG

car·riage /ˈkærɪdʒ/ noun
1 one of the parts of a train, in which people sit
2 a vehicle pulled by horses

car·ri·er bag /ˈkærɪə ˌbæg/ noun
a bag made of plastic or paper, used for carrying things that you have bought in a shop

car·rot /ˈkærət/ noun
a long orange root that is eaten as a vegetable ⇨ see picture on page 199

car·ry /ˈkærɪ/ verb (present participle **carrying**, past **carried**)
1 to take something somewhere: He carried the food to the table. | Can you carry the baby and I'll carry the shopping bags. ⇨ see picture on page 207
2 **carry on** to continue: They carried on talking. | Carry on **with** your homework.
3 **carry something out** to do or finish something: The soldiers carried out their orders.

car·toon /kɑːˈtuːn/ noun
1 a film made using drawings or models, not real people
2 a funny drawing in a newspaper

car·ton /ˈkɑːtn/ noun
a plastic or stiff paper box for holding food or drink: a carton **of** apple juice ⇨ see picture at CONTAINER

carve /kɑːv/ verb (present participle **carving**, past **carved**)
1 to cut wood or stone into shapes: He carved the figure of a woman from a piece of wood.
2 to cut cooked meat into pieces: She carved the chicken. ⇨ see pictures at KNIFE and on page 198

case /keɪs/ noun
1 one example of something: This is a typical case **of** bad planning. | In some cases it may be necessary to talk to a child's parents.
2 **in case** because something might happen: I'll take some biscuits in case we get hungry.
3 **in that case** as this is true: "It's raining." "In that case we'll need coats."
4 a question that is decided in a court of law: a court case dealing with cruelty to animals
5 a large strong bag for carrying clothes in, for example on holiday: I'll

just take my case up to my room.
⇨ same meaning SUITCASE

cash[1] /kæʃ/ noun (no plural)
1 coins and paper money: Are you paying by cash?
2 money: I'm short of cash.

cash[2] verb
to get cash in return for a cheque: I cashed a cheque at the bank this morning.

cash dis·pens·er /ˈkæʃ dɪˌspensəʳ/ noun
British a machine in a wall where you can get money from your bank account ⇨ same meaning CASHPOINT

cash·ier /kæˈʃɪəʳ/ noun
a person who takes and gives out money in a bank or shop

cash·point /ˈkæʃpɔɪnt/ noun
British a machine in a wall where you can get money from your bank account ⇨ same meaning CASH DISPENSER

cashpoint
withdrawing cash

cash reg·is·ter /ˈkæʃ ˌredʒɪstəʳ/ noun
a machine in a shop that shows how much you should pay

cas·sette /kəˈset/ noun
a small plastic container holding a TAPE that plays music when fitted into a special machine

cas·tle /ˈkɑːsl/ noun
a large strong building built in the past so that no one could attack the people inside

castle

cas·u·al /ˈkæʒuəl/ adjective
1 relaxed and not worried about things: His casual attitude to homework annoyed me.
2 casual clothes are clothes that you wear at home, not at work or school

cat /kæt/ *noun*
a small animal that people often keep as a pet

cat·a·logue /'kætəlɒg/ *noun*
1 a book containing details of things you can buy from a shop or business
2 a list of all the objects in a place: *There was a catalogue of the books in the library.*

catch[1] /kætʃ/ *verb (past* **caught** /kɔːt/)
1 to stop something that is moving in the air and hold it: *The dog caught the ball in its mouth.* ⇨ see picture on page 207
2 to take hold of someone or something after trying to get them: *The police finally caught the thief.* | *How many fish did you catch?*
3 catch the bus, train, etc to get on a bus, train, etc to go somewhere: *I caught the train to London.*
4 to get an illness: *She caught a cold.*
5 to be attached to something or stuck on something: *My shirt caught on the fence and tore.*
6 catch up to come up behind someone and get to the same place: *I tried, but I couldn't catch up with you.*

catch[2] *noun*
when you catch something: *That was a good catch!*

cat·e·gor·y /'kætɪgəri/ *noun (plural* **categories**)
a group of people or things that are like one another: *The books are divided into two main categories.*

cat·er·pil·lar /'kætə,pɪlər/ *noun*
the young form of some insects, that looks like a WORM with many legs

ca·the·dral /kə'θiːdrəl/ *noun*
an important large church

Cath·o·lic /'kæθəlɪk/ *noun*
a Christian belonging to the church whose leader is the Pope

cat·tle /'kætl/ *plural noun*
large animals kept on farms for their meat and milk

caught /kɔːt/
the past tense and past participle of the verb **catch**

cau·li·flow·er /'kɒlɪ,flaʊər/ *noun*
a vegetable with green leaves around the outside and a hard white centre ⇨ see picture on page 199

cause[1] /kɔːz/ *verb (present participle* **causing**, *past* **caused**)
to make something happen: *The heavy rain caused the flood.* | *We still don't know what caused the computer to crash.*

cause[2] *noun*
1 a person or thing that makes something happen: *What was the cause of the accident?*
2 an idea you believe in or care about very strongly: *I am willing to give money for a good cause.*

cau·tion /'kɔːʃn/ *noun (no plural)*
care taken to avoid danger: *Drive with caution.*

cau·tious /'kɔːʃəs/ *adjective*
taking care to avoid danger: *She is cautious about giving her address to strangers.* ⇨ opposite RECKLESS

cave /keɪv/ *noun*
a hollow place under the ground or in the side of a mountain or rock

CD /,siː 'diː/ *noun*
a small round piece of hard plastic that music or information is recorded on ⇨ same meaning COMPACT DISC

CD play·er /,siː 'diː ,pleɪər/ *noun*
a special machine for playing music CDs ⇨ see picture on page 197

cease /siːs/ *verb (present participle* **ceasing**, *past* **ceased**)
to stop: *Her mother never ceases talking about her troubles.*

cease·less /'siːsləs/ *adjective*
never stopping

cei·ling /'siːlɪŋ/ *noun*
the roof of a room

cel·e·brate /'selɪbreɪt/ *verb (present participle* **celebrating**, *past* **celebrated**)
to show that you are happy about something by having a special meal or party: *She had a party to celebrate her birthday.*

cel·e·bra·tion /,selɪ'breɪʃn/ *noun*
a special meal or party that you have because something good has happened: *There were great celebrations at the beginning of the year 2000.*

cell /sel/ *noun*
1 a small room in which a prisoner is kept

2 a very small part of a plant or an animal.

cel·lar /'selər/ noun
a room under the ground in a house, used especially for storing things in ⇨ compare BASEMENT ⇨ see picture on page 204

cel·lo /'tʃeləʊ/ noun
a musical instrument like a large VIOLIN that you hold between your knees

Cel·si·us /'selsɪəs/ noun (no plural)
a measure of temperature. Water freezes at 0 degrees Celsius and boils at 100 degrees Celsius

ce·ment /sɪ'ment/ noun (no plural)
a powder that becomes hard like stone when mixed with water and can then be used in building

cem·e·tery /'semɪtrɪ/ noun (plural cemeteries)
an area of land where dead bodies are put into the ground

cent /sent/ noun
a small coin used in some countries. There are 100 cents in a dollar

Cen·ti·grade /'sentɪgreɪd/ noun (no plural)
a measure of temperature that is the same as CELSIUS

cen·ti·me·tre /'sentɪ,miːtər/ noun
a measure of length: The pencil was 12 centimetres long.

cen·tral /'sentrəl/ adjective
in the middle of something: He worked in central London.

cen·tre /'sentər/ noun
1 the middle of something: Put the flowers in the centre of the table.
2 a place where a lot of people come with a special purpose: The doctors worked at the Health Centre. I Have you seen the new shopping centre?

cen·tu·ry /'sentʃərɪ/ noun (plural centuries)
a period of 100 years: This house was built two centuries ago.

ce·re·al /'sɪərɪəl/ noun
1 a crop such as wheat or rice
2 breakfast food that is made from grain and usually eaten with milk

cer·e·mo·ny /'serɪmənɪ/ noun (plural ceremonies)
a number of special actions done and special words spoken in a particular order to mark an important public, social, or religious event: a wedding ceremony

cer·tain /'sɜːtn/ adjective
1 sure: I am certain he told me to come at two o'clock. I I'm not certain when the bus will arrive.
2 some: You cannot smoke in certain restaurants.

cer·tain·ly /'sɜːtnlɪ/ adverb
1 without doubt: You've certainly got a lot of books. I Chris certainly spends a lot of money on clothes.
2 used when you agree to something: "Will you help me, please?" "Certainly."

cer·tif·i·cate /sə'tɪfɪkət/ noun
an official document that shows that you have done something: Please send copies of your certificates.

chain¹ /tʃeɪn/ noun
a number of metal rings joined together: She wore a gold chain around her neck. ⇨ see picture at BICYCLE

chain² verb
to use a chain to tie something to something else: I chained my bicycle to the fence.

chairs

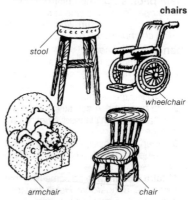

stool

wheelchair

armchair   chair

chair /tʃeər/ noun
1 a piece of furniture you sit on, with four legs and a back ⇨ compare SOFA, STOOL
2 a chairperson

chair·per·son /'tʃeə,pɜːsn/ noun
also **chair·man** /'tʃeəmən/ someone who controls a meeting

chair·wom·an /'tʃeəwʊmən/ noun
a woman who controls a meeting

chalk /tʃɔːk/ noun
1 (no plural) a soft white substance found in the ground
2 a piece of this substance used for writing or drawing ⇨ see picture on page 205

chal·lenge [1] /'tʃælɪndʒ/ verb (present participle **challenging**, past **challenged**)
1 to offer to fight or play a game against someone: *Their school challenged ours **to** a football match.*
2 to test or question someone: *I did not think he was right, so I challenged him.*

challenge [2] noun
1 a test of ability: *To build a bridge in a month was a real challenge.*
2 an offer to fight or play against someone

cham·pagne /ʃæm'peɪn/ noun (no plural)
an alcoholic drink with a lot of bubbles in it

cham·pi·on /'tʃæmpɪən/ noun
a person who is the best at something, especially a sport or game

cham·pi·on·ship /'tʃæmpɪənʃɪp/ noun
a competition to find who is the best at something: *Our team won the swimming championship.*

chance /tʃɑːns/ noun
1 a time that you use to do something: *I haven't had a chance to read my letter.* | *Parents will have a chance to look round the school.*
2 (no plural) when something happens that has not been planned: *I met him **by** chance.*
3 when it is possible that something will happen: *There is a chance **that** I will be chosen for the team.*
4 **take a chance** to do something that might be dangerous: *He is taking a chance by driving his car so fast.*

change [1] /tʃeɪndʒ/ verb (present participle **changing**, past **changed**)
1 to become or to make something different: *This town has changed since I was a child.* | *The leaves change colour in the autumn.* | *You've changed your hair.*
2 to stop having or doing one thing and start something else instead: *She took the dress back to the shop and changed it for a smaller one.* | *You will have to change planes in Amsterdam.*
3 **get changed** to put on different clothes: *She got changed when she arrived home from school.*
4 **change your mind** to make a new decision that is opposite to the one before: *I was planning to go to the cinema but I've changed my mind.*

change [2] noun
1 when something has changed: *You will see many changes in the village since last year.*
2 (no plural) money that you get back when you give too much for something: *I gave him a pound and he gave me 20 pence change.*
3 **for a change** as something different from usual: *Let's eat in a restaurant tonight for a change.*

chan·nel /'tʃænl/ noun
1 a narrow piece of flowing water: *The English Channel is between France and England.*
2 a company that broadcasts on television: *There's a good programme on Channel 5 this evening.*

cha·os /'keɪɒs/ noun (no plural)
a state when there is no order or control: *After the bomb explosion the town was **in** chaos.*

chap·ter /'tʃæptə⁰/ noun
a part of a book: *Open your books at Chapter 3.*

char·ac·ter /'kærɪktə⁰/ noun
1 what a person, place, or thing is like: *He has a strong but gentle character.* | *The new buildings have changed the character of the city.*
2 a person in a book, film, or play

charge [1] /tʃɑːdʒ/ verb (present participle **charging**, past **charged**)
1 to ask for an amount of money for something: *The restaurant charged us £20 **for** the wine.*
2 to say officially that a person has done something wrong: *He was charged **with** stealing a car.*
3 to run or hurry: *The little boy charged into the room.*

charge [2] noun
1 a price you pay for something: *In the hotel there was a charge **for** the use of the telephone.*
2 **be in charge** to control someone or

something: *Ask Mr Davis. He's in charge.* | *I'm in charge of the children until their mother comes home.*
3 take charge to take control of someone or something: *Mrs Williams will take charge of the first lesson after lunch.*
4 an official statement that a person has done wrong: *He's in court on a murder charge.*

char·i·ty /'tʃærətɪ/ *noun*
1 (*plural* **charities**) an organization that collects money from people and then gives money, food, etc to those who need it
2 (*no plural*) money or help given to people who need it: *She is too proud to accept charity.*

charm[1] /tʃɑːm/ *verb*
nice behaviour that makes people like you: *His smile charmed her.*

charm[2] *noun*
1 (*no plural*) pleasing behaviour that makes people like you: *He had great charm. Everyone liked him.*
2 a thing that brings good luck

charm·ing /'tʃɑːmɪŋ/ *adjective*
very pleasant or attractive

chart /tʃɑːt/ *noun*
1 a large piece of paper with information on it in pictures and writing
2 a map of the sea or the stars

chase[1] /tʃeɪs/ *verb* (*present participle* **chasing**, *past* **chased**)
to follow someone quickly: *The boy chased the dog.*

chase[2] *noun*
when something follows someone or something quickly to catch them: *He caught the dog after a long chase.*

chat[1] /tʃæt/ *verb* (*present participle* **chatting**, *past* **chatted**)
to talk in a friendly way: *We chatted together for a while.*

chat[2] *noun*
a friendly talk: *We had a chat.*

chat·ter /'tʃætər/ *verb*
to talk a lot, especially about things that are not important

cheap /tʃiːp/ *adjective*
costing not very much money: *A bicycle is much cheaper than a car.* ⇨ opposite EXPENSIVE

cheat[1] /tʃiːt/ *adjective*
to do something that is not fair or honest: *He always cheats when he plays hide-and-seek.*

cheat[2] *noun*
a person who is not fair or honest

check[1] /tʃek/ *verb*
1 to make sure that something is correct, true, or safe: *Did you check the door to see if it is locked?*
2 check in to say that you have arrived: *You must check in at the airport an hour before the plane leaves.*

check[2] *noun*
1 a careful look to make sure that something is correct, true, or safe: *The police are doing a check on cars and lorries.*
2 a pattern of squares: *The material had red and white checks on it.* ⇨ see picture at PATTERN
3 *American* a printed piece of paper that you write on to pay for things (*British* **cheque**)

check·out /'tʃekaʊt/ *noun*
a place in a shop where you pay for goods

cheek /tʃiːk/ *noun*
one of the two soft parts on each side of your face under your eyes ⇨ see picture at HEAD

cheek·y /'tʃiːkɪ/ *adjective*
not polite or respectful: *Don't be so cheeky.*

cheer[1] /tʃɪər/ *verb*
1 to shout because you are pleased: *The crowd cheered when the film stars arrived.*
2 cheer someone up to make someone happy: *I tried to cheer her up by buying her a gift.*
3 cheer up to start feeling happy: *Cheer up! We'll be going soon.*

cheer[2] *noun*
a shout of happiness or support: *Let's give three cheers for the winning team.*

cheer·ful /'tʃɪəfəl/ *adjective*
happy and feeling good

cheese /tʃiːz/ *noun*
a solid food made from milk

chem·i·cal[1] /'kemɪkl/ *noun*
a substance, especially one made by or used in chemistry

A
B
C
D
E
F
G
H
I
J
K
L
M
N
O
P
Q
R
S
T
U
V
W
X
Y
Z

chemical² *adjective*
made by chemistry

chem·ist /'kemɪst/ *noun*
1 a person who makes and sells medicines
2 chemist's *British* a shop where medicines and some goods for the house can be bought ⇨ see picture on page 201
3 a person who studies chemistry

chem·is·try /'kemɪstrɪ/ *noun* (*no plural*)
the science that studies substances like gases, metals, liquids, etc, what they are made of, and how they behave

cheque /tʃek/ *noun*
British a printed piece of paper that you write on to pay for things (*American* **check**)

cher·ry /'tʃerɪ/ *noun* (*plural* **cherries**)
a small round fruit with red or black skin that grows on trees ⇨ see picture on page 199

chess

board

chess /tʃes/ *noun* (*no plural*)
a game that you play by moving different shaped pieces on a board of black and white squares ⇨ see picture on page 197

chest /tʃest/ *noun*
the front of your body between your shoulders and your stomach

chest of drawers /ˌtʃest əv 'drɔːz/ *noun* (*plural* **chests of drawers**)
a large piece of furniture with several drawers

chew /tʃuː/ *verb*
to break up food in your mouth with your teeth

chew·ing gum /'tʃuːɪŋ ɡʌm/ *noun* (*no plural*)
a sweet substance that you chew but do not swallow

chick /tʃɪk/ *noun*
a young bird, especially a young chicken

chick·en /'tʃɪkɪn/ *noun*
a bird that people keep for its eggs and meat

chief¹ /tʃiːf/ *adjective*
most important: *Our chief concern is for the safety of the children.*

chief² *noun*
the leader of a group or organization: *the chief of police*

chief·ly /'tʃiːflɪ/ *adverb*
mainly: *He kept animals – chiefly cattle, with some pigs.*

child /tʃaɪld/ *noun* (*plural* **children** /'tʃɪldrən/)
1 a young person older than a baby but not yet fully grown
2 a son or daughter: *They have three children.* ⇨ look at SON

child·hood /'tʃaɪldhʊd/ *noun*
the time when you are a child

child·ish /'tʃaɪldɪʃ/ *adjective*
an adult who is childish behaves in a silly way, like a small child: *Stop being so childish.*

chil·dren /'tʃɪldrən/
the plural of **child**

chime /tʃaɪm/ *verb* (*present participle* **chiming**, *past* **chimed**)
to make a sound like a bell: *The clock chimed three o'clock.* ⇨ same meaning RING

chim·ney /'tʃɪmnɪ/ *noun*
a wide pipe that allows smoke from a fire to go up and out of a building ⇨ see picture at ROOF

chim·pan·zee /ˌtʃɪmpæn'ziː/ *noun*
an African animal like a monkey but without a tail ⇨ see picture on page 195

chin /tʃɪn/ *noun*
the part of your face below your mouth ⇨ see picture at HEAD

chi·na /'tʃaɪnə/ *noun* (*no plural*)
cups, plates, etc that are made from baked clay

chip¹ /tʃɪp/ *noun*
1 a small space or crack where a part has broken off something: *My cup has a chip in it.* ⇨ see picture at BROKEN
2 *British* a long thin piece of potato cooked in oil (*American* **french fry**):

We'll have fish and chips for supper.
⇨ see picture at FAST FOOD

3 *American* a very thin piece of cooked potato that you buy in a packet and eat cold (*British* **crisp**)

4 a very small piece of metal or plastic used in computers to store information and make the computer work

chip [2] verb (*present participle* **chipping,** *past* **chipped**)
to break a small piece off something hard: *He chipped the cup when he dropped it.*

chirp /tʃɜːp/ *noun*
a short high sound made by some birds and insects

choco·late /'tʃɒklət/ *noun*
1 (*no plural*) a sweet brown food made from COCOA
2 a small sweet covered in chocolate: *He gave her a box of chocolates.*

choice /tʃɔɪs/ *noun*
1 different things from which you can choose: *I've got to make a choice between the two jobs.* | *If you had a choice, where would you want to live?*
2 the person or thing that you have decided to choose: *Her choice of dress surprised me.*
3 a variety of things from which you can choose: *There's a wide choice of colours.* | *You will have a choice of five questions in the test.*

choir /'kwaɪər/ *noun*
a group of people who sing together: *the school choir*

choke /tʃəʊk/ *verb* (*present participle* **choking,** *past* **choked**)
to be unable to breathe because of something in your throat: *She choked on a piece of meat.*

choose /tʃuːz/ *verb* (*present participle* **choosing,** *past tense* **chose** /tʃəʊz/, *past participle* **chosen** /'tʃəʊzn/)
to decide from two or more things or people the one you want: *The students had to choose between geography and history.* | *They chose Roy to be the team's captain.*

chop [1] /tʃɒp/ *verb* (*present participle* **chopping,** *past* **chopped**)
also **chop up** to cut something with a sharp knife or an AXE: *She was chopping onions and peppers.*
⇨ see picture on page 198

chop [2] *noun*
a piece of meat with a bone, cut from the side of an animal's body

chop

chopping wood

cho·rus /'kɔːrəs/ *noun* (*plural* **choruses**)
1 a part of a song that is repeated
2 a group of singers

chose /tʃəʊz/
the past tense of the verb **choose**

cho·sen /'tʃəʊzn/
the past participle of the verb **choose**

chris·ten·ing /'krɪsnɪŋ/ *noun*
the Christian ceremony at which a baby is given its name

Chris·tian /'krɪstʃən, -tɪən/ *noun*
a person who follows the teachings of Jesus Christ

Chris·ti·an·i·ty /ˌkrɪstɪ'ænɪtɪ/ *noun* (*no plural*)
the religion based on the teachings of Jesus Christ

Chris·tian name /'krɪstʃən ˌneɪm/ *noun*
a person's first name, not their family name

Christ·mas /'krɪsməs/ *noun*
December 25th, the day when Christians celebrate the birth of Jesus Christ and people give presents

chuck·le /'tʃʌkl/ *verb* (*present participle* **chuckling,** *past* **chuckled**)
to laugh quietly: *He chuckled at the funny story.*

chunk /tʃʌŋk/ *noun*
a large piece of something: *I cut off a chunk of cheese.*

church /tʃɜːtʃ/ *noun* (*plural* **churches**)
a building in which Christians meet and pray

ci·gar /sɪ'ɡɑːr/ *noun*
a thick brown stick of tobacco leaves rolled together for smoking

cig·a·rette /ˌsɪɡə'ret/ *noun*
a thin stick made of tobacco rolled in white paper for smoking

A B C D E F G H I J K L M N O P Q R S T U V W X Y Z

cin·e·ma /'sɪnəmə/ noun
a building in which you can see films

cir·cle¹ /'sɜːkl/ noun
1 a round shape or ring: *They sat in a circle round the fire.* ⇨ see picture at SHAPE
2 a group of people who like the same things: *She has a large circle **of** friends.*

circle² verb
to draw a circle round something: *Circle the correct answer.*

cir·cu·lar /'sɜːkjʊləʳ/ adjective
1 in the shape of a circle: *He sat at a circular table.*
2 going to different places and ending where you started: *We walked along a circular path.*

cir·cu·late /'sɜːkjʊleɪt/ verb (present participle **circulating**, past **circulated**)
to move around a place or system: *Blood circulates **round** your body.*

cir·cu·la·tion /ˌsɜːkjʊ'leɪʃn/ noun (no plural)
the movement of blood round your body

cir·cum·fer·ence /sə'kʌmfrəns/ noun
the length around the outside edge of a round object

cir·cum·stan·ces /'sɜːkəmstənsɪz/ plural noun
1 in/under the circumstances after what has happened: *In the circumstances I think I should stay at home.*
2 in/under no circumstances never: *Under no circumstances should you leave this house!*

cir·cus /'sɜːkəs/ noun
a show given by people and trained animals, often in a large tent

cit·i·zen /'sɪtɪzn/ noun
a person who lives in a country or town and has particular rights there

city /'sɪti/ noun (plural **cities**)
a very large town

ci·vil·ian /sɪ'vɪljən/ noun
a person who is not in the army, navy, etc

civ·i·li·za·tion /ˌsɪvɪlaɪ'zeɪʃn/ noun
the fact that a society has laws, government, and education

civ·i·lize /'sɪvɪlaɪz/ verb (present participle **civilizing**, past **civilized**)
to change the way that people live together, by making laws and having government and education

civ·il ser·vice /ˌsɪvəl 'sɜːvɪs/ noun
the different government organizations, and the people who work for them

civ·il war /ˌsɪvəl 'wɔːʳ/ noun
a war between two groups of people who live in the same country

claim¹ /kleɪm/ verb
1 to say that something is true: *He claimed **that** he hadn't done it, but I didn't believe him.*
2 to ask for something that is yours: *This coat was left behind after the party, but no one has been back to claim it.*

claim² noun
1 something that you say is true: *I don't believe his claim about how rich he is.*
2 something that you ask for: *They made a claim **for** higher pay.*

clang /klæŋ/ verb
to make a loud sound like metal being hit: *The gate clanged shut.*

clap /klæp/ verb (present participle **clapping**, past **clapped**)
to make a sound by hitting your hands together to show that you like something: *When the singer finished, we clapped.* ⇨ same meaning APPLAUD

clash¹ /klæʃ/ verb
1 to fight or argue with someone: *The police clashed **with** the angry crowd.*
2 if colours clash, they look wrong together: *His shirt clashed **with** his coat.*
3 if two events clash, they happen at the same time: *I couldn't go to the wedding as it clashed **with** my holiday.*

clash² noun (plural **clashes**)
1 a fight or argument: *There were clashes **between** the two armies at the border.*
2 a loud noise made by metal objects hitting each other: *the clash of weapons.*

clasp¹ /klɑːsp/ verb
to hold something tightly: *He clasped my hand.* ⇨ same meaning GRIP

clasp² noun
a small metal object used to fasten a bag, belt, piece of jewellery, etc: *The clasp on my bag has broken.* ⇨ compare BUCKLE

class /klɑːs/ noun (plural **classes**)
1 a group of people who learn

together: *She was in a class of thirty students.*
2 the social group that you belong to: *He comes from a working-class family.*
3 a group of people or things of the same kind: *Cats belong to one class of animals, fish to another.*

clas·sic /ˈklæsɪk/ *noun*
a book or film that is very good and that people have liked for a long time: *The film 'Casablanca' is a classic.*

clas·si·cal /ˈklæsɪkl/ *adjective*
classical music or art is serious and important: *I prefer rock music to classical music.*

class·room /ˈklɑːsruːm/ *noun*
a room in which a class meets for a lesson

clat·ter /ˈklætər/ *noun*
to make the loud noise of hard things hitting something: *The pans clattered to the floor.*

clause /klɔːz/ *noun*
a group of words that contains a verb. The sentence 'As I was walking home, I met my friend' contains two clauses. 'As I was walking home' is one clause and 'I met my friend' is the other ⇨ compare SENTENCE

claw[1] /klɔː/ *noun*
1 one of the sharp hard points on the foot of a bird or animal
2 the hand of a CRAB or LOBSTER

claw[2] *verb*
to tear something or try to get something, using claws or hands: *She clawed at his sleeve.*

clay /kleɪ/ *noun (no plural)*
soft sticky earth used for making containers and bricks

clean[1] /kliːn/ *adjective*
not dirty: *Haven't you got a clean shirt? | My hands are clean.*

clean[2] *verb*
to make something clean: *Have you cleaned the kitchen?*

clean·er /ˈkliːnər/ *noun*
a person who cleans houses or other buildings as their job

clear[1] /klɪər/ *adjective*
1 easy to understand, see, read, or hear: *She spoke in a clear voice. | Are the instructions clear?*
2 easy to see through: *clear water | a clear glass bottle*
3 not blocked or covered: *The road is clear now.*
4 not possible to doubt: *Hugh made it quite clear that he was not interested.*

clear[2] *verb*
1 to make a table, floor, etc tidy by removing things from it: *I'll just clear the dishes* **from** *the table.*
2 clear something up (a) to tidy a place by putting things where they should be: *Jimmy, can you clear those toys up?* **(b)** to explain something that you did not understand: *I think he will be able to clear up the mystery.*
3 clear up if the weather clears up, it becomes brighter: *I hope the weather clears up before Sunday.*

clear·ly /ˈklɪəli/ *adverb*
1 in a way that is easy to understand, see, or hear: *Please speak more clearly; we can't hear you.*
2 without any doubt: *Clearly, the situation is more of a problem than we thought. | He clearly thought that it was her fault.*

clerk /klɑːk/ *noun*
a person whose job is to keep the records or accounts in an office or organization

clev·er /ˈklevər/ *adjective*
quick at learning and understanding things
cleverly *adverb*: *She dealt with the problem very cleverly.*

click[1] /klɪk/ *noun*
a short sharp sound: *I heard the click of a key in the lock.*

click[2] *verb*
1 to make a short sharp sound: *The door clicked shut.*
2 to press a button on your computer MOUSE, with your CURSOR pointing at a particular part of the screen: *Now click* **on** *that box.*

cli·ent /ˈklaɪənt/ *noun*
a person who pays someone for help or advice

cliff /klɪf/ *noun*
an area of high steep rock, often close to the sea ⇨ see picture on page 193

cli·mate /ˈklaɪmət/ *noun (no plural)*
the weather that a place usually has

climate

a place with a tropical climate

a place with a polar climate

climb¹ /klaɪm/ *verb*

to go up something: *The two boys climbed the tree.* ⇨ see picture on page 193

climb² *noun*

when you climb or travel up: *It's a long climb to the top of the hill.*

cling /klɪŋ/ *verb (past* **clung** /klʌŋ/*)*

to hold on tightly to something: *The baby monkey clung to its mother.*

clin·ic /ˈklɪnɪk/ *noun*

a place where people go to see a doctor

clip¹ /klɪp/ *noun*

a small metal object used for fastening things: *The documents were held together with a clip.*

clip² *verb (present participle* **clipping**, *past* **clipped**)

to hold things with a clip: *A small card was clipped to the letter.*

cloak·room /ˈkləʊkruːm/ *noun*

1 a room where you leave hats, coats, etc

2 *British* a toilet in a public building

clock /klɒk/ *noun*

a piece of equipment that tells you what the time is ⇨ compare WATCH ⇨ see picture on page 205

clock·wise /ˈklɒkwaɪz/ *adverb*

in the same direction as the hands of a clock ⇨ compare ANTICLOCKWISE

close¹ /kləʊs/ *adjective*

1 near: *I live close to the shops.* I *They were staying in a hotel close to the beach.*

2 **close to something** almost something: *The temperature is close to 35 degrees.*

3 careful: *We kept a close watch on the children.*

4 if people are close, they like each other very much: *Peter and John are close friends.*

close² /kləʊz/ *verb (present participle* **closing**, *past* **closed**)

1 to shut something: *Please close the door.*

2 to stop being open for business: *What time does the bank close?* ⇨ opposite OPEN

close³ /kləʊz/ *noun (no plural)*

the end of an activity or period of time: *It's time to bring the meeting to a close.*

closed /kləʊzd/ *adjective*

1 shut: *Keep your eyes closed.* I *The window was closed because it was raining.* ⇨ see picture at AJAR

2 not open to the public: *The shops were closed on Sundays.*

cloth /klɒθ/ *noun*

1 *(no plural)* material made of wool, cotton, etc: *a suit made of grey cloth* ⇨ same meaning MATERIAL, FABRIC

2 a piece of cloth used for a particular purpose: *He polished the surface with a soft cloth.* ⇨ look at CLOTHES

clothes /kləʊðz/ *plural noun*

things such as shirts, skirts, or trousers that people wear: *I need some new clothes.* I *You need to wear old clothes for this job.* ⇨ see picture on page 203

NOTE: **Cloth** is **not** the singular of **clothes** (look at the entry for **cloth** above). The word **clothes** is always plural and does not have a singular form. People usually use the name of the thing they are talking about, e.g. *a shirt, a dress,* etc when there is only one.

cloth·ing /ˈkləʊðɪŋ/ *noun (no plural)*

clothes that people wear: *warm winter clothing*

cloud /klaʊd/ *noun*

a mass of very small drops of water floating in the sky: *Storm clouds moved closer.*

cloud·y /ˈklaʊdɪ/ *adjective*

if the weather is cloudy, the sky is full of clouds: *It is a cloudy day.* ⇨ see picture on page 194

clown /klaʊn/ noun
a person who wears funny clothes and tries to make people laugh

club /klʌb/ noun
1 a group of people who meet each other because they share an interest: *I belong to a chess club.* | *She's a member of the local drama club.*
2 a large heavy stick

clue /kluː/ noun
something that helps you find the answer to a difficult question: *Police are looking for clues to help them catch the killer.*

clum·si·ly /'klʌmzɪli/ adverb
in a clumsy way: *She climbed down clumsily.*

clum·sy /'klʌmzi/ adjective (**clumsier**, **clumsiest**)
often dropping, breaking, or hitting things accidentally: *At thirteen she was clumsy and shy.*

clung /klʌŋ/
the past tense and past participle of the verb **cling**

clutch /klʌtʃ/ verb
to hold something tightly: *She clutched her baby in her arms.*

cm
a short way of writing the word **centimetre**: *It's 10 cm long.*

coach[1] /kəʊtʃ/ noun (plural **coaches**)
1 someone who gives special lessons to a team or person: *Mr Jones is our football coach*
2 British a bus with comfortable seats for long journeys: *We're going on a coach tour of Europe.*
3 a covered vehicle with four wheels pulled by horses

coach[2] verb
to give a person or team special lessons: *He coached her for the English examination.* | *She coaches the tennis team.*

coal /kəʊl/ noun (no plural)
a hard black material dug out of the ground and burned to give heat

coarse /kɔːs/ adjective
rough, not smooth or even: *a coarse woollen blanket*

coast /kəʊst/ noun
the land next to the sea: *She lives in a town on the south coast.*

coast·line /'kəʊstlaɪn/ noun
the edge of the land: *From the ship, they saw the rocky coastline.*

coat /kəʊt/ noun
1 a piece of clothing that you wear over your clothes to keep you warm when you go outside: *Put your coat on if you're going outside.* ⋄ see picture on page 203
2 a covering of something spread over a surface: *I'll give the walls a coat of paint.*
3 an animal's fur, wool, or hair: *The dog had a thick glossy coat.*

coat hang·er /'kəʊt ˌhæŋəʳ/ noun
a specially shaped piece of wood or plastic on which you hang clothes in a cupboard

coax /kəʊks/ verb
to persuade someone to do something by talking to them gently and kindly: *She coaxed him to take the medicine.* | *We coaxed her into eating something.*

cob·web /'kɒbweb/ noun
the thin net that a SPIDER makes to catch flies and insects

cock /kɒk/ noun
British a male chicken

co·coa /'kəʊkəʊ/ noun (no plural)
1 a brown powder made from the seeds of a tree, from which chocolate is made
2 a hot drink made from this powder: *a cup of cocoa*

co·co·nut /'kəʊkənʌt/ noun
an extremely large nut that is white inside and contains juice

cod /kɒd/ noun (plural **cod**)
a sea fish used for food

code /kəʊd/ noun
a way of using words, letters, numbers, etc to keep messages secret: *The letter was written in code and I could not understand it.*

cof·fee /'kɒfi/ noun
1 (no plural) a drink made from a brown powder from the seeds of the coffee tree
2 British a cup of this drink: *Two coffees, please!*

cof·fin /'kɒfin/ noun
a box that is made to hold a dead body

coil[1] /kɔɪl/ verb
to twist a rope, wire, etc into a round shape

coil² *noun*
a piece of rope, wire, etc that has been twisted into a round shape: *a coil of rope*

coin /kɔɪn/ *noun*
a piece of money made of metal ⇨ compare BANK NOTE

co·in·ci·dence /kəʊˈɪnsɪdəns/ *noun*
a surprising situation when two similar events happen by chance: *What a coincidence that I was in London at the same time as you!*

cold¹ /kəʊld/ *adjective*
with a low temperature: *Would you like a cold drink?* | *It's very cold outside.* ⇨ opposite HOT

cold² *noun*
1 an illness of the nose and throat: *I've got a cold.*
2 (*no plural*) cold weather: *I don't like the cold.* ⇨ opposite HEAT

col·lapse /kəˈlæps/ *verb* (*present participle* **collapsing**, *past* **collapsed**)
to fall down suddenly: *The old man collapsed in the street.* | *The roof of the house collapsed.*

collars

collar / collar

col·lar /ˈkɒlər/ *noun*
1 the part of a shirt or coat that goes round your neck: *The collar of his shirt was dirty.*
2 a leather or metal band put round the neck of an animal

col·lect /kəˈlekt/ *verb*
1 to bring or put things together: *I collect stamps from all over the world.* | *Can someone collect all the books?*
2 *British* to come to take someone or something away: *He collected the children from school.*
3 to get money from people: *I'm collecting for the blind.*

4 to come together in a place: *A crowd had collected to watch the ceremony.*

col·lec·tion /kəˈlekʃən/ *noun*
a group of similar things that have been brought together: *He had a large collection of old coins.*

col·lege /ˈkɒlɪdʒ/ *noun*
a place where people study after they have left school

col·lide /kəˈlaɪd/ *verb* (*present participle* **colliding**, *past* **collided**)
if two things collide, they hit each other with great force: *The two trains collided.* | *In the fog, her car collided with a lorry.*

col·li·sion /kəˈlɪʒən/ *noun*
a violent crash: *a collision between two trains*

co·lon /ˈkəʊlɒn/ *noun*
the sign (:), which in this book comes before an example

colo·nel /ˈkɜːnl/ *noun*
an officer in the army

col·o·ny /ˈkɒlənɪ/ *noun* (*plural* **colonies**)
a country that is under the control of another country

col·our¹ /ˈkʌlər/ *noun*
the quality that makes things look green, red, yellow, etc: *"What colour is her hair?" "It's black."* | *My favourite colour is yellow.*

> NOTE: The word **colour** is not usually used in sentences describing the colour of something, e.g. *Her dress is red.* | *He has brown hair.*

colour² *verb*
to put colour onto something: *The little boy is colouring the picture in his book.*

col·our·ful /ˈkʌləfəl/ *adjective*
with a lot of bright colours: *She always wears colourful clothes.*

col·umn /ˈkɒləm/ *noun*
1 a large post used to support a part of a building
2 something with a narrow shape: *a column of smoke*
3 a list of numbers or words: *Can you add up this column of figures?*

comb¹ /kəʊm/ *noun*
a piece of plastic, metal, etc with a row of pointed parts that you use to make your hair tidy

comb [2] *verb*
to tidy your hair with a comb: *Have you combed your hair?*

com·bi·na·tion /ˌkɒmbɪˈneɪʃn/ *noun*
two or more separate things that are used or put together: *The painting had a wonderful combination of colours.* | *His character is a combination of strength and kindness.*

com·bine /kəmˈbaɪn/ *verb* (*present participle* **combining**, *past* **combined**)
to join or mix two or more things together: *The two small shops combined to make one large one.* | *I want a job that combines my computer skills with my languages.*

come /kʌm/ *verb* (*present participle* **coming**, *past* **came** /keɪm/, *past participle* **come**)
1 to move towards the person speaking: *Come here, Mary.* | *Are you coming with me?*
2 to arrive at a place: *He was tired when he came home from work.*
3 come about to happen: *This situation should never have come about.*
4 come across someone or something to meet someone or find something by chance: *I came across an old friend I hadn't seen for years.*
5 come back to return from a place: *When is Jane coming back from New York?*
6 come down to become lower in price, amount, number, etc: *We will buy a new computer when the price comes down a little.*
7 come from somewhere to have been born in a place or have lived there a long time: *I come from Glasgow.*
8 Come on! used when telling someone to hurry or to come with you: *Come on Helen or we're going to be late!*
9 come off to become removed from something: *My shoe has come off.* | *A button has come off my shirt.*

com·e·dy /ˈkɒmədɪ/ *noun* (*plural* **comedies**)
a funny play, film, book, etc: *The film is a comedy and it's very funny.* ⇨ compare TRAGEDY

com·fort [1] /ˈkʌmfət/ *noun*
a feeling of being relaxed and calm, not worried or in pain: *These shoes were designed for comfort.* | *Now you can sit in comfort and watch the show.*

comfort [2] *verb*
to be kind to someone or help them when they are in pain or trouble: *She comforted the crying baby.*

com·fort·a·ble /ˈkʌmftəbl/ *adjective*
1 pleasant to wear, sit in, or be in: *This is a very comfortable chair.*
2 with no pain or worries: *I feel more comfortable knowing that you are in the house.* ⇨ opposite UNCOMFORTABLE

com·ic [1] /ˈkɒmɪk/ *adjective*
making people laugh; funny: *He gave a comic performance.*

comic [2] *noun*
a magazine for children that tells a story in pictures ⇨ see picture on page 197

com·ma /ˈkɒmə/ *noun*
the sign (,) used in writing to divide up a sentence

com·mand [1] /kəˈmɑːnd/ *verb*
1 to order someone to do something: *The officer commanded his men to attack.*
2 to give orders to people: *A general is a man who commands a large number of soldiers.*

command [2] *noun*
1 an order given to someone: *Don't shoot until your officer gives the command.*
2 (*no plural*) control of a group of people or a situation: *Who is in command?*

com·ment [1] /ˈkɒment/ *noun*
something that someone says about something: *He made rude comments about the other guests.*

comment [2] *verb*
to say something about something: *He commented on the bad road.*

com·men·ta·ry /ˈkɒməntrɪ/ *noun* (*plural* **commentaries**)
a description of an event that is being broadcast on television or radio

com·men·ta·tor /ˈkɒmənteɪtəʳ/ *noun*
someone who describes an event while it is happening: *a radio commentator*

com·merce /ˈkɒmɜːs/ *noun* (*no plural*)
the business of buying and selling goods

com·mer·cial /kəˈmɜːʃl/ *adjective*
related to the buying and selling of goods

com·mit /kəˈmɪt/ *verb* (*present participle* **committing**, *past* **committed**)
to do something wrong: *He said he hadn't committed the murder.*

com·mit·tee /kəˈmɪtɪ/ *noun*
a group of people chosen to study something, plan, and make decisions: *She's **on** a research committee in the science department.*

com·mon /ˈkɒmən/ *adjective*
1 happening often or found everywhere: *That is a common spelling mistake.* | *Red buses are quite common in London.* ⇨ opposite RARE
2 shared by or belonging to two or more people: *We both had a common interest.*

common sense /ˌkɒmən ˈsens/ *noun* (*no plural*)
the ability to think about things in a reasonable way and make good decisions: *It's just common sense to take warm clothes on holiday in winter.*

com·mu·ni·cate /kəˈmjuːnɪkeɪt/ *verb* (*past participle* **communicating**, *past* **communicated**)
to speak or write to someone: *If you know English you can communicate **with** a lot of people.* | *We communicated by letter.*

com·mu·ni·ca·tion /kəˌmjuːnɪˈkeɪʃn/ *noun*
1 (*no plural*) the act of speaking or writing to someone and being understood by them: *Communication between people who speak different languages is difficult.*
2 **communications** (*plural noun*) the different ways of sending information between places, such as computers, telephones, radio, etc

com·mu·ni·ty /kəˈmjuːnətɪ/ *noun* (*plural* **communities**)
all the people living in one place: *All the children in our community go to the same school.*

com·mut·er /kəˈmjuːtəʳ/ *noun*
a person who travels a long way to work each day

com·pact disc /ˌkɒmpækt ˈdɪsk/ *noun*
a small round piece of hard plastic that music or information is recorded on ⇨ same meaning CD

com·pan·ion /kəmˈpænjən/ *noun*
a person you are with, often a friend: *He was my travelling companion for many months.*

com·pa·ny /ˈkʌmpənɪ/ *noun*
1 (*plural* **companies**) a business that buys, makes, and sells things: *I work for a computer company.*
2 (*no plural*) the fact that someone is with you: *They obviously enjoy each other's company.*

com·par·a·tive /kəmˈpærətɪv/ *noun, adjective*
a word or a form of a word that shows that something is bigger, smaller, better, worse, etc than something else. The comparative form of 'big' is 'bigger' and the comparative of 'happy' is 'happier' ⇨ compare SUPERLATIVE

com·pare /kəmˈpeəʳ/ *verb* (*present participle* **comparing**, *past* **compared**)
to decide in what way things are similar or different: *People are always comparing me **to** my sister.* | *We compared the prices in the shop **with** the prices in the market.*

com·pa·ri·son /kəmˈpærɪsn/ *noun*
when someone compares two things or people: *They studied a comparison of the crime figures in Detroit and Chicago.* | *My shoes are small **in** comparison **with** my sister's.*

com·part·ment /kəmˈpɑːtmənt/ *noun*
1 a small space inside something larger: *a luggage compartment*
2 a room in a train

com·pass /ˈkʌmpəs/ *noun* (*plural* **compasses**)
an instrument with a metal needle that always points north

compass

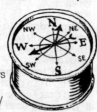

com·pel /kəmˈpel/ *verb* (*present participle* **compelling**, *past* **compelled**)
to force someone to do something: *The floods compelled us to turn back.*

com·pete /kəmˈpiːt/ *verb* (*present participle* **competing**, *past* **competed**)
to try to win a race, prize, etc: *Five children competed in the race.* | *He competed **with** the rest of the class for the prize.*

com·pe·ti·tion /ˌkɒmpəˈtɪʃn/ *noun*
a test of who is best at something: *She came first in a drawing competition.* | *There was strong competition **between** the teams.*

com·pet·i·tor /kəm'petɪtə^r/ noun
a person who tries to win something: *Two of the competitors didn't arrive in time for the race.*

com·plain /kəm'pleɪn/ verb
something that you say when you are not pleased about something: *We complained **about** the bad food.* I *Local children complained **that** there was nowhere for them to play.*

com·plaint /kəm'pleɪnt/ noun
something you say when you are annoyed or unhappy about something: *There have been several complaints **about** the rail service.*

com·plete¹ /kəm'pli:t/ adjective
1 whole and with nothing left out: *the complete works of Shakespeare* I *I now have a complete set of dishes.*
⇨ opposite INCOMPLETE
2 used to emphasize what you are saying: *This is a complete waste of time.* I *The news came as a complete surprise.*

complete² verb (present participle **completing**, past **completed**)
to finish doing or making something: *They have completed the new school building.* I *He never completed the course of study.*

com·plete·ly /kəm'pli:tlɪ/ adverb
totally, in every way: *I completely forgot about your birthday.*

com·pli·cat·ed /'kɒmplɪkeɪtɪd/ adjective
difficult to understand and with many parts or details: *She asked us to solve a very complicated problem.* I *The instructions are much too complicated.*

com·pli·ment¹ /'kɒmplɪmənt/ noun
something nice said about someone
⇨ opposite INSULT

com·pli·ment² /'kɒmplɪment/ verb
to say something nice to someone or to praise them: *She complimented Mary **on** passing all her exams.*

com·pose /kəm'pəʊz/ verb (present participle **composing**, past **composed**)
1 be composed of to be formed from different parts: *Water is composed of hydrogen and oxygen.*
2 to write or make up a poem or a piece of music: *Nyman composed the music for the film 'The Piano'.*

com·pos·er /kəm'pəʊzə^r/ noun
a person who writes music

com·po·si·tion /ˌkɒmpə'zɪʃn/ noun
a story, poem, piece of music, etc that you have written

com·pound /'kɒmpaʊnd/ noun
a group of buildings and the land around them

com·pre·hen·sive school
/ˌkɒmprɪ'hensɪv ˌsku:l/ noun
a school for children over the age of eleven that teaches students of all abilities

com·pul·so·ry /kəm'pʌlsərɪ/ adjective
something that is compulsory must be done because of a rule or law: *Learning science is compulsory at our school.*

com·put·er /kəm'pju:tə^r/ noun
a machine that can store and use large amounts of information: *All our data is kept on computer.* I *Oh no! My computer's just crashed.*

computer game /kəm'pju:tə ˌgeɪm/ noun
a game played on a computer ⇨ see picture on page 197

con·cen·trate /'kɒnsəntreɪt/ verb (present participle **concentrating**, past **concentrated**)
to keep your thoughts and attention on something: *Are you concentrating **on** your work?* I *With all this noise, it is hard to concentrate.*

con·cern¹ /kən's3:n/ noun
worry: *He shows no concern for his children.*

concern² verb
1 to affect or involve someone: *This letter concerns you.* I *What we are planning doesn't concern Barry.*
2 to be about someone or something: *The story concerns a man who lived in Russia a long time ago.*
3 to worry someone: *The drug problem concerns most parents.*

con·cerned /kən's3:nd/ adjective
1 worried: *I'm very concerned **about** my mother's illness.* I *She was concerned for their safety.*
2 as far as I'm concerned used when you are giving your opinion: *As far as I'm concerned, the whole idea is silly.*

A B C D E F G H I J K L M N O P Q R S T U V W X Y Z

con·cern·ing /kənˈsɜːnɪŋ/ preposition
about: I have a question concerning the car.

con·cert /ˈkɒnsət/ noun
a performance of music

con·clude /kənˈkluːd/ verb (present participle **concluding**, past **concluded**)
1 to decide that something is true from what you have learned: When I had heard the story, I concluded **that** he had told me the truth.
2 to finish something: She concluded her speech with a joke.

con·clu·sion /kənˈkluːʒn/ noun
a judgement or decision that you reach after some thought: I came to the conclusion **that** he had forgotten.

con·crete /ˈkɒnkriːt/ noun (no plural)
a grey powder mixed with sand and water, that becomes very hard and is used for building

con·demn /kənˈdem/ verb
1 to say very strongly that you do not approve of someone or something: She knew that people would condemn her **for** leaving her children.
2 to give someone a punishment for a crime

con·di·tion /kənˈdɪʃn/ noun
1 the state of someone or something: The car is in very good condition. | Weather conditions are bad today.
2 something that must happen before something else happens: One of the conditions **for** getting into college was that I had to learn English.

con·duct¹ /kənˈdʌkt/ verb
1 to do or organize something: The children conducted an experiment.
2 to lead someone: He conducted us on a tour of the castle.

con·duct² /ˈkɒndʌkt/ noun (no plural)
the way you behave: That's not the sort of conduct we expect of our pupils.
⇨ same meaning BEHAVIOUR

con·duc·tor /kənˈdʌktəʳ/ noun
1 a person who controls a group of people playing music
2 British a person who sells tickets on a bus or train

cone /kəʊn/ noun
a round shape that is pointed at one end, like the end of a sharp pencil ⇨ see picture at SHAPE

con·fe·rence /ˈkɒnfərəns/ noun
a meeting of people to find out what they think about a subject: He is at a doctors' conference.

con·fess /kənˈfes/ verb
to tell someone about things you have done wrong: She confessed to the teacher that she had stolen some money.

con·fes·sion /kənˈfeʃn/ noun
a speech or piece of writing saying what you have done wrong: He made a confession.

con·fi·dence /ˈkɒnfɪdəns/ noun (no plural)
a feeling that you are sure that you can do something well: She plays the piano well but doesn't have the confidence to play to others.

con·fi·dent /ˈkɒnfɪdənt/ adjective
feeling sure you can do something well: I was confident that I had passed the examination. | She's quite confident **about** her new job.

con·firm /kənˈfɜːm/ verb
to say definitely that something is true or will happen: The doctor confirmed that she had a broken leg.

con·fir·ma·tion /ˌkɒnfəˈmeɪʃn/ noun (no plural)
a statement that something is true or will happen

con·flict¹ /ˈkɒnflɪkt/ noun
a fight or argument: There was a conflict **between** the two countries.

con·flict² /kənˈflɪkt/ verb
to not be the same: His story conflicts **with** what he said before.

con·fuse /kənˈfjuːz/ verb (present participle **confusing**, past **confused**)
1 to make someone feel they cannot think clearly or understand something: His explanations really confused me.
2 to think wrongly that one person or thing is someone or something else: It's easy to confuse Sue **with** her sister.

con·fus·ion /kənˈfjuːʒn/ noun (no plural)
when you do not know what to think or do: There was confusion **over** the new rules.

con·grat·u·late /kənˈgrætʃʊleɪt/ verb
to say you are pleased about a happy event: I congratulated them **on** the birth of their baby.

con·grat·u·la·tions /kənˌgrætʃʊ'leɪʃnz/
an expression of happiness or admiration for something someone has done: *Congratulations **on** your new job!*

con·junc·tion /kən'dʒʌŋkʃən/ *noun*
a word such as 'and' or 'but' that joins two parts of a sentence

con·nect /kə'nekt/ *verb*
to join two or more things together: *Could you connect the hose **to** the tap?*

con·nec·tion /kə'nekʃən/ *noun*
1 a relationship between two or more things, ideas, etc: *Scientists eventually discovered the connection **between** smoking and lung cancer.*
2 the joining of two or more things: *Check the pipes for any leaks around the connections.*

con·quer /'kɒŋkəʳ/ *verb*
to win a war: *The Ottoman Empire conquered Egypt in 1517.*

con·quest /'kɒŋkwest/ *noun*
when a person or country wins control: *The Spanish conquest of the Incas took place in South America.*

con·science /'kɒnʃəns/ *noun*
1 the feeling inside you that tells you if something is right or wrong
2 a guilty conscience a feeling that you have done something wrong

con·scious /'kɒnʃəs/ *adjective*
awake and knowing what is happening around you: *He is badly hurt but still conscious.* ⇨ opposite UNCONSCIOUS

con·sent[1] /kən'sent/ *noun (no plural)*
permission to do something: *We need your parent's written consent.*

consent[2] *verb*
to agree to something: *Her father consented **to** her marriage.*

con·se·quence /'kɒnsɪkwəns/ *noun*
something that happens as a result of something else: *Air pollution can have bad consequences for people's health.*

con·se·quent·ly /'kɒnsɪkwəntlɪ/ *adverb*
happening as a result of something else: *We talked most of the night and consequently felt very tired the next morning.*

con·ser·va·tion /ˌkɒnsə'veɪʃn/ *noun*
(no plural)
the saving and protecting of animals or plants: *He is involved in the conservation of trees.*

con·ser·va·tive /kən'sɜːvətɪv/ *adjective*
not liking changes or new ideas: *He has a conservative attitude to education.*

con·sid·er /kən'sɪdəʳ/ *verb*
to think about something: *I'm considering changing my essay.* I *Have you ever considered moving abroad?*

con·sid·er·a·tion /kənˌsɪdə'reɪʃn/ *noun*
(no plural)
1 thought and attention: *They gave the plan careful consideration.*
2 attention to other people's feelings and needs: *Jeff never shows any consideration **for** his mother's feelings.*

con·sist /kən'sɪst/ *verb*
consist of to be made up of: *The soup consists of carrots, potatoes, and onions.*

con·so·nant /'kɒnsənənt/ *noun*
a written letter, or the sound of a letter, that is not a, e, i, o, or u. ⇨ compare VOWEL

con·stant /'kɒnstənt/ *adjective*
happening all the time: *The younger children are kept under constant supervision.*

con·sti·tu·tion /ˌkɒnstɪ'tjuːʃn/ *noun*
a set of laws in a country, state, club, etc

con·sti·tu·tion·al /ˌkɒnstɪ'tjuːʃnəl/
adjective
allowed by, limited by, or relating to the constitution: *There are constitutional limits on the Queen's power.*

con·struct /kən'strʌkt/ *verb*
to build or make something: *The city plans to construct a new bridge over the river.*

con·struc·tion /kən'strʌkʃən/ *noun*
(no plural) the process of building something: *A construction company is building a new road.*

con·sul /'kɒnsl/ *noun*
a person whose job is to help people who come from the same country that he or she comes from

con·sult /kən'sʌlt/ *verb*
to talk to someone or look at a book in order to get information: *Consult your doctor if the headaches continue.*

con·sume /kən'sjuːm/ *verb (present participle* **consuming***, past* **consumed***)*
to use energy, goods, time, etc:

Expensive cars can consume a lot of fuel.

con·sump·tion /kən'sʌmpʃən/ *noun* (*no plural*)

the amount of energy, gas, etc that someone or something uses: *We have a plan to reduce water consumption.*

con·tact[1] /'kɒntækt/ *noun* (*no plural*)

1 the fact that you are talking or writing to someone, or having a relationship with them: *We don't have much contact **with** my husband's family.*

2 when two people or things touch against each other: *The fire started when two wires came into contact.*

contact[2] *verb*

to talk or write to someone: *She contacted me as soon as she arrived.*

contact lens /'kɒntækt ˌlenz/ *noun* (*plural* **contact lenses**)

a small round piece of plastic that you put in your eye to help you see clearly

con·tain /kən'teɪn/ *verb*

to have something inside: *We also found a purse containing £32.* | *This book contains all the information I need.*

containers

a tube of toothpaste

a jar of honey

a can of cat food　*a carton of milk*

a box of chocolates

a bottle of orange juice

a packet of pasta

con·tain·er /kən'teɪnər/ *noun*

something you can put things into, for example a box or bottle

con·tent /kən'tent/ *adjective*

happy: *Gary seems content **to** sit around and watch TV all day.*

con·tent·ed /kən'tentɪd/ *adjective*

happy: *My father seems more contented in his new job.*

con·tents /'kɒntents/ *plural noun*

the things that are inside something: *The contents of the box fell onto the floor.*

con·test /'kɒntest/ *noun*

a competition: *Tonight's contest is bound to be exciting.*

con·ti·nent /'kɒntɪnənt/ *noun*

one of the large areas of land on Earth, for example Africa or Australia

con·ti·nen·tal /ˌkɒntɪ'nentl/ *adjective*

relating to a continent

con·tin·u·al /kən'tɪnjuəl/ *adjective*

happening often or all the time: *continual arguments* | *She was in continual pain.*

con·tin·ue /kən'tɪnjuː/ *verb* (*present participle* **continuing**, *past* **continued**)

1 to keep happening or doing something without stopping: *She continued to look at them in silence.* | *The fighting continued for three days.*

2 to start again after stopping: *The play will continue in 15 minutes.*

3 to go further in the same direction: *The road continues on down the valley.*

con·tin·u·ous /kən'tɪnjuəs/ *adjective*

never stopping: *These plants need a continuous supply of fresh water.*

con·tract /'kɒntrækt/ *noun*

a written agreement between two people or companies that says what each one must do for the other

con·tra·ry[1] /'kɒntrəri/ *noun* (*no plural*)

on the contrary used for saying that the opposite of what was just said is true: *"You must be tired." "On the contrary, I feel wide awake."*

contrary[2] *adjective*

contrary to something not agreeing with something: *He passed the examination, contrary to what I expected.*

con·trast[1] /'kɒntrɑːst/ *noun* (*no plural*)

a difference: *There's a big contrast **between** rich people and poor people.*

con·trast[2] /kən'trɑːst/ *verb*

to compare two things and find the

differences between them: *The book contrasts life in the city* **with** *life on a farm.*

con·trib·ute /kən'trɪbjuːt/ *verb (present participle* **contributing**, *past* **contributed**)
to give money or help: *We all contributed money to buy Richard's present.*

con·tri·bu·tion /ˌkɒntrɪ'bjuːʃn/ *noun*
money or help that is offered or given: *Peter collected all the contributions* **to** *the school magazine.*

con·trol [1] /kən'trəʊl/ *noun*
1 the power or authority to make someone or something do what you want: *Peter and Rachel have no control* **over** *their son.*
2 out of control not controlled by anyone: *The horse went out of control and the rider fell to the ground.*
3 lose control of something to stop being able to make something do what you want: *He lost control of the car and it crashed.*

control [2] *verb (present participle* **controlling**, *past* **controlled**)
to make someone or something do what you want: *He wasn't a bad teacher but he couldn't control the class.*

con·ve·ni·ence /kən'viːnɪəns/ *noun*
the quality of being useful, helpful, or easy: *My mother likes the convenience of living close to the shops.* ⇨ opposite INCONVENIENCE

con·ve·ni·ent /kən'viːnɪənt/ *adjective*
1 helpful, useful, or suitable for your needs: *It would be more convenient for me to pay by cheque.*
2 near and easy to get to: *The school is very convenient, just down the street.* ⇨ opposite INCONVENIENT

con·vent /'kɒnvənt/ *noun*
1 a place where women who lead a religious life live ⇨ compare MONASTERY
2 a school or college run by these women

con·ver·sa·tion /ˌkɒnvə'seɪʃn/ *noun*
a talk between two or more people: *I had a long conversation* **with** *your teacher.* | *a telephone conversation*

con·ver·sion /kən'vɜːʃn/ *noun*
a change from one use to another or from one religion to another: *his recent conversion* **to** *Islam.*

con·vert /kən'vɜːt/ *verb*
to change something into something else: *The company is converting the building* **into** *a school.*

con·vict [1] /kən'vɪkt/ *verb*
to decide in a law court that someone is guilty of something: *He was convicted* **of** *murder.*

con·vict [2] /'kɒnvɪkt/ *noun*
a person who has been sent to prison for doing something wrong

con·vince /kən'vɪns/ *verb (present participle* **convincing**, *past* **convinced**)
1 to make a person believe something: *He convinced me* **that** *he was telling the truth.*
2 be convinced that to be completely sure about something: *I was convinced that I was doing the right thing.*

cook [1] /kʊk/ *verb*
to make food ready to eat by using heat: *He's cooking dinner for me tonight.*

cook [2] *noun*
a person who prepares food for eating: *Sarah is a very good cook.* | *He works as a cook in a hotel near here.* ⇨ see picture on page 200

cook·er /'kʊkə'/ *noun*
British a piece of equipment for cooking food: *a gas cooker*

cook·e·ry /'kʊkəri/ *noun (no plural)*
British the study or activity of preparing food for eating: *cookery lessons*

cook·ie /'kʊki/ *noun*
American a dry thin cake that is usually sweet (*British* **biscuit**)

cook·ing /'kʊkɪŋ/ *noun (no plural)*
1 the activity of preparing food: *Cooking is fun.*
2 food made in a particular way or by a particular person: *Sue's cooking is always good.*

cool [1] /kuːl/ *adjective*
1 slightly cold: *a cool breeze* | *The room was cool after the sun had gone down.*
2 calm: *Although he was nervous about the exam he tried to look cool.*

cool [2] *verb*
1 to make something slightly colder or to become slightly colder: *Leave the cake to cool.* | *They opened the windows to cool the room.*

A B C D E F G H I J K L M N O P Q R S T U V W X Y Z

2 cool down (a) to become slightly colder: *Let the engine cool down.* **(b)** to become calmer: *I'll discuss it with her again when she's cooled down a bit.*

co·op·e·rate /kəʊ'ɒpəreɪt/ *verb* (*present participle* **cooperating**, *past* **cooperated**)

to work together with someone else to get something done: *If we all cooperate we'll finish this by five o'clock.*

co·op·e·ra·tion /kəʊˌɒpə'reɪʃn/ *noun* (*no plural*)

willingness to work together: *Thank you for your cooperation.*

co·ope·ra·tive /kəʊ'ɒprətɪv/ *adjective*

willing to help other people: *Ned has always been very cooperative in the past.* ⇨ opposite UNCOOPERATIVE

cop·per /'kɒpər/ *noun* (*no plural*)

a red-gold metal

cop·y[1] /'kɒpɪ/ *verb* (*present participle* **copying**, *past* **copied**)

1 to make or do something exactly the same as something else: *Copy the sums from the blackboard.*

2 to cheat by writing exactly the same thing as someone else: *The teacher saw him copying in the history test.*

copy[2] *noun* (*plural* **copies**)

1 something that is exactly the same as something else: *Please send a copy of this letter to Mr Brown.*

2 one magazine, book, or newspaper from the many that have been produced: *Have you got another copy of this book?*

cord /kɔːd/ *noun*

a piece of thin rope

core /kɔːr/ *noun*

1 the central or most important part of something: *Now we are getting to the core of the problem.*

2 the hard central part of an apple or PEAR

cork /kɔːk/ *noun*

1 (*no plural*) a light substance that comes from the outside part of the stem of a tree

2 a piece of this put in the top of a wine bottle to keep the liquid in

corn /kɔːn/ *noun* (*no plural*)

British the seed of grain plants such as wheat

cor·ner /'kɔːnər/ *noun*

the place where two lines, walls, streets, etc meet each other: *The table stood in the corner of the room.* | *His house is on the corner of School Road and the High Street.*

corn·flakes /'kɔːnfleɪks/ *plural noun*

a breakfast food made from MAIZE, that is usually eaten with milk and sugar

cor·po·ra·tion /ˌkɔːpə'reɪʃn/ *noun*

a large business

corpse /kɔːps/ *noun*

the dead body of a person

cor·rect[1] /kə'rekt/ *adjective*

right, with no mistakes: *a correct answer* | *"Your name is Ives?" "Yes, that's correct."* ⇨ opposite INCORRECT

correct[2] *verb*

1 to show that something is wrong and make it right: *I've corrected your homework.* | *Correct my pronunciation if it's wrong.*

2 to make something work the way it should: *These glasses will help to correct your vision.*

cor·rec·tion /kə'rekʃən/ *noun*

a change that makes something right or better: *He made several corrections to the letter.*

cor·re·spond /ˌkɒrɪ'spɒnd/ *verb*

1 to have the same value or effect as something else: *The French 'baccalauréat' roughly corresponds to British 'A levels'.*

2 to write to someone and receive letters from them: *She corresponded with him regularly for years.*

cor·re·spon·dence /ˌkɒrɪ'spɒndəns/ *noun* (*no plural*)

letters sent by people to each other

cor·re·spon·dent /ˌkɒrɪ'spɒndənt/ *noun*

1 someone who writes and receives letters

2 someone who sends news from another country to a newspaper or television company: *a foreign correspondent*

cor·ri·dor /'kɒrɪdɔːr/ *noun*

a long narrow part of a building with doors into rooms on each side of it: *Go down the corridor, to the third room on the left.*

cos·met·ics /kɒz'metɪks/ plural noun
substances that you put on your face to make you look prettier

cost¹ /kɒst/ noun
1 the money that you spend on something: *The cost of books has gone up.*
2 something needed, given, or lost in order to get something else: *War is never worth the terrible cost in human life.*
3 at all costs whatever happens: *We must avoid war at all costs.*

cost² verb (past **cost**)
to have a particular amount as a price: *How much did that bag cost?* | *These trousers only cost me ten pounds!*

cost·ly /'kɒstlɪ/ adjective
costing a lot of money: *The ring was very costly.* ⇨ same meaning EXPENSIVE

cos·tume /'kɒstjuːm/ noun
clothes worn for a special reason, or to represent a country or time in history: *They all wore national costume.*

co·sy /'kəʊzɪ/ adjective
warm and comfortable: *a cosy little house*

cot /kɒt/ noun
British a bed with high sides, for a baby ⇨ see picture at BED

cottage

cot·tage /'kɒtɪdʒ/ noun
a small attractive house in the country

cot·ton /'kɒtn/ noun (no plural)
1 a plant grown in hot countries for the white threads that cover its seeds
2 thread or cloth made from the cotton plant: *She bought a cotton dress.* ⇨ see picture at REEL

cotton-wool /ˌkɒtn 'wʊl/ noun (no plural)
British soft white material made from cotton and used for cleaning the skin, wounds, etc

couch /kaʊtʃ/ noun (plural **couches**)
a long seat on which you can sit or lie ⇨ same meaning SOFA

cough¹ /kɒf/ noun
a sharp noise made when you send air out of your throat and mouth suddenly: *Billy had a bad cough, so his mother took him to the doctor.*

cough² verb
to push air out from your throat and mouth with a sudden rough sound: *He was coughing all night.*

could /kəd; strong kʊd/ verb
1 the word for 'can' in the past: *Could you understand what she was saying?* | *I could see him through the window.*
2 used when saying what might happen: *It could take weeks for the package to arrive.*
3 used as a polite way of asking someone something: *Could you help me, please?*

couldn't /'kʊdnt/
could not: *I couldn't see because it was dark.*

could've /'kʊdəv/
could have: *He could've told me he was going to be late.*

coun·cil /'kaʊnsl/ noun
a group of people who are chosen to make laws or decisions in a town or city: *The town council will decide where to plant the trees.*

coun·cil·lor /'kaʊnsələʳ/ noun
a member of a council

count¹ /kaʊnt/ verb
1 to say numbers in the right order: *He can count from one to ten.*
2 to find out how many things there are in a group: *She counted the books. There were fourteen of them.*
3 to have value or importance: *He felt that his opinion didn't count.*
4 count on someone or something to depend on someone or something: *You can always count on me to help you.*

count² noun (no plural)
1 when you add everything together to get a total: *At the last count, I'd visited 15 countries.*
2 lose count to forget the total of something: *I've lost count of how many people I've invited.*

coun·ter /'kaʊntər/ noun
1 the place in a shop or bank where you go to be served
2 a small round piece of plastic or wood used in playing games

count·less /'kaʊntləs/ adjective
very many: She's had countless boyfriends.

coun·try /'kʌntrɪ/ noun
1 (plural **countries**) an area ruled by one government: France and Germany are European countries.
2 (no plural) the land that is not a town: He lives in the country.

coun·try·side /'kʌntrɪsaɪd/ noun (no plural)
land outside towns and cities: She loves the English countryside.

coun·ty /'kaʊntɪ/ noun (plural **counties**)
a part of a country: Devon is a county in the southwest of England.

cou·ple /'kʌpl/ noun
1 (no plural) two things usually thought of together: I waited for a couple **of** hours.
2 two people who are married, live together, or have a close relationship: We've invited three other couples to dinner.

cou·pon /'ku:pɒn/ noun
a piece of paper that can be exchanged for goods or money: Collect three coupons for a free pen.

cour·age /'kʌrɪdʒ/ noun (no plural)
willingness to do dangerous and frightening things: The soldier showed great courage in the battle. ⇨ same meaning BRAVERY

cou·ra·geous /kə'reɪdʒəs/ adjective
brave: She is a courageous person.

course /kɔ:s/ noun
1 **of course** definitely or as you would expect: Of course I'll still love you when you're old. | "Can I borrow your pen?" "Of course."
2 a set of lessons: What course are you taking at college?
3 one part of a meal: We have three courses: soup, meat and vegetables, and fruit. | What would you like for your main course?
4 the path or direction that something takes: The course of the river was marked on the map. | The plane had to change course and go another way.

5 (no plural) the way that something happens or the time when something is happening: During the course **of** the journey, we saw a lot of new places. | The war changed the course of history.

court /kɔ:t/ noun
1 a place where it is decided if someone is guilty of a crime or not: She had to appear **in** court to explain what she saw.
2 an open space where games are played: a tennis court
3 a king or queen and all the people who live with him or her

cour·te·ous /'kɜ:tɪəs/ adjective
polite: He was a courteous young man.

cour·te·sy /'kɜ:təsɪ/ noun (no plural)
polite behaviour

court·yard /'kɔ:tjɑ:d/ noun
an open space surrounded by walls or buildings

cous·in /'kʌzn/ noun
someone whose parent is the sister or brother of your parent

cov·er[1] /'kʌvər/ verb
1 to put something over something else: She covered the table **with** a cloth.
2 to be spread over a particular area or surface: Snow covered the ground. | Your boots are covered **with** mud!
3 to include or deal with something: His talk covered British history between the wars.
4 **cover something up (a)** to place something over something else to protect or hide it: Cover the furniture up before you start painting. **(b)** to stop people finding out the truth about something: She tried to cover up the news about her sister.

cov·er[2] noun
1 something that you put over something else: Put a cover over the bowl.
2 the outside of a book or magazine
3 **take cover** to shelter or hide from something: We took cover under a tree.

cow /kaʊ/ noun
a large female animal that is kept on farms for its milk: He kept a herd of cows.

cow·ard /'kaʊəd/ noun
someone who avoids pain or danger because they are not brave

cow·ard·ly /'kaʊədlɪ/ *adjective*
behaving in a way that shows you are not brave: *That was a cowardly thing to do.* ⇨ opposite BRAVE

cow·boy /'kaʊbɔɪ/ *noun*
a man who rides a horse and looks after cattle in America

crab /kræb/ *noun*
a sea-animal with ten legs and a hard shell ⇨ see picture on page 195

crack¹ /kræk/ *verb*
1 to break, or to break something, so that lines appear on the surface: *I've cracked this plate.* | *The ice is starting to crack.*
2 to make a sudden loud noise, like something breaking

crack² *noun*
1 a thin line on something where it has been damaged: *A crack appeared in the wall.* ⇨ see picture at BROKEN
2 a very narrow space between two things: *Sunlight shone through a crack in the curtains.*
3 a sharp noise: *I heard a crack of thunder.*

cracked /krækt/ *adjective*
with a crack or cracks on the surface: *One of these cups is cracked.*

cra·dle /'kreɪdl/ *noun*
a bed for a baby which can be moved from side to side ⇨ compare COT

craft /krɑːft/ *noun*
1 a job or trade needing skill, especially skill with your hands: *He knew the craft of making furniture.*
2 (*plural* **craft**) a boat or plane

crafts·man /'krɑːftsmən/ *noun* (*plural* **craftsmen** /-mən/)
someone whose job needs a lot of skill, especially skill with their hands

craft·y /'krɑːftɪ/ *adjective*
a crafty person is good at getting what they want by deceiving people

cram /kræm/ *verb* (*present participle* **cramming**, *past* **crammed**)
to force people or things into a small space: *Lots of people were crammed into the bus.*

crane /kreɪn/ *noun*
a tall machine for lifting heavy things

crash¹ /kræʃ/ *noun* (*plural* **crashes**)
1 an accident in which vehicles hit each other: *a car crash*
2 a loud noise, like something large falling over: *The tray fell to the floor with a crash.*

crash² *verb*
1 if a car, plane, etc crashes, it has an accident and hits something: *The car crashed into the tree.*
2 if a computer crashes, it stops working suddenly ⇨ same meaning GO DOWN
3 to make a sudden loud noise: *We listened to the waves crashing against the rocks.*

crash hel·met /'kræʃ ˌhelmɪt/ *noun*
a hard hat that you wear to protect your head when you ride a MOTORBIKE

crate /kreɪt/ *noun*
a big strong box: *a crate of fruit*

crawl /krɔːl/ *verb*
to move along the floor on your hands and knees: *The baby crawled towards his father.*

cray·on /'kreɪən/ *noun*
a soft coloured pencil ⇨ see picture on page 205

cra·zy /'kreɪzɪ/ *adjective* (**crazier**, **craziest**)
1 very strange and not reasonable: *He's crazy to drive his car so fast.*
2 **be crazy about someone or something** to like someone or something very much: *He's crazy about her.*

creak /kriːk/ *verb*
to make a noise when pushed, stepped on, or sat on: *The door creaked as she opened it.*

cream¹ /kriːm/ *noun* (*no plural*)
1 the thick part of milk that you can eat with other foods: *I love strawberries and cream.*
2 a thick liquid that you put on your skin: *She's trying a new face cream.*

cream² *adjective, noun*
a yellowish-white colour

cre·ate /krɪ'eɪt/ *verb* (*present participle* **creating**, *past* **created**)
to make something new: *Her behaviour is creating problems for the school.* | *The government wants to create more jobs.*

cre·a·tion /krɪ'eɪʃn/ *noun*
1 (*no plural*) when something is made: *the creation of a United Europe*
2 something that has been made: *the artist's latest creation*

A B C D E F G H I J K L M N O P Q R S T U V W X Y Z

cre·a·tive /krɪ'eɪtɪv/ adjective
good at making new and interesting things

crea·ture /'kri:tʃəʳ/ noun
an animal or insect

cred·it[1] /'kredɪt/ noun (no plural)
1 attention that you get for doing something good: Mum gave all the credit to James, even though I helped him.
2 a way of buying things in which you pay for them later: We bought the furniture **on** credit.
3 **be in credit** to have money in a bank account

credit[2] verb
to add money to a bank account

credit card /'kredɪt ˌkɑːd/ noun
a small plastic card that allows you to buy things without using coins and notes. You pay for the goods later

creep /kri:p/ verb (past **crept** /krept/)
to move slowly and quietly: She crept downstairs in the dark.

crept /krept/
the past tense and past participle of the verb **creep**

crest /krest/ noun
the top of a hill, mountain, or wave: We climbed to the crest **of** the hill.

crew /kru:/ noun
the people who work on a ship or plane

crick·et /'krɪkɪt/ noun
1 a ball game played by two teams of eleven players each ⇨ see picture on page 196
2 a small brown insect that jumps and makes a loud noise

cried /kraɪd/
the past tense and past participle of the verb **cry**

cries /kraɪz/
1 the plural of the noun **cry**
2 the form of the verb **cry** that you use with 'he', 'she', or 'it' in the present tense

crime /kraɪm/ noun
1 an action that is wrong and can be punished by the law: Killing people is a crime. ⇨ compare SIN
2 **commit a crime** to do something wrong that can be punished by the law

crim·i·nal /'krɪmɪnl/ noun
someone who has done something that

is against the law: The prison contains 325 criminals.

crim·son /'krɪmzən/ adjective, noun
a deep red colour, like the colour of blood

cri·sis /'kraɪsɪs/ noun (plural **crises** /'kraɪsiːz/)
a time when something serious, very worrying, or dangerous happens: She's good at keeping calm in a crisis.

crisp[1] /krɪsp/ adjective
1 firm, dry, and easily broken: Keep the biscuits in a tin so that they stay crisp.
2 firm and fresh: He was eating a nice crisp apple.

crisp[2] noun
British a very thin piece of cooked potato that you buy in a packet and eat cold (American **chip**): I bought a packet of crisps. ⇨ compare CHIP

crit·ic /'krɪtɪk/ noun
a person whose job is to write about art, music, a film, etc and say if it is good or bad

crit·i·cal /'krɪtɪkl/ adjective
1 looking for faults: She was very critical **of** my work.
2 very important: The next part is critical **to** the plan's success.

crit·i·cis·m /'krɪtɪsɪzəm/ noun
when you say what you think is bad about someone or something: I listened to her criticism in silence.

crit·i·cize /'krɪtɪsaɪz/ verb (present participle **criticizing**, past **criticized**)
to say what is wrong with someone or something: She's always criticizing me.

croc·o·dile /'krɒkədaɪl/ noun
a large animal with a long body, a hard skin, and sharp teeth, that lives in or near rivers in hot countries ⇨ see picture on page 195

crook /krʊk/ noun
a person who is not honest

crook·ed /'krʊkɪd/ adjective
1 bent, twisted, or not straight: Her hat was crooked.
2 not honest

crop /krɒp/ noun
a plant that is grown as food: We had a good crop **of** apples this year.

cross [1] /krɒs/ noun (plural **crosses**)
  1 a shape (X) with four arms that meet in the centre
  2 a post on which people were left to die as a punishment in ancient times

cross [2] verb
  1 to go from one side of something to the other: They crossed the road.
  2 if you cross your arms or legs, you put one arm or leg over the other

cross [3] adjective
  angry: Why are you cross **with** me?

cross·ing /ˈkrɒsɪŋ/ noun
  a place where you can safely cross a road, river, etc

cross·roads /ˈkrɒsrəʊdz/ plural noun
  a place where two roads meet and cross each other

cross·word /ˈkrɒswɜːd/ noun
  a game in which you have to guess words, the letters of which fit into a pattern of squares down and across the page

crouch /kraʊtʃ/ verb
  to make your body come close to the ground by bending your knees: She crouched by the fire to get warm.

crow /krəʊ/ noun
  a large black bird with a low hard cry

crowd [1] /kraʊd/ noun
  a large number of people: There was a crowd **of** people waiting at the station. | A crowd gathered to watch the parade.

crowd [2] verb
  to come together in a large group: They all crowded round the teacher.

crowd·ed /ˈkraʊdɪd/ adjective
  full of people: I don't like the market; it's too crowded.

crown /kraʊn/ noun
  a special hat made of gold, beautiful stones, etc, worn by a king or queen

cru·ci·fix /ˈkruːsɪfɪks/ noun (plural **crucifixes**)
  a cross with a figure of Jesus on it

crude /kruːd/ adjective
  1 in a natural or raw condition: Crude oil has to be made pure before it can be used.
  2 rude: a crude joke

cru·el /ˈkruːəl/ adjective
  liking to hurt other people or animals: He is cruel **to** animals ⇨ opposite KIND

cru·el·ty /ˈkruːəltɪ/ noun (no plural)
  actions that cause pain to a person or animal: He wanted to stop cruelty to animals.

cruise

a cruise to the tropical islands

cruise [1] /kruːz/ noun
  a long sea journey for pleasure

cruise [2] verb
  if a boat or vehicle cruises, it moves steadily but not very fast: A boat cruised past on the lake.

crumb /krʌm/ noun
  a very small piece of something such as bread or cake

crum·ble /ˈkrʌmbl/ verb (present participle **crumbling**, past **crumbled**)
  to break into small pieces: The old stone wall is crumbling.

crum·ple /ˈkrʌmpl/ verb
  to press or crush something so that it becomes smaller and bent: Don't sit on that shirt – you'll crumple it. | She crumpled the piece of paper she was holding.

crunch /krʌntʃ/ verb
  1 to crush food with the teeth making a noise: The dog crunched **on** the bone.
  2 to make a noise that sounds like something being crushed: The stones crunched under the car tyres.

crush /krʌʃ/ verb
  to press something so hard that it breaks or is damaged: Wine is made by crushing grapes.

crust /krʌst/ noun
  the hard part on the outside of bread

crutch /krʌtʃ/ noun (plural **crutches**)
  a piece of wood or metal that supports a person who cannot walk well: I hurt my ankle and had to use crutches for several days.

A B C D E F G H I J K L M N O P Q R S T U V W X Y Z

cry [1] /kraɪ/ verb (past **cried**)
 1 to shout something loudly: *The boy cried for help.* | *"Stop!" she cried.*
 2 to produce water from your eyes, usually because you are sad: *She began to cry when she heard of her friend's death.*

cry [2] noun (plural **cries**)
 a loud shout: *There was a loud cry from the next room.* | *We woke to hear cries of "Fire!"*

cub /kʌb/ noun
 a young bear, lion, TIGER, or FOX

cube /kju:b/ noun
 a solid shape with six equal square sides ⇨ see picture at SHAPE

cuck·oo /'kʊku:/ noun
 a bird that makes a sound like its name

cu·cum·ber /'kju:kʌmbər/ noun
 a long thin green vegetable that is usually eaten without cooking ⇨ see picture on page 199

cud·dle /'kʌdl/ verb (present participle **cuddling**, past **cuddled**)
 to put your arms around someone and hold them close to you: *She cuddled her little boy.*

cuff /kʌf/ noun
 the end of an arm of a shirt, dress, etc

cul·ti·vate /'kʌltɪveɪt/ verb (present participle **cultivating**, past **cultivated**)
 to prepare land and use it for growing plants or crops

cul·ti·va·tion /ˌkʌltɪ'veɪʃn/ noun (no plural)
 when land is prepared and used for growing plants or crops

cul·ture /'kʌltʃər/ noun
 1 the beliefs, customs, and way of life of a particular society: *The students were learning about American culture.*
 2 (no plural) art, music, and the theatre: *Paris is full of culture.*

cun·ning /'kʌnɪŋ/ adjective
 clever and good at deceiving people

cup /kʌp/ noun
 1 a container, usually with a handle, that you can drink from, or the liquid it contains: *She handed me a cup and saucer.* | *Would you like a cup of tea?*
 2 a prize, shaped like a bowl, usually made of silver or gold: *The school cricket team won the cup.*

cup·board /'kʌbəd/ noun
 a piece of furniture with shelves and a door in which you keep clothes, plates, or food ⇨ see picture on page 205

cure [1] /kjʊər/ verb (present participle **curing**, past **cured**)
 to make someone better when they have been ill: *I hope the doctor can cure the pain in my shoulder.*

cure [2] noun
 a medicine or treatment for making someone better when they have been ill: *Scientists are trying to find a cure for cancer.*

cu·ri·os·i·ty /ˌkjʊərɪ'ɒsətɪ/ noun (no plural)
 the wish to know something or learn about something: *Children are full of curiosity about the world around them.*

cu·ri·ous /'kjʊərɪəs/ adjective
 wanting to know about things or people: *Aren't you curious about where she was last night?*
 curiously adverb: *"But what happened?" John asked curiously.*

curl [1] /kɜːl/ verb
 1 to roll or bend something in a round or curved shape: *She curled her hair.*
 2 **curl up** to lie or sit with your arms and legs close to your body: *She curled up in front of the fire.*

curl [2] noun
 a piece of hair that curves around

curl·y /'kɜːlɪ/ adjective
 curly hair has lots of twists in it ⇨ see picture on page 202

cur·rant /'kʌrənt/ noun
 a small dried GRAPE

cur·ren·cy /'kʌrənsɪ/ noun (plural **currencies**)
 the money used in a country: *Can I pay in British currency on the boat?*

cups

mug

cup

glass

saucer

cur·rent[1] /'kʌrənt/ *adjective*
happening or being used right now: *Why does he want to change his current job?*

current[2] *noun*
a flow of water, electricity, or air: *Don't swim in the river; the current is very fast.*

cur·ry /'kʌrɪ/ *noun (plural* **curries**)
an Indian food of meat, vegetables, or fish, cooked in a thick hot-tasting liquid: *I'll have a chicken curry, please.*

curse[1] /kɜːs/ *verb*
1 to wish that something unpleasant will happen to someone: *He cursed the person who had stolen his money.*
2 to speak angry words: *He cursed when he hit his head on the shelf.*

curse[2] *noun*
1 something that you say which shows anger or hate, or which uses bad words
2 put a curse on someone to say magical words that are intended to make something unpleasant happen to someone: *The witch put a curse on the prince and he turned into a frog.*

cur·sor /'kɜːsəʳ/ *noun*
a mark you can move on a computer screen that shows where you are writing

cur·tain /'kɜːtn/ *noun*
a piece of hanging cloth that can be pulled across to cover a window ⬦ compare BLIND ⬦ see picture on page 204

curve[1] /kɜːv/ *noun*
something that bends like part of a circle: *There was a curve in the road.*

curve[2] *verb (present participle* **curving**, *past* **curved**)
to bend or move in the shape of a circle: *The river curved round the hill.*

cush·ion /'kʊʃn/ *noun*
a bag filled with soft material to sit on or rest against ⬦ compare PILLOW

cus·tard /'kʌstəd/ *noun (no plural)*
a thick sweet yellow liquid that you pour over some fruit and sweet foods

cus·tom /'kʌstəm/ *noun*
a special way of doing something that a person or group of people has: *It's the custom for the bride's father to pay for the wedding.*

cus·tom·er /'kʌstəməʳ/ *noun*
a person who buys things from a shop

cus·toms /'kʌstəmz/ *plural noun*
a place where officials check what is in your bags when you leave or enter a country

cut[1] /kʌt/ *verb (present participle* **cutting**, *past* **cut**)
1 to divide or damage something with a knife or something sharp: *She cut the apple in half.* I *He cut his leg, and it was bleeding.*
2 to make something shorter: *Could you cut my hair for me?*
3 to reduce something a lot, especially prices, time, or money: *The college will cut the number of students on the course.*
4 to use something sharp to remove one part from something bigger: *She cut a piece of cake.*
5 cut down to make something fall to the ground by cutting it: *We'll have to cut down that tree.*
6 cut something off (a) to stop or disconnect something: *They've cut the gas off!* **(b)** to separate a person or place from the other people or places near them: *Snow has cut off many villages.*
7 cut something up to cut something into pieces: *Could you cut up the chicken?*
8 cut something out to remove something by cutting it: *She cut a picture out of the newspaper.*

cut[2] *noun*
1 an opening or wound made by something sharp: *I have a cut on my arm.*
2 a reduction in size, number, or amount: *There has been a cut in the education budget.*

cutlery

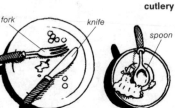

fork   knife   spoon

cut·le·ry /'kʌtlərɪ/ *noun (no plural)*
knives, forks, and spoons used for eating

cy·ber·space /ˈsaɪbəspeɪs/ *noun (no plural)*
all the connections between computers around the world, thought of as a real place where information, messages, etc can exist: *We didn't meet in San Francisco – we met in cyberspace.*

cy·cle[1] /ˈsaɪkl/ *noun*
a bicycle ⇨ same meaning BIKE

cycle[2] *verb (present participle* **cycling,** *past* **cycled)**
to ride a bicycle: *He cycles to school every day.* ⇨ see picture on page 196

cy·clist /ˈsaɪklɪst/ *noun*
a person who rides a bicycle

cyl·in·der /ˈsɪlɪndər/ *noun*
a long round shape like a tube or a pencil ⇨ see picture at SHAPE

D, d /diː/
the fourth letter of the English alphabet

'd /d/
1 had: *He'd* (=he had) *eaten all the cake.* | *I'd* (=I had) *already asked him three times.*
2 would: *I'd* (=I would) *buy a new car if I had enough money.* | *Ask her if she'd* (=she would) *like to go with us.*

dad /dæd/ *noun*
father: *Hey, Dad! Look at this.*

dad·dy /'dædɪ/ *noun*
used by and to small children to mean father

daf·fo·dil /'dæfədɪl/ *noun*
a yellow flower that appears in the spring

daft /dɑːft/ *adjective*
British silly: *That was a daft idea.*

dag·ger /'dægəʳ/ *noun*
a knife used as a weapon ⟡ compare SWORD

dai·ly /'deɪlɪ/ *adjective, adverb*
happening or done every day: *Take the medicine twice daily.* ⟡ compare WEEKLY

dair·y /'deərɪ/ *noun* (*plural* **dairies**)
a place where milk is kept and foods are made from milk

dai·sy /'deɪzɪ/ *noun* (*plural* **daisies**)
a small wild flower that is white with a yellow centre

dal·ma·tian /dæl'meɪʃn/ *noun*
a white dog with black spots

dam¹ /dæm/ *noun*
a wall built to hold back water

dam² ** *verb* (*present participle* **damming, *past* **dammed**)
to build a dam across something: *There is a plan to dam the river.*

dam

dam·age¹ /'dæmɪdʒ/ *noun* (*no plural*)
harm done to something: *Was there any damage to your car?*

damage² *verb*
to harm something: *Both cars were badly damaged in the accident.*

damp /dæmp/ *adjective*
slightly wet: *My clothes are still damp from the rain.*

dance¹ /dɑːns/ *verb* (*present participle* **dancing**, *past* **danced**)
to move to music: *We danced all night at the party.*

dance² *noun*
1 a set of movements you do to music: *They're learning a new dance.*
2 a party where there is dancing: *Are you going to the dance?*

danc·er /'dɑːnsəʳ/ *noun*
someone who dances, especially as their job

dan·de·li·on /'dændɪlaɪən/ *noun*
a yellow flower that grows wild

dan·druff /'dændrʌf/ *noun* (*no plural*)
very small white pieces of loose skin in a person's hair

dan·ger /'deɪndʒəʳ/ *noun*
1 (*no plural*) a situation in which you may be harmed: *Danger! Do not enter.* | *I had a sudden feeling that Ben was in danger.*
2 something that can cause harm: *Does she understand the dangers of smoking?*

dan·ger·ous /'deɪndʒərəs/ *adjective*
likely to harm people: *He is a dangerous driver.* | *It's dangerous to walk alone at night around here.*

dare /deəʳ/ *verb* (*present participle* **daring**, *past* **dared**)
1 to be brave enough to do something: *He didn't dare tell his dad what he had done.*
2 how dare you used when you are angry about what someone has done or said: *How dare you speak to me like that!*
3 don't you dare used when you are angry with someone and are telling them not to do something: *Don't you dare touch that!*
4 dare someone to do something to try to persuade someone to do something to show they are not afraid: *I dare you to jump.*

daren't /deənt/
dare not: *I daren't talk to him.*

dark¹ /dɑːk/ *adjective*

1 a dark place is one where there is not much light or no light: *Turn on the light; it's dark in here.* | *It was getting dark, so we hurried home.* ⋄ opposite LIGHT

2 of a deep colour, nearer black than white: *She has dark hair.* | *He wore a dark suit.* ⋄ opposite LIGHT, PALE

dark² *noun (no plural)*
when there is no light: *We couldn't see in the dark.* | *Make sure you are home before dark* (=before it is night).

dark·ness /'dɑːknɪs/ *noun (no plural)*
when there is no light: *The room was in darkness* (=was dark).

dar·ling /'dɑːlɪŋ/
a name you call someone you love: *Come on darling, or we'll be late.*

dart /dɑːt/ *verb*
to move suddenly and quickly: *A mouse darted across the floor.*

darts
dart
board

darts /dɑːts/ *noun (no plural)*
a game in which you throw small objects with sharp points at a board with numbers on it

dash¹ /dæʃ/ *verb*
to move quickly: *She dashed out of the room.*

dash² *noun (plural dashes)*
the sign (–) used in writing to separate two parts of a sentence

da·ta /'deɪtə, 'dɑːtə/ *noun (no plural)*
facts and information

da·ta·base /'deɪtəbeɪs/ *noun*
a large amount of information stored in a computer system

date /deɪt/ *noun*
1 the day of the month, or the year: *"What date is your birthday?" "It's April 2nd."* | *Please write today's date.*

2 an arrangement to meet someone you like in a romantic way: *I've got a date tonight.*

3 a small sweet brown fruit

4 out of date old-fashioned

5 up to date modern

daugh·ter /'dɔːtər/ *noun*
your female child: *They have three daughters and one son.* ⋄ look at SON

daughter-in-law /'dɔːtər ɪn lɔː/ *noun*
(*plural* **daughters-in-law**)
the wife of your son

dawn

dawn

dusk

dawn /dɔːn/ *noun*
the start of the day when the sun rises ⋄ same meaning DAYBREAK

day /deɪ/ *noun*
1 (*no plural*) the time when it is light: *The days get longer in the summer.* ⋄ opposite NIGHT

2 24 hours: *It hasn't stopped raining for days.* | *"What day is it today?" "It's Tuesday."*

3 a day off a day when you do not have to go to work or school: *She's having a day off.*

4 one day, some day at a time in the future: *Some day I'll be rich.*

5 the other day a few days ago: *I went there the other day.*

6 these days at the present time: *Everyone seems so busy these days.*

day·break /'deɪbreɪk/ *noun (no plural)*
the start of the day when the light first appears: *We left the house at daybreak.* ⋄ same meaning DAWN

day·dream /'deɪdriːm/ *verb*
to imagine nice things, especially things you would like to happen in the future

day·light /'deɪlaɪt/ *noun (no plural)*
the light of the day: *We want to travel in daylight* (=before night comes).

day·time /'deɪtaɪm/ *noun (no plural)*
the time when it is light ⋄ opposite NIGHT-TIME

dead[1] /ded/ *adjective*
not living: *My grandfather has been dead for ten years.* ⋄ opposite ALIVE, LIVING

dead[2] *noun*
the dead dead people: *After the battle, they counted the dead.* ⋄ opposite the LIVING

dead·ly /'dedli/ *adjective*
likely to cause death: *The murderer used a deadly poison.* ⋄ compare FATAL

deaf /def/ *adjective*
not able to hear: *I'm deaf in my right ear.*

deal[1] /di:l/ *noun*
1 a business arrangement: *They have just signed a new deal with their record company.*
2 a good deal, a great deal a lot: *There's a good deal of work to do.* | *He knows a great deal more than I do about computers.*

deal[2] *verb* (*past* **dealt** /delt/)
1 deal with something to take the correct action to achieve something: *I will deal with your questions now* (=answer them). | *Someone has already dealt with that problem.*
2 deal with someone to do business with someone: *We've been dealing with that company for years.*

deal·er /'di:lə^r/ *noun*
a person whose job is to buy and sell a particular thing: *He's a car dealer.*

dealt /delt/
the past tense and past participle of the verb **deal**

dear[1] /dɪə^r/ *adjective*
1 loved: *She is a very dear friend.*
2 used at the start of a letter to someone: *Dear Sue, Thank you for your gift.*
3 British costing a lot of money: *I can't afford to buy those shoes; they're too dear.* ⋄ same meaning EXPENSIVE

dear[2]
a word you use when you are surprised, annoyed, or disappointed: *Oh dear! I've forgotten something.*

death /deθ/ *noun*
the end of someone's life: *The death of his father was very sad for us all.* | *Morioni lived in London until his death.*

de·bate[1] /dɪ'beɪt/ *noun*
a public talk at which people give opinions about a subject: *I'm going to a debate about crime and punishment.*

debate[2] *verb* (*present participle* **debating**, *past* **debated**)
to talk about something so that you can make a decision: *We're just debating whether to go or not.*

debt /det/ *noun*
1 money that you owe: *She doesn't have enough money to pay her debts.*
2 be in debt to owe money

dec·ade /'dekeɪd/ *noun*
a period of ten years

de·cay[1] /dɪ'keɪ/ *verb*
to be slowly destroyed by natural processes: *The dead sheep was starting to decay.* ⋄ same meaning ROT

de·cay[2] *noun* (no plural)
when something decays: *Brushing your teeth helps prevent tooth decay.*

de·ceit /dɪ'si:t/ *noun* (no plural)
when someone deliberately makes you believe something that is not true

de·ceive /dɪ'si:v/ *verb* (*present participle* **deceiving**, *past* **deceived**)
to deliberately make someone believe something that is not true: *He had managed to deceive us all.*

De·cem·ber /dɪ'sembə^r/ *noun*
the 12th month of the year

de·cent /'di:snt/ *adjective*
good: *Make sure you eat a decent breakfast.*

de·cide /dɪ'saɪd/ *verb* (*present participle* **deciding**, *past* **decided**)
to choose what to do: *I decided to go home.* | *She decided that the dress was too expensive.*

dec·i·mal /'desɪml/ *noun*
a number less than one that is shown by a point (.) followed by numbers. For example, a quarter is shown by the decimal 0.25

de·ci·sion /dɪ'sɪʒn/ *noun*
a choice: *They couldn't make a decision about where to go on holiday.* | *Brett's sudden decision to join the army surprised everyone.*

deck /dek/ *noun*
a part of a ship, bus, etc where you sit or stand: *Can we sit on the top deck of the bus?*

A B C D E F G H I J K L M N O P Q R S T U V W X Y Z

dec·la·ra·tion /ˌdekləˈreɪʃn/ *noun*
an official statement: *The country made a declaration of war.*

de·clare /dɪˈkleər/ *verb (present participle* **declaring**, *past* **declared**)
to say in public what you think or decide: *The judge declared that he was not guilty.*

de·cline¹ /dɪˈklaɪn/ *verb (present participle* **declining**, *past* **declined**)
1 when the number or quality of something becomes lower: *The number of teachers has declined.*
2 to refuse to do something: *He declined to answer*

decline² *noun*
a decrease in the number or quality of something

decorating a cake

decorate

decorating a bedroom

dec·o·rate /ˈdekəreɪt/ *verb (present participle* **decorating**, *past* **decorated**)
1 to put paint or paper on the walls of a house: *We're decorating the bathroom.*
2 to make something look more attractive by adding things to it: *She's decorating the cake.*

dec·o·ra·tion /ˌdekəˈreɪʃn/ *noun*
an attractive thing that is added to something to improve its appearance

dec·o·ra·tor /ˈdekəreɪtər/ *noun*
a person whose job is to put paint or paper on the walls of houses

de·crease¹ /dɪˈkriːs/ *verb (present participle* **decreasing**, *past* **decreased**)
to become less or fewer: *The number of children in the school has decreased this year.* ⇨ opposite INCREASE

de·crease² /ˈdiːkriːs/ *noun (no plural)*
when something decreases: *There has been a decrease in the number of babies being born.* ⇨ opposite INCREASE

deep

shallow   *deep*

deep /diːp/ *adjective*
1 going down a long way: *The water is not very deep here.* | *Jim has a deep cut on his leg.* ⇨ opposite SHALLOW
2 with a low sound: *John has a deep voice.*
3 strong or dark in colour: *She has deep blue eyes.*
4 felt strongly: *She has a deep love for her son.*

deep·ly /ˈdiːpli/ *adverb*
very strongly: *I care deeply about this problem.* | *She is deeply in love with him.*

deer /dɪər/ *noun*
an animal that can run fast. The male deer has horns that look like tree branches

de·feat¹ /dɪˈfiːt/ *verb*
to beat someone in a war, game, etc: *Manchester United defeated them by three goals to one.*

defeat² *noun*
when someone is defeated: *It was another defeat for the team.* ⇨ opposite VICTORY

de·fence /dɪˈfens/ *noun (no plural)*
when people defend themselves or other people: *The weapons are for the defence of our country.*

de·fend /dɪˈfend/ *verb*
to fight in order to protect someone or something: *He said he used the knife to defend himself.* ⇨ compare ATTACK

de·fi·ant /dɪˈfaɪənt/ *adjective*
not doing what someone tells you to do, and not showing respect: *He was still defiant, even after being punished.*

def·i·nite /ˈdefɪnət/ *verb*
not going to change: *Let's fix a definite*

date for the next meeting. I *We do not have definite plans yet.*

def·i·nite ar·ti·cle /ˌdefɪnət ˈɑːtɪkl/ *noun*
the word **the**

def·i·nite·ly /ˈdefɪnətlɪ/ *adverb*
without any doubt: *I'm definitely going to come.* I *That was definitely the best film I've seen all year.*

def·i·ni·tion /ˌdefɪˈnɪʃn/ *noun*
the meaning of a word, as it is explained in a dictionary

de·fy /dɪˈfaɪ/ *verb (present participle* **defying**, *past* **defied**)
to refuse to obey someone and show no respect for them: *She defied her parents' wishes and went to the party.*

de·gree /dɪˈgriː/ *noun*
1 a measurement used for temperatures or angles: *an angle of 45 degrees* (45°) I *a temperature of 30 degrees* (30°)
2 a document stating that a person has completed their period of study and passed examinations at university: *She has a degree **in** history.*

de·lay[1] /dɪˈleɪ/ *noun*
a time of waiting before something can happen: *We are sorry about the delay.*

delay[2] *verb*
1 to wait until later to do something: *Don't delay – call her now.*
2 to make something late: *Our flight was delayed by bad weather.*

de·lete /dɪˈliːt/ *verb (present participle* **deleting**, *past* **deleted**)
to remove a piece of information from a computer: *Are you sure you want to delete this file?*

de·lib·er·ate /dɪˈlɪbrət/ *adjective*
a deliberate action is planned or intended: *The attack was deliberate.*

de·lib·er·ate·ly /dɪˈlɪbrətlɪ/ *adverb*
intending to do something: *I didn't do it deliberately – it was an accident.*

del·i·cate /ˈdelɪkət/ *adjective*
easily harmed, damaged, or broken: *Be careful with that glass; it's delicate.*

del·i·ca·tes·sen /ˌdelɪkəˈtesn/ *noun*
a shop that sells special or unusual food especially food from other countries
⇨ see picture on page 201

de·li·cious /dɪˈlɪʃəs/ *adjective*
very good to eat: *She cooked us a delicious meal.*

de·light[1] /dɪˈlaɪt/ *noun (no plural)*
great happiness: *Jenny laughed with delight.*

delight[2] *verb*
to give great happiness to someone: *She gave a performance that delighted the audience.*

de·light·ed /dɪˈlaɪtɪd/ *adjective*
very pleased: *We are delighted **with** the news.*

de·light·ful /dɪˈlaɪtfəl/ *adjective*
very nice or attractive: *It's a delightful book for children.*

de·liv·er /dɪˈlɪvəʳ/ *verb*
1 to take something to the place where it should go: *He's out delivering newspapers.*
2 **deliver a baby** to help a baby come out of its mother's body

de·liv·er·y /dɪˈlɪvərɪ/ *noun (plural* **deliveries**)
the act of taking something to the place where it should go: *They offer free delivery for pizzas.*

de·mand[1] /dɪˈmɑːnd/ *verb*
to say in a very strong and firm way that you want something: *"Give me my book at once!" she demanded.* I *He demanded an explanation.*

demand[2] *noun*
1 when someone says what they want in a very strong and firm way: *The workers made a demand **for** more money.*
2 **in demand** wanted by a lot of people: *His books are in demand at the moment.*

de·moc·ra·cy /dɪˈmɒkrəsɪ/ *noun (plural* **democracies**)
a government or country where everyone has an equal right to choose their leaders, by voting

de·mol·ish /dɪˈmɒlɪʃ/ *verb*
to destroy something completely: *The houses were demolished in a few days.*

dem·o·li·tion /ˌdeməˈlɪʃn/ *noun (no plural)*
the act of destroying a building completely

dem·on·strate /ˈdemənstreɪt/ *verb (present participle* **demonstrating**, *past* **demonstrated**)
1 to show something clearly: *He demonstrated how the new machine works.*

2 to walk through the streets in a group to show that you are angry about something or do not agree with something

demonstration

giving a demonstration

dem·on·stra·tion /ˌdemən'streɪʃn/ noun
1 when you show how to do something: *She gave a cookery demonstration.*
2 a group of people walking together to show that they are angry about something or do not agree with something

den /den/ noun
a place in which a wild animal lives

den·im /'denɪm/ noun (no plural)
a strong cloth, usually blue in colour, that is used to make JEANS

dense /dens/ adjective
thick: *a dense forest*

den·tist /'dentɪst/ noun
a person whose job is to treat people's teeth: *I need to go to the dentist.* ⇨ see picture on page 200

den·tures /'dentʃəz/ plural noun
teeth that are not real

de·ny /dɪ'naɪ/ verb (present participle **denying**, past **denied**)
to say that something is not true: *He denied that he had cheated in the test.* ⇨ opposite ADMIT

de·o·do·rant /diːˈəʊdərənt/ noun (no plural)
a liquid that people put under their arms, to stop their body smelling bad

de·part /dɪ'pɑːt/ verb
to leave: *The next train for Paris will depart from Platform 2.* ⇨ opposite ARRIVE

de·part·ment /dɪ'pɑːtmənt/ noun
a part of a business, company, government, etc

department store /dɪ'pɑːtmənt ˌstɔːʳ/ noun
a shop that is divided into several parts, each of which sells different types of goods ⇨ see picture on page 201

de·par·ture /dɪ'pɑːtʃəʳ/ noun
when a person, plane, train, etc leaves a place: *You need to be at the airport an hour before departure.* ⇨ opposite ARRIVAL

de·pend /dɪ'pend/ verb
1 it depends used when you are not sure about something: *"How long will the journey take?" "I don't know, it depends."*
2 depend on someone to need the help of someone: *He's very ill and depends on his wife to look after him.*

de·pen·dant /dɪ'pendənt/ noun
someone, especially a child, who depends on another person for money, food, etc: *Do you have any dependants?*

de·pen·dent /dɪ'pendənt/ adjective
needing someone or something to help or support you: *Young children are dependent on their mothers.* ⇨ opposite INDEPENDENT

de·pos·it¹ /dɪ'pɒzɪt/ verb
to put money into a bank account

deposit² noun
1 part of the cost of something that you pay at once so that the thing will not be sold to someone else: *We put down a deposit on a new car.*
2 money that is added to a bank account

dep·ot /'depəʊ/ noun
a place where goods or vehicles are stored

de·press /dɪ'pres/ verb
to make someone feel very sad: *I can't watch the news because it depresses me.*

de·pressed /dɪ'prest/ adjective
very sad: *She's depressed.*

de·press·ing /dɪ'presɪŋ/ adjective
causing you to feel sad: *The story was very depressing.*

de·pres·sion /dɪ'preʃn/ noun (no plural)
a feeling of great sadness

depth /depθ/ *noun*
the distance to the bottom of something: *The river has a depth of 10 metres.*

dep·u·ty /'depjʊtɪ/ *noun* (*plural* **deputies**)
a person who is second in importance in a business, school, or organization

de·scend /dɪ'send/ *verb*
to go down: *He slowly descended the steps of the plane.*

de·scen·dant /dɪ'sendənt/ *noun*
someone who is related to a person who lived a long time ago

de·scribe /dɪ'skraɪb/ *verb* (*present participle* **describing**, *past* **described**)
to say what someone or something is like: *She described the hotel and the beach.*

de·scrip·tion /dɪ'skrɪpʃən/ *noun*
an account of what someone or something is like: *He gave a clear description of the child.*

des·ert /'dezət/ *noun*
a large empty area of land where it is hot and dry

de·sert·ed /dɪ'zɜːtɪd/ *adjective*
a place that is deserted has no people in it: *At night the streets are deserted.*

de·serve /dɪ'zɜːv/ *verb* (*present participle* **deserving**, *past* **deserved**)
if you deserve something, you should get it because of your behaviour: *You deserve a holiday after all your hard work.*

de·sign[1] /dɪ'zaɪn/ *noun*
1 a pattern: *The plate has a design of blue flowers.*
2 a drawing of how to make something: *Have you seen the designs for the new house?*

design[2] *verb*
to make a drawing as a plan for something: *The architects are designing a new building.*

de·sign·er /dɪ'zaɪnə^r/ *noun*
a person whose job is to think of and plan how something will be made: *He's a fashion designer.*

de·sire[1] /dɪ'zaɪə^r/ *noun*
a strong feeling that you want something very much: *Children show the desire for knowledge. | He has a strong desire to succeed.*

desire[2] *verb* (*present participle*

desiring, *past* **desired**)
to want something very much

desk /desk/ *noun*
a table for writing on, often with drawers for keeping books, pens, etc ⇨ see picture on page 205

de·spair[1] /dɪ'speə^r/ *noun*
a feeling of great sadness and of being without hope

despair[2] *verb*
to have no hope

des·per·ate /'desprət/ *adjective*
wanting or needing something very much: *I was desperate for the school holidays to start. | She made a desperate attempt to escape.*

de·spise /dɪ'spaɪz/ *verb* (*present participle* **despising**, *past* **despised**)
to hate a person or thing because you think they are not worth anything

de·spite /dɪ'spaɪt/ *preposition*
although something is true: *Despite the bad weather, we enjoyed our holiday. | She still liked him despite the way he behaved.*

des·sert /dɪ'zɜːt/ *noun*
a sweet dish that you eat at the end of a meal ⇨ same meaning PUDDING

des·ti·na·tion /ˌdestɪ'neɪʃn/ *noun*
the place you are travelling to: *What is your destination?*

de·stroy /dɪ'strɔɪ/ *verb*
to break or spoil something completely: *The building was destroyed by fire.*

de·struc·tion /dɪ'strʌkʃən/ *noun* (*no plural*)
when something is destroyed: *She was upset about the destruction of the old buildings.*

de·tail /'diːteɪl/ *noun*
1 one fact or piece of information about something: *Tell me all the details of the plan.*
2 in detail paying attention to all the facts: *We must talk about it in detail.*

de·tect /dɪ'tekt/ *verb*
to discover or notice something

de·tec·tive /dɪ'tektɪv/ *noun*
a special police officer who tries to discover who has done a crime

de·ter·gent /dɪ'tɜːdʒənt/ *noun*
powder or liquid that you use for washing clothes or dishes

A B C **D** E F G H I J K L M N O P Q R S T U V W X Y Z

de·te·ri·o·rate /dɪ'tɪərɪəreɪt/ *verb*
(*present participle* **deteriorating**, *past* **deteriorated**)
to get worse: *Her health has deteriorated.*

de·ter·mi·na·tion /dɪˌtɜːmɪˈneɪʃn/ *noun*
(*no plural*)
a strong wish to do something, even when it is difficult: *Her determination to go to university made her study hard.*

de·ter·mined /dɪ'tɜːmɪnd/ *adjective*
wanting to do something very much so that nothing can stop you: *I'm determined to win.*

de·test /dɪ'test/ *verb*
to hate someone or something very much: *He detested having his photograph taken.*

de·vel·op /dɪ'veləp/ *verb*
1 to grow: *He is developing **into** one of the country's best players.* | *The insect develops wings at a later stage.*
2 to make something grow or improve: *There are plans to develop industry in the area.*
3 to begin to happen or exist: *Clouds are developing in the distance.*
4 to treat the film from a camera with special chemicals so that you can see the picture: *Can you take this film to be developed?*

de·vel·op·ing coun·try
/dɪˌveləpɪŋ ˈkʌntrɪ/ *noun* (*plural* **developing countries**)
a country that is just starting to have modern industries

de·vel·op·ment /dɪ'veləpmənt/ *noun*
1 (*no plural*) when someone or something grows or improves: *Good food is necessary for a child's development.* | *He is interested in the development **of** new technology.*
2 a new event that changes a situation: *Here is news of the latest developments.*

de·vice /dɪ'vaɪs/ *noun*
a piece of equipment or tool that you use for a particular purpose: *a device for measuring electricity*

dev·il /'devəl/ *noun*
a bad spirit who some people believe causes bad things in the world

de·vote /dɪ'vəʊt/ *verb* (*present participle* **devoting**, *past* **devoted**)
devote yourself to something to give all your time or thoughts to something: *She devoted herself to her work.*

dew /djuː/ *noun* (*no plural*)
small drops of water that form on the ground or on plants during the night

di·ag·o·nal /daɪˈægənl/ *noun*
a straight line that goes between the opposite corners of a square or other shape, dividing it into two parts

di·a·gram /'daɪəgræm/ *noun*
a plan or picture drawn to explain an idea, or to show how something works: *He showed me a diagram **of** a car engine.*

dial¹ /'daɪəl/ *noun*
a round part of a clock, watch, instrument, etc with numbers on it: *She looked at the dial to check her speed.*

dial² *verb* (*present participle* **dialling**, *past* **dialled**)
to turn the dial or press the numbers of a telephone in order to telephone someone: *She dialled Jane's number.*

di·a·lect /'daɪəlekt/ *noun*
a form of language that is spoken in one part of a country ⇨ compare ACCENT

di·am·e·ter /daɪˈæmɪtər/ *noun*
a straight line that divides a circle in half

di·a·mond /'daɪəmənd/ *noun*
a very hard bright clear stone that is worth a lot of money and is worn in jewellery

di·a·per /'daɪəpər/ *noun*
American a piece of cloth that is put between a baby's legs and fastened at the waist (*British* **nappy**)

di·ar·rhoe·a /ˌdaɪəˈriːə/ *noun* (*no plural*)
an illness in which a person's waste is like water and comes out often

di·a·ry /'daɪərɪ/ *noun* (*plural* **diaries**)
a book in which you write about the things that happen or will happen to you each day

dice /daɪs/ *noun* (*plural* **dice**)
a small square block with a different number of spots on each side from 1 to 6 that is used in games

dic·tate /dɪk'teɪt/ *verb* (*present participle* **dictating**, *past* **dictated**)
to say something for someone else to write down: *I dictated a letter **to** my secretary.*

dic·ta·tion /dɪkˈteɪʃn/ noun
a language test in which you must write what the teacher says without making mistakes

dic·ta·tor /dɪkˈteɪtəʳ/ noun
a very strong ruler, usually one who is not fair and who uses soldiers to control people

dic·tion·ary /ˈdɪkʃənrɪ/ noun (plural **dictionaries**)
a book that tells you what words mean and how to spell them

did /dɪd/ verb
the past tense of the verb **do**: *"Did you go there?" "Yes, I did."*

didn't /ˈdɪdnt/
did not: *You didn't enjoy the film, did you?*

die /daɪ/ verb (present participle **dying**, past **died**)
1 to stop living: *She died **of** cancer last year.*
2 be dying for something to want something very much: *I'm dying for a cup of tea.*

di·et /ˈdaɪət/ noun
1 the kind of food that you eat: *She has a healthy diet.*
2 the food you eat when you are controlling the types of food you eat because you want to be thinner or because you are ill: *You are not allowed to eat sugar on this diet.*
3 go on a diet to eat less food than usual, or different types of food, because you want to become thinner

dif·ference /ˈdɪfrəns/ noun
1 a way in which things are not the same: *There isn't much difference **between** the two books.* | *The two coats look the same but there's a big difference **in** price.* ⇨ opposite SIMILARITY
2 make a big difference to have a good effect on someone or something: *Exercise can make a big difference **to** how you feel.*
3 make no difference to have no importance or effect: *It makes no difference what you say. I've already decided.*

dif·ferent /ˈdɪfrənt/ adjective
not the same: *I don't like that dress – I want a different one.* | *Life here is totally different to life at home.* | *My ideas are different **from** yours.* ⇨ opposite SAME

NOTE: Use **different from** to talk about two things that are not the same: *He was different from his friends.* In British English, you can also say **different to**: *The village in the past was different to what it is like today.* Note that many teachers think this use is wrong. In American English, you can also say **different than**: *The United States is different than Poland.*

dif·fi·cult /ˈdɪfɪkəlt/ adjective
hard to do or understand: *He finds English very difficult.* | *We had a difficult test at school today.* ⇨ opposite EASY

dif·fi·cul·ty /ˈdɪfɪkəltɪ/ noun (plural **difficulties**)
when something is not easy to do: *David's having difficulty finding a job.* | *The old lady got out of her chair **with** difficulty.*

dig /dɪg/ verb   dig
(present participle **digging**, past **dug** /dʌg/)
to move earth or make a hole in the ground: *The children were digging a hole in the sand.*

digging the garden

di·gest /daɪˈdʒest/ verb
to break down food in your stomach so that your body can use it: *Some babies cannot digest cow's milk.*

di·gi·tal /ˈdɪdʒɪtl/ adjective
1 using a system in which information is shown in the form of numbers: *a digital recording*
2 giving information in the form of numbers: *a digital watch*

dig·ni·fied /ˈdɪgnɪfaɪd/ adjective
serious and calm and respected by other people: *She is a dignified old lady.*

dig·ni·ty /ˈdɪgnətɪ/ noun (no plural)
calm and serious behaviour that makes people respect you: *Although she is very poor she has not lost her dignity.*

A B C **D** E F G H I J K L M N O P Q R S T U V W X Y Z

dim /dɪm/ adjective
not very bright: There was only a dim light in the corner of the room.

din /dɪn/ noun (no plural)
loud noise: What a din the children are making!

din·ing room /'daɪnɪŋ ruːm/ noun
a room with a table where you can eat meals

din·ner /'dɪnər/ noun
the largest meal of the day, eaten in the evening or in the middle of the day ⬦ compare LUNCH, TEA, SUPPER

dip /dɪp/ verb (present participle **dipping**, past **dipped**)
to put something into a liquid and then take it out again: She dipped her hand **in** the water. ⬦ see picture on page 198

di·plo·ma /dɪ'pləʊmə/ noun
a piece of paper given to someone to show that they have passed an examination

di·rect[1] /dɪ'rekt, daɪ-/ adjective
going straight from one place to another: We took a direct flight to Paris.

direct[2] verb
to tell someone the way to go or what to do: I directed the traveller **to** the hotel.

di·rec·tion /dɪ'rekʃn, daɪ-/ noun
the way that someone or something is going or pointing: Which direction are you going, north or south?

di·rect·ly /dɪ'rektlɪ, daɪ-/ adverb
with no other person, process, etc between: John sat directly behind me.

di·rec·tor /dɪ'rektər, daɪ-/ noun
1 a person who controls a business: He's one of the directors of the company.
2 someone who tells actors and other people what to do in a film or play

di·rec·to·ry /dɪ'rektərɪ, daɪ-/ noun (plural **directories**)
a book that tells you where people live or what their telephone numbers are: a telephone directory

dirt /dɜːt/ noun (no plural)
something such as dust or soil that stops something being clean: He had dirt all over his face.

dirt·y /'dɜːtɪ/ adjective
with dirt on: My shoes were dirty. ⬦ opposite CLEAN

dis·a·bled /dɪs'eɪbəld/ adjective
not able to move or use a part of your body well

dis·ad·van·tage /ˌdɪsəd'vɑːntɪdʒ/ noun
something that makes things more difficult for you: It can be a disadvantage not owning a car. ⬦ opposite ADVANTAGE

dis·a·gree /ˌdɪsə'griː/ verb (past **disagreed**)
to have a different opinion from someone else: I'm afraid I disagree **with** you. | We always disagree **about** politics. ⬦ opposite AGREE

dis·a·gree·ment /ˌdɪsə'griːmənt/ noun
when you do not agree with someone: Mum and Dad had a disagreement **over** money. | We've had some disagreements but we're still friends.

dis·ap·pear /ˌdɪsə'pɪər/ verb
to go away or to suddenly not be seen: The boy disappeared round the corner. ⬦ opposite APPEAR

dis·ap·point /ˌdɪsə'pɔɪnt/ verb
to be less interesting or less nice than you expected, and so make you sad: I'm sorry to disappoint you but we can't go on holiday this year.

dis·ap·point·ed /ˌdɪsə'pɔɪntɪd/ adjective
sad because something is not as good or as nice as you expected: He was disappointed **that** Kerry couldn't come.

dis·ap·point·ing /ˌdɪsə'pɔɪntɪŋ/ adjective
not as good or as nice as you expected: It was a disappointing meal.

dis·ap·point·ment /ˌdɪsə'pɔɪntmənt/ noun
the feeling you have when something is disappointing: Brian felt disappointment **at** not being chosen for the team.

dis·ap·prov·al /ˌdɪsə'pruːvəl/ noun (no plural)
the feeling or opinion that someone or something is bad or wrong ⬦ opposite APPROVAL

dis·ap·prove /ˌdɪsə'pruːv/ verb (present participle **disapproving**, past **disapproved**)
to not like someone or something because you think they are bad or wrong: My mother disapproves **of** my friends. ⬦ opposite APPROVE

di·sas·ter /dɪˈzɑːstəʳ/ *noun*
something very bad, especially something that happens to a lot of people and causes a lot of damage or harm: *The earthquake was a disaster in which hundreds of people died.*

disc /dɪsk/ *noun*
1 a round flat object in the shape of a circle
2 a record for playing music

dis·ci·pline /ˈdɪsɪplɪn/ *noun (no plural)*
the training of people so that they will obey orders and control their own feelings and behaviour: *Soldiers have to learn discipline in the army.* | *There is a high level of discipline in the school.*

disc jock·ey /ˈdɪsk ˌdʒɒkɪ/ *noun*
also **DJ** a person whose job is to play records on the radio, or at parties, etc
⇨ see picture at JOCKEY

dis·co /ˈdɪskəʊ/ *noun*
a place where people dance to popular music

dis·count /ˈdɪskaʊnt/ *noun*
an amount of money taken away from the price of something: *Sales start Monday with discounts of 20 per cent.*

dis·cour·age /dɪsˈkʌrɪdʒ/ *verb (present participle* **discouraging**, *past* **discouraged**)
to try to stop someone doing something: *We discourage smoking in our offices.* ⇨ opposite ENCOURAGE

dis·cov·er /dɪsˈkʌvəʳ/ *verb*
to find something, or to learn about something for the first time: *Columbus discovered America.* | *Did you discover who sent you the flowers?*

dis·cov·e·ry /dɪsˈkʌvərɪ/ *noun (plural* **discoveries**)
something discovered: *Scientists have made an important new discovery.*

di·scrim·i·na·tion /dɪˌskrɪmɪˈneɪʃn/ *noun*
unfair treatment of people because of the colour of their skin, where they come from, etc

dis·cuss /dɪsˈkʌs/ *verb*
to talk about something: *I want to discuss your work* **with** *you.*

dis·cus·sion /dɪsˈkʌʃn/ *noun*
a talk about something: *We had a discussion* **about** *responsibility in class yesterday.*

dis·ease /dɪˈziːz/ *noun*
an illness, especially a serious one that continues for a long time

dis·grace /dɪsˈgreɪs/ *noun (no plural)*
when people are very angry with you because of something that you have done: *Harry left the school* **in** *disgrace.*

dis·grace·ful /dɪsˈgreɪsfəl/ *adjective*
very bad and wrong: *Her attitude is disgraceful.*

dis·guise¹ /dɪsˈgaɪz/ *verb (present participle* **disguising**, *past* **disguised**)
to make yourself look like someone else so that people do not know who you are: *He disguised himself* **as** *a priest.*

disguise² *noun*
something that you wear to make you look like someone else so that people do not know who you are: *The glasses were part of her disguise.*

dis·gust¹ /dɪsˈgʌst/ *verb*
to make you feel that something is very bad or unpleasant: *The smell disgusted me.*

disgust² *noun (no plural)*
a strong feeling of not liking something or finding it unpleasant: *Everyone looked at him* **with** *disgust.*

dis·gust·ing /dɪsˈgʌstɪŋ/ *adjective*
very bad and unpleasant: *The medicine tasted disgusting.*

dish /dɪʃ/ *noun (plural* **dishes**)
1 a container like a large bowl, used for cooking or serving food
2 do the dishes to wash the dirty plates, etc after a meal

dis·hon·est /dɪsˈɒnɪst/ *adjective*
not honest: *You can't trust him – he's dishonest.*

dish·wash·er /ˈdɪʃˌwɒʃəʳ/ *noun*
a machine that washes dirty plates, etc

dis·in·fec·tant /ˌdɪsɪnˈfektənt/ *noun (no plural)*
a chemical used to clean things thoroughly ⇨ see picture at FIRST AID

disk /dɪsk/ *noun*
a flat piece of plastic used for storing computer information

disk drive /ˈdɪsk draɪv/ *noun*
a piece of equipment in a computer that is used to pass information to or from a disk

A
B
C
D
E
F
G
H
I
J
K
L
M
N
O
P
Q
R
S
T
U
V
W
X
Y
Z

dis·like[1] /dɪsˈlaɪk/ *verb* (*present participle* **disliking**, *past* **disliked**)
to not like someone or something: *Why do you dislike her so much?*

dislike[2] *noun*
a feeling of not liking someone or something

> NOTE: The verb **dislike** is not often used in ordinary conversation because it is rather formal. People usually say that they **don't like** something, rather than that they **dislike** it, e.g. *I don't like her.* | *He doesn't like swimming.*

dis·loy·al /dɪsˈlɔɪəl/ *adjective*
not loyal ⇨ opposite LOYAL

dis·may /dɪsˈmeɪ/ *noun* (no plural)
when you feel very disappointed and surprised by something: *Amanda read her exam results **with** dismay.*

dis·miss /dɪsˈmɪs/ *verb*
1 to send someone away: *Classes will be dismissed early tomorrow.*
2 to tell someone they must leave their job because they have done something wrong

dis·o·be·di·ence /ˌdɪsəˈbiːdɪəns/ *noun* (no plural)
the act of refusing to obey someone ⇨ opposite OBEDIENCE

dis·o·be·di·ent /ˌdɪsəˈbiːdɪənt/ *adjective*
not willing to obey: *He is a disobedient child.* ⇨ opposite OBEDIENT

dis·o·bey /ˌdɪsəˈbeɪ/ *verb*
to refuse to do what someone tells you to do: *She would never disobey her parents.* ⇨ opposite OBEY

dis·or·gan·ized /dɪsˈɔːɡənaɪzd/ *adjective*
not arranged or planned very well: *The meeting was completely disorganized.*

a window display

dis·play[1] /dɪˈspleɪ/ *verb*
to show something so that many people can see it: *The artist's pictures were displayed on the wall.*

display[2] *noun*
1 a show of something: *There was a display of the children's work.*
2 **on display** being shown for many people to see

dis·pos·al /dɪˈspəʊzl/ *noun* (no plural)
when someone gets rid of something: *The council has plans for the safe disposal of dangerous chemicals.*

dis·pose /dɪˈspəʊz/ *verb*
dispose of something to get rid of something: *How did the killer dispose of the body?*

di·spute /dɪˈspjuːt/ *noun*
a serious argument: *There was a dispute **between** the two countries.*

dis·sat·is·fied /dɪˈsætɪsfaɪd/ *adjective*
not pleased with something: *We were very dissatisfied **with** the food at the restaurant.* ⇨ opposite SATISFIED

dissolve

dis·solve /dɪˈzɒlv/ *verb* (*present participle* **dissolving**, *past* **dissolved**)
to mix completely with a liquid: *Sugar dissolves **in** water.* | *Dissolve the powder **in** water.*

dis·tance /ˈdɪstəns/ *noun*
1 the amount of space between two places: *What's the distance between London and Paris?*
2 **in the distance** far away: *That's our house in the distance.*

dis·tant /ˈdɪstənt/ *adjective*
far away: *He could just hear the distant sound of traffic.*

dis·tinct /dɪˈstɪŋkt/ *adjective*
1 different or separate: *There are two distinct languages in the area.*
2 clearly seen, heard, or understood: *A distinct smell of burning came from the kitchen.*

dis·tinct·ly /dɪˈstɪŋktlɪ/ adverb
very clearly: *I distinctly remember telling you to finish your homework first.*

diver

dis·tin·guish /dɪˈstɪŋgwɪʃ/ verb
1 to see the difference between things: *You are old enough to distinguish between good and bad.*
2 to be able to see, hear, or taste something, although it is difficult to do this: *It was dark and I could just distinguish their faces.*

dis·tin·guished /dɪˈstɪŋgwɪʃt/ adjective
successful and respected by many people: *She is a distinguished scientist.*

dis·tress[1] /dɪˈstres/ noun (no plural)
a feeling of sadness, pain, or trouble: *The child was lost and crying in distress.*

distress[2] verb
to make someone sad or upset

dis·tress·ing /dɪˈstresɪŋ/ adjective
making you feel sad or upset: *The news of her death was extremely distressing.*

dis·trib·ute /dɪˈstrɪbjuːt/ verb (present participle **distributing**, past **distributed**)
to give or send something to different people or places: *The teacher distributed the books to the children.*

dis·trict /ˈdɪstrɪkt/ noun
a part of a country, city, or area

dis·turb /dɪˈstɜːb/ verb
1 to interrupt someone and stop them working, thinking, sleeping, etc: *Please don't disturb me while I'm working.*
2 to make someone feel worried or upset: *We were very disturbed by these events.*
3 to change or move something: *Someone had disturbed the papers on his desk.*

dis·turb·ance /dɪˈstɜːbəns/ noun
a noisy event in which people fight or cause trouble: *There has been a disturbance in the street.*

ditch /dɪtʃ/ noun (plural **ditches**)
a deep narrow place for water to go along, especially by the side of a road or field

dive /daɪv/ verb (present participle **diving**, past **dived**)
to jump into water with your head first: *He dived into the lake.* | *She dived to the bottom of the river.*

div·er /ˈdaɪvəʳ/ noun
someone who goes under water wearing special instruments to help them breathe

di·vide /dɪˈvaɪd/ verb (present participle **dividing**, past **divided**)
1 to separate into pieces or parts: *The road divided into two.* | *The class divided into groups.*
2 also **divide up** to share something: *We divided the money between us.* | *Her belongings were divided up among her grandchildren.*
3 to find how many times a number will go into a bigger number: *If you divide 39 by 3, the answer is 13.*

di·vine /dɪˈvaɪn/ adjective
from a god or like a god

div·ing board /ˈdaɪvɪŋ ˌbɔːd/ noun
a special board, often high above the ground, that you stand on before jumping into water

di·vi·sion /dɪˈvɪʒn/ noun
1 when something is divided into two or more parts: *We learned about the division of Germany after the war.*
2 (no plural) the process of finding how many times a number will go into a bigger number
3 a part of something: *Which division of the company do you work in?*

di·vorce[1] /dɪˈvɔːs/ verb (present participle **divorcing**, past **divorced**)
to arrange legally to stop being someone's wife or husband: *They're getting divorced.*

divorce[2] noun
a legal agreement to stop being someone's wife or husband

DIY /ˌdiː aɪ ˈwaɪ/ noun (no plural)
also **do-it-yourself** painting or building things in your house yourself instead of paying a painter, builder, etc to do it for you

A
B
C
D
E
F
G
H
I
J
K
L
M
N
O
P
Q
R
S
T
U
V
W
X
Y
Z

diz·zy /'dɪzɪ/ *adjective*

feeling as if you are going to fall and as if things are moving when they are not: *I feel dizzy when I look out of a high window.*

DJ /,di:'dʒeɪ/ *noun*

also **disc jockey** a person whose job it is to play records on the radio or at parties, etc ⇨ see picture at JOCKEY

do[1] /duː/ *verb*

1 to perform an action or job: *I must do some work.* | *What are you doing?* | *I'm doing the gardening.*

2 do well to be a success: *He has done well in school this year.*

3 do someone good to make someone feel better or more healthy: *A holiday will do you good.*

4 do something up to fasten something: *Do up your coat.* | *Just let me do up my zip and I'll come.*

5 to do with about or relating to someone or something: *Her job's to do with looking after old people.* | *The lecture is to do with new scientific theories.*

6 How do you do? a polite greeting used when you meet someone for the first time. The reply is also "How do you do?": *"Mother, this is Dr Jones." "How do you do, Dr Jones?" "How do you do?"*

7 What do you do? used when you ask someone what their job is: *"What do you do?" "I'm a politician."*

8 could do with to want or need something: *The baby could do with some sleep.* | *I could do with a drink.*

9 do without something to live or continue without a particular thing: *I couldn't do without your help.*

10 What have you done with something? used to ask where something is or where someone has put it: *What have you done with my book?*

11 do as you are told to do what someone such as a parent tells you to do

present tense	
singular	*plural*
I **do**	We **do**
You **do**	You **do**
He/She/It **does**	They **do**

past tense	
singular	*plural*
I **did**	We **did**
You **did**	You **did**
He/She/It **did**	They **did**

present participle	**doing**
past participle	**done**
negative short forms	**don't, doesn't, didn't,**

(you can find each of these words in its own place in the dictionary)

NOTE: Compare the verbs **do** and **make**. Use **do** when you are talking about an action or activity, e.g. *to do some work, to do the shopping.* Use **make** when you are talking about producing something or doing what is needed to make something exist, e.g. *to make a cake, to make a noise,* or when you are talking about plans, decisions, or communicating with people, e.g. *to make a decision, to make a choice, to make a statement, to make a joke.*

do[2] *verb*

1 used with **not** before another verb, to say that something is not so: *I do not agree with you.* | *He doesn't* (=does not) *have a car.*

2 used with another verb, to ask a question: *Do you like dancing?* | *Did you find the answer?*

3 used with **not**, to tell someone not to do something: *Do not lean out of the window.* | *Don't* (=do not) *do that!*

4 used to make the meaning of another verb stronger: *You do talk a lot!* | *You do believe me, don't you?*

5 used instead of repeating a verb: *"Do you agree?" "Yes, I do."* (=I do agree)

dock[1] /dɒk/ *noun*

a place where goods are taken on and off ships

dock[2] *verb*

when a ship docks, it arrives at a dock

doc·tor /'dɒktəʳ/ *noun*

a person who looks after people's health: *I'll go to the doctor tomorrow.* | *You should see a doctor about that cough.* ⇨ see picture on page 200

doc·u·ment /ˈdɒkjʊmənt/ *noun*
a piece of paper with something official written on it

doc·u·men·tary /ˌdɒkjʊˈmentrɪ/ *noun* (*plural* **documentaries**)
a film giving information and facts about something

dodge /dɒdʒ/ *verb* (*present participle* **dodging**, *past* **dodged**)
1 to move quickly to one side to avoid something: *He tried to hit me but I managed to dodge.*
2 to avoid something you should not avoid: *He dodged the question* (=did not answer it).

does /dəz; *strong* dʌz/ *verb*
the part of the verb **do** that we use with **he**, **she**, and **it**: *Does she have a job?*

doesn't /ˈdʌznt/
does not: *She doesn't like school.*

dog /dɒg/ *noun*
an animal that is sometimes used to protect buildings. Many people keep dogs as pets

do-it-your·self /ˌduː ɪt jɔːˈself/ *noun* (*no plural*)
also **DIY** painting or building things in your house yourself instead of paying a painter, builder, etc to do it for you

doll /dɒl/ *noun*
a toy made to look like a person, especially a baby, woman, or girl

dol·lar /ˈdɒləʳ/ *noun*
dollars are the money used in America and some other countries

dol·phin /ˈdɒlfɪn/ *noun*
a large grey sea animal with a long pointed nose

dolphin

dome /dəʊm/ *noun*
a high round roof

do·mes·tic /dəˈmestɪk/ *adjective*
1 in the home or about the home: *Cleaning and cooking are domestic jobs.*
2 happening in one country and not involving any others: *There are many domestic flights every day in the US.*
⇨ compare INTERNATIONAL
3 a domestic animal lives in someone's home or on a farm: *Dogs are domestic animals.*

dom·i·nate /ˈdɒmɪneɪt/ *verb* (*present participle* **dominating**, *past* **dominated**)
to have power and control over someone or something

dom·i·noes /ˈdɒmɪnəʊz/ *plural noun*
a game played with small flat pieces of wood with spots on

do·nate /dəʊˈneɪt/ *verb* (*present participle* **donating**, *past* **donated**)
to give something to a person or an organization that needs help: *Our school donated £500 to charity.*

do·na·tion /dəʊˈneɪʃn/ *noun*
something, especially money, that you give to help a person or organization: *She made a donation to the hospital.*

done[1] /dʌn/
the past participle of the verb **do**: *Have you done your homework?*

done[2] *adjective*
finished: *The work is nearly done.*

don·key /ˈdɒŋkɪ/ *noun*
an animal like a small horse with long ears

do·nor /ˈdəʊnəʳ/ *noun*
someone who gives something to help a person or organization

don't /dəʊnt/
do not: *I don't want to go.* | *Don't touch that!*

door

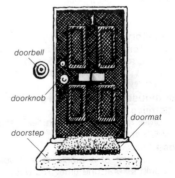

door /dɔːʳ/ *noun*
1 the flat piece of wood, metal, etc that shuts the entrance to a building or room: *Can you open the door for me?* | *Please lock the door when you leave.*

2 the entrance to a building or room: *You go **through** this door and turn to the left.*

3 answer the door to open the door when someone knocks

4 door to door going from one house or building to another: *The police went door to door asking if anyone had seen anything suspicious.*

5 next door in the building or room next to a place: *He lives next door **to** my parents* (=in the house next to theirs).

6 at the door waiting beside the door for someone to open it: *Is there someone at the door?*

door·bell /'dɔːbel/ *noun*
a button by a door that you push to make a sound so that someone inside knows you are there: *I'll ring the doorbell in case someone is at home.* ⇨ see picture at DOOR

door·knob /'dɔːnɒb/ *noun*
a round handle on a door that you use when you open and close it ⇨ see picture at DOOR

door·mat /'dɔːmæt/ *noun*
a small piece of thick material beside a door, for you to clean your shoes on ⇨ see picture at DOOR

door·step /'dɔːstep/ *noun*
1 a step in front of the door of a house ⇨ see picture at DOOR
2 on your doorstep very close to where you live: *The beach is right on our doorstep.*

door·way /'dɔːweɪ/ *noun*
an opening where there is a door: *He stood in the doorway.*

dor·mi·tory /'dɔːmɪtrɪ/ *noun* (plural **dormitories**)
a large room with beds for people to sleep in: *There were six children in her dormitory at school.*

dor·mouse /'dɔːmaʊs/ *noun* (plural **dormice** /'dɔːmaɪs/)
a small mouse that lives in fields and sleeps in the winter

dose /dəʊs/ *noun*
the amount of a medicine that you should take at one time: *The dose is two spoonfuls every four hours.*

dot /dɒt/ *noun*
a small round mark: *On the map, towns were marked by a red dot. I The stars look like dots of light in the sky.*

doub·le [1] /'dʌbl/ *adjective, adverb*
1 twice as much: *I'll pay you double if you finish the work quickly.*
2 used before a number or letter happening twice: *My telephone number is six, double five, double eight (65588).*
3 with two parts that are the same: *We went through the double doors into the room.*
4 made for two people: *a double bed* ⇨ compare SINGLE

double [2] *verb* (present participle **doubling**, past **doubled**)
1 to become twice as big or twice as much: *Sales of our new car have doubled.*
2 to make something twice as big or twice as much: *By moving to a new job I doubled my income.*

doubt [1] /daʊt/ *verb*
to not be sure if something is true or will happen: *I doubt **if** he will pass the examinations. I I doubt **that** they will come.*

doubt [2] *noun*
1 the feeling of not being sure about something: *I have doubts **about** whether he is the best man for the job.*
2 no doubt very probably: *No doubt we'll see you again soon.*

doubt·ful /'daʊtfəl/ *adjective*
not likely: *It's doubtful whether she'll succeed.*

doubt·less /'daʊtləs/ *adverb*
very likely to happen or be true: *He will doubtless arrive on the next train. I There will doubtless be someone at the party who you know.*

dough /dəʊ/ *noun* (no plural)
a soft mixture of flour and water that is cooked to make bread

dough·nut /'dəʊnʌt/ *noun*
a small round sweet cake that is cooked in oil

dove /dʌv/ *noun*
a white bird that people think of as a sign of peace

down [1] /daʊn/ *adverb, preposition*
1 in or to a lower place: *Sit down, please. I The children ran down the hill. I I must put these bags down.* ⇨ opposite UP ⇨ see picture on page 208
2 to a lower level or number: *Sales went down last year.* ⇨ opposite UP
3 in or towards the south: *Gail's driving*

down to London to see her brother.
⇨ opposite UP
4 written on paper: *Write this down so you don't forget it.*
5 along or towards the far end of something: *We walked down the beach.* | *They live down the road.*

down² *adjective*
1 sad: *Andrew was feeling down.*
2 behind in a game by a particular number of points: *We were down by six points halfway through the game.*
3 when a computer is down, it is not working

down·hill /ˌdaʊnˈhɪl/ *adjective, adverb*
to or towards the bottom of a hill: *The ball rolled downhill.* ⇨ opposite UPHILL

downstairs (upstairs)

upstairs

downstairs

down·stairs /ˌdaʊnˈsteəz/ *adjective, adverb*
in or towards a lower part of a house: *Run downstairs and answer the door.* | *They have a downstairs bathroom.* ⇨ opposite UPSTAIRS

down·wards /ˈdaʊnwədz/ *adverb*
to a lower place or position: *Nina looked downwards.* ⇨ opposite UPWARDS

doze /dəʊz/ *verb* (*present participle* **dozing**, *past* **dozed**)
1 to sleep lightly for some time: *Graham dozed for an hour.*
2 doze off to go to sleep without meaning to: *I dozed off watching television.*

doz·en /ˈdʌzn/ *noun*
1 twelve: *Emma bought a dozen eggs.*
2 dozens very many: *There were dozens of people there.*

Dr /ˈdɒktər/
the short way of writing the word 'doctor' when you are writing someone's name: *Dr Brown*

drag /dræg/ *verb* (*present participle* **dragging**, *past* **dragged**)
to pull something heavy along behind you ⇨ see picture on page 207

dra·gon /ˈdrægən/ *noun*
an animal in stories that has fire coming out of its mouth

drain¹ /dreɪn/ *noun*
a pipe that takes dirty water away ⇨ see picture at PAVEMENT

drain² *verb*
to flow away, or to make water flow away: *Some farmers have to drain their fields.* | *The water drained away slowly.* ⇨ see picture on page 198

drain·ing board /ˈdreɪnɪŋ bɔːd/ *noun*
the place where you leave plates to dry after they have been washed

drain·pipe /ˈdreɪnpaɪp/ *noun*
a pipe on the outside of a building that takes away dirty water or water from the roof

dra·ma /ˈdrɑːmə/ *noun* (*no plural*)
1 acting and plays: *She's studying drama.*
2 excitement: *I like the drama of a big storm.*

dra·mat·ic /drəˈmætɪk/ *adjective*
exciting: *He told a dramatic story.*

drank /dræŋk/
the past tense of the verb **drink**

draught /drɑːft/ *noun*
air blowing into a room: *There was a cold draught under the door.*

draughts /drɑːfts/ *plural noun*
a game played by two people using 24 round pieces on a board of black and white squares

draw¹ /drɔː/ *verb* (*past* **drew** /druː/, *past participle* **drawn** /drɔːn/)
1 to make a picture, especially with a pencil or pen: *I like drawing.* | *Why not draw a picture of your sister?*
2 to take something out of a place: *He drew a gun from his pocket.* | *I need to draw some money out of the bank.*
3 to end a game or match with an equal result, so that no one wins: *We drew with the London team.*
4 to move in a particular direction:

*A car drew **into** our drive.*

5 draw the curtains to pull curtains across so that they cover or do not cover a window

6 draw a conclusion to decide if something is true or not, after thinking about it

7 draw up if a vehicle draws up, it stops: *A car drew up beside me.*

draw² *noun*

a game or a result where no one wins because both sides are equal: *The match was a draw.*

drawer /drɔːʳ/ *noun*

a part of a piece of furniture, used for keeping things in, which can be pulled out and pushed in ⇨ see picture on page 205

draw·ing /ˈdrɔːɪŋ/ *noun*

1 (*no plural*) the making of pictures with pencils or pens: *She's very good at drawing.*

2 a picture done by pen or pencil: *She had done a drawing **of** her mother.*

drawing pin /ˈdrɔːɪŋ pɪn/ *noun*

a small pin with a round flat top that is used for fixing things to a wall

drawn /drɔːn/

the past participle of the verb **draw**

dread·ful /ˈdredfəl/ *adjective*

very bad or unpleasant: *There's been a dreadful accident. I I've had a dreadful day – everything seems to have gone wrong.* ⇨ same meaning AWFUL, TERRIBLE

dread·ful·ly /ˈdredfəli/ *adverb*

1 very badly: *The children behaved dreadfully.*

2 very: *She was dreadfully upset.*

dream¹ /driːm/ *verb* (*present participle* **dreaming**, *past* **dreamt** /dremt/ *or* **dreamed** /driːmd/)

1 to imagine things while you are asleep: *I dreamt **about** you last night.*

2 to imagine something nice: *He dreamed **of** becoming famous.*

dream² *noun*

1 something that you imagine while you are asleep: *I had a strange dream last night.*

2 something nice that you imagine or that you want to do: *It is their dream to visit Australia.*

dreamt /dremt/

the past tense and past participle of the verb **dream**

drear·y /ˈdrɪəri/ *adjective*

boring and not attractive: *It was a dreary afternoon.*

drench /drentʃ/ *verb*

to make someone or something completely wet: *I was drenched in the storm.*

dress¹ /dres/ *verb*

1 to put clothes on yourself or someone else: *She washed and dressed and ate her breakfast. I Can you dress the children for me?*

2 clothes of a particular type or for a particular purpose: *Dress warmly – it's cold outside.*

3 be dressed to be wearing clothes: *They arrived before I was dressed. I She was dressed **in** red (=wearing red clothes).*

4 get dressed to put on clothes: *It will only take a minute to get dressed.*

5 dress up (a) to put on special clothes for an important occasion: *It's just a small party; there's no need to dress up.* **(b)** to wear special clothes for fun or as a game: *She dressed up **as** a witch with a tall black hat.*

dress² *noun*

1 (*plural* **dresses**) a piece of clothing covering the body and legs that is worn by women and girls ⇨ see picture on page 203

2 (*no plural*) clothes of a certain type or for a particular purpose: *You must wear formal dress to the dinner this evening.*

dress·er /ˈdresəʳ/ *noun*

a piece of furniture with shelves for showing plates

dress·ing /ˈdresɪŋ/ *noun* (*no plural*)

a cold liquid made with oil and put on SALADS

dressing gown /ˈdresɪŋ ˌɡaʊn/ *noun*

a piece of clothing like a coat that you wear on top of the clothes that you sleep in

dressing ta·ble /ˈdresɪŋ ˌteɪbl/ *noun*

a table with a mirror on top, used for sitting at while you brush your hair, etc

drew /druː/

the past tense of the verb **draw**

dried /draɪd/

the past tense and past participle of the verb **dry**

drift /drɪft/ *verb*
to move slowly on water or through the air: *A boat drifted **down** the river.*

drill[1] /drɪl/ *noun*
a machine for making holes in something hard ⇨ see picture on page 204

drill[2] *verb*
to make a hole in something with a drill: *I drilled a hole **in** the wall to put up a shelf.*

drink[1] /drɪŋk/ *verb* (*present participle* **drinking**, *past tense* **drank** /dræŋk/, *past participle* **drunk** /drʌŋk/)
1 to take liquid into your mouth and swallow it: *Would you like something to drink?* | *He drank some coffee.*
2 to drink alcohol, especially too much: *You should never drink and drive.*

drink[2] *noun*
a liquid that you can swallow: *Can I have a drink?* | *I'd like a drink **of** water.*

drip /drɪp/ *verb* (*present participle* **dripping**, *past* **dripped**)
1 to produce small drops of liquid: *The tap was dripping.*
2 to fall as small drops: *Sweat was dripping from his face.*

drive[1] /draɪv/ *verb* (*present participle* **driving**, *past tense* **drove** /drəʊv/, *past participle* **driven** /ˈdrɪvn/)
to make a vehicle move in the direction you want: *Can you drive?* | *I drove to town yesterday.*

drive[2] *noun*
1 a journey in a car: *It's only a short drive to the village.*
2 a short road that goes to one house only: *He left his car in the drive.*

driv·en /ˈdrɪvn/
the past participle of the verb **drive**

driv·er /ˈdraɪvəʳ/ *noun*
a person who is driving a vehicle or who drives a vehicle as their job: *a train driver*

driv·ing li·cence /ˈdraɪvɪŋ ˌlaɪsns/ *noun*
an official piece of paper that shows you are allowed to drive a car

driv·ing test /ˈdraɪvɪŋ ˌtest/ *noun*
an examination that you must pass before you are allowed to drive a car

droop /druːp/ *verb*
to hang down: *The flowers drooped because of lack of water.*

drop[1] /drɒp/ *verb* (*present participle* **dropping**, *past* **dropped**)
1 to let something you are holding fall to the ground: *She dropped the plate.* | *The dog dropped the stick at my feet.* ⇨ see picture on page 207
2 to fall: *The bottle rolled off the table and dropped to the floor.*
3 drop in on someone to visit someone when they are not expecting you

drop[2] *noun*
a small amount of liquid: *Drops **of** rain ran down the window.*

drought /draʊt/ *noun*
a time when no rain falls and the land becomes very dry

drove /drəʊv/
the past tense of the verb **drive**

drown /draʊn/ *verb*
to die under water because you cannot breathe

drow·sy /ˈdraʊzi/ *adjective*
wanting to sleep: *This medicine can make you feel drowsy.*

drug /drʌg/ *noun*
1 a medicine
2 something that people take to change the way they feel or behave. Many drugs are not allowed by law: *He took drugs when he was young.*

drum[1] /drʌm/ *noun*
1 a round musical instrument that you play by hitting it with your hand or a stick
2 a metal container for oil, water, etc

drum[2] *verb* (*present participle* **drumming**, *past* **drummed**)
to make music on a drum by hitting it

drunk[1] /drʌŋk/ *adjective*
having had too much alcohol and so not able to control your behaviour: *You're drunk!*

drunk[2]
the past participle of the verb **drink**

drunk·en /ˈdrʌŋkən/ *adjective*
caused by too much alcohol: *drunken behaviour*

dry[1] /draɪ/ *adjective*
1 having no water in something or on something: *This coat will keep you dry in the rain.*
2 without any rain: *The weather tomorrow will be dry.*

A B C D E F G H I J K L M N O P Q R S T U V W X Y Z

dry[2] *verb* (*past* **dried**)
  1 to become dry: *The clothes dried quickly outside.*
  2 to make something dry: *I just need to dry my hair.*

dry-clean·er's /ˌdraɪ ˈkliːnəz/ *noun*
  a shop that cleans clothes in a special way without using water

dual car·riage·way /ˌdjuːəl ˈkærɪdʒweɪ/ *noun*
  a wide road with two lines of traffic moving in each direction and a narrow piece of land in the centre

duch·ess /ˈdʌtʃɪs/ *noun* (*plural* **duchesses**)
  the title of a woman from a very important family in Britain: *the Duchess of York* ⇨ compare DUKE

duck

duck   duckling

duck[1] /dʌk/ *noun*
  a bird that swims on water and is used for its eggs, meat, and feathers

duck[2] *verb*
  to suddenly move your head or body down because you do not want to be hit or seen: *He had to duck his head to get through the doorway.* | *He ducked down behind the wall.*

duck·ling /ˈdʌklɪŋ/ *noun*
  a young duck ⇨ see picture at DUCK[1]

due /djuː/ *adjective*
  1 **be due** to be expected to happen or arrive at a particular time: *The train is due at 5 o'clock.* | *My library books are due back tomorrow.*
  2 **be due to do something** to be going to do something: *We're due to leave on the 17th.*
  3 needing to be paid: *The rent is due at the end of the month.*
  4 **be due for something** if someone is due for something, it is the time they should have it: *The baby is due for a feed.*
  5 **due to** because of: *This shop is closed due to illness.*

du·et /djuːˈet/ *noun*
  a song or piece of music for two people

dug /dʌg/
  the past tense and past participle of the verb **dig**

duke /djuːk/ *noun*
  the title of a man from a very important family in Britain: *the Duke of York* ⇨ compare DUCHESS

dull /dʌl/ *adjective*
  1 not bright or light: *It was a dull cloudy day.*
  2 not interesting or clever: *He gave a dull speech.* | *What a dull party.*

dumb /dʌm/ *adjective*
  not able to speak. This word offends many people

dum·my /ˈdʌmɪ/ *noun* (*plural* **dummies**)
  British a small rubber object that you put in a baby's mouth to stop it crying

dump[1] /dʌmp/ *verb*
  1 to drop something and leave it: *We dumped our bags on the floor.*
  2 to get rid of something that you do not want: *Illegal chemicals had been dumped in the river.*

dump[2] *noun*
  a place where things can be left when people do not want them any more

dune /djuːn/ *noun*
  a hill of sand

dun·ga·rees /ˌdʌŋɡəˈriːz/ *plural noun*
  trousers with a piece of material at the top that covers your chest ⇨ see picture on page 203

dun·geon /ˈdʌndʒən/ *noun*
  a dark prison under the ground

dur·ing /ˈdjʊərɪŋ/ *preposition*
  1 all the time that something is going on: *They swim every day during the holidays.* | *You need to water plants more often during the summer.*
  2 at some time when something else is happening: *He fell asleep during the lesson.* | *Her grandfather died during the night.*

dusk /dʌsk/ *noun* (*no plural*)
  the time in the evening when the sun has just gone down ⇨ see picture at DAWN

dust[1] /dʌst/ *noun* (*no plural*)
  extremely small pieces of dirt carried in the air

dust² *verb*
to clean dust from something: *She dusted the table.*

dust·bin /'dʌstbɪn/ *noun*
a large metal or plastic container that people keep outside their houses and in which they put things they want to get rid of ⇨ compare BIN

dust·er /'dʌstər/ *noun*
a cloth you use to clean dust from furniture

dust·man /'dʌstmən/ *noun* (*plural* **dustmen** /-mən/)
a person whose job is to take away the things inside DUSTBINS

dust·pan /'dʌstpæn/ *noun*
a flat container that you use to carry away dust after you have swept the floor: *Have you got a dustpan and brush?*

dust·y /'dʌstɪ/ *adjective*
covered in dust

du·ty /'djuːtɪ/ *noun* (*plural* **duties**)
1 something you must do because it is right: *You have a duty to look after your family.* | *Everyone has a duty to pay taxes.*

2 off duty, on duty if someone such as a policeman or doctor is off duty, they are not working. If they are on duty, they are working

du·vet /'djuːveɪ/ *noun*
a thick warm cover with feathers inside it that you put on a bed ⇨ compare BLANKET

DVD /ˌdiː viː 'diː/ *noun*
a small round piece of hard plastic that pictures and sounds are recorded on. You use it on a computer

dwarf /dwɔːf/ *noun*
1 a plant or animal that is much smaller than usual
2 a person who is very small because of a medical problem. This word offends many people

dye¹ /daɪ/ *verb* (*present participle* **dyeing**, *past* **dyed**)
to give a different colour to something: *She dyed her hair black.*

dye² *noun*
a liquid or powder that is used to change the colour of things

dy·na·mite /'daɪnəmaɪt/ *noun* (*no plural*)
a substance used to make explosions

A
B
C
D
E
F
G
H
I
J
K
L
M
N
O
P
Q
R
S
T
U
V
W
X
Y
Z

Ee

E, e /iː/
the fifth letter of the English alphabet

each /iːtʃ/
1 every one separately: *Each child has an exercise book for their work.* | *The tickets are £10 each.*

2 each other used to show that each of two people do something to the other person: *The two brothers help each other.* | *Karen and Mark kissed each other.*

ea·ger /ˈiːgəʳ/ adjective
very keen to do something: *The girl was eager to show me her photographs.*

eagerly adverb: *"Can I come?" she asked eagerly.*

ea·gle /ˈiːgl/ noun
a large bird that lives in mountain areas and kills small animals for food

eagle
beak
wing

ear /ɪəʳ/ noun
1 one of the parts of your body with which you hear ⇨ see picture at HEAD

2 the top part of a plant such as wheat, where the seed is

ear·ache /ˈɪəreɪk/ noun
pain inside your ear: *She's got earache.*

ear·ly /ˈɜːlɪ/ adjective, adverb
1 before the usual or agreed time: *You're early! It's only five o'clock.* | *The plane landed ten minutes early.*

2 near the beginning of the day or a period of time: *It often rains in the early morning.* | *Do you get up early?*
⇨ opposite LATE ⇨ look at SOON

earn /ɜːn/ verb
1 to get money for work you do: *He earns a lot of money.*

2 to get something that you deserve because you have worked hard: *You've earned a good rest.*

ear·ring /ˈɪərɪŋ/ noun
a piece of jewellery you wear on your ear ⇨ see picture at JEWELLERY

earth /ɜːθ/ noun (no plural)
1 also **Earth** the world in which we live: *The Earth goes round the sun once a year.* | *I thought it was the most beautiful place on earth.*

2 the substance on the ground in which plants can grow: *She planted the seeds in the wet earth.* ⇨ same meaning SOIL

earth·quake /ˈɜːθˌkweɪk/ noun
a strong and sudden shaking of the ground

ease¹ /iːz/ noun (no plural)
1 with ease if you do something with ease, it is easy for you: *He passed the examination with ease.*

2 at ease feeling comfortable and sure of yourself: *The other children were friendly and made her feel at ease in her new school.*

ease² verb (present participle **easing**, past **eased**)
to make something better: *The medicine eased the pain.*

ea·sel /ˈiːzl/ noun
a frame used to hold a picture that is being painted ⇨ see pictures at ARTIST and on page 197

eas·i·ly /ˈiːzɪlɪ/ adverb
without difficulty: *I can easily be there by tomorrow.*

east /iːst/ adjective, adverb
1 the direction from which the sun comes up in the morning: *Our house faces east.* | *She lived on the east coast of the island.*

2 east wind a wind that comes from the east

Eas·ter /ˈiːstəʳ/ noun
a special Sunday in March or April when Christians remember Christ's death and his return to life

Easter egg /ˈiːstər eg/ noun
a chocolate egg eaten at Easter

east·ern /ˈiːstən/ adjective
in or of the east: *There will be high temperatures in eastern parts of the country.*

east·wards /ˈiːstwədz/ adverb
towards the east: *They travelled eastwards.*

eas·y /ˈiːzɪ/ adjective
not difficult: *I can answer all these questions – they're too easy.* | *Jane*

needs a book that is easy to understand. ⟡ opposite DIFFICULT, HARD

eat /iːt/ *verb (past tense* **ate** /et, eɪt/, *past participle* **eaten** /ˈiːtn/)
  1 to put food into your mouth and swallow it: *Have you eaten your breakfast yet?*
  2 to have a meal: *What time did you eat?*

ech·o¹ /ˈekəʊ/ *verb*
  if a sound echoes, you hear it again: *Our voices echoed in the empty room.*

echo² *noun (plural* **echoes**)
  a sound that you hear again: *We could hear the echo of our voices in the cave.*

e·clipse /ɪˈklɪps/ *noun*
  a short time when you cannot see the light from the sun or moon because it is blocked by the moon or Earth

e·co·nom·ic /ˌiːkəˈnɒmɪk, ˌekə-/ *adjective*
  relating to industry and trade: *The country's economic problems can be solved.*

e·co·nom·i·cal /ˌiːkəˈnɒmɪkl, ˌekə-/ *adjective*
  using time, money, etc without wasting it: *We need an economical way of heating the school.*

e·con·o·my /ɪˈkɒnəmi/ *noun (plural* **economies**)
  the system by which a country's industry and trade are controlled: *The new tax laws will help the economy.*

edge /edʒ/ *noun*

edge

  1 the part which is furthest from the centre: *The edge of the plate is painted red.* | *She was standing at the water's edge.*
  2 the sharp cutting part of a knife or tool

climbing on the edge of a cliff

  3 **on edge** nervous and worried: *His exam results are tomorrow so he's a bit on edge.*

e·di·tion /ɪˈdɪʃn/ *noun*
  a book, magazine, or newspaper that appears at a particular time

ed·i·tor /ˈedɪtər/ *noun*
  a person who prepares books or newspapers for printing

ed·u·cate /ˈedjʊkeɪt/ *verb (present participle* **educating**, *past* **educated**)
  to teach someone, especially in a school or a college: *He's well educated.* | *Children should be educated **about** the dangers of smoking.*

ed·u·ca·tion /ˌedjʊˈkeɪʃn/ *noun (no plural)*
  teaching and learning: *The government believes in the importance of education.*

ed·u·ca·tion·al /ˌedjʊˈkeɪʃnəl/ *adjective*
  helping you to learn: *She bought him an educational toy.*

eel /iːl/ *noun*
  a long fish shaped like a snake

ef·fect /ɪˈfekt/ *noun*
  a result: *Eating too many sweets can have a bad effect **on** your teeth.*

ef·fec·tive /ɪˈfektɪv/ *adjective*
  getting the result you want: *These pills are an effective cure for a headache.*

ef·fi·cient /ɪˈfɪʃnt/ *adjective*
  working well, quickly, and without waste: *He is a very efficient worker.* | *We bought the most efficient heating system.*

ef·fort /ˈefət/ *noun*
  the physical or mental energy that you need to do something: *With a great effort he pushed open the door.* | *Please put more effort into your school work.*

EFL /ˌiː ef ˈel/ *noun*
  the teaching of English to people who speak a different language

e.g. /ˌiː ˈdʒiː/
  a short way of writing or saying 'for example': *You can try many different sports on this holiday, e.g. sailing, tennis, and swimming.*

egg

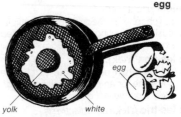

yolk   *white*

egg /eg/ *noun*
  1 a round object usually with a hard

shell from which a baby bird, snake, fish, or insect comes

2 an egg from a bird such as a chicken that is eaten as food: *We had eggs for breakfast.*

eight /eɪt/
the number 8

eigh·teen /eɪˈtiːn/
the number 18

eighth /eɪtθ/ *adjective*
8th

eigh·ty /ˈeɪtɪ/
the number 80

ei·ther /ˈaɪðəʳ, ˈiːðəʳ/
1 one or the other of two people or things: *You can have either tea or coffee.*
2 used in sentences with 'not' to say that something else is also true: *I haven't been to America, or to England either.*

e·lab·orate /ɪˈlæbrət/ *adjective*
full of detail, with a large number of parts

e·las·tic /ɪˈlæstɪk/ *adjective*
able to go back into shape after being stretched or pulled: *Rubber is an elastic substance.*

elastic band /ɪˌlæstɪk ˈbænd/ *noun*
a thin circle of rubber that is used to hold things together

el·bow /ˈelbəʊ/ *noun*
the part in the middle of your arm that bends

el·der·ly /ˈeldəlɪ/ *adjective*
an elderly person is old: *My aunt is rather elderly and needs a lot of care.*

el·dest /ˈeldɪst/ *adjective*
oldest of three or more people: *His eldest sister is a doctor.*

e·lect /ɪˈlekt/ *verb*
to choose someone for an official position by voting: *Clinton was elected President in 1992 and 1996.*

e·lec·tion /ɪˈlekʃən/ *noun*
a time when people vote to choose someone for an official position: *Which party won the last election?*

e·lec·tric /ɪˈlektrɪk/ *adjective*
using electricity to work: *He plays an electric guitar.*

e·lec·tri·cal /ɪˈlektrɪkl/ *adjective*
relating to or using electricity: *The cooker isn't working because of an electrical fault.*

e·lec·tri·cian /ɪˌlekˈtrɪʃn, ˌelɪk-/ *noun*
a person whose job is to fit and repair electrical machines

e·lec·tri·ci·ty /ɪˌlekˈtrɪsətɪ, ˌelɪk-/ *noun*
(*no plural*)
power that is sent through wires and is used for lighting, heating, and making machines work

e·lec·tron·ics /ɪˌlekˈtrɒnɪks, ˌelɪk-/
the study of making equipment that uses electricity, such as televisions and computers

el·e·gant /ˈelɪgənt/ *adjective*
moving and dressing in an attractive way: *She always wears elegant clothes.*

el·e·ment /ˈelɪmənt/ *noun*
1 one of the very simple substances from which everything is made: *Gold and iron are elements.*
2 a part of a whole: *Honesty is an important element of the job.*

el·e·men·tary /ˌelɪˈmentrɪ/ *adjective*
simple and easy: *She was practising some elementary exercises on the piano.*

el·e·phant /ˈelɪfənt/ *noun*
a large grey animal with a very long nose that lives in hot countries ⇨ see picture on page 195

el·e·va·tor /ˈeləveɪtəʳ/ *noun*
American a machine that carries people or things between the floors of a tall building (*British* **lift**)

e·lev·en /ɪˈlevn/
the number 11

e·lev·enth /ɪˈlevənθ/ *adjective*
11th

elf /elf/ *noun* (*plural* **elves** /elvz/)
a small imaginary creature with pointed ears

else /els/ *adverb*
1 other, different, or instead: *If you don't like eggs I can cook something else.* | *She was wearing someone else's coat.*
2 more, or as well: *Would you like something else to eat?* | *He needs someone else to help him.*
3 or else used to say what the result

will be if you do not do something: *He has to pay or else he will be in trouble.*

NOTE: Use **else** after words that begin **any-**, **every-**, **no-**, and **some**: *Do you know anyone else we could invite?* | *It's cold and wet here but I don't know what it's like everywhere else.* | *I have nothing else to say.* You can also use **else** after question words like **how**, **what**, and **who**: *He must be angry. Why else would he have shouted like that?*

else·where /els'weə^r/ *adverb*
in or to some other place: *They left the village and went elsewhere.* | *Snow is expected elsewhere in the area.*

elves /elvz/ *noun*
the plural of the word **elf**

e-mail¹ /'iː meɪl/ *noun*
also **email** a message written on one person's computer and sent to someone else's computer: *I had several e-mails today.*

e-mail² *verb*
also **email** to send a message from your computer to another person's computer: *I e-mailed him to tell him the time the party would start.*

em·bar·rass /ɪm'bærəs/ *verb*
to make someone feel nervous or silly: *I'm sorry – I didn't mean to embarrass you.*

em·bar·rassed /ɪm'bærəst/ *adjective*
feeling nervous or silly: *I feel so embarrassed when I think of what I said.*

NOTE: **1** People feel **embarrassed** about small things that they have done which make them appear silly to other people, such as forgetting someone's name or going to a party in the wrong type of clothes. If someone is sorry because they have done something very bad and important, they feel **ashamed**, not **embarrassed**. **2** Do not confuse **embarrassed** (=feeling uncomfortable or nervous) and **embarrassing** (=making someone feel like this): *It was an embarrassing mistake.* | *We all felt very embarrassed.*

em·bar·rass·ing /ɪm'bærəsɪŋ/ *adjective*
making you feel nervous or silly: *He asked several embarrassing questions.*

em·bar·rass·ment /ɪm'bærəsmənt/ *noun* (*no plural*)
the way you feel when something embarrasses you: *He couldn't hide his embarrassment* **at** *his children's rudeness.*

em·bas·sy /'embəsɪ/ *noun* (*plural* **embassies**)
a place in another country where people work for their government to represent their own country

em·brace /ɪm'breɪs/ *verb* (*present participle* **embracing**, *past* **embraced**)
to hold someone in your arms to show that you love them: *The child embraced his parents.* | *The couple embraced.*

em·broi·der·y /ɪm'brɔɪdərɪ/ *noun* (*no plural*)
beautiful patterns made with a needle and thread on cloth: *The top of her dress is covered with embroidery.*

em·er·ald /'emərəld/ *noun*
a bright green stone that is very valuable

e·merge /ɪ'mɜːdʒ/ *verb* (*present participle* **emerging**, *past* **emerged**)
to come or appear from somewhere hidden: *The baby birds emerged* **from** *their eggs.*

e·mer·gen·cy /ɪ'mɜːdʒənsɪ/ *noun* (*plural* **emergencies**)
a sudden dangerous event that needs to be dealt with very quickly: *The hospital has to treat emergencies such as car accidents.* | *In an emergency, phone the police.*

em·i·grant /'emɪgrənt/ *noun*
a person who leaves their own country in order to live in another country
➪ compare IMMIGRANT

em·i·grate /'emɪgreɪt/ *verb* (*present participle* **emigrating**, *past* **emigrated**)
to leave your own country to go and live in another country: *Her family emigrated to Australia.*

em·i·gra·tion /ˌemɪ'greɪʃn/ *noun* (*no plural*)
the act of leaving your own country to go and live in another country
➪ compare IMMIGRATION

A
B
C
D
E
F
G
H
I
J
K
L
M
N
O
P
Q
R
S
T
U
V
W
X
Y
Z

e·mir /'emɪə^r/ *noun*
a Muslim ruler, especially in Asia and parts of Africa

e·mo·tion /ɪ'məʊʃn/ *noun*
a strong feeling such as love, hate, or anger: *Her voice was trembling with emotion.* I *Julie was able to express her emotions more easily than her husband.*

e·mo·tion·al /ɪ'məʊʃnəl/ *adjective*
having strong feelings that you show, sometimes by crying

em·pe·ror /'empərə^r/ *noun*
a ruler of a big country or several countries

em·pha·size /'emfəsaɪz/ *verb* (*present participle* **emphasizing**, *past* **emphasized**)
to show that something is important: *He emphasized the need for hard work.* I *My teacher always emphasized the importance of grammar.* ⟡ same meaning STRESS

em·pire /'empaɪə^r/ *noun*
a group of countries ruled by one government: *the British Empire*

em·ploy /ɪm'plɔɪ/ *verb*
to give someone a job: *She is employed as a teacher.* I *The hospital employs hundreds of people.*

em·ploy·ee /ɪm'plɔɪ-iː/ *noun*
a person who works for someone else: *There are ten employees in his firm.*

em·ploy·er /ɪm'plɔɪə^r/ *noun*
a person or group that pays people to work for them

em·ploy·ment /ɪm'plɔɪmənt/ *noun* (*no plural*)
work that you do to get money: *Students start looking for employment when they leave college.* ⟡ opposite UNEMPLOYMENT

em·press /'emprɪs/ *noun*
a female ruler of a country or several countries, or the wife of an EMPEROR

emp·ty¹ /'emptɪ/ *adjective*
with nothing inside: *The house is empty; no one is living there.* I *Your glass is empty – would you like another drink?* ⟡ opposite FULL

empty² *verb* (*past* **emptied**)
also **empty out** to take everything out of something: *He emptied the bottle.* I *I found your old shoes when I was emptying out the cupboard.* ⟡ opposite FILL

en·a·ble /ɪ'neɪbl/ *verb* (*present participle* **enabling**, *past* **enabled**)
to make someone able to do something: *The new machines enable us to work very fast.*

en·close /ɪn'kləʊz/ *verb* (*present participle* **enclosing**, *past* **enclosed**)
1 to put something in an envelope with a letter: *I enclosed a photograph of the baby with my letter.*
2 to surround something completely: *A high wall enclosed the garden.*

en·cour·age /ɪn'kʌrɪdʒ/ *verb* (*present participle* **encouraging**, *past* **encouraged**)
to give praise and support to someone so that they will do something: *I encouraged her to start playing tennis.* ⟡ opposite DISCOURAGE

en·cour·age·ment /ɪn'kʌrɪdʒmənt/ *noun* (*no plural*)
praise and support given to someone so that they will feel confident: *Her parents gave her lots of encouragement.*

en·cour·ag·ing /ɪn'kʌrɪdʒɪŋ/ *adjective*
giving you hope or making you feel confident: *The doctor gave us some encouraging news.*

en·cy·clo·pe·di·a /ɪnˌsaɪklə'piːdɪə/ *noun*
a book that gives you knowledge about a lot of different things

end¹ /end/ *noun*
1 the point where something finishes, or the last part of something: *When you get to the end of this road, turn right.* I *At the end of the lesson, we went home.* I *We're going on holiday at the end of August.* ⟡ opposite BEGINNING
2 in the end after a very long time, when you almost thought something was not going to happen: *We walked for hours, but in the end we found the house.*

straw

empty

full   empty

end² *verb*

1 to finish: *The party ended at midnight.* | *Lucy decided to end her relationship with Jeff.* ⇨ opposite BEGIN

2 end up to finish in a particular way or place although you did not want to: *We ended up going by bus.*

end·ing /'endɪŋ/ *noun*
the end of a story, film, or play: *The book had a happy ending.*

end·less /'endləs/ *adjective*
not pleasant and seeming never to end: *There is endless work to do when you have children in the house.*

en·e·my /'enəmi/ *noun (plural **enemies**)*
a person or country that is not friendly to you or that wants to fight or harm you: *He's **made** a lot of enemies at school.* | *Jake and Paul have been enemies for years.*

en·er·get·ic /ˌenə'dʒetɪk/ *adjective*
very active: *My children are very energetic.*

en·er·gy /'enədʒi/ *noun (no plural)*
1 the ability to be active and do a lot without feeling tired: *I have no energy left after playing football all day.* | *She came back from her holiday full of energy and enthusiasm.*
2 the power that makes machines work or that gives heat: *Some people say that we should use the energy of the sun to heat our buildings.*

en·gaged /ɪn'geɪdʒd/ *adjective*
1 if you are engaged to someone, you have promised to marry them: *They got engaged last year.*
2 *British* if a telephone number is engaged, the telephone is already being used: *I tried to ring her but her phone was engaged.*

en·gage·ment /ɪn'geɪdʒmənt/ *noun*
1 an agreement to marry someone: *My brother has just told me about his engagement to Anne.*
2 an arrangement to meet someone: *I'm unable to come because I have another engagement.*

en·gine /'endʒɪn/ *noun*
a machine that uses petrol, oil, gas, electricity, or steam and makes things work or move: *a car engine*

en·gi·neer /ˌendʒɪ'nɪər/ *noun*
a person who is trained to plan and build machines, roads, bridges, etc

en·gi·neer·ing /ˌendʒɪ'nɪərɪŋ/ *noun (no plural)*
the science or job of an engineer: *He is studying engineering at college.*

En·glish /'ɪŋglɪʃ/ *noun*
1 the language that is spoken in Great Britain, the United States, Canada, Australia, etc
2 the English *(plural)* the people of England

en·joy /ɪn'dʒɔɪ/ *verb*
1 to get pleasure and happiness from something: *She enjoys listening to music.* | *Did you enjoy the film?*
2 enjoy yourself to be happy and have a good time: *Did you enjoy yourself at the wedding?*

en·joy·a·ble /ɪn'dʒɔɪəbl/ *adjective*
giving pleasure or happiness: *We had an enjoyable weekend at the beach.*

en·joy·ment /ɪn'dʒɔɪmənt/ *noun (no plural)*
pleasure: *I get a lot of enjoyment from playing sports.*

en·large /ɪn'lɑːdʒ/ *verb (present participle **enlarging**, past **enlarged**)*
to make something bigger: *I want to enlarge this photograph.*

e·nor·mous /ɪ'nɔːməs/ *adjective*
very large: *Mr and Mrs Smith have an enormous house with seven bedrooms.* | *We have an enormous amount of work to do before the school holidays.*

e·nor·mous·ly /ɪ'nɔːməsli/ *adverb*
very much: *I like Jane enormously.*

e·nough /ɪ'nʌf/ *adjective, adverb*
as much as is needed: *There is enough food for three people.* | *This bag isn't big enough for all my books.* | *The water isn't warm enough for us to swim.*

en·quire /ɪn'kwaɪər/ *verb*
another spelling of **inquire**

en·qui·ry /ɪn'kwaɪəri/ *noun (plural **enquiries**)*
another spelling of **inquiry**

en·ter /'entər/ *verb*
1 to go or come in to a particular place: *She unlocked the door and entered the house.* | *Everyone stopped talking when he entered.*
2 to become part of an organization or group: *He decided to enter college.* | *I*

A B C D **E** F G H I J K L M N O P Q R S T U V W X Y Z

She's hoping to enter the medical profession.

3 to start to take part in something: *She entered the race and won.* | *Do you want to enter this competition?*

4 to write down information or include it on a computer: *Please enter your name on the form.*

en·ter·tain /ˌentəˈteɪn/ *verb*

1 to make people laugh or to interest people: *He entertained us with stories about life in Italy.*

2 to give food and drink to guests

en·ter·tain·er /ˌentəˈteɪnəʳ/ *noun*

a person whose job is to entertain others, for example by telling jokes

en·ter·tain·ing /ˌentəˈteɪnɪŋ/ *adjective*

amusing and interesting

en·ter·tain·ment /ˌentəˈteɪnmənt/ *noun* (no plural)

activities that make people laugh or that interest people: *For entertainment we watch television.*

en·thu·si·as·m /ɪnˈθjuːzɪæzəm/ *noun* (no plural)

a strong feeling of being interested in something or wanting to do something: *His friends all share his enthusiasm for football.*

en·thu·si·as·tic /ɪnˌθjuːzɪˈæstɪk/ *adjective*

very keen on something or interested in it: *She was enthusiastic about going to America.*

en·tire /ɪnˈtaɪəʳ/ *adjective*

whole or complete: *The entire class will be there.* | *I've spent the entire day cleaning my room.*

en·trance /ˈentrəns/ *noun*

a place where you go in to a building: *Where's the entrance to the hospital?*

en·try /ˈentri/ *noun* (plural **entries**)

1 (no plural) when you enter a place: *They gained entry through a window.*

2 (no plural) the right to enter a building or country: *The sign says 'No Entry'.* | *The travellers were refused entry to the country.*

3 a piece of work that someone sends to be judged in a competition: *The winning entry was a photo of children playing.*

envelope

stamp

Mr. J. Thomas
49, Ledsham Road,
Manchester M6 4RJ

letter

envelope

en·vel·ope /ˈenvələʊp, ˈɒnvələʊp/ *noun*

a folded paper cover for a letter

en·vi·ous /ˈenvɪəs/ *adjective*

wishing you had something that belongs to someone else: *She was envious of my new car.* ⬦ same meaning JEALOUS

en·vi·ron·ment /ɪnˈvaɪərənmənt/ *noun*

1 the world of land, sea, and air that you live in: *Cutting down too many trees destroys the environment.*

2 the conditions of the society around you: *Children need a happy home environment.*

en·vy [1] /ˈenvi/ *noun* (no plural)

the feeling of wanting something that someone else has got: *He looked with envy at Al's new car.* ⬦ same meaning JEALOUSY

envy [2] *verb* (past **envied**)

to wish that you had what someone else has got: *I envy John – he seems so happy.*

ep·i·dem·ic /ˌepɪˈdemɪk/ *noun*

an illness that spreads quickly to a lot of people

e·qual [1] /ˈiːkwəl/ *adjective*

the same in size, number, or value: *Divide the cake into four equal parts.* | *Women want equal pay to men.*

equal [2] *verb* (present participle **equalling**, past **equalled**)

1 to be the same as something else in number or amount: *Three and five equals eight* $(3 + 5 = 8)$.

2 to be as good as someone or something else: *None of us can equal Sarah – she's always top of the class.*

equal [3] *noun*

a person who has the same ability and rights as someone else: *All people should be treated as equals by the law.*

e·qual·i·ty /ɪˈkwɒlətɪ/ *noun (no plural)*
when people have the same rights and advantages: *Women want equality with men.*

e·qua·tor /ɪˈkweɪtəʳ/ *noun*
an imaginary line that runs round the middle of the Earth from east to west

e·quip /ɪˈkwɪp/ *verb (present participle* **equipping**, *past* **equipped**)
to give someone things that are useful for doing something: *The government wants to equip schools* **with** *more modern computers.*

e·quip·ment /ɪˈkwɪpmənt/ *noun (no plural)*
the things that are used for a particular activity: *We need to buy some camping equipment before our holiday.* I *She was looking at an expensive piece of electrical equipment.*

e·rect¹ /ɪˈrekt/ *adjective*
in a straight upright position: *She held her head erect.*

erect² *verb*
to fit something together and make it stand upright: *They erected the tent.*

er·rand /ˈerənd/ *noun*
a short journey made to do something useful or to buy something

er·ror /ˈerəʳ/ *noun*
a mistake: *The doctor's error was very serious.*

e·rupt /ɪˈrʌpt/ *verb*
if a VOLCANO erupts, it sends out fire and smoke

escalator

es·ca·la·tor /ˈeskəleɪtəʳ/ *noun*
a set of moving stairs that can take you up or down without you having to walk

es·cape¹ /ɪˈskeɪp/ *verb (present participle* **escaping**, *past* **escaped**)
to get free from a place where you are kept by force: *He escaped* **from** *prison.*

escape² *noun*
when someone escapes from a place: *The prisoner made his escape at night.*

es·cort¹ /ɪˈskɔːt/ *verb*
to go with someone in order to protect them: *A group of soldiers escorted the President.*

es·cort² /ˈeskɔːt/ *noun*
people, cars, planes, etc that travel with someone to protect them: *The slow-moving vehicle has a police escort.*

ESL /ˌiː es ˈel/ *noun*
the teaching of English to students who do not speak English but who are living in a country where people speak English

es·pe·cial·ly /ɪˈspeʃlɪ/ *adverb*
1 more than usual: *She is especially good at science.* I *These chairs are especially suitable for people with back problems.*
2 most of all: *I would like a bicycle, especially a blue one.* I *Everyone is excited about our trip, especially Sam.*

es·say /ˈeseɪ/ *noun*
a piece of writing on a subject: *She wrote an essay* **on** *'My Family'.*

es·sen·tial /ɪˈsenʃəl/ *adjective*
important and necessary: *If you travel abroad, it is essential* **that** *you have the right papers.* I *Good food is essential* **for** *good health.*

es·tab·lish /ɪˈstæblɪʃ/ *verb*
to start a company, organization, system, situation, etc: *The school was established in 1922.*

es·tate /ɪˈsteɪt/ *noun*
a large piece of land, usually with a house or group of buildings on it

estate a·gent /ɪˈsteɪt ˌeɪdʒənt/ *noun*
British a person whose job is to arrange the buying and selling of houses and land

es·ti·mate¹ /ˈestɪmeɪt/ *verb (present participle* **estimating**, *past* **estimated**)
to make a reasonable guess about the size or amount of something: *They estimated* **that** *the house cost £1 million.*

es·ti·mate² /'estɪmət/ *noun*
a guess about the size or amount of something

etc /et'setrə/
used after a list of things to say that more similar things could be added: *There are lots of things to buy – tea, sugar, bread, etc.*

eu·ro /'jʊərəʊ/ *noun*
euros are money that can be used in many European countries

Eu·ro·pe·an¹ /ˌjʊərə'piːən/ *adjective*
from or connected with a country in Europe

European² *noun*
a person from a country in Europe

e·vac·u·ate /ɪ'vækjʊeɪt/ *verb* (*present participle* **evacuating,** *past* **evacuated**)
to move people from a dangerous place to a safer place

eve /iːv/ *noun*
the night or day before a religious holiday or before another event: *Christmas Eve* | *On the eve of the election there were riots.*

e·ven¹ /'iːvn/ *adverb*
1 used to show when something is surprising or unusual: *Even Peter helped us and he's usually very lazy.* | *He hadn't even remembered my birthday.*
2 used when you are comparing two things to make the second seem stronger: *Yesterday it rained hard and today it's raining even harder.*

even² *adjective*
1 flat and smooth: *The table has an even surface.*
2 an even amount does not change much: *We are travelling at an even speed.*
3 equal: *He won the first game and I won the second, so we're even.*

eve·ning /'iːvnɪŋ/ *noun*
the end of the afternoon and the early part of night

e·ven·ly /'iːvənli/ *adverb*
equally: *Divide the sweets evenly among the three boys.*

even num·ber /ˌiːvn 'nʌmbər/ *noun*
a number that can be divided exactly by two, for example 2, 4, or 6

e·vent /ɪ'vent/ *noun*
something that happens, often something important or unusual: *What events do you remember from the last five years?*

e·ven·tual·ly /ɪ'ventʃəli/ *adverb*
after a period of time: *I looked everywhere for my glasses and eventually found them under my chair.*

ev·er /'evər/ *adverb*
1 at any time: *Have you ever been to Jamaica?* | *Nothing ever makes Carol angry.*
2 **ever since** since a particular time in the past: *I have lived here ever since I was a child.*

ev·ery /'evrɪ/
each one: *I have read every book he has written.* | *Every student will take the test.*

ev·ery·bod·y /'evrɪbɒdɪ/
every person: *Everybody wants to watch the match.* | *Everybody who passed the test received a prize.*

NOTE: Remember that **everybody** and **everyone** are singular words, like **he** or **she**, so you must use them with a singular verb ending: *Everyone knows that sugar is bad for your teeth.*

---

ev·ery·day /ˌevrɪ'deɪ/ *adjective*
usual or ordinary: *Problems are part of everyday life.*

ev·ery·one /'evrɪwʌn/
every person: *She likes everyone in her class.* | *Everyone agreed that the concert was a success.* ⇨ look at EVERYBODY

ev·ery·thing /'evrɪθɪŋ/
all things: *I got everything I needed in the market.*

ev·ery·where /'evrɪweər/ *adverb*
in or to every place: *I looked everywhere for my watch, but I couldn't find it.* ⇨ compare NOWHERE

ev·i·dence /'evɪdəns/ *noun* (*no plural*)
words or facts that show something to be true: *You say that John took your book, but have you any evidence of that?*

ev·i·dent /'evɪdənt/ *adjective*
easy to notice or understand: *Her love of animals is evident.* | *It was evident*

that he was not telling the truth.
⇨ same meaning OBVIOUS

e·vil /'i:vl/ *adjective*
morally bad, or causing harm: *In the film, the good queen saves the child from an evil enemy.*

ex·act /ɪgˈzækt/ *adjective*
completely correct: *Can you tell me the exact time?*

ex·act·ly /ɪgˈzæktlɪ/ *adverb*
1 used to say that something is completely correct: *We got home at exactly six o'clock.* | *I don't know exactly where she lives.*
2 used to agree with someone: *"So you think we should spend more on education?" "Exactly."*

ex·ag·ger·ate /ɪgˈzædʒəreɪt/ *verb*
(*present participle* **exaggerating**, *past* **exaggerated**)
to make something seem bigger, better, worse, etc than it really is: *He exaggerated when he said the dog was the size of a horse.*

ex·am /ɪgˈzæm/ *noun*
an official test of knowledge in a subject: *When do you take your history exam?*

ex·am·i·na·tion /ɪgˌzæmɪˈneɪʃn/ *noun*
1 an official test of knowledge in a subject: *Please arrive on time for all examinations.*
2 a careful look at someone or something: *He was given a thorough examination by the doctor.* | *On closer examination, the painting was found to be a copy.*

ex·am·ine /ɪgˈzæmɪn/ *verb* (*present participle* **examining**, *past* **examined**)
1 to look at someone or something closely and carefully: *The doctor examined my ears.*
2 to ask someone questions to be sure that they know something

ex·am·ple /ɪgˈzɑːmpl/ *noun*
1 something that you mention because it is typical of the kind of thing you are talking about: *Can anyone give me an example of a verb?* | *This painting is a good example of African art.*
2 for example used to give an example of something that makes your meaning clearer: *Prices are going up. For example, meat costs a lot more now.*

ex·as·pe·rate /ɪgˈzɑːspəreɪt/ *verb* (*present participle* **exasperating**, *past* **exasperated**)
to annoy someone

ex·ceed /ɪkˈsiːd/ *verb*
to be more than a particular amount: *The total cost should not exceed £200.*

ex·cel·lent /'eksələnt/ *adjective*
very good: *This is excellent work, Peter.*

ex·cept /ɪkˈsept/
not including a particular thing, person, or fact: *I've washed all the clothes except your shirt.* | *Everyone went to the show except **for** Scott.* | *I have some earrings just like that except **that** they are silver.*

ex·cep·tion /ɪkˈsepʃn/ *noun*
1 something that is different from what is usually expected: *Most children like sweets, but she is the exception – she won't eat them!*
2 with the exception of except: *They'd all been there before with the exception of Jim.*

ex·cep·tion·al /ɪkˈsepʃənəl/ *adjective*
of unusually high ability: *Jill is an exceptional student.*

ex·cep·tion·ally /ɪkˈsepʃənlɪ/ *adverb*
unusually or especially: *This has been an exceptionally cold winter.*

ex·cess /'ekses/ *noun* (*plural* **excesses**) *adjective*
more than is usual or allowed: *You have to pay for excess luggage on a plane.*

ex·change[1] /ɪksˈtʃeɪndʒ/ *verb* (*present participle* **exchanging**, *past* **exchanged**)
to give something to someone in return for something else: *This skirt is too small. Can I exchange it for a larger one?* | *We exchanged phone numbers.*

exchange[2] *noun*
1 when you give something to someone and they give you something else: *The two countries are planning an exchange **of** prisoners.*
2 in exchange in the place of something that you give to someone: *I gave him the book in exchange **for** a CD.*

exchange rate /ɪksˈtʃeɪndʒ reɪt/ *noun*
the value of a country's money compared to the money of another country

A B C D E F G H I J K L M N O P Q R S T U V W X Y Z

ex·cite /ɪkˈsaɪt/ *verb (present participle* **exciting**, *past* **excited**)
to make someone feel very happy and interested, because something good is going to happen: *The games excited the children and they all started to shout.*

ex·cit·ed /ɪkˈsaɪtɪd/ *adjective*
feeling very happy and interested, because something good is going to happen: *The kids are really excited **about** our trip to California.*

ex·cite·ment /ɪkˈsaɪtmənt/ *noun (no plural)*
the way you feel when you are excited: *The crowd's excitement grew near the end of the match.*

ex·cit·ing /ɪkˈsaɪtɪŋ/ *adjective*
making you feel very happy and interested: *I heard your exciting news about winning the prize.*

ex·claim /ɪkˈskleɪm/ *verb*
to speak loudly and suddenly in surprise: *"Look – there's James on the television!" exclaimed Peter.*

ex·cla·ma·tion /ˌekskləˈmeɪʃn/ *noun*
a sound, word, or phrase that you say suddenly and loudly because you are surprised or angry

exclamation mark /ˌekskləˈmeɪʃn ˌmɑːk/ *noun*
the sign (!) used in writing to show a strong feeling like surprise, or when calling someone

ex·clude /ɪkˈskluːd/ *verb (present participle* **excluding**, *past* **excluded**)
to not allow someone to be included in something or to enter a place: *We had to exclude John **from** the team because of his leg injury. | Women are excluded from the club.* ⇨ opposite INCLUDE

ex·clud·ing /ɪkˈskluːdɪŋ/
not including: *The shop is open every day, excluding Sundays.* ⇨ opposite INCLUDING

ex·cuse[1] /ɪkˈskjuːz/ *verb (present participle* **excusing**, *past* **excused**)
1 excuse me used to get someone's attention, leave a group of people, or say sorry for doing something slightly rude: *Excuse me, but have you got the time, please? | Excuse me, I'll be back in a minute.*
2 to not be angry or upset about something: *She excused him **for** being late. | Please excuse this untidy room.*
3 to give someone permission not to do something or to leave: *The teacher excused her **from** going to the school's sports day.*

ex·cuse[2] /ɪkˈskjuːs/ *noun*
a reason given to explain a mistake or bad behaviour: *Have you any excuse **for** not finishing the work on time? | I'm sure Mike has an excuse for why he didn't pay you yesterday.*

ex·e·cute /ˈeksɪkjuːt/ *verb (present participle* **executing**, *past* **executed**)
to kill someone as a punishment decided by law

ex·e·cu·tion /ˌeksɪˈkjuːʃn/ *noun*
the killing of a person when it is a punishment decided by law

ex·er·cise[1] /ˈeksəsaɪz/ *noun*
1 physical activity that you do in order to stay strong and healthy: *Running is good exercise. | You can do special exercises to strengthen your back.*
2 a set of questions given in school to help students practise something: *Please do exercises 3 and 4.*

exercise[2] *verb (present participle* **exercising**, *past* **exercised**)
to do physical activities so that you stay strong and healthy: *The doctor told him to exercise more.*

exercise book /ˈeksəsaɪz ˌbʊk/ *noun*
a book with empty pages in which students do their work for school

ex·haust[1] /ɪɡˈzɔːst/ *verb*
to make someone very tired: *The long journey exhausted her.*

exhaust[2] *noun*
1 also **exhaust pipe** a pipe that lets waste gas out of the back of a car
2 (*no plural*) the waste gas that is produced when an engine is working

ex·haust·ed /ɪɡˈzɔːstɪd/ *adjective*
very tired: *I'm exhausted from not getting enough sleep.*

ex·haust·ing /ɪɡˈzɔːstɪŋ/ *adjective*
making you very tired: *Looking after babies is exhausting.*

ex·hib·it /ɪɡˈzɪbɪt/ *verb*
to show things in public: *She exhibited her paintings at our school.*

exhibition

an exhibition in an art gallery

ex·hi·bi·tion /ˌeksɪˈbɪʃn/ *noun*
a public show of objects, for example paintings: *We went to an art exhibition.*

ex·ile¹ /ˈeksaɪl/ *noun*
1 in exile someone who is in exile is not allowed to live in their own country as a punishment: *After the revolution, they had to live in exile in Europe.*
2 a person who is living in exile

exile² *verb (present participle* **exiling,** *past* **exiled)**
to send a person away from their own country as a punishment

ex·ist /ɪgˈzɪst/ *verb*
to be real, present, or alive: *The house where I was born no longer exists.* I *Some insects exist just in this small area of forest.*

ex·ist·ence /ɪgˈzɪstəns/ *noun (no plural)*
the state of being real or alive: *The elephant is the largest land animal* **in** *existence.*

ex·it /ˈeksɪt/ *noun*
the way out of a place: *Where is the exit?*

ex·pand /ɪkˈspænd/ *verb*
to become larger or make something larger: *The business has expanded from one office to four.*

ex·pan·sion /ɪkˈspænʃən/ *noun*
an increase in size

ex·pect /ɪkˈspekt/ *verb*
1 to think that something will happen: *Do you expect to win the race?* I *The car cost more than I expected.*
2 be expecting someone or something to feel sure that someone or something will arrive, often because you have arranged it: *We're expecting the Johnsons for lunch.*
3 to ask strongly for someone to do

something: *Visitors to the hospital are expected not to smoke.*
4 be expecting, be expecting a baby when a woman is expecting, a baby is developing inside her

ex·pe·di·tion /ˌekspəˈdɪʃn/ *noun*
a long difficult journey, usually to find out something: *They are planning an expedition to the North Pole.*

ex·pel /ɪkˈspel/ *verb (present participle* **expelling,** *past* **expelled)**
to force someone to leave a school, group, or country: *Two pupils were expelled for stealing.*

ex·pense /ɪkˈspens/ *noun*
money spent on something: *I made a list of my travelling expenses.* I *Having a car is a big expense.*

ex·pen·sive /ɪkˈspensɪv/ *adjective*
costing a lot of money: *It is expensive to travel by plane.* ⇨ opposite CHEAP

ex·pe·ri·ence¹ /ɪkˈspɪərɪəns/ *noun*
1 something that happens to you: *The accident was an experience she will never forget.* I *She told me about her first experience* **of** *travelling abroad.*
2 *(no plural)* knowledge or skill that you get from doing a job: *She is a teacher with 5 years of experience.*

experience² *verb (present participle* **experiencing,** *past* **experienced)**
to have something happen to you: *We are experiencing some problems with our computers.*

ex·pe·ri·enced /ɪkˈspɪərɪənst/ *adjective*
having a lot of knowledge and skill because you have done something for a long time: *He is a very experienced pilot.*

ex·per·i·ment¹ /ɪkˈsperɪmənt/ *noun*
a careful test done to see if something is true: *He did a scientific experiment for the class.*

ex·per·i·ment² /ɪkˈsperɪment/ *verb*
to do a careful test to see if something is true: *We experimented by putting oil and water together, and we saw that they did not mix.*

ex·pert¹ /ˈekspɜːt/ *noun*
a person who has special skill in something or knowledge of something: *Paul is an expert* **in** *modern art.* I *Professor Robins is an expert* **on** *ancient Egypt.*

A B C D E F G H I J K L M N O P Q R S T U V W X Y Z

expert[2] *adjective*
having special skill or knowledge of something: *I need some expert advice.*

ex·plain /ɪk'spleɪn/ *verb*
to make something easy to understand, or to give the reason for something: *Can you explain what this word means?* | *I explained to him that I'd missed the bus.*

ex·pla·na·tion /ˌeksplə'neɪʃn/ *noun*
something that makes something easy to understand, or gives the reason for it: *He gave an explanation of how to use the program.*

ex·plode /ɪk'spləud/ *verb* (*present participle* **exploding**, *past* **exploded**)
to break into pieces with a loud noise and a lot of force: *A bomb exploded there last night.*

ex·plo·ra·tion /ˌeksplə'reɪʃn/ *noun*
a journey to a place to learn about it: *He liked to read about the exploration of space.*

ex·plore /ɪk'splɔːr/ *verb* (*present participle* **exploring**, *past* **explored**)
to find out about a place by travelling through it: *We spent a week exploring the Oregon coastline.*

ex·plor·er /ɪk'splɔːrər/ *noun*
a person who travels into a new area to find out about it

ex·plo·sion /ɪk'spləuʒn/ *noun*
when something explodes: *The explosion damaged three houses.*

ex·plo·sive[1] /ɪk'spləusɪv/ *adjective*
something that is explosive can cause an explosion

explosive[2] *noun*
a substance that causes an explosion

ex·port[1] /ɪk'spɔːt/ *verb*
to send goods to another country to be sold: *India exports cloth.* ⇨ compare IMPORT

ex·port[2] /'ekspɔːt/ *noun*
a product that is sold to another country: *Fruit is one of South Africa's exports.* ⇨ compare IMPORT

ex·pose /ɪk'spəuz/ *verb* (*present participle* **exposing**, *past* **exposed**)
to show something that is usually covered: *You shouldn't expose your skin to the sun.*

ex·press[1] /ɪk'spres/ *verb*
to show a feeling or thought by saying or doing something: *He wanted to express his thanks but he could not think of the best words.* | *It can be difficult to express how you feel about someone.*

express[2] *adjective*
going or sent very quickly: *I sent it by express mail.*

express[3] *noun*
also **express train** a fast train that makes only a few stops on its journey

ex·pres·sion /ɪk'spreʃn/ *noun*
1 a word or group of words with a particular meaning: *You shouldn't use that expression – it's not polite.* | *"Mustn't grumble," my father said. It was an expression he often used.*
2 the look on someone's face: *She came back with a cheerful expression.*

ex·qui·site /ɪk'skwɪzɪt/ *adjective*
very beautiful or delicate: *It was an exquisite piece of jewellery.*

ex·tend /ɪk'stend/ *verb*
1 to reach or stretch over an area: *The garden extends all the way to the river.*
2 to make something larger or longer: *The headmaster extended our holiday by four days.* | *The club is being extended to make a new dance area.*

ex·ten·sion /ɪk'stenʃən/ *noun*
a part added to make something longer or bigger: *They built an extension onto the school, so now we have two more classrooms.*

ex·ten·sive /ɪk'stensɪv/ *adjective*
spreading over a large area: *The school has extensive playing fields.*

ex·tent /ɪk'stent/ *noun*
the size or limit of something: *What is the extent of the damage?*

ex·te·ri·or[1] /ɪk'stɪərɪər/ *adjective*
on the outside of something: *We painted the exterior walls of the house.* ⇨ opposite INTERIOR

exterior[2] *noun*
the outside part of something: *The exterior of the building needed repairs.* ⇨ opposite INTERIOR

ex·ter·nal /ɪk'stɜːnl/ *adjective*
outside a place, person, or thing: *He had no external signs of injury.* ⇨ opposite INTERNAL

ex·tin·guish /ɪkˈstɪŋgwɪʃ/ *verb*
to make a fire stop burning

ex·tra /ˈekstrə/ *adjective, adverb*
more than usual, necessary, or expected: *Can I have extra time to finish my work?* | *This hotel charges extra for a room with a bath.* | *I want a large pizza with extra cheese.*

extra·or·di·nary /ɪkˈstrɔːdnrɪ/ *adjective*
very unusual or strange: *I heard an extraordinary story the other day.* | *Ellington had an extraordinary musical talent.*

ex·trav·a·gance /ɪkˈstrævəgəns/ *noun*
when someone spends too much money

ex·trav·a·gant /ɪkˈstrævəgənt/ *adjective*
spending too much money: *She's very extravagant – she spends all her money on clothes.*

ex·treme /ɪkˈstriːm/ *adjective*
1 very great: *As a policeman, he was sometimes in extreme danger.*
2 at the furthest end or edge of something: *She lives in the extreme north of the country.*

ex·treme·ly /ɪkˈstriːmlɪ/ *adverb*
very: *I'm extremely grateful for your help.*

eye /aɪ/ *noun*
1 the part of your head with which you see ⇨ see picture at HEAD
2 keep an eye on someone or something to watch people or things to make sure that they are safe: *Can you keep an eye on my house while I'm away?*
3 in someone's eyes in someone's opinion: *In her eyes, he's perfect.*
4 see eye to eye to agree with someone completely: *My father and I have never seen eye to eye.*
5 a small hole in a needle through which you put thread

eye·brow /ˈaɪbraʊ/ *noun*
the hairy line above your eye ⇨ see picture at HEAD

eye·lash /ˈaɪlæʃ/ *noun*
one of the hairs that grow on your eyelids ⇨ see picture at HEAD

eye·lid /ˈaɪlɪd/ *noun*
either of the pieces of skin that shut over your eye ⇨ see picture at HEAD

eye·sight /ˈaɪsaɪt/ *noun (no plural)*
your ability to see: *You need perfect eyesight to be a pilot.*

F, f /ef/
1 the sixth letter of the English alphabet
2 another way of writing FAHRENHEIT. For example, *32°F* means the same as *32 degrees* FAHRENHEIT

fa·ble /'feɪbl/ *noun*
a story that teaches people a lesson about how to behave

fab·ric /'fæbrɪk/ *noun*
cloth used for making things such as clothes: *The dress was made of woollen fabric.*

fab·u·lous /'fæbjʊləs/ *adjective*
very good or nice: *We had a fabulous holiday.* ⇨ same meaning WONDERFUL

face¹ /feɪs/ *noun*
1 the front part of your head, with your eyes, nose, and mouth
2 the part of a clock or watch that has numbers on it

face² *verb (present participle* **facing***, past* **faced***)*
1 if a person, building, object, etc faces someone or something, they have their front turned towards them: *Our house faces the park.* | *Dan turned to face me.*
2 to deal with a difficult situation or someone you want to avoid: *I knew he was angry and I could not face him.* | *You must face the fact that you are ill.*

fa·cil·i·ties /fə'sɪlətiz/ *plural noun*
rooms, equipment, etc used for a particular purpose: *The school has very good sports facilities.*

fact /fækt/ *noun*
1 something that you know is true or something that you know has happened: *It is a fact that plants need water.* | *We can't comment until we know all the facts.*
2 **in fact** used when you add information to something you have already said, or to emphasize that something is true: *I don't know him very well – in fact, I've only met him once.* | *They told me it would be cheap but in fact it cost me nearly £500.*

fac·tory /'fæktri/ *noun (plural* **factories***)*
a place where things are made by machines: *Harry works in a car factory.*

fade /feɪd/ *verb (present participle* **fading***, past* **faded***)*
to become less bright, or to make something less bright: *Years of sunlight had faded the carpet.*

Fah·ren·heit /'færənhaɪt/ *noun (no plural)*
a measure of temperature. Water freezes at 32 degrees Fahrenheit and boils at 212 degrees Fahrenheit

fail /feɪl/ *verb*
1 to not succeed: *Doctors failed to save the girl's life.* | *The crops have failed because of lack of rain.* ⇨ opposite SUCCEED
2 to not pass an examination: *I failed my vocabulary test.*
3 **fail to do something** to not do something that people expect or need: *Our flight failed to arrive on time.* ⇨ opposite SUCCEED

fail·ure /'feɪljəʳ/ *noun*
someone or something that does not succeed: *The plan was a failure.* | *I always felt a bit of a failure at school.* ⇨ opposite SUCCESS

faint¹ /feɪnt/ *adjective*
1 not strong or clear: *I heard a faint sound in the distance.* | *I could see the path by the faint light of the moon.*
2 **a faint possibility, chance, hope, etc** a very small possibility, chance, hope, etc: *There's still a faint hope that they might be alive.*

faint² *verb*
to suddenly become unconscious for a short time

fair¹ /feəʳ/ *adjective*
1 equal for everyone: *I try to be fair to all my children.* | *It's not fair – I want one too!* ⇨ opposite UNFAIR
2 good, but not very good: *His writing is good, but his reading is only fair.*
3 fair hair or skin is light in colour ⇨ opposite DARK

fair² *noun*
a place where people, especially children, go and pay money to ride on special machines and play games in order to win prizes

fair·ly /'feəli/ *adverb*
more than slightly, but less than very:

I'm fairly happy with the result. I *He speaks French fairly well.* ➪ same meaning QUITE

fai·ry /'feərɪ/ *noun (plural* **fairies)**
in stories, a very small person with wings who can do magic things

fairy tale /'feərɪ teɪl/ *noun*
a story for children about magic people or events

faith /feɪθ/ *noun*
1 (*no plural*) belief in something or someone: *I have faith* **in** *you; I am sure you will do well.*
2 (*no plural*) belief and trust in God
3 a religion: *She belongs to the Jewish faith.*

faith·ful /'feɪθfəl/ *adjective*
being loyal to someone who can trust you: *She is a faithful friend.*

faith·ful·ly /'feɪθfəlɪ/ *adverb*
Yours faithfully used to end a formal letter that begins Dear Sir or Dear Madam

fall¹ /fɔːl/ *verb*
(*past tense* **fell** /fel/, *past participle* **fallen** /'fɔːlən/)
1 to move or drop towards the ground: *The leaves are falling* **from** *the trees.* I *Rain was falling.* I *She fell* **down** *the stairs.* I *I fell* **off** *my bicycle.* ➪ see picture on page 207

fall

falling off a ladder

2 to go down to a lower level or amount: *House prices are falling.* I *Temperatures may fall below zero tonight.*
3 **fall apart** to break into pieces: *These old shoes are falling apart.*
4 **fall asleep** to start to sleep: *I fell asleep in front of the fire.*
5 **fall for something** to be tricked into thinking that something is true: *I can't believe he fell for that old story.*
6 **fall for someone** to start to feel love for someone: *She's fallen for a boy in her class.*
7 **fall in love with someone** to start to love someone

8 **fall out with someone** to have an argument and stop being friendly with someone: *They're always falling out with each other.*
9 **fall over** to fall to the ground: *I fell over on the ice.*
10 **fall to pieces** to break into pieces: *When I sat on the old chair it fell to pieces.*

fall² *noun*
1 the act of falling to the ground: *He had a bad fall and hurt himself.*
2 when an amount or level becomes lower: *There was a sudden fall* **in** *prices.*
3 *American* the season between summer and winter, when the leaves fall off the trees (*British* **autumn**)

fall·en /'fɔːlən/
the past participle of the verb **fall**

false /fɔːls/ *adjective*
1 not true: *He gave the police false information.*
2 not real: *He had a set of false teeth.*

fame /feɪm/ *noun (no plural)*
when someone is known and admired by a lot of people

fa·mil·i·ar /fə'mɪlɪər/ *adjective*
1 easy to recognize because you have seen or heard something often before: *This song sounds familiar.*
2 **be familiar with something** to know about something: *Are you familiar with this type of computer?*

fam·ily /'fæmlɪ/ *noun (plural* **families)**
a group of people who are related, especially a father and mother and their children: *Ned comes from a family of four* (=with four people in it). I *Do you know the family next door?*

family tree /ˌfæmlɪ 'triː/ *noun*
a drawing that shows how a group of people are related to each other

fam·ine /'fæmɪn/ *noun*
a time when there is not enough food for people to eat

fam·ous /'feɪməs/ *adjective*
known about and admired by a lot of people: *This town is famous* **for** *its beautiful buildings.* I *She's a famous singer.*

fan¹ /fæn/ *noun*
1 an instrument for moving air around to make you less hot
2 someone who likes a particular

person or thing very much: *I'm a fan of his music.* | *a football fan*

fan[2] *verb* (*present participle* **fanning**, *past* **fanned**)
to make the air around you move: *She fanned herself with the newspaper to cool her face.*

fan·cy /ˈfænsɪ/ *verb* (*present participle* **fancying**, *past* **fancied**)
1 to want something: *Do you fancy fish for dinner?* | *I fancy a walk.*
2 to find someone sexually attractive: *I really fancy Dan.*

fan·tas·tic /fænˈtæstɪk/ *adjective*
very good, attractive, enjoyable, etc: *You look fantastic in that dress.* | *We had a fantastic holiday in New Orleans.*
⇨ same meaning GREAT

far[1] /fɑːr/ *adverb* (**farther** *or* **further**, **farthest** *or* **furthest**)
1 a long distance from a place: *How far is it to London?* | *Let's see who can jump the farthest.* ⇨ opposite NEAR, CLOSE
2 very much: *I'm far too tired to go out.* | *You can't carry that box – it's far too heavy.* | *Our new car is far better than the old one.*
3 as far as to a place: *He only drove as far as the end of the road.*
4 far away a very long distance from a place: *I don't see my brother very often – he lives too far away.*
5 so far until now: *We haven't had any problems so far.*

far[2] *adjective*
1 a long way away from something else: *We can walk if it's not far.*
⇨ opposite NEAR, CLOSE
2 most distant from where you are: *She was on the far side of the room.*

NOTE: Use **far** in questions, in negative sentences, and after **too**, **as**, and **so**: *How far is it to your house?* | *It isn't far.* | *It's too far to walk.* | *We drove as far as the next town.* | *We didn't mean to walk so far.* In other types of sentences use **a long way**: *We walked a long way.* | *It's a long way from the school to my house.*

fare /feər/ *noun*
the amount of money that you have to pay to travel on a bus, train, plane, etc: *Train fares are going up again.*

farm /fɑːm/ *noun*
an area of land on which people grow food or keep animals

farm·er /ˈfɑːmər/ *noun*
a person who owns or works on a farm

farm·house /ˈfɑːmhaʊs/ *noun*
the main house on a farm

farm·ing /ˈfɑːmɪŋ/ *noun* (*no plural*)
the job of growing food or keeping animals

farm·yard /ˈfɑːmjɑːd/ *noun*
the piece of ground next to farm buildings

far·ther /ˈfɑːðər/
a comparative of **far**

far·thest /ˈfɑːðɪst/
a superlative of **far**

fas·ci·nate /ˈfæsɪneɪt/ *verb* (*present participle* **fascinating**, *past* **fascinated**)
to interest someone very much: *Her new toy fascinates Jill.*

fas·ci·na·tion /ˌfæsɪˈneɪʃn/ *noun* (*no plural*)
very strong interest in something: *The children watched with fascination.*

fash·ion /ˈfæʃn/ *noun*
1 the way of dressing or doing something that is liked by many people at a particular time: *She always buys the newest fashions.*
2 in fashion liked by many people now: *These ideas are in fashion.*
3 out of fashion no longer liked by many people: *Hats are out of fashion.*

fash·ion·a·ble /ˈfæʃnəbl/ *adjective*
liked by many people at a particular time: *She loves fashionable clothes.*
⇨ opposite UNFASHIONABLE

fast[1] /fɑːst/ *adjective*
1 moving, happening, or done quickly: *He is a fast runner.* | *What's the fastest way to get to the airport?*
2 a clock or watch that is fast shows a time that is later than the real time
⇨ opposite SLOW

fast[2] *adverb*
1 quickly: *He can run fast.* ⇨ opposite SLOWLY
2 fast asleep sleeping very well: *The baby is fast asleep.*

3 firmly or tightly: *The boat stuck fast in the mud.*

fast³ *verb*

to eat no food, usually for religious reasons ➪ compare STARVE

fas·ten /'fɑːsn/ *verb*

to join or tie together two sides of something so that it is closed: *She fastened her coat.* | *Can you fasten my necklace for me?*

fasteners

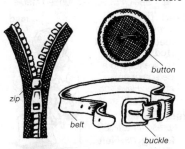

button

zip

belt

buckle

fas·ten·er /'fɑːsnə^r/ *noun*

something used to join or tie things together

fast food

chips

hotdog

sandwich

hamburger

pizza

fast food /ˌfɑːst 'fuːd/ *noun* (*no plural*)

hot food such as HAMBURGERS that are made and served quickly ➪ see picture on page 201

fat¹ /fæt/ *adjective*

1 a fat person weighs too much: *She worries a lot about getting fat.* ➪ opposite SLIM, THIN

2 thick or wide: *He's reading a big fat book.* ➪ opposite THIN

fat² *noun*

1 the substance under the skin of people and animals that helps to keep them warm

2 an oily substance contained in some foods: *Julie was trying to eat less fat and more fruit and vegetables.*

fa·tal /'feɪtl/ *adjective*

causing someone to die: *He was involved in a fatal car accident.* ➪ compare DEADLY

fate /feɪt/ *noun* (*no plural*)

a power that some people believe causes things to happen to you during your life: *I believe fate brought us together.*

fa·ther /'fɑːðə^r/ *noun*

your male parent

Father Christ·mas /ˌfɑːðə 'krɪsməs/ *noun*

an imaginary old man in red clothes who brings presents at Christmas

father-in-law /'fɑːðər ɪn lɔː/ *noun* (*plural* **fathers-in-law**)

the father of your wife or husband

fault /fɔːlt/ *noun*

1 **be someone's fault** if a bad thing is your fault, you made it happen: *I'm sorry – it's all my fault.* | *It's not my fault we missed the bus.*

2 a problem with something that stops it working: *There must be a fault in the engine.*

fault·less /'fɔːltləs/ *adjective*

with no faults or mistakes: *Yasmin spoke faultless Spanish.*

fault·y /'fɔːltɪ/ *adjective*

not working correctly: *We have a faulty wire in the telephone.*

fa·vour /'feɪvə^r/ *noun*

1 something kind done for someone: *May I* **ask** *you a favour?* | *Will you* **do** *me a favour and lend me some money?*

2 **be in favour of something** to agree with and support something: *I'm not in favour of the plan.* | *Are you in favour of changing the law?*

fa·vour·a·ble /'feɪvrəbl/ *adjective*

good and suitable: *We need favourable weather to take the boat out.*

fa·vour·ite /'feɪvrɪt/ *adjective*

liked best of all: *Orange is my favourite colour.* | *Who's your favourite actor?*

A B C D E F G H I J K L M N O P Q R S T U V W X Y Z

fax /fæks/ *noun*

1 also **fax machine** a machine, joined to a telephone, that you use for sending copies of letters or pictures to another place

a fax machine

2 a letter, picture, etc that you get on a fax machine

fear[1] /fɪəʳ/ *noun*

1 the feeling of being afraid: *He was shaking with fear.* | *I have a fear of snakes.*

2 a feeling of being worried in case something bad has happened or is going to happen: *You cannot live in fear.*

fear[2] *verb*

1 to worry because you think that something bad had happened or is going to happen: *He feared that his children would not be safe.*

2 to be afraid of someone or something: *The head teacher was feared by many of the students.*

fear·ful /ˈfɪəfəl/ *adjective*
afraid: *Everyone is fearful of getting the disease.*

fear·less /ˈfɪələs/ *adjective*
not afraid of anything: *He is a fearless soldier.* ⇨ compare BRAVE

feast[1] /fiːst/ *noun*
a large meal of good food for a special reason

feast[2] *verb*
to eat a large meal of good food

fea·ther /ˈfeðəʳ/ *noun*
one of the things that covers a bird, like a thin stick with soft hairs

fea·ture /ˈfiːtʃəʳ/ *noun*

1 an important, interesting, or typical part of something: *The new car has some extra safety features.*

2 a part of your face, especially your eyes, nose, or mouth

Feb·ru·a·ry /ˈfebrʊəri/ *noun*
the second month of the year

fed /fed/
the past tense and past participle of the verb **feed**

fed·e·ral /ˈfedərəl/ *adjective*
with several states or countries that are joined under one government but which also decide some things on their own

fed up /ˌfed ˈʌp/ *adjective*
annoyed or bored and wanting something to change: *I'm fed up with staying at home all day.*

fee /fiː/ *noun*
money that you pay to a doctor, school, etc

fee·ble /ˈfiːbl/ *adjective*
very weak: *His voice sounded feeble.*

feed /fiːd/ *verb*
(*present participle* **feeding**, *past* **fed** /fed/)
to give food to a person or an animal: *Have you fed the cat?*

feed

feeding a baby

feel /fiːl/ *verb*
(*present participle* **feeling**, *past* **felt** /felt/)

1 to have a particular feeling: *I feel happy.* | *Do you feel cold?* | *John felt ill after lunch.*

2 to touch something with your fingers to see what it is like: *Feel this cloth – it's so smooth.*

3 to notice something touching you: *He loved to feel the sand between his toes.*

4 to have an opinion because of your feelings rather than facts: *I feel sure she will agree.*

5 feel like something to want something: *I feel like having something to eat.*

6 feel for someone to have sympathy for someone: *She is very unhappy, and I feel for her.*

7 feel sorry for someone to feel sad about something that has happened to someone else

feel·ing /ˈfiːlɪŋ/ *noun*

1 something that you experience in your body or your mind: *I had a sudden feeling of tiredness.* | *It was a wonderful feeling to be home again.*

2 an opinion about something: *What is her feeling about having the party on Saturday?*

3 hurt someone's feelings to upset someone

feet /fiːt/ *noun*
1 the plural of **foot**
2 **on your feet** standing up: *I've been on my feet all day.*
3 **put your feet up** to rest: *You've had a tiring day; why not put your feet up?*

fell /fel/
the past tense of the verb **fall**

fel·low¹ /'feləʊ/ *noun*
a man

fellow² *adjective*
from the same place as you or doing the same thing as you: *She likes her fellow students.* I *Her fellow competitors were all very friendly.*

felt /felt/
the past tense and past participle of the verb **feel**

felt tip /'felt tɪp/ *noun*
also **felt tip pen** a type of thick coloured pen ⇨ see picture on page 205

fe·male¹ /'fiːmeɪl/ *adjective*
belonging to the sex that gives birth to young ones: *a female spider* ⇨ opposite MALE

female² *noun*
a person or animal that belongs to the sex that gives birth to young ones ⇨ opposite MALE

fem·i·nine /'femɪnɪn/ *adjective*
like a woman or typical of a woman: *Diane loved pretty feminine things.* ⇨ opposite MASCULINE

fence /fens/ *noun*
a thin wall made of wood or wire

fern /fɜːn/ *noun*
a green plant that has no flowers and grows in places that are wet and without much sun

fe·ro·cious /fə'rəʊʃəs/ *adjective*
extremely violent, angry, or ready to attack: *He had a ferocious dog in the back garden.*

fer·ry /'feri/ *noun* (plural **ferries**)
a boat that takes people or things across an area of water: *A ferry crosses the river every hour.*

fer·tile /'fɜːtaɪl/ *adjective*
fertile land or soil produces a lot of good crops or plants: *His farm is on fertile land.*

fer·ti·liz·er /'fɜːtɪlaɪzəʳ/ *noun*
something that you put on the soil to make crops grow better

fes·ti·val /'festɪvl/ *noun*
1 a set of special events of a particular type: *The film festival starts next week.* I *a music festival*
2 a time when people celebrate, especially a religious event

fetch /fetʃ/ *verb*
to go somewhere and bring someone or something back with you: *Could you fetch the children* **from** *school?* I *Run upstairs and fetch my glasses for me.*

fetch
fetching a stick

NOTE: Compare the verbs **fetch** and **bring**. If you **bring** something to a place, you have it with you when you go there. If you **fetch** something, you go and get it from somewhere else and then have it with you when you come back: *Please bring a bottle of wine to the party* (=come to the party with a bottle of wine). I *Can you fetch me some milk when you go to the shop* (=go and get it from the shop and come back with it).

fete /feɪt/ *noun*
British an outdoor event with games, competitions, and goods for sale, to collect money for a special purpose

fe·ver /'fiːvəʳ/ *noun*
an increase of heat in your body, caused by illness: *She has a fever and I'm giving her plenty of water and orange juice.*

few /fjuː/
1 **a few** a small number of people, things, etc: *Can I ask you a few questions?* I *We can wait a few more minutes.* I *Why not invite a few* **of** *your friends?*
2 not many: *In the 1950s few people had television.* I *The people were friendly but few* **of** *them spoke English.* ⇨ opposite MANY
3 **quite a few** a rather large number of things or people: *I've read quite a few of her books.*

A B C D E F G H I J K L M N O P Q R S T U V W X Y Z

fi·an·cé /fiː'ɒnseɪ/ *noun*
a man who has promised to marry a particular woman: *Her fiancé is called George.*

fi·anc·ée /fiː'ɒnseɪ/ *noun*
a woman who has promised to marry a particular man: *His fiancée is called Susan.*

fib /fɪb/ *noun*
a lie: *Are you telling a fib?*

fi·bre /'faɪbər/ *noun*
a thin thread used for making cloth

fic·tion /'fɪkʃən/ *noun (no plural)*
books and stories about imaginary people and events: *He writes children's fiction.*

field /fiːld/ *noun*
a piece of ground, usually with a fence or wall round it, used for growing crops or keeping animals: *There were several fields of wheat beside the road.*

fierce /fɪəs/ *adjective*
very violent, angry, or ready to attack: *Fierce dogs guarded the house.* | *She turned round looking fierce.*

fif·teen /fɪf'tiːn/
the number 15

fif·teenth /fɪf'tiːnθ/ *adjective*
15th

fifth /fɪfθ/ *adjective, noun*
1 5th
2 one of five equal parts

fif·ti·eth /'fɪftɪ-əθ/ *adjective*
50th

fif·ty /'fɪftɪ/
the number 50

fig /fɪg/ *noun*
a sweet fruit that is full of small seeds

fight¹ /faɪt/ *verb (past fought* /fɔːt/*)*
1 to use your body or weapons to try to hurt or kill someone: *He fought against them in the war.* | *Two men were fighting in the street.*
2 to have an argument with someone: *The boys are always fighting over what to watch on TV.*

fight² *noun*
1 a determined attempt to do something: *Many people agree with the fight to save the rainforest.*
2 when two people or groups fight each other with their bodies or weapons: *The two boys had a fight.*

fig·ure /'fɪgər/ *noun*
1 a written number such as 3, 5, or 8
2 a shape, especially the shape of a human body: *I could see a tall figure near the door.* | *She has a good figure* (=her body is very attractive).

file¹ /faɪl/ *noun*
1 a cover or container for documents ⇨ see picture on page 205
2 a document or set of information in a computer that is stored under a particular name: *I've deleted that file.*
3 a tool with a rough edge that you use for making things smooth: *a nail file*

file² *verb (present participle filing, past filed)*
1 to store documents or information in a particular order or a particular place: *Can you file these reports please?*
2 to make something smooth using a file: *She was filing her nails.*
3 to walk in a line one behind the other: *The children filed into the classroom.*

fil·ing cab·i·net /'faɪlɪŋ ˌkæbɪnət/ *noun*
a tall narrow piece of furniture with drawers where important documents are kept

fill /fɪl/ *verb*
1 also **fill up** to make something full: *I filled the glass with water.* | *Crowds of people soon filled the streets.* ⇨ opposite EMPTY
2 also **fill up** to become full: *The room filled with smoke.* | *The hole he had dug was filling up with water.* ⇨ opposite EMPTY
3 fill something in to give the written information you are asked for on an official piece of paper: *Fill in the answers to these questions.*

fill·ing /'fɪlɪŋ/ *noun*
a small amount of a substance that is put in a hole in your tooth

filling sta·tion /'fɪlɪŋ ˌsteɪʃn/ *noun*
a place where you go to buy petrol for your car

film¹ /fɪlm/ *noun*
1 a story that is told using sound and moving pictures, shown in a cinema or on television (*American* **movie**): *Have you seen any good films recently?*
2 the roll of thin plastic that makes photographs when you put it into a camera

film[2] *verb*
to make a film of something: *He filmed the football match.*

film star /'fɪlm stɑːʳ/ *noun*
a famous person who acts in films

fil·ter[1] /'fɪltəʳ/ *noun*
a thing that gas or liquid is put through to remove substances that are not wanted

filter[2] *verb*
to clean a liquid or gas using a filter

filth·y /'fɪlθɪ/ *adjective*
very dirty: *His clothes are filthy.*

fin /fɪn/ *noun*
a part on the side of a fish that helps it to swim ⇨ see picture at FISH

fi·nal[1] /'faɪnl/ *adjective*
last in a series, or coming at the end of something: *Did you read the final part of the story? | They scored a goal in the final minutes of the game.*

final[2] *noun*
the last and most important game in a competition, to decide who will win: *the World Cup Final*

fi·nal·ly /'faɪnl-ɪ/ *adverb*
1 after a long time: *When she finally arrived it was too late. | We finally left after waiting two hours.*
2 a word you use when you come to the last thing you want to say: *Finally, let me thank you all for your help.*

fi·nance[1] /'faɪnæns/ *noun (no plural)*
the controlling of large sums of money, for example by a bank, a company, or a government

finance[2] *verb (present participle financing, past financed)*
to give someone the money for something: *The government will finance the building of the new roads.*

fi·nan·cial /faɪ'nænʃəl/ *adjective*
connected with money: *I need financial advice.*

find /faɪnd/ *verb (past found /faʊnd/)*
1 to see or get something after you have been looking for it: *I can't find my keys. | Have you found a job yet?* ⇨ opposite LOSE
2 to learn or discover something: *I want to find the answer to her question. | I soon found that it was quicker to go by bus.*

3 **find someone guilty** to say that someone is guilty of a crime: *The court found him guilty of murder.*
4 **find something out** to discover the facts about something: *I never found out her name. | I need to find out more about what subjects I can study.*

fine[1] /faɪn/ *adjective*
1 very nice or of high quality: *He gave a fine performance in the film.*
2 good enough: *"What do you want for lunch?" "A sandwich would be fine, thanks."*
3 very well, happy, or healthy: *"How are you?" "Fine, thank you."*
4 with the sun shining, or without rain: *Let's hope the fine weather lasts over the weekend.*
5 very thin: *There was a fine layer of dust on everything.*

fine[2] *noun*
money that you pay as a punishment after doing something wrong

fine[3] *verb (present participle fining, past fined)*
to make someone pay money as a punishment: *Robert was fined £50 for driving too fast.*

fin·ger /'fɪŋgəʳ/ *noun*
one of the five long parts on your hand ⇨ see picture at HAND

fin·ger·nail /'fɪŋgəneɪl/ *noun*
one of the hard flat parts that cover the top end of your fingers ⇨ see picture at HAND

fin·ger·print /'fɪŋgəprɪnt/ *noun*
a mark made by the lines on the ends of your fingers ⇨ see picture at HAND

fin·ger·tip /'fɪŋgətɪp/ *noun*
the end of one of your fingers

fin·ish[1] /'fɪnɪʃ/ *verb*
1 to complete something or to stop doing something: *I finish work at 5 o'clock. | I've finished reading the newspaper.* ⇨ opposite BEGIN, START
2 to end: *The game finished at four o'clock.* ⇨ opposite BEGIN, START
3 **finish something off** to complete something: *I'm just finishing off a letter.*
4 **finish something up** to eat or drink all the rest of something: *Do you want to finish up that cake?*
5 **finish with something** to stop using something because you no longer

A B C D E F G H I J K L M N O P Q R S T U V W X Y Z

need it: *Have you finished with that pen?*

finish² *noun* (no plural)
the end of something: *The meal was horrible from start to finish.* ⇨ opposite START

fir /fɜːʳ/ *noun*
a tree with leaves shaped like needles that do not fall off in winter

fire¹ /faɪəʳ/ *noun*
1 heat and flames that burn and destroy things: *The building was destroyed by fire.* ⇨ see picture on page 193
2 a pile of burning coal or wood used to make a room warm: *I like to sit in front of the fire.*
3 catch fire to begin to burn: *Mary knocked the candle over and the tablecloth caught fire.*
4 on fire burning: *The house is on fire.*
5 set fire to something to make something burn: *An angry crowd set fire to the shops.*

fire² *verb*
to shoot with a gun: *Someone fired at the President's car.*

fire a·larm /faɪər ə,lɑːm/ *noun*
a bell that rings to warn you when a building starts to burn

fire bri·gade /faɪə brɪ,geɪd/ *noun*
British a group of people whose job is to stop dangerous fires

fire en·gine /faɪər ,endʒɪn/ *noun*
a vehicle used by the fire brigade that has water and special equipment for stopping fires ⇨ see picture on page 206

fire es·cape /faɪər ɪ,skeɪp/ *noun*
a set of stairs on the outside of a building that you use to escape when there is a fire

fire ex·tin·guish·er /faɪər ɪk,stɪŋgwɪʃəʳ/ *noun*
a metal container with water or chemicals inside for putting on a fire to stop it burning

fire-fight·er /faɪə,faɪtəʳ/ *noun*
a person whose job is to stop dangerous fires

fire-man /faɪəmən/ *noun* (plural **firemen** /-mən/)
a man whose job is to stop dangerous fires ⇨ see picture on page 200

fire-place /faɪəpleɪs/ *noun*
the part of the wall of a room where you have a fire

fire sta·tion /faɪə ,steɪʃn/ *noun*
the building where people and equipment stay until they are needed to fight a fire

fire-wood /faɪəwʊd/ *noun* (no plural)
wood for burning on a fire

fireworks

fire-work /faɪəwɜːk/ *noun*
a thing that explodes and makes pretty patterns of light and colour in the sky

firm¹ /fɜːm/ *adjective*
1 not soft: *I need a firm bed to sleep on.* | *Choose the firmest tomatoes.*
2 making sure that people obey you: *The teacher was firm **with** the children.*
3 a firm grip, a firm hold a strong way of holding something: *He took my arm in a firm grip.*

firm² *noun*
a group of people who work together in a business: *She's worked for the same firm for years.* ⇨ same meaning COMPANY

firm·ly /fɜːmlɪ/ *adverb*
in a way that shows strong control: *She told him firmly that he must wait.*

first /fɜːst/ *adjective, adverb*
1 before anyone or anything else: *It's his first year at school.* | *She came first in the competition.* | *It's the first day of the month.* ⇨ opposite LAST
2 happening or done before other similar events or actions: *I first visited America two years ago.* | *Welles made his first film at the age of 25.* ⇨ opposite LAST
3 first of all (a) before doing anything else: *First of all, can you tell me your*

name? **(b)** used when you are talking about something that happened before a lot of other things: *First of all we had dinner, then we went to the cinema, and then we went home.*

4 at first at the start of something: *At first I didn't enjoy school, but now I like it.* ⇨ look at FIRSTLY

first aid

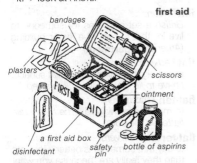

bandages
plasters
scissors
ointment
FIRST AID
a first aid box
disinfectant
safety pin
bottle of aspirins

first aid /ˌfɜːst 'eɪd/ *noun (no plural)*
simple help that you give to an ill or wounded person before the doctor comes

first-class /ˌfɜːst 'klɑːs/ *adjective*
of the best or most expensive type: *He bought a first-class train ticket.*

first floor /ˌfɜːst 'flɔːr/ *noun*
British the floor of a building just above the one that is level with the ground ⇨ compare GROUND FLOOR

first·ly /'fɜːstlɪ/ *adverb*
a word you use when you are making the first of several points: *Firstly, let me thank everyone for coming here this evening.* ⇨ opposite LASTLY

NOTE: **Firstly** does **not** mean 'in the beginning'. Use **at first** instead: *At first I didn't like my job, but then I started to enjoy it.*

first name /'fɜːst neɪm/ *noun*
the name or names that come before your family name: *"What is your first name, Mrs James?" "It's Anne. I'm Mrs Anne Jones."* ⇨ compare SURNAME

fish¹ /fɪʃ/ *noun (plural* **fish** *or* **fishes)**
a creature that lives in water and can swim, and which people eat as food

fish² *verb*
1 to try to catch fish: *Dad's fishing **for** salmon.*

fish

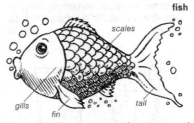

scales
gills
fin
tail

2 go fishing to go to a place to try and catch fish ⇨ see picture on page 193

fish·er·man /'fɪʃəmən/ *noun (plural* **fishermen** /-mən/)
a person who catches fish for sport or as a job ⇨ see picture on page 200

fish·ing rod /'fɪʃɪŋ ˌrɒd/ *noun*
a long stick with string at the end used for catching fish

fish·mon·ger /'fɪʃmʌŋgər/ *noun*
1 a person who owns or works in a shop that sells fish
2 fishmonger's a shop that sells fish

fist /fɪst/ *noun*
a hand with the fingers closed tightly together: *He hit me with his fist.*

fit¹ /fɪt/ *verb (present participle* **fitting**, *past* **fitted)**
1 to be the right size and shape for someone or something: *The trousers don't fit him; they're too small.* | *This lid doesn't fit very well.*
2 to find space to put someone or something: *We can't fit any more people in the car.*
3 to put a piece of equipment in the place where it will be used: *He fitted a telephone in my office.*
4 fit in to be accepted by other people in a group: *The new student didn't fit in.*

fit² *adjective*
1 suitable and good enough: *This food is not fit **for** your visitors.*
2 healthy and strong, especially because you exercise a lot: *I want to get fit.* | *Jogging helps her keep fit.* ⇨ opposite UNFIT

five /faɪv/
the number 5

fix /fɪks/ *verb*
1 to repair something: *Can you fix my bicycle?*
2 to arrange an exact time, place, price, or limit: *We haven't fixed a day for the party yet.*

3 *British* to fasten something firmly to something else: *He fixed a picture to the wall.*

fizzy

fizzy water   *still water*

fiz·zy /ˈfɪzɪ/ *adjective*
a fizzy drink contains BUBBLES of gas

flag /flæg/ *noun*
a piece of cloth with a special pattern on it, used as the sign of a country, club, etc ⇨ see picture at HOLE

flag·pole /ˈflæɡpəʊl/ *noun*
a tall pole at the top of which you hang a flag

flake /fleɪk/ *noun*
a small thin piece of something that has broken off a larger piece: *Flakes of paint fell from the ceiling.*

flame /fleɪm/ *noun*
1 a bright piece of burning gas that you see in a fire
2 in flames burning: *The house was in flames.*

flap¹ /flæp/ *verb* (*present participle* **flapping**, *past* **flapped**)
if a bird flaps its wings, it moves them up and down

flap² *noun*
a piece of something that hangs down over an opening: *I tore the flap on my shirt pocket.*

flash¹ /flæʃ/ *noun*
1 a sudden bright light: *There was a flash of lightning.*
2 a light on a camera that you use when you take a photograph inside a building
3 in a flash very quickly: *I'll be back in a flash.*

flash² *verb*
to shine brightly for a moment, or to make a light shine brightly for a moment: *The driver flashed his headlights.*

flask /flɑːsk/ *noun*
a special type of bottle for keeping hot

drinks hot, or cold drinks cold: *a flask of coffee*

flat¹ /flæt/ *adjective*
1 smooth and level without any raised places: *The house has a flat roof.* | *Lay the paper on a flat surface.*
2 a flat tyre does not have enough air inside

flat² *noun*
British a set of rooms for someone to live in, that is part of a larger building (*American* **apartment**)

flat³ *adverb*
in a straight position along a flat surface: *I have to lie flat on my back to sleep.*

flat·ten /ˈflætn/ *verb*
to make something flat: *The heavy rain flattened the corn.*

flat·ter /ˈflætər/ *verb*
to say that someone is better, nicer, etc than they really are, because you want something from them: *He was flattering her, saying how beautiful she was.*

flat·ter·y /ˈflætərɪ/ *noun* (*no plural*)
nice things that you say to someone, because you want something from them

fla·vour /ˈfleɪvər/ *noun*
a taste: *Which flavour do you want, chocolate or vanilla?*

flea /fliː/ *noun*
a very small jumping insect that drinks blood from animals and people

flee /fliː/ *verb* (*present participle* **fleeing**, *past* **fled** /fled/)
to leave a place very quickly in order to escape from danger: *When they saw the police, they turned and fled.*

fleece /fliːs/ *noun*
1 the wool of a sheep
2 a type of soft material, or a coat made from it

fleet /fliːt/ *noun*
a group of ships or all the ships in a navy: *We could see a fleet of fishing boats out at sea.*

flesh /fleʃ/ *noun* (*no plural*)
the soft part of your body that covers your bones ⇨ compare SKIN

flew /fluː/
the past tense of the verb **fly**

flight /flaɪt/ *noun*
a journey on a plane: *She was on a*

flight from New York to Paris. | What time is the next flight to Edinburgh?

fling /flɪŋ/ *verb (past* **flung** /flʌŋ/)
to throw or move something with force: *She flung her arms around his neck.*

flip·per /ˈflɪpəʳ/ *noun*
1 a wide flat part of the body that some sea animals have and which helps them swim
2 a wide flat plastic shoe that you wear to help you swim fast under water

flirt /flɜːt/ *verb*
to behave in a way that is intended to get sexual attention: *He flirts **with** all the women.*

float /fləʊt/ *verb*
to stay on the surface of a liquid: *A boat floats on water.* ⇨ opposite SINK ⇨ see picture at SINK

flock /flɒk/ *noun*
a group of sheep, goats, or birds ⇨ compare HERD

flood[1] /flʌd/ *noun*
a great quantity of water covering a place that is usually dry: *The floods destroyed many homes.*

flood[2] *verb*
to cover a place with water: *The river flooded the fields.*

flood·light /ˈflʌdlaɪt/ *noun*
a very strong light used at night to show the outside of buildings, or at sports events

floor /flɔːʳ/ *noun*
1 the part of a room that you walk on: *The room has a wooden floor. | She was sweeping the kitchen floor.*
2 all the rooms on the same level of a building: *We live on the third floor.*

floor·board /ˈflɔːbɔːd/ *noun*
a long narrow piece of wood used to make floors

flop·py disk /ˌflɒpɪ ˈdɪsk/ *noun*
a piece of plastic that you can put into a computer and on which information can be stored ⇨ compare HARD DISK

flor·ist /ˈflɒrɪst/ *noun*
1 a person who sells flowers in a shop
2 **florist's** a shop that sells flowers ⇨ see picture on page 201

flour /flaʊəʳ/ *noun (no plural)*
powder made from wheat, used for making bread, cakes, etc

flour·ish /ˈflʌrɪʃ/ *verb*
to be successful or grow well: *The garden is flourishing.*

flow[1] /fləʊ/ *verb*
if a liquid flows, it moves along in a steady way: *The river flows through the town.*

flow[2] *noun (no plural)*
a steady continuous movement of something: *He tried to stop the flow **of** blood. | The flow of cars through the city never stops.*

flow·er /ˈflaʊəʳ/ *noun*
the part of a plant that holds the seeds and that is usually pretty and brightly coloured: *A vase of flowers stood on the table.*

flow·er·bed /ˈflaʊəbed/ *noun*
an area of earth with flowers planted in it

flow·er·pot /ˈflaʊəpɒt/ *noun*
a container in which you grow plants

flown /fləʊn/
the past participle of the verb **fly**

flu /fluː/ *noun*
an illness that makes you weak and hot and makes your body hurt: *Three of the teachers have got flu.*

flu·ent /ˈfluːənt/ *adjective*
speaking a language easily and well: *He speaks fluent English.*

fluff /flʌf/ *noun (no plural)*
soft pieces that come off wool, fur, feathers, etc

flu·id[1] /ˈfluːɪd/ *noun*
a liquid: *The doctor advised her to rest and drink plenty of fluids.*

fluid[2] *adjective*
able to move or flow like a liquid

flush /flʌʃ/ *verb*
1 to clean a toilet by making water go down it: *He flushed the toilet and washed his hands.*
2 to become red in the face because you are ashamed, angry, etc: *Billy flushed and looked down.*

flute /fluːt/ *noun*
a musical instrument like a pipe that you hold to your mouth sideways and blow

flute
flute

A
B
C
D
E
F
G
H
I
J
K
L
M
N
O
P
Q
R
S
T
U
V
W
X
Y
Z

flut·ter /ˈflʌtəʳ/ verb
to move or wave in the air quickly: Dead leaves fluttered to the ground. I A flag was fluttering in the wind.

fly¹ /flaɪ/ verb (present participle **flying**, past tense **flew** /fluː/, past participle **flown** /fləʊn/)
1 to move through the air: Birds were flying above the trees. I The plane flew from Paris to Rome.
2 to control a plane: Bill's learning to fly.
3 to run or move quickly: She flew out of the house. I Timmy flew down the stairs and out of the door.

fly² noun (plural **flies**)
a small flying insect

fly·ing sau·cer /ˌflaɪ-ɪŋ ˈsɔːsəʳ/ noun
a space vehicle that some people think carries creatures from another world

fly·o·ver /ˈflaɪəʊvəʳ/ noun
British a bridge that carries one road over another road

foal /fəʊl/ noun
a very young horse

foam /fəʊm/ noun (no plural)
a mass of very small bubbles on the surface of something: white foam on the tops of the waves

fog /fɒg/ noun (no plural)
thick cloud close to the ground that makes it difficult to see: Drivers are warned that there is fog and they should drive with care. ⇨ compare MIST

fog·gy /ˈfɒgi/ adjective
if it is foggy, there is fog: It was really foggy last night. ⇨ compare MISTY ⇨ see picture on page 194

fold¹ /fəʊld/ verb
1 to turn part of something over another part: He folded the letter and put it in an envelope. I She folded her clothes and put them on a chair.
2 fold your arms to bend your arms so that they are resting across your chest
3 also **fold up** to bend or close something so that it is smaller: Fold up the ironing board when you are finished.

fold² noun
a line made in paper or cloth when you bend one part of it over another

fold·er /ˈfəʊldəʳ/ noun
a large piece of hard paper that is folded so you can keep documents in it

folk /fəʊk/ adjective
folk music, art, dancing, etc is traditional and typical of the ordinary people of a particular country or area

fol·low /ˈfɒləʊ/ verb
1 to walk, drive, etc behind someone: If you follow me, I'll show you to the office. I A woman walked into the room followed by three children.
2 to go in the same direction as a road, river, etc: Follow the road as far as the church.
3 to happen immediately after something else: I heard a shout followed by a loud crash.
4 to understand something: I didn't follow what you were saying.
5 to do what someone tells you to do: Did you follow the instructions on the box?
6 follow in someone's footsteps to do the same as someone else did in the past: He's following in his father's footsteps and becoming a doctor.

fol·low·ing /ˈfɒləʊɪŋ/ adjective
the following day, week, year, etc the next day, week, year, etc: He was sick in the evening but he was better the following day. I We leave on Friday and return the following Monday.

fond of /ˈfɒnd ɒv/ adjective
be fond of someone or something to like someone or something a lot: I'm very fond of you.

food /fuːd/ noun (no plural)
things that you eat: How much do you spend on food? I I love Chinese food.

fool¹ /fuːl/ noun
1 a silly person ⇨ same meaning IDIOT
2 make a fool of yourself to do something embarrassing in front of other people

fool² verb
1 to trick or deceive someone: He fooled me into giving him money. I Don't be fooled into believing their promises.
2 fool about to behave in a silly way: Stop fooling about!

fool·ish /ˈfuːlɪʃ/ adjective
not reasonable or wise: He was a vain foolish man.

foot

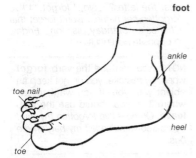

ankle

toe nail

heel

toe

foot /fʊt/ *noun* (*plural* **feet** /fiːt/)
1 the part of your body that you stand on
2 **on foot** walking: *They set out on foot to explore the city.*
3 the bottom of something: *I waited at the foot of the hill.*
4 a measure of length equal to 12 inches: *The man was six feet tall.*

foot·ball /'fʊtbɔːl/ *noun*
1 (*no plural*) a game played by two teams who each try to kick a ball into a net ⇨ see picture on page 196
2 a ball filled with air used for playing the game of football ⇨ see picture on page 197

foot·ball·er /'fʊtbɔːləʳ/ *noun*
a man whose job is to play football

football pitch /'fʊtbɔːl ˌpɪtʃ/ *noun* (*plural* **football pitches**)
a piece of land where people play football

foot·path /'fʊtpɑːθ/ *noun*
a narrow path for people to walk on, especially in the country

footprint

foot·print /'fʊtprɪnt/ *noun*
the mark made by a foot or shoe: *We left footprints in the snow.*

foot·step /'fʊtstep/ *noun*
the sound of someone walking: *I heard footsteps behind me.*

for /fəʳ; *strong* fɔːʳ/ *preposition*
1 meant to be given to or used by someone or something: *Here's a letter for you.* | *I'm making some curtains for the bedroom.* | *She goes to a school for girls.*
2 meant to be used in this way: *That's a knife for cutting bread.*
3 used for showing how far or how long: *She has lived in this town for many years.* | *I waited for three hours.* ⇨ look at AGO
4 used to show who is helped by someone or something: *She did some work for her father.* | *Let me lift that box for you.*
5 towards a place: *She got on the train for London.* | *I was leaving for church when you called.*
6 at a price of: *She bought the dress for £35.* | *I received a cheque for £50.*
7 with the meaning of: *What is the word for 'tree' in your language?*
8 supporting or liking someone or something: *The government is for the plan.* | *I'm for getting a pizza – what about you?*
9 by or at a particular time: *We'll be home for Christmas.*
10 because of something: *He won a prize for singing.* | *They were punished for their bad behaviour.*
11 used to show who a feeling is about: *I'm very pleased for you.*

for·bid /fə'bɪd/ *verb* (*present participle* **forbidding**, *past tense* **forbade** /fə'bæd, fə'beɪd/, *past participle* **forbidden** /fə'bɪdn/)
to tell someone they must not do something: *I forbid you to see that man again.* | *It is forbidden to smoke in school.* ⇨ opposite ALLOW, PERMIT

force¹ /fɔːs/ *noun*
1 (*no plural*) power or strength: *The police used force to break up the demonstration.* | *The force of the explosion threw me to the ground.*
2 a group of people who have been trained to do military or police work: *the armed forces* | *Both of her sons are in the police force.*
3 **by force** using violent physical action

force² *verb (present participle* **forcing**, *past* **forced**)

1 to make someone do something they do not want to do: *He forced me to see a doctor.*

2 to use your strength to make something move: *Firefighters had to force the door open.*

fore·cast¹ /ˈfɔːkɑːst/ *noun*

something that says what is likely to happen in the future: *Did you see the weather forecast?*

forecast² *verb (past* **forecast** *or* **forecasted**)

to say what is likely to happen: *They've forecast more rain.*

fore·head /ˈfɔːhed, ˈfɒrəd/ *noun*

the top part of your face, above your eyes but below your hair ⇨ see picture at HEAD

for·eign /ˈfɒrɪn/ *adjective*

of or from a country that is not your country: *Can you speak a foreign language? | He likes foreign cars.*

for·eign·er /ˈfɒrɪnəʳ/ *noun*

a person who comes from a country that is not your country

fore·man /ˈfɔːmən/ *noun (plural* **foremen** /-mən/)

the person who is the leader of a group of workers

for·est /ˈfɒrɪst/ *noun*

an area where a lot of trees grow together ⇨ compare WOOD ⇨ see picture on page 193

for·ev·er /fərˈevəʳ/ *adverb*

for all time in the future: *I shall love you forever.*

for·gave /fəˈgeɪv/

the past tense of the verb **forgive**

forge /fɔːdʒ/ *verb (present participle* **forging**, *past* **forged**)

to make a copy of something in order to deceive people: *Police say the money is forged.*

for·ge·ry /ˈfɔːdʒərɪ/ *noun*

1 (*no plural*) the crime of making a copy of something in order to deceive people: *He went to prison for forgery.*

2 (*plural* **forgeries**) a copy that is intended to deceive people

for·get /fəˈget/ *verb (present participle* **forgetting**, *past* **forgot** /fəˈgɒt/, *past participle* **forgotten** /fəˈgɒtn/)

to not remember something: *"Did you post the letter?" "No, I forgot." | I've forgotten her name. | Don't forget that Charles's birthday is on Friday.*
⇨ opposite REMEMBER

NOTE: You can use the verb **forget** when, by mistake, you do not keep an object with you. If you want to say where it is, you should use the verb **leave**: *Oh no – I've forgotten my bag!* compared with *I've left my bag on the bus.*

for·get·ful /fəˈgetfəl/ *adjective*

often forgetting things: *Bill is getting forgetful in his old age.*

for·give /fəˈgɪv/ *verb (present participle* **forgiving**, *past* **forgave** /fəˈgeɪv/, *past participle* **forgiven** /fəˈgɪvn/)

to not be angry with someone, although they have done something wrong: *Please forgive me – I didn't mean to be rude. | I knew my mother would forgive me.*

for·got /fəˈgɒt/

the past tense of the verb **forget**

for·got·ten /fəˈgɒtn/

the past participle of the verb **forget**

fork¹ /fɔːk/ *noun*

1 an instrument with a handle and three or four points at the end, that you use to eat food ⇨ see picture at CUTLERY

2 a tool with three or four points at the end, used to dig the ground

3 a place where a road or a river divides into two: *Past the bridge, there's a fork in the road where you should turn left.*

fork² *verb*

if a road or river forks, it divides into two parts

form¹ /fɔːm/ *noun*

1 a type of something: *The country has a new form of government. | Trains are usually a safe form of transport.*

2 an official piece of paper with spaces where you write information: *Please fill in the form (=write information in the spaces).*

3 *British* a school class: *Her oldest son is in the sixth form.*

4 a shape: *She had a birthday cake in the form of the number 18.*

form[2] *verb*

1 to start to appear or exist: *Ice was forming on the roads.* | *These rocks were formed over 400 million years ago.*

2 to make a particular shape: *The children formed a circle.* | *Fold the paper in half to form a triangle.*

3 to start an organization or group: *We want to form a computer club at school.*

4 to make or produce something: *You form the adverb of the word 'quick' by adding '-ly' to the end.*

form·al /'fɔːml/ *adjective*

suitable for an official or important occasion: *I received a formal letter from her office.* | *It's a formal event so you should wear formal clothes.* ⇨ opposite INFORMAL

for·mer[1] /'fɔːmə[r]/ *noun*

the former the first of two people or things that you are mentioning: *Britain has agreements with both Germany and Italy, but its agreement with the former will soon change.* ⇨ opposite the LATTER

former[2] *adjective*

at an earlier time but not any more: *The former President of the United States was at the meeting.* | *Her former husband is a friend of mine.*

for·mer·ly /'fɔːməli/ *adverb*

in the past: *The shop was formerly owned by his family.*

for·mu·la /'fɔːmjʊlə/ *noun (plural* **formulas** *or* **formulae** /'fɔːmjʊliː/)

a list of the substances used to make something: *He developed a new formula for the drug.*

fort /fɔːt/ *noun*

a strong building where soldiers lived in the past and where people could go to be safe from attack

for·ti·eth /'fɔːtɪ-əθ/ *adjective*

40th

fort·night /'fɔːtnaɪt/ *noun*

British two weeks: *We're going on holiday for a fortnight.* | *The meetings take place once a fortnight.* ⇨ look at TIME

for·tu·nate /'fɔːtʃənət/ *adjective*

lucky: *We were fortunate enough to get tickets for the show.* ⇨ opposite UNFORTUNATE

for·tu·nate·ly /'fɔːtʃənətli/ *adverb*

happening because of good luck: *Fortunately, we arrived in time to help.* ⇨ opposite UNFORTUNATELY

for·tune /'fɔːtʃuːn/ *noun*

1 *(no plural)* luck or chance: *I had the good fortune to get a job.*

2 a very large amount of money: *He made a fortune by selling houses.*

3 tell someone's fortune to tell someone what is going to happen to them in the future

for·ty /'fɔːti/

the number 40

for·ward[1] /'fɔːwəd/ *adverb*

1 also **forwards** in the direction that is in front of you: *I leaned forward to hear what she was saying.* ⇨ opposite BACKWARDS

2 look forward to something to think about something that is going to happen and feel pleased about it: *I'm looking forward to meeting you.*

forward[2] *adjective*

1 in the direction that is in front of you: *Forward movement was blocked by a barrier.* ⇨ opposite BACKWARD

fought /fɔːt/

the past tense and past participle of the verb **fight**

foul /faʊl/ *adjective*

very unpleasant or dirty: *A foul smell was coming from the room.*

found[1] /faʊnd/

the past tense and past participle of the verb **find**

found[2] *verb*

to start an organization: *He founded the school in 1954.*

foun·da·tions /faʊn'deɪʃnz/ *plural noun*

the parts of the walls of a building that are under the ground

foun·tain /'faʊntən/ *noun*

a structure that sends water high into the air

fountain

fountain pen /'faʊntən pen/ *noun*

a pen that is filled with ink

A B C D E **F** G H I J K L M N O P Q R S T U V W X Y Z

four /fɔːʳ/
the number 4

four·teen /fɔːˈtiːn/
the number 14

four·teenth /fɔːˈtiːnθ/ *adjective*
14th

fourth /fɔːθ/ *adjective, noun*
1 4th
2 one of four equal parts

fowl /faʊl/ *noun*
a bird such as a chicken that is kept for food

fox /fɒks/ *noun (plural* **foxes***)*
a wild animal like a dog, with dark red fur and a thick tail ⇨ see picture on page 195

frac·tion /ˈfrækʃən/ *noun*
a division or part of a number, such as ¹/₄ or ¹/₂

frac·ture¹ /ˈfræktʃəʳ/ *verb (present participle* **fracturing***, past* **fractured***)*
to crack or break something, especially a bone: *He fractured his leg during training.*

fracture² *noun*
a crack or break in something hard such as bone

fra·gile /ˈfrædʒaɪl/ *adjective*
easy to break or damage: *The bowl was beautiful but it was fragile.*

frag·ment /ˈfrægmənt/ *noun*
a small piece broken off something: *Fragments of glass lay on the floor.*

fra·grance /ˈfreɪgrəns/ *noun*
a sweet or pleasant smell: *The fragrance of flowers filled the air.* ⇨ same meaning PERFUME

fra·grant /ˈfreɪgrənt/ *adjective*
with a nice sweet smell: *Grow fragrant plants near your front door.* ⇨ compare SMELLY

frail /freɪl/ *adjective*
weak and not healthy: *Tom is a frail old man now.*

frame¹ /freɪm/ *noun*
1 the main structure of a building, vehicle, or piece of furniture: *The bicycle frame was damaged in the accident.*
2 a piece of wood or metal round the edges of a picture, window, mirror, etc: *She's painted the window frames yellow.*
3 the part of a pair of glasses that goes over your nose and ears and holds the glass

frame² *verb*
to put a wood or metal frame around the edges of a picture

franc /fræŋk/ *noun*
francs are the money used in France and some other countries

frank /fræŋk/ *adjective*
honest and not afraid to say what is true: *Mark and I have always been frank with each other.*

frank·ly /ˈfræŋklɪ/ *adverb*
1 used when saying what you really think about something: *Frankly, I think you're wasting your time.*
2 in an honest way: *They talked very frankly about their problems.*

fraud /frɔːd/ *noun*
the crime of deceiving people in order to get money

fray /freɪ/ *verb*
if cloth or rope frays, its threads become loose at the edges: *Her sleeve was starting to fray.*

freak /friːk/ *noun*
an unkind word for a person or animal that is very strange

freck·le /ˈfrekl/ *noun*
a very small brown spot on a person's skin

free¹ /friː/ *adjective*
1 able to do what you like, or not controlled by others: *You are free to leave at any time. | Feel free to ask questions.*
2 not costing any money: *I had a free ticket to the concert.*
3 not working or busy: *Are you free this evening?*
4 not being used by anyone else: *Excuse me, is this seat free?*
5 **free of charge** not costing any money: *Our help is free of charge.*
6 **free time** time when you are not busy or working and can do what you want: *I don't seem to have had any free time lately.*
7 **set someone free** to allow someone to leave a prison

free² *verb (past* **freed***)*
to let a person or an animal leave a place where they have been kept as a prisoner: *They freed the birds from the cages.*

free[3] *adverb*
1 without having to pay any money: *Children under 12 travel free.*
2 not controlled by someone or held in a particular position: *He held my arm, but I pulled it free.*

free·dom /'fri:dəm/ *noun (no plural)*
being able to do what you want without being a prisoner and without being under another person's control: *Teachers are given complete freedom in the way they teach.*

freeze /fri:z/ *verb (present participle* **freezing**, *past* **froze** /frəʊz/, *past participle* **frozen** /'frəʊzn/)*
1 to become very cold and change from a liquid into a solid: *When water freezes it becomes ice.*
2 to feel very cold: *If you don't put a coat on, you'll freeze.*

freez·er /'fri:zər/ *noun*
a machine that keeps food very cold, so that it keeps for a long time ⇨ see picture at FROZEN

freez·ing /'fri:zɪŋ/ *adjective*
very cold: *I'm freezing! | It's freezing outside.*

freezing point /'fri:zɪŋ ˌpɔɪnt/ *noun (no plural)*
the temperature at which water changes to become ice

French fry /ˌfrentʃ 'fraɪ/ *noun*
American a long thin piece of potato cooked in oil (*British* **chip**)

fre·quent /'fri:kwənt/ *adjective*
happening often: *They make frequent trips abroad. | Her teacher is worried about her frequent absences from class.*
frequently *adverb*: *The trains are frequently late.*

fresh /freʃ/ *adjective*
1 fresh food is in good condition because it has been picked, prepared, etc a short time ago: *I bought some fresh fish. | It is important to eat fresh fruit and vegetables.*
2 new and different: *Write your answer on a fresh sheet of paper.*
3 **fresh air** air outside that feels pleasant and not hot: *I'm going for a walk to get some fresh air.*

Fri·day /'fraɪdeɪ, -dɪ/ *noun*
the fifth day of the week after Thursday and before Saturday

fridge /frɪdʒ/ *noun*
a piece of electrical equipment like a cupboard, in which you keep food cold ⇨ same meaning REFRIGERATOR ⇨ see picture on page 204

fried[1] /fraɪd/
the past tense and past participle of the verb **fry**

fried[2] *adjective*
cooked in hot oil: *fried eggs*

friend /frend/ *noun*
1 a person who you know well and who you like and trust: *Lee is a friend of mine. | Martha went to London with some friends.*
2 **make friends** to start to know someone and be their friend: *He is shy and finds it hard to make friends* **with** *other people.*

friend·ly /'frendlɪ/ *adjective*
behaving in a pleasant kind way like a friend: *a friendly smile | The local people are very friendly* **towards** *tourists.* ⇨ opposite UNFRIENDLY

friend·ship /'frendʃɪp/ *noun*
the state of being friends: *Their friendship began in college.*

fright /fraɪt/ *noun (no plural)*
1 a feeling of fear: *I had a horrible fright when your dog rushed at me.*
2 **give someone a fright** to make someone feel afraid suddenly

fright·en /'fraɪtn/ *verb*
to make someone afraid: *The noise frightened me.*

fright·ened /'fraɪtnd/ *adjective*
afraid: *He's frightened* **of** *snakes.*

fright·en·ing /'fraɪtnɪŋ/ *adjective*
making you afraid: *It was a frightening film.*

fringe /frɪndʒ/ *noun*
1 *British* hair that goes in a line across the top of your face, above your eyes ⇨ see picture on page 202
2 threads that hang in a straight line around the edge of something

fro /frəʊ/ *adverb*
to and fro first in one direction and then in the opposite direction: *He was walking to and fro in front of the house.*

A B C D E F G H I J K L M N O P Q R S T U V W X Y Z

frog /frɒg/ *noun*
a small brown or green animal that lives in water and has long legs for jumping

frog

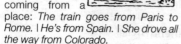

from /frəm; *strong* frɒm/
1 starting at or coming from a place: *The train goes from Paris to Rome.* | *He's from Spain.* | *She drove all the way from Colorado.*
2 used to show how far away something is: *The town is 10 miles from here.* | *We live five miles from the airport.*
3 given or sent by someone: *This letter is from my uncle.* | *Who is the present from?* | *I got a phone call from Ernie today.*
4 starting now and going on in the future: *From now on Mr Collins will be teaching this class.*
5 used for showing that someone or something is moved, separated, or taken away: *He pulled his shoes out from under the bed.* | *If you subtract 10 from 24 you are left with 14.* ⇨ see picture on page 208
6 made of something: *Bread is made from flour.*
7 because of something: *She was crying from the pain.*

front[1] /frʌnt/ *noun*
1 the side opposite the back of something: *She was sitting at the front of the class.* | *The magazine had a picture of a film star on the front.* ⇨ opposite BACK, REAR
2 in front of something near something in the direction that it faces or moves: *I'll meet you in front of the cinema.* ⇨ see picture on page 208

front[2] *adjective*
at or in the front of something: *He got in the front seat of the car.* ⇨ opposite BACK

front door /ˌfrʌnt 'dɔːr/ *noun*
the door at the front of the house that you use when you enter the house

fron·tier /'frʌntɪər/ *noun*
the dividing line between two countries: *The town was on the frontier **between** France and Spain.* ⇨ same meaning BORDER

frost /frɒst/ *noun* (*no plural*)
a white powder of ice that forms on outdoor surfaces in cold weather: *The trees were white with frost.*

frown /fraʊn/ *verb*
to look as if you are angry or thinking very hard by bringing your EYEBROWS together so that lines appear at the top of your face: *Mel frowned and pretended to ignore me.*

froze /frəʊz/
the past tense of the verb **freeze**

frozen

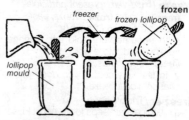

freezer · frozen lollipop · lollipop mould

fro·zen[1] /'frəʊzn/
the past participle of the verb **freeze**

frozen[2] *adjective*
frozen food is kept at a very low temperature so that it stays safe to eat

fruit /fruːt/ *noun* (*no plural*)
the part of a plant that carries the seeds and is often sweet and good to eat: *Would you like some fruit – an apple or an orange?* | *There was a bowl of fruit on the table.* ⇨ see picture on page 199

fruit juice /'fruːt dʒuːs/ *noun* (*no plural*)
a drink made by pressing fruit and getting liquid from it

fry /fraɪ/ *verb* (*past* **fried**)
to cook something in hot oil: *I'll fry us some eggs.*

fry·ing pan /'fraɪ-ɪŋ ˌpæn/ *noun*
a wide flat pan used for cooking food in hot oil ⇨ see picture at PAN

ft
a short way of writing the words **foot** and **feet** when they are used for measuring things: *He's 6ft tall.*

fuel /'fjuːəl/ *noun*
a substance such as gas, coal, or oil that burns to give heat, light, or power

ful·fil /fʊl'fɪl/ *verb* (*present participle* **fulfilling**, *past* **fulfilled**)
to do what you have promised or are expected to do: *He fulfilled his promise*

of taking them all to America for a holiday.

full /fʊl/ adjective

1 also **full up** containing as much as possible: *My cup is full.* | *The train was full, so we had to wait for the next one.* | *We found a box full of old letters.* | *The restaurant is full up.* ⇨ opposite EMPTY ⇨ see picture at EMPTY

2 having had as much as you want to eat: *I couldn't eat any more – I'm full.*

3 complete or whole: *What's your full name and address?* | *You have our full support.*

4 **be full of something** to contain a lot of something: *The streets were full of people.*

full stop /ˌfʊl 'stɒp/ noun

the sign (.) used in writing to show the end of a sentence, or after a short form of a word

full-time /ˌfʊl 'taɪm/ adverb

if you work or study full-time, you work or study for the whole week, usually from Monday to Friday: *She has a full-time job.* ⇨ compare PART-TIME

fun /fʌn/ noun (no plural)

1 things that you do for pleasure or to enjoy yourself: *The children had fun at the party.*

3 **make fun of someone** to laugh at someone in a cruel way or to make other people laugh at them

func·tion[1] /'fʌŋkʃən/ noun

the purpose of someone or something, or the job that they do: *The function of a chairman is to lead and control meetings.*

function[2] verb

to work: *This machine isn't functioning well.*

fund /fʌnd/ noun

an amount of money collected for a particular reason: *We have a fund to build a new church.*

fu·ne·ral /'fjuːnərəl/ noun

a ceremony in which the body of a dead person is burned or put into the ground

fun·fair /'fʌnfeər/ noun

a place where people go to enjoy themselves by paying to ride on special machines and by playing games for small prizes

fun·gus /'fʌŋgəs/ noun (plural **fungi** /'fʌŋgaɪ, -dʒaɪ/)

a plant such as a MUSHROOM that has no leaves or flowers

fun·nel /'fʌnl/ noun

1 a tube that is wide at the top and narrow at the bottom, used for pouring things into a container

2 a pipe through which smoke leaves a ship or an engine

fun·ny /'fʌni/ adjective

1 amusing and making you laugh: *He told a very funny joke.* | *She looks funny in that hat.*

2 strange or unusual: *What's that funny smell?*

fur /fɜːr/ noun (no plural)

the soft hair on some animals, sometimes used to make clothes: *It's got lovely soft fur.* | *a fur coat*

fu·ri·ous /'fjʊəriəs/ adjective

very angry: *Dad will be furious if we're late.*

fur·nace /'fɜːnɪs/ noun

a large container with a hot fire inside, used for melting metals or producing power or heat

fur·nish /'fɜːnɪʃ/ verb

to put furniture in a place: *It costs a lot of money to furnish a house.*

fur·ni·ture /'fɜːnɪtʃər/ noun (no plural)

objects such as chairs, tables, and beds that you use in a house

---

NOTE: Remember that the noun **furniture** has no plural: *We've hired a van to move all our furniture to the new house.* | *There were only three pieces of furniture in the room.*

---

fur·ry /'fɜːri/ adjective

covered in fur: *She had a furry rabbit.* ⇨ compare HAIRY

fur·ther /'fɜːðər/

a comparative of **far**

fur·thest /'fɜːðɪst/

a superlative of **far**

fu·ry /'fjʊəri/ noun (no plural)

very great anger: *There was a look of fury on his face.* ⇨ same meaning RAGE

fuss[1] /fʌs/ noun (no plural)

1 worry or excitement about something that is not important: *What is all the fuss about?*

2 make a fuss to cause trouble, especially by complaining

3 make a fuss of someone to be very kind to someone and give them a lot of attention: *She always makes a fuss of her grandchildren.*

fuss ² *verb*

to behave nervously, worrying about things that are not important: *Stop fussing; we'll be home soon.*

fus·sy /ˈfʌsɪ/ *adjective* (**fussier, fussiest**)

1 very careful about which things you choose because you only like a few things: *He's very fussy about his food.*

2 thinking too much about small things that are not important

fu·ture ¹ /ˈfjuːtʃəʳ/ *noun* (no plural)

1 the future the time that will come or things that have not happened yet: *What are your plans for the future?*

2 in future after now: *I'll be more careful in future.*

3 in the near future soon: *I'm hoping to go to France in the near future.*

future ² *adjective*

happening or existing in the future: *protecting the environment for future generations*

future tense /ˌfjuːtʃə ˈtens/ *noun*

the form of a verb that you use when you are talking about the future. For example, in English 'I will go' is in a future tense

Gg

G, g /dʒiː/
1 the seventh letter of the English alphabet
2 a short way of writing the word **gram**: *It weighs 150g.*

gad·get /'gædʒɪt/ *noun*
a small useful tool: *a gadget for squeezing lemons | kitchen gadgets*

gain /geɪn/ *verb*
1 to get or achieve something good: *She's gaining good experience in the job.*
2 to increase: *The baby's gaining weight.*

gal·ax·y /'gæləksɪ/ *noun* (*plural* **galaxies**)
a very big group of stars in space: *One day, people might be able to travel to other galaxies.*

gale /geɪl/ *noun*
a very strong wind: *There was a gale blowing outside.*

gal·le·ry /'gælərɪ/ *noun* (*plural* **galleries**)
a room or building where people can go and look at paintings, photographs, etc: *an art gallery* ⇨ see picture at EXHIBITION

gal·lon /'gælən/ *noun*
a measure of liquid that is equal to eight PINTS: *a gallon of oil*

gal·lop /'gæləp/ *verb*
if a horse gallops, it runs very fast: *The horses were too tired to gallop any further.*

gam·ble ¹ /'gæmbl/ *verb* (*present participle* **gambling**, *past* **gambled**)
to try to win money by guessing the result of a horse race, a game, etc: *It's illegal to gamble in many US states.*

gamble ² *noun*
when you do something and hope you will get something good, although you know that something bad might happen instead: *It was a gamble to turn up at the game without a ticket.*

gam·bler /'gæmblər/ *noun*
someone who gambles regularly

game /geɪm/ *noun*
1 a sport or activity that has rules, in which you play against another person or team in order to win: *What card games do you play? | a game of chess | We're going to watch the ball game tonight. | computer games*
2 **give the game away** to accidentally tell someone something that should be a secret

Game·boy /'geɪmbɔɪ/ *noun*
trademark a small computer on which you play games

game·show /'geɪmʃəʊ/ *noun*
a television programme in which people play games to win money or prizes

gang ¹ /gæŋ/ *noun*
1 a group of criminals or people who cause trouble: *a gang of bank robbers*
2 a group of people who are friends: *I'm going out with the gang tonight.*
3 a group of people who work together, especially doing hard physical work: *A gang of workmen were digging up the road.*

gang ² *verb*
gang up on someone if people gang up on someone, they behave as a group and treat the other person very badly: *All the other kids in the class ganged up on her.*

gang·ster /'gæŋstər/ *noun*
a member of a group of violent criminals

gaol /dʒeɪl/ *noun*
another spelling of **jail**

gap /gæp/ *noun*
1 a space between two things or between two parts of something: *He has a gap between his two front teeth. | There was a small gap in the fence.*
2 a difference between two groups, amounts, or situations: *the gap between rich and poor*
3 something that makes a situation seem not complete: *There's been a gap in my life since my father died.*
4 a period of time when nothing happens or is said: *a gap in the conversation*

gar·age /'gærɑːʒ/ *noun*
1 a building where you keep your car ⇨ see picture on page 204
2 a place where cars are repaired
3 a place where you buy petrol for your car

gar·bage /'gɑːbɪdʒ/ *noun* (*no plural*)
American waste material such as old food, dirty paper, etc (*British* **rubbish**)

gar·den /'gɑːdn/ noun
an area of land next to a house or in a public place where flowers, trees, vegetables, etc are grown: *The kids were playing in the garden.*

gar·den·er /'gɑːdnər/ noun
someone who works in a garden, as a job or because they enjoy it: *She works as a gardener in the local park.* ⇨ see picture on page 200

gar·den·ing /'gɑːdnɪŋ/ noun (no plural)
work that someone does in a garden, for example growing flowers: *Do you enjoy gardening?*

gar·lic /'gɑːlɪk/ noun (no plural)
a small plant with a strong taste, used in cooking

gar·ment /'gɑːmənt/ noun
a piece of clothing: *woollen garments*

gas /gæs/ noun
1 (no plural) a substance that you cannot see or feel, that burns and is used for cooking and heating: *a gas cooker*
2 (no plural) also **gasoline** (American) a liquid that you put into a car to make it go (British **petrol**): *We need to fill up with gas before we set off.*
3 (plural **gases**) a substance like air that you cannot see or feel: *Oxygen is a gas.*

gasp[1] /gɑːsp/ verb
1 to take a short quick breath, especially because you are very surprised: *The crowd gasped **with** astonishment.*
2 to take quick deep breaths, because you do not have enough air: *I came out of the water gasping **for** air.*

gasp[2] noun
a short quick breath, or the sound it makes: *a gasp of surprise*

gas sta·tion /'gæs ˌsteɪʃn/ noun
American a place where you buy PETROL for your car (British **petrol station**)

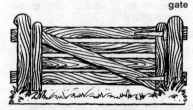

gate

gate /geɪt/ noun
1 a door in a fence or outside wall, that you can open and close: *Don't forget to close the gate.*
2 the place at an airport where you get on a plane: *Flight AF113 to Paris is now boarding at Gate 23.*

gath·er /'gæðər/ verb
1 to come together as a group in one place: *A crowd gathered outside the hotel.*
2 also **gather up** to collect things into one pile or place: *She gathered up her school books.*

gath·er·ing /'gæðərɪŋ/ noun
a group of people who all meet in one place: *a family gathering*

gauge /geɪdʒ/ noun
a piece of equipment for measuring an amount of something: *a fuel gauge*

gave /geɪv/
the past tense of the verb **give**

gaze /geɪz/ verb (present participle **gazing**, past **gazed**)
to look at someone or something for a long time: *He gazed **into** her eyes.*

GCSE /ˌdʒiː siː es 'iː/ noun
an examination taken by students in the UK, usually at the age of 15 or 16. There is a separate examination for each subject: *I've got seven GCSEs.*

gear /gɪər/ noun
a part of an engine or machine that turns power into movement, especially in a car: *My bike has got 24 gears.* | *He changed into third gear.*

geese /giːs/
the plural of **goose**

gel /dʒel/ noun (no plural)
1 a thick liquid that you put on your hair to make it stay in the right position
2 a thick liquid that you can use instead of soap when you have a SHOWER

gem /dʒem/ noun
a stone that is very valuable and can be made into jewellery

gen·der /'dʒendər/ noun
someone's gender is the fact that they are male or female

gene /dʒiːn/ noun
the part of a CELL of a living thing that controls its development and that is passed from the parent to the young person, animal, or plant: *Brothers and sisters share some of the same genes.*

gen·er·al [1] /ˈdʒenrəl/ *adjective*
1 relating to or true of most people or places: *The general opinion is that children should not work long hours.*
2 including the main parts of something, not its details: *a general introduction to computers*
3 relating to the whole of something, not its parts: *Regular exercise can help your general health.*
4 **in general** usually or in most situations: *The students are very happy here in general.*

general [2] *noun*
a very important officer who controls an army

general e·lec·tion /ˌdʒenrəl ɪˈlekʃən/ *noun*
when the people of a country vote to choose their government

general knowl·edge /ˌdʒenrəl ˈnɒlɪdʒ/ *noun (no plural)*
knowledge about a lot of different things: *a general knowledge quiz*

gen·eral·ly /ˈdʒenrəli/ *adverb*
usually or mainly: *She's generally a very cheerful person.*

general pub·lic /ˌdʒenrəl ˈpʌblɪk/ *noun*
the general public all the ordinary people in a country: *3,000 tickets went on sale to the general public.*

gen·er·ate /ˈdʒenəreɪt/ *verb (present participle* **generating***, past* **generated***)*
to produce or make something such as heat or power: *We still use coal to generate electricity.*

gen·e·ra·tion /ˌdʒenəˈreɪʃn/ *noun*
all the people born around the same time: *Women of my generation didn't go to college.* I *the younger generation*

gen·e·ra·tor /ˈdʒenəreɪtəʳ/ *noun*
a machine that produces electricity

gen·e·ros·ity /ˌdʒenəˈrɒsəti/ *noun (no plural)*
when someone is willing to give money, help, presents, etc to someone else: *Thank you for your generosity.*

gen·er·ous /ˈdʒenərəs/ *adjective*
willing to give money, help, presents, etc to someone else: *It was very generous of you to pay for the tickets.*
⬦ opposite MEAN

ge·net·ic /dʒəˈnetɪk/ *adjective*
relating to or caused by GENES: *genetic diseases*

ge·ni·us /ˈdʒiːniəs/ *noun (plural* **geniuses***)*
someone who is extremely clever or good at something: *She's a musical genius.*

gen·tle /ˈdʒentl/ *adjective*
1 careful not to hurt or damage anyone or anything: *a kind, gentle old man.*
2 not loud, strong, or rough: *a gentle breeze*

gen·tle·man /ˈdʒentlmən/ *noun (plural* **gentlemen** /-mən/***)*
1 a man who is polite and behaves well towards other people: *He's a real gentleman!*
2 a polite word for a man: *Ask the gentleman if he would like any help.*

gen·tly /ˈdʒentli/ *adverb*
in a kind way, being careful not to hurt, damage, or upset someone or something: *The boy held the kitten gently.* I *She kissed him gently on the cheek.*

Gents /dʒents/ *noun*
the Gents a public toilet for men: *He's gone to the Gents.* ⬦ compare LADIES

gen·u·ine /ˈdʒenjuɪn/ *adjective*
real or true: *She seems upset but I'm not sure if it's genuine.*

gen·u·ine·ly /ˈdʒenjuɪnli/ *adverb*
used for emphasizing that something is real or true: *She's genuinely worried about you.*

ge·og·ra·phy /dʒɪˈɒgrəfi/ *noun (no plural)*
the study of the countries of the world and natural things such as the sea, mountains, and weather

ge·ol·o·gy /dʒɪˈɒlədʒi/ *noun (no plural)*
the study of rocks and how they were formed

ge·om·e·try /dʒɪˈɒmətri/ *noun (no plural)*
the mathematical study of lines, angles, and shapes

germ /dʒɜːm/ *noun*
a very small living thing that grows in dirty places and can cause illnesses: *Keep your cooking equipment clean and free of germs.*

A B C D E F **G** H I J K L M N O P Q R S T U V W X Y Z

ges·ture[1] /ˈdʒestʃərʳ/ *noun*

a movement you make with your hand, arms, head, etc to show someone what you want or how you feel

gesture[2] *verb* (*present participle* **gesturing**, *past* **gestured**)

to move your hand, arms, head, etc in order to show someone what you want or how you feel: *He gestured for me to come over to him.*

get /get/ (*present participle* **getting**, *past* **got** /gɒt/, *past participle* (*British*) **got** /gɒt/ (*American*) **gotten** /ˈgɒtn/)

1 to obtain or buy something: *Where did you get that CD player?* | *I have to get a birthday card for my mother.*

2 to receive or be given something: *I got a letter from Jo this morning.* | *She got a real surprise when she saw him standing there.*

3 to go and bring something or someone: *Could you get me a glass of water, please?* | *The girl got a couple of plates **from** the kitchen.* | *She went to get the children from school.*

4 to become: *He suddenly got really angry with me.* | *Put your coat on – it's getting cold.* | *It was getting late.*

5 to reach a particular place or position: *What time did you get **to** school this morning?* | *Give me a call when you get there.*

6 get away to leave a place or escape from somewhere or someone: *Four prisoners managed to get away.*

7 get away with something to not be punished for something you have done wrong, or not be seen doing it: *I'm not going to let him get away with swearing at me!*

8 get back to return to a place you have been away from, especially your home: *She got back very late last night.* | *When will you get back from your vacation?*

9 get off to leave something such as a bus or train: *You should get off at the next stop.*

10 get on to climb onto something such as a bicycle, bus, or train: *The passengers all got on the train.*

11 get on with someone also **get along with someone** to have a friendly relationship with someone: *The students in this class get on with each other very well.*

12 get up to stand up after you have been lying or sitting down, especially from your bed after you have been asleep: *What time do you usually get up in the morning?* | *He got up and walked over to the door.*

ghet·to /ˈgetəʊ/ *noun* (*plural* **ghettoes**)

a part of a city where a lot of very poor people live

ghost /gəʊst/ *noun*

the form of a dead person that some people believe can be seen or heard: *Do you believe in ghosts?*

gi·ant[1] /ˈdʒaɪənt/ *noun*

a very big strong man in children's stories

giant[2] *adjective*

very big: *There was a giant TV screen in the stadium.*

gift /gɪft/ *noun*

1 something that you give to someone as a present, for example because it is their birthday: *a store selling gifts and candy* ⇨ see picture on page 201

2 a special ability to do something: *He has a real gift **for** music.*

gi·gan·tic /dʒaɪˈgæntɪk/ *adjective*

extremely big: *A gigantic statue stood in the middle of the square.* ⇨ same meaning HUGE

gig·gle /ˈgɪgl/ *verb* (*present participle* **giggling**, *past* **giggled**)

to laugh in a silly way: *A group of kids were giggling at the back of the classroom.*

gills /gɪlz/ *noun*

the part of a fish, near its head, that it breathes through ⇨ see picture at FISH

gin·ger[1] /ˈdʒɪndʒəʳ/ *noun* (*no plural*)

1 a plant with a strong-tasting root that is used in cooking

2 a colour between orange and brown

ginger[2] *adjective*

with a colour between orange and brown: *a man with a ginger beard*

gi·raffe /dʒɪˈrɑːf/ *noun*

a tall African animal with a long thin neck and big brown spots on its fur

girl /gɜːl/ *noun*

a female child: *A little girl was sitting on the doorstep.* | *They have two children, a girl and a boy.*

girl·friend /'gɜːlfrend/ noun
1 a girl or woman that you are having a romantic relationship with: *I'm going out with my girlfriend tonight.*
2 a girl or woman who is the friend of another girl or woman

give /gɪv/ verb (present participle **giving**, past **gave** /geɪv/, past participle **given** /'gɪvn/)
1 to put something into someone's hand: *I gave her a piece of candy.* | *Could you give me that TV guide?*
2 to let someone have something: *Dad gave me five dollars for washing his car.* | *Who did they give the job to?*
3 to do a particular thing: *She gave her grandmother a kiss.* | *Give me a call later in the week.*
4 to tell someone facts, details, or ideas: *Did you give John the message?* | *Let me give you some advice.*
5 **give something away (a)** to let someone have something and not expect to be paid for it: *We're giving away hundreds of free gifts.* **(b)** to let someone know something that should be a secret: *He was accused of giving away government secrets to another country.*
6 **give something back** to return something to the person who owns it: *I'll give you back your disk next week.*
7 **give in** to say you will do something that you were not willing to do before: *Sue finally gave in and said she would take the kids to the beach.*
8 **give something off** to produce something such as heat, a smell, or a signal: *The factory was giving off clouds of thick black smoke.*
9 **give something out** to give something to each of several people: *The teacher asked Maisie to give out the books.*
10 **give something up** to stop doing or having something that you enjoy, for example because it will make you healthier: *Her father was trying to give up smoking.*

gla·ci·er /'glæsɪər/ noun
a large area of ice that moves very slowly over the ground: *This valley was formed by a glacier millions of year ago.*

glad /glæd/ adjective
pleased and happy about something: *I am glad you can come to the party.*

glad·ly /'glædlɪ/ adverb
if you do something gladly, you are pleased to do it: *I'll gladly walk home with you.*

glance¹ /glɑːns/ verb (present participle **glancing**, past **glanced**)
to look quickly at someone or something: *She glanced at her watch.*

glance² noun
a quick short look

glare¹ /gleər/ verb (present participle **glaring**, past **glared**)
to look at someone angrily: *She just glared at me and then walked away.*

glare² noun
1 an angry look: *She gave him a glare.*
2 unpleasant brightness: *the glare of the sun*

glar·ing /'gleərɪŋ/ adjective
1 glaring lights are very bright, so that your eyes hurt if you look at them: *the car's glaring headlights*
2 a glaring mistake is very bad and very noticeable

glasses

glass /glɑːs/ noun
1 (no plural) a clear hard substance used for windows and bottles
2 (plural **glasses**) a cup made of glass, without a handle: *a glass of water* ⇨ see picture at CUP
3 **glasses** (plural noun) specially shaped pieces of glass or plastic that you wear in front of your eyes, to help you see better: *He wears glasses for reading.* | *a pair of glasses* ⇨ see picture on page 202

gleam /gliːm/ verb
to shine: *The river gleamed in the moonlight.*

glide /glaɪd/ verb (present participle **gliding**, past **glided**)
to move or walk smoothly: *He watched her gliding around the room.*

glider

gli·der /'glaɪdəʳ/ *noun*
an aircraft without an engine

glim·mer[1] /'glɪməʳ/ *verb*
to give a weak light: *They could see the lights glimmering in the distance.*

glimmer[2] *noun*
1 a weak light
2 a very small sign that something exists: *a glimmer of hope*

glimpse[1] /glɪmps/ *noun*
a very quick look: *I only caught a glimpse of his face.*

glimpse[2] *verb (present participle* **glimpsing**, *past* **glimpsed**)
to see something very quickly, usually by chance

glis·ten /'glɪsn/ *verb*
if something glistens, it shines because it has water or oil on it: *Mother's eyes glistened with tears.* | *His back glistened with sweat.*

glit·ter[1] /'glɪtəʳ/ *verb*
to shine brightly with many small points of light: *The sea glittered in the sun.*

glitter[2] *noun (no plural)*
the excitement of being with many rich and famous people: *the glitter of Hollywood*

glo·bal warm·ing /ˌgləʊbl 'wɔːmɪŋ/ *noun (no plural)*
an increase in temperatures around the world, because gases caused by POLLUTION trap the sun's heat

globe /gləʊb/ *noun*
1 a ball with a map of the world on it
2 the Earth: *Her days of travelling the globe are over.*

gloom·i·ly /'gluːmɪli/ *adverb*
sadly and without hope

gloom·y /'gluːmi/ *adjective* (**gloomier**, **gloomiest**)
1 a gloomy place is rather dark and unpleasant: *It's rather gloomy in here – I'll put the light on.*
2 sad, because there seems to be no chance that things will improve: *There's no need to look so gloomy!*

glo·ri·ous /'glɔːrɪəs/ *adjective*
1 deserving great honour or success: *He said they should be proud of their country's glorious history.*
2 extremely enjoyable or beautiful: *We had an absolutely glorious time.* | *a glorious sunset*

glo·ry /'glɔːri/ *noun (no plural)*
fame and respect that is given to someone who has done something very good

glove /glʌv/ *noun*
a piece of clothing that you wear on your hand, with separate parts for each finger: *a pair of gloves*

glow[1] /gləʊ/ *verb*
1 to shine softly: *The fire glowed in the dark.*
2 to look very happy or pleased: *She was glowing with pride.*

glow[2] *noun*
1 a soft light: *the glow of the dying fire*
2 **a glow of pleasure, pride, etc** a strong feeling of pleasure, etc

glue[1] /gluː/ *noun (no plural)*
a substance used for sticking things together ⇨ see picture on page 205

glue[2] *verb (present participle* **glueing** *or* **gluing**, *past* **glued**)
to stick something with glue: *She glued the pieces together.*

glum /glʌm/ *adjective*
sad: *Try not to look so glum!*
glumly *adverb:* *"No," he said glumly.*

GM /ˌdʒiː 'em/ *adjective*
genetically modified; used to describe foods that contain GENES that have been deliberately changed

GMT /ˌdʒiː em 'tiː/ *noun (no plural)*
Greenwich Mean Time; the time in London, used as an international measure

gnaw /nɔː/ *verb*
to bite something for a long time: *A rat had gnawed a hole in the box.*

go[1] /gəʊ/ *verb (past* **went** /went/, *past participle* **gone** /gɒn/)
1 to move or travel somewhere: *They went to India last year.* | *"Where's Jane?" "She went that way."* | *They've gone shopping.* | *The others went on*

the bus. | She's gone to get the children from school.

2 to leave a place: Hurry up – the train goes in five minutes. | Let's go!

3 if something goes in a particular place, you keep it in that place: That chair goes in the kitchen.

4 to become: His hair is going grey.

5 if a machine is going, it is working: My watch won't go since it fell in the bath.

6 if a problem goes, it disappears or stops: Has your headache gone yet?

7 be going to if you are going to do something, you will do it. If something is going to happen, it will happen: I'm going to get a new bike. | I think it's going to rain.

8 go away to leave: She's gone away for a few months.

9 go down if a computer goes down, it stops working ⇨ same meaning CRASH

10 go out to leave a building: She's just gone out.

11 go up to increase: Prices have gone up a lot.

12 go well, go badly if something goes well, it is a success. If it goes badly, it is not a success: The concert went very well.

13 how did it go? used to ask how successful something was: How did your interview go?

go² noun (plural **goes**)
   1 a try: Let me have a go.
   2 a turn in a game: It's your go.

goal /gəʊl/ noun
   1 the space between two posts that you try to get the ball into, in games like football
   2 a point that you win when the ball goes into the goal: We won by three goals to one.
   3 something that you want to do: Her goal is to have her own business.

gnaw

gnawing a bone

goal·keeper /ˈgəʊlkiːpəʳ/ noun
   the player in games like football who tries to stop the ball before it goes into the GOAL

goat /gəʊt/ noun
   an animal like a sheep with long hair under its chin

god /gɒd/ noun
   1 (no plural) the spirit who, especially in the Christian, Muslim, and Jewish religions, is believed to be the maker and ruler of the world: He believes that if it is God's will, it will happen.
   2 any spirit or creature that people pray to and that is believed to control the world

god·dess /ˈgɒdes/ noun
   a female god

gog·gles /ˈgɒglz/ plural noun
   GLASSES that you wear to protect your eyes

gold /gəʊld/ noun (no plural)
   1 a yellow metal that costs a lot of money: a gold ring
   2 the colour of this metal

gold·en /ˈgəʊldən/ adjective
   the colour of gold: She had golden hair.

golf /gɒlf/ noun (no plural)
   a game in which you use a special stick to hit a small hard ball into holes in the ground ⇨ see picture on page 196

gone /gɒn/
   the past participle of the verb **go**

NOTE: Look at the difference between **been** and **gone**. If you have **been** to a place, you have travelled there and returned. If you have **gone** to a place, you have travelled there but you have not yet returned: Liz has gone to Spain (=she is in Spain now). | Liz has been to Spain (=she went there and now she has returned).

gong /gɒŋ/ noun
   a flat piece of metal that is hung up and hit with a stick to make a noise

good¹ /gʊd/ adjective (**better**, **best**)
   1 of a high standard or quality: It's a very good school.
   2 pleasant: Have a good time! | a good party
   3 successful: She's good at languages. | He's good with babies.

A
B
C
D
E
F
G
H
I
J
K
L
M
N
O
P
Q
R
S
T
U
V
W
X
Y
Z

good

4 useful or suitable for a particular purpose: *This game's really good **for** teaching numbers.*
5 good children are well-behaved: *They were really good.*
6 kind: *He's been very good **to** me.*
7 Good for you! used to show that you approve of what someone has done: *"I told him what I thought." "Good for you!"*

good² *noun*
1 goods (*plural noun*) things like food or clothes that are bought and sold
2 do you good if something does you good, it makes you feel better: *A walk will do you good.*
3 for good for always: *She's left her job for good.*
4 no good useless: *This pen's no good.* | *It's no good complaining.*
5 what's the good of? what's the advantage in doing something?: *What's the good of having a car if you can't drive?*

good af·ter·noon /ˌgʊd ˌɑːftəˈnuːn/
a greeting used in the afternoon

good·bye /ˌgʊdˈbaɪ/
a word you use when you leave someone or when someone leaves you ⇨ compare HELLO

good eve·ning /ˌgʊd ˈiːvnɪŋ/
a greeting used in the evening

good-look·ing /ˌgʊd ˈlʊkɪŋ/ *adjective*
someone who is good-looking is attractive: *He's very good-looking.*

good morn·ing /ˌgʊd ˈmɔːnɪŋ/
a greeting used in the morning

good·ness /ˈgʊdnɪs/ *noun*
1 a word used in phrases that show you are surprised or annoyed: *Goodness me!*
2 (*no plural*) the part of food that makes you healthy: *Most of the goodness in an apple is just under the skin.*

good·night /ˌgʊdˈnaɪt/
an expression you use to say goodbye when you are going home at night or before you go to bed

goose /guːs/ *noun* (*plural* **geese** /giːs/)
a large white bird like a large duck

gor·geous /ˈgɔːdʒəs/ *adjective*
very nice or beautiful: *Her dress was absolutely gorgeous.* ⇨ same meaning LOVELY

go·ril·la /gəˈrɪlə/ *noun*
an animal like a very large monkey ⇨ see picture on page 195

gosh /gɒʃ/
something you say when you are surprised: *Gosh! What are you doing here?*

gos·sip¹ /ˈgɒsɪp/ *noun*
1 (*no plural*) conversations about other people's private lives: *You shouldn't listen to gossip.*
2 a person who likes to talk about people's private lives: *Be careful what you say to her – she's a real gossip.*

gossip² *verb*
to talk about other people's private lives: *What are you two gossiping about?*

got /gɒt/
1 the past tense of the verb **get**
2 *British* the past participle of the verb **get** ⇨ look at HAVE

got·ten /ˈgɒtn/
American the past participle of the verb **get**

gov·ern /ˈgʌvn/ *verb*
to control and rule a country and its people: *The country was governed by the army for several years.*

gov·ern·ment /ˈgʌvəmənt/ *noun*
the people who control what happens in a country

gov·er·nor /ˈgʌvənəʳ/ *noun*
a person who controls a state or prison

gown /gaʊn/ *noun*
a long dress: *a beautiful evening gown*

grab /græb/ *verb* (*present participle* **grabbing**, *past* **grabbed**)
to take hold of something quickly and roughly: *Someone tried to grab my bag.*

grace /greɪs/ *noun* (*no plural*)
1 an attractive way of moving: *She dances with such grace.*
2 a short prayer before or after a meal: *Who's going to **say** grace?*

grace·ful /ˈgreɪsfəl/ *adjective*
moving in an attractive and smooth way: *a graceful dancer*

gra·cious /ˈgreɪʃəs/ *adjective*
1 kind, polite, and pleasant: *a gracious smile.*
2 Gracious! Good Gracious! a phrase used when you are surprised: *Gracious! Is that the time?*

grade[1] /greɪd/ *noun*

1 a level or quality: *They complained about having to work with low-grade materials.*

2 a mark you get for an examination or piece of work at school

3 in the American school system, one of the years you spend at school: *He's in fourth grade.*

grade[2] *verb (present participle* **grading**, *past* **graded)**

to put things into groups according to size, quality, etc: *We grade the apples into different sizes.*

grad·u·al /ˈgrædʒʊəl/ *adjective*

happening slowly: *There's been a gradual improvement in his work.*

grad·u·ate[1] /ˈgrædʒʊeɪt/ *verb (present participle* **graduating**, *past* **graduated)**

to finish studying and pass your last examinations at university or college: *She graduated from a French university.* | *He graduated in history.*

grad·u·ate[2] /ˈgrædʒʊət/ *noun*

someone who has passed their last examinations at university or college

grain /greɪn/ *noun*

1 *(no plural)* the seeds of a crop such as wheat or rice: *He lifted the heavy sacks of grain onto the truck.*

2 a seed of wheat, rice, etc: *A few grains of maize still lay on the ground.*

3 a very small piece of a substance such as sand or salt: *a few grains of salt*

4 *(no plural)* the natural pattern of lines on a piece of wood

gram /græm/ *noun*

a measure of weight. There are 1,000 grams in a kilogram

gram·mar /ˈgræmər/ *noun (no plural)*

the rules of a language: *English grammar*

gram·mat·i·cal /grəˈmætɪkl/ *adjective*

correct according to the rules of language: *'I aren't' is not grammatical.*

grand /grænd/ *adjective*

very large and impressive: *He lives in a rather grand house.*

grand·child /ˈgrænˌtʃaɪld/ *noun (plural* **grandchildren** /ˈgrænˌtʃɪldrən/)

the child of your son and daughter

grand·daugh·ter /ˈgrændɔːtər/ *noun*

the daughter of your son or daughter

grand·fa·ther /ˈgrænfɑːðər/ *noun*

the father of one of your parents

grand·moth·er /ˈgrænmʌðər/ *noun*

the mother of one of your parents

grand·par·ent /ˈgrænpeərənt/ *noun*

the parent of your mother or father

grand·son /ˈgrænsʌn/ *noun*

the son of your son or daughter

gran·ny /ˈgræni/ *noun (plural* **grannies)**

a grandmother

grant[1] /grɑːnt/ *noun*

an amount of money that is officially given to someone for a specific purpose: *He was hoping to receive a government grant to help set up his business.*

grant[2] *verb*

1 to give or allow someone something, often officially: *He was granted an extra week to finish the work.*

2 take something for granted to expect something to happen, without thinking about it: *You can't take it for granted that you'll pass the exam – it's hard work.*

grape /greɪp/ *noun*

GRAPES are small juicy fruits that are eaten or used to make wine: *a bunch of grapes* ⇨ see picture on page 199

grape·fruit /ˈgreɪpfruːt/ *noun*

a fruit like a large orange, that is yellow and not sweet ⇨ see picture on page 199

graph

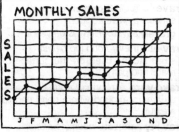

graph /grɑːf/ *noun*

a picture or line that shows information about quantities or levels

graph-pa·per /ˈgrɑːf ˌpeɪpər/ *noun (no plural)*

paper with squares on it for making graphs

A B C D E F G H I J K L M N O P Q R S T U V W X Y Z

grasp /grɑːsp/ *verb*
1 to take hold of something firmly: *He grasped the rope and pulled himself up.*
2 to understand something: *She just can't grasp what I'm saying.*

grass /grɑːs/ *noun (no plural)*
a common plant with thin leaves that covers the ground: *We sat on the grass and had a drink.*

grass·hopper /'grɑːsˌhɒpəʳ/ *noun*
an insect with strong back legs, that jumps around

gras·sy /'grɑːsɪ/ *adjective*
covered with grass

grate¹ /greɪt/ *noun*
a metal frame that holds the wood or coal in a fire

grate² *verb (present participle* **grating**, *past* **grated**)
to cut food into small thin pieces by rubbing it against a tool with a rough surface, called a **grater**: *Can you grate these carrots for me?* ➪ see picture on page 198

grate·ful /'greɪtfəl/ *adjective*
feeling that you want to thank someone: *I'm so grateful to you.* | *He was grateful for their help.* ➪ opposite UNGRATEFUL

grat·i·tude /'grætɪtjuːd/ *noun (no plural)*
the feeling of wanting to thank someone: *He expressed his gratitude to everyone involved.*

grave¹ /greɪv/ *noun*
a hole in the ground where a dead body is put

grave² *adjective (* **graver**, **gravest**)
serious: *a grave accident*
gravely *adverb*: *He was gravely ill.*

grav·el /'grævl/ *noun (no plural)*
small stones used on the surface of roads and paths

grave·yard /'greɪvjɑːd/ *noun*
an area of ground where dead people are put

grav·i·ty /'grævətɪ/ *noun (no plural)*
1 the force that makes things fall to the ground when they are dropped
2 the fact that something is serious: *the gravity of the situation*

gra·vy /'greɪvɪ/ *noun (no plural)*
a liquid that is made with meat juices and poured over meat and other food

graze¹ /greɪz/ *verb (present participle* **grazing**, *past* **grazed**)
1 to eat grass: *The cattle were grazing by the river.*
2 to cut the surface of your skin by rubbing it against something: *He grazed his knee when he fell.*

graze² *noun*
a wound made by grazing your skin

grease¹ /griːs/ *noun (no plural)*
oil or fat: *The food was covered in grease and tasted horrible.*

grease² *verb*
to put oil or fat on something: *Grease the baking tin before adding the cake mixture.*

greas·y /'griːsɪ/ *adjective (* **greasier**, **greasiest**)
covered with oil or fat: *The food there was always very greasy.* | *Wait a minute – my hands are greasy.*

great /greɪt/ *adjective*
1 large in amount or size: *She had great difficulty in doing her homework.* | *There were great piles of rubbish everywhere.*
2 important or famous: *one of our greatest poets*
3 very good: *It was a great party.* | *I feel great.*
4 **great big** very big: *a great big dog*

great-grand·child /ˌgreɪt 'græn̩tʃaɪld/ *noun (plural* **great-grandchildren** /-ˌtʃɪldrən/)
the son or daughter of your GRANDCHILD

great-grand·daugh·ter /ˌgreɪt 'grændɔːtəʳ/ *noun*
the daughter of your GRANDCHILD

great-grand·fa·ther /ˌgreɪt 'grænfɑːðəʳ/ *noun*
the father of your grandmother or grandfather

great-grand·moth·er /ˌgreɪt 'grænmʌðəʳ/ *noun*
the mother of your grandmother or grandfather

great-grand·son /ˌgreɪt 'grænsʌn/ *noun*
the son of your GRANDCHILD

great·ly /'greɪtlɪ/ *adverb*
very much: *She greatly admired his poems.*

greed /griːd/ *noun (no plural)*
the feeling that you want more of something than you need

greed·y /ˈgriːdɪ/ *adjective* (**greedier**, **greediest**)

wanting more of something than you need: *Don't be so greedy – leave some for the others.*

green¹ /griːn/ *adjective*

1 the colour of leaves and grass: *She wore a green dress.*

2 covered with grass and trees: *Cities need more green areas.*

3 relating to the protection of the environment: *Green issues have become increasingly important.*

green² *noun* (*no plural*)

the colour of leaves and grass: *She was dressed in green.*

green·house gas /ˈgriːnhaʊs gæs/ *noun*

greenhouse gases are gases, caused by POLLUTION, that trap the sun's heat and make the Earth's temperature rise

greet /griːt/ *verb*

to welcome someone with words or actions: *He greeted her **with** a smile.*

greet·ing /ˈgriːtɪŋ/ *noun*

1 what you say or do when you meet someone: *We said good morning but our greeting was not returned.*

2 a friendly message that you send to someone, for example on their birthday: *Christmas greetings*

grew /gruː/

the past tense of the verb **grow**

grey /greɪ/ *adjective, noun*

the colour that is a mixture of black and white, like clouds when it is raining: *He wore a grey suit.* | *She was dressed in grey.*

grid·lock /ˈgrɪdlɒk/ *noun* (*no plural*)

when the roads are so full of traffic that nothing can move

grief /griːf/ *noun* (*no plural*)

great sadness: *She hid her grief when her son died.*

grieve /griːv/ *verb* (*present participle* **grieving**, *past* **grieved**)

to feel very sad, because someone you love has died

grill¹ /grɪl/ *verb*

British to cook meat, fish, etc under direct heat

grill

a barbecue grill

grill² *noun*

British a piece of equipment in which you cook things under direct heat: *Toast the bread under the grill.*

grim /grɪm/ *adjective*

1 serious and worrying: *grim news*

2 a place that is grim is very unpleasant or unattractive

grin¹ /grɪn/ *verb* (*present participle* **grinning**, *past* **grinned**)

to smile widely: *He grinned **with** pleasure as he received his prize.*

grin² *noun*

a wide smile: *She had a big grin on her face.*

grind /graɪnd/ *verb* (*past* **ground** /graʊnd/)

grind

1 to crush something so that it becomes powder: *This is where we grind the grain into flour.*

2 to make something smooth or sharp by rubbing it on a hard surface

grinding pepper

grip¹ /grɪp/ *verb* (*past participle* **gripping**, *past* **gripped**)

to hold something very tightly: *She gripped his hand in fear.* ⇨ same meaning CLUTCH

grip² *noun*

a tight hold: *She kept a firm grip **on** her bag.*

groan¹ /grəʊn/ *verb*

to make a long deep noise because you are in pain or are unhappy: *He groaned **with** pain.* ⇨ same meaning MOAN

A B C D E F **G** H I J K L M N O P Q R S T U V W X Y Z

groan[2] *noun*
the noise you make when you groan: *There was a groan from the class when the teacher told them about the test.*

gro·cer /ˈgrəʊsəʳ/ *noun*
1 a person who sells groceries
2 **grocer's** a GROCERY

gro·cer·ies /ˈgrəʊsəriz/
foods and other goods that you use in the house, for example sugar, tea, tinned meat, and soap

gro·cer·y /ˈgrəʊsəri/ *noun*
a shop where you can buy groceries

groom /gruːm/ *noun*
a man who is getting married: *The groom wore a dark blue suit.* ⇨ same meaning BRIDEGROOM ⇨ compare BRIDE

grope /grəʊp/ *verb* (*present participle* **groping**, *past* **groped**)
to use your hands to look for something that you cannot see: *He groped for his matches in the dark.*

ground[1] /graʊnd/ *noun*
1 (*no plural*) the surface of the earth: *They sat down on the ground.*
2 (*no plural*) soil or land: *The ground was hard and full of stones – nothing could grow there.*
3 a piece of land used for a particular purpose: *a football ground*
4 **grounds** (*plural noun*) the land around a large building

ground[2]
the past tense and past participle of the verb **grind**

ground floor /ˌgraʊnd ˈflɔːʳ/ *noun*
the floor of a building on the same level as the ground

ground·nut /ˈgraʊndnʌt/ *noun*
a nut that grows in a soft shell under the ground: *groundnut oil* ⇨ same meaning PEANUT

group /gruːp/ *noun*
1 a number of people or things together: *A group of girls was waiting outside the school.*
2 a small number of people who sing and play music together

grow /grəʊ/ *verb* (*past* **grew** /gruː/, *past participle* **grown** /grəʊn/)
1 to get bigger or taller: *Haven't you grown!* | *The sunflowers have grown a lot this week.*

2 to become greater or stronger: *Fears were growing for his safety.* | *His reputation continues to grow.*
3 to plant crops, flowers, or trees and care for them: *Over here we're growing beans and peas.*
4 if you grow your hair, you let it get longer. If you grow a BEARD, you let it develop
5 to become: *My uncle is growing old.*
6 **grow out of something** to become too big or too old for something: *My daughter's grown out of all her dresses.*
7 **grow up** to change from being a child to being an adult: *What do you want to do when you grow up?*

growl[1] /graʊl/ *verb*
if a dog growls, it makes a low angry noise: *The dog growled at anyone who came near its owner.*

growl[2] *noun*
the noise made by a dog when it growls

grown /grəʊn/
the past participle of the verb **grow**

grown-up[1] /ˌgrəʊn ˈʌp/ *adjective*
1 no longer a child: *Her children are all grown-up now.*
2 behaving like an adult: *Try to be a bit more grown-up.*

grown-up[2] *noun*
an adult: *Can we have all the grown-ups over here, please?* ⇨ same meaning ADULT

growth /grəʊθ/ *noun*
1 (*no plural*) an increase in size, amount, or strength: *a growth in food production* | *the growth of the company*
2 a swelling caused by disease

grub /grʌb/ *noun*
the young form of an insect, without wings

grub·by /ˈgrʌbi/ *adjective*
rather dirty: *Those shorts look a bit grubby.*

grudge /grʌdʒ/ *noun*
a bad feeling that you have towards someone because of something that happened in the past: *I don't think he bears any grudge against you.*

grum·ble /ˈgrʌmbl/ *verb* (*past participle* **grumbling**, *past* **grumbled**)
to complain continuously: *She kept grumbling about the cost of the food.*

grump·y /'grʌmpɪ/ *adjective*
bad-tempered: *Oh, don't be so grumpy!*

grunt¹ /grʌnt/ *verb*
to make a short low noise, like a pig

grunt² *noun*
a short low noise like the noise made by a pig

guar·an·tee¹ /ˌgærən'tiː/ *noun*
1 a promise that something will definitely happen: *I want a guarantee **that** they'll be safe.*
2 a written promise by the maker of an article to repair it or give you another one if it goes wrong: *This one's got a two-year guarantee.*

guarantee² *verb* (*past* **guaranteed**)
1 to promise that something will definitely happen: *He guaranteed **that** he would do it today.*
2 to promise to repair an article if it goes wrong: *How long was the TV guaranteed for?*

guard¹ /gɑːd/ *verb*
1 to protect someone or something by staying near and watching them: *They bought a dog to guard the house when they're out.*
2 to watch someone so that they do not escape: *He was heavily guarded.*

guard² *noun*
1 a person who guards someone or something: *a prison guard*
2 **be on guard, be on your guard** to be careful, so that nothing bad can happen
3 **be on guard, stand guard** to stand near a building ready to protect it: *There was a policeman on guard outside.*

guard

a prison guard

guard·i·an /'gɑːdɪən/ *noun*
a person who looks after a child because the child's parents are dead or away

gua·va /'gwɑːvə/ *noun*
a small fruit that is pink inside, with many seeds

guer·ril·la /gə'rɪlə/ *noun*
a member of a military organization who fights in a small group

guess¹ /ges/ *verb*
to give an answer that you feel may be right, although you are not sure: *I don't know how old she is but I'd guess around 40.* | *Guess what happened next!*

guess² *noun* (*plural* **guesses**)
an answer that you think is right, although you are not sure: *If you don't know the answer, have a guess.*

guest /gest/ *noun*
1 someone who visits your home: *We're having guests for dinner tonight.*
2 someone who is staying in a hotel

guid·ance /'gaɪdns/ *noun* (*no plural*)
help and advice: *I haven't done this before so I'd be grateful for some guidance.*

guide¹ /gaɪd/ *verb* (*present participle* **guiding**, *past* **guided**)
to lead someone somewhere: *She guided us through the narrow streets.* | *He took her arm to guide her.*

guide² *noun*
1 a person who shows you around a place of interest or helps you to travel in a dangerous area: *They had a guide to show them the city.*
2 a book that teaches you about something: *a guide **for** parents* | *a guide **to** British birds*

guide book /'gaɪd bʊk/ *noun*
a book that gives information about a place

guilt /gɪlt/ *noun* (*no plural*)
1 the bad feeling you have when you know you have done something wrong: *She doesn't seem to have any sense of guilt.*
2 the fact that a person has done something illegal: *The court was convinced of his guilt.* ⬦ opposite INNOCENCE

guilt·y /'gɪltɪ/ *adjective* (**guiltier**, **guiltiest**)
1 looking or feeling upset because you have done something wrong: *He had a really guilty look on his face.*
2 if you are guilty, you have done something illegal: *He was found guilty **of** stealing the money.* ⬦ opposite INNOCENT

gui·tar /gɪ'tɑːr/ *noun*
a musical instrument with strings, used a lot in modern music ⬦ see picture on page 197

A
B
C
D
E
F
G
H
I
J
K
L
M
N
O
P
Q
R
S
T
U
V
W
X
Y
Z

gulf /gʌlf/ *noun*
a narrow piece of sea with land on three sides of it: *The Persian Gulf*

gulp¹ /gʌlp/ *verb*
to swallow food or drink quickly: *He gulped down the water.*

gulp² *noun*
the action of swallowing: *He drank it in one gulp.*

gum /gʌm/ *noun*
1 your gums are the parts of your mouth where your teeth grow
2 (*no plural*) CHEWING GUM

gun /gʌn/ *noun*
a weapon that fires BULLETS

gush /gʌʃ/ *verb*
to flow quickly in large quantities: *He turned on the tap and water gushed out.*

gust /gʌst/ *noun*
a sudden strong wind: *A gust **of** wind blew the leaves along.*

gut·ter /'gʌtəʳ/ *noun*
1 the area along the edge of a road, where water can flow away ⇨ see picture at PAVEMENT

2 an open pipe along the edge of a roof, where water can flow away

guy /gaɪ/ *noun*
an informal word for a man: *He's such a nice guy!*

gym /dʒɪm/ *noun*
1 a room or club where you can exercise using special equipment
2 (*no plural*) gymnastics: *a gym class*

gymnast

gym·nast /'dʒɪmnæst/ *noun*
someone who is trained in gymnastics

gym·nas·tics /dʒɪmˈnæstɪks/ *plural noun*
the sport of doing exercises that show physical strength and control ⇨ see picture on page 196

H, h /eɪtʃ/
the eighth letter of the English alphabet

hab·it /'hæbɪt/ noun
something that you always do, often without thinking about it: *She has a habit of biting her fingernails.*

hack /hæk/ verb
hack into to use a computer to enter someone else's computer system: *John managed to hack into the company's computer network.*

had /əd, həd; *strong* hæd/
the past tense and past participle of the verb **have**

had·dock /'hædək/ noun (no plural)
a sea fish used for food

hadn't /'hædnt/
had not: *I hadn't finished making dinner when everyone arrived.*

hail¹ /heɪl/ noun (no plural)
drops of hard icy rain: *We had a hail storm yesterday.*

hail² verb
to rain with hard icy drops: *It's hailing.*

hail·stone /'heɪlstəʊn/ noun
a hard icy drop of rain

hair /heəʳ/ noun
1 one of the thin threads that grow on the head and skin of people and animals: *There's a hair in my soup!*
2 (no plural) a lot of these threads together, for example on your head: *I must get my hair cut.* ⇨ see picture at HEAD
3 **make your hair stand on end** to make you feel very afraid

hair·brush /'heəbrʌʃ/ noun (plural **hairbrushes**)
a brush you use on your hair to make it smooth ⇨ see picture at BRUSH¹

hair·cut /'heəkʌt/ noun
1 the style in which your hair is cut: *I like your new haircut.*
2 **have a haircut** to have your hair cut: *I must have a haircut.*

hair·dress·er /'heə,dresəʳ/ noun
1 a person whose job is to wash, cut, and shape your hair ⇨ see picture on page 200
2 **hairdresser's** a shop where you go to get your hair cut

hair·dry·er /'heə,draɪəʳ/ noun
a machine that you use to dry your hair after washing it

hair·style /'heəstaɪl/ noun
the style in which your hair is cut or arranged: *I like your new hairstyle.*

hair·y /'heəri/ adjective (**hairier**, **hairiest**)
with a lot of body hair: *My uncle's got a hairy chest.* ⇨ compare FURRY

half /hɑːf/ noun (plural **halves** /hɑːvz/)
1 one of the two equal parts of something: *I had half the apple and my brother had the other half.* I *We had half each.*
2 **in half** into two equal pieces: *I cut the apple in half.*
3 **half past 2, half past 3, etc** 30 minutes after 2 o'clock, 3 o'clock, etc: *I'll see you at half past three.*

half-price /,hɑːf 'praɪs/ adjective
costing half the usual amount: *half-price tickets*

half term /,hɑːf 'tɜːm/ noun
British a short holiday, usually for a week, in the middle of a school TERM

half time /,hɑːf 'taɪm/ noun (no plural)
the middle point in a game or match when the players stop to rest

half·way /,hɑːf'weɪ/ adverb
in the middle between two places or things: *I live halfway between London and Guildford.*

hall /hɔːl/ noun
1 a large room or building: *The children were in the school hall.*
2 the room just inside the front door of a house: *Hang your coat in the hall.*

hal·lo /hæ'ləʊ/
also **hello, hullo** the usual word that you say when you meet someone or begin to talk on the telephone: *Hallo John.* I *Hello, my name's Sarah.*

Hal·low·e'en /,hæləʊ'iːn/ noun
the last night in October, when children dress in strange clothes, and visit people's houses to ask for sweets or to play tricks on them

halt[1] /hɔːlt/ *verb*
to stop: *The policemen halted all the traffic.* | *The truck had halted and was blocking the road.*

halt[2] *noun (no plural)*
a stop: *The car came to a halt.*

halve /hɑːv/ *verb (present participle* **halving**, *past* **halved**)
to divide something into two equal pieces: *James and I halved the apple.*

ham /hæm/ *noun (no plural)*
meat from a pig's leg that has had salt added to stop it going bad

ham·burg·er /'hæmbɜːgəʳ/ *noun*
a flat round piece of cooked meat eaten between two pieces of bread ⇨ see picture at FAST FOOD

ham·mer[1] /'hæməʳ/ *noun*
a tool with a heavy metal part and a long handle, used for knocking nails into things, breaking things, or making something flat ⇨ see picture on page 204

hammer[2] *verb*
to hit something with a hammer

ham·ster /'hæmstəʳ/ *noun*
a small animal like a mouse that keeps its food in its mouth and that children sometimes keep as a pet

hand

wrist
fingernail
palm
finger
fingerprint
thumb

hand[1] /hænd/ *noun*
1 the part of your body at the end of your arm, with which you hold things: *She held out her hand and I gave her some of my sweets.* | *She ran her hand through her hair.*
2 by hand not by machine: *This toy was made by hand.*
3 give someone a hand to help someone: *Will you give me a hand **with** the cleaning?*
4 hand in hand holding each other by the hand: *They were walking hand in hand.*

5 the part of a clock that moves to show the time: *When the minute hand points to twelve and the hour hand points to three, it's three o'clock.*

hand[2] *verb*
1 to give something to someone using your hands: *Hand me that plate, please.* | *She handed the letter **to** John.*
2 hand something in to give something to someone, usually to a teacher: *Please hand in your books at the end of the lesson.*
3 hand things out to give one thing to each person: *Hand out the pencils.*

hand·bag /'hændbæg/ *noun*
a small bag used by women to carry money and personal things ⇨ see picture at BAG

hand·cuffs /'hændkʌfs/ *plural noun*
two metal rings used for holding a prisoner's hands together

hand·ful /'hændfʊl/ *noun*
1 a small number or amount: *There were only a handful **of** people in the room.*
2 the amount that you can hold in your hand: *a handful **of** rice*
3 someone, especially a child who is difficult to deal with

hand·i·cap[1] /'hændɪkæp/ *noun*
something that makes it difficult for you to do something: *Not being able to speak the language is a real handicap if you are travelling in France.*

handicap[2] *verb (present participle* **handicapping**, *past* **handicapped**)
to make it difficult for someone to do something: *She has been handicapped by her illness.* | *Rescue efforts were handicapped by the darkness.*

hand·ker·chief /'hæŋkətʃɪf/ *noun*
a piece of cloth or thin soft paper used for drying your nose or eyes

han·dle[1] /'hændl/ *noun*
the part of a tool or instrument that you hold in your hand

handle[2] *verb (present participle* **handling**, *past* **handled**)
1 to hold or touch something: *Please don't handle the fruit.*
2 to control someone or something: *I find it hard to handle difficult customers.*

han·dle·bars /'hændl,bɑːz/ *plural noun*
the parts of a bicycle that you hold when you ride it ⇨ see picture at BICYCLE

hand·some /ˈhænsəm/ *adjective*
a handsome man is attractive to look at:
*The bride was beautiful, the groom
handsome.* ⇨ same meaning GOOD-
LOOKING ⇨ look at BEAUTIFUL

hands-on /ˌhændz ˈɒn/ *adjective*
used to describe experience or training
that you get from doing something
rather than studying it

hand·writ·ing /ˈhændˌraɪtɪŋ/ *noun* (*no
plural*)
1 writing done by hand with a pen or
pencil
2 the style of someone's writing: *I
recognized her handwriting.*

hand·y /ˈhændɪ/ *adjective* (**handier,
handiest**)
1 near and easy to reach: *This house is
handy for the market.*
2 useful: *It's very handy having a car.*

hang /hæŋ/ *verb*
1 (*past* **hung**) to fix something at the
top so that the lower part is free: *I hung
my coat up on a hook.*
2 (*past* **hanged**) to kill someone,
usually as a punishment, by dropping
them from above the ground with a
rope around their neck
3 **hang about** to stand and do nothing
or to wait around without any reason: *He
was hanging about outside my house.*
4 **hang on** to wait: *Hang on – I want to
talk to you.*
5 **hang on to something** to hold
something tightly: *Hang on to your hat;
it's very windy.*

hang·er /ˈhæŋər/ *noun*
a specially shaped piece of wire, plastic,
or wood for hanging clothes on

hap·pen /ˈhæpən/ *verb*
1 if an event or situation happens, it
starts to exist and continues for a period
of time: *The accident happened outside
my house.*
2 **happen to do something** to do
something by chance: *If you happen to
see her will you give her a message?*

NOTE: If an event **occurs** or **happens**,
it is not planned: *The explosion
happened on Friday evening.* If an
event **takes place** it is the result of a
plan or arrangement: *The wedding will
take place on June 6th.*

hap·pen·ing /ˈhæpənɪŋ/ *noun*
an event: *a strange happening*

hap·pi·ly /ˈhæpɪlɪ/ *adverb*
feeling happy: *They were laughing
happily.* ⇨ opposite UNHAPPILY

hap·pi·ness /ˈhæpɪnəs/ *noun* (*no plural*)
pleasure: *They've had years of
happiness together.*

hap·py /ˈhæpɪ/ *adjective* (**happier,
happiest**)
1 very pleased: *I am happy to see you
again.*
2 full of happiness: *It was a very happy
time.* | *Happy Birthday!* ⇨ opposite
UNHAPPY

har·bour /ˈhɑːbər/ *noun*
an area of water next to the land where
ships can shelter safely

hard[1] /hɑːd/ *adjective* (**harder,
hardest**)
1 firm like rock or metal, and difficult to
press down, break, or cut: *This ground
is too hard to dig.* ⇨ opposite SOFT
2 difficult to do or understand: *a hard
exam* ⇨ opposite EASY

hard[2] *adverb* (**harder, hardest**)
very much or a lot: *It's raining hard.* | *Are
you working hard?*

hard cop·y /ˌhɑːd ˈkɒpɪ/ *noun* (*no
plural*)
information from a computer that is
printed onto paper: *Reading something
on screen is never as easy as reading
hard copy.*

hard disk /ˌhɑːd ˈdɪsk/ *noun*
a part of a computer on which you can
store information ⇨ compare FLOPPY DISK

hard·en /ˈhɑːdn/ *verb*
to become firm: *Give the paint time to
dry and harden.*

hard-heart·ed /ˌhɑːd ˈhɑːtɪd/ *adjective*
not caring about other people's feelings:
She's a very hard-hearted woman.
⇨ opposite KIND-HEARTED

hard·ly /ˈhɑːdlɪ/ *adverb*
1 almost not: *It was so dark that I could
hardly see.*
2 **hardly ever** almost never: *He hardly
ever eats meat.*

hare /heər/ *noun*
an animal like a large rabbit that has
long ears and long back legs and can
run very fast

harm¹ /hɑːm/ noun (no plural)
1 hurt: *Modern farming methods have done a lot of harm to the countryside.*
2 come to no harm to not be hurt or damaged: *We left the dog outside last night but she came to no harm.*
3 there's no harm in ... there is nothing bad in ...: *There's no harm in asking him for a job.*

harm² verb
to hurt someone or something: *Our dog won't harm you.*

harm·ful /'hɑːmfəl/ adjective
dangerous: *Smoking is harmful to your health.*

harm·less /'hɑːmləs/ adjective
not dangerous: *The products are harmless to the environment.* | *The grass snake is harmless.*

harsh /hɑːʃ/ adjective
very unpleasant or cruel: *Three years in jail was a harsh punishment.*
harshly adverb: *He spoke to the child harshly.*

har·vest¹ /'hɑːvɪst/ noun
1 the time when the crops are collected: *It's harvest time.*
2 the amount of food collected during the harvest: *The harvest was good this year.*

harvest² verb
to collect a crop: *The herb is harvested in parts of Morocco.*

has /əz, həz; strong hæz/
the part of the verb **have** that we use with **he**, **she**, and **it**: *She has three children.*

hasn't /'hæznt/
has not: *Hasn't he finished yet?*

haste /heɪst/ noun
speed in doing something, when you do not have enough time: *In my haste I forgot my coat.*

hast·i·ly /'heɪstɪli/ adverb
quickly or in a hurry

hast·y /'heɪstɪ/ adjective (**hastier**, **hastiest**)
done in a hurry: *He ate a hasty lunch.*

hat /hæt/ noun
a piece of clothing that you wear on your head: *She was wearing a huge red hat.*

hatch /hætʃ/ verb
to come out of an egg: *The chickens hatched this morning.*

hate /heɪt/ verb (present participle **hating**, past **hated**)
not to like someone or something at all: *I hate snakes.* ⬦ opposite LOVE

ha·tred /'heɪtrɪd/ noun (no plural)
also **hate** a very strong feeling of not liking someone or something: *She looked at me with an expression of hatred.* ⬦ opposite LOVE

haul /hɔːl/ verb
to lift or pull something with difficulty: *They hauled the boat up onto the shore.*

haunt /hɔːnt/ verb
if the spirit of a dead person haunts a place, it appears there often: *People say that the old house is haunted.*

have /əv, həv; strong hæv/
1 a word that helps another word to say that something happened in the past: *We have been to the shops.* | *When I arrived she had already gone away.*
2 to own, to hold, or to keep: *Do you have a car?* | *I haven't any money.* | *He has two sisters.* | *I have a good job.* You can use **have got** instead of the verb: *Have you got a car?* | *I haven't got any money.* | *He's got two sisters.* | *I've got a good job.*
3 to feel or experience something, especially a pain: *She has a headache.* You can use **have got** instead of **have** with this meaning: *She's got a headache.*

hats

hats

helmet

woollen hat

baseball cap

4 to do something: *I have my breakfast at 8 o'clock on Tuesday.* | *I think I'll have a swim.*

present tense	
singular	*plural*
I **have** (I've)	We **have** (We've)
You **have** (You've)	You **have** (You've)
He/She/It **has** (He's/She's/It's)	They **have** (They've)

past tense	
singular	*plural*
I **had** (I'd)	We **had** (We'd)
You **had** (You'd)	You **had** (You'd)
He/She/It **had** (He'd/She'd/It'd)	They **had** (They'd)

present participle	**having**
past participle	**had**
negative short forms	**haven't, hasn't, hadn't**

For the pronunciations of all these words, find them at their place in the dictionary.

haven't /ˈhævnt/
have not: *I haven't seen that film.*

have to /ˈhæv tuː/ *verb*
also **have got to** must: *We have to leave now, so that we can catch the bus.* | *We've got to go straight away.*

hawk /hɔːk/ *noun*
a large bird that kills small animals and birds for food

hay /heɪ/ *noun (no plural)*
dry grass fed to cattle

haz·ard /ˈhæzəd/ *noun*
a danger: *The wooden stairs were a fire hazard.*

haz·ard·ous /ˈhæzədəs/ *adjective*
dangerous: *Running at night can be hazardous.*

haze /heɪz/ *noun (no plural)*
thin clouds that stop you seeing clearly: *A haze of tobacco smoke hung over the room.*

haz·y /ˈheɪzɪ/ *adjective* (**hazier, haziest**)
not clear: *It was hazy and we couldn't see the mountains.*

he /ɪ, hɪ; *strong* hiː/
the male person or animal that has already been mentioned or is already

known about: *He is my brother.* | *Be careful of that dog – he bites.*

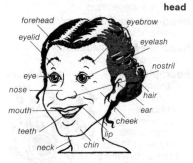

head

forehead *eyebrow* *eyelid* *eyelash* *eye* *nostril* *nose* *hair* *mouth* *ear* *cheek* *teeth* *lip* *neck* *chin*

head [1] /hed/ *noun*
1 the top part of your body, that has your eyes, mouth, brain etc in it: *He turned his head and looked at me.*
2 your brain: *His head's full of ideas.*
3 the most important position of something: *She sat at the head of the table.*
4 someone who controls a group of people: *He's the head of a large firm.*
5 the front: *At the head of the line of cars was a bus.*
6 the teacher who controls a school
➪ same meaning HEADTEACHER
7 keep your head to stay calm: *She was able to keep her head in a crisis.*
8 lose your head to do things without thinking because you are too afraid or angry

head [2] *verb*
1 to be at the top of a list or group of people or things: *The list was headed by some famous names.*
2 to hit a ball with your head
3 head for something, head towards something to go towards something: *I'm heading for home.*

head·ache /ˈhedeɪk/ *noun*
a pain in your head: *I've got a headache.*

head·first /ˌhedˈfɜːst/ *adverb*
with your head in front and the rest of your body following: *He fell headfirst down the stairs.*

head·ing /ˈhedɪŋ/ *noun*
something written at the top of a piece of writing

head·light /ˈhedlaɪt/ *noun*
also **head·lamp** /ˈhedlæmp/ one of the big lights at the front of a car

A B C D E F G **H** I J K L M N O P Q R S T U V W X Y Z

head·line /'hedlaɪn/ noun
words printed in large letters at the top of a newspaper story

head·mas·ter /hed'mɑːstər/ noun
a male HEADTEACHER

head·mis·tress /hed'mɪstrɪs/ noun
a female HEADTEACHER

head·phones /'hedfəʊnz/ plural noun   headphones
a piece of equipment that you wear over your ears to listen to music or a radio ⇨ see picture on page 197

head·quar·ters /hed'kwɔːtəz/ plural noun
the main office of a business or other group

head·teach·er /hed'tiːtʃər/ noun
the teacher who controls a school ⇨ same meaning HEAD

heal /hiːl/ verb
to make something healthy again or become healthy again: The wound on my arm has healed.

health /helθ/ noun (no plural)
how well your body is: His health is not good.

health·y /'helθi/ adjective (**healthier, healthiest**)
1 strong and well in your body: healthy children | a healthy plant
2 good for your body: It is healthy to eat fruit. ⇨ opposite UNHEALTHY

heap¹ /hiːp/ noun
a number of things put untidily on top of each other: A heap of old clothes was lying in the corner. ⇨ same meaning PILE

heap² verb
to put a lot of things on top of each other: He heaped his plate with food. ⇨ same meaning PILE

hear /hɪər/ verb (past **heard** /hɜːd/)
1 to notice sounds through your ears: I heard the rain on the roof.
2 to be given information about something: I heard that he was ill.
3 hear from someone to get news of someone: Have you heard from John recently?

4 have heard of someone or something to know about someone or something: I've never heard of her.

hear·ing /'hɪərɪŋ/ noun (no plural)
your ability to hear: My hearing is getting worse.

heart /hɑːt/ noun
1 the part of your body in your chest that pushes the blood round your body
2 your feelings: He has a kind heart.
3 the middle: in the heart **of** the forest
4 a shape like the shape of a heart
5 break someone's heart to make someone very unhappy
6 by heart so that you can remember something perfectly: At school we learned lots of poems by heart.
7 lose heart to have less courage and hope: When pursued they lost heart and surrendered.
8 take heart to have more hope or feel more confident: If you've been struggling, take heart – there are better days ahead.
9 with a heavy heart sadly
10 with all your heart with deep feeling: I love you with all my heart.

heart·beat /'hɑːtbiːt/ noun
the movement or sound of someone's heart

heart·brok·en /'hɑːt,brəʊkən/ adjective
very unhappy

heart·less /'hɑːtləs/ adjective
cruel or unkind: How can you be so cruel and heartless?

heat¹ /hiːt/ noun
1 (no plural) the feeling of something hot: The heat of the sun made her feel ill.
2 a race run earlier than the main race, to decide who will run in the main race
3 (no plural) hot weather: I hate the heat. ⇨ opposite COLD

heat² verb
to make something hot: It's expensive to heat big rooms.

heat·er /'hiːtər/ noun
a machine for making air or water hotter

heat·ing /'hiːtɪŋ/ noun (no plural)
a system for keeping rooms warm

heav·en /'hevn/ noun
a place where people think God or the gods live, and good people will go after they die ⇨ compare HELL

heav·y /'hevɪ/ adjective **heavier, heaviest**

1 weighing a lot: This bag is too heavy to carry. ⇨ opposite LIGHT

2 great in amount: heavy rain | heavy traffic ⇨ opposite LIGHT

3 a heavy sleeper someone who sleeps deeply

4 a heavy smoker someone who smokes a lot

heavy met·al /ˌhevɪ 'metl/ noun (no plural)

a type of very loud ROCK MUSIC

hec·tare /'hektɑːʳ, 'hekteəʳ/ noun

a measure of land, equal to 10,000 square metres

he'd /hiːd/

1 he had: He'd met her before.

2 he would: He said he'd tell me tomorrow.

hedge /hedʒ/ noun

a row of small trees planted between fields or along roads to make a wall: The hedge needs trimming.

heel /hiːl/ noun

1 the back part of your foot ⇨ see picture at FOOT

2 the part of a shoe or sock that surrounds your heel

height /haɪt/ noun

how tall or far from the ground something is: He measured the height of the bridge.

heir /eəʳ/ noun

a person who gets money or property when someone dies

held /held/

the past tense and past participle of the verb **hold**

hel·i·cop·ter /'helɪkɒptəʳ/ noun

a flying machine with long thin parts that move round on top ⇨ see picture on page 206

he'll /hiːl/

he will: He'll be here soon.

hell /hel/ noun

a place where bad people are believed to go after they die ⇨ compare HEAVEN

hel·lo /həˈləʊ/

also **hallo, hullo** the usual word that you say when you meet someone or begin to talk on the telephone: Hello, Jane!

hel·met /'helmɪt/ noun

a hard hat that you wear to stop your head being hurt ⇨ see picture at HAT

help¹ /help/ verb

1 to do something for someone: Could you help me move this box?

2 cannot help something cannot stop or control something: I couldn't help laughing when I saw his funny hat.

3 help yourself to take what you want: Help yourself **to** a drink.

help² noun

someone or something that makes things easier or better for someone else: If you want any help, just ask me. | She's been a great help.

help·ful /'helpfəl/ adjective

doing something to help someone else: She's so kind and helpful.

help·ing /'helpɪŋ/ noun

the amount of food on a plate: Would you like another helping **of** soup?

help·less /'helpləs/ adjective

not able to do things for yourself: It's a crime to hurt helpless animals.

hem /hem/ noun

the bottom edge of a skirt, shirt, etc when turned under: I'll let down the hem of that dress for you.

hen /hen/ noun

an adult female chicken

her /əʳ, həʳ; strong hɜːʳ/

1 the female person or animal that has already been mentioned or is already known about: Give her the book. | I had a letter from her.

2 belonging to a woman or girl: Her baby was sleeping in her arms.

herb /hɜːb/ noun

a plant used for medicine or for giving a special taste to food

herd¹ /hɜːd/ noun

a group of animals of the same kind: He owns a large herd **of** cattle. ⇨ compare FLOCK

herd² verb

to make a group of people or animals move in a particular direction

here /hɪəʳ/ adverb

1 at or to this place: Come here and sit by me. ⇨ compare THERE

2 here and there in different places: There were a few colourful boats here and there on the water.

A
B
C
D
E
F
G
H
I
J
K
L
M
N
O
P
Q
R
S
T
U
V
W
X
Y
Z

3 here you are a phrase used when you are giving something to someone

he·ro /ˈhɪərəʊ/ *noun* (*plural* **heroes**)
1 a man who does something that is very good or very brave
2 a person you admire very much: *Che Guevara's my hero.*

he·ro·ic /hɪˈrəʊɪk/ *adjective*
very brave

her·o·ine /ˈherəʊɪn/ *noun*
a woman who does something that is very good or very brave

hers /hɜːz/
something belonging to a woman or girl: *My hand touched hers.*

her·self /əˈself; *strong* həˈself/
1 the same girl or woman as the subject of the sentence: *She locked herself in the bedroom.*
2 used to give the word 'she' a stronger meaning: *She had once hoped that she herself would become an artist.*
3 by herself alone or without help: *She went for a walk by herself.* | *Did she make that all by herself?*

he's /hiːz/
he is: *He's a doctor.*

hes·i·tate /ˈhezɪteɪt/ *verb* (*present participle* **hesitating**, *past* **hesitated**)
to stop what you are doing for a short time: *He hesitated before he answered because he didn't know what to say.*

hes·i·ta·tion /ˌhezɪˈteɪʃn/ *noun*
a short stop or wait before you do something because you are not sure: *His answer came without a moment's hesitation.*

hi /haɪ/
a friendly word that you use when you meet someone

hic·cups /ˈhɪkʌps/ *noun*
sudden loud sounds in your throat that you sometimes make for a short time after eating or drinking too quickly

hide¹ /haɪd/ *verb* (*present participle* **hiding**, *past* **hid** /hɪd/, *past participle* **hidden** /ˈhɪdn/)
1 to put something in a place where no one can see it or find it: *Where did you hide the money?*
2 to go to a place where no one can see or find you: *I hid behind the door, so that no one would see me.*

3 to not tell people about something: *She hid her feelings.*

hide² *noun*
1 the skin of an animal
2 *British* a place from where you watch animals without being seen

hide-and-seek /ˌhaɪd ən ˈsiːk/ *noun* (*no plural*)
a children's game in which one child hides and the others have to find him or her

hi-fi /ˈhaɪ faɪ/ *noun*
a machine that plays CDs, records, and tapes

high /haɪ/ *adjective*
1 tall, or far from the ground: *The highest mountain in Africa is Mount Kilimanjaro.* | *It is nearly 20,000 feet high.*
2 costing a lot of money: *They charge high prices.*
3 stronger, greater, or larger than usual: *There was a high wind.* | *The car was travelling at high speed when the accident happened.*
4 near the top of a set of sounds that the ear can hear: *She has a very high voice.* ⊃ opposite (all meanings) LOW

high·er ed·u·ca·tion /ˌhaɪər edjʊˈkeɪʃn/ *noun* (*no plural*)
study after you have left school, for example at university or college

high·lands /ˈhaɪləndz/ *plural noun*
an area that has a lot of hills, or is high up in the hills: *the Scottish Highlands*

High·ness /ˈhaɪnəs/ *noun* (*plural* **Highnesses**)
a way of talking to or about some members of the royal family: *His Royal Highness, the Prince of Wales*

high school /ˈhaɪ skuːl/ *noun*
a school for children between 11 and 18 years old

high street /ˈhaɪ striːt/ *noun*
the main road in a town, where there are a lot of shops

high-tech /ˌhaɪ ˈtek/ *adjective*
using the most modern ways of doing things in business and industry: *He bought a new high-tech camera.*

high tide

low tide   high tide

high tide /ˌhaɪ ˈtaɪd/ noun
the time when the sea is very high up the shore ➪ opposite LOW TIDE

high·way /ˈhaɪweɪ/ noun
a main road

hi·jack /ˈhaɪdʒæk/ verb
to use violence or threats in order to take control of a plane, train, etc

hi·jack·er /ˈhaɪdʒækəʳ/ noun
a person who uses violence or threats in order to take control of a plane, train, etc

hill /hɪl/ noun
a piece of ground higher than usual, or a small mountain ➪ see picture on page 193

him /ɪm; strong hɪm/
the male person or animal that has already been mentioned or is already known about: Give him the book. | I had a letter from him.

him·self /ɪmˈself; strong hɪmˈself/
1 the same man or boy as the subject of the sentence: Peter bought himself some new clothes.
2 used to give the word 'he' a stronger meaning: He told me so himself.
3 **by himself** alone or without help: He stayed at home by himself. | He repaired the roof all by himself.

hin·der /ˈhɪndəʳ/ verb
to make it more difficult for someone to do something: Bad weather hindered the rescue attempts.

Hin·du /ˈhɪnduː/ noun
a person who follows the main religion of India

Hin·du·is·m /ˈhɪnduːɪzəm/ noun (no plural)
the main religion of India

hinge /hɪndʒ/ noun
a piece of metal that holds a door or lid

in place, but lets it open: We need a new hinge on that door.

hint¹ /hɪnt/ verb
to say something in a way that is not direct: He hinted that he was looking for another job.

hint² noun
1 something said in a way that is not direct: When she said she was tired, it was a hint that she wanted us to go.
2 a piece of useful advice: Here are some helpful hints for cleaning stains off clothes.

hip /hɪp/ noun
the part of your body where your legs join your bottom

hip·po·pot·a·mus /ˌhɪpəˈpɒtəməs/ noun (plural **hippopotamuses**)
a large African animal with short legs, a big mouth, and thick hairless skin, that lives near rivers

hire¹ /haɪəʳ/ verb (present participle **hiring**, past **hired**)
to pay for the use of something or for someone's help: He hired a car for two days.

NOTE: Use **hire** only when you are talking about paying to use something for a short time: We hired a car for the holiday. You use **rent** when talking about longer periods of time, e.g. you rent a house to live in, you do not hire it.

hire² noun (no plural)
the use of something that you hire: There were boats **for** hire.

his /ɪz; strong hɪz/
1 belonging to a man or boy: He sat drinking his coffee.
2 something belonging to a man or boy: My hand touched his.

hiss¹ /hɪs/ verb
to make a sound like a continuous 's' by forcing air out through your teeth: The snake hissed angrily.

hiss² noun (plural **hisses**)
a sound like a continuous 's'

his·tor·ic /hɪˈstɒrɪk/ adjective
important in the past: This was a historic meeting between the two leaders.

his·tor·i·cal /hɪˈstɒrɪkl/ adjective
in or about the past: Her historical novels are famous.

A B C D E F G H I J K L M N O P Q R S T U V W X Y Z

his·to·ry /'hɪstrɪ/ *noun (no plural)*
1 things that happened in the past
2 the study of things that happened in the past: *We have history twice a week.*

hit¹ /hɪt/ *verb (present participle* **hitting**, *past* **hit**)
to touch something suddenly and with a lot of force: *He hit me in the face.* I *She hit her head on the low roof.*

hit² *noun*
1 when something touches, reaches, or damages something: *I got a direct hit with my first shot.*
2 a song or film that is popular and successful: *That song was a hit last year.*

hitchhike

hitch·hike /'hɪtʃhaɪk/ *verb (present participle* **hitchhiking**, *past* **hitchhiked**)
to stand beside a road and ask for free rides in other people's cars

hitch·hik·er /'hɪtʃhaɪkəʳ/ *noun*
someone who is hitchhiking

HIV /,eɪtʃ aɪ 'viː/ *noun (no plural)*
1 a VIRUS that can cause the serious illness AIDS
2 **be HIV positive** to have HIV

hive /haɪv/ *noun*
also **beehive** a box made for BEES to live in

hoard¹ /hɔːd/ *verb*
to collect and store things but not use them: *She hoards her money – she never spends it.*

hoard² *noun*
a large amount of something that has been stored: *She has hidden a small hoard of money in a tin can.*

hoarse /hɔːs/ *adjective*
a hoarse voice sounds rough, as if the speaker's throat hurts: *His voice was hoarse after talking for an hour.*

hob·by /'hɒbɪ/ *noun (plural* **hobbies**)
an activity that you enjoy doing in your free time: *He works in a bank, but his hobby is building model boats.*

hock·ey /'hɒkɪ/ *noun (no plural)*
a game played by two teams who use curved sticks to hit a ball into a net

hold¹ /həʊld/ *verb (past* **held** /held/)
1 to have something in your hand or arms: *He was holding a knife.* ⇨ see picture on page 207
2 to keep something in a particular position: *Can you hold the picture up for a minute, please?*
3 to have something inside: *The first cage held a lion.*
4 to be able to have a particular amount inside: *This bottle holds one litre.*
5 to arrange and make something happen: *We're holding a party next week.*
6 to have a particular job or position: *He holds an important position at the bank.*
7 **hold someone back** to stop someone from moving forwards: *The police tried to hold the crowd back.*
8 **hold a conversation** to talk to someone
9 **hold your breath** to stop breathing for a short time: *You have to hold your breath under water.*
10 **hold the line** to wait for a short time when you are talking on the telephone: *Hold the line. I'll see if I can find the manager.*
11 **hold on** to wait for a short time: *Could you hold on, please? I'll see if he's in.*

hold² *noun*
1 the place on a ship where goods are stored
2 **get hold of, take hold of** to take something in your hand and keep it there: *He took hold of the rope and pulled.*

hold-up /'həʊld ʌp/ *noun*
1 a delay: *I'm sorry I'm late – there was a hold-up near the bridge.*
2 an attempt to rob someone by threatening them with a gun: *There were no fewer than eight bank hold-ups last month.*

hole
hole
flag

hole /həʊl/ *noun*
an empty space or opening in something: *I fell into a hole in the road.*

hol·i·day /'hɒlɪdeɪ, -dɪ/ *noun*
1 a time when you do not work or go to school: *Next Friday is a holiday.*
2 on holiday not at school or work: *I'm on holiday next week*
3 go on holiday to go to another place for a short time to have a rest from school or work

hol·low /'hɒləʊ/ *adjective*
something that is hollow has an empty space inside: *This bee nests within hollow stems and insect holes.*
⇨ opposite SOLID ⇨ see picture at SOLID

ho·ly /'həʊlɪ/ *adjective*
1 connected with God or religion: *the holy city of Mecca*
2 very good or religious: *Some of the people living alone in the woods are holy men.*

home[1] /həʊm/ *noun*
1 the place where someone lives: *Her home is far away, so we don't often see her.*
2 a place where a particular group of people or animals are cared for: *I was brought up in a children's home.*
3 at home in your own house: *I stayed at home to read.*

home[2] *adjective*
1 connected with or belonging to the place where someone lives or is based: *Blackpool is my home town.*
2 playing on your own sports field and not that of the other team: *The home team scored two more goals.*

home[3] *adverb*
to or at your own house: *Let's go home. | Is Mum home yet?*

home·less /'həʊmləs/ *adjective*
homeless people have nowhere to live: *We're going to open a centre for homeless young people.*

home-made /ˌhəʊm 'meɪd/ *adjective*
made in someone's house, not in a factory or shop: *Try some of my home-made jam.*

home·sick /'həʊmsɪk/ *adjective*
sad because you are away from home: *I felt homesick living in Paris by myself.*

home·work /'həʊmwɜːk/ *noun* (no plural)
work that a teacher gives you to do at home: *Have you done your homework yet?*

hon·est /'ɒnɪst/ *adjective*
not lying, stealing, or cheating: *You have an honest face.* ⇨ opposite DISHONEST

hon·est·ly /'ɒnɪstlɪ/ *adverb*
1 without lying, stealing, or cheating: *If I can't get the money honestly, I'll have to think of something else.*
2 used to show that you are telling the truth: *I honestly don't mind working late tonight.*
3 Honestly! a word used to show that you are annoyed: *Honestly! What a stupid thing to do.*

hon·es·ty /'ɒnɪstɪ/ *noun* (no plural)
honest behaviour: *He was praised for his honesty when he returned the money.*

hon·ey /'hʌnɪ/ *noun* (no plural)
sweet sticky liquid that is made by BEES and that people can eat

hon·ey·moon /'hʌnɪmuːn/ *noun*
a holiday taken by a man and a woman who have just got married

hon·our /'ɒnəʳ/ *noun* (no plural)
1 great respect: *He won the 100 metres in great style to bring honour to the country.*
2 in honour of someone, in someone's honour done to show respect for someone: *I have cooked a special meal in honour of our visitors.*

hood /hʊd/ *noun*
1 a piece of cloth on a coat or other piece of clothing that you can pull up to cover your head and neck
2 the covering of an open car: *It's raining. Put the hood up.*
3 *American* the metal covering over the engine of a car (*British* **bonnet**)

A B C D E F G H I J K L M N O P Q R S T U V W X Y Z

hoof /huːf/ noun (plural **hooves** /huːvz/)
the foot of a horse, cow, sheep, or goat

hook /hʊk/ noun
1 a bent piece of metal or hard plastic for hanging something on or for catching something: *He hung his coat on the hook behind the door.* | *I need some more fish hooks.*
2 off the hook with the telephone RECEIVER lifted so that the telephone will not ring

hoo·li·gan /ˈhuːlɪɡən/ noun
a noisy violent young person who causes trouble by fighting and breaking things

hoo·ray /hʊˈreɪ/
also **hurray** a shout that shows that you are very happy or pleased: *Hooray! We've won!*

hoot¹ /huːt/ verb
to make a loud noise with the horn of a vehicle, as a warning

hoot² noun
1 the sound made by a car's horn
2 the sound made by an OWL
3 a shout of laughter

hoo·ver¹ /ˈhuːvər/ noun
trademark a machine that cleans the floor by sucking up dirt ⇨ same meaning VACUUM CLEANER

hoover² verb
to clean the floor using a machine that sucks up dirt: *Most days I hoover the floor after breakfast.*

hooves /huːvz/
the plural of the word **hoof**

hop¹ /hɒp/ verb (present participle **hopping**, past **hopped**)
1 when people hop, they jump on one foot
2 when a small bird or animal hops, it jumps with both legs together

hop² noun
1 a small jump
2 a very short journey in a plane: *We'll do the final hop from Cairo to Luxor the following day.*

hope¹ /həʊp/ verb (present participle **hoping**, past **hoped**)
to want something to happen and to think it probably will happen: *I hope to go to college.* | *Is she coming? I hope so.* | *I hope not.*

hope² noun
1 an idea that something will happen as you want it to: *Hopes of reaching an agreement are fading.*
2 someone or something that could make everything happen as you want it to: *You're my last hope.*
3 give up hope, lose hope to stop thinking that everything will happen as you want it to: *Don't lose hope.*
4 hope for the best to hope that everything will be all right in the end

hope·ful /ˈhəʊpfəl/ adjective
feeling that something will happen as you want it to: *He was hopeful that a decision could be made before March.*

hope·ful·ly /ˈhəʊpfəlɪ/ adverb
1 if everything goes well: *Hopefully, we'll be there by dinner time.*
2 in a hopeful way: *The dog waited hopefully beside the table for some food.*

hope·less /ˈhəʊpləs/ adjective
1 with no sign of something getting better: *The economy is in a hopeless mess!* | *I knew the situation was hopeless.*
2 very bad or without skill: *I'm hopeless at science.*

ho·ri·zon /həˈraɪzn/ noun
the line between the land or sea and the sky: *I could see a ship on the horizon.*

hor·i·zon·tal /ˌhɒrɪˈzɒntl/ adjective
in a flat position, parallel to the ground: *Make sure the shelf is horizontal.* ⇨ compare VERTICAL

horns

horn

horn

horn /hɔːn/ noun
1 one of the two hard pieces sticking out from the heads of some animals
2 an instrument on a car, bus, etc that gives a short loud sound as a warning: *He sounded his horn.* | *The taxi blew its horn.*
3 a musical instrument that you blow into

hor·ri·ble /ˈhɒrəbl/ adjective
very unpleasant: There was a horrible accident here yesterday. | It was one of the most horrible afternoons of my life.
⇨ same meaning TERRIBLE, DREADFUL

hor·rid /ˈhɒrɪd/ adjective
unpleasant: The rooms were fine, but the food was horrid.

hor·ri·fic /hɒˈrɪfɪk/ adjective
very shocking and unpleasant: It was a horrific accident.

hor·ri·fy /ˈhɒrɪfaɪ/ verb (present participle **horrifying**, past **horrified**)
to shock someone or make them feel fear: I was horrified by the news.

hor·ror /ˈhɒrəʳ/ noun (no plural)
great fear and shock: His feelings are of horror and disgust.

horse /hɔːs/ noun
a large animal that people ride on and use for pulling heavy things

horse·back /ˈhɔːsbæk/ noun
on horseback riding on a horse

horse·rid·ing /ˈhɔːsraɪdɪŋ/ noun (no plural)
the sport of riding horses ⇨ see picture on page 193

horse-shoe /ˈhɔːs-ʃuː/ noun
a piece of metal shaped like a half circle that is fixed to a horse's foot

hose /həʊz/ noun
a long piece of tube that bends easily, used for getting water from one place to another

hos·pi·tal /ˈhɒspɪtl/ noun
a building where people who are ill get treatment: He's been **in** hospital for a week.

hos·pi·tal·i·ty /ˌhɒspɪˈtæləti/ noun (no plural)
kind attention given to visitors: The people of your village showed me great hospitality.

host /həʊst/ noun
a person who has invited other people to their house for a social event: Mr Brown was our host at the party.

hos·tage /ˈhɒstɪdʒ/ noun
a person taken and kept as a prisoner by someone to force other people to do something: They released three of the hostages yesterday.

hos·tel /ˈhɒstl/ noun
a building where students or other people living away from home can eat and sleep

hos·tess /ˈhəʊstes/ noun
a woman who has invited people to her house for a social event: They thanked their hostess, Mrs Brown.

hos·tile /ˈhɒstaɪl/ adjective
not friendly: His attitude towards me was hostile.

hot /hɒt/ adjective (**hotter, hottest**)
1 high in temperature: The sun is very hot. | Here is some hot tea for you.
⇨ opposite COLD
2 with a strong burning taste: Pepper makes food taste hot. ⇨ opposite MILD

hot dog /ˌhɒt ˈdɒg/ noun
a SAUSAGE that you eat between two pieces of bread ⇨ see picture at FAST FOOD

ho·tel /həʊˈtel/ noun
a building where people can pay for a room to sleep in and for meals

hound /haʊnd/ noun
a dog used for hunting or racing

hour /aʊəʳ/ noun
1 a measure of time equal to 60 minutes: I took two hours to finish my homework.
2 a particular time of day or night: Trains don't run at this hour of the night.
3 a time when you usually do a particular thing: Our business hours are 9.30–5.30. | I went shopping in my lunch hour.
4 for hours for a long time: I've been waiting here for hours.
5 in an hour after one hour has passed: I'll meet you in an hour.
6 on the hour at one o'clock, two o'clock, etc: The trains leave on the hour.

house /haʊs/ noun
a building that people live in

house·hold /ˈhaʊshəʊld/ noun
all the people who live in a house together

house·keep·er /ˈhaʊskiːpəʳ/ noun
someone who is paid to clean, cook, and look after your house for you

house·wife /ˈhaʊswaɪf/ noun (plural **housewives** /-waɪvz/)
a married woman who works in the house for her family

hov·er /ˈhɒvəʳ/ *verb*
to stay in the air in one place: *The hawk hovered above the field, looking for a mouse.*

hov·er·craft
/ˈhɒvəkrɑːft/ *noun*

a type of boat
that travels over
land and water
by floating on
air: *We went to*
France by
hovercraft.

hovercraft

how /haʊ/ *adverb*
1 in what way: *How do you open this box?*
2 used in questions about time, amount, or size: *How much money did you pay? | How many children are there in the school? | How old are you?*
3 **how is, how are** used to ask about someone's health: *How is your mother? | How are you?*
4 **How do you do?** a polite greeting used when you meet someone for the first time
5 used to make something you say stronger: *How beautiful those flowers are!*

how·ev·er /haʊˈevəʳ/ *adverb*
1 in whatever way: *She goes swimming every day, however cold it is.*
2 but: *I don't think we can do it – however, we'll try. | He smiled at me happily. He might, however, have been less happy if he had known what I thought of him.*

howl¹ /haʊl/ *verb*
to make a long loud crying sound: *The dog howled when it was shut in the house. | Wind howled round the house.*

howl² *noun*
a long loud cry

hud·dle /ˈhʌdl/ *verb (present participle* **huddling,** *past* **huddled)**
to move close to the other people in a small group: *We huddled round the fire to keep warm.*

hug¹ /hʌg/ *verb (present participle* **hugging,** *past* **hugged)**
to put your arms round someone and hold them because you love them: *He hugged his daughter.* ⇨ same meaning CUDDLE

hug² *noun*
when you hug someone: *He gave her a hug.* ⇨ same meaning CUDDLE

huge /hjuːdʒ/ *adjective*
very large: *He eats a huge amount of food.* ⇨ same meaning ENORMOUS

hul·lo /həˈləʊ/
also **hallo, hello** the usual word you say when you meet someone or begin to talk on the telephone

hum /hʌm/ *verb (present participle* **humming,** *past* **hummed)**
1 to make a low steady noise
2 to sing with your lips closed: *She was humming a tune.*

hum·an¹ /ˈhjuːmən/ *adjective*
belonging or relating to people: *Human rights cannot be ignored. | There is nothing more complex than the human mind.*

human² *noun*
also **human be·ing** /ˌhjuːmən ˈbiːɪŋ/ a man, woman, or child, not an animal

hum·ble /ˈhʌmbl/ *adjective*
1 thinking that you are not better or more important than other people: *He's a brilliant player, but still a very humble, likeable person.*
2 simple or poor: *Welcome to my humble home.*

hu·mor·ous /ˈhjuːmərəs/ *adjective*
funny or making you laugh: *She's always making humorous remarks.*

hu·mour /ˈhjuːməʳ/ *noun (no plural)*
the ability to laugh at things or to make others laugh: *He doesn't have a sense of humour.*

hump /hʌmp/ *noun*
1 a large lump, for example on a CAMEL's back
2 a small hill or raised part in a road

hun·dred /ˈhʌndrəd/
1 *(plural* **hundred)** the number 100: *a hundred years ago | three hundred people*
2 **hundreds** a very large number of people or things: *We received hundreds of letters.*

hun·dredth /ˈhʌndrədθ/ *adjective*
100th

hung /hʌŋ/
the past tense and past participle of the verb **hang**

hun·ger /'hʌŋgəʳ/ noun (no plural)
the feeling of wanting or needing to eat:
The best way to prevent hunger is to eat a lot of bread and fatty foods.
⇨ compare THIRST

hun·gry /'hʌŋgrɪ/ adjective
wanting or needing food: *Can I have an apple? I'm hungry.* ⇨ compare THIRSTY

hunt /hʌnt/ verb
1 to look for and kill animals or birds for food or sport
2 hunt for something to try to find something: *I hunted everywhere for that book.*

hunt·er /'hʌntəʳ/ noun
a person who looks for and kills animals or birds, usually for food

hurl /hɜːl/ verb
to throw something with force: *He hurled a brick through the window.*

hur·ray /huˈreɪ/
also **hooray** a shout that shows that you are very happy or pleased: *We've won! Hurray!*

hur·ri·cane /'hʌrɪkən/ noun
a bad storm with a very strong wind

hur·ry [1] /'hʌrɪ/ verb (past **hurried**)
1 to move quickly or do something quickly: *We need to hurry or we'll be late.*
2 hurry up to do something more quickly: *I wish you'd hurry up!*

hurry [2] noun
be in a hurry to try to do things quickly because you do not have much time: *You always seem to be in a hurry.*

hurt [1] /hɜːt/ verb (past **hurt**)
1 to damage part of a person's body or

bring pain to them: *I fell over and hurt myself.* | *Sorry – did I hurt you?*
2 to cause you pain: *My feet hurt.*
3 to make someone unhappy: *I didn't mean to hurt him.*
4 hurt someone's feelings to make someone unhappy or upset: *I tried not to hurt her feelings.*

hurt [2] adjective
1 damaged or feeling pain: *He was badly hurt.*
2 unhappy: *She's hurt because you haven't visited her.*

hus·band /'hʌzbənd/ noun
the man that a woman is married to
⇨ compare WIFE

hush /hʌʃ/ noun (no plural)
complete and peaceful silence:
Suddenly a hush fell over the room.

hut /hʌt/ noun
a small building often made of wood

hy·dro·gen /'haɪdrədʒən/ noun (no plural)
a very light gas

hy·e·na /haɪˈiːnə/ noun
a wild animal like a large dog

hymn /hɪm/ noun
a religious song

hype /haɪp/ noun (no plural)
when something is talked about on television, in newspapers etc to make it sound good or important: *The media hype surrounding the event is incredible.*

hy·phen /'haɪfn/ noun
the sign (-) used to join two words or parts of words: *half-price*

A
B
C
D
E
F
G
H
I
J
K
L
M
N
O
P
Q
R
S
T
U
V
W
X
Y
Z

I i

I, i /aɪ/
the ninth letter of the English alphabet

I /aɪ/ (plural **we**)
the person who is speaking: *I want to go home.* | *My friend and I went to the cinema.* | *I'm* (=I am) *very glad to see you.* | *I've* (=I have) *been waiting a long time.* | *I'll* (=I will or I shall) *wait a little longer.* | *When I'd* (=I had) *written the story, I read it to a friend.* | *I thought that I'd* (=I had) *missed the bus but I hadn't* (=I had not).

ice /aɪs/ *noun* (no plural)
water that is so cold that it has become hard: *He put some ice in his drink.* | *There was ice on the roads this morning.*

ice·berg
/'aɪsbɜːɡ/ *noun*
a very large piece
of ice floating in
the sea

ice-cream
/ˌaɪs 'kriːm/ *noun*
(no plural)
a sweet food
made from milk
that has been
frozen: *I ate some
chocolate ice
cream.*

ice cube /'aɪs kjuːb/ *noun*
a small square piece of ice that you put in a drink to make it cold

ice skate¹ /'aɪs skeɪt/ *noun*
a special shoe that you wear for moving or dancing on ice

ice skate² *verb* (present participle **ice skating**, past **ice skated**)
to move or dance across ice wearing special shoes ⇨ see picture on page 196

i·ci·cle /'aɪsɪkl/ *noun*
a long thin piece of ice that hangs down from something: *There were icicles hanging from the edge of the roof.*

ic·ing /'aɪsɪŋ/ *noun* (no plural)
a mixture of sugar and water put on top of cakes

i·con /'aɪkɒn/ *noun*
a small picture on a computer screen that you can choose to make the computer do something

ic·y /'aɪsɪ/ *adjective*
1 very cold: *an icy wind*
2 covered with ice: *It's dangerous to drive on icy roads.* ⇨ see picture on page 194

I'd /aɪd/
1 I had: *I'd already left by the time she arrived.* | *I wish I'd been there – it must have been fun.*
2 I would: *I'd like a cup of coffee, please.* | *I'd leave now if I were you.*

i·dea /aɪˈdɪə/ *noun*
1 a thought or plan that you form in your mind: *I have an idea: why don't we have a party?* | *Where did you get your idea **for** the book?*
2 have no idea not to know something: *"What time is it?" "I've no idea."* | *I had no idea **that** you had a brother.*

i·deal /aɪˈdɪəl/ *adjective*
the best that something could be: *This book is an ideal Christmas present.* | *It's an ideal place for a picnic.*

i·den·ti·cal /aɪˈdentɪkl/ *adjective*
exactly the same: *Your shoes are identical **to** mine.* | *The four houses were identical.*

i·den·ti·fi·ca·tion /aɪˌdentɪfɪˈkeɪʃn/ *noun* (no plural)
official documents that show who you are: *Have you any identification with you?*

i·den·ti·fy /aɪˈdentɪfaɪ/ *verb* (past **identified**)
to say who someone is or what something is: *Can you identify the man in the picture?*

i·den·ti·ty /aɪˈdentətɪ/ *noun* (plural **identities**)
who someone is: *The police do not know the identity **of** the dead man.*

id·i·om /'ɪdɪəm/ *noun*
a group of words that have a special meaning when they are used together. For example 'have cold feet' is an idiom that means to start to feel that you are not brave enough to do something

id·i·ot /'ɪdɪət/ *noun*
a silly person ⇨ same meaning FOOL

i·dle /ˈaɪdl/ adjective
1 not working or being used: We can't leave this expensive machinery lying idle.
2 lazy: Come on, you idle people! Let's do something!

i·dol /ˈaɪdl/ noun
1 a famous person who is loved and admired by many people
2 an image or object that people pray to as a god

i.e. /ˌaɪ ˈiː/
used when you want to explain the exact meaning of something: The film is only for adults, i.e. people over 18.

if /ɪf/
1 used for saying that something might happen: You will catch the bus if you go now. | If you get the right answer, you win a prize. | What will you do if you don't get into college?
2 used when talking about different things that might happen: I don't know if he will come or not. | I wonder if John's home yet. ⬦ same meaning WHETHER
3 used when you are talking about something that always happens: I always visit them if I go to the city.
4 as if used when you are describing something: It looks as if it's going to rain. | He talks to me as if I'm stupid.
5 if I were you used when you are giving advice to someone: If I were you, I'd buy a cheaper car.
6 do you mind if a polite way of asking someone if you can do something: Do you mind if I take this chair?

ig·no·rance /ˈɪɡnərəns/ noun (no plural)
when people do not have facts or information about something: My mistake was caused by ignorance.

ig·no·rant /ˈɪɡnərənt/ adjective
not knowing facts or information that you should know: We went on, ignorant **of** the dangers. | She is very ignorant **about** her own country.

ig·nore /ɪɡˈnɔːr/ verb (present participle **ignoring**, past **ignored**)
to not pay any attention to someone or something: I tried to tell her but she ignored me.

I'll /aɪl/
I will or I shall: I'll come with you. | I'll be late if I don't leave now.

ill /ɪl/ adjective
1 not healthy: She can't go to work because she's ill.
2 be taken ill to become ill suddenly: He was taken ill last night.

il·le·gal /ɪˈliːgl/ adjective
not allowed by law: It is illegal to steal things. ⬦ opposite LEGAL
illegally adverb: He owned a gun illegally.

il·le·gi·ble /ɪˈledʒəbl/ adjective
not possible to read: His writing is illegible. ⬦ opposite LEGIBLE

il·lit·e·rate /ɪˈlɪtərət/ adjective
not able to read or write

ill·ness /ˈɪlnəs/ noun
(plural **illnesses**) when you are ill: She's had all the usual childhood illnesses. | He suffered from mental illness.

il·lus·trate /ˈɪləstreɪt/ verb (present participle **illustrating**, past **illustrated**)
to add pictures to a book or magazine: The book was illustrated with colour photographs.

il·lus·tra·tion /ˌɪləˈstreɪʃn/ noun
a picture in a book or magazine

I'm /aɪm/
I am: I'm very pleased to meet you. | I'm a student.

im·age /ˈɪmɪdʒ/ noun
1 the way a person or organization appears to other people: The company wants to change its image.
2 a picture you see through a camera, on television, or in a mirror
3 a picture of someone or something that you have in your mind: She had a clear image **of** how he would look in twenty years' time.

i·ma·gi·na·ry /ɪˈmædʒɪnəri/ adjective
not real and existing only in your mind: He wrote a story about an imaginary world.

i·ma·gi·na·tion /ɪˌmædʒɪˈneɪʃn/ noun
(no plural)
the ability that you have to form pictures or ideas in your mind: You didn't really see it; it was just your imagination.

i·ma·gine /ɪˈmædʒɪn/ verb (present participle **imagining**, past **imagined**)
1 to make a picture in your mind of someone or something: I tried to

A B C D E F G H I J K L M N O P Q R S T U V W X Y Z

imagine what life was like a hundred years ago.
2 to have a wrong idea about something: *No one is out there; you're imagining things.*

im·i·tate /ˈɪmɪteɪt/ *verb* (*present participle* **imitating**, *past* **imitated**)
to copy someone: *She imitated the way her teacher talked.*

im·i·ta·tion /ˌɪmɪˈteɪʃn/ *noun*
a copy of something: *This isn't a real gun; it's only an imitation.*

im·ma·ture /ˌɪməˈtjʊəʳ/ *adjective*
behaving in a way that is only suitable for someone much younger ⇨ opposite MATURE

im·me·di·ate /ɪˈmiːdɪət/ *adjective*
happening or done now, with no delay: *I need an immediate answer.*

im·me·di·ate·ly /ɪˈmiːdɪətlɪ/ *adverb*
now, with no delay: *Open the door immediately!*

im·mense /ɪˈmens/ *adjective*
very large: *He made an immense amount of money in business.* ⇨ same meaning ENORMOUS

im·mense·ly /ɪˈmenslɪ/ *adverb*
very much: *I enjoyed the concert immensely.*

im·mi·grant /ˈɪmɪɡrənt/ *noun*
a person from another country who comes to your country to live

im·mi·gra·tion /ˌɪmɪˈɡreɪʃn/ *noun* (no plural)
when people come to a country in order to live there: *The government wants to control immigration.* ⇨ compare EMIGRATION

im·mor·al /ɪˈmɒrəl/ *adjective*
morally bad: *Being cruel to people is immoral.* ⇨ opposite MORAL

im·mu·nize /ˈɪmjʊnaɪz/ *verb* (*present participle* **immunizing**, *past* **immunized**)
to protect someone from an illness by giving them a weak form of it

im·pa·tient /ɪmˈpeɪʃnt/ *adjective*
not being able to wait calmly for something to happen because you want it to happen now: *It's no use getting impatient – dinner won't be ready for another hour.* ⇨ opposite PATIENT

im·per·a·tive /ɪmˈperətɪv/ *noun*
the form of a verb that you use when you are telling someone to do something. In the sentence 'Come here!', 'come' is in the imperative

im·po·lite /ˌɪmpəˈlaɪt/ *adjective*
rude in the way you speak or behave towards other people: *She worried that her questions might seem impolite.* ⇨ opposite POLITE

im·port¹ /ɪmˈpɔːt/ *verb*
to bring goods into a country to be sold or used: *We import cars **from** other countries.* ⇨ compare EXPORT

im·port² /ˈɪmpɔːt/ *noun*
something that is imported: *Machinery is one of our main imports.* ⇨ compare EXPORT

im·por·tance /ɪmˈpɔːtəns/ *noun* (no plural)
great value or power: *We all agree on the importance **of** a good education.*

im·por·tant /ɪmˈpɔːtənt/ *adjective*
1 very useful or valuable: *We had an important meeting today.* | *It is important to explain the subject clearly.*
2 an important person is powerful

im·pos·si·ble /ɪmˈpɒsəbl/ *adjective*
not able to be done or happen: *It's impossible to sleep with all this noise.* | *I can't do this crossword; it's impossible.* ⇨ opposite POSSIBLE

im·press /ɪmˈpres/ *verb*
to make someone feel admiration: *He was trying to impress me.* | *I was very impressed by your work.*

im·pres·sion /ɪmˈpreʃn/ *noun*
1 the way something seems to you: *My impression is that she is not telling the truth.* | *What was your first impression of Richard?*
2 **make an impression on someone** to make someone remember you, usually with admiration

im·pres·sive /ɪmˈpresɪv/ *adjective*
very good and causing admiration: *He gave an impressive performance.*

im·pris·on /ɪmˈprɪzn/ *verb*
to put someone in prison: *He was imprisoned for two years.*

im·pris·on·ment /ɪmˈprɪznmənt/ *noun* (no plural)
the state of being in prison: *He was given two years' imprisonment.*

im·prove /ɪmˈpruːv/ verb (present
participle **improving**, past **improved**)
to become better, or to make
something better: *Her English is
improving.* | *I want to improve my
tennis.*

im·prove·ment /ɪmˈpruːvmənt/ noun
when something is better than it was, or
is better than something else: *There has
been an improvement **in** Danny's
school work.* | *This school is an
improvement **on** my last one.*

im·pulse /ˈɪmpʌls/ noun
a sudden wish to do something: *He had
an impulse to take a day's holiday and
go to the beach.* | *Jenny bought the
dress **on** impulse.*

im·pul·sive /ɪmˈpʌlsɪv/ adjective
doing things without thinking about
them carefully first: *It was rather an
impulsive decision.*

in¹ /ɪn/ preposition
1 used to show where someone or
something is: *They were sitting in the
kitchen.* | *The knife is in the top drawer.* |
He lived in Spain for 15 years. ⇨ see
picture on page 208
2 used to say when something
happened: *The house was built in
1950.* | *It's his birthday in June.*
3 during or after a period of time: *I'll be
ready in a few minutes.* | *We finished the
whole project in a week.*
4 included as part of something: *He
talked about the environment in his
speech.* | *All the people in the story
were American.*
5 using a particular way of speaking or
writing: *She spoke in a quiet voice.* | *The
words were written in pencil.* | *They
were talking in French.*
6 wearing something: *Who's the
woman in the black dress?*
7 arranged in a particular way: *We
stood in a line.* | *Put the words in
alphabetical order.*

in² adverb
1 so that something is inside or
surrounded by something: *She opened
the washing machine and put his
clothes in.* | *He picked up a glass and
poured some water in.*
2 at home or in the place where you
work: *I came round to see you but you
weren't in.* ⇨ opposite OUT

in·ac·cu·rate /ɪnˈækjʊrət/ adjective
not correct: *The answer is inaccurate.*
⇨ opposite ACCURATE

in·ad·e·quate /ɪnˈædɪkwət/ adjective
not enough or not good enough: *The
food was inadequate **for** ten people.*
⇨ opposite ADEQUATE

in·ap·pro·pri·ate /ˌɪnəˈprəʊpriət/
adjective
not suitable or right: *It was an
inappropriate present **for** a child.*
⇨ opposite APPROPRIATE
inappropriately adverb: *She was
inappropriately dressed for such a
formal occasion.*

in·ca·pa·ble /ɪnˈkeɪpəbl/ adjective
not able to do something: *Since her
accident she has been incapable **of**
working.* ⇨ opposite CAPABLE

inch /ɪntʃ/ noun (plural **inches**)
a measure of length, equal to 2.54
CENTIMETRES. There are 12 inches in a
foot: *The snow was 5 inches deep.*

in·ci·dent /ˈɪnsɪdənt/ noun
an event or something that happens

in·ci·den·tal·ly /ˌɪnsɪˈdentli/ adverb
used when you are adding more
information to something you have just
said, or when you have just
remembered an interesting fact: *I saw
Peter the other day. Incidentally, he
wants us to come over for lunch next
week.*

in·clined /ɪnˈklaɪnd/ adjective
be inclined to do something to be
likely to do something, or to want to do
something: *He's inclined to get angry
when someone does not agree with
him.*

in·clude /ɪnˈkluːd/ verb (present
participle **including**, past **included**)
1 to have something as part of a
whole: *The price of the holiday includes
food.* | *The group included several
women.*
2 to make someone or something part
of a larger group: *I included my uncle in
my list of people to invite.*
⇨ opposite EXCLUDE

in·clud·ing /ɪnˈkluːdɪŋ/ preposition
used to show that someone or
something is part of a larger group:
*There were twenty people in the room,
including the teacher.* ⇨ opposite
EXCLUDING

A B C D E F G H I J K L M N O P Q R S T U V W X Y Z

in·come /'ɪŋkʌm, -kəm/ *noun*
all the money you receive: *There are many people who live on low incomes.*

in·come tax /'ɪŋkəm ˌtæks/ *noun (no plural)*
money taken by the government from what people earn

incomplete

an incomplete jigsaw puzzle

in·com·plete /ˌɪnkəm'pliːt/ *adjective*
not finished: *The work is incomplete.* | *He wrote an incomplete sentence.* ⇨ opposite COMPLETE

in·con·ve·ni·ence [1] /ˌɪnkən'viːnɪəns/ *noun*
something that causes you problems or difficulty: *I hope that the delay won't cause you any inconvenience.*

inconvenience [2] *verb (present participle* **inconveniencing**, *past* **inconvenienced**)
to cause problems or difficulties for someone: *Am I inconveniencing you by staying here?*

in·con·ve·ni·ent /ˌɪnkən'viːnɪənt/ *adjective*
causing problems or difficulty: *I hope this isn't an inconvenient time for me to visit you.* ⇨ opposite CONVENIENT

in·cor·rect /ˌɪnkə'rekt/ *adjective*
wrong: *That is an incorrect spelling.* ⇨ opposite CORRECT

incorrectly *adverb: You answered the question incorrectly.*

in·crease [1] /ɪn'kriːs/ *verb (present participle* **increasing**, *past* **increased**)
1 to become more in amount or number: *My wages have increased this year.* | *The noise increased suddenly.*
2 to make something more in amount or number: *My employer has increased my wages.* | *Smoking increases your*

chances of getting cancer. ⇨ opposite DECREASE

in·crease [2] /'ɪŋkriːs/ *noun*
a rise in number, level, or amount: *There has been an increase in profits this year.* ⇨ opposite DECREASE

in·creas·ing·ly /ɪn'kriːsɪŋlɪ/ *adverb*
more and more: *It's becoming increasingly difficult to find work.*

in·cred·i·ble /ɪn'kredəbl/ *adjective*
1 very good: *What incredible luck!*
2 very large in amount: *She won an incredible amount of money.*
3 very strange or difficult to believe: *He told us an incredible story.* ⇨ same meaning AMAZING

in·deed /ɪn'diːd/ *adverb*
1 used to add more information to support a statement: *I don't know where Sam is. Indeed, I haven't seen him for weeks.*
2 *British* used when you want to make the meaning of 'very' even stronger: *He runs very fast indeed.* | *Thank you very much indeed.*

in·def·i·nite /ɪn'defɪnət/ *adjective*
an indefinite period of time has no definite end arranged for it: *I am staying for an indefinite time.*

indefinitely *adverb: She has moved to Spain and plans to be there indefinitely*

in·de·pen·dence /ˌɪndɪ'pendəns/ *noun (no plural)*
1 the quality of being able to look after yourself: *Old people want to keep their independence.*
2 the state of being free from the control of another country: *America declared its independence in 1776.*

in·de·pen·dent /ˌɪndɪ'pendənt/ *adjective*
1 confident, free, and not needing to ask people for help, money, or permission to do something: *Although she is young, she is very independent.*
2 not controlled by another government or organization: *India became independent from Britain in 1947.*

in·dex /'ɪndeks/ *noun (plural* **indexes** *or* **indices** /'ɪndɪsiːz/)
a list in a book that tells you what can be found in the book, and on what page

index fin·ger /'ɪndeks ˌfɪŋgər/ *noun*
the finger that is next to your thumb

in·di·cate /'ɪndɪkeɪt/ verb (present participle **indicating**, past **indicated**)
1 if facts indicate something, they show that it exists or is likely to be true: *Research indicates **that** women live longer than men.*
2 to point at something: *Please indicate which one you have chosen. | Indicating a chair, he said, "Please sit down."*

in·di·ca·tion /ˌɪndɪ'keɪʃn/ noun
a sign that something exists or is likely to be true: *Did he give you any indication of when the work will be finished?*

in·di·ca·tor /'ɪndɪkeɪtər/ noun
British one of the two lights on a car that are used to show that the car is going to turn left or right

in·di·ces /'ɪndɪsiːz/
a plural of **index**

in·di·rect /ˌɪndɪ'rekt, ˌɪndaɪ-/ adjective
1 not directly caused by something or relating to something: *The accident was an indirect result of the heavy rain. | She made some indirect criticism of students' work.*
2 not using the shortest or straightest way to get to a place: *We took an indirect route to avoid traffic.* ⇨ opposite DIRECT

in·di·vid·u·al[1] /ˌɪndɪ'vɪdʒʊəl/ noun
one person, considered separately from the society that they live in: *The rights of the individual must be protected.*

individual[2] adjective
for one person only: *The children had individual desks.*
individually adverb: *The children were taught individually, not in a group.*

in·door /'ɪndɔːr/ adjective
inside a building: *If it rains, we play indoor games. | The school has an indoor swimming pool.* ⇨ opposite OUTDOOR

in·doors /ɪn'dɔːz/ adverb
into or inside a building: *Let's stay indoors today. | It's raining – let's go indoors.* ⇨ opposite OUTDOORS

in·dus·tri·al /ɪn'dʌstrɪəl/ adjective
connected with industry or with a lot of industries: *Britain is an industrial nation.*

in·dus·try /'ɪndəstrɪ/ noun (plural **industries**)
the making of goods, especially in factories: *What are the important industries in the town?*

in·fant /'ɪnfənt/ noun
a baby or young child

in·fect /ɪn'fekt/ verb
to give an illness to someone: *One of the women at work had a cold and infected everyone else.*

in·fec·tion /ɪn'fekʃən/ noun
an illness: *She has a throat infection.*

in·fec·tious /ɪn'fekʃəs/ adjective
an infectious illness can be passed from one person to another: *Flu is an infectious illness.*

in·fe·ri·or /ɪn'fɪərɪər/ adjective
worse than other things: *Larry's work is inferior **to** Ben's.* ⇨ opposite SUPERIOR

in·fi·nite /'ɪnfɪnət/ adjective
very large or great and having no limit: *Infinite space surrounds the Earth.*

in·fi·nit·ely /'ɪnfɪnətlɪ/ adverb
very much: *I feel infinitely better after my holiday.*

in·fin·i·tive /ɪn'fɪnɪtɪv/ noun
the part of a verb that is used with the word **to**. In the sentence 'I want to go.', 'to go' is the infinitive form of the verb 'go'

in·flate /ɪn'fleɪt/ verb (present participle **inflating**, past **inflated**)
to fill something with air: *The machine quickly inflates the tyres.*

inflate

inflating a ball

in·flu·ence[1] /'ɪnflʊəns/ noun
1 to have the power to change what a person thinks or does: *Her parents have a strong influence **on** her.*
2 **be a bad influence on someone** to make someone behave badly because of how you behave
3 **be a good influence on someone** to make someone behave in a better way than usual because of how you behave

influence[2] verb (present participle **influencing**, past **influenced**)

to have an effect on the way someone behaves, thinks, or develops: *I do not want to influence your decision.*

in·flu·en·tial /ˌɪnfluˈenʃl/ adjective

important and having the power to change people or things: *He is an influential politician in the city.* | *They published an influential arts magazine.*

in·flu·en·za /ˌɪnfluˈenzə/ noun (no plural)

FLU

in·form /ɪnˈfɔːm/ verb

to tell someone about something: *The teacher informed us **that** the school would be closed for one day next week.* | *Please inform the library **of** the books you need.*

in·for·mal /ɪnˈfɔːməl/ adjective

happening or done in an easy friendly way and not according to rules: *We had an informal meeting at my house.* | *His classes are quite informal but we learn a lot.* ⇨ opposite FORMAL

in·for·ma·tion /ˌɪnfəˈmeɪʃn/ noun (no plural)

facts: *Could you give me some information **about** the times of the buses?* | *The book contains information **on** a lot of different subjects.* | *For further information, phone the number given.*

NOTE: Remember that the noun **information** does not have a plural: *I get a lot of information from the Internet.*

in·gre·di·ent /ɪnˈgriːdiənt/ noun

1 something that you add when you are cooking something: *Flour, milk, and eggs are the main ingredients.*

2 one of the qualities that together produce a particular situation: *the ingredients **of** a good marriage*

in·hab·it /ɪnˈhæbɪt/ verb

be inhabited by someone or something if a place is inhabited by people or animals, people or animals live there: *The island is inhabited mainly by sheep.* | *The country is inhabited by 20 million people.*

in·hab·i·tant /ɪnˈhæbɪtənt/ noun

a person who lives in a place: *The town has only 250 inhabitants.*

in·her·it /ɪnˈherɪt/ verb

to receive something from someone when they die: *He inherited the farm **from** his parents.*

in·her·i·tance /ɪnˈherɪtəns/ noun

money or other things that you receive from a person after they have died

i·ni·tial[1] /ɪˈnɪʃl/ adjective

at the beginning: *The initial plan was to build a new hospital, but now the council has decided to repair the old one.* | *Her initial anxiety about the party was quickly replaced by enjoyment.* ⇨ same meaning FIRST

initial[2] noun

the first letter of a name, used to represent the name: *His name is John Smith, so he has the initials J. S. on his suitcase.*

i·ni·tial·ly /ɪˈnɪʃl-i/ adverb

at the beginning of something: *It may seem strange initially but you'll soon get used to your new job.* | *He was employed initially as a temporary worker.*

in·ject /ɪnˈdʒekt/ verb

to put a drug into your body using a special needle

in·jec·tion /ɪnˈdʒekʃən/ noun

an act of putting a drug into your body using a special needle: *The nurse gave me an injection.*

in·jure /ˈɪndʒəʳ/ verb (present participle **injuring**, past **injured**)

to harm or wound a person or animal: *Two people were injured in the accident.* | *I injured myself playing football.* ⇨ same meaning HURT

in·ju·ry /ˈɪndʒəri/ noun (plural **injuries**)

a wound: *She had serious injuries after a car accident.*

in·jus·tice /ɪnˈdʒʌstɪs/ noun

1 a situation in which people are not treated fairly: *He was determined to fight injustice.* ⇨ opposite JUSTICE

2 do someone an injustice to judge someone in an unfair way

ink /ɪŋk/ noun (no plural)

a coloured liquid used for writing or printing

inn /ɪn/ *noun*

a small hotel, especially one in the countryside: *The travellers stopped to eat at an inn.*

in·ner /'ɪnəʳ/ *adjective*

on the inside or close to the centre of something: *The central corridor led to several inner rooms.* I *The telephone code for inner London had changed.* ⇨ opposite OUTER

in·no·cence /'ɪnəsns/ *noun* (*no plural*)

the fact of not being guilty of a crime ⇨ opposite GUILT

in·no·cent /'ɪnəsnt/ *adjective*

having done nothing bad or wrong: *Nobody would believe that I was innocent.* I *She was found innocent of murder.* ⇨ opposite GUILTY

in·quire /ɪn'kwaɪəʳ/ *verb* (*present participle* **inquiring**, *past* **inquired**)

to ask for information about something: *He inquired about the times of trains to London.*

in·quir·y /ɪn'kwaɪərɪ/ *noun* (*plural* **inquiries**)

1 a question asking for information about something: *There have been a lot of inquiries about the new bus service.*
2 make inquiries to ask for information: *I'll make inquiries about who left their coat behind.*

in·quis·i·tive /ɪn'kwɪzɪtɪv/ *adjective*

wanting to know too many things, especially about other people

ins

a short way of writing the word **inches**: *It is 6 ins long.*

in·sane /ɪn'seɪn/ *adjective*

1 extremely silly, dangerous, or unreasonable: *He must be insane to drive his car so fast.*
2 with a serious mental illness ⇨ opposite SANE

in·sect /'ɪnsekt/ *noun*

a very small creature such as a fly that has six legs

in·sert /ɪn's3ːt/ *verb*

to put something into something else: *He inserted the key in the lock.*

insert
keyhole
key
inserting a key

in·side¹ /ɪn'saɪd/ *noun*

the inside the inner part of something: *The outside of an orange is bitter, but the inside is sweet.* I *Have you seen the inside of the house?* ⇨ opposite OUTSIDE

inside² *adverb, preposition*

in or into something: *She put the money inside her bag.* I *Don't stand out there in the sun – come inside.* ⇨ opposite OUTSIDE

inside³ /ɪn'saɪd/ *adjective*

the part that is near the centre or that is not outside: *The inside walls of the house are painted white.* I *The story was on an inside page of the newspaper.* ⇨ opposite OUTSIDE

inside out /ˌɪnsaɪd 'aʊt/ *adverb*

with the parts that are usually inside on the outside: *You're wearing your socks inside out.*

in·sist /ɪn'sɪst/ *verb*

1 to say firmly that something is true, especially when other people think it is not: *He insists that he is right.*
2 to say something that must happen or be done: *I insist that you stop doing that.* I *She insisted on seeing the manager.*

in·spect /ɪn'spekt/ *verb*

to look at something carefully, to see if there is anything wrong: *He inspected the car before he bought it.*

in·spec·tion /ɪn'spekʃən/ *noun*

a careful look to see if there is anything wrong with something

in·spec·tor /ɪn'spektəʳ/ *noun*

1 an official whose job is to visit places and see if there is anything wrong with them: *He works as a school inspector.* I *A health inspector visited the restaurant.*
2 a police officer of middle rank

in·spire /ɪn'spaɪəʳ/ *verb* (*present participle* **inspiring**, *past* **inspired**)

to make someone want to do something, especially by giving them new ideas: *He inspired me to write a poem.*

in·stall /ɪn'stɔːl/ *verb*

to put a piece of equipment somewhere and connect it so that it can be used: *We have installed a telephone in the office.* I *He's installing some new software.*

in·stal·ment /ɪn'stɔːlmənt/ *noun*
1 one of several amounts of money that you pay over a period of time: *She paid for her car in instalments.*
2 one part of a long story that is told in several parts on television, in a magazine, etc

in·stance /'ɪnstəns/ *noun*
for instance for example: *She has a lot of friends. For instance, 30 people came to her party.*

in·stant¹ /'ɪnstənt/ *adjective*
1 happening or working with no delay: *The new shop was an instant success.*
2 very quick to prepare: *I have instant coffee or tea. Which would you like?*

instant² *noun*
a moment: *He waited for an instant before answering the question.*

in·stant·ly /'ɪnstəntlɪ/ *adverb*
with no delay

in·stead /ɪn'sted/ *adverb*
replacing someone or something else: *I didn't have a pen, so I used a pencil instead.* | *Can you come on Saturday instead of Sunday?*

in·stinct /'ɪnstɪŋkt/ *noun*
a force or ability that makes you do things without thinking about them or learning them: *Cats kill birds by instinct.*

in·sti·tute /'ɪnstɪtjuːt/ *noun*
an organization that does scientific or educational work

in·sti·tu·tion /ˌɪnstɪ'tjuːʃn/ *noun*
a large organization such as a university, a hospital, or a bank

in·struct /ɪn'strʌkt/ *verb*
1 **instruct someone to do something** to tell someone that they must do something: *I've been instructed to wait here.* | *Police officers were instructed to search the house.*
2 to teach someone something

ins·truc·tion /ɪn'strʌkʃn/ *noun*
a piece of information that tells you how to do something: *Read the instructions before you use the machine.*

in·struc·tor /ɪn'strʌktər/ *noun*
a person who teaches a skill or an activity: *He's a swimming instructor.*

in·stru·ment /'ɪnstrʊmənt/ *noun*
1 a small tool used for doing a particular thing: *medical instruments*
2 an object used for making music: *He plays several instruments, including the piano and violin.*

in·sult¹ /ɪn'sʌlt/ *verb*
to be rude to someone and offend them: *How dare you insult my wife like that!*

in·sult² /'ɪnsʌlt/ *noun*
something rude said to offend someone: *He shouted insults at the boys.* ⟡ opposite COMPLIMENT

in·sur·ance /ɪn'ʃʊərəns/ *noun (no plural)*
money paid to a company which then agrees to pay an amount of money if something bad happens to you or your property: *All drivers must have car insurance.*

in·sure /ɪn'ʃʊər/ *verb (present participle **insuring**, past **insured**)*
to pay money for insurance: *The house is insured against fire.*

in·tel·li·gence /ɪn'telɪdʒəns/ *noun (no plural)*
the ability to learn and understand things: *The test should not be too difficult for someone of average intelligence.*

in·tel·li·gent /ɪn'telɪdʒənt/ *adjective*
quick to learn and understand things: *She is a very intelligent child.*

in·tend /ɪn'tend/ *verb*
to plan to do something: *What do you intend to do today?*

in·ten·tion /ɪn'tenʃn/ *noun*
1 something that you plan to do: *His intention is to become World Champion.*
2 **have no intention of doing something** to not intend to do something

in·ter·act·ive /ˌɪntər'æktɪv/ *adjective*
involving reactions between a computer program and the person using it

in·terest¹ /'ɪntrəst/ *noun*
1 (*no plural*) a wish to know more about something: *We both have an interest in music.*
2 **lose interest** to stop being interested: *Kelly lost interest in the film halfway through.*
3 something you do or study because you enjoy it: *Her interests are music and sport.* ⟡ same meaning HOBBY
4 (*no plural*) money that you earn by keeping money in the bank

interest² *verb*
to make someone want to know more about something: *Her story interested me.* | *a book that might interest you*

in·terest·ed /ˈɪntrəstɪd/ *adjective*
wanting to do something or know more about something: *He's very interested in history.* I *Are you interested in coming with us?*

in·terest·ing /ˈɪntrəstɪŋ/ *adjective*
making you want to pay attention: *It was an interesting story.* I *There were a lot of interesting people on the tour.* ⇨ opposite BORING

in·ter·fere /ˌɪntəˈfɪəʳ/ *verb* (present participle **interfering**, past **interfered**)
1 to deliberately become involved in a situation where you are not wanted or needed: *Just go away and stop interfering!* I *It's better not to interfere in their arguments.*
2 interfere with something to stop something from continuing or developing successfully: *Don't let sports interfere with your schoolwork.*

in·te·ri·or[1] /ɪnˈtɪərɪəʳ/ *noun* (no plural)
the inside of something: *His car has a brown leather interior.* ⇨ opposite EXTERIOR

interior[2] *adjective*
on the inside of something: *The interior walls of the house where white.* ⇨ opposite EXTERIOR

in·ter·me·di·ate /ˌɪntəˈmiːdɪət/ *adjective*
on the middle level between two other levels: *I'm going to a class in intermediate Spanish.*

in·ter·nal /ɪnˈtɜːnl/ *adjective*
of or on the inside: *She has internal injuries from the accident.* ⇨ opposite EXTERNAL

in·ter·na·tion·al /ˌɪntəˈnæʃnəl/ *adjective*
for or by many countries: *An international agreement was signed by ten countries.* I *an international airport* ⇨ compare DOMESTIC, NATIONAL

In·ter·net /ˈɪntənet/ *noun*
the Internet a system that allows people using computers around the world to exchange information: *Are you on the Internet yet?*

in·ter·pret /ɪnˈtɜːprɪt/ *verb*
to say the words of one language in the words of another language: *She spoke good German and said she would interpret for me.* ⇨ compare TRANSLATE

in·ter·pre·ta·tion /ɪnˌtɜːprɪˈteɪʃn/ *noun*
a way of explaining or understanding information, someone's actions, etc: *Their interpretation of the evidence was very different from ours.*

in·ter·pret·er /ɪnˈtɜːprɪtəʳ/ *noun*
a person who changes the spoken words of one language into another language

in·ter·rupt /ˌɪntəˈrʌpt/ *verb*
to say something when someone else is already speaking and cause them to stop: *It's rude to interrupt.* I *I didn't mean to interrupt you.*

in·ter·rup·tion /ˌɪntəˈrʌpʃn/ *noun*
something that stops you from continuing what you are doing for a while: *I couldn't work because there were so many interruptions.*

in·ter·val /ˈɪntəvəl/ *noun*
1 a time or space between things: *The theatre opened again after an interval of two years.*
2 at intervals happening regularly with a period of time or space between: *There were trees at intervals along the road.*

in·ter·view[1] /ˈɪntəvjuː/ *noun*
1 a meeting to decide if a person is suitable for a job: *I've got an interview for a new job.*
2 a meeting at which a famous person is asked about their life, opinions, etc

interview[2] *verb*
1 to talk to someone to see if they are suitable for a job
2 to ask a famous person questions about their life, opinions, etc

in·to /ˈɪntə, -tʊ; *strong* ˈɪntuː/ *preposition*
1 so as to be inside or in something: *They went into the house.* I *He fell into the water.* ⇨ see picture on page 208
2 involved in an activity: *I want to go into business for myself.*
3 changed so as to be in a different shape, form, situation, etc: *She made the material into a dress.* I *He cut the cake into six pieces.* I *They're going to move Ian into a different class.*
4 used when dividing one number by another number: *Five into twenty goes four times.*

in·tran·si·tive /ɪnˈtrænsətɪv/ *adjective*
an intransitive verb does not have an object and the action is not done to a person or thing. In the sentence 'When he had finished, he sat down', 'finish' and 'sit' are intransitive verbs ⇨ compare TRANSITIVE

in·tro·duce /ˌɪntrə'djuːs/ verb (present participle **introducing**, past **introduced**)
1 to cause two people to meet each other for the first time, and tell each person the name of the other person: *He introduced his friend **to** me.*
2 to make a change, plan, etc happen or exist for the first time: *The company introduced a new policy on smoking.*

in·tro·duc·tion /ˌɪntrə'dʌkʃən/ noun
1 (no plural) when you make a change, plan, etc happen or exist for the first time: *The introduction of the new law meant that people's rights were protected.*
2 a piece of writing at the beginning of a book that tells you what the rest of the book is about

in·vade /ɪn'veɪd/ verb (present participle **invading**, past **invaded**)
to attack and enter a country or place with an army: *The army invaded the city.*

in·va·lid[1] /'ɪnvəlɪd/ noun
a person who is weak because they are ill: *He helps to look after his grandfather who is an invalid.*

in·val·id[2] /ɪn'vælɪd/ adjective
not suitable or correct: *His ticket was invalid.* ⇨ opposite VALID

in·va·sion /ɪn'veɪʒn/ noun
an occasion when an army attacks and enters a country or place in order to control it: *The invasion of Normandy took place during the Second World War.*

in·vent /ɪn'vent/ verb
to think of and plan something completely new that did not exist before: *Alexander Graham Bell invented the telephone in 1876.*

in·ven·tion /ɪn'venʃən/ noun
1 something completely new that has just been thought of and made: *She loves inventions such as the fax machine and e-mail.*
2 (no plural) when something new is invented: *The invention of the computer has changed the way business is done.*

in·ven·tor /ɪn'ventər/ noun
a person who thinks of and plans something completely new

in·vert·ed com·mas /ɪn,vɜːtɪd 'kɒməz/
the signs (' ') or (" "), used in writing to show what someone says

in·vest /ɪn'vest/ verb
to give money to a bank, business, etc so that you can get a profit later

in·ves·ti·gate /ɪn'vestɪgeɪt/ verb (present participle **investigating**, past **investigated**)
to try to get information about someone or something by looking, asking questions, etc: *The police are investigating the crime.*

in·ves·ti·ga·tion /ɪn,vestɪ'geɪʃn/ noun
to try to get information about something such as a crime or problem: *There will be an investigation **into** the cause of the accident.*

in·vis·i·ble /ɪn'vɪzəbl/ adjective
not able to be seen: *Air is invisible.* ⇨ opposite VISIBLE

in·vit·a·tion /ˌɪnvɪ'teɪʃn/ noun
an offer, in words or writing, of a chance to do something or to go somewhere: *Did you get an invitation **to** the party?*

in·vite /ɪn'vaɪt/ verb (present participle **inviting**, past **invited**)
to ask someone to come to your house, to go out with you, etc: *She invited us **to** her party.*

NOTE: People do not usually use the verb **invite** when they are asking you if you want to go somewhere or do something. Instead they say things like "Would you like to come to dinner at my house?" or "Do you want to come to a party tonight?"
(NOTE: **Never** say "I invite you ..." Say "I'd like to invite you ...")

in·volve /ɪn'vɒlv/ verb (present participle **involving**, past **involved**)
1 to include or affect someone or something: *The accident involved four cars.* | *These changes will involve everyone in the school.*
2 to include something as a necessary part of something else: *The job will involve a lot of hard work.*
3 to make someone take part in something: *Schools are trying to involve parents more **in** their children's education.*

in·volved /ɪn'vɒlvd/ adjective
be involved in something to take part in something: *Al did not want to get involved in their argument.* | *She is involved in politics.*

peak

In the Countryside

mountain

hill

forest

waterfall

cabin

cliff

climbing

wood

lake

horseriding

canoeing

path

fishing

tent

rucksack

sleeping bag

fire

logs

stream

icy

windy

rainy

snowy

winter

spring

autumn

summer

stormy

foggy

cloudy

sunny

polar bear

seal

squirrel

crab

fox

badger

camel

lion

zebra

panda

gorilla

elephant

chimpanzee

jaguar

snake

koala

rhinoceros

crocodile

kangaroo

turtle

octopus

penguin

shark

Sports

swimming

athletics

football

horse racing

basketball

tennis

ice skating

cricket

cycling

golf

rugby

judo

surfing

snooker

gymnastics

skiing

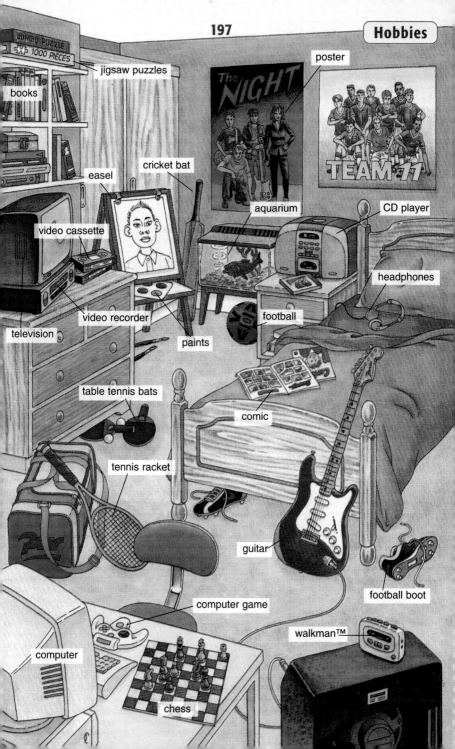

jigsaw puzzles

books

poster

cricket bat

easel

aquarium

CD player

video cassette

headphones

video recorder

football

television

paints

table tennis bats

comic

tennis racket

guitar

football boot

computer game

computer

walkman™

chess

mix

sprinkle

mash

pour

spread

peel

squeeze

roll

grate

slice

carve

knead

dip

drain

whip

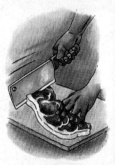

chop

apple

strawberries

orange

avocado

cherries

lime

lemon

melon

pineapple

plums

banana

grapes

pear

grapefruit

blackberries

mushrooms

onion

green beans

carrot

sprouts

pumpkin

lettuce

aubergine

cabbage

cucumber

tomato

peas

potato

asparagus

artichoke

cauliflower

peppers

mechanic

dentist

actress

cook

fisherman

carpenter

taxi driver

nurse

gardener

builder

hairdresser

fireman

pilot

vet

model

journalists

baker

doctor

printer

bookshop

shoe shop

toy shop

jeweller's

gift shop

pet shop

department store

fast food restaurant

supermarket

clothes shop

record shop

phone box

bank

post office

chemist's

delicatessen

bakery

florist's

TICKETS

tall
medium-height
short
skinny
plump
slim

curly hair
fringe
plait
long straight hair
wrinkles
beard
moustache
ponytail
glasses
grey hair

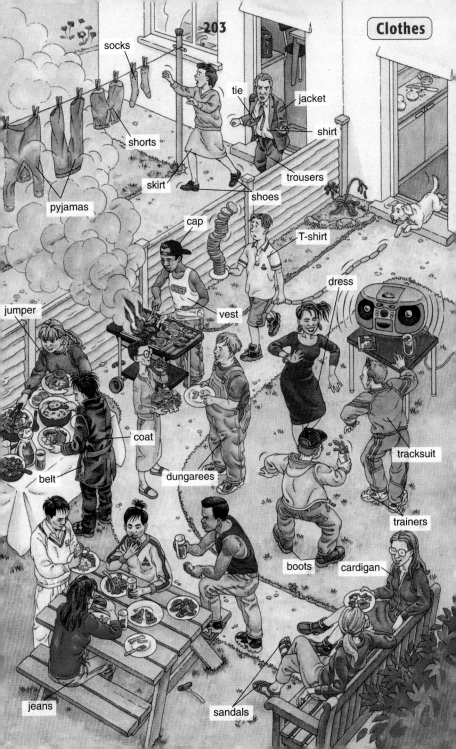

Clothes

socks
shorts
pyjamas
skirt
shoes
tie
jacket
shirt
trousers
cap
T-shirt
vest
dress
jumper
coat
dungarees
tracksuit
belt
trainers
boots
cardigan
jeans
sandals

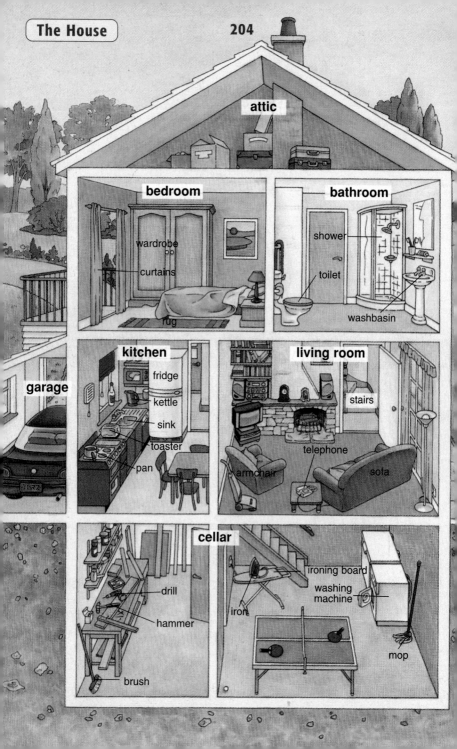

attic

bedroom

wardrobe

curtains

rug

bathroom

shower

toilet

washbasin

garage

kitchen

fridge

kettle

sink

toaster

pan

living room

stairs

telephone

armchair

sofa

cellar

drill

hammer

iron

brush

ironing board

washing machine

mop

in·ward /ˈɪnwəd/ *adjective*
1 towards the middle or the inside of something ⇨ opposite OUTWARD
2 not shown to other people: *I had an inward feeling of happiness.*

in·wards /ˈɪnwədz/ *adverb*
towards the middle or the inside of something: *She turns her toes inwards when she walks* | *The door swings inwards.* ⇨ opposite OUTWARDS

iron

iron

ironing a shirt

i·ron[1] /ˈaɪən/ *noun*
1 (*no plural*) a hard grey metal
2 an instrument that is heated and then used to make clothes smooth ⇨ see picture on page 204

iron[2] *verb*
to press clothes with a hot iron to make them smooth: *Will you iron my shirt?*

iron[3] *adjective*
made of the metal iron: *The gate has iron bars.*

i·ron·ing /ˈaɪənɪŋ/ *noun* (*no plural*)
do the ironing to press clothes with a hot iron to make them smooth ⇨ see picture on page 204

ironing board /ˈaɪənɪŋ ˌbɔːd/ *noun*
a narrow board on which you use an iron to press clothes smooth

ir·reg·u·lar /ɪˈregjʊləʳ/ *adjective*
1 having a shape or surface that is not even or smooth: *His face had irregular features.*
2 an irregular noun or verb does not change its form in the same way as most nouns and verbs. 'Child' and 'person' are irregular nouns. ⇨ opposite REGULAR

ir·ri·gate /ˈɪrɪgeɪt/ *verb* (*present participle* **irrigating**, *past* **irrigated**)
to make water flow onto dry land so that crops can grow

ir·ri·ga·tion /ˌɪrɪˈgeɪʃn/ *noun* (*no plural*)
when water is supplied for dry land so that crops can grow

ir·ri·tate /ˈɪrɪteɪt/ *verb* (*present participle* **irritating**, *past* **irritated**)
1 to annoy someone: *The noise of the children was irritating me.*
2 to make a part of your body hurt slightly: *The sun irritates my eyes.*

PREPOSITIONS

1 The boy is hiding **in** the tree above his friend.
2 The dog is wading **across** the stream.
3 There is a man leaning **against** a tree.
4 The girl and her dog are running **around** the fountain.
5 The woman and her son are walking **away from** the park.
6 The boy is hiding from his friends **behind** a tree.
7 There is a boy standing **below** the branch of the tree.
8 A child is standing **between** his parents.
9 There is a woman standing **by** the merry-go-round.
10 A boy is going **down** the slide.
11 Two boys are building a castle **in** the sand.
12 Two people are standing **in front of** the ice cream van.
13 The man is standing **beside** his son.
14 The boy is falling **into** the lake.
15 The couple are sitting **on** a bench.
16 A boy is climbing **onto** the ice cream van.
17 A dog is drinking **from** the lake.
18 Two children are sitting **opposite** each other on the seesaw.
19 A boy is climbing **out** of the paddle boat.
20 An old man is walking **over** the bridge.
21 A boy is cycling **past** the merry-go-round.
22 Two people are jogging **through** the park.
23 A little boy is running **towards** his mother.
24 A squirrel is sitting **under** the slide.
25 A boy is climbing **up** the steps of the slide.

A B C D E F G H I J K L M N O P Q R S T U V W X Y Z

is /əz; *strong* ɪz/ *verb*
the part of the verb **be** that you use with
he, **she**, and **it**: *She is Peter's sister.* |
Where is my key? | *He's* (=he is) *her
brother.* | *That boy's* (=boy is) *in my
class.* | *He isn't* (=is not) *very clever.*

Is·lam /ˈɪzlɑːm/ *noun*
the religion started by Mohammed

island

is·land /ˈaɪlənd/ *noun*
a piece of land surrounded by water:
Britain and Japan are islands.

isn't /ˈɪznt/
is not: *She isn't coming.* | *It's a lovely
day, isn't it?* | *Isn't he attractive?*

i·so·lat·ed /ˈaɪsəˌleɪtɪd/ *adjective*
far from other places: *He lives on an
isolated farm.* | *Not many people visit
this isolated spot.*

is·sue[1] /ˈɪʃuː/ *verb* (*present participle*
issuing, *past* **issued**)
1 to make an official statement: *The
government issued a warning about the
new drug.*
2 to provide someone with something:
*The teacher issued paper and pencils to
all the children.* | *The team was issued
with new shoes.*

issue[2] *noun*
1 a subject or problem that many
people think is important: *They were
discussing the issue **of** health care.*
2 a magazine or newspaper that is
printed for a particular day, week, or
month: *Have you got the latest issue **of**
Vogue?*

it /ɪt/
1 the thing or animal that the sentence
is about: *I've lost my book, and I can't
find it anywhere.* | *It's* (=it is) *not in my
room.* | *It was an interesting film.*
2 used when you are talking about the
weather, time, and dates: *It is very hot
today.* | *It's nearly four o'clock.* | *It is
Thursday, September 2nd.*
3 used when you are talking about an

event or a fact: *It's a long way to the
town.* | *"What's that noise?" "It's a car."*
4 used when you are asking or saying
who is there: *"Who is it?" "It's me,
Peter."* | *"What's that?" "It's a vegetable."*

itch[1] /ɪtʃ/ *verb*
to have an annoying feeling on your skin
that makes you want to rub it: *The
insect bite itched all night.*

itch[2] *noun*
an annoying feeling on your skin that
makes you want to rub it: *I've got an
itch on my back.*

itch·y /ˈɪtʃɪ/ *adjective*
if your skin is itchy, it itches: *That red
patch on my skin is very itchy.*

it'd /ˈɪtəd/
1 it would: *It'd be lovely to see you.* |
I'd do it if I thought it'd help.
2 it had: *It'd taken us two hours to get
there.* | *It would have been nicer if it'd
been sunnier.*

i·tem /ˈaɪtəm/ *noun*
a single thing in a group, list, etc: *There
was an interesting item in the
newspaper today.* | *On the desk there
were two books, a pen, and some other
items.*

it'll /ˈɪtl/
it will: *It'll soon be the holidays.* | *It'll be
dark before they get back.*

it's /ɪts/
1 it is: *It's very nice to meet you.*
2 it has: *It's stopped raining.* ⇨ look at ITS

its /ɪts/
belonging to it: *She gave the cat its
food.* | *The dog hurt its foot.* | *The tree
has lost all of its leaves.*

NOTE: Do not confuse **its** (=belonging
to it) with **it's** (=it is or it has) which is
spelled with a **'**.

it·self /ɪtˈself/
the same thing or animal as the one that
the sentence is about: *The cat was
washing itself.* | *Your body will try to
defend itself against disease.*

I've /aɪv/
I have: *I've got two sisters.* | *I've never
been here before.*

i·vo·ry /ˈaɪvərɪ/ *noun* (*no plural*)
the hard yellow substance taken from
the long tooth of an ELEPHANT

J, j /dʒeɪ/
the tenth letter of the English alphabet

jab¹ /dʒæb/ *verb* (*present participle*
jabbing, *past* **jabbed**)
to push something pointed into or
toward something else: *She jabbed the
needle into my arm.* | *He kept jabbing his
finger into my back until I turned round.*

jab² *noun*
a quick sharp push: *I felt a jab in my
back.*

jack·et /dʒækɪt/ *noun*
a short coat ⇨ see picture on page 203

jag·ged /dʒægɪd/ *adjective*
rough, with many sharp points: *I cut
myself on the jagged edge of the tin.* |
There are jagged rocks along the coast.

jag·u·ar /dʒægjʊəʳ/ *noun*
a large wild cat with spots on its fur
⇨ see picture on page 195

jail /dʒeɪl/ *noun*
prison: *The man was sent to jail.*

jam¹ /dʒæm/ *verb* (*present participle*
jamming, *past* **jammed**)
1 to press things or people tightly
together into a place: *I managed to jam
all my clothes **into** one case.* | *She
jammed the letter into her pocket.*
2 if a machine, door, gun, etc jams, or
if you jam it, it no longer works properly:
*I've jammed the lock and I can't open
the door.* | *The brakes jammed on her
bicycle.*
3 to fill a place with people or things so
nothing can move: *The streets were
jammed **with** cars.*

jam² *noun*
1 (*no plural*) a sweet food made of fruit
boiled with sugar, usually eaten with
bread
2 a lot of people or things pressed so
tightly together in a particular place so
that nothing can move: *We were stuck
in a traffic jam.*

jan·gle /dʒæŋgl/ *verb* (*present participle*
jangling, *past* **jangled**)
to make a sharp noise like metal hitting
metal: *She jangled her keys in her
pocket.*

Jan·u·a·ry /dʒænjʊərɪ/ *noun*
the first month of the year

jar /dʒɑːʳ/ *noun*
a round glass container with a lid, used
for storing food: *a jam jar* | *a jar of honey*
⇨ see picture at CONTAINER

jav·e·lin
/dʒævlɪn/ *noun*
a long pointed
stick that is
thrown as a sport

jaw /dʒɔː/ *noun*
either of the two
bones in your
face that hold
your teeth

javelin

throwing a javelin

jazz /dʒæz/ *noun*
(*no plural*)
a kind of music with a strong beat: *Do
you like listening to jazz?*

jeal·ous /dʒeləs/ *adjective*
1 unhappy because you want
something that someone else has: *I
was very jealous **of** Sarah's new
bicycle.* | *It makes me jealous seeing all
my sister's new clothes.* ⇨ same
meaning ENVIOUS
2 unhappy or angry because you think
that someone will stop loving you and
start loving someone else: *Her husband
gets jealous if she talks to other men.*

jeal·ous·y /dʒeləsɪ/ *noun* (*no plural*)
1 the unhappy feeling that you have
when you want something that
someone else has ⇨ same meaning
ENVY
2 the angry or unhappy feeling that you
have when you think that someone will
stop loving you and start loving
someone else

jeans /dʒiːnz/
trousers made of a strong cotton cloth,
usually blue: *I bought a new pair of
jeans.* ⇨ see picture on page 203

jeep /dʒiːp/ *noun*
trademark a large strong car that can be
used on rough roads

jeer /dʒɪəʳ/ *verb*
to laugh rudely at someone or shout
unkind things: *The crowd jeered **at** the
speaker.*

jel·ly /dʒelɪ/ *noun*
(*plural* **jellies**) a soft sweet DESSERT
made with fruit and sugar

jel·ly·fish /'dʒelɪˌfɪʃ/ noun (plural
jellyfish or **jellyfishes**)
a soft sea creature that can sting

jerk ¹ /dʒɜːk/ verb
1 to pull something suddenly and
quickly: *She jerked the rope but it
wouldn't move.*
2 to move with a sudden movement:
*Her hand jerked and she dropped her
drink.*

jerk ² noun
a short hard pull or sudden movement:
The bus started with a jerk.

jer·sey /'dʒɜːzɪ/ noun
a piece of clothing, usually made
of wool, that covers the top part of
your body. ⇨ same meaning SWEATER,
JUMPER

Je·sus /'dʒiːzəs/
also **Jesus Christ** the man on whose
life and teaching Christianity is based

jet /dʒet/ noun
1 a narrow stream of gas, air, or liquid
that comes out of a small hole: *The
firefighter sent jets of water into the
burning house.*
2 a kind of plane that can go very fast

Jew /dʒuː/ noun
a person who follows the religion of
Judaism

jew·el /'dʒuːəl/ noun
a valuable stone that is worn as
decoration: *She wore beautiful jewels
round her neck.*

earrings   ring   **jewellery**

bracelet   necklace

jew·el·lery /'dʒuːəlrɪ/ noun (no plural)
things such as rings, gold, etc that
people wear for decoration

Jew·ish /'dʒuːɪʃ/ adjective
belonging to a group of people whose
religion is Judaism

jig·saw puz·zle /'dʒɪɡsɔː ˌpʌzl/ noun
a game in which you must fit together
many small pieces to make one big
picture ⇨ see pictures at INCOMPLETE and
on page 197

jin·gle /'dʒɪŋɡl/ verb (present participle
jingling, past **jingled**)
to make a noise like small bells: *The
coins jingled in his pocket.*

job /dʒɒb/ noun
1 work that you are paid to do: *"What
is your job?" "I'm a teacher."* | *I got a job
as a waitress.* ⇨ look at WORK
2 a piece of work or duty that must be
done: *My mother does all the jobs
about the house.* | *My job is to take the
dog for a walk.*
3 **make a good or bad job of
something** British to do something well
or badly: *Sarah made a good job of her
essay.*

jockey   **jockey**

disc jockey (DJ)

jock·ey /'dʒɒkɪ/ noun
a person who rides in horse races

jog ¹ /dʒɒɡ/ verb (present participle
jogging, past **jogged**)
to run slowly, usually for exercise: *She
jogs around the park every morning.*
⇨ see picture on page 207

jog ² noun (no plural)
a slow steady run, that you do as
exercise: *Let's go for a jog.*

join ¹ /dʒɔɪn/ verb
1 to become a member of something:
He joined the army. | *Trevor joined the
BBC in 1969.*
2 to connect or fasten things together:
*Tie a knot to join those two pieces of
rope.* | *This road joins the two villages.*
3 to come together; meet: *Where do
the two roads join?*
4 to go and do something together
with someone else: *Will you join me for*

dinner? | I am joining my family for
Christmas.

5 join hands if people join hands, they
hold each other's hands: *We all joined
hands and danced round in a circle.*

6 join in to take part in an activity, a
game, etc: *We all joined in the singing. |
We're going to play football; do you
want to join in?*

joint[1] /dʒɔɪnt/ *noun*
  1 a place where two bones in your
body meet: *Her joints ached and she
felt sick.*
  2 a place where two things are joined
together: *One of the joints between the
pipes was leaking.*
  3 *British* a large piece of meat for
cooking, usually with a bone in it

joint[2] *adjective*
  shared by two or more people: *We wrote
it together; it was a joint effort. | His sons
are joint owners of the business. | We
have a joint bank account.*
  jointly *adverb*: *We paid for the car
jointly.*

joke[1] /dʒəʊk/ *noun*
  1 something that you say or do to
make people laugh: *Our teacher told us
a funny joke. | Do you know any jokes?*
  2 play a joke on someone to do
something funny to someone to make
other people laugh: *Let's play a joke on
Michael.*

joke[2] *verb (present participle* **joking**,
past **joked**)
  to say things to make people laugh: *I
didn't mean that seriously – I was only
joking.*

jolt[1] /dʒəʊlt/ *noun*
  1 a sudden shake or movement: *The
train started with a jolt.*
  2 a sudden shock: *Her resignation
gave me a bit of a jolt.*

jolt[2] *verb*
  to move with sudden rough shakes:
The bus jolted along the mountain road.

jot /dʒɒt/ *verb (present participle* **jotting**,
past **jotted**)
  jot something down to write
something down quickly: *I jotted down
her address on my newspaper.*

jour·nal /'dʒɜːnl/ *noun*
  1 a serious newspaper or magazine for
a special subject: *She works for a
leading medical journal.*

2 a record of the things you do each
day ⇨ same meaning DIARY

jour·nal·is·m /'dʒɜːnl-ɪzəm/ *noun (no
plural)*
  the job or activity of being a journalist

jour·nal·ist /'dʒɜːnl-ɪst/ *noun*
  a person who writes about the news for
newspapers or magazines, or who
records information about the news for
television or radio ⇨ see picture on
page 200

jour·ney /'dʒɜːni/ *noun*
  a trip, usually a long one: *How long is
the journey to the coast? | My journey
to work usually takes about an hour.*

joy /dʒɔɪ/ *noun*
  1 *(no plural)* great happiness: *She was
full of joy when her baby was born. | To
Beth's surprise and joy, she was
awarded first prize.*
  2 something that gives great
happiness: *The joys and sorrows of
bringing up a family.*

joy·ful /'dʒɔɪfəl/ *adjective*
  very happy: *Her birthday was a joyful
occasion.*

joy·stick /'dʒɔɪstɪk/ *noun*
  a handle that you use to control
something in a computer game

Ju·da·is·m /'dʒuːdeɪ-ɪzəm/ *noun (no
plural)*
  the JEWISH religion

judge[1] /dʒʌdʒ/ *noun*
  1 the official person in control of a court
who decides how criminals should be
punished: *The judge sent him to prison
for two years.*
  2 a person who decides who has won
a competition

judge[2] *verb (present participle* **judging**,
past **judged**)
  1 to form an opinion about something
or someone: *How can you judge which
dictionary to buy? | It's harder to judge
distances when you're driving in the
dark.*
  2 to decide who or what is the winner
of a competition: *Who is judging the
poetry competition?* ⇨ compare DECIDE

judge·ment /'dʒʌdʒmənt/ *noun*
  1 the ability to make reasonable
decisions about situations and people: *I
thought his remarks showed his good
judgement.*
  2 *(no plural)* what you decide after

A
B
C
D
E
F
G
H
I
J
K
L
M
N
O
P
Q
R
S
T
U
V
W
X
Y
Z

ju·do /'dʒuːdəʊ/ noun (no plural)
a fighting sport in which you try to throw the other person to the ground ⇨ see picture on page 196

jug /dʒʌg/ noun
a container with a handle, for holding and pouring liquids: I'll fetch a jug of water.

jug·gle /'dʒʌgl/ **juggle**
verb (present participle **juggling**, past **juggled**)
to throw several things into the air and keep them moving by throwing and catching them quickly

juggling balls

juice /dʒuːs/ noun
(no plural)
the liquid that comes from fruit or vegetables: Can I have a glass of orange juice?

juic·y /'dʒuːsɪ/ adjective
having a lot of juice: Those plums were very juicy.

Ju·ly /dʒʊ'laɪ/ noun
the seventh month of the year

jum·ble¹ /'dʒʌmbl/ noun (no plural)
a lot of things that are mixed together in an untidy way: There was a jumble of clothes on the floor.

jumble² verb (present participle **jumbling**, past **jumbled**)
to mix things together in an untidy way: The clothes were all jumbled up in the drawer.

jum·bo jet /'dʒʌmbəʊ ˌdʒet/ noun
a large plane that can carry a lot of people

jump¹ /dʒʌmp/ verb
1 to push yourself up in the air or over something using your legs: The children jumped up and down with excitement. | The horse jumped over the fence. | Boys were diving and jumping off the bridge into the river.

2 to move quickly or suddenly in a particular direction: Paul jumped up to answer the door. | She jumped into bed.
3 to move suddenly because of fear or surprise: That noise made me jump.
4 jump at something to quickly accept the chance to do something: Ruth jumped at the chance to study in Paris.

jump² noun
when you push yourself off the ground or over something using your legs: He got over the fence in one jump.

jump·er /'dʒʌmpə'/ noun
a piece of clothing, usually made of wool, that covers the top part of your body ⇨ same meaning SWEATER, JERSEY ⇨ see picture on page 203

junc·tion /'dʒʌŋkʃən/ noun
a place where roads or railway lines meet: Turn left at the junction.

June /dʒuːn/ noun
the sixth month of the year

jungle

jun·gle /'dʒʌŋgl/ noun
a thick forest in a hot country with large plants that grow close together

ju·nior /'dʒuːnjə'/ adjective
lower in importance or position: He is a junior member of the company. ⇨ opposite SENIOR

junior school /'dʒuːnjə ˌskuːl/ noun
a school in Britain for children who are between seven and eleven years old

junk /dʒʌŋk/ noun (no plural)
old things that you do not want or cannot use: That room is full of junk. ⇨ compare RUBBISH

jury /'dʒʊərɪ/ noun (plural **juries**)
a group of people in a court who decide if someone is guilty or not: The jury listened carefully to the case.

just[1] /dʒʌst/ *adverb*

1 only: *It happened just a few weeks ago.* | *"Who was there?" "Just me and Elaine."* | *I play tennis just for fun.*

2 a very short time ago: *I've just got home.* | *You've just missed the bus.*

> NOTE: British people usually use **just**[1] (2), **already**, and **yet** with the present perfect tense (=the tense with **have** + the past participle) and not with the simple past tense: *He had just heard the news.* | *I've already seen that film.* | *Have you finished yet?*

3 exactly: *You look just like your Dad.* | *I have just enough money to buy a stamp.*

4 now, or at a particular moment: *The telephone rang just as I was leaving.* | *I'm just making some coffee – would you like some?*

5 used to emphasize something you are saying: *I just couldn't believe the news.* | *Just sit down and shut up!*

6 used to be polite when asking or telling someone something: *Could I just use your phone for a minute?*

7 just about almost: *She walks to school just about every day.* | *I am just about finished.*

8 just a minute, just a second a phrase used when you want to ask someone to wait for a short time: *"Can I speak to Mr Jones?" "Just a minute, please. I'll find him for you."* | *Just a second – I can't find my keys.*

just[2] *adjective*

fair and right: *He received a just punishment.*

jus·tice /'dʒʌstɪs/ *noun* (no plural)

1 treatment of people that is fair and right: *She is fighting for justice.* ⋄ opposite INJUSTICE

2 the system of law in a country

K, k /keɪ/
the eleventh letter of the English alphabet

kan·ga·roo /ˌkæŋɡəˈruː/ *noun*
an Australian animal that jumps along on its large back legs and keeps its young in a special pocket of skin ⇨ see picture on page 195

ka·ra·te /kəˈrɑːtɪ/ *noun (no plural)*
a Japanese sport in which you fight using your hands and legs

keen /kiːn/ *adjective*
1 wanting to do something very much: *He was keen to see the new film.*
2 be keen on someone or something to like someone or something very much or be very interested in them: *Are you keen on swimming?*

keep /kiːp/ *verb (past kept /kept/)*
1 to continue to have something and not give it to someone, sell it, or get rid of it: *You can keep the book – I don't need it any more.* | *I kept all her letters through the years.*
2 to stay in the same place or state: *I wish you would keep still for a moment.* | *This blanket should help you keep warm.*
3 to make someone or something stay in a place or state: *Do you want me to keep the windows open?* | *My work's been keeping me very busy.*
4 keep doing something to continue doing something or repeat an action many times: *She kept making the same mistake.* | *If he keeps on growing like this he'll be taller than his dad.*
5 to store something in a particular place: *Where do you keep the tea?*
6 to stay fresh: *Milk only keeps for a few days.*
7 keep a secret not to tell a secret
8 keep off something to stay off or away from a place: *Notices told us to keep off the grass.*
9 keep someone up to make someone stay awake and out of bed: *Your loud music is keeping me up.*

10 keep up to move as fast as a person or thing: *I can't keep up with you when you walk so fast.*

ken·nel /ˈkenl/ *noun*
a small house for a dog to sleep in

kept /kept/
the past tense and past participle of the verb **keep**

kerb /kɜːb/ *noun*
a line of raised stones separating the path at the side of a road from the road ⇨ see picture at PAVEMENT

ketch·up /ˈketʃʌp/ *noun (no plural)*
a thick red liquid made from TOMATOES, eaten with food to give a pleasant taste

ket·tle /ˈketl/ *noun*
a container with a lid and handle used for boiling and pouring water: *Let's put the kettle on and make tea.* ⇨ see picture on page 204

key /kiː/ *noun*
1 something that you put into a lock in order to open a door, start a car, etc: *I can't find my car keys.* ⇨ see picture at INSERT
2 one of the things that you press on a computer to produce letters or numbers
3 one of the narrow black and white bars on some musical instruments, such as a piano, that you press to make a musical sound ⇨ see picture at PIANO
4 the key the most important part of a plan or action: *Exercise is the key to a healthy body.*

key·board /ˈkiːbɔːd/ *noun*
a set of keys on a computer or a musical instrument such as a piano that you press to produce letters or sounds

key·hole /ˈkiːhəʊl/ *noun*
the part of a lock that a key fits into ⇨ see picture at INSERT

kg
a short way of writing the word kilogram: *She bought 2 kg of flour.*

kha·ki /ˈkɑːkɪ/ *adjective, noun*
a green-brown or yellow-brown colour

kick¹ /kɪk/ *verb*
1 to hit someone or something with your foot: *He kicked the ball over the fence.*

2 to move your legs strongly: *The baby kicked happily.*

3 kick off to start a football match

4 kick someone out to force someone to leave a place: *They kicked Dan out of the club.*

kick² *noun*

1 a quick hard hit with your foot: *If the door won't open, give it a kick.*

2 a feeling of pleasure or excitement: *I get a kick **out of** ice skating.*

kid /kɪd/ *noun*

1 a child

2 a young goat

kid·nap /'kɪdnæp/ *verb* (*present participle* **kidnapping**, *past* **kidnapped**)

to take someone away and ask for money in return for bringing them back safely

kid·nap·per /'kɪdnæpə^r/ *noun*

a person who kidnaps someone

kid·ney /'kɪdnɪ/ *noun*

one of the two parts inside your body that remove waste liquid from your blood

kill /kɪl/ *verb*

to make a plant, animal, or person die: *Ten people were killed in the train crash.* | *The cat kept killing birds.* ⇨ compare MURDER

kil·ler /'kɪlə^r/ *noun*

a person, animal, or thing that kills: *The police are searching for the killer.*

ki·lo /'kiːləʊ/ *noun*

a short way of writing or saying **kilogram**: *a kilo of sugar*

kil·o·byte /'kɪləbaɪt/ *noun*

a unit for measuring computer information

kil·o·gram, kil·o·gramme /'kɪləgræm/ *noun*

a measure of weight equal to 1000 grams

kil·o·me·tre /'kɪləmiːtə^r, kɪ'lɒmɪtə^r/ *noun*

a measure of length equal to 1000 metres

kin /kɪn/ *noun* (*no plural*)

people in your family: *His next of kin (=his closest relative) was told about his death.*

kind¹ /kaɪnd/ *noun*

a type of person or thing: *She is the kind of woman who helps people.* | *What kind of pizza do you want?* ⇨ same meaning TYPE, SORT

kind² *adjective*

helpful, caring, and wanting to do things that make other people happy: *She was kind **to** me when I was unhappy.* | *It's very kind of you to help me.* ⇨ opposite UNKIND, CRUEL

NOTE: Remember that if you use the singular of **kind¹** it must be followed by a singular noun, and the plural **kinds** must be followed by a plural noun, e.g. *this kind of car, these kinds of cars.*

kind-heart·ed /ˌkaɪnd 'hɑːtɪd/ *adjective*

caring and kind: *a kind-hearted person* ⇨ opposite HARD-HEARTED

kindly *adverb*: *She kindly offered to drive me home.*

kind·ness /'kaɪndnəs/ *noun* (*no plural*)

being kind or doing kind things: *Thank you very much for your kindness.*

king /kɪŋ/ *noun*

a male ruler of a country, especially one who is a member of a royal family: *The King **of** Spain visited the UK.* ⇨ compare QUEEN

king·dom /'kɪŋdəm/ *noun*

a country ruled by a king or queen

kiss¹ /kɪs/ *verb*

to touch someone with your lips as a sign of love or as a greeting: *He kissed his wife goodbye.*

kiss² *noun* (*plural* **kisses**)

when someone kisses you: *He **gave** his daughter a kiss.*

kit /kɪt/ *noun*

1 (*no plural*) British all the things that you need for doing a particular sport: *I've forgotten my football kit.*

2 a set of small pieces from which to make something: *We made a model plane out of a kit.*

kitch·en /'kɪtʃɪn/ *noun*

a room used for preparing and cooking food ⇨ see picture on page 204

kite /kaɪt/ *noun*
a toy with a light frame covered with plastic or cloth that flies in the air on the end of a long string

kite

kit·ten /'kɪtn/ *noun*
a young cat

kit·ty /'kɪti/ *noun*
(*plural* **kitties**)
a child's word for a cat

Kleen·ex /'kliːneks/ *noun*
trademark a piece of soft thin paper used especially for cleaning your nose

km
a short way of writing the word **kilometre**

knead /niːd/ *verb*
to press a mixture of flour and water with your hands so that it becomes ready to cook to make bread: *Knead the dough for three minutes.* ⇨ see picture on page 198

knee /niː/ *noun*
1 the joint in the middle of your leg where the leg bends
2 on your knee on the top part of your leg when you are sitting down: *The baby sat on my knee.*

knee·cap /'niːkæp/ *noun*
the bone at the front of your knee

kneel /niːl/ *verb* (*past* **knelt** /nelt/)
also **kneel down** to bend your legs and rest on your knees: *She knelt down to pray.*

knew /njuː/
the past tense of the verb **know**

knick·ers /'nɪkəz/ *plural noun*
British a piece of underwear that a woman or girl wears between the waist and the top of the legs ⇨ same meaning PANTS

knife /naɪf/ *noun* (*plural* **knives** /naɪvz/)
a blade with a handle used for cutting something or as a weapon ⇨ see picture at CUTLERY

knight /naɪt/ *noun*
1 a soldier of the Middle Ages trained to fight on a horse
2 in Britain, a man who is given a special honour and whose name then has 'Sir' in front of it

knit /nɪt/ (*present participle* **knitting**, *past* **knitted** *or* **knit**)
to make clothes by joining wool or another thread with long needles or on a special machine: *She's knitting some clothes for her baby.* ⇨ compare SEW

knit·ting nee·dle /'nɪtɪŋ ˌniːdl/ *noun*
a long thin stick that you use to knit clothes ⇨ see picture at NEEDLE

knob /nɒb/ *noun*
1 a round handle on a door or a drawer
2 a round control button on a machine

knock¹ /nɒk/ *verb*
1 to hit a door or window with your hand to get someone's attention: *I knocked on the door.*
2 to hit something so that it moves or falls: *He knocked the glass off the table.* | *Careful you don't knock the camera.*
3 knock something down to destroy or remove a building: *They knocked down the houses to build a shopping centre.*
4 knock someone down to hit someone with a car, bus, etc so that they fall to the ground: *She was knocked down by a bus.*
5 knock someone out to make someone go to sleep or become unconscious: *Those sleeping pills really knocked me out.*

knock² *noun*
the sound made by hitting something: *There was a loud knock at the door.*

knot¹ /nɒt/ *noun*
1 a fastening made by tying two ends of string or rope together: *She tied her belt with a knot.*

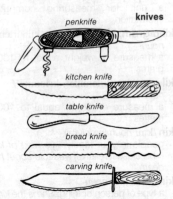

penknife

knives

kitchen knife

table knife

bread knife

carving knife

2 a mass of hairs or threads accidentally twisted together: *I can't get the knots out of my hair.*

3 a measure of the speed of a ship, about 1,853 metres every hour

knot² *verb (present participle* **knotting**, *past* **knotted**)

to tie together two ends or pieces of rope or string

know /nəʊ/ *verb (past* **knew** /njuː/, *past participle* **known** /nəʊn/)

1 to have information or facts about something in your mind: *She doesn't know your address.* I *He knows a lot* **about** *cars.* I *Did you know* **that** *Mary went to Portugal yesterday?*

2 to be sure about something: *I know* **that** *I won't get the job.* I *I knew you'd say that.* I *The boy stared at him uncertainly, not knowing whether to believe him.*

3 to have learned and be able to use a language or skill: *Do you know French?* I *I taught him everything he knows.*

4 to have experience of a person or a place: *I know Mary well.* I *Do you know London?*

5 I know a phrase used to show you agree with someone: *"It's a bad idea." "I know."* I *"Those shoes are ugly." "I know – they're awful."*

6 you know a phrase used when you want to explain something more clearly: *It's the building on the left. You know, the new one.*

NOTE: Compare **know**, **learn**, and **teach**. If you know something, you already have the facts or information about it: *She knows a lot about computers.* If you **learn** something, you discover facts about something or discover how to do something, either on your own or with a teacher: *He's learning to drive.* I *The children are learning maths at school.* If you **teach** someone something, you help them learn something by giving them help and information: *She taught me to play the piano.* I *He teaches the older children history.*

knowl·edge /ˈnɒlɪdʒ/ *noun (no plural)*
understanding or information that you have in your mind: *His knowledge* **of** *languages is excellent.* I *Our knowledge* **about** *how the brain works is increasing.*

knowl·edge·a·ble /ˈnɒlɪdʒəbl/ *adjective*
having a lot of information or understanding about something: *She's very knowledgeable* **about** *horses.*

known /nəʊn/
the past participle of the verb **know**

knuck·le /ˈnʌkl/ *noun*
one of the joints in your fingers

ko·a·la /kəʊˈɑːlə/ *noun*
an Australian animal like a small bear ⇨ see picture on page 195

Ko·ran /kɔːˈrɑːn/
the holy book of the MUSLIMS

A B C D E F G H I J K L M N O P Q R S T U V W X Y Z

L, l /el/

1 the twelfth letter of the English alphabet
2 a short way of writing the word **litre** or **litres**: *a 2l bottle of beer*

lab /læb/ *noun*
a LABORATORY

labels

label

label

label

la·bel¹ /'leɪbl/ *noun*
a piece of paper fixed to something, that gives you information about it: *Put a label on the box to say what's inside.* | *Always read the instructions on the label.*

label² *verb (present participle **labelling**, past **labelled**)*
to put or fix a label on something: *Make sure you label the package clearly.*

la·bor·a·tory /lə'bɒrətrɪ/ *noun (plural **laboratories**)*
also **lab** a room or building in which scientific work is done

la·bour¹ /'leɪbər/ *noun (no plural)*
1 hard work, especially work that you do with your hands: *Her beautiful home was the result of many years of labour.* | *The job involves a lot of physical labour.*
2 the workers in a country or factory: *We don't have enough labour to finish the job.*

labour² *verb*
to work hard: *He laboured **over** the report for hours.*

la·bour·er /'leɪbərər/ *noun*
a person who does hard work with their hands: *a farm labourer* ⇨ compare WORKER

lace /leɪs/ *noun (no plural)*
a type of cloth made from thin thread

with a pattern of holes in it: *My dress has lace around the neck and sleeves.*

lack¹ /læk/ *noun (no plural)*
when you do not have something or do not have enough of it: *The plants died through lack **of** water.* | *She was exhausted from lack of sleep.*

lack² *verb*
to not have something or to not have enough of something: *She lacked the strength to lift the box.* | *The only thing he lacks is experience.*

lad·der /'lædər/ *noun*
two long pieces of wood or metal joined together by shorter pieces that form steps for climbing: *I need a ladder to reach the roof.*

la·den /'leɪdn/ *adjective*
carrying something, especially a large amount: *The lorry was laden **with** boxes of fruit.*

la·dies /'leɪdɪz/ *noun*
1 the plural of **lady**
2 **the Ladies** *British* a public toilet for women: *She's gone to the Ladies.* ⇨ compare GENTS

la·dle /'leɪdl/ *noun*
a big deep spoon with a long handle used for serving liquids

la·dy /'leɪdɪ/ *noun (plural **ladies**)*
1 a woman: *Good afternoon ladies and gentlemen.*
2 a title given to a woman of a high social rank

la·ger /'lɑːgər/ *noun*
1 a kind of light beer
2 a glass or bottle of light beer: *Two lagers, please.*

laid /leɪd/
the past tense and past participle of the verb **lay** ⇨ look at LAY¹

lain /leɪn/
the past participle of the verb **lie** ⇨ look at LAY¹

lake /leɪk/ *noun*
a big area of water with land all round it ⇨ compare POND ⇨ see picture on page 193

lamb /læm/ *noun*
a young sheep

lame /leɪm/ *adjective*
not able to walk easily, usually because of an injured leg or foot: *My horse is lame, so I can't ride her.*

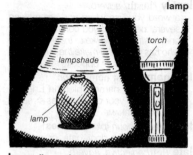

lamp

lampshade

torch

lamp

lamp /læmp/ *noun*
an object that produces light and stands on a table, shelf, etc: *a bedside lamp*

lamp-post /'læmp-pəʊst/ *noun*
a tall pole with a light at the top by the side of a road

lamp·shade /'læmpʃeɪd/ *noun*
a cover put over a lamp to make it less bright or to make it look attractive

land¹ /lænd/ *noun*
1 (*no plural*) an area of ground, especially when it is used for buildings or farming: *Farmers own most of the land round here.*
2 (*no plural*) the dry part of the Earth not covered by the sea: *They reached land after six weeks at sea.*
3 a country: *He wants to travel to foreign lands.*

land

a plane landing

a plane taking off

land² *verb*
to arrive somewhere after a journey by plane: *We landed at Rome at six in the evening.* ⬦ opposite TAKE OFF

land·ing /'lændɪŋ/ *noun*
1 the space at the top of a set of stairs

in a building: *The bedroom opens onto the landing.*
2 when a plane comes down from the air onto the ground: *The plane made a safe landing.*

land·la·dy /'lændleɪdɪ/ *noun* (*plural* **landladies**)
a woman who owns a building that she lets other people use or live in, in return for money

land·lord /'lændlɔːd/ *noun*
a man who owns a building that he lets other people use or live in, in return for money

land·scape /'lænd,skeɪp/ *noun* (*no plural*)
an area of land, used especially when talking about the way it looks: *The beauty of the New England landscape in autumn.*

lane /leɪn/ *noun*
1 a narrow road: *We walked down the lane past the farm.*
2 one of the parts that a main road is divided into by painted lines

lan·guage /'læŋgwɪdʒ/ *noun*
the words that people use in speaking and writing: *People in different countries speak different languages. | I am studying the English language.*

lan·tern /'læntən/ *noun*
a light in a glass case, often with a handle

lap¹ /læp/ *noun*
1 the flat surface formed by the upper parts of your legs when you are sitting down: *Susan's little girl sat on her lap.*
2 the distance once around a track, or between two ends of a swimming pool

lap² *verb* (*present participle* **lapping**, *past* **lapped**)
also **lap up** when an animal laps a liquid, it uses its tongue to drink it: *The cat lapped up its milk.*

laptop

a laptop computer

lap·top /'læptɒp/ *noun*
a small computer that you can carry with you

large /lɑːdʒ/ *adjective*
big: *They need a large house because they have nine children.* | *Order us a large pizza.* | *He earns large amounts of money.* ⇨ opposite SMALL

la·ser /'leɪzəʳ/ *noun*
a piece of equipment that produces a very strong, very narrow line of light, used in some machines or in medical operations: *a laser printer* | *He needs laser surgery on his eye.*

lash /læʃ/ *noun* (*plural* **lashes**)
one of the hairs that grow on the parts of your eye that touch when you shut your eyes ⇨ same meaning EYELASH

last[1] /lɑːst/
1 most recent: *I saw my friend last week, but I haven't seen him this week.* | *I haven't been to London since last Christmas.* | *The last time we played tennis, you won.*
2 coming at the end after all the others: *The last girl who came in was Mary.* | *This is my last chance.* | *When does the last bus leave?* ⇨ opposite FIRST
3 the last person or thing is the only one that remains: *Can I have the last piece of cake?*

last[2] *adverb*
1 most recently before now: *When I last saw him, he was just a boy.* | *When did you last go shopping?*
2 after everything or everyone else: *They told her they would interview her last.* | *Mix together flour, butter, and sugar, and add the eggs last.*

last[3] *verb*
1 to continue to happen for a period of time: *Our holiday lasted ten days.* | *The hot weather lasted for the whole of June.*
2 to stay in good condition or stay the same: *Good shoes last longer.* | *She was very angry yesterday, but her anger didn't last.*
3 to be enough for a particular amount of time: *Two loaves of bread will last us for two days.*

last·ing /'lɑːstɪŋ/ *adjective*
continuing for a long time: *We want to have a lasting relationship.*

last·ly /'lɑːstlɪ/ *adverb*
a word you use when you are making several points and you come to the last one: *Lastly, I would like to thank everyone who has worked to make the new school such a success.* ⇨ opposite FIRSTLY

last name /'lɑːst neɪm/ *noun*
your family's name which, in English, comes after your other names ⇨ same meaning SURNAME

latch /lætʃ/ *noun* (*plural* **latches**)
a fastening for a door, gate, or window

late /leɪt/ *adjective, adverb*
1 after the usual, agreed, or expected time: *I was late for school.* | *I may not be home until late.* | *Our flight arrived two hours late.*
2 near the end of a period of time: *The house was built in the late 19th century.* | *He began the work in late May.*
3 near the end of the day: *It's getting late. We'd better go home.*

late·ly /'leɪtlɪ/ *adverb*
in the recent past: *Have you seen him lately?* ⇨ same meaning RECENTLY

lat·er /'leɪtəʳ/ *adverb*
1 after the present time: *I'll do it later.*
2 **later on** at some time in the future: *Your plans may cause some problems later on.*

lat·est /'leɪtɪst/ *adjective*
1 most recent: *Have you heard the latest news?*
2 **at the latest** used to emphasize that something must happen or be done before a particular time: *Please arrive by 9 o'clock at the latest* (=and no later).

Lat·in /'lætɪn/ *noun* (*no plural*)
the language of the ancient Romans: *A few children still study Latin at school.*

lat·i·tude /'lætɪtjuːd/ *noun* (*no plural*)
the position north or south of the middle of the Earth ⇨ compare LONGITUDE

lat·ter /'lætəʳ/ *noun*
the latter the second of two people or things that have just been mentioned: *You can use glass or plastic, but the latter* (=plastic) *is cheaper.* ⇨ opposite THE FORMER

laugh[1] /lɑːf/ *verb*
1 to make a sound that shows you are pleased, happy, or think something is funny: *It was so funny we couldn't stop laughing.* | *No one ever laughs at my*

jokes. | *He burst out laughing* (=started laughing suddenly).

2 laugh at someone or something to say unkind things about someone or something, or tell jokes about them: *They'll laugh at you if you wear that awful coat.*

laugh[2] *noun*
the sound you make when you find something funny: *We had a good laugh at his story.*

laugh·ter /'lɑːftə^r/ *noun* (*no plural*)
the act or sound of laughing: *We could hear laughter from next door.*

launch /lɔːntʃ/ *verb*
1 to start something new: *The hospital is launching a campaign to buy new equipment.*
2 to put a ship into the water or to send a spaceship into space

laun·der·ette /ˌlɔːndə'ret/ *noun*
a shop where you pay to wash your clothes and sheets in a machine

laun·dry /'lɔːndrɪ/ *noun* (*no plural*)
clothes and sheets that need washing or have just been washed

la·va /'lɑːvə/ *noun* (*no plural*)
very hot liquid rock that comes out of the top of a VOLCANO ⇨ see picture at VOLCANO

lav·a·tory /'lævətrɪ/ *noun* (*plural* **lavatories**)
a room with a toilet in it: *I need to go to the lavatory.* ⇨ same meaning TOILET

law /lɔː/ *noun*
1 a rule made by the government, that all people must obey: *There is a law against driving too fast.*
2 the law the whole system of laws in a country: *Will I be breaking the law* (=doing something illegal) *if I do that?* | *Driving without a seatbelt is against the law* (=not allowed).
3 by law according to the law: *Young children are not allowed to work by law.*

law·ful /'lɔːfəl/ *adjective*
allowed by the law ⇨ same meaning LEGAL ⇨ opposite ILLEGAL

lawn /lɔːn/ *noun*
an area of short grass outside a house or in a park

lawn mow·er /'lɔːn ˌməʊə^r/ *noun*
a machine for cutting the grass in a garden or park

law·yer /'lɔːjə^r/ *noun*
a person whose job is to give advice about the law and speak for people in court

lay[1] /leɪ/ *verb* (*past* **laid** /leɪd/)
1 to put something on a surface: *She laid her coat over a chair.* | *He laid the baby on the bed.*
2 lay the table to arrange knives, forks, plates, and other things on a table ready for a meal
3 to make eggs and send them out of the body: *The hen laid three eggs.*

> NOTE: Do not confuse the verb **lay** (past tense and past participle **laid**) with the verb **lie** (past tense **lay**, past participle **lain**). **Lay**[1] means 'to put something down' and is **always** used with an object: *She laid the clothes on the bed.* **Lie** means 'to have your body flat on something' and is **never** used with an object: *She lay on her bed.* There is another verb **lie** (past tense and past participle **lied**) which means 'to say something that is not true' and is also used without an object: *He lied to me.*

lay[2]
the past tense of the verb **lie**

lay·er /'leɪə^r/ *noun*
a covering that is spread on top of something or in between two things: *This cake has got a layer of chocolate in the middle.* | *There was a layer of dust on the furniture.*

la·zy /'leɪzɪ/ *adjective* (**lazier**, **laziest**)
not wanting to work: *Eva's the laziest girl in the class.*

lb (*plural* **lbs**)
a short way of writing the word **pound** or **pounds** weight: *1lb flour* | *3lbs potatoes*

lead[1] /liːd/ *verb* (*past* **led** /led/)
1 to show someone the way, usually by going in front: *You lead and we'll follow.* | *He led his horse to the barn.*
2 if a road or a path leads to a place, it goes there: *This path leads to the church.*
3 to go in front of a group of people or vehicles: *He's going to lead the climb up Mount Everest.* | *The English team was leading at half time.*

4 to be winning a game or competition: *We were leading 2 to 1 with ten minutes to play.*

5 to be more successful than others at something: *Our company leads the world in making cars.*

6 lead to something to cause something to happen: *The new factory has led to new jobs.*

7 lead a ... life to experience a particular kind of life: *She led a very lonely life.*

lead² /liːd/ *noun*

1 a position in front of the others: *The Spanish runner now has a lead of 50m.*

2 be in the lead to be winning in a game or competition: *Lewis is still in the lead after 3 laps.*

3 *British* a piece of rope, leather, etc, used to hold an animal: *Please keep your dog on a lead.*

lead³ /led/ *noun*

1 (*no plural*) a heavy soft grey metal: *The old house had lead pipes.*

2 the part inside a pencil that you write with

lead·er /ˈliːdəʳ/ *noun*
a person who leads other people: *He is one of the leaders of the community.*

lead·er·ship /ˈliːdəʃɪp/ *noun* (*no plural*)

1 the position of leader: *Smith took over the leadership of the party.*

2 the qualities necessary in a leader: *The United States needs strong leadership.*

lead·ing /ˈliːdɪŋ/ *adjective*
most important: *Julia Roberts plays the leading role in the film.*

leaf /liːf/ *noun* (*plural* **leaves** /liːvz/)
one of the green flat parts of a plant or tree that grow out of a branch or stem: *The leaves of this tree change colour in autumn.* ⇨ see picture at ROSE

leaf·let /ˈliːflət/ *noun*
a piece of paper with an advertisement or information printed on it

league /liːg/ *noun*

1 a group of people or teams that play against each other in a competition: *Manchester United are top of the Football League.*

2 a group of people or countries that have joined together to work for a special purpose

leak¹ /liːk/ *noun*
a hole or crack through which gas or liquid may accidentally pass in or out: *There's a leak in the pipes.*

leak

leak² *verb*
if something leaks, there is a hole or crack in it through which gas or liquid accidentally passes in or out: *The roof leaks and the rain's coming in.*

a leaking bucket

leak·y /ˈliːkɪ/ *adjective* (**leakier, leakiest**)
having a hole or crack so that liquid or gas accidentally escapes: *The roof is leaky and the rain comes in.*

lean¹ /liːn/ *verb* (*past* **leaned** or **leant** /lent/)

1 to bend forwards, sideways, or backwards: *Don't lean out of the window because you might fall out.* | *She leaned forward to kiss him.*

2 to put something against another thing to support it: *She leant her bicycle against the wall.*

3 to rest your body against something: *Joe was leaning on the fence.* ⇨ see picture on page 207

lean² *adjective*
not containing very much fat: *She bought some lean meat.*

leant /lent/
the past tense and past participle of the verb **lean**

leap¹ /liːp/ *verb* (*past* **leaped** or **leapt** /lept/)
to jump high into the air or over something: *The dog leapt over the fence.*

leap² *noun*
a big jump up into the air or over something: *With one leap she crossed the stream.*

leap year /ˈliːp jɪəʳ/ *noun*
a year, once every four years, in which the month of February has 29 days instead of 28 days: *The years 1984 and 1988 were leap years.*

learn /lɜːn/ *verb* (*past* **learned** or **learnt** /lɜːnt/)

1 to get knowledge of something or

the ability to do something: *I learned to drive when I was 18.* | *I am learning English.*

2 to get to know something so well that you can easily remember it: *She learnt the poem and said it in front of the class.* ⇨ look at KNOW

learn·er /'lɜːnəʳ/ *noun*
a person who is learning: *She's a slow learner.*

learnt /lɜːnt/
the past tense and past participle of the verb **learn**

least /liːst/
1 at least (a) not less than a particular number or amount: *At least 150 people were killed in the earthquake.* **(b)** used before changing something you just said: *His name is Paul – at least I think it is.*

2 less than anything or anyone else: *Do it the way that takes the least time.* | *Which one is the least expensive?* | *They arrived when I least expected them* (=when I did not expect them at all). ⇨ opposite MOST

3 least of all especially not: *I don't like any of them, least of all Debbie.*

4 not in the least not at all: *I'm not in the least interested in what she says.*

leath·er /'leðəʳ/ *noun* (*no plural*)
the skin of dead animals used for making things such as shoes and bags: *a leather belt*

leave¹ /liːv/ *verb* (*present participle* **leaving**, *past* **left** /left/)
1 to go away from a place or person: *The train leaves in five minutes.* | *She left Australia for Britain.* | *What time did you leave the office?*

2 to put something in a place: *Just leave those letters on my desk please.*

3 to let a thing stay in a particular place or state: *Why did you leave the windows open?* | *Leave the dishes – I'll wash them later.*

4 also **leave behind** to forget to take something with you when you leave a place: *I think I left my books at home.* ⇨ look at FORGET

5 leave someone alone to stop worrying or annoying someone: *Go away and leave me alone!*

6 leave something alone used to tell someone not to touch or move something: *Leave the dog alone.* |

Leave those cakes alone or there won't be enough for tea.

7 leave someone or something out to not include a person or thing: *I left out a really important idea.* | *They left me out of the team.*

8 to give something to someone after you die: *My aunt left me her house.* ⇨ compare INHERIT

9 be left, be left over to remain after everything else has been taken away or used: *Is there any coffee left?*

leave² *noun* (*no plural*)
a period of time away from work: *The soldiers had six weeks leave.*

leaves /liːvz/
the plural of the word **leaf** ⇨ see picture at TREE

lec·ture¹ /'lektʃəʳ/ *noun*
a talk given to teach a large number of people: *The students have lectures every day.*

lecture² *verb*
to talk to a group of people about a particular subject: *She lectures on Shakespeare at Edinburgh University*

led /led/
the past tense and past participle of the verb **lead**

ledge /ledʒ/ *noun*
a narrow shelf, such as the one at the bottom of a window

leek /liːk/ *noun*
a long green and white vegetable

left¹ /left/
the past tense and past participle of the verb **leave**

left² *noun* (*no plural*)
the opposite side to the hand that most people write with: *The school is on the left of the road and his house is on the right.* ⇨ opposite RIGHT

left³ *adjective, adverb*
on or towards the left: *Jim's broken his left leg.* | *Turn left at the corner.* ⇨ opposite RIGHT

left-hand·ed /ˌleft ˈhændɪd/ *adjective*
using your left hand for jobs such as writing ⇨ opposite RIGHT-HANDED

left·o·vers /'leftəʊvəz/ *noun* (*plural*)
food that has not been eaten during a meal

leg /leg/ *noun*
1 one of the two parts of your body

that you use for walking: *Dogs have four legs.* | *She broke her leg skiing.*

2 one of the parts on which chairs, tables, etc stand: *The chair has a broken leg.*

le·gal /'li:gl/ *adjective*
allowed by the law: *Drinking alcohol is legal in Britain.* ⇨ opposite ILLEGAL

le·gend /'ledʒənd/ *noun*
1 a story about people who lived in the past, that may not be true
2 a very famous person: *Elvis Presley was a legend in rock music.*

le·gi·ble /'ledʒəbl/ *adjective*
clear enough to read: *Her writing is not very legible.* ⇨ opposite ILLEGIBLE

lei·sure /'leʒər/ *noun (no plural)*
the time when you are not at work and can do things that you enjoy: *What do you do in your leisure time?*

lem·on /'lemən/ *noun*
a yellow fruit with a sour taste that grows on trees in hot countries ⇨ see picture on page 199

lem·on·ade /ˌleməˈneɪd/ *noun (no plural)*
a sweet drink made from lemons

lend /lend/ *verb (past lent /lent/)*
1 to let someone use or have something for a time, after which they must give it back: *Can you lend me that book for a few days?* | *I've lent my bike to Tom.* ⇨ look at BORROW
2 if a bank lends you money, you borrow the money and then pay it back with an extra amount included

length /leŋθ/ *noun (no plural)*
how long something is from one end to the other: *He caught a fish that was ten feet **in** length.* | *What length is the room?*

length·en /'leŋθən/ *verb*
to make something longer: *I need to lengthen this dress.* ⇨ opposite SHORTEN

length·y /'leŋθɪ/ *adjective*
continuing for a long time: *He gave a lengthy speech.*

lens /lenz/ *noun (plural lenses)*
a curved piece of glass used for making things look bigger, smaller, or clearer

lent /lent/
the past tense and past participle of the verb **lend**

len·til /'lentl/ *noun*
an orange, green, or brown round seed that can be cooked and eaten

leopard

leop·ard /'lepəd/ *noun*
a large wild cat in Africa and Asia that has yellow fur with black spots

less[1] /les/ *adverb*
1 not so much or to a smaller degree: *There's a less expensive seat towards the back.* | *You take the bag that is less heavy.* | *I definitely walk less since I've owned a car.*
2 less and less continuing to become smaller in amount: *It seems like we have less and less money every month.* ⇨ opposite (**1** and **2**) MORE

less[2]
a smaller amount or a smaller amount of something: *I live less **than** a mile from here.* | *She spends less **of** her time playing with the children now.* | *You ought to eat less salt.*

less·en /'lesn/ *verb*
1 to make something less: *The medicine will lessen the pain.*
2 to become less: *The rain lessened and finally stopped.*

les·son /'lesn/ *noun*
a time when someone teaches you a subject or skill: *We have a history lesson this afternoon.* | *I am **taking** piano lessons.*

let /let/ *verb (present participle letting, past let)*
1 to allow someone to do something or to have something: *My mother wouldn't let me go to the film.* | *They won't let people in without a ticket.* | *I let her have £10.*
2 let's used when you ask someone to do something with you: *Let's go down to the river and swim.* | *I'm hungry – let's eat.*
3 let go to stop holding something: *Hold the ladder for me and don't let go.* | *Let go **of** my arm!*

4 let someone know to tell someone about something: *Let me know what time you'll be arriving.* | *I need to let her know that I'm going out.*

5 let someone down to make someone feel disappointed, especially by not doing what you promised: *You've let us down by not working for your exam.*

6 to allow someone to use a house or some land in return for money: *They let their house to another family when they went away.*

let·ter /'letər/ *noun*

1 one of the signs such as A, a, B, b, G, and g that we use to write words: *You should start a sentence with a capital letter.*

2 a written message sent to someone, for example by post: *I'm writing a letter to a friend.* ⇨ look at YOURS ⇨ see picture at ENVELOPE

letter box /'letə bɒks/ *noun* (*plural* **letter boxes**)

1 a hole or box in the front of a building into which letters are delivered

2 a box in the street or post office in which letters are put to be sent through the mail ⇨ same meaning POSTBOX

let·tuce /'letɪs/ *noun*

a vegetable with large green leaves that are eaten without cooking ⇨ see picture on page 199

lev·el¹ /'levəl/ *noun*

1 the amount, degree, or number of something: *People are worried about the high level of pollution in the air.*

2 the height or position of something: *Hold out your arm at the same level as your shoulder.*

level² *adjective*

1 flat with no area that is higher or lower: *We need a level piece of ground to play football on.*

2 at the same height or position as something else: *He bent down so that his head was level with the little boy's.*

level³ *verb* (*present participle* **levelling**, *past* **levelled**)

to make something flat: *I'm going to level the ground to make a lawn.*

level cross·ing /ˌlevəl 'krɒsɪŋ/ *noun*

a place where a railway crosses a road and traffic has to wait for trains to pass

le·ver¹ /'liːvər/ *noun*

1 a bar that you use to lift something heavy by putting one end under the object and pushing down on the other end

2 a handle on a machine that you push or pull to work the machine

lever² *verb*

to move something with a lever: *I levered the lid off the box with a stick.*

li·a·ble /'laɪəbl/ *adjective*

be liable to do something to be likely to do something: *He's liable to get angry if people keep him waiting.* | *The forest is so dry it's liable to burn quickly if anyone starts a fire.*

li·ar /'laɪər/ *noun*

someone who tells lies

lib·e·ral /'lɪbərəl/ *adjective*

willing to understand and accept the different behaviour or ideas of other people

lib·er·ty /'lɪbəti/ *noun* (*no plural*)

being free to do what you want without having to ask permission: *They fought for their liberty.*

li·brar·i·an /laɪˈbreərɪən/ *noun*

a person who works in a library

li·bra·ry /'laɪbrəri/ *noun* (*plural* **libraries**)

a place where you can borrow or look at books: *There's a very good library in the next town.*

lice /laɪs/

the plural of **louse**

li·cence /'laɪsns/ *noun*

a piece of paper showing that the law allows you to do something, such as drive a car: *The policeman asked to see my driving licence.*

li·cense /'laɪsns/ *verb* (*past participle* **licensing**, *past* **licensed**)

to give official permission for someone to own or do something: *He is licensed to drive buses and private coaches.*

lick /lɪk/ *verb*

to touch something with your tongue: *She licked the stamps and stuck them on the letter.* | *The dog jumped up and licked her face.*

lid /lɪd/ *noun*

a cover for a box, pan, or other container, that can be taken off: *Where's the lid for this jar?* ⇨ same meaning TOP

A
B
C
D
E
F
G
H
I
J
K
L
M
N
O
P
Q
R
S
T
U
V
W
X
Y
Z

lie¹ /laɪ/ *verb* (*present participle* **lying**, *past* **lay** /leɪ/, *past participle* **lain** /leɪn/)

to have your body flat on something or to get into this position: *He was lying on the bed.* | *She lay **down** on the floor.* | *Lie down and rest for a while.* ⇨ look at LAY

lie² *verb* (*present participle* **lying**, *past* **lied**)

to say things that are not true: *I would never lie **to** you.* | *She lied to him **about** her age.* ⇨ look at LAY

lie³ *noun* (*plural* **lies**)

something said that is not true: *Why did he **tell** her a lie?*

lieu·ten·ant /lefˈtenənt/ *noun*

an officer of middle rank in the army or the navy

life /laɪf/ *noun*

1 (*plural* **lives** /laɪvz/) the period of time during which someone is alive: *She had lived in the same village all her life.* | *It was the happiest day of my life.*

2 all the experiences and activities that are typical of a particular way of living: *Life in New York is exciting.* | *According to his book, the life of a rock star is not a happy one.*

3 (*no plural*) activity and movement: *The children were jumping about and full of life.* | *There were no signs of life in the house.*

4 (*no plural*) living things such as people, animals, and plants: *She is studying the island's plant life.*

lighthouse   lifeboat

life·boat /ˈlaɪfbəʊt/ *noun*

a boat used for saving people who are in danger at sea

life jack·et /ˈlaɪf ˌdʒækɪt/ *noun*

a piece of clothing that you wear around your upper body to make you float in water

life·style /ˈlaɪfstaɪl/ *noun*

the way in which you live, including the conditions you live in, the things you own, and the things you do: *They had a healthy lifestyle.* | *My lifestyle changed when I went to college.*

life·time /ˈlaɪftaɪm/ *noun*

the time in which someone is alive: *In my father's lifetime there have been many changes in the village.* | *During her lifetime she experienced two world wars.*

lift¹ /lɪft/ *verb*

to take something in your hands and raise it higher: *Can you lift the other end of the table?* | *Lift me up so I can see over the fence.* ⇨ see picture on page 207

lift² *noun*

1 *British* a machine that carries people or things between the floors of a tall building (*American* **elevator**)

2 give someone a lift to take someone somewhere in a vehicle: *He sometimes gives me a lift to school.*

lift-off /ˈlɪft ɒf/ *noun*

the moment when a space vehicle rises up into the air at the beginning of its journey

light¹ /laɪt/ *noun*

1 (*no plural*) the energy from the sun, a LAMP, etc that allows you to see: *There's more light near the window.* | *The light from her torch showed us the way.*

2 a thing that gives out light: *Turn off the lights when you go to bed.*

light² *adjective*

1 pale and not dark in colour: *She wore a light blue dress* ⇨ opposite DARK

2 not weighing very much: *The box is quite light and easy to lift.* | *You take the light bag and I'll take the heavy one.* ⇨ opposite HEAVY

3 not having much force or power: *I heard a light tap on the window.* | *There was a light wind.*

4 not great in amount: *The traffic was very light this evening.*

light³ *verb* (*past* **lit** /lɪt/ *or* **lighted**)

1 to start burning or to make something start burning: *Will you light the fire for me?* | *He lit a cigarette.*

2 to produce light in a place: *The room was lit by two lamps.*

light bulb /'laɪt bʌlb/ *noun*
the round glass part of an electric light

light·en /'laɪtn/ *verb*
to make something light or lighter in weight or colour

light·er /'laɪtəʳ/ *noun*
an object that makes a small flame for lighting a cigarette

light·house /'laɪthaʊs/ *noun (plural* **lighthouses** /-haʊzɪz/)
a tall building with a powerful light that acts as a signal for ships ⇨ see picture at LIFEBOAT

light·ing /'laɪtɪŋ/ *noun (no plural)*
the system that gives light to a place: *We need more lighting in this office.*

light·ly /'laɪtlɪ/ *adverb*
with only a small amount of weight or force: *She touched me lightly on the arm.*

light·ning /'laɪtnɪŋ/ *noun (no plural)*
a sudden bright light in the sky during a storm

like¹ /laɪk/ *verb (present participle* **liking**, *past* **liked**)
to enjoy something, or think that someone or something is pleasant: *I like bananas.* | *Do you like dancing?* | *Pam didn't like to walk home late at night.* | *Jenny didn't like the film very much.*

like²
1 in the same way as someone or something: *I wish I could sing like her.*
2 with the same qualities as someone or something: *Mary's dress is red, like mine.*
3 in a way that makes you think something is true: *They looked like they were used to being outdoors.*

like·a·ble /'laɪkəbl/ *adjective*
friendly and easy to like: *He's a likeable man.*

like·ly /'laɪklɪ/ *adjective*
probably or almost definitely: *The train is likely to be late.* | *She is the girl most likely to win the prize.* ⇨ opposite UNLIKELY

like·wise /'laɪkwaɪz/ *adverb*
in the same way: *We respect his wishes and we hope you will do likewise.*

lik·ing /'laɪkɪŋ/ *noun*
have a liking for something to like something: *He has a liking for fast cars.*

lil·y /'lɪlɪ/ *noun (plural* **lilies**)
a plant with large white or coloured flowers

limb /lɪm/ *noun*
an arm or leg

lime /laɪm/ *noun*
1 a green fruit with a sour taste ⇨ see picture on page 199
2 (*no plural*) a white substance used for making CEMENT

lim·it¹ /'lɪmɪt/ *noun*
1 the greatest amount, number, or distance that is allowed or possible: *There is a limit to the amount of money I can afford.* | *There is a 30 mile an hour speed limit in the town.*
2 the edge or furthest point of something: *The fence shows the limit of the field.*

limit² *verb*
to keep something from going past a particular point, level, or amount: *The government limits the amount of money you can take out of the country.* | *They are going to limit the number of children they have.*

limp¹ /lɪmp/ *adjective, adverb*
not firm or stiff: *When flowers are dying, their stems become limp.* | *Her body went limp as she fell to the floor unconscious.*

limp² *verb*
to walk with difficulty because one leg or foot has been hurt: *He limped off the football field.*

limp³ *noun*
a way of walking when one leg or foot is hurt: *She walked with a limp.*

line¹ /laɪn/ *noun*
1 a long very narrow mark: *Write on the lines of the paper.* | *Draw a straight line across the top.*
2 a row of people or things: *A line of people were outside the cinema waiting to get in.* | *There was a line of trees along the side of the road.*
3 a long piece of string or rope: *Can you fetch the clothes off the washing line (=line for drying washed clothes)?*

line² *verb (present participle* **lining**, *past* **lined**)
1 to form a line or row: *People lined the streets to see the Queen.*

2 to cover the inside of something with another material: *The box was lined **with** soft paper.*

lin·en /ˈlɪnɪn/ *noun (no plural)*

1 a kind of cloth like thick strong cotton
2 things made of cloth that you use in your home, for example sheets

lin·ing /ˈlaɪnɪŋ/ *noun*

the cloth covering the inside of a piece of clothing, bag, or container: *The lining of my coat is torn.*

link¹ /lɪŋk/ *noun*

1 something that connects two or more things, events, people, or ideas: *There's a new rail link **between** the two towns.* | *Britain is developing closer links **with** Europe.*
2 one ring of a chain

link² *verb*

to join two things or places together: *The two towns are linked by a railway.*

li·on /ˈlaɪən/ *noun*

a dangerous wild animal like a big cat, that lives in Africa ⇨ see picture on page 195

li·on·ess /ˈlaɪənes/ *noun (plural lionesses)*

a female lion

lip /lɪp/ *noun*

one of the edges of your mouth: *He kissed her on the lips.* ⇨ see picture at HEAD

lip·stick /ˈlɪpstɪk/ *noun (no plural)*

a coloured substance that women sometimes put on their lips: *Does she use lipstick?*

liq·uid¹ /ˈlɪkwɪd/ *noun*

a substance that can be poured, such as water, milk, or oil

liquid² *adjective*

in the form of a liquid: *a bottle of liquid soap*

list¹ /lɪst/ *noun*

a lot of names or things you must do, written down one under another: *I must make a list of things to pack.* | *a shopping list*

list² *verb*

to write or say things as a list: *I listed the things I wanted to buy.*

Bill didn't hear his friend because he was listening to music.

lis·ten /ˈlɪsn/ *verb*

to pay attention to what someone is saying or what you hear: *Listen! There's a strange noise in the engine.* | *Have you listened **to** those tapes yet?* | *I told him not to do it but he wouldn't listen.*

NOTE: When you use **listen** and you want to say who the person or thing is that you hear, you should use **listen to**: *Listen to me.* | *We were listening to music.* | *She is listening to the radio.*

lit /lɪt/

the past tense and past participle of the verb **light**

lit·era·ture /ˈlɪtrətʃərʳ/ *noun (no plural)*

good books and writing, including plays and poems: *She's studying French literature at University.* | *We're doing Shakespeare in our English Literature course.*

li·tre /ˈliːtərʳ/ *noun*

a measure of liquid: *The bottle holds a litre **of** beer.*

litter

lit·ter /ˈlɪtərʳ/ *noun (no plural)*

waste paper and other things lying on the ground: *There was litter everywhere on the streets of the town.* ⇨ compare RUBBISH

litter bin /ˈlɪtə bɪn/ *noun*

a large container in a public place for people to put their waste paper in

lit·tle [1] /ˈlɪtl/ *adjective*
1 small: *It's only a little house.* | *The mother was carrying her little girl.*
⇨ opposite BIG
2 a little bit a small amount: *Can I have a little bit of sugar?*
3 short in time or distance: *I will wait a little while and then call her again.* | *Anna walked a little way down the road with him.*

little [2]
1 only a small amount of something: *She eats very little.* | *I have very little money at the moment.*
2 a little some, but not much: *I feel a little better today.* | *Put a little salt on the meat.* | *She knows a little English.*

live [1] /lɪv/ *verb* (*present participle* **living**, *past* **lived**)
1 to be alive or to stay alive: *Is your grandmother still living?* | *Plants can't live without light.*
2 to have your home in a place: *I live in London.* | *Where does Shirin live?*
3 live on something to keep alive by eating something or by earning some money: *Cows live on grass.* | *I can live on very little money.*

live [2] /laɪv/ *adjective*
1 not dead: *He feeds his snake live rats.*
2 done or performed for people who are present and watching: *The restaurant has live music tonight.*

live·ly /ˈlaɪvlɪ/ *adjective*
very active: *It was a lively party.* | *a lively group of children*

liv·er /ˈlɪvəʳ/ *noun*
1 a part inside your body that cleans your blood
2 the liver of an animal eaten as food

lives /laɪvz/
the plural of **life**

liv·ing [1] /ˈlɪvɪŋ/ *adjective*
alive: *She has no living relatives*
⇨ opposite DEAD

living [2] *noun*
1 (*no plural*) the way in which you earn money: *"What does he do for a living?" "He's a builder."*
2 the living people who are alive
⇨ opposite the DEAD

living room /ˈlɪvɪŋ ruːm/ *noun*
the main room in a house in which people sit and do things together ⇨ see picture on page 204

liz·ard /ˈlɪzəd/

lizard

noun
an animal that has four short legs, a long tail, and a skin like a snake

'll /l/ *verb*
1 will: *She'll do it tomorrow.* | *It'll be sunny soon.*
2 shall: *We'll see you soon.* | *I'll be there after lunch.*

load [1] /ləʊd/ *noun*
things that are carried, especially on a vehicle: *The lorry was carrying a load of bananas.*

load [2] *verb*
1 to put things onto a vehicle: *We loaded the car with shopping.*
⇨ opposite UNLOAD
2 to put BULLETS in a gun or film in a camera

loaf /ləʊf/ *noun* (*plural* **loaves** /ləʊvz/)
bread that has been baked in one large piece: *I need to buy a loaf of bread.*
⇨ see picture at BREAD

loan [1] /ləʊn/ *noun*
an amount of money that you borrow from a person or bank: *I asked the bank for a loan.*

loan [2] *verb*
to let someone borrow something, especially money

loathe /ləʊð/ *verb* (*present participle* **loathing**, *past* **loathed**)
to hate very much: *I loathe washing dishes.*

loaves /ləʊvz/
the plural of **loaf**

lob·by /ˈlɒbɪ/ *noun* (*plural* **lobbies**)
a large room inside the entrance of a building: *Wait for me in the hotel lobby.*

lob·ster /ˈlɒbstəʳ/ *noun*
a sea animal that people eat, with a shell, a tail, eight legs, and two large CLAWS

lo·cal /ˈləʊkl/ *adjective*
in the area near a place, especially near where you live: *My children go to the local school.*
locally *adverb*: *Do you live locally?*

lo·ca·tion /ləʊˈkeɪʃn/ *noun*
a particular place or position: *The map shows the location of the church.*

lock¹ /lɒk/ *noun*

an object that keeps a door, gate, or drawer shut and that can only be opened with a key

lock² *verb*

1 to close a door, gate, or drawer using a key in the lock: *Did you remember to lock the door?*

2 lock up to make a building safe by closing all the doors with keys: *Don't forget to lock up when you go out.* ⇨ opposite (**1** and **2**) UNLOCK

lock·er /'lɒkə'/ *noun*

a small cupboard, often with a lock, for keeping things in: *She left her clothes in a locker and went for a swim in the pool.*

lo·cust /'ləʊkəst/ *noun*

an insect that flies in large groups and eats crops in fields

locust

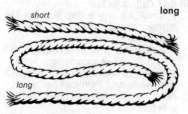

lodge /lɒdʒ/ *verb*

(*present participle* **lodging**, *past* **lodged**)

to pay to live in a room in someone else's house: *He's lodging with friends.*

lodg·er /'lɒdʒə'/ *noun*

British someone who pays to live in a room in someone else's house

loft /lɒft/ *noun*

a room or space at the top of a house inside the roof ⇨ same meaning ATTIC

log¹ /lɒg/ *noun*

a large piece of wood from a tree: *Put another log on the fire.* ⇨ see picture on page 193

log² *verb*

1 log on to do the things necessary so that you can start using a computer

2 log off to do the things necessary so that you can stop using a computer

lol·li·pop /'lɒlɪpɒp/ *noun*

a sweet made from boiled sugar or frozen juice on the end of a stick ⇨ see picture at FROZEN

lone·ly /'ləʊnlɪ/ *adjective*

unhappy because you are alone: *He was lonely without his wife.*

short   long

long

long¹ /lɒŋ/ *adjective*

measuring a great distance, length, or time: *Julie has got long hair.* I *It takes a long time to walk to school.* ⇨ opposite SHORT ⇨ see picture on page 202

long² *adverb*

1 for a long time: *Have you been waiting long?*

2 at a long time before or after a particular event: *The farm was sold long **before** you were born.* I *It happened long **after** they were married.*

3 as long as, so long as having the condition that: *You can go out as long as you promise to be back before 9.*

long³ *verb*

to want something very much: *I longed **for** a bicycle.* I *She longed **to** go home.*

long-dis·tance /ˌlɒŋ 'dɪstəns/ *adjective*

between places that are a long way from each other: *I need to make a long-distance telephone call.*

long·ing /'lɒŋɪŋ/ *noun (no plural)*

a strong feeling of wanting something

lon·gi·tude /'lɒndʒɪtjuːd/ *noun (no plural)*

a position on the Earth shown on maps as the distance east or west of a line that goes from the top of the Earth to the bottom ⇨ compare LATITUDE

look¹ /lʊk/ *verb*

1 to turn your eyes towards something so that you can see it: *She looked **at** me angrily.* I *He was sitting looking out of the window.* ⇨ look at WATCH

2 to seem to be something: *That dog looks dangerous.* I *You look tired.*

3 Look! said when you are annoyed or want someone to notice something: *Look! I don't want to argue with you, but I think you've made a mistake.*

4 look as if, look like to seem likely: *It looks as if we're going to miss the plane.*

5 What does someone look like?

used to ask someone to describe the appearance of someone or something: *"What does your sister look like?" "She's tall and she's got dark hair."*

6 look after someone or something to take care of someone or something: *She looked after my dog while I was on holiday.* I *We look after Rodney's children until he gets home from work.*

7 look for someone or something to try to find someone or something: *I'm looking for my key.*

8 look forward to something to feel happy because you are going to do something that you will enjoy: *We're looking forward to the party.* I *I'm looking forward to meeting you.*

9 look something up to find a piece of information in a book: *Did you look up that word in the dictionary?*

look² *noun*
1 **have a look, take a look** to look at something: *Have a look **at** this book.* I *Let me take a look at the map.*
2 the expression on someone's face: *He gave me an angry look.*
3 the way something appears: *Mr Flynn had a tired look in his eyes.*
4 **looks** (*plural noun*) how attractive someone is: *She worries about her looks.* I *Good looks* (=beauty) *are not as important as kindness.*

loom /luːm/ *noun*
a machine on which cloth is made from threads

loop /luːp/ *noun*
a ring made by something like rope or string crossing itself: *She put a loop of rope around the cow's neck.*

loose /luːs/ *adjective*
1 not firmly fixed or joined: *My shirt button is loose.* I *There is a loose screw here.*
2 loose clothes are big and do not fit tightly: *These trousers are loose – I must have lost weight.* ➪ opposite (**1** and **2**) TIGHT
3 free from control: *The dog's loose.*

loos·en /ˈluːsn/ *verb*
to become less tight or make something less tight: *I need to loosen my belt after eating all that.* ➪ opposite TIGHTEN

lord /lɔːd/
1 a title in Britain for a man with high social rank

2 the Lord in CHRISTIANITY, God or Jesus Christ

lor·ry /ˈlɒrɪ/ *noun* (*plural* **lorries**)
a large vehicle for carrying heavy goods on the road ➪ same meaning TRUCK ➪ see picture on page 206

lose /luːz/ *verb* (*present participle* **losing**, *past* **lost** /lɒst/)
1 to not know where something is: *I've lost my watch.* ➪ opposite FIND
2 to not have something important that you had before: *He lost his job last week.*
3 to not win a game, argument, war, etc: *Our team lost the football match.* ➪ opposite WIN
4 to have less of something than before: *She has lost a lot of weight.*
5 **lose your temper** to become angry
6 **lose your way** to go in the wrong direction and not know where you are

los·er /ˈluːzəʳ/ *noun*
someone who loses

loss /lɒs/ *noun* (*plural* **losses**)
1 the act of losing something, or something that you have lost: *His death was a great loss to us.* I *The loss of her job was a shock.*
2 an amount of money that you have lost: *The company made a big loss this year.*

lost¹ /lɒst/
the past tense and past participle of the verb **lose**

lost² *adjective*
not knowing where you are: *He went for a walk and got lost.*

lost prop·er·ty /ˌlɒst ˈprɒpətɪ/ *noun* (no plural)
things that people have lost: *We went to the lost property office at the station.*

lot /lɒt/
a lot, lots a large amount or number: *There was a lot **of** mud on the ground.* I *I picked lots **of** flowers.* ➪ look at MUCH, MANY

lo·tion /ˈləʊʃn/ *noun*
a liquid that you put on your skin to make it soft or protect it: *Put this lotion on to stop your skin from being burned by the sun.*

lot·te·ry /ˈlɒtərɪ/ *noun* (*plural* **lotteries**)
a competition in which you can win a prize if you have a ticket with the right number on it

loud /laʊd/ *adjective*
making a lot of noise: *The radio's rather loud – please turn it down.* | *I heard a loud bang.* ⋄ opposite QUIET

loud·speak·er /laʊd'spiːkəʳ/ *noun*
something that makes your voice sound louder: *The police called to him through a loudspeaker.*

lounge /laʊndʒ/ *noun*
a room in a house or hotel with comfortable chairs

louse /laʊs/ *noun* (*plural* **lice** /laɪs/)
a small insect that lives on the skin and in the hair of people and animals

lou·sy /'laʊzɪ/ *adjective*
very bad: *What a lousy day I've had!*

lov·a·ble /'lʌvəbl/ *adjective*
easy to love: *She's a very lovable child.*

love[1] /lʌv/ *verb* (*present participle* **loving**, *past* **loved**)
1 to have the very strong feeling that you have for a member of your family: *Mothers and fathers love their children.*
2 to like someone very much in a romantic or sexual way: *I love you.*
3 to like something or enjoy doing something very much: *Maria loves reading.* | *I love chocolate.* ⋄ opposite HATE

love[2] *noun* (*no plural*)
1 the feeling you have for someone you love: *Her love **for** her husband kept her strong.* ⋄ opposite HATRED
2 when you like or enjoy something very much: *She has a great love **of** music.* ⋄ opposite HATRED
3 Love a word used at the end of a letter to someone you love or someone in your close family
4 fall in love to begin to love someone of the opposite sex: *He fell in love **with** a dancer.*

love af·fair /'lʌv ə,feəʳ/ *noun*
a romantic or sexual relationship between two people

love·ly /'lʌvlɪ/ *adjective*
beautiful, pleasant, or enjoyable: *You look lovely in that dress.* | *I need a lovely cool drink.* | *I had a lovely evening.*

lov·er /'lʌvəʳ/ *noun*
1 a person that you have a romantic or sexual relationship with
2 a person who enjoys something: *He is an art lover.*

lov·ing /'lʌvɪŋ/ *adjective*
showing that you love someone: *He gave her a loving kiss.*

low /ləʊ/ *adjective*
1 not high or not far above the ground: *The room had a low ceiling.* | *He threw the ball too low.*
2 small in number or amount: *Their prices are very low.* | *Temperatures in the west will be lower than yesterday.*
3 below an accepted standard: *She got a very low grade in English.*
4 not high in sound: *She has a low voice.* ⋄ opposite HIGH

low·er /'ləʊəʳ/ *verb*
to reduce something in amount, strength, etc: *We're lowering prices.* | *Can you lower your voice* (=speak less loudly), *please.* ⋄ opposite RAISE

lower case /,ləʊə 'keɪs/ *noun* (*no plural*)
letters written in their small form, for example a, b, d, g, r, etc ⋄ compare CAPITAL, UPPER CASE

low tide /,ləʊ 'taɪd/ *noun*
the time when the sea is very low and far from the shore ⋄ opposite HIGH TIDE ⋄ see picture at HIGH TIDE

loy·al /'lɔɪəl/ *adjective*
giving strong support to a person, idea, etc without changing the way you feel even if bad things happen: *She is a loyal friend.* | *He stays loyal **to** Arsenal Football Club.* ⋄ opposite DISLOYAL

loy·al·ty /'lɔɪəltɪ/ *noun* (*no plural*)
the quality of being loyal: *His loyalty **to** his friends is well known.*

LP /,el 'piː/ *noun*
a record that plays for about 25 minutes on each side

Ltd /'lɪmɪtɪd/
British used after the name of a company to show that the group of people who own it would not lose all their money if the company failed: *Jones Brothers Ltd*

luck /lʌk/ *noun* (*no plural*)
the good and bad things that happen to you by chance, especially good things: *Have you had any luck finding a job?* | ***Good** luck with your exam tomorrow.* | *We've had some **bad** luck recently.*

luck·y /'lʌkɪ/ *adjective*
having or bringing good luck: *If you're lucky, you might still get tickets.* | *You're*

lucky **to** *have such good friends.*
⇨ opposite UNLUCKY

lug·gage /'lʌgɪdʒ/ *noun (no plural)*
the bags, containers, and other things
you take with you when you travel

> NOTE: Remember that the noun
> **luggage** has no plural: *I've just got
> these two suitcases; that's all my
> luggage.* | *She didn't have much
> luggage.*

luke·warm /ˌluːkˈwɔːm/ *adjective*
not very warm but not cold

lump /lʌmp/ *noun*
1 a hard piece of something, without a
special shape: *A lump of clay was on
the table.*
2 a swelling on a person's body: *I've
got a lump on my head where I hit it on
the door.*

lump·y /'lʌmpɪ/ *adjective*
full of lumps, usually when you do not
want them: *I'm sleeping on a lumpy
bed.*

lu·na·tic /'luːnətɪk/ *noun*
someone who behaves in a very
strange and dangerous way: *You
lunatic! You nearly drove straight into
me.*

lunch /lʌntʃ/ *noun (plural* **lunches***)*
the meal that you eat in the middle of
the day: *Have you **had** lunch yet?*

lunch·time /'lʌntʃtaɪm/ *noun (no plural)*
the time at which you have lunch

lung /lʌŋ/ *noun*
one of the two parts inside your chest
with which you breathe

lurk /lɜːk/ *verb*
to wait in hiding, especially in order to
do something bad: *There's someone
lurking behind that bush.*

lux·u·ri·ous /lʌgˈzjʊərɪəs/ *adjective*
very comfortable and expensive

lux·u·ry[1] /'lʌkʃərɪ/ *noun*
1 *(no plural)* a very enjoyable situation
in which you are very comfortable or
have a lot of expensive things: *They live
in luxury in a very big house.*
2 *(plural* **luxuries***)* something that you
do not really need, but that is very
pleasant: *Foreign holidays are a real
luxury.*

luxury[2] *adjective*
very expensive and of very good quality:
a luxury hotel | *luxury cars*

ly·ing /'laɪ-ɪŋ/
the present participle of the verb **lie**

lyr·ics /'lɪrɪks/
the words of a popular song

A
B
C
D
E
F
G
H
I
J
K
L
M
N
O
P
Q
R
S
T
U
V
W
X
Y
Z

Mm

M, m /em/
1 the thirteenth letter of the English alphabet
2 a short way of writing the word **metre** or **metres**: *14m*

'm /m/ *verb*
am: *I'm hungry.* | *I'm a student.*

mac /mæk/ *noun*
British a MACKINTOSH

ma·chine /məˈʃiːn/ *noun*
an instrument made up of many parts, used to do particular work: *I have a new sewing machine.*

ma·chine-gun /məˈʃiːn gʌn/ *noun*
a gun that fires a lot of BULLETS very quickly

ma·chin·e·ry /məˈʃiːnəri/ *noun (no plural)*
machines, or the parts inside a machine: *The machinery is controlled by computers.*

mack·in·tosh /ˈmækɪntɒʃ/ *noun (plural* **mackintoshes**)
British also **mac** a light coat that keeps out the rain

mad /mæd/ *adjective*
1 extremely silly or dangerous: *No one would be mad enough to take a boat out in this weather.*
2 to make someone angry: *She was mad with him for being late.*
3 mentally ill
4 **mad about someone or something** liking someone or something very much: *He's mad about football.*
5 **drive someone mad** to annoy someone very much: *That noise is driving me mad.*
6 **like mad** very hard or fast: *If you run like mad, you might catch the train.* | *We've been working like mad to get the school play ready.*

mad·am /ˈmædəm/ *noun*
a polite way of speaking or writing to a woman who you do not know ⬦ look at YOURS

made /meɪd/
the past tense and past participle of the verb **make**

mad·ly /ˈmædli/ *adverb*
1 in a wild way: *She rushed madly from room to room.*
2 **be madly in love** to love someone very much in a romantic way

mag·a·zine /ˌmægəˈziːn/ *noun*
a book with paper covers containing stories, articles, and pictures, that you buy every week or every month ⬦ compare COMIC

ma·gic /ˈmædʒɪk/ *noun (no plural)*
1 a special power that makes strange or good things happen: *He turned the thread into gold by magic.*
2 clever or strange tricks done to entertain people

ma·gic·al /ˈmædʒɪkl/ *adjective*
1 very enjoyable in a special way: *It was a magical evening.*
2 done using magic: *He claimed to have magical powers.*

ma·gi·cian /məˈdʒɪʃn/ *noun*
a person who does clever or strange tricks to entertain people

mag·net /ˈmægnɪt/ *noun*
a piece of iron that draws other pieces of iron towards it

magnet

mag·net·ic /mægˈnetɪk/ *adjective*
having the power of a magnet

mag·nif·i·cent /mægˈnɪfɪsnt/ *adjective*
very good or beautiful: *What a magnificent building!*

mag·ni·fy /ˈmægnɪfaɪ/ *verb (present participle* **magnifying**, *past* **magnified**)
to make something look larger than it really is: *The photo shows the bacteria magnified 150 times.*

mag·ni·fy·ing glass /ˈmægnɪfaɪɪŋ ˌglɑːs/ *noun*
a curved piece of glass with a handle, that makes things appear larger than they really are

maid /meɪd/ *noun*
a woman who is paid to work in someone's house, for example cleaning or cooking

maid·en name /ˈmeɪdn ˌneɪm/ *noun*
the family name of a woman before she marries and takes her husband's name

mail /meɪl/ *noun (no plural)*
letters and parcels that you send by post ⇨ same meaning POST

main /meɪn/ *adjective*
most important: *The main road into town crosses the river. | Coffee is the country's main export.*

main·ly /ˈmeɪnli/ *adverb*
mostly: *That hospital is mainly for older people.*

main·tain /meɪnˈteɪn/ *verb*
1 to make something continue in the same way or to the same standard as before: *We need to maintain good relations with our customers..*
2 to keep something in good condition: *It is expensive to maintain an old house.*

main·te·nance /ˈmeɪntənəns/ *noun (no plural)*
keeping something in good condition: *He took a course to learn about car maintenance.*

maize /meɪz/ *noun (no plural)*
also **corn** a tall plant with yellow seeds that are used for food

ma·jes·tic /məˈdʒestɪk/ *adjective*
very big, important, or impressive: *We visited the majestic temples of Bangkok.*

ma·jes·ty /ˈmædʒəsti/ *noun (plural majesties)*
Your Majesty, Her Majesty, His Majesty used when you are talking to or about a king or queen: *Her Majesty the Queen will arrive at 10 o'clock.*

ma·jor¹ /ˈmeɪdʒəʳ/ *adjective*
very important or large: *Our car needs major repairs.* ⇨ opposite MINOR

major² *noun*
an officer in the army

ma·jor·i·ty /məˈdʒɒrəti/ *noun (no plural)*
most of the things or people in a group: *The majority of children in our class have brown eyes.* ⇨ opposite MINORITY

make /meɪk/ *verb (present participle making, past* **made** /meɪd/)
1 to produce something: *He made a model plane out of wood. | I'll make some coffee. | She's making a film for TV.* ⇨ look at DO
2 to do something: *We need to make a decision. | Billy made a mistake. | Can I make a suggestion?* ⇨ look at DO
3 to cause something to happen: *Sarah always makes me laugh. | Ice is making the roads dangerous. | That music makes me want to dance.*
4 to force someone to do something: *I don't like milk, but she made me drink it. | The teacher made me write the correct spelling twenty times.*
5 to earn: *I don't make enough money to have expensive holidays.*
6 to be a particular number or amount when added together: *Two and two make four. | If you include us, that makes eight people for lunch.*
7 **make the bed** to tidy a bed by making the sheets and covers straight
8 **make it** to arrive somewhere by the time you need to be there: *Even if we hurry we won't make it. | We just made it to the hospital on time.*
9 **make sure** to check something so that you can be sure: *Make sure you lock the door.*
10 **make something out** to see, hear, or understand something with difficulty: *I could just make out the shape of the house in the darkness. | Can you make out what the sign says?*
11 **make something up** to think of and tell other people a story that is not true: *He made up that story about being a policeman.*
12 **make up your mind** to decide something: *I've made up my mind to go to Spain this summer.*

make-up /ˈmeɪk ʌp/ *noun (no plural)*
substances that people put on their faces to make themselves look more attractive: *Ginny put on her make-up.*

ma·lar·i·a /məˈleəriə/ *noun (no plural)*
a serious illness caused by the bite of a MOSQUITO

male¹ /meɪl/ *adjective*
belonging to the sex that cannot have babies: *The male bird is brightly coloured.* ⇨ opposite FEMALE

male² *noun*
a male person or animal ⇨ opposite FEMALE

mam·mal /ˈmæml/ *noun*
an animal that drinks its mother's milk when it is young, for example a cow, a lion, or a human

A B C D E F G H I J K L M N O P Q R S T U V W X Y Z

man /mæn/ *noun*
1 (*plural* **men** /men/) a fully grown human male ⬦ compare WOMAN
2 (*plural* **men**) a human being: *Men have lived here for thousands of years.*
3 (*no plural*) all humans: *Man uses animals in many ways.*

man·age /'mænɪdʒ/ *verb* (*present participle* **managing**, *past* **managed**)
1 to succeed in doing something: *He managed to avoid an accident.* I *Jenny managed to pass her driving test the third time she tried.*
2 to control a business or activity: *The horse was difficult to manage.* I *He used to manage a rock band.*

man·age·ment /'mænɪdʒmənt/ *noun* (*no plural*)
1 the people who control a business or how they control it: *We're meeting the management tomorrow.* I *The failure was due to poor management.*
2 the control of something such as a business or money: *traffic management*

man·ag·er /'mænɪdʒər/ *noun*
someone who manages a bank, shop, restaurant, etc or who controls a group of people in a company

mane /meɪn/ *noun*
the long hair on the necks of some animals

man·go /'mæŋgəʊ/ *noun* (*plural* **mangoes**)
a sweet juicy yellow or green fruit with one large seed, from a tree that grows in hot countries

man·kind /mæn'kaɪnd/ *noun* (*no plural*)
all humans

man-made /,mæn 'meɪd/ *adjective*
made by people, not grown or produced in the earth: *Plastic is a man-made material.*

man·ner /'mænər/ *noun*
1 the way in which something is done or happens: *Why are you talking in such a strange manner?*
2 **manners** (*plural noun*) the way you behave and speak: *It's bad manners to eat like that.*

man·sion /'mænʃən/ *noun*
a large house

man·tel·piece /'mæntlpiːs/ *noun*
a shelf above the place where a fire is in a room

man·u·al [1] /'mænjʊəl/ *adjective*
done with your hands, not by machine: *manual work*

manual [2] *noun*
a book that tells you how to do something: *She bought a computer manual.*

man·u·fac·ture [1] /,mænjʊ'fæktʃər/ *verb* (*present participle* **manufacturing**, *past* **manufactured**)
to make things in large numbers in a factory using machines: *The company that manufactured the drug was based in Switzerland.*

manufacture [2] *noun* (*no plural*)
the making of things in large numbers

man·u·fac·tur·er /,mænjʊ'fæktʃərər/ *noun*
a company or industry that makes large quantities of goods: *The fridge was sent back to the manufacturers.*

man·y /'menɪ/ (**more, most**)
1 a large number of people, things, or places: *Not many of the children can read.* I *There aren't many tickets left.* I *You've eaten too many chocolates already.*
2 **How many?** used in questions asking about the number of people or things there are: *How many people were there?* I *How many brothers and sisters do you have?* ⬦ opposite FEW

map

reading a map

map /mæp/ *noun*
a drawing of a town, a country, or an area: *Have you got a map of Scotland?*

mar·ble /'mɑːbl/ *noun*
1 (*no plural*) a hard stone that can be made smooth and shiny and is used in making buildings
2 a small glass or stone ball used in a game

March /mɑːtʃ/ noun
the third month of the year

march[1] verb
1 to walk with regular steps like a soldier
2 to walk somewhere quickly: *She marched out of the room in anger.*

march[2] noun (plural **marches**)
an event in which many people walk together to complain about something: *They went on a march to protest against the war.*

mar·ga·rine /ˌmɑːdʒəˈriːn/ noun (no plural)
a soft food like BUTTER made from animal or vegetable fats

mar·gin /ˈmɑːdʒɪn/ noun
the space at each edge of a page without writing or printing

mark[1] /mɑːk/ noun
1 a spot or dirty area that spoils the appearance of something: *You have a mark on your shirt.*
2 a spot on the surface of something: *Our dog has a white mark on its ear.*
3 British a figure or letter given by a teacher to say how good someone's work is: *The teacher gave me a good mark for my essay.*

mark[2] verb
1 to put words or signs on something to give information about it: *The door was marked 'Private'.*
2 to read through a piece of work and say how good it is: *The teacher marked our examination papers.*
3 to put a spot or line on something, that spoils it: *She marked her dress sitting on the grass.*

mar·ket /ˈmɑːkɪt/ noun
1 a place, often outside, where many people come to buy and sell goods
2 **be on the market** to be ready to be sold: *Their house has been on the market for six months.*

mar·ma·lade /ˈmɑːməleɪd/ noun (no plural)
a kind of JAM usually made from oranges, that people sometimes eat at breakfast

mar·riage /ˈmærɪdʒ/ noun
1 the occasion when a man and woman become husband and wife in a legal ceremony: *The marriage took place in church.* ⇨ same meaning WEDDING
2 the relationship between a husband and wife: *They have had a long and happy marriage.*

mar·ried /ˈmærɪd/ adjective
1 having a husband or wife: *He is a married man.*
2 **get married** to become husband and wife in a legal ceremony: *They've just got married.*

mar·ry /ˈmæri/ verb (past **married**)
1 to become someone's husband or wife: *I am going to marry John.*
2 to perform the ceremony in which two people become husband and wife: *They were married by a priest.*

marsh /mɑːʃ/ noun (plural **marshes**)
an area of low wet soft ground

mar·vel·lous /ˈmɑːvələs/ adjective
extremely good or enjoyable: *It is a marvellous film.* ⇨ same meaning GREAT, FANTASTIC

mas·cu·line /ˈmæskjʊlɪn/ adjective
like a man or typical of a man: *He had a dark masculine face.* ⇨ opposite FEMININE

mash /mæʃ/ verb
to crush food to make it soft: *Mash the potatoes with a fork.* ⇨ see picture on page 198

mask /mɑːsk/ noun
a cover for all or part of your face: *The doctor wore a mask over his mouth and nose.*

mass /mæs/ noun (plural **masses**)
1 a large quantity of something with no special shape: *Before the rain, the sky was a mass of clouds.*
2 British a large number or amount of something: *I've got masses of homework.*

mas·sa·cre[1] /ˈmæsəkəʳ/ verb (present participle **massacring** /ˈmæsəkrɪŋ/, past **massacred**)
to kill a large number of people in a violent and cruel way

massacre[2] noun
the cruel killing of many people

mas·sive /ˈmæsɪv/ adjective
very large: *There was a massive ship on the ocean.* ⇨ same meaning HUGE, ENORMOUS

mass me·di·a /ˌmæs ˈmiːdɪə/ noun
all the newspapers, radio, and television that give news and information to the public

mast /mɑːst/ *noun*

1 a tall length of wood or metal that supports the sails of a ship

2 a metal post that sends out radio or television signals

mas·ter[1] /ˈmɑːstəʳ/ *noun*

1 a man in control of people or animals: *The dog obeyed his master.*

2 a man of great skill or ability: *The painting is the work of a master.*

master[2] *verb*

to learn how to do something well: *It takes years to master a new language.*

mat /mæt/ *noun*

a small piece of rough strong material used as a floor covering ⇨ compare CARPET, RUG

match[1] /mætʃ/ *noun*

1 a short stick of wood that produces a flame when you rub it against a rough surface: *I need a box of matches.*

2 a game or sports event: *We have a tennis match today.* | *Are you going to the football match?*

3 something that is the same size, shape, colour etc as something else: *That skirt's a perfect match for your blue skirt.*

match[2] *verb*

to be like something else in size, shape, colour, etc: *These shoes do not match my dress.* | *The carpet matches the curtains.*

mate[1] /meɪt/ *noun*

1 *British* a friend, or a person you work with: *He's a mate of mine.*

2 one of a male and female pair of animals or birds

mate[2] *verb* (*present participle* **mating**, *past* **mated**)

when animals mate they have sex to produce babies: *Birds mate in the spring.*

ma·te·ri·al /məˈtɪəriəl/ *noun*

1 anything from which something can be made: *Building materials are expensive.*

2 (*no plural*) cloth used for making clothes, curtains etc: *I used some blue cotton material to make the curtains.* ⇨ same meaning FABRIC

math·e·mat·i·cal /ˌmæθəˈmætɪkl/ *adjective*

relating to or using mathematics

math·e·mat·ics /ˌmæθəˈmætɪks/ *noun*

also **maths** the study or science of numbers, shapes, etc

maths /mæθs/ *noun*

mathematics

mat·i·nee /ˈmætɪneɪ/ *noun*

an afternoon showing of a play or film

mat·ter[1] /ˈmætəʳ/ *noun*

1 an important event or subject that you must think about or deal with: *I have an important matter to talk to you about.* | *You do realize this is a serious matter, don't you.* | *I'm not very interested in financial matters.*

2 What's the matter? What is wrong?: *What's the matter **with** the radio?* | *What's the matter – are you ill?*

3 as a matter of fact used when you are giving a surprising or unexpected answer to someone: *"Do you know Liz?" "Yes, as a matter of fact we're cousins."*

4 no matter used when you are having difficulty changing a situation: *No matter how hard she pulled, the door would not open.* | *We'll finish the job no matter how long it takes.*

5 (*no plural*) the material that everything is made of

matter[2] *verb*

to be important: *It doesn't matter if I miss this bus, I can walk.* | *Money is the only thing that matters to him.*

mat·tress /ˈmætrəs/ *noun* (*plural* **mattresses**)

the large soft part of a bed that you lie on

ma·ture[1] /məˈtjʊəʳ/ *adjective*

behaving in a responsible way like an adult: *She's very mature for her age.* ⇨ opposite IMMATURE

mature[2] *verb* (*present participle* **maturing**, *past* **matured**)

1 to become fully grown or developed

2 to begin to behave in a responsible way like an adult: *Pat's matured since going to college.*

max·i·mum[1] /ˈmæksɪməm/ *adjective*

the maximum amount, quantity, speed, etc is the largest that is possible or allowed: *What's the car's maximum speed?* ⇨ opposite MINIMUM

maximum[2] *noun*

the largest amount, number, size, etc that is possible: *I can swim a maximum of one mile.* ⇨ opposite MINIMUM

May /meɪ/ *noun*
the fifth month of the year

may *verb*
1 used to show that something is possible but is not sure to happen: *He may come tonight, or he may wait until tomorrow.* | *We may not have enough money to buy tickets.*
2 to be allowed to do something: *Please may we go home now?* | *May I borrow your pen?*

may·be /'meɪbɪ/ *adverb*
used to say that something may be true or may happen: *"Are you coming to the party?" "Maybe – I don't know yet."* | *Maybe Anna has already left.* ⇨ same meaning PERHAPS

mayor /meəʳ/ *noun*
someone who is elected to lead the government of a city or town

me /miː/
1 the person who is speaking: *She handed the book to me.* | *Can you see me?*
2 me too used when you agree with someone: *"I'm hungry." "Me too."*

meal /miːl/ *noun*
the food you eat at one time, or the time that it is eaten: *We always* **have** *a meal together in the evening.*

mean¹ /miːn/ *verb (past* **meant** /ment/*)*
1 to have a particular meaning: *What does this mean in English?* | *The red light means stop.*
2 mean to do something to plan or want to do something: *I meant to give you this book today, but I forgot.* | *She didn't mean to upset you.*
3 mean a lot to someone to be very important to someone: *His work means a lot to him.*

mean² *adjective*
1 *British* not willing to spend money: *He's so mean he didn't even get his son a birthday present.* ⇨ opposite GENEROUS
2 unkind: *Don't be mean to your little sister.*

mean·ing /'miːnɪŋ/ *noun*
what you should understand from something you see, read, or hear: *A dictionary is a book that gives the meanings* **of** *words.*

means /miːnz/ *noun (plural* **means**)
1 a way of doing something, or a thing used to do something: *We'll use any means we can to find the money.* | *The car is her main means of transport.*
2 by all means used to say that you are very willing for something to happen: *"May I borrow your paper?" "By all means."*
3 by no means not at all: *The results are by no means certain.*
4 the money that someone has and can use: *He wants to go to college, but his family haven't the means to help him.*

meant /ment/
the past tense and past participle of the verb **mean**

mean·time /'miːntaɪm/ *noun (no plural)*
in the meantime in the time between two things happening or while something is happening: *I'll phone for a taxi and in the meantime you pack your case.*

mean·while /'miːnwaɪl/ *adverb*
in the time before something happens or while something else is happening: *They'll arrive in a few minutes. Meanwhile, we'll have a cup of tea.*

mea·sure¹ /'meʒəʳ/ *noun*
1 an amount of something, or a way of measuring size, weight, etc: *A metre is a measure of length.*
2 an official action for dealing with a problem: *Strong measures are needed to stop crime.*

measure

measure² *verb (present participle* **measuring***, past* **measured***)*
to find out the size, weight, or amount of something: *He measured the width of the room.*

mea·sure·ment /'meʒəmənt/ *noun*
a number showing how long, tall, wide, etc something is

meat /miːt/ *noun (no plural)*
the parts of an animal's body used as food: *I gave up eating meat a few months ago.*

me·chan·ic /mɪˈkænɪk/ *noun*
a person who has trained to make or repair machines ⇨ see picture on page 200

me·chan·i·cal /mɪˈkænɪkl/ *adjective*
relating to machines or done by machine: *The car needs repairing – it has a mechanical problem.*
mechanically /-klɪ/ *adverb*: *Most of the work is done mechanically.*

medal

med·al /ˈmedl/ *noun*
a piece of metal, usually round or shaped like a cross, given to honour someone who has done something special

med·i·cal /ˈmedɪkl/ *adjective*
relating to medicine and the job of treating people who are ill: *He is a medical student.*

medi·cine /ˈmedsɪn/ *noun*
1 (*no plural*) the study of treating and understanding illnesses
2 something that you drink or eat when you are ill, to help you to get better

me·di·um /ˈmiːdɪəm/ *adjective*
of middle size or amount: *She is of medium height.* ⇨ see picture on page 202

meet /miːt/ *verb* (*past* **met** /met/)
1 to be in the same place at the same time as someone else and to speak to them: *I met my teacher in the street today.* | *Let us meet at your house tonight.*
2 to see and talk to someone for the first time: *I would like you to meet my father.*

meet·ing /ˈmiːtɪŋ/ *noun*
an occasion when people meet to talk about something: *Many people came to the meeting.*

mel·o·dy /ˈmelədɪ/ *noun* (*plural* **melodies**)
a song or tune

mel·on /ˈmelən/ *noun*
a large juicy fruit with a thick green or yellow skin ⇨ see picture on page 199

melt /melt/ *verb*
to change from a solid to a liquid by heat: *The ice is melting in the sun.* | *Melt the chocolate in a pan.*

mem·ber /ˈmembər/ *noun*
a person who belongs to a group, club, or organization: *He is a member of the football team.*

Mem·ber of Par·lia·ment /ˌmembər əv ˈpɑːləmənt/ *noun* (*plural* **Members of Parliament**)
also **MP** a person who has been elected to speak in Parliament for a particular area of the country

mem·ber·ship /ˈmembəʃɪp/ *noun* (*no plural*)
the fact of being a member of a group or organization, or all the people who are members: *Membership costs £20 a year.*

mem·o·ry /ˈmemərɪ/ *noun* (*plural* **memories**)
1 (*no plural*) the ability to remember things: *She has a good memory for faces.*
2 something that you can remember from the past: *I have happy memories of that summer.*

men /men/
the plural of **man**

men·ace /ˈmenɪs/ *noun*
someone or something that causes danger or is annoying: *The insects are a menace in the summer.*

mend

mending an ornament

mend /mend/ *verb*
to repair or fix something that is broken or damaged: *Can you mend the hole in my shirt, Mum?* ⇨ compare REPAIR

men·tal /'mentl/ *adjective*
1 done with your mind: *This will need a lot of mental effort.*
2 relating to illness of the mind: *She works in a mental hospital*
mentally *adverb*: *He is mentally ill.*

men·tion /'menʃən/ *verb*
to speak or write about something in a few words with no details: *On the telephone he mentioned that he had been ill.*

men·u /'menjuː/ *noun*
1 a list of food that you can choose to eat in a restaurant
2 a list of different choices shown on a computer

mer·cy /'mɜːsɪ/ *noun (no plural)*
kind treatment, and being willing not to punish someone: *The man asked for mercy from the judge.*

mere·ly /'mɪəlɪ/ *adverb*
only: *Don't get angry with me – I was merely making a suggestion.*

mer·it [1] /'merɪt/ *noun*
a good quality

merit [2] *verb*
to deserve something: *His work merits a prize.*

mer·maid /'mɜːmeɪd/ *noun*
a creature in children's stories with the body of a girl and the tail of a fish

mer·ri·ly /'merɪlɪ/ *adverb*
in a happy way: *They were laughing merrily.*

mer·ry /'merɪ/ *adjective* (**merrier, merriest**)
happy and having fun: *Have a merry Christmas!*

merry-go-round

merry-go-round /'merɪ gəʊ ˌraʊnd/ *noun*
a big machine that children can ride on for pleasure while it turns round and round

mess [1] /mes/ *noun*
1 when a place looks dirty and untidy: *Your room is in a mess.* | *Don't make a mess in the kitchen.*
2 a situation in which there are a lot of problems and difficulties: *His personal life is a mess.*

mess [2] *verb*
1 **mess something up** to make something dirty or untidy: *I've just cleaned the floor, and you've messed it up again!*
2 **mess about, mess around** to play or do silly things instead of working: *Stop messing about and finish your work.*

mes·sage /'mesɪdʒ/ *noun*
a piece of information that one person sends to another: *There's a message **for** you **from** your Mum.* | *"Janet just phoned." "Did she leave a message?"*

mes·sen·ger /'mesɪndʒəʳ/ *noun*
someone who takes messages to other people

mess·y /'mesɪ/ *adjective* (**messier, messiest**)
1 untidy or dirty: *What a messy room!*
2 a messy situation is difficult and unpleasant to deal with: *They had a messy divorce!*

met /met/
the past tense and past participle of the verb **meet**

met·al /'metl/ *noun*
a hard substance such as iron, tin, gold, etc

me·tal·lic /mə'tælɪk/ *adjective*
made of metal or like metal: *The car was painted metallic blue.*

me·ter /'miːtəʳ/ *noun*
a machine used for measuring the amount of something used: *an electricity meter* | *The taxi driver turned off his meter and said "£5.40 please".*

meth·od /'meθəd/ *noun*
a way of doing something: *We use new methods **of** teaching languages.* | *What method **of** payment do you use?*

me·tre /'miːtəʳ/ *noun*
a measure of length equal to 100 CENTIMETRES: *The room was 4 metres long.*

met·ric /'metrɪk/ *adjective*
using the system of measuring that uses metres, grams, and litres

mi·aow[1] /mɪˈaʊ/ *verb*
to make the long high sound that a cat makes

miaow[2] *noun*
the long high sound that a cat makes

mice /maɪs/
the plural of the word **mouse**

mi·cro·phone /ˈmaɪkrəfəʊn/ *noun*
a piece of equipment used to record sounds or make them louder

mi·cro·scope /ˈmaɪkrəskəʊp/ *noun*

microscope

an instrument that helps you to see very small things by making them look much bigger: *She looked at some cells **under** a microscope.*

mi·cro·wave /ˈmaɪkrəweɪv/ *noun*
a machine that cooks food very quickly using electrical waves instead of heat

mid·day /ˌmɪdˈdeɪ/ *noun (no plural)*
twelve o'clock in the middle of the day: *She arrived just before midday.* ⇨ same meaning NOON

middle[1] /ˈmɪdl/ *noun*
the centre of something: *Please stand **in the** middle **of** the room.* | *I woke in the middle of the night.* | *Look at this old photo – that's me in the middle.*

middle[2] *adjective*
in the centre: *There are three shops there – the baker's is the middle one.* | *Shall we sit in the middle row?*

middle-aged /ˌmɪdl ˈeɪdʒd/ *adjective*
between about 40 and 60 years old

middle school /ˈmɪdl skuːl/ *noun*
a school in Britain for children between the ages of 8 and 12

mid·night /ˈmɪdnaɪt/ *noun (no plural)*
12 o'clock at night

might[1] /maɪt/ *verb*
1 the past tense of the verb **may**: *I asked if I might borrow the book.* | *I thought it might rain, so I took an umbrella.*
2 used to show that something is possible, but is not sure to happen: *I might come and see you tomorrow.* | *I*

might be wrong but I think he's French. | *He might not be able to go.*

might[2] *noun (no plural)*
strength and power: *He tried with all his might to open the door, but it stayed shut.*

might·y /ˈmaɪti/ *adjective* (**mightier, mightiest**)
strong and powerful: *He gave it a mighty push and it fell.*

mi·grate /maɪˈɡreɪt/ *verb (present participle* **migrating**, *past* **migrated**)
1 birds and fish that migrate travel to a warmer part of the world in winter and return in spring
2 to move in large numbers from one place to another: *People migrate to find work.*

mi·gra·tion /maɪˈɡreɪʃn/ *noun*
moving to another place: *Many people study the migration of birds.*

mild /maɪld/ *adjective*
1 not too severe or serious: *He's got a mild cold.*
2 mild weather is not very cold or very hot: *It's mild today.*
3 mild food is not strong in taste: *I had a mild curry.* ⇨ opposite HOT

mile /maɪl/ *noun*
a measure of length equal to 1760 yards or 1.6 kilometres

mil·i·tary /ˈmɪlɪtri/ *adjective*
used by the army, navy, etc or relating to war: *He works in a military hospital.*

milk[1] /mɪlk/ *noun (no plural)*
the white liquid that comes from female animals as food for their babies: *We drink cows' milk.* | *I'd like a glass of milk.* | *Would you like some milk in your coffee?*

milk[2] *verb*
to get milk from an animal: *They use a machine to milk the cows.*

milk·man /ˈmɪlkmən/ *noun (plural* **milkmen** /-mən/)
in Britain, a person who takes milk to people's houses each morning

mill /mɪl/ *noun*
1 a place where wheat and other crops are made into flour
2 a large factory where things such as cloth are made on machines: *She works in a cotton mill.*

mil·len·ni·um /mɪˈleniəm/ *noun*
a period of time equal to 1000 years, or

the time when a new 1000-year period begins

mil·li·me·tre /ˈmɪlɪmiːtəʳ/ noun
a measure of length equal to 1/1000 of a metre: 60 millimetres

mil·lion /ˈmɪljən/ noun
1 (plural million) the number 1,000,000
2 millions a very large number: I've heard that song millions of times.

mil·lion·aire /ˌmɪljəˈneəʳ/ noun
a person who is very rich

mime¹ /maɪm/ verb (present participle miming, past mimed)
to entertain people by using actions and movements instead of words to tell a story

mime² noun (no plural)
the use of movements without words to tell a story: He's really good at mime.

mim·ic¹ /ˈmɪmɪk/ verb (present participle mimicking, past mimicked)
to copy someone's speech or actions in order to make people laugh: He mimicked the teacher's voice.

mimic² noun
a person who is good at copying the way someone else speaks and moves

mince¹ /mɪns/ verb (present participle mincing, past minced)
to cut food up into very small pieces

mince² noun (no plural)
British meat that has been cut into very small pieces: Add the mince to the pan with the onions.

mind¹ /maɪnd/ noun
1 your thoughts or the part of your brain used for thinking and imagining things: Her mind is full of dreams about becoming famous. | I keep going over the problem in my mind.
2 change your mind to decide to do something different: I was going to leave tomorrow but I've changed my mind.
3 make up your mind to decide: I can't make up my mind which film to go and see.
4 take your mind off something to make you stop thinking about something: I need a holiday to take my mind off all my problems.
5 out of your mind mentally ill or behaving very strangely

mind² verb
1 to be annoyed or upset about

something: Do you mind if I smoke? | It was raining but we didn't mind.
2 not mind doing something to be willing to do something: I don't mind driving if you're tired.
3 do you mind, would you mind a polite way of asking someone to do something: Do you mind if I use your phone. | Would you mind moving your bag, please?
4 Mind out! used to warn someone to get out of the way of something dangerous: Mind out – there's a car coming!
5 never mind used to tell someone not to worry, or that something is not important: "I've just broken a glass." "Never mind – they weren't expensive." | "I'm sorry I'm so late." "Never mind – we haven't started yet."

mine¹ /maɪn/
something that belongs to the person speaking: That bicycle is mine; I bought it yesterday. | Can I borrow your radio? Mine's broken.

mine² noun
1 a deep hole in the ground from which people dig out coal, iron, gold, etc
2 a kind of bomb that is put just under the ground or in the sea and explodes when it is touched

mine³ verb (present participle mining, past mined)
1 to dig something out of the ground: They were mining for silver.
2 to put bombs in the ground or the sea

min·er /ˈmaɪnəʳ/ noun
a person who works under the ground digging out coal, iron, gold, etc

min·e·ral /ˈmɪnərəl/ noun
1 a natural substance like iron, coal, or salt that has formed under the ground
2 a substance such as iron or CALCIUM that is found naturally in some foods and is good for your health

mineral wa·ter /ˈmɪnərəl ˌwɔːtəʳ/ noun (no plural)
water that comes from under the ground and has minerals in it

min·ia·ture /ˈmɪnətʃəʳ/ adjective
very small: There is a miniature railway for the children to ride on.

min·i·mum¹ /ˈmɪnɪməm/ noun
the smallest possible amount, number,

or size: *You must get **a** minimum **of** 40 questions right to pass the examination.* | *What's the minimum I can pay a month?* ⇨ opposite MAXIMUM

min·i·mum² *adjective*
the minimum number or amount is the smallest that is possible or needed: *The minimum pass mark in the examination is 40 out of 100.* ⇨ opposite MAXIMUM

min·is·ter /'mɪnɪstər/ *noun*
1 an important person in the government
2 a Christian priest

min·is·try /'mɪnɪstrɪ/ *noun* (*plural* **ministries**)
a part of the government: *She works in the Ministry **of** Defence.*

mi·nor /'maɪnər/ *adjective*
small and not very important: *We made a few minor changes to the plan.* | *She had minor injuries.* ⇨ opposite MAJOR

mi·nor·i·ty /maɪ'nɒrətɪ/ *noun* (*plural* **minorities**)
a small part of a larger group: *Only a minority **of** the children were noisy; the rest were quiet.* ⇨ opposite MAJORITY

mint /mɪnt/ *noun*
1 a type of sweet
2 (*no plural*) a plant with a strong fresh smell and taste used in cooking

mi·nus /'maɪnəs/
less: *10 minus 2 is 8 (10 – 2 = 8).* ⇨ compare PLUS

min·ute¹ /'mɪnɪt/ *noun*
1 a period of time equal to 60 seconds. There are 60 minutes in an hour: *The plane will land **in** fifteen minutes.* | *The train arrived at four minutes **past** eight.* | *It's three minutes **to** ten.*
2 **in a minute** very soon: *I'll be ready in a minute*
3 **just a minute** used to ask someone to wait for a short period of time: *Just a minute – I'll get some money.*
4 **this minute** used to tell someone to do something immediately: *Come here this minute!*

mi·nute² /maɪ'njuːt/ *adjective*
very small: *His writing is minute.* ⇨ same meaning TINY

mir·a·cle /'mɪrəkl/ *noun*
1 something lucky that happens that you did not expect or think was possible: *It was a miracle you weren't killed!*

2 an action or event that does not seem possible and that people believe is caused by God

mi·rac·u·lous /mɪ'rækjʊləs/ *adjective*
surprising and very good: *Her recovery from the illness was miraculous.*

miraculously *adverb*: *Miraculously, no one was killed.*

mir·ror /'mɪrər/ *noun*
a flat piece of glass with a shiny back in which you can see yourself: *She looked at herself **in the** mirror.*

mis·be·have /ˌmɪsbɪ'heɪv/ *verb* (*present participle* **misbehaving**, *past* **misbehaved**)
to behave badly: *The teacher was angry because the children were misbehaving.*

mis·chief /'mɪstʃɪf/ *noun* (*no plural*)
bad behaviour, especially by children: *She was a lively child and full of mischief.*

mis·chie·vous /'mɪstʃɪvəs/ *adjective*
a mischievous child behaves badly but not in a way that makes people angry: *She's a mischievous little girl.*

mis·e·ra·ble /'mɪzrəbl/ *adjective*
1 very unhappy: *I'm feeling miserable. I'm tired, cold, and very hungry.*
2 making people unhappy: *What miserable weather!*

mis·e·ry /'mɪzərɪ/ *noun* (*no plural*)
great unhappiness: *The programme showed the misery of the people who had lost their homes in the fire.*

mis·for·tune /mɪs'fɔːtʃən/ *noun*
bad luck or something bad that happens to you: *He had the misfortune to lose his job.*

Miss /mɪs/ *noun* (*plural* **Misses**)
the title of a girl or woman who is not married: *Have you seen Miss Johnson?* ⇨ compare MRS, MS

miss /mɪs/ *verb*
1 to feel sad when someone is not there: *We shall all miss you when you go away.* | *I really missed Paula after she had left.*
2 to not do or not have something: *I'll have to miss the meeting tomorrow.* | *I'm really hungry – I missed breakfast.*
3 to arrive too late to catch a bus, train, etc: *Hurry or we'll miss the train.*
4 to not hit or catch something: *He*

threw the ball to me, but I missed it and it landed on the ground. I He shot at me but missed.

5 miss something out to not include something: *You've missed your telephone number out. I I hope we haven't missed out anyone on the list.*

mis·sile /ˈmɪsaɪl/ *noun*
something that is thrown or fired to harm or damage something else: *Bottles and other missiles were thrown at the police.*

miss·ing /ˈmɪsɪŋ/ *adjective*
not in the correct place and not able to be found: *A book is missing from my desk. I Police are still searching for the missing child.*

mis·sion·ary /ˈmɪʃənri/ *noun (plural* **missionaries)**
a person who goes to another country to teach others about his or her religion

mist /mɪst/ *noun*
thin cloud near the ground: *There was a mist over the river.* ⇨ compare FOG

mis·take [1] /mɪˈsteɪk/ *noun*
1 something that is not correct: *You have made a mistake here – this 3 should be 5.*
2 by mistake without planning to do something: *Jake took his dad's pen by mistake.*

mistake [2] *verb (present participle* **mistaking,** *past* **mistook** /mɪˈstʊk/, *past participle* **mistaken** /mɪˈsteɪkən/)
1 to think that something is correct when it is not: *I was mistaken when I told you she was a teacher. She's a doctor.*
2 mistake someone for someone else to wrongly think that one person is a different person: *I am sorry; I mistook you for someone I know.*

mist·y /ˈmɪsti/ *adjective*
having a lot of thin cloud near the ground: *It was a misty morning.* ⇨ compare FOGGY

mit·ten /ˈmɪtn/ *noun*
a piece of clothing to cover your hand, with one part to cover your four fingers and another part for your thumb ⇨ compare GLOVE

mix /mɪks/ *verb*
1 to put different things together to make something new: *Mix the butter and flour together. I Oil and water don't mix.* ⇨ see picture on page 198

2 mix someone up with to think that a person is someone else: *It's easy to mix him up with his brother.*
3 mix things up to change the way things are arranged so that there is no order: *Someone has mixed up my papers.*

mix·ture /ˈmɪkstʃər/ *noun*
a number of different things or people put together: *This tea is a mixture of two different types. I People are a mixture of good and bad.*

mm
the short way of writing the word **millimetre** or **millimetres**: *60 mm*

moan [1] /məʊn/ *verb*
to make a low sound of pain: *The child lay moaning gently.*

moan [2] *noun*
a low sound of pain: *He gave a moan of pain.*

mo·bile phone
/ˌməʊbaɪl ˈfəʊn/ *noun*
a telephone that you can carry with you

mobile phone

mock /mɒk/ *verb*
to laugh unkindly at someone: *You shouldn't mock the way he walks.*

mod·el [1] /ˈmɒdl/ *noun*
1 a small copy of something: *He is making a model of an aeroplane.*
2 a person who wears new clothes at special shows or for photographs so that people will see the clothes and want to buy them ⇨ see pictures at ARTIST and on page 200

model [2] *verb (present participle* **modelling,** *past* **modelled)**
to do the job of wearing new clothes at special shows or for photographs so that people will see the clothes and want to buy them: *Kate is modelling a black leather suit designed by Armani.*

model [3] *adjective*
a model car, train, etc is a very small copy of a car, train, etc: *He was painting his model soldiers.*

mo·dem /ˈməʊdem/ *noun*
a piece of electronic equipment that sends information from one computer along a telephone wire to another computer

mod·e·rate /'mɒdərət/ *adjective*
neither high nor low, fast nor slow, large nor small: *The train travelled at a moderate speed.* | *We're looking for a house with a moderate-sized garden.*

mod·ern /'mɒdn/ *adjective*
new and in the style that is popular now: *She was reading a book about modern history.* | *I like modern art.* ⇨ opposite OLD-FASHIONED

mod·est /'mɒdɪst/ *adjective*
not talking too much about the things that you do well: *She is very modest about the prizes she has won.*

moist /mɔɪst/ *adjective*
slightly wet: *His eyes were moist with tears.*

mois·ture /'mɔɪstʃə^r/ *noun (no plural)*
small drops of water: *The sun dries the moisture on the ground.*

mole /məʊl/ *noun*
1 a small animal that lives in holes under the ground
2 a small round dark spot on someone's skin

mol·e·cule /'mɒlɪkjuːl/ *noun*
the smallest part into which a substance can be broken without changing its form

mole·hill /'məʊl hɪl/ *noun*
a small pile of earth thrown up by a MOLE when it is digging

mo·ment /'məʊmənt/ *noun*
1 a very short time: *I'll be back in a moment.* | *She paused for a moment before answering.*
2 at any moment very soon: *He might come back at any moment.*
3 at the moment now: *At the moment I have a very good job.*
4 for the moment happening now, but not definitely happening in the future: *The rain has stopped for the moment.*

mon·arch /'mɒnək/ *noun*
a king or queen

mon·ar·chy /'mɒnəki/ *noun (plural monarchies)*
a country that is ruled by a king or queen

mon·as·tery /'mɒnəstri/ *noun (plural monasteries)*
a place where MONKS live

Mon·day /'mʌndeɪ, -di/ *noun*
the first day of the week after Sunday and before Tuesday

mon·ey /'mʌni/ *noun (no plural)*
1 coins and paper notes that have a fixed value and are used for buying and selling things: *I haven't got much money.* | *She spends a lot of money on clothes.*
2 make money to earn money or make a profit: *John's business is making a lot of money.*

mon·i·tor /'mɒnɪtə^r/ *noun*
a piece of equipment with a screen that shows information or pictures from a computer

monk /mʌŋk/ *noun*
one of a group of men who live together and have given their lives to a religion ⇨ compare NUN

mon·key /'mʌŋki/ *noun*
an animal that is like a small person in shape but has a long tail and lives in trees

mo·not·o·nous /mə'nɒtənəs/ *adjective*
always the same and never interesting: *My job is rather monotonous.*

mon·soon /mɒn'suːn/ *noun*
the heavy rain that falls at a particular time of year in parts of Asia

mon·ster /'mɒnstə^r/ *noun*
a large ugly frightening creature in stories

month /mʌnθ/ *noun*
one of the 12 parts into which a year is divided ⇨ look at TIME

month·ly /'mʌnθli/ *adjective, adverb*
happening every month or once a month: *We have a monthly meeting.*

mon·u·ment /'mɒnjʊmənt/ *noun*
something that is built to help people to remember an important person or event

moo /muː/ *verb*
to make the noise that a cow makes

mood /muːd/ *noun*
the way you feel at any one time: *She is in a good mood (=feeling happy).* | *Why are you in such a bad mood (=feeling annoyed)?*

moon /muːn/ *noun*
the large round object that shines in the sky at night ⇨ compare SUN

moon·light /'muːnlaɪt/ *noun (no plural)*
the light from the moon

moor[1] /mʊəʳ/ noun
an area of open land covered with rough grass or low bushes

moor[2] verb
to tie up a boat

mop[1] /mɒp/ noun
a long stick with thick threads on the end that you use to wash the floor ⇨ see picture on page 204

mop[2] verb (present participle **mopping**, past **mopped**)
to wash the floor using a wet mop

mo·ped /ˈməʊped/ noun
a vehicle with two wheels and a small engine

moped

riding a moped

mor·al[1] /ˈmɒrəl/ adjective
relating to what is right and wrong: He believes we have a moral duty to help the poor.

moral[2] noun
1 a lesson about what is right and wrong that you learn from a story or an event: The moral of the story was that we should be kind to other people.
2 **morals** (plural noun) the set of ideas about what is right and wrong that you use when deciding how to live your life

more[1] /mɔːʳ/ adverb
1 to a greater degree: This book is much more interesting than his last one. | Could you speak more quietly? ⇨ opposite LESS
2 happening for longer or more often: She goes out more now that she has a car. ⇨ opposite LESS
3 **not any more** no longer happening or true: They don't live here any more.
4 **once more** again: Read that page once more, please.

more[2]
1 a larger amount or number: We spend more of our money on food these days. | In some bars orange juice costs more **than** beer. ⇨ opposite LESS
2 another thing or amount added to what you have already: Would you like some more tea? | I have to make a few more phone calls.
3 **more and more** continuing to become greater in amount: He got more and more angry.
6 **more or less** about or almost: The holiday will cost £600, more or less.

morn·ing /ˈmɔːnɪŋ/ noun
the time from when the sun rises until the middle part of the day ⇨ compare AFTERNOON, EVENING, NIGHT

Mos·lem /ˈmɒzləm/ noun
also **Muslim** a follower of the religion that believes in the teachings of Mohammed as written in the Koran

mosque /mɒsk/ noun
a building in which Muslims worship

mosque

mos·qui·to /məˈskiːtəʊ/ noun (plural **mosquitoes**)
a flying insect that drinks blood from people and animals and can carry illnesses from one person to another

moss /mɒs/ noun (no plural)
a bright green plant that grows in a thick mass on wet ground, trees, and stones

most[1] /məʊst/ adverb
1 used before many adjectives and adverbs to show that something is the best, worst, biggest, smallest, etc: Anna is one of the most beautiful girls I know. | I forgot to tell you the most important thing.
2 more than anyone or anything else: I like dark chocolate most. | I love all my family, but I love my Mum most **of all**. ⇨ opposite LEAST

most[2]
1 almost all of a group of people or things: Most people go on holiday in July and August. | Most **of** the kids I know love ice cream.

NOTE: Use **most** when you are talking about people or things in general: Most children like sweets. | Most people have a television. Use **most of** when you are talking about a particular group of people or things: Most of the people he works with are friendly. | I've read most of her books.

A B C D E F G H I J K L M N O P Q R S T U V W X Y Z

2 more than anyone or anything else: *Ricardo's restaurant gives you the most food for your money.* | *Whoever scores most will win.* ⇨ opposite LEAST

3 at most, at the most not more than a particular amount or number: *It will take an hour at the most.*

4 make the most of something to use something in the best way possible: *We've only got two days here – let's make the most of them.*

most·ly /ˈməʊstlɪ/ *adverb*
1 usually: *When I go to London, it's mostly on business.*
2 almost all: *The people at the party were mostly students.*

moth /mɒθ/ *noun*
an insect like a BUTTERFLY that flies at night

moth·er /ˈmʌðəʳ/ *noun*
a female parent: *Her mother is a teacher.*

mother-in-law /ˈmʌðər ɪn lɔː/ *noun*
(*plural* **mothers-in-law**)
the mother of your wife or husband

mo·tion /ˈməʊʃn/ *noun* (*no plural*)
the process of moving or the way that something moves: *You must not get off the train when it is in motion.*

mo·tion·less /ˈməʊʃnləs/ *adjective*
not moving: *The cat sat motionless, waiting for the mouse to move.*

mo·tive /ˈməʊtɪv/ *noun*
a reason for doing something: *Police are questioning everyone who had a motive for killing the man.*

mo·tor /ˈməʊtəʳ/ *noun*
an engine that makes things move or work

motorbike

riding a motorbike

mo·torbike /ˈməʊtəbaɪk/ *noun*
a large heavy vehicle with two wheels worked by an engine ⇨ see picture on page 206

mo·tor·boat /ˈməʊtəbəʊt/ *noun*
a small boat with an engine

mo·tor·cy·cle /ˈməʊtəsaɪkl/ *noun*
also **motorbike** a large heavy vehicle with two wheels worked by an engine

mo·tor·ist /ˈməʊtərɪst/ *noun*
a person who drives a car

mo·tor·way /ˈməʊtəweɪ/ *noun*
in Britain, a wide road built for vehicles to travel fast for long distances

mould [1] /məʊld/ *noun*
1 (*no plural*) a greenish-white substance that grows on old food and in cold wet buildings
2 a container that you pour liquid into so that the liquid will take its shape when it becomes solid: *a jelly mould* ⇨ see picture at FROZEN

mould [2] *verb*
to make something into a particular shape: *You can mould clay with your fingers.*

mould·y /ˈməʊldɪ/ *adjective* (**mouldier, mouldiest**)
covered with mould: *The bread has **gone** (=become) mouldy.*

mound /maʊnd/ *noun*
a pile of earth that looks like a small hill

Mount /maʊnt/ *noun*
used in the names of mountains: *Mount Everest is the highest mountain in the world.*

mount *verb*
1 also **mount up** to become larger in size or amount
2 to get onto a horse or bicycle

mountain

peak

moun·tain /ˈmaʊntɪn/ *noun*
a very high hill: *There were mountains in the distance.* ⇨ see picture on page 193

mountain bike /ˈmaʊntɪn baɪk/ *noun*
a strong bicycle with wide thick tyres

mourn /mɔːn/ *verb*
to be very sad because someone you

love has died: *She mourned for her dead child.*

mourn·ing /'mɔːnɪŋ/ *noun (no plural)*
1 a feeling of great sadness because someone has died
2 in mourning dressed in black clothes or behaving in a way that shows how sad you are at someone's death

mouse /maʊs/ *noun (plural* **mice** /maɪs/)
a small animal with a long tail that lives in houses or in fields ⇨ compare RAT

mous·tache /mə'stɑːʃ/ *noun*
the hair that grows above a man's mouth ⇨ compare BEARD ⇨ see picture on page 202

mouth /maʊθ/ *noun*
1 the opening in your face through which you speak and take in food ⇨ see picture at HEAD
2 the place where a river meets the sea

mouth·ful /'maʊθfʊl/ *noun*
the amount of food or drink that fills your mouth at one time: *That was a wonderful meal. I enjoyed every mouthful.*

move /muːv/ *verb (present participle* **moving**, *past* **moved**)
1 to change from one position or place to another: *Sit still and don't move.* | *She could hear someone moving **around** in the kitchen.*
2 to change the position of something or to take something from one place and put it in another: *I can't move my legs.* | *Could you move your car, please?*
3 to go to a new place to live or work: *He has moved to New York.* | *I moved **house** (=went to live in a different house) last week.*
4 move in to start to live in a new home: *We should be able to move in next week.*
5 move out to leave the home you have been living in in order to live somewhere else: *Mr Smith moved out last week.*

move·ment /'muːvmənt/ *noun*
a change in position from one place to another: *Suddenly I saw a movement behind the curtain.* | *The dancer's movements were very graceful.*

mov·ie /'muːvi/ *noun*
American a story that is told using

ound and moving pictures, shown in a cinema or on television (*British* **film**)

mow /məʊ/ *verb (present participle* **mowing**, *past* **mowed**, *past participle* **mown** /məʊn/)
to cut grass with a machine

MP /ˌem 'piː/ *noun*
also **Member of Parliament** a person who has been elected to speak in Parliament for a particular area of the country

MP3 /ˌem piː 'θriː/ *noun*
a piece of music on the INTERNET that you can put on your own computer

Mr /'mɪstər/ *noun*
a word put before a man's name: *This is Mr Brown.*

Mrs /'mɪsɪz/ *noun*
a word put before a married woman's name: *This is Mrs Brown.* ⇨ compare MISS, MS

Ms /mɪz, məz/ *noun*
a word put before the name of a woman who does not wish to call herself 'Miss' or 'Mrs': *My name is Ms Smith.*

much¹ /mʌtʃ/
1 by a large amount: *She's much cleverer than I am.* | *Dad's feeling much better now.* | *The fair this year was much more fun than last year.* | *He is not much older* (=only slightly older) *than I am.*
2 very much used to emphasize something you are saying: *Thank you very much.*
3 more than you need or want: *He talks too much.*
4 not much not very often: *I don't see her much because she lives so far away.*

much²
1 a lot or a large amount of something: *We haven't got much time.* | *Do you get much chance to travel in your job?*

NOTE: **Much** (1) is used in questions and in negative sentences: e.g. *How much does it cost?* | *It doesn't cost much.* For other types of sentences use **a lot of** instead: *It cost a lot of money.* | *He has a lot of work to do.*

2 how much used to ask about the amount or cost of something: *How much milk is left?* | *I wonder how much that shirt costs.*

3 as much as the same amount as someone or something: *We haven't got as much money as the Browns.*

mud /mʌd/ *noun* (*no plural*)
wet earth that is soft and sticky

mud·dle [1] /'mʌdl/ *noun*
having everything mixed up and in the wrong place: *She was in such a muddle she couldn't even remember what day it was.*

muddle [2] *verb* (*present participle* **muddling** , *past* **muddled**)
1 to put everything in the wrong place: *My papers were all muddled.*
2 to make someone think that they do not understand something: *All these different instructions just muddle me.*

mud·dy /'mʌdɪ/ *adjective* (**muddier** , **muddiest**)
covered with wet earth: *Take those muddy boots off!*

mues·li /'mjuːzlɪ/ *noun* (*no plural*)
a breakfast food of nuts, grain, and fruit that you eat with milk

mug /mʌg/ *noun*
a big cup with straight sides ⇨ see picture at CUP

mule /mjuːl/ *noun*
an animal that has a DONKEY and a horse as parents

mul·ti·ply /'mʌltɪplaɪ/ *verb* (*present participle* **multiplying** , *past* **multiplied**)
to add a number to itself a particular number of times. For example, 2 multiplied by 3 is 6 (2 x 3 = 6) ⇨ compare DIVIDE

mum /mʌm/ *noun*
British a word you call your mother: *Mum, can I borrow some money?* | *My mum's a teacher.*

mum·ble /'mʌmbl/ *verb* (*present participle* **mumbling** , *past* **mumbled**)
to speak in a way that is difficult to hear or understand: *He mumbled something to me but I couldn't hear what he said.*

mum·my /'mʌmɪ/ *noun* (*plural* **mummies**)
British a word for mother used by and to children

mumps /mʌmps/ *noun* (*no plural*)
an illness that causes swelling in the neck

mur·der [1] /'mɜːdər/ *verb*
to kill a person on purpose when it is against the law ⇨ compare KILL

murder [2] *noun*
the crime of killing someone on purpose

mur·der·er /'mɜːdərər/ *noun*
a person who kills someone on purpose when it is against the law ⇨ compare KILLER

mur·mur [1] /'mɜːmər/ *verb*
to speak very softly: *The child murmured in her sleep.*

murmur [2] *noun*
a soft low sound made by someone's voice: *She answered in a low murmur.*

mus·cle /'mʌsl/ *noun*
one of the parts of your body under your skin that make you strong and help you to move

mu·se·um /mjuːˈziːəm/ *noun*
a building in which you can see old, interesting, or beautiful things: *the Museum of Modern Art*

mush·room /'mʌʃruːm/ *noun*
a brown plant with a short stem and round top that can be eaten ⇨ see picture on page 199

mu·sic /'mjuːzɪk/ *noun* (*no plural*)
1 the pleasant sounds made by voices or by instruments: *What kind of music do you like?* | *That's my favourite **piece of** music.*
2 a set of written marks representing music

mu·sic·al /'mjuːzɪkl/ *adjective*
1 relating to music: *The shop sells musical instruments.*
2 good at singing or playing music: *She is very musical.*

mu·si·cian /mjuːˈzɪʃn/ *noun*
a person who plays an instrument or writes music

Mus·lim /'mʊzlɪm/ *noun*
also **Moslem** a follower of the religion that believes in the teachings of Mohammed as written in the Koran

must /məst; *strong* mʌst/ *verb*
1 used with another verb to show what is necessary or what has to be done: *I must go or I'll be late.* | *All passengers must wear seatbelts.*
2 used to show that you think something is very likely or definite: *It is very late; it must be nearly midnight.* |

I can't open the door – somebody must have locked it.

mus·tard /'mʌstəd/ *noun* (no plural)
a hot-tasting yellow SAUCE, usually eaten with meat

must·n't /'mʌsnt/ *verb*
must not: *You mustn't be late for school.* | *You mustn't tell anyone – it's a secret.*

must've /'mʌstəv/
must have: *Jane doesn't seem to be here. She must've left.*

mut·ter /'mʌtəʳ/ *verb*
to speak in a low voice that is difficult to hear: *He's always muttering to himself.*

my /maɪ/
belonging to the person speaking: *I hurt my knee when I fell off my bicycle.* | *I tried not to let my feelings show.*

my·self /maɪˈself/
1 the same person as the one who is speaking: *I looked at myself in the mirror.* | *I made myself a cup of coffee.*
2 used to give the word 'I' a stronger meaning: *I made this shirt myself.*

mys·te·ri·ous /mɪˈstɪərɪəs/ *adjective*
very strange, and difficult to explain or understand: *He died suddenly of a mysterious illness.*

mys·te·ry /'mɪstərɪ/ *noun* (plural **mysteries**)
a strange thing that is difficult to explain or understand: *"Who had taken the money?" "It was a mystery."*

A
B
C
D
E
F
G
H
I
J
K
L
M
N
O
P
Q
R
S
T
U
V
W
X
Y
Z

N, n /en/

the fourteenth letter of the English alphabet

nag /næg/ *verb* (*present participle* **nagging**, *past* **nagged**)

to keep complaining to someone because you want them to do something: *Stop nagging me! I'll tidy my room later.*

nail¹ /neɪl/ *noun*

1 a thin pointed piece of metal with one flat end that you use to join pieces of wood together ⇨ compare SCREW

2 one of the hard flat parts at the end of your fingers and toes: *Stop biting your nails!*

nail² *verb*

to fasten or fix something with a nail: *Will you nail the sign on the door?*

na·ked /ˈneɪkɪd/ *adjective*

not wearing any clothes: *The children ran around the garden naked.* ⇨ same meaning NUDE

name¹ /neɪm/ *noun*

1 the word that you use when speaking to or about a person or thing: *My name is Jane Smith. | What is the name of this town?*

2 make a name for yourself to become well known: *She's made a name for herself as an artist.*

name² *verb* (*present participle* **naming**, *past* **named**)

to give a name to someone or something: *They named the baby Ann.*

name·ly /ˈneɪmlɪ/ *adverb*

that is: *There is only one problem, namely how to get more money.*

nan·ny /ˈnænɪ/ *noun* (*plural* **nannies**)

a woman who is paid to live with a family and look after the children

nap /næp/ *noun*

a short sleep during the day: *He always has a nap in the afternoon.*

nap·kin /ˈnæpkɪn/ *noun*

a square of cloth or paper used at meals to keep your clothes, hands, and mouth clean

nap·py /ˈnæpɪ/ *noun* (*plural* **nappies**)

British a piece of cloth or thick paper that a baby wears between its legs and round its bottom (*American* **diaper**): *The baby has a wet nappy – will you change it?*

narrow

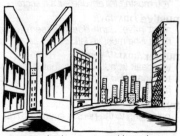

a narrow street   a wide road

nar·row /ˈnærəʊ/ *adjective*

small from one side to the other: *The gate is too narrow for cars to go through.* ⇨ opposite WIDE

nas·ty /ˈnɑːstɪ/ *adjective* (**nastier**, **nastiest**)

1 not pleasant to see, taste, smell, etc: *This medicine has a nasty taste.*

2 not kind in behaviour: *Don't be nasty to your sister.* ⇨ same meaning HORRIBLE

na·tion /ˈneɪʃn/ *noun*

all the people belonging to a country and living under its government: *The whole nation supported the government. | The show features artists from 90 different nations.*

na·tion·al /ˈnæʃnəl/ *adjective*

of or belonging to a country: *Next Monday is a national holiday.*

national an·them /ˌnæʃnəl ˈænθəm/ *noun*

the official song of a country, sung on special days and occasions: *Rise, please, for the national anthem.*

na·tion·al·i·ty /ˌnæʃəˈnælətɪ/ *noun* (*plural* **nationalities**)

the fact of belonging to a particular country: *London attracts visitors of many different nationalities.*

na·tive¹ /ˈneɪtɪv/ *noun*

a person born in the place you are talking about: *Mary is a native of Australia.*

native [2] *adjective*
your native country, town etc is the place where you were born: *She's a native of Australia.*

nat·u·ral/'nætʃərəl/ *adjective*
1 not made by people or machines: *Cotton is a natural fabric.*
2 usual or expected: *It's natural to feel nervous before an exam.* ⇨ same meaning NORMAL

nat·u·ral·ly/'nætʃərəli/ *adverb*
1 not made or caused by anyone: *Her hair is naturally straight.*
2 without looking or sounding different from usual: *She talked quite naturally even though she was frightened.*
3 as you would expect: *Naturally you must talk to your parents before you decide.* ⇨ same meaning OF COURSE

na·ture/'neɪtʃər/ *noun*
1 (*no plural*) the world and everything in it that people have not made, for example weather, plants, and animals: *These mountains are one of nature's loveliest sights.*
2 the character of a person or thing: *Peter has a happy nature.* | *It was not in his nature to be cruel.*

naugh·ty/'nɔːti/ *adjective* (**naughtier, naughtiest**)
used about children who are not well behaved: *Don't do that, you naughty boy!*
naughtily *adverb*: *He's been behaving very naughtily.*

na·val/'neɪvl/ *adjective*
connected with the ships that are used in war: *That is a South African naval vessel.*

nav·i·gate/'nævɪgeɪt/ *verb* (*present participle* **navigating** *past* **navigated**)
to find the direction a ship or car should go in, using a map or other instruments: *He navigated the plane through the low cloud.*

nav·i·ga·tion/ˌnævɪ'geɪʃn/ *noun* (*no plural*)
when you decide which direction to go in or which road to take when you are travelling somewhere: *Navigation is difficult on the river because of the rocks.*

nav·i·ga·tor/'nævɪgeɪtər/ *noun*
the person on a ship or plane who plans and says where it should go

na·vy/'neɪvi/ *noun* (*plural* **navies**)
the part of a country's military organization that uses ships for fighting: *My son is in the navy.* ⇨ compare ARMY, AIRFORCE

navy blue/ˌneɪvi 'bluː/
a dark blue colour

near/nɪər/ *adjective, adverb, preposition*
not far: *Our school is very near.* | *My aunt lives quite near.* | *He sat in a chair near the window.*

near·by/nɪə'baɪ/ *adjective, adverb*
close to a place: *We swim in a nearby river.* | *Is the school nearby?*

near·ly/'nɪəli/ *adverb*
1 almost: *We have nearly finished.*
2 **not nearly** not at all: *I haven't got nearly enough money to buy the shoes I want.*

neat/niːt/ *adjective*
1 clean and well arranged: *She always kept her room neat and tidy.*
2 careful and tidy: *He has nice neat writing.*
neatly *adverb*: *Her mattress and blankets were neatly rolled up.*

neat·ness/'niːtnəs/ *noun* (*no plural*)
the quality of being neat: *He believed in order, method, neatness in everything.*

ne·ces·sa·ry/'nesəsri, 'nesəseri/ *adjective*
which you need or must have: *Good food is necessary **for** good health.* ⇨ opposite UNNECESSARY
necessarily *adverb*: *Change is not necessarily a bad thing.*

ne·ces·si·ty/nə'sesəti/ *noun* (*plural* **necessities**)
something that you need or must have, for example food: *We are giving them basic necessities such as flour, sugar, and salt.*

neck/nek/ *noun*
1 the part of your body between your head and shoulders ⇨ see picture at HEAD
2 the narrow part at the end of something: *the neck of a bottle*
3 **up to your neck in something** involved with something that is difficult or unpleasant: *The President is up to his neck in the country's troubles.*

neck·lace/'nekləs/ *noun*
a piece of jewellery that you wear

A
B
C
D
E
F
G
H
I
J
K
L
M
N
O
P
Q
R
S
T
U
V
W
X
Y
Z

around your neck ⇨ see picture at
JEWELLERY

need¹ /niːd/ noun
  1 something that you want or must
  have: *The needs of a very small baby
  are simple.*
  2 in need without enough food or
  money: *We're collecting money for
  children in need.*
  3 in need of something wanting or
  needing something: *After working so
  hard I felt in need of a good holiday.*

need² verb
  1 to want something that is necessary:
  *I need a hammer and some nails to
  mend this chair.*
  2 need to do something to have to
  do something because it is necessary:
  *You need to see a doctor as soon as
  you can.*
  **3 need not do something, needn't
  do something** used when saying that it
  is not necessary to do something: *You
  needn't phone me until next week.*

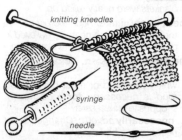

needles

knitting kneedles

syringe

needle

nee·dle /ˈniːdl/ noun
  1 a thin piece of pointed metal with a
  hole at one end for thread, used to SEW
  something
  2 a long thin pointed piece of plastic or
  metal used to make clothes from wool:
  I bought a pair of knitting needles.

need·less /ˈniːdləs/ adjective
  needless to say as expected:
  *Needless to say, it rained the day we
  wanted to go for a walk.*

need·n't /ˈniːdnt/ verb
  need not: *You needn't do it if you don't
  want to.*

neg·a·tive¹ /ˈnegətɪv/ adjective
  saying or meaning 'no': *He gave me a
  negative answer.*

negative² noun
  the piece of film from which a
  photograph can be made

ne·glect¹ /nɪˈglekt/ verb
  to not give enough attention or care to
  someone or something: *The animals
  were thin and ill because the farmer had
  neglected them.*

neglect² noun (no plural)
  when someone or something does not
  get enough attention or care: *He was
  shocked at my neglect of my parental
  duties.*

ne·glect·ed /nɪˈglektɪd/ adjective
  not well cared for or looked after:
  *Families in the area offered to adopt the
  neglected animals.*

ne·go·ti·ate /nɪˈgəʊʃieɪt/ verb
  to talk about something in order to
  reach an agreement: *The government
  has failed to negotiate an agreement.*

neigh¹ /neɪ/ verb
  to make the long loud sound that a
  horse makes

neigh² noun
  the long loud sound that a horse
  makes

neighbour

neighbours talking over the garden fence

neigh·bour /ˈneɪbər/ noun
  someone who lives near you: *He's a
  loving family man and a kind and
  considerate neighbour.* | *I'll borrow a
  ladder from my next-door neighbour.*

neigh·bour·hood /ˈneɪbəhʊd/ noun
  the small area around a place and the
  people living there: *You will find several
  shops in the neighbourhood.*

neigh·bour·ing /ˈneɪbərɪŋ/ adjective
  near to a place: *There's a bus going to
  the town and the neighbouring villages.*

nei·ther /ˈnaɪðər, ˈniːðər/
  1 not one and not the other of two
  people or things: *Neither boy could
  swim, but they both wanted to learn.*
  2 used in negative expressions when

you are saying that two or more things are not true: *He wanted grandchildren but neither his son **nor** his daughter had given him any.*

neph·ew /'nefju:/ *noun*
the son of your brother or sister ⇨ compare NIECE

nerve /nɜ:v/ *noun*
1 a very small part in your body like a thread that carries feelings and messages to and from your brain
2 nerves great excitement and worry: *She's always full of nerves before a race.*
3 get on someone's nerves to make someone annoyed: *That loud music is really getting on my nerves.*

ner·vous /'nɜ:vəs/ *adjective*
1 worried or afraid: *She's nervous **about** travelling alone.*
2 related to the nerves in your body: *The disease can damage the heart and nervous system.*

nest /nest/ *noun*
the home built by a bird or by some animals and insects: *We had a swallow's nest in the garden.*

net /net/ *noun*
1 (*no plural*) material with open spaces between knotted thread, string, or wire: *There were net curtains at the window.*
2 a piece of this material used for a particular purpose: *a football net* I *a fishing net*

net·ball /'netbɔ:l/ *noun* (*no plural*)
a game usually played by seven girls or women in which a ball is thrown into two high rings at opposite ends of a court

net·tle /'netl/ *noun*
a wild plant with leaves that can hurt you

net·work /'netwɜ:k/ *noun*
a large group of lines, wires, etc that cross or meet each other: *This is one of a network of canals that run off the Saigon River.*

neu·tral [1] /'nju:trəl/ *adjective*
not supporting any of the countries or people who are in a war or argument: *Iran remained neutral in the Gulf war.*

neutral [2] *noun*
the position of the GEARS of a car when the engine does not turn the wheels: *Start the car **in** neutral.*

nev·er /'nevər/ *adverb*
not ever or not at any time: *I'll never forget her kindness.* I *My brother never lets me ride his bicycle.* ⇨ opposite ALWAYS

nev·er·the·less /ˌnevəðə'les/ *adverb*
but or yet: *It is safer to wear seat belts when driving. Nevertheless, many people do not wear them.* I *In August, we'll mark the 800th anniversary of the birth of a little-known but nevertheless interesting Scottish king, Alexander II.*

new /nju:/ *adjective*
1 recently made, bought, or thought of: *We've got a new car.* I *He'll bring a lot of new ideas to the job.* ⇨ opposite OLD
2 not seen, known, or experienced before: *I'm learning a new language – Russian.* I *He's starting at his new school on Tuesday.*
3 new to something without a lot of experience or knowledge of something: *I'm new to the Web, so I'm just finding my way around.*

new·com·er /'nju:kʌmər/ *noun*
a person who has recently come to a place or has recently started an activity: *She's a newcomer to the city.*

new·ly /'nju:li/ *adverb*
recently: *The house was newly built.*

news /nju:z/ *noun* (*used with a singular verb*)
information about things that have just happened: *We can listen to the news on the radio.* I *Have you any news of your family?*

news·a·gent /'nju:zeɪdʒənt/ *noun*
1 a person who has a shop selling newspapers and magazines: *I buy sweets and magazines from the newsagent round the corner.*
2 newsagent's a shop selling newspapers, magazines, and sweets

news·pa·per /'nju:speɪpər/ *noun*
a set of sheets of paper containing news and advertisements, that is sold every day or week: *I always buy an evening newspaper.*

New Year's Day /ˌnju: jɪəz 'deɪ/ *noun*
January 1st

New Year's Eve /ˌnju: jɪəz 'i:v/ *noun*
December 31st

next[1] /nekst/ *adjective*
   1 nearest: *There was music coming from the next room.*
   2 coming after the present one: *I'll see you next week.*

next[2] *adverb*
   1 just after something: *What did he do next?*
   2 used when you are talking about the following part in a story or instructions: *He packed his bag, and next he put on his coat.*
   3 beside: *Come and sit next to me.*

next-door /ˌnekst ˈdɔːr/ *adjective*
   in the next room or building: *I get on well with my next-door neighbours.*

nib /nɪb/ *noun*
   the pointed part of a pen out of which the ink comes

nib·ble /ˈnɪbl/
   verb (*present participle* **nibbling**, *past* **nibbled**)
   to take small bites of food: *She was nibbling a piece of bread.*

nibble

nibbling some cheese

nice /naɪs/
   adjective (**nicer, nicest**)
   1 pleasant or good: *Have a nice time at the party.* | *It was a nice summer's day.*
   2 kind and friendly: *What a nice person!*
   nicely *adverb*: *He was nicely dressed.*

nick·name /ˈnɪkneɪm/ *noun*
   a name given informally to someone that is not their real name: *John's nickname is 'Tiny' because he is very small.*

niece /niːs/ *noun*
   the daughter of your brother or sister
   ⇨ compare NEPHEW

night /naɪt/ *noun*
   1 the time when it is dark and the sun cannot be seen: *It rained during the night.* | *Nurses often have to work at night.*
   2 the evening: *We're going to a play on Saturday night.*
   3 by night during the night: *In the desert they travelled by night.*
   4 the other night a few nights ago

night·ie /ˈnaɪti/ *noun*
   a type of loose dress that women and girls wear in bed

night·mare /ˈnaɪtmeər/ *noun*
   a dream that makes you very afraid: *I had the same terrible nightmare again and again.*

night-time /ˈnaɪt-taɪm/ *noun*
   the time each day when it is dark
   ⇨ opposite DAYTIME

night watch·man /ˌnaɪt ˈwɒtʃmən/ *noun*
   a person who guards buildings at night

nil /nɪl/ *noun*
   nothing or zero: *Their team won the game four–nil (=4–0).*

nine /naɪn/
   the number 9

nine·teen /naɪnˈtiːn/
   the number 19

nine·teenth /naɪnˈtiːnθ/ *adjective*
   19th

ninet·i·eth /ˈnaɪnti-əθ/ *adjective*
   90th

nine·ty /ˈnaɪnti/
   the number 90

ninth /naɪnθ/ *adjective*
   9th

nip /nɪp/ *verb* (*present participle* **nipping** *past* **nipped**)
   to bite someone: *Your dog has just nipped my leg!*

no /nəʊ/ *adverb*
   1 used to refuse something, to show that something is not true, or that you do not agree with something. It can also be used to accept or agree with a negative statement: *"Would you like some tea?" "No, thanks."* | *"Is that where you're working now?" "No, I'm with the medical team."* | *"Don't forget." "No dear, I won't."*
   2 not any: *There are no children in the classroom.*

no·ble /ˈnəʊbl/ *adjective* (**nobler, noblest**)
   1 belonging to an old important family
   2 showing courage to help others: *I understand that I am asking a lot of you, but I believe it is in a noble cause.*

no·bod·y /ˈnəʊbədi/
   also **no one** no person: *I knocked on*

*the door but nobody answered. |
Nobody liked him.*

nod[1] /nɒd/ *verb (present participle*
nodding, *past* **nodded**)
to bend your head forward and then up,
to show that you agree or as a greeting:
*She nodded when I asked if she liked
the film.*

nod[2] *noun*
a movement of your head forward and
then up: *He greeted me with a nod.*

noise /nɔɪz/ *noun*
a sound, often loud and unpleasant:
*Planes make a lot of noise. | My car's
making strange noises.* ⇨ compare
SOUND

nois·i·ly /'nɔɪzɪlɪ/ *adverb*
in a way that makes a lot of noise: *He
put his book down noisily.*

nois·y /'nɔɪzɪ/ *adjective*
making a lot of noise: *"What a noisy
class you are!" said the teacher.*
⇨ opposite QUIET

no·mad /'nəʊmæd/ *noun*
a member of a group of people who
travel about instead of living in one
place

no·mad·ic /nəʊ'mædɪk/ *adjective*
not living in one place, but moving from
one place to another

none /nʌn/
not any: *None of the pupils knew the
answer. | I've eaten all the bread and
there is none left.*

non·sense /'nɒnsəns/ *noun (no plural)*
1 something that has no sense or
meaning: *You're talking nonsense.*
2 a word you use if you strongly believe
that something is silly or not true: *"This
book is too difficult for me." "Nonsense!"*

non-stop /,nɒn 'stɒp/ *adjective, adverb*
without stopping: *We took a non-stop
flight from London to Singapore.*

noo·dles /'nuːdlz/ *plural noun*
long thin pieces of food made from flour,
water, and eggs, that you cook by
boiling them in water: *a plate of noodles*

noon /nuːn/ *noun (no plural)*
12 o'clock in the middle of the day: *At
noon, the sun is high in the sky.* ⇨ same
meaning MIDDAY

no one /nəʊ wʌn/
also **nobody** no person: *There's no one
I'd ever tell this to, except you.*

nor /nɔːʳ/
a word used between two choices after
the words neither or not: *Neither Anna
nor Maria likes cooking.*

nor·mal /'nɔːml/ *adjective*
usual or expected: *It's normal to feel
tired after working so hard.*

nor·mal·ly /'nɔːməlɪ/ *adverb*
usually: *Normally I get up at seven
o'clock, but today I got up at nine
o'clock. | The village shop was full of
customers on a normally quiet public
holiday.*

north /nɔːθ/ *noun, adjective, adverb*
the direction that is on the left when you
look towards the rising sun: *Manchester
is in the north of England. | The north
part of the house doesn't get a lot of
sun. | Birds fly north in summer.*

north-east /,nɔːθ 'iːst/ *noun, adjective,
adverb*
the direction that is in the middle
between north and east: *the forests of
north-east Amazonia*

north-east·ern /,nɔːθ 'iːstən/ *adjective*
in or from the north-east part of a
country or area: *a city in north-eastern
Uganda*

north·ern /'nɔːðən/ *adjective*
in or from the north part of a country or
area: *We're going on holiday in northern
Italy.*

North Pole /,nɔːθ 'pəʊl/ *noun*
the most northern point of the Earth

north-west /,nɔːθ 'west/ *noun,
adjective, adverb*
the direction that is in the middle
between north and west

north-west·ern /,nɔːθ 'westən/
adjective
in or from the north-west part of a
country or area

nose /nəʊz/ *noun*
1 the part of your face through which
you breathe and with which you smell
⇨ see picture at HEAD
2 turn up your nose at something to
think that something is not good or
important enough for you
3 under someone's nose right in
front of someone: *I looked for my pen
everywhere and it was under my nose
all the time!*

nos·tril /ˈnɒstrɪl/ *noun*
one of the two holes in your nose through which you breathe ⇨ see picture at HEAD

not /nɒt/ *adverb*
used to make a word or statement have the opposite meaning: *I'm not going home now.* | *It's red, not pink.*

note¹ /nəʊt/ *noun*
1 a single sound in music
2 a short written message: *I'll write a note to thank her for the party.*
3 a few words written down to help you remember something: *Please make a note of my new address.*
4 a piece of paper money: *I handed her a ten pound note.*

note² *verb (present participle* **noting**, *past* **noted)**
1 to pay attention to something so that you remember it: *Please note that the shop will close on Saturdays.*
2 note something down to write something down so that you remember it: *He noted down our new address.*

note·book /ˈnəʊtbʊk/ *noun*
a book in which you write things that you need to remember ⇨ see picture on page 205

note·pa·per /ˈnəʊtˌpeɪpəʳ/ *noun*
paper for writing letters on: *He tore off a sheet of notepaper.*

noth·ing /ˈnʌθɪŋ/
1 not any thing: *There is nothing in this box – it's empty.* | *She said nothing about her holiday.*
2 for nothing for no money: *If you buy the table, you can have the chairs for nothing.*

no·tice¹ /ˈnəʊtɪs/ *noun*
a written or printed paper that is put in a public place and gives information to people: *The notice on the door said that the library was closed.*

notice² *verb (present participle* **noticing**, *past* **noticed)**
to see, hear, or smell something: *The prisoner noticed that the door was open and ran away.* | *Did you notice the funny smell in the room?*

no·tice·a·ble /ˈnəʊtɪsəbl/ *adjective*
easily recognized or seen: *The hole in your trousers is not noticeable – no one will see it.*

notice board

notice board /ˈnəʊtɪs ˌbɔːd/ *noun*
a board fixed to a wall on which you put notices telling people about things: *I read on the notice board that I had passed my exams.* ⇨ see picture on page 205

no·to·ri·ous /nəˈtɔːrɪəs/ *adjective*
famous because of being so bad: *He was a notorious criminal.*

nought /nɔːt/ *noun*
the number 0: *When we write a thousand (1000), we write three noughts after the one.* ⇨ look at O

noun /naʊn/ *noun*
a word that is the name of a person, place, animal, thing, quality, or idea. In the sentence 'The boy threw a stone at the dog', 'boy', 'stone', and 'dog' are nouns

nov·el /ˈnɒvl/ *noun*
a long written story, usually about characters or events that are not real: *I have written the first five chapters of my novel.*

nov·el·ist /ˈnɒvəlɪst/ *noun*
a person who writes novels

No·vem·ber /nəʊˈvembəʳ/ *noun*
the 11th month of the year

now /naʊ/ *adverb*
1 at the present time: *We used to live in a village, but now we live in a city.* | *I must go now – I can't wait any longer.*
2 used to get someone's attention or to start talking about something else: *Now, children, open your books at page 6.*

no·where /ˈnəʊˌweəʳ/ *adverb*
not anywhere: *We looked for the key everywhere but it was nowhere to be found (=we couldn't find it anywhere).* | *He had nowhere to sleep, so he slept on the street.*

nu·cle·ar /'njuːklɪə^r/ *adjective*
relating to or using the power made by splitting or joining atoms: *We must do everything to avoid nuclear war.* | *They're building a nuclear power plant in the north.*

nu·cle·us /'njuːklɪəs/ *noun* (*plural* **nuclei** /'njuːklɪaɪ/)
the central part of something, for example, an atom

nude /njuːd/ *adjective*
not wearing any clothes ⇨ same meaning NAKED

nudge¹ /nʌdʒ/ *verb* (*present participle* **nudging**, *past* **nudged**)
to push someone lightly, usually with your elbow: *She nudged me when it was time to go.*

nudge² *noun*
a gentle push, usually given with your elbow: *He gave her a nudge.*

nui·sance /'njuːsns/ *noun* (*no plural*)
someone or something that makes you annoyed or worried: *What a nuisance! I've missed my train.*

numb /nʌm/ *adjective*
not able to feel anything: *My feet were numb with cold.*

num·ber¹ /'nʌmbə^r/ *noun*
1 a figure such as 1, 2, or 3
2 a group of numbers that you use to telephone someone: *Can you give me her number?*
3 more than one person or thing in a group: *Birds gather in large numbers beside the river.*
4 a number of several: *A number of people asked me where I had bought my hat.*

number² *verb*
to give a figure or number to something: *Number the pages from 1 to 100.*

numb·ered /'nʌmbəd/ *adjective*
with a number: *Seats in a cinema are usually numbered.*

number-plate /'nʌmbə ˌpleɪt/ *noun*
a sign at the front and back of a vehicle that shows its number: *The number-plate was F360 XJB.*

nu·me·ral /'njuːmərəl/ *noun*
a sign used to represent a number. For example 3, 11, and 29 are numerals

nu·me·rous /'njuːmərəs/ *adjective*
many: *Your work has numerous mistakes in it.*

nun /nʌn/ *noun*
one of a group of women who live together and have given their lives to a religion ⇨ compare MONK

nurse¹ /nɜːs/ *noun*
a person, often a woman, who is trained to help doctors and look after people who are ill or old: *She works as a nurse in a hospital.* ⇨ see picture on page 200

nurse² *verb* (*present participle* **nursing**, *past* **nursed**)
to care for sick people: *She nursed her mother when she was ill.*

nur·sery /'nɜːsrɪ/ *noun* (*plural* **nurseries**)
1 a place where young children are taken care of while their parents are at work
2 the room in a house in which young children play and sleep

nursery rhyme /'nɜːsrɪ ˌraɪm/ *noun*
a short well-known song for young children

nursery school /'nɜːsrɪ skuːl/ *noun*
a school for young children between three and five years old

nut /nʌt/ *noun*
1 the dried fruit of a tree, with a hard shell
2 a shaped piece of metal with a hole in it that is used with a BOLT to fasten things together

ny·lon /'naɪlɒn/ *noun* (*no plural*)
a strong material, made by machines, and used to make clothes: *She was dressed in a blue nylon nightdress.*

A B C D E F G H I J K L M N O P Q R S T U V W X Y Z

O, o /əʊ/

1 the fifteenth letter of the English alphabet

2 used in speech to represent the number zero, for example when you are giving a telephone number: *The number is 60275* (=six o two seven five)

oak /əʊk/ *noun*

1 a big tree with hard wood

2 (*no plural*) the wood of this tree: *an oak table*

oar /ɔːʳ/ *noun*

a pole with a flat end, used to move a boat through water

oasis

o·a·sis /əʊˈeɪsɪs/ *noun* (*plural* **oases** /əʊˈeɪsiːz/)

a place in the desert where there is water and where trees can grow

oath /əʊθ/ *noun* (*plural* **oaths** /əʊðz/)

a very serious promise: *She took an oath to tell the truth in court.*

oats /əʊts/ *plural noun*

a type of grain that is used as food

o·be·di·ence /əʊˈbiːdɪəns/ *noun* (*no plural*)

behaviour in which you do what people tell you to do: *Mrs Jones expects obedience from all her pupils.* ⇨ opposite DISOBEDIENCE

o·be·di·ent /əʊˈbiːdɪənt/ *adjective*

willing to do what people tell you to do: *She's an obedient child.* ⇨ opposite DISOBEDIENT

obediently *adverb*: *She went to bed obediently at 7 o'clock.*

obey /əʊˈbeɪ/ *verb*

to do what someone tells you to do: *You should obey your teacher.* | *I always obey instructions as carefully as possible.* ⇨ opposite DISOBEY

ob·ject¹ /ˈɒbdʒɪkt/ *noun*

1 a thing that you can see or touch: *What is that big red object over there?*

2 a purpose: *The object of this exercise is to find out how many people like cats more than dogs.*

3 a word used in grammar to describe the person or thing that usually follows the verb in a sentence. In the sentence 'Jane bought the bread', 'bread' is the object

ob·ject² /əbˈdʒekt/ *verb*

to say that you do not like or do not agree with something: *She objected to our plan.* | *"But we'll be going in at midnight," I objected. "No-one will see us."*

ob·jec·tion /əbˈdʒekʃən/ *noun*

something that you say or feel about something you do not like or do not agree with: *She had strong objections to working on Sundays.*

ob·li·ga·tion /ˌɒblɪˈɡeɪʃn/ *noun*

something that you must do because it is your duty: *We have an obligation to encourage children to eat as healthily as possible.*

ob·lige /əˈblaɪdʒ/ *verb* (*present participle* **obliging,** *past* **obliged**)

to make it necessary for someone to do something: *It was raining so hard that I was obliged to stay at home.* | *I felt obliged to tell her the truth.*

ob·long /ˈɒblɒŋ/ *noun*

a shape with four straight sides and four equal angles that is longer than it is wide ⇨ same meaning RECTANGLE

ob·ser·va·tion /ˌɒbzəˈveɪʃn/ *noun* (*no plural*)

1 careful watching: *Mary is very ill and is going into hospital for observation.*

2 under observation watched carefully, especially by the police or in a hospital: *The police kept him under observation.*

ob·serve /əbˈzɜːv/ *verb* (*present participle* **observing,** *past* **observed**)

to watch someone or something carefully: *Children can learn to do things by observing other people.*

ob·sta·cle /ˈɒbstəkl/ *noun*
something that makes it difficult for you to move or that causes a problem: *Cars were driving slowly because the storm had left many obstacles in the road.* | *The major obstacle that he faces is financial.*

ob·sti·nate /ˈɒbstɪnət/ *adjective*
having a strong will and not willing to change your ideas easily: *She is an obstinate child – she won't eat unless she wants to.* ⇨ same meaning STUBBORN

ob·struct /əbˈstrʌkt/ *verb*
1 to block a road, path, or entrance: *Do not obstruct this entrance.*
2 to try to stop something from happening: *They are accused of obstructing justice because they helped the prisoners to escape.*

obstruction

ob·struc·tion /əbˈstrʌkʃən/ *noun*
something that blocks the way: *The accident caused an obstruction on the road.*

ob·tain /əbˈteɪn/ *verb*
to get something: *I haven't been able to obtain the book that you wanted.*

ob·vi·ous /ˈɒbvɪəs/ *adjective*
clear and easy to see or understand: *It is obvious to anyone who has met her that she is very clever.*
obviously *adverb*: *She is obviously upset.*

oc·ca·sion /əˈkeɪʒn/ *noun*
1 a time when something happens: *I've spoken to him on several occasions.*
2 a special event: *I only wear a tie on special occasions.*

oc·ca·sion·al /əˈkeɪʒnəl/ *adjective*
happening from time to time: *He paid us an occasional visit.*
occasionally *adverb*: *We go to the cinema occasionally.*

oc·cu·pa·tion /ˌɒkjʊˈpeɪʃn/ *noun*
1 a job: *"What is your occupation?" "I'm a doctor."*
2 something that you do in your free time: *Reading is one of her favourite occupations.*

oc·cu·py /ˈɒkjʊpaɪ/ *verb* (*present participle* **occupying**, *past* **occupied**)
1 to live in a place: *Three families occupy that big house.*
2 to fill a position or space: *His CDs occupy a lot of space.*
3 to keep someone busy: *This game will keep the children occupied all afternoon.*
4 **occupy yourself** to use time to do something: *He occupied himself **with** his computer.*

oc·cur /əˈkɜːr/ *verb* (*present participle* **occurring**, *past* **occurred**)
1 to happen: *What time did the accident occur?* ⇨ look at HAPPEN
2 **occur to someone** to come into someone's mind: *That idea has never occurred to me before.* | *It occurred to him that he should take his aunt to the station.*

o·cean /ˈəʊʃn/ *noun*
a very large sea: *the Atlantic Ocean*

o'clock /əˈklɒk/ *adverb*
a word used to tell what time it is: *"It's four o'clock."*

Oc·to·ber /ɒkˈtəʊbər/ *noun*
the 10th month of the year

oc·to·pus /ˈɒktəpəs/ *noun* (*plural* **octopuses**)
a sea creature with a soft body and eight long legs ⇨ see picture on page 195

odd /ɒd/ *adjective*
1 strange or unusual: *It's odd that he hasn't telephoned me.*
2 **odd number** a number that cannot be divided exactly by two. For example, 13 and 15 are odd numbers ⇨ compare EVEN NUMBER

odds and ends /ˌɒdz ənd ˈendz/
various different small things that are not very important or useful: *There was a box full of odds and ends.*

of /əv; *strong* ɒv/
1 forming part of something or belonging to something: *the wheels of a car* | *the streets of London*
2 a word that shows a relationship between people or things: *a friend of mine* | *the colour of her hair*

3 containing: *a cup of tea* | *a bag of sweets* | *a room full of people*

4 a word used in expressions that show amounts: *Have some of my sweets.* | *a pound of butter* | *a piece of cake* | *a group of people*

5 made from: *a bar of steel*

6 about: *I often think of you.*

7 used in dates: *the 12th of June*

off[1] /ɒf/ *adverb, preposition*

1 away from something: *Can you pull this lid off?* | *One of my buttons has fallen off.* | *He fell off the chair.*

2 not on: *All the lights were off.* | *Switch the computer off.* ⇨ opposite (**1** and **2**) ON

3 away to another place: *He drove off.* | *She went off without saying goodbye.*

4 not working: *He's off for three days.*

5 **off your food** not hungry because you are ill

off[2] *adjective*

food that is off is old and no longer good to eat: *This milk is off.*

of·fence /əˈfens/ *noun*

1 something that is wrong or against the law: *It is an offence to ride a bicycle at night without lights.*

2 **take offence** to feel unhappy or angry about something someone says to you: *She took offence when I asked her how old she was.*

of·fend /əˈfend/ *verb*

to make someone feel unhappy or angry: *I offended him by not answering his letter.* ⇨ same meaning UPSET

of·fer[1] /ˈɒfəʳ/ *verb*

1 to show someone that you want to give them something: *I offered James some of my chocolates.*

2 to tell or show someone that you are willing to help them: *She offered to help her mother with the shopping.*

offer[2] *noun*

1 an act of showing that you are happy to help with something: *Thank you for your offer of help.*

2 the amount of money that you say you will pay for something: *They made us a good offer for the house.*

of·fice /ˈɒfɪs/ *noun*

a place where people work: *She works in an office.*

of·fi·cer /ˈɒfɪsəʳ/ *noun*

1 a person in the army, navy, etc who can give orders to other people

2 a person who has an important job in the government, or an official organization: *a police officer* | *a prison officer*

of·fi·cial[1] /əˈfɪʃl/ *adjective*

approved by someone in power: *I received an official letter.* | *We are waiting for the official report to be published.*

official[2] *noun*

a person who has an important job, especially in the government or an organization: *He was an official in the Department of Health.*

of·ten /ˈɒfn/ *adverb*

1 many times: *I often go to bed early.* | *He often writes his own songs.*

2 **how often?** used to ask how many times something happens: *How often does it rain here?* | *How often do you go to the cinema?*

oh /əʊ/

something you say when you feel surprised, happy, annoyed, etc: *Oh, no! I've missed the bus.*

oil[1] /ɔɪl/ *noun* (no plural)

thick liquid that comes from under the ground or under the sea, used for cooking, burning, or for making machines work smoothly: *You need to check the oil in your car every few weeks.*

oil[2] *verb*

to put oil on something to make it work more smoothly: *You should oil your bike more often.*

oil paint /ˈɔɪl peɪnt/ *noun*

a special paint with oil in it, used by artists to paint pictures

oil paint·ing /ˈɔɪl ˌpeɪntɪŋ/ *noun*

a picture painted with oil paints

oil rig /ˈɔɪlrɪg/ *noun*

oil rig

a large structure with equipment for getting oil from under the ground or under the sea: *He works **on** an oil rig.*

oil-well /ˈɔɪl wel/ *noun*

a big hole that is made in the ground to get oil out

oint·ment /ˈɔɪntmənt/ *noun*
an oily substance that you rub on your skin for medical reasons ⇨ see picture at FIRST AID

OK /əʊˈkeɪ/ *adjective, adverb*
1 a word used to say you agree: *"Shall we go for a walk?" "OK."*
2 all right: *"How is your mother?" "She's OK."*

o·kay /əʊˈkeɪ/
another way of writing **OK**

old /əʊld/ *adjective*
1 having lived a long time: *My grandmother is very old.* ⇨ opposite YOUNG
2 the word we use to show our age: *How old are you? | I am eleven years old.*
3 having been used for a long time or having existed for a long time: *She was wearing old clothes. | The building was very old.* ⇨ opposite NEW
4 having existed for a long time: *We are very old friends – we've known each other since we were children.*

old-fash·ioned /ˌəʊld ˈfæʃnd/ *adjective*
not modern: *My clothes are all old-fashioned. | His parents have old-fashioned ideas.* ⇨ opposite MODERN

ol·ive /ˈɒlɪv/ *noun*
a small green or black fruit, eaten as a vegetable or used for making oil

ol·ive oil /ˌɒlɪv ˈɔɪl/ *noun (no plural)*
oil made from olives and used in cooking

O·lym·pic Games /əˌlɪmpɪk ˈɡeɪmz/
also **Olympics** an international sports competition that takes place every four years

ome·lette /ˈɒmlɪt/ *noun*
also **omelet** a mixture of eggs cooked in a flat shape in oil: *He was eating a cheese omelette.*

o·mit /əˈmɪt/ *verb (present participle* **omitting***, past* **omitted***)*
to not include someone or something: *You have omitted my name from the list. | If you like you can omit the salt.*

on /ɒn/
1 used to show where something is: *I put the glass on the shelf.* ⇨ see picture on page 208
2 working or in use: *Is the kitchen light on?*
3 covering a part of your body: *He had a big coat on. | She looks very nice with her hat on.* ⇨ opposite (**2** and **3**) OFF
4 used with days or dates, to show when something happens: *The party is on March the 12th. | I'll see you on Monday.*
5 inside a bus, train, or plane, or travelling by bicycle: *I saw Jane on the bus. | We watched that film on a plane.*
6 further or more: *I stopped to look at a map and then drove on.*
7 used to show that when one thing happened, another happened: *On arriving* (=when she arrived), *she telephoned her mother.*
8 being shown: *What's on television tonight* (=what programmes are being shown)?
9 **on foot** walking: *Let's go on foot.*
10 **on the left, on the right** at the left or right side of something: *There was a cinema on the left and a church on the right.*

once /wʌns/ *adverb*
1 one time: *I have been to America only once. | We go shopping once a week.*
2 some time ago: *My grandmother was a teacher once.*
3 when: *It was easy once I learnt how to do it.*
4 **at once** now; straight away: *We must leave at once.*
5 **at once** at the same time: *You can't do three different things at once.*
6 **once more** one more time: *Try ringing the bell once more – perhaps they're in the garden and didn't hear.*
7 **once or twice** only a few times: *"Have you ever been to a football match?" "Once or twice."*
8 **once upon a time** an expression used at the beginning of some children's stories meaning 'a long time ago'

one /wʌn/
1 the number 1
2 a single thing or person: *Have you any books on farming? – I'd like to borrow one* (=a book on farming). *| That girl has only got one sock on.*
3 a particular day, evening etc in the past, or at some time in the future: *John telephoned me one day last week. | Let's go for a drink one evening.*
4 the same: *They all ran in one direction.*

A B C D E F G H I J K L M N **O** P Q R S T U V W X Y Z

5 *formal* any person: *One should try to help other people.*

6 one another used to show that two people do the same thing to each other: *The two boys hit one another.* | *Mark and Sarah like one another* (=Mark likes Sarah and Sarah likes Mark).

one·self /wʌnˈself/
1 *formal* used in sentences with 'one' to speak or write about the same person: *One cannot blame oneself all the time.*
2 by oneself alone: *Sometimes it's nice to be by oneself.*

one-way /ˈwʌn weɪ/ *adjective*
moving only in one direction or allowing movement only in one direction: *Because of the accident there was only one-way traffic on the main road.* | *It was a one-way street.*

on·ion /ˈʌnjən/ *noun*
a round white or red vegetable with a strong smell and taste that is often used in cooking: *Slice the onions and put them in the frying pan.* ⇨ see picture on page 199

on·ly ¹ /ˈəʊnlɪ/ *adjective, adverb*
1 being the one person or thing of a particular kind: *She is the only girl in her family; all the other children are boys.*
2 and nothing more or no one else: *You can only have one piece of cake.* | *This room is for teachers only.*
3 just: *We're only trying to help.*
4 an only child a child with no brothers or sisters: *Only children are often very lonely.*
5 only just almost not: *This box is very heavy; I can only just lift it.*

only ²
but: *I'd love to come with you, only I have to stay at home and help my mother.*

on·to /ˈɒntə, -tʊ; *strong* ˈɒntuː/
to a place: *He climbed onto a rock.* ⇨ see picture on page 208

on·wards /ˈɒnwədz/ *adverb*
forward in time or space: *They hurried onwards.* | *From Monday onwards I shall be in another class.*

ooze /uːz/ *verb (present participle* **oozing**, *past* **oozed**)
to move or flow slowly: *The blood oozed from his knee.*

o·pen ¹ /ˈəʊpən/ *adjective*
1 not shut: *She's not asleep; her eyes are open* ⇨ see picture at AJAR
2 ready for business: *Is the bank open yet?* ⇨ opposite (**1** and **2**): CLOSED
3 not surrounded by other things: *We drove through open country.*
4 in the open air outside: *We ate our lunch in the open air.*

open ² *verb*
1 to make something open: *Open your books at page three.*
2 to become open: *The door opened and a man came in.*
3 to begin business: *The shop doesn't open until 10 o'clock.* ⇨ opposite (**1**, **2**, and **3**): CLOSE

o·pen·er /ˈəʊpənəʳ/ *noun*
an instrument for opening things: *a tin opener* | *a bottle opener*

o·pen·ing /ˈəʊpənɪŋ/ *noun*
a hole or space in something: *There was an opening **in** the fence.*

opera

performing an opera

op·era /ˈɒprə/ *noun*
a type of play that has songs and music instead of spoken words: *I enjoy a night **at the** opera.*

op·e·rate /ˈɒpəreɪt/ *verb (present participle* **operating**, *past* **operated**)
1 to make something work: *Do you know how to operate this machine?*
2 to work: *How does this machine operate?*
3 to cut open the body of someone who is ill in order to remove or repair an unhealthy part: *The doctors operated **on** her stomach.*

op·e·ra·tion /ˌɒpəˈreɪʃn/ *noun*
when doctors cut open the body of someone who is ill in order to remove or repair an unhealthy part: *She needs an operation **on** her stomach.*

op·e·ra·tor /ˈɒpəreɪtər/ noun

1 a person who works for a telephone company and who you can ring for help or information

2 a person whose job is to control a machine

3 a company that does a particular type of business: *The nightclub operator reported a 49 per cent increase in profits.*

o·pin·ion /əˈpɪnjən/ noun

what someone thinks about something: *He asked his father's opinion about his plans.* I *In my opinion* (=I think)*, you're wrong.* ⇨ same meaning VIEW

op·po·nent /əˈpəʊnənt/ noun

someone who is on the opposite side in a game or competition: *We beat our opponents at football.*

op·por·tu·ni·ty /ˌɒpəˈtjuːnəti/ noun (plural **opportunities**)

a chance to do something: *You can use the Internet to look for new job opportunities.*

op·pose /əˈpəʊz/ verb (present participle **opposing**, past **opposed**)

to be against something or not agree with something: *At first she opposed her husband's interest in politics.* I *My mother is opposed to the new plan.*

op·po·site [1] /ˈɒpəzɪt/ noun

a person or thing that is as different as possible from another. For example, 'high' is the opposite of 'low'

opposite [2] adjective

1 as different as possible: *The buses went in opposite directions – one went south and the other went north.*

2 on the other side of an area or road: *The library is on the opposite side of the road from the school.*

opposite [3] preposition

in a position on the other side of an area or road: *The library is opposite the school.* ⇨ see picture on page 208

op·ti·cian /ɒpˈtɪʃn/ noun

a person who tests your eyes and makes and sells glasses

op·ti·mist /ˈɒptɪmɪst/ noun

a person who always believes that good things will happen in the future ⇨ opposite PESSIMIST

op·ti·mist·ic /ˌɒptɪˈmɪstɪk/ adjective

believing that good things will happen in the future: *I'm optimistic that we'll win the game.* ⇨ opposite PESSIMISTIC

op·tion /ˈɒpʃn/ noun

something that you can choose to do: *If you like the car and you like the price then it's a very attractive option.* I *The weather was bad and it was becoming too dark for the pilots, leaving them no option but to land* (=they couldn't do anything but land).

op·tion·al /ˈɒpʃnəl/ adjective

if something is optional, you can choose to have it or do it, but you do not have to: *Games are optional at our school* (=you don't have to do them if you don't want to).

or /ər; strong ɔːr/

used when giving a choice between two or more things: *Do you want tea or coffee?*

o·ral /ˈɔːrəl/ adjective

spoken, not written: *We took an oral exam.*

or·ange [1] /ˈɒrɪndʒ/ noun

1 a round sweet juicy fruit with a thick skin ⇨ see picture on page 199

2 the colour of this fruit, between red and yellow: *The sky turned a brilliant orange.*

orange [2] adjective

something that is orange has the colour between red and yellow: *She wore an orange dress.*

or·bit [1] /ˈɔːbɪt/ noun

the path of one thing moving around another in space, for example the Earth moving round the sun

orbit

orbiting the Earth

orbit [2] verb

to move in a circle round something in space, for example the Earth or the moon: *The spaceship orbited the moon.*

A B C D E F G H I J K L M N O P Q R S T U V W X Y Z

orchard

or·chard /ˈɔːtʃəd/ *noun*
a field where fruit trees grow

or·ches·tra /ˈɔːkɪstrə/ *noun*
a large group of people who play musical instruments together

or·der¹ /ˈɔːdəʳ/ *noun*
1 something you must do because your parents or people in authority tell you to: *Go upstairs and tidy your room. That's an order!* | *Soldiers must obey orders.*
2 (*no plural*) a special way in which things are arranged or placed: *in alphabetical order* (=words and letters arranged in a system that starts at A and finishes at Z) | *Here are the reasons for giving you the job, in order of importance* (=starting with the most important and finishing with the least important).
3 in order to so that something can happen or someone can do something: *He stood on a chair in order to* (=so that he could) *reach the top shelf.*
4 keep things in order to keep things arranged tidily: *Try to keep these papers in order.*
5 out of order not working: *The telephone is out of order.*

order² *verb*
1 to tell someone to do something: *The judge ordered her to pay back the money she had stolen.*
2 to ask a shop to get something for you: *I've ordered a new table but it won't arrive until next week.*
3 to ask a waiter to bring you something in a restaurant: *I've ordered two coffees.*

or·di·na·ri·ly /ˈɔːdnərɪlɪ/ *adverb*
usually: *Storms ordinarily do not last over four or five hours.*

or·di·na·ry /ˈɔːdnərɪ/ *adjective*
1 not special, unusual, or different from other things: *I thought they were very normal, ordinary people.*

2 out of the ordinary unusual or strange: *Did you notice anything out of the ordinary at school today?*

ore /ɔːʳ/ *noun*
a type of rock or earth in which metal is found: *iron ore*

organ

playing the organ

or·gan /ˈɔːgən/ *noun*
1 a part of an animal or a plant that has a special purpose: *The disease spread from her liver to her other internal organs.*
2 a large musical instrument that has long pipes and is often played in a church
3 an electronic instrument with a KEYBOARD like a piano

or·gan·i·za·tion /ˌɔːgənaɪˈzeɪʃn/ *noun*
1 a large group that a lot of people, countries etc belong to, so they can meet and do something together: *the National Organization for Women* | *the North Atlantic Treaty Organization*
2 (*no plural*) the way in which you organize or plan something: *Good organization makes your work easier.*

or·gan·ize /ˈɔːgənaɪz/ *verb* (*present participle* **organizing**, *past* **organized**)
1 to plan and make all the arrangements for an event: *Did you organize the wedding by yourself or did your parents help you?*
2 to put things in order: *I must organize my CDs, because I can never find the one I want.*

or·gan·ized /ˈɔːgənaɪzd/ *adjective*
1 tidy and carefully arranged: *Her desk is always very organized.*
2 good at planning and doing things: *John is very organized – he always does his work well and quickly.*

or·i·gin /ˈɒrɪdʒɪn/ *noun*
1 the place that someone or

something comes from: *The way he talks shows that he has Irish origins* (=comes from Ireland).

2 the beginning or cause of something: *There are many different theories about the origin of the universe.*

o·rig·i·nal /əˈrɪdʒɪnəl/ *adjective*
1 first or earliest: *Who was the original owner of this house?*
2 new and different: *He had an original idea for a computer game.*
3 existing first and not copied: *This is the original painting, and this is the copy.*

o·rig·i·nal·ly /əˈrɪdʒɪnəli/ *adverb*
first or in the beginning: *I wonder who lived in this house originally*

or·na·ment /ˈɔːnəmənt/ *noun*
something that people have because it is beautiful, not because it is useful: *Their house is full of little ornaments.*

or·phan /ˈɔːfn/ *noun*
a child whose mother and father are dead

or·phan·age /ˈɔːfənɪdʒ/ *noun*
a home for children whose parents are dead

os·trich /ˈɒstrɪtʃ/ *noun* (*plural* **ostriches**)
a very large African bird with long legs that runs fast but cannot fly

oth·er /ˈʌðər/
1 not the same: *I sleep in this room, and my brother sleeps in the other room.* | *Alice didn't like the dress, so she asked to see some others.*
2 the remaining thing or person: *These two pens are mine but you can have all the others.* | *I can take Peter and Mary but all the others will have to go by bus.*
3 **other people** people in general, not including you: *I don't care what other people think.*
4 **the other day** not many days ago: *I saw John the other day.*

oth·er·wise /ˈʌðəwaɪz/ *adverb*
1 if not: *You should go now, otherwise you'll miss the bus.*
2 not including that: *I've just got to comb my hair, but otherwise I'm ready.*
3 differently: *We choose our employees on merit alone. We would be mad to do otherwise* (=to do something different).

ouch /aʊtʃ/
something you say when something hurts you slightly

ought to /ˈɔːt tuː/ *verb*
used to show what you think someone should do: *She ought to look after her children a bit better.*

ounce /aʊns/ *noun*
a measure of weight equal to 28.35 grams. There are 16 ounces (=16 oz) in one pound.

our /aʊər/ *adjective*
belonging to us: *We put our books in our bags.*

ours /aʊəz/
something that belongs to us: *Ours was one of the many houses she worked in.* | *No country in the world is richer than ours.*

our·selves /aʊəˈselvz/
1 the same people as the subject of the sentence: *We could see ourselves in the mirror.* | *We bought a lot of things for ourselves.*
2 **by ourselves** without help from anyone: *We painted the bedroom by ourselves.*
3 **by ourselves** alone, without anyone else: *Our mother never lets us go to the cinema by ourselves.*

out /aʊt/ *adverb*
1 not in a place; away from a place: *Shut the gate or the dog will get out.*
2 not at home or not at work: *My father is out this morning, but he will be in this afternoon.* ⇨ opposite (**1** and **2**): IN
3 not shining: *The lights were out and the house was dark.*
4 loudly: *He called out but nobody heard him.* | *He made the workers line up and shout out their names.*
5 **out of** away from something: *She took the keys out of her bag.* | *He walked out of the room.* ⇨ see picture on page 208

out·door /ˈaʊtdɔːr/ *adjective*
happening outside or used outside: *Wear your outdoor shoes.* | *We held an outdoor party on my birthday.* ⇨ opposite INDOOR

out·doors /aʊtˈdɔːz/ *adverb*
also **out-of-doors** outside in the open air: *It's a nice day; let's play outdoors.* ⇨ opposite INDOORS

out·er /ˈaʊtər/ *adjective*
on the outside or edge of something, far away from the middle: *The outer walls of the house are made of brick.* |

A B C D E F G H I J K L M N O P Q R S T U V W X Y Z

I worked in the outer office and saw very few people. ⇨ opposite INNER

out·fit /'aʊtfɪt/ *noun*
a set of clothes, especially for a special purpose: *I want to buy a new outfit for her wedding.*

out·grow /aʊt'grəʊ/ *verb* (*past* **outgrew** /aʊt'gruː/, *past participle* **outgrown** /aʊt'grəʊn/)
to grow too big for your clothes: *Jack has outgrown his coat, so I need to buy him a bigger one.*

out·ing /'aʊtɪŋ/ *noun*
a short trip to enjoy yourself, usually in a group: *We're going for a family outing tomorrow.*

out·line /'aʊtlaɪn/ *noun*
a line showing the shape of something: *He drew the outline of a house.*

out-of-date /ˌaʊt əv 'deɪt/ *adjective*
old or no longer useful: *He gave us out-of-date information about the times of the buses.* ⇨ compare OLD-FASHIONED

out-of-doors /ˌaʊt əv 'dɔːz/ *adverb*
another way of saying **outdoors**

out·side [1] /'aʊtsaɪd/ *noun*
the outer part or surface of something: *The outside of the house was painted white.* ⇨ opposite INSIDE

out·side [2] /aʊt'saɪd/ *adverb*
out of a building or room, but near it: *He opened the door and went outside.* I *He left his bicycle outside.* ⇨ opposite INSIDE

outside [3] /'aʊtsaɪd/ *preposition*
out of a building or room, but still near it: *I'll meet you outside the cinema.* I *He was talking to his friends outside the house.* ⇨ opposite INSIDE

out·skirts /'aʊtskɜːts/ *plural noun*
the parts of a town that are not in the centre: *We live on the outskirts of the city*

out·stand·ing /aʊt'stændɪŋ/ *adjective*
very good: *She was an outstanding pupil.* ⇨ same meaning EXCELLENT

out·ward /'aʊtwəd/ *adjective*
1 relating to how someone seems to be: *There were no outward signs that she was upset.*
2 going away from a place or towards the outside: *She took an outward flight to Switzerland.* ⇨ opposite INWARD

out·wards /'aʊtwədz/ *adverb*
towards the outside or away from the middle: *The door opens outwards.* ⇨ opposite INWARDS

o·val /'əʊvəl/ *noun*
a shape like an egg ⇨ see picture at SHAPE

ov·en /'ʌvn/ *noun*
a piece of equipment that you cook food inside, shaped like a metal box with a door: *Pre-heat the oven to 250 degrees Fahrenheit before you put the dish inside.*

o·ver [1] /'əʊvər/ *adverb*
1 across to the other side: *We can cross over when the traffic stops.*
2 down to a lying position: *He knocked the glass over and it broke.* I *She fell over.*
3 from the start to the finish: *Think it over before you decide.* I *Read this letter over and tell me if there are any mistakes.*
4 finished: *When we arrived the film was already over.*
5 remaining or not used: *Did you spend all the money I gave you or did you have any over?*
6 **over and over again** many times: *I've told you over and over again that you mustn't play near the road.*
7 **over there** used when you are pointing to a place that is not near you: *I'll sit here and you sit over there.*

over [2] *preposition*
1 above: *The lamp is hanging over the table.*
2 covering; on top of: *My father went to sleep with a newspaper over his face.*
3 from one side to the other: *He jumped over the wall.* ⇨ see picture on page 208
4 more than or older than: *Only children over 11 can attend the school.*
5 **all over** everywhere: *They travelled all over the world.*

o·ver·all /'əʊvərɔːl/ *noun*
1 a piece of clothing that you put over other clothes to keep them clean
2 **overalls** (*plural noun*) loose trousers with a top part that you wear over other clothes to keep them clean

o·ver·board /'əʊvəbɔːd/ *adverb*
over the side of a boat into the water: *He fell overboard.*

o·ver·coat /ˈəʊvəkəʊt/ *noun*
a warm coat that you wear outside when it is cold

overflow

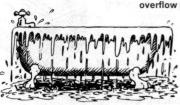

an overflowing bath

o·ver·flow /ˌəʊvəˈfləʊ/ *verb*
to flow over the edge of something: *The bath overflowed because I forgot to turn the water off.*

o·ver·head /ˌəʊvəˈhed/ *adverb*
over your head or in the sky: *Birds were flying overhead.*

o·ver·hear /ˌəʊvəˈhɪəʳ/ *verb (past* **overheard** /ˌəʊvəˈhɜːd/)
to hear something that other people are saying when they do not know you are listening: *I overheard them talking about me.*

o·ver·look /ˌəʊvəˈlʊk/ *verb*
1 to be higher than something, so that you can look down on it: *Our house overlooks the sea.*
2 not to see or notice something: *You have overlooked several of my mistakes.*

o·ver·night /ˌəʊvəˈnaɪt/ *adjective, adverb*
for the whole night: *We stayed overnight with my sister.*

o·ver·seas /ˌəʊvəˈsiːz/ *adjective, adverb*
to, in, or from places across the sea from your own country: *My brother lives overseas.* I *overseas students*

o·ver·sleep /ˌəʊvəˈsliːp/ *verb (past* **overslept** /ˌəʊvəˈslept/)
to sleep longer than you had wanted to: *I was late for school this morning because I overslept.*

o·ver·take /ˌəʊvəˈteɪk/ *verb (present participle* **overtaking**, *past* **overtook** /ˌəʊvəˈtʊk/)
to pass another person or vehicle going in the same direction: *Don't try to overtake on narrow roads.*

o·ver·weight /ˌəʊvəˈweɪt/ *adjective*
too fat: *The doctor told her she was*

overweight *and should do more exercise.*

owe /əʊ/ *verb (present participle* **owing**, *past* **owed**)
1 if you owe money to someone, you have not yet paid them for something or returned the money that you borrowed: *I owe John £10 because he paid for my ticket.* I *I can pay you £20 now but I'll have to owe you the rest.*
2 to feel grateful to someone for something: *I owe a lot to my mother for teaching me to cook so well.*

ow·ing to /ˈəʊɪŋ tuː/
because of: *They arrived late, owing to the traffic.*

owl /aʊl/ *noun*
a large bird that flies at night and kills small animals for food

own¹ /əʊn/
1 belonging to you: *I like writing with my own pen.* I *That bicycle isn't his own; it belongs to his brother.*
2 on your own alone, with no one else with you or helping you: *I was on my own all afternoon.* I *Did you write this story on your own?*

own² *verb*
to have something that belongs to you: *Who owns this house?*

own·er /ˈəʊnəʳ/ *noun*
a person who owns something: *Who is the owner of this car?*

ox /ɒks/ *noun*
a large type of male cow that is used for work on farms

ox·y·gen /ˈɒksɪdʒən/ *noun (no plural)*
a gas in the air that people must breathe in order to live

oz
a short way of writing the word **ounce** or **ounces**

o·zone /ˈəʊzəʊn/ *noun (no plural)*
a gas high above the surface of the Earth

ozone-friend·ly /ˈəʊzəʊn ˌfrendlɪ/ *adjective*
not harmful to the OZONE LAYER: *ozone-friendly products*

ozone lay·er /ˈəʊzəʊn ˌleɪəʳ/ *noun (no plural)*
a layer of OZONE that protects the Earth from the bad effects of the sun

Pp

P, p /piː/
the sixteenth letter of the English
alphabet

pace¹ /peɪs/ *noun*
(*no plural*) the speed at which you move
forwards, especially when running or
walking: *They walk at a very fast pace.*

pace² *verb* (*present participle* **pacing**,
past **paced**)
to walk slowly backwards and forwards,
especially when you are waiting or
worried

pack

packing a suitcase

pack¹ /pæk/ *verb*
1 to put things into boxes, bags, etc in
order to take them somewhere: *We're
going to Greece tomorrow and I haven't
even started packing yet.* | *She packed
her bags and left.*
2 if a crowd packs a place there are a
lot of people there, so the place is too
full: *Thousands of people packed the
stadium.*
3 pack up to finish work: *I think I'll
pack up and go home early.*

pack² *noun*
1 several things packed together in
order to sell, carry, or send them: *We
bought a pack of chocolate bars.*
2 *British* a large bag that you carry on
your back
3 a set of cards for playing a game: *a
pack of cards*
4 a group of animals that hunt
together: *a pack of wild dogs*

pack·age /ˈpækɪdʒ/ *noun*
a parcel: *The postman brought a
package for you.*

packed /pækt/
adjective
full of people

package

pack·et /ˈpækɪt/
noun
a small box in
which goods are
packed: *He
opened a packet
of cigarettes.*
⇨ see picture at CONTAINER

pack·ing /ˈpækɪŋ/ *noun*
when you put things into cases, boxes,
etc in order to take them somewhere:
*I'll do my packing the night before we
leave.*

pact /pækt/ *noun*
an important agreement between two
countries

pad¹ /pæd/ *noun*
1 a thick piece of soft material used to
protect or clean a part of your body or a
wound
2 a number of sheets of paper stuck
together at one edge: *I need a writing
pad.*

pad² *verb* (*present participle* **padding**,
past **padded**)
to protect something or make it warmer
or more comfortable by covering or
filling it with soft material: *The jacket is
padded at the shoulders.*

pad·dle¹ /ˈpædl/ *noun*
a pole with a flat part at one or both ends,
used to move a boat through water

paddle² *verb* (*present participle*
paddling, *past* **paddled**)
1 to move a boat through the water
using a paddle
2 *British* to walk about in water that is
not very deep: *The children paddled in
the sea.*

pad·dy /ˈpædɪ/ *noun*
also **paddy field** a field for growing rice

pad·lock /ˈpædlɒk/ *noun*
a small lock that you can put on a door,
bicycle, etc

page /peɪdʒ/ *noun*
one of the sheets of paper in a book or
newspaper: *The book has 120 pages.* |
There's a picture on the next page.

paid /peɪd/
the past tense and past participle of the
verb **pay**

A B C D E F G H I J K L M N O P Q R S T U V W X Y Z

pain /peɪn/ *noun*
1 the feeling you have when part of your body hurts: *I've got a bad pain in my leg.* | *Are you **in** pain (=feeling pain)?*
2 a pain, a pain in the neck a very annoying person or thing: *He's a real pain when he's tired.*
3 (*no plural*) feelings of sadness: *Divorce causes great pain for children.*

pain·ful /ˈpeɪnfəl/ *adjective*
causing pain: *Her ankle was swollen and painful.* ⇨ opposite PAINLESS

pain·kill·er /ˈpeɪnˌkɪləʳ/ *noun*
a medicine that helps to stop pain

pain·less /ˈpeɪnləs/ *adjective*
causing no pain ⇨ opposite PAINFUL

paint¹ /peɪnt/ *noun*
1 (*no plural*) a liquid that you put on a surface to make it a particular colour: *Terry bought a can of yellow paint to decorate the kitchen walls.*
2 paints a set of small tubes or blocks of paint used for painting pictures: *She brought a box of paints to school.* ⇨ see pictures at ARTIST and on page 197

paint² *verb*
1 to put paint on a surface: *He painted the door green.*
2 to make a picture of someone or something using paint: *She loves painting the sea.*

paint·brush /ˈpeɪntbrʌʃ/ *noun* (*plural* **paintbrushes**)
a brush that you use for painting ⇨ see picture at BRUSH

paint·er /ˈpeɪntəʳ/ *noun*
1 a person who paints buildings as a job
2 a person who paints pictures ⇨ see picture at ARTIST

paint·ing /ˈpeɪntɪŋ/ *noun*
a painted picture: *A large painting hung on the wall.* ⇨ see picture at ARTIST

pair /peəʳ/ *noun*
1 two things of the same kind that are usually used together: *I can't find a pair **of** socks.*
2 something with two parts joined and used together: *I'd like to buy this pair **of** trousers.* | *Use a pair of scissors to open the pack.*
3 two people who do something together or are closely connected: *Jenny and her husband make a lovely pair.*

pal /pæl/ *noun*
a friend

pal·ace /ˈpælɪs/ *noun*
a large building in which a king or queen lives

pale /peɪl/ *adjective*
1 having a light skin colour, especially because you are ill or frightened: *She was very pale after her illness.*
2 not light or bright: *His shirt is pale green.* ⇨ opposite DARK

palm¹ /pɑːm/ *noun*
1 a tall tree with no branches and a group of large leaves at the top
2 the flat part inside your hand: *He put the insect on the palm of his hand.* ⇨ see picture at HAND

pam·phlet /ˈpæmflɪt/ *noun*
a thin book with a paper cover that gives you information about something

pans

saucepan   *frying pan*

pan /pæn/ *noun*
a round container, especially one with a handle, that is used for cooking

pan·cake /ˈpænkeɪk/ *noun*
a very thin flat cake cooked in a pan

pan·da /ˈpændə/ *noun*
a large black and white animal like a bear that comes from China ⇨ see picture on page 195

pane /peɪn/ *noun*
a single piece of glass in a window: *Who broke this pane **of** glass?*

pan·el /ˈpænl/ *noun*
1 a flat piece of wood used in a door or on a wall
2 a group of speakers who are chosen to talk about something or answer questions: *A panel of experts will discuss the subject.*

pan·ic¹ /ˈpænɪk/ *noun* (*no plural*)
a sudden feeling of great fear that makes you lose control of yourself: *There was panic when the fire started.*

panic² verb (present participle **panicking**, past **panicked**)
to feel a sudden fear that makes you lose control of yourself: *The crowd panicked at the sound of guns.*

panic-strick·en /'pænɪk ˌstrɪkən/ adjective
very afraid and not able to think clearly

pant /pænt/ verb
to breathe hard and quickly, especially because you are doing something that needs a lot of effort: *He was panting when he reached the top of the hill.*

pant·ies /'pæntɪz/ plural noun
American a piece of clothing that you wear under other clothes from below your waist to the top of your legs (British **pants**)

pan·to·mime /'pæntəmaɪm/ noun
a funny play for children produced at Christmas in Britain, usually telling a traditional story

pants /pænts/ plural noun
1 British a piece of clothing that you wear under other clothes from below your waist to the top of your legs (American **panties**)
2 American a piece of clothing that covers the lower half of your body and has a separate part for each leg (British **trousers**)

pa·per /'peɪpər/ noun
1 (no plural) thin material used for writing or drawing on: *I haven't got any writing paper.* | *He wrote her phone number down on* **a piece of paper.**
2 a newspaper: *Here's today's paper.*
3 papers official pieces of paper that give information about who you are and what you are allowed to do: *At the airport they asked for his papers.*

pa·per·back
/'peɪpəbæk/ noun
a book with a stiff paper cover

paper clip
/'peɪpə klɪp/ noun
a small curved piece of wire used to hold sheets of paper together

par·a·chute
/'pærəʃuːt/ noun
a large piece of

parachute

cloth that fills with air and lets someone fall slowly to earth from a plane

pa·rade¹ /pə'reɪd/ noun
when people celebrate by walking in a large group down the street

parade² verb (present participle **parading**, past **paraded**)
to walk in a large group down the street to celebrate something: *The people paraded through the town.*

par·a·dise /'pærədaɪs/ noun (no plural)
1 HEAVEN
2 a place or situation that makes you feel completely happy: *Paradise for me is lying on the beach all day.*

par·af·fin /'pærəfɪn/ noun (no plural)
British oil that can be burned cooking and lighting

par·a·graph /'pærəɡrɑːf/ noun
a group of sentences that begins on a new line and deals with one particular idea: *Read from your book, starting at the second paragraph.*

par·al·lel /'pærəlel/ adjective
running side by side, but always the same distance away from each other: *The railway runs parallel* **to** *the road.* | *The children stood in two parallel lines.*

par·a·lyse /'pærəlaɪz/ verb (present participle **paralysing**, past **paralysed**)
to make someone lose the ability to move their body or part of their body: *The climber was paralysed in a fall and couldn't walk.*

pa·ral·y·sis /pə'ræləsɪs/ noun (no plural)
when you lose the ability to move part of your body

par·cel /'pɑːsl/ noun
something covered in paper and tied for posting or carrying: *She sent a parcel of books to her brother.* ⇨ same meaning PACKAGE

par·don /'pɑːdn/ noun (no plural)
a word used to ask someone to say something again, because you did not hear them the first time: *"It's four o'clock." "Pardon?" "I said, it's four o'clock."*

par·ent /'peərənt/ noun
a father or mother: *My parents live in London.*

par·ish /'pærɪʃ/ noun (plural **parishes**)
an area looked after by one Christian priest or served by one church

park[1] /pɑːk/ *noun*
a large piece of ground in a town, usually covered in grass and used by the public for pleasure: *Let's go for a walk in the park.*

park[2] *verb*
to stop a car and leave it in a particular place for a period of time: *She parked the car near the bank.* | *You can't park there.*

park·ing /'pɑːkɪŋ/ *noun (no plural)*
1 when you park a car
2 **No parking** a phrase used on a sign to show that you are not allowed to leave your car in a particular place

parking me·ter /'pɑːkɪŋ ˌmiːtəʳ/ *noun*
a small machine at the side of the street into which you put money to pay for parking a car next to it

par·lia·ment /'pɑːləmənt/ *noun*
a group of people chosen by the people of a country to make laws: *She was elected to Parliament last year.*

par·rot /'pærət/ *noun*
a brightly coloured bird with a short curved beak

pars·ley /'pɑːslɪ/ *noun (no plural)*
a small plant with strong-tasting leaves, that can be used in cooking

part[1] /pɑːt/ *noun*
1 a piece of something such as an object, area, period of time, etc: *Which part of the town do you live in?* | *The front part of the car was damaged.* | *I only saw the first part of the programme on TV last night.*
2 one of the pieces that something is made of: *I need some new parts for my car.*
3 a character represented by an actor in a play or film: *James played the part of the soldier.* | *The play has some good parts for children.*
4 **take part in something** to do an activity with other people: *He took part in lots of sports at school.*
5 to some degree but not completely: *Her success was due in part to good luck.*

part[2] *verb*
1 to pull two sides of something so that they separate: *He parted the curtains and looked out of the window.*
2 **part with something** to give away something that you like a lot: *She hates parting with her old toys.*

par·tial /'pɑːʃl/ *adjective*
not complete: *The meeting was only a partial success.*

par·tial·ly /'pɑːʃəlɪ/ *adverb*
not completely: *He is only partially to blame for the problem.*

par·tic·i·pant /pɑːˈtɪsɪpənt/ *noun*
a person who takes part in an activity: *Participants on the course are expected to work hard.*

par·tic·i·pate /pɑːˈtɪsɪpeɪt/ *verb*
(*present participle* **participating**, *past* **participated**)
to take part in an activity: *I'd like to thank everyone who participated in tonight's show.*

par·ti·ci·ple /'pɑːtɪsɪpl/ *noun*
the form of a verb, usually ending in '-ing' or '-ed', that is used to form some verb tenses. For example, the past participle of 'discover' is 'discovered' and the present participle is 'discovering'

par·tic·u·lar /pəˈtɪkjʊləʳ/ *adjective*
1 this one and not others: *On that particular day, I wasn't feeling well.* | *I haven't seen that particular film.*
2 special or important: *Did you have a particular reason for choosing this book?* | *You should pay particular attention to spelling.*
3 **in particular** especially: *He likes sports, and football in particular.* | *Is there anything in particular I can help you with?*

par·tic·u·lar·ly /pəˈtɪkjʊləlɪ/ *adverb*
especially: *It is particularly hot today.* | *He is particularly worried about his maths exam.*

part·ly /'pɑːtlɪ/ *adverb*
to some degree but not completely: *The accident was partly my fault.*

part·ner /'pɑːtnəʳ/ *noun*
1 someone that you dance with or play a game with: *Take your partners for the next dance.*
2 one of the owners of a business
3 the person who you are married to or who you live with

part-time /ˌpɑːt ˈtaɪm/ *adjective*
working during only a part of the usual working time: *I work part-time at the library.*

A B C D E F G H I J K L M N O P Q R S T U V W X Y Z

par·ty /ˈpɑːtɪ/ noun (plural **parties**)

1 a social occasion when people eat, drink, and enjoy themselves: *Will you come to my birthday party on Saturday? | She's **having** a party next week.*

2 a group of people who are doing something together: *Our teacher is taking a party of children to the museum.*

3 a group of people with the same opinions in politics: *Are you a member of a political party?*

pass¹ /pɑːs/ verb

1 to go past a person or a thing: *She waved at me as she passed my house. | I pass the park every morning on my way to school.*

2 to give something to someone: *Pass the salt, please.*

3 when time passes, it goes by: *Time passes very slowly when you're waiting.*

4 to kick, throw, or hit a ball to someone in your own team during a game: *Johnson passes the ball to Eliot and Eliot scores!*

5 to succeed in a test or examination: *I'm having a party when I pass my driving test!*

6 pass away to die: *I was sorry to hear that your aunt had passed away.*

7 pass out to suddenly become unconscious: *He always passes out at the sight of blood.*

8 pass something on to give someone information that someone has told you: *I will pass the message on to her.*

pass² noun (plural **passes**)

1 a successful result in an examination: *In this class there were seven passes.*

2 when someone kicks, throws, or hits a ball to another person in their own team

3 a high mountain road: *The Khyber Pass*

4 a paper allowing you to go somewhere or have something: *I showed my pass to the man at the factory gate, and was allowed in.*

pas·sage /ˈpæsɪdʒ/ noun

1 a long narrow space in a building that connects different rooms: *The bathroom is at the end of the passage on the left.* ⇨ same meaning CORRIDOR

2 a short part of a piece of written work: *He read a passage from the book to the rest of the class.*

pas·sen·ger /ˈpæsɪndʒəʳ/ noun

a person who rides in a car, bus, train, etc, but does not drive it: *There were ten passengers in the bus.*

pass·er·by /ˌpɑːsə ˈbaɪ/ noun (plural **passers-by**)

a person who walks past a place in the street: *A passer-by told me the time.*

pas·sion /ˈpæʃn/ noun

a very strong deep feeling, especially of love or anger: *She spoke with passion about human rights.*

pas·sion·ate /ˈpæʃnət/ adjective

with very strong deep feelings: *He is passionate about caring for animals.*

pas·sive /ˈpæsɪv/ adjective

having the action done by someone. For example, in the sentence 'The ball was kicked by John', 'was kicked' is a passive verb ⇨ opposite ACTIVE

pass·port /ˈpɑːspɔːt/ noun

a small book that has your photograph and facts about you and which you must have if you are going to another country

past¹ /pɑːst/ adjective

having happened or existed before the present time: *I've been ill for the past two weeks. | There is no point in worrying about past mistakes.* ⇨ compare NEXT

past² preposition

1 up to and further than something: *He drove past the school.* ⇨ see picture on page 208

2 more than a particular time: *It's just past four o'clock. | It's ten past nine.*

past³ noun (no plural)

1 the past (a) all the time that has already gone: *Farming is much easier now than it was in the past.* **(b)** the past tense: *What's the past of 'to go'?*

2 a person's life until now: *I don't know anything about his past.* ⇨ compare (**1**, **2**, and **3**): FUTURE

past⁴ adverb

up to and further than a particular place: *Hal drove past without stopping.*

pas·ta /ˈpæstə/ noun (no plural)

an Italian food made from flour and water, eaten with vegetables, meat, cheese etc

paste[1] /peɪst/ *noun (no plural)*
  1 a type of thick glue that is used for sticking paper
  2 a soft wet mixture that can be spread over something

paste[2] *verb (present participle* **pasting**, *past* **pasted)**
  to stick something onto something else with paste

past par·ti·ci·ple /ˌpɑːst ˈpɑːtɪsɪpl/ *noun*
  the part of a verb that is used to show an action done or happening in the past. For example, 'done' and 'walked' are the past participles of the verbs 'do' and 'walk'

pas·try /ˈpeɪstrɪ/ *noun*
  1 (*plural* **pastries**) a small sweet cake
  2 (*no plural*) a mixture of flour, fat, and water that you bake and use to make PIES

past tense /ˌpɑːst ˈtens/ *noun*
  one of the forms of a verb that show past time. For example, the past tense of 'call' is 'called'

pas·ture /ˈpɑːstʃəʳ/ *noun*
  land covered with grass, used for cattle and sheep

pat[1] /pæt/ *verb (present participle* **patting**, *past* **patted)**
  to touch something gently several times with your open hand: *She patted the dog.*

pat[2] *noun*
  a light friendly touch with your open hand: *She gave the boy a pat on the head.*

patch[1] /pætʃ/ *noun (plural* **patches**)
  1 a piece of material used for covering a hole in something
  2 a small area of something that looks different from the rest: *There were wet patches on the wall.*

patch[2] *verb*
  to put a piece of material over a hole or a worn place in order to repair it: *You can patch a bicycle tyre with a piece of rubber.*

path /pɑːθ/ *noun (plural* **paths** /pɑːðz/)
  a track for walking on: *There was a narrow path through the forest.* ⇨ see picture on page 193

pa·tience /ˈpeɪʃns/ *noun (no plural)*
  the ability to deal with difficulties or wait for something for a long time without getting angry or upset: *You need a lot of patience to be a teacher.*

pa·tient[1] /ˈpeɪʃnt/ *adjective*
  able to deal with difficulties or wait for something calmly and without getting upset or angry: *I know your leg hurts; just be patient until the doctor arrives.* ⇨ opposite IMPATIENT

patient[2] *noun*
  someone who is getting medical treatment: *There are 150 patients in this hospital.*

pa·ti·o /ˈpætɪəʊ/ *noun*
  an outdoor area with a hard surface near a house where you can sit, eat, relax, etc

pa·trol[1] /pəˈtrəʊl/ *noun*
  1 when police officers, guards, or soldiers go regularly round an area or building to make sure there is no crime or trouble
  2 on patrol patrolling an area or building: *Police are on patrol in the town.*

patrol[2] *verb (present participle* **patrolling**, *past* **patrolled)**
  to go round an area or building in order to protect it: *Every hour a policeman patrolled our street.*

pat·ter /ˈpætəʳ/ *verb*
  to make a light knocking noise: *The rain pattered on the roof.*

pattern
spotted   striped
checked   zigzag

pat·tern /ˈpætn/ *noun*
  1 an arrangement of shapes, lines, and colours: *The dress has a pattern of flowers on it.*
  2 the regular way in which something

happens, develops, or is done: *There is a pattern to the crimes.*

3 a shape that you copy if you want to make something, especially a piece of clothing: *a dress pattern*

pause¹ /pɔːz/ *noun*
a short time when you stop what you are doing: *There was a pause in the conversation when Mary came in.*

pause² *verb* (*present participle* **pausing**, *past* **paused**)
to stop for a short time: *When he reached the top of the hill he paused for a minute to rest.*

pave /peɪv/ *verb* (*present participle* **paving**, *past* **paved**)
to cover a road, path, etc with a hard level surface

pavement   *kerb*   *drain*   *gutter*   **pavement**

pave·ment /'peɪvmənt/ *noun*
British a path made of flat stones at the side of a road for people to walk on (*American* **sidewalk**)

paw /pɔː/ *noun*
the foot of an animal such as a dog or cat: *The dog has a thorn in his paw.*

pay¹ /peɪ/ *verb* (*present participle* **paying**, *past* **paid** /peɪd/)
1 to give someone money for something you are buying from them or for work they have done for you: *She paid **for** the coffee and stood up.* | *Most people **get** paid monthly.* | *Dad paid me £2 to wash the car.*
2 pay attention to listen or watch carefully: *Pay attention **to** the story, children.* | *Sorry, I wasn't paying attention. What did you say?*
3 pay someone back to return the money you have borrowed from someone: *Can I borrow £10? I'll pay you back next week.*

pay² *noun* (*no plural*)
the money that you receive for work that you have done: *The job is interesting but the pay is quite low.*

pay·ment /'peɪmənt/ *noun*
1 (*no plural*) the act of paying: *This money is in payment for your work.*
2 an amount of money that you pay: *I have to **make** monthly payments for rent.*

pay phone

pay phone

/'peɪ fəʊn/ *noun*
a public telephone that you pay to use by putting coins or a card in it

PC /ˌpiː 'siː/ *noun*
also **personal computer** a small computer that is used by one person

pea /piː/ *noun*
a very small round green vegetable ⇨ see picture on page 199

peace /piːs/ *noun* (*no plural*)
1 quiet and calm: *I love the peace of this village.* | *Go away and leave me in peace.*
2 a time when there is no war or fighting: *There has been peace in the area for six years now.*

peace·ful /'piːsfəl/ *adjective*
1 quiet and calm: *I spent a peaceful day at the beach.*
2 not violent: *A peaceful crowd marched to the city centre.*

peach /piːtʃ/ *noun* (*plural* **peaches**)
a juicy fruit with one large seed and a soft yellow or pink skin

pea·cock /'piːkɒk/ *noun*
a large bird with a long brightly coloured tail covered with blue-green spots

peak /piːk/ *noun*
1 the time when someone or something is most successful: *She is at the peak of her career.*
2 the pointed top of a hill or mountain ⇨ see pictures at MOUNTAIN and on page 193
3 the front part of a hat that sticks forward over your eyes

peal /piːl/ *noun*
1 the loud sound of bells
2 long loud sounds that follow each other: *There were peals of laughter from the audience.*

peel

peeling an orange

pea·nut /ˈpiːnʌt/ *noun*
a small nut that grows under the ground and which you can eat

peanut but·ter /ˌpiːnʌt ˈbʌtə^r/ *noun (no plural)*
a soft food made from crushed peanuts that is usually eaten on bread

pear /peə^r/ *noun*
a sweet juicy yellow or green fruit that is narrow at one end and wide at the other ➪ see picture on page 199

pearl /pɜːl/ *noun*
a small round white object, found in the shell of a sea creature and used to make expensive jewellery: *She was wearing a pearl necklace.*

peas·ant /ˈpeznt/ *noun*
a person who lives in the country and works on their own small piece of land

peb·ble /ˈpebl/ *noun*
a small stone

peck /pek/ *verb*
if a bird pecks something, it takes a small quick bite: *The hens pecked at the corn.*

pe·cu·li·ar /prˈkjuːlɪə^r/ *adjective*
strange or unusual, especially in a way that worries you: *A peculiar smell was coming from the room.* | *The fish had a rather peculiar taste.* ➪ same meaning ODD

ped·al¹ /ˈpedl/ *noun*
a part of a machine that you move with your foot: *a bicycle pedal* ➪ see pictures at BICYCLE and PIANO

pedal² *verb (present participle* **pedalling**, *past* **pedalled**)
to move a bicycle by pushing the pedals with your feet: *We pedalled slowly up the hill.*

pe·des·tri·an /pəˈdestrɪən/ *noun*
a person walking: *This bridge is for pedestrians only.*

pedestrian cross·ing /pəˌdestrɪən ˈkrɒsɪŋ/ *noun*
a special place in the road where people who are walking can cross safely

peel¹ /piːl/ *noun (no plural)*
the outside part of a fruit or vegetable: *Apples have red or green peel.*

peel² *verb*
to take off the outside part of a vegetable or fruit: *Please would you peel this orange for me?* | *She is peeling potatoes.* ➪ see picture on page 198

peep¹ /piːp/ *verb*
to look at something quickly and secretly: *I peeped through the window to see if she was there.* ➪ compare GLANCE

peep² *noun*
a quick or secret look: *He took a peep at the back of the book to check the answer.*

peer /pɪə^r/ *verb*
to look very hard or carefully at something: *She was peering **at** the notice which was in very small print.*

peg /peg/ *noun*
1 a short piece of wood, metal, etc fixed to a wall, on which you can hang clothes
2 a small piece of plastic or wood that you use to fasten clothes to a washing line

pen /pen/ *noun*
1 a long narrow object that is filled with ink and is used to write or draw with ➪ compare PENCIL ➪ see picture on page 205
2 a small area surrounded by a fence, in which farm animals are kept

pen·al·ty /ˈpenltɪ/ *noun (plural* **penalties**)
1 a punishment for breaking a law or rule: *What is the penalty **for** dangerous driving?*
2 a punishment given to a player or team not obeying the rules of a game or sport
3 in football, a chance to kick the ball into the GOAL because the other team has broken the rules

pence /pens/ *noun*
a plural of the word **penny**

pen·cil /ˈpensəl/ *noun*
a long narrow object made of wood and filled with a black substance used for writing or drawing ➪ compare PEN

A
B
C
D
E
F
G
H
I
J
K
L
M
N
O
P
Q
R
S
T
U
V
W
X
Y
Z

pen·e·trate /'penɪtreɪt/ verb (present participle **penetrating**, past **penetrated**)
to go into or through something that is difficult to enter: *The sun penetrated through the thick clouds.* | *He gradually penetrated into the thick forest.*

pen friend /'pen frend/ noun
British a person in another country who you write to and who writes to you

pen·guin /'peŋgwɪn/ noun
a large black and white Antarctic sea bird, that cannot fly but uses its wings for swimming ⇨ see picture on page 195

pen·knife /'pen,naɪf/ noun (plural **penknives** /-,naɪvz/)
a small folding knife that you can carry in your pocket ⇨ see picture at KNIFE

pen·ny /'penɪ/ noun (plural **pence** /pens/ or **pennies**)
a British coin. There are 100 pence in a pound

pen·sion /'penʃən/ noun
money given to a person regularly when they are too old to work: *He lives on his pension now that he's retired.*

pen·sion·er /'penʃənəʳ/ noun
a person who has stopped work and is receiving a pension

peo·ple /'piːpl/ noun
the plural of the word **person**: *I like the people I work with.* | *There were lots of people at the party.*

pep·per /'pepəʳ/ noun
1 (no plural) a powder made from the seeds of a particular plant and used to give food a hot taste ⇨ see picture at GRIND
2 a hollow red or green vegetable that can be eaten raw or used in cooking ⇨ see picture on page 199

pep·per·mint /'pepəmɪnt/ noun
1 (no plural) oil from a plant with a special strong taste used in sweets and TOOTHPASTE
2 a sweet that tastes of peppermint

per /pəʳ; strong pɜːʳ/ preposition
for each or during each: *How much do you earn per week?* | *The fruit costs 70 pence per kilo.*

per cent /pə 'sent/ noun
out of a hundred. Per cent can also be written as %: *Sixty per cent of the pupils are boys.*

perch /pɜːtʃ/ verb
to sit on something narrow: *Birds perched **on** the branch.* | *She perched on the edge of the chair.*

per·fect¹ /'pɜːfɪkt/ adjective
1 without any faults or bad points: *We went to the beach and had a perfect day.*
2 without any mistakes: *She speaks perfect French.*
3 exactly right for a particular purpose: *The rug is perfect **for** the living room.*

per·fect² /pə'fekt/ verb
to make something very good or perfect: *They worked hard to perfect their dance.*

per·fect³ /'pɜːfɪkt/ noun
the form of a verb made by adding the verb 'have' to the past participle, for example 'Someone has stolen my car'

per·fec·tion /pə'fekʃən/ noun (no plural)
when something is perfect: *I'll do my best but don't expect perfection.*

per·fect·ly /'pɜːfɪktlɪ/ adverb
1 completely or very: *You know perfectly well what I mean.*
2 very well, without any mistakes or bad points: *The house suits us perfectly.*

per·form /pə'fɔːm/ verb
1 to do something to entertain people: *They're performing a new play tonight.*
2 to work well: *This car performs well in bad weather.*

per·form·ance /pə'fɔːməns/ noun
1 when people perform a play, concert, etc: *It was an excellent performance of the play.*
2 your ability to do something well: *Her performance in the test was very good.*

per·form·er /pə'fɔːməʳ/ noun
a person who performs in public, for example an actor or singer

per·fume /'pɜːfjuːm/ noun
1 a liquid with a strong pleasant smell that you put on your skin: *What perfume are you wearing?*
2 a sweet or pleasant smell

per·haps /pə'hæps/ adverb
used to say that something may be true or may happen: *Perhaps our team will win.* | *Sarah's late – perhaps she missed the bus.* ⇨ same meaning MAYBE

pe·ri·od /'pɪərɪəd/ noun
a length of time: *There were long periods when we didn't hear from him.* |

She will be in Australia for a period of four weeks.

per·ish /ˈperɪʃ/ *verb*
formal to die: *The crops perished because there was no rain.*

perm /pɜːm/ *noun*
a treatment with chemicals that changes the shape of your hair

per·ma·nent /ˈpɜːmənənt/ *adjective*
continuing for a long time or for always: *Jim now has a permanent job.*
⇨ compare TEMPORARY

per·mis·sion /pəˈmɪʃn/ *noun (no plural)*
when you are allowed to do something: *Did you get permission to use her computer?*

per·mit[1] /pəˈmɪt/ *verb (present participle* **permitting**, *past* **permitted**)
to allow someone to do something: *You are not permitted to bring food into the library.*

per·mit[2] /ˈpɜːmɪt/ *noun*
an official piece of paper saying that you are allowed to do something

per·son /ˈpɜːsn/ *noun (plural* **people** /ˈpiːpl/ *or* **persons**)
a man, woman, or child: *She's a lovely person.* | *You're just the person I want to talk to.*

NOTE: **1** The usual plural of **person** is **people**. **Persons** is very formal and is used only in official notices and ANNOUNCEMENTS, e.g. *Would all persons wishing to buy tickets please come to the tourist office.* **2** Do **not** say 'all people'. Use **everyone** or **everybody** instead.

per·son·al /ˈpɜːsnəl/ *adjective*
belonging to or relating to you: *We work together, but she's also a personal friend.* | *These are my personal letters.*

per·son·al·i·ty /ˌpɜːsəˈnælətɪ/ *noun (plural* **personalities**)
1 the character of a particular person: *She has a loveable personality.*
2 a well-known person: *He is a television personality.*

per·son·al·ly /ˈpɜːsnəlɪ/ *adverb*
used when you are giving your own opinion about something: *Personally, I think he is dishonest, but many people*
trust him.* | *Personally, I believe it is a bad idea.*

per·suade /pəˈsweɪd/ *verb (present participle* **persuading**, *past* **persuaded**)
to talk with someone and give them reasons until they agree with what you say: *He persuaded her **to** go to school, even though she did not want to.* | *I persuaded her to buy the dress.*

per·sua·sion /pəˈsweɪʒn/ *noun (no plural)*
the act of persuading someone: *After a lot of persuasion, she agreed to go.*

pes·si·mist /ˈpesɪmɪst/ *noun*
a person who always thinks that something bad will happen ⇨ opposite OPTIMIST

pes·si·mis·tic /ˌpesɪˈmɪstɪk/ *adjective*
always believing that something bad will happen ⇨ opposite OPTIMISTIC

pest /pest/ *noun*
1 an animal that is harmful or annoying: *Insects which eat crops are pests.*
2 a person who annoys you

pes·ter /ˈpestər/ *verb*
to annoy someone by asking them for something all the time: *Stop pestering me – I'll clean my room tomorrow!*

pet /pet/ *noun*
1 an animal that you look after and keep in your house for company: *She has two cats as pets.* ⇨ see picture on page 201
2 **teacher's pet** a student who the teacher particularly likes

pet·al /ˈpetl/ *noun*
one of the brightly coloured parts of a flower ⇨ see picture at ROSE

pe·ti·tion /pəˈtɪʃn/ *noun*
a letter signed by a lot of people and sent to a government or other official group in order to ask for something or complain about something: *Thousands of people signed the petition asking for a local hospital to be built.*

pet·rol /ˈpetrəl/ *noun (no plural)*
British a liquid used in cars to make the engine work (American **gas**)

petrol sta·tion /ˈpetrəl ˌsteɪʃn/ *noun*
British a place where you take your car to fill it with petrol (American **gas station**)

pet·ti·coat /ˈpetɪkəʊt/ *noun*
a piece of clothing that a girl or woman wears under a skirt or dress

phan·tom /ˈfæntəm/ *noun*
a GHOST

phar·ma·cist /ˈfɑːməsɪst/ *noun*
a person who prepares and sells medicines ⬦ compare CHEMIST

phar·ma·cy /ˈfɑːməsi/ *noun (plural* **pharmacies***)*
a shop or part of a shop that sells medicines

phase /feɪz/ *noun*
one part of the process by which something develops

phi·los·o·pher /fɪˈlɒsəfəʳ/ *noun*
a person who studies philosophy

phi·los·o·phy /fɪˈlɒsəfi/ *noun (no plural)*
the study of life and what it means, how we should live, or what knowledge is: *She's studying philosophy at university.*

phone[1] /fəʊn/ *noun*
also **telephone** a piece of equipment you use to speak to someone who is in another place: *Can I use your phone, please?* | *Could you answer the phone?* | *You can book tickets for the film by phone.*

phone[2] *verb (present participle* **phoning***, past* **phoned***)*
also **telephone** to speak to someone by phone: *I phoned my parents to tell them the news.* | *Has Anna phoned yet?*

phone book /ˈfəʊn bʊk/ *noun*
a book that contains the names, addresses, and telephone numbers of the people in an area

phone box /ˈfəʊn bɒks/ *noun (plural* **phone boxes***)*
a small structure in the street where there is a telephone you can pay to use ⬦ see picture on page 201

phone call /ˈfəʊn kɔːl/ *noun*
when you speak to someone on the telephone: *I need to make a quick phone call.*

phone num·ber /ˈfəʊn ˌnʌmbəʳ/ *noun*
the number that you need to ring when you want to talk to someone on the telephone: *What's your phone number?*

pho·net·ic /fəˈnetɪk/ *adjective*
using special signs to show the sounds you make when speaking: *This dictionary uses a phonetic alphabet to show you how to pronounce words.*

pho·net·ics /fəˈnetɪks/ *noun*
the study of the sounds you make when speaking

pho·to /ˈfəʊtəʊ/ *noun*
a photograph: *She took a photo of the garden.*

pho·to·copy[1] /ˈfəʊtəkɒpi/ *noun (plural* **photocopies***)*
a copy of a piece of writing made on a special machine: *Here's a photocopy of the letter.*

photocopy[2] *verb (present participle* **photocopying***, past* **photocopied***)*
to make a copy of a piece of writing using a special machine

pho·to·graph[1] /ˈfəʊtəgrɑːf/ *verb*
to take a photograph of someone or something: *He has photographed many film stars.*

photograph[2] *noun*
a picture made by a camera: *She's taking photographs of the children.*

pho·tog·ra·pher
/fəˈtɒgrəfəʳ/ *noun*
a person who takes photo-graphs, especially as their job

photographer

pho·tog·ra·phy
/fəˈtɒgrəfi/ *noun (no plural)*
the art or business of taking pictures using a camera: *The programme had wonderful photography of wild animals.*

taking a photograph

phras·al verb /ˌfreɪzl ˈvɜːb/ *noun*
a verb that contains more than one word and has a special meaning, such as 'look something up' or 'show off'

phrase /freɪz/ *noun*
a group of words that does not make a whole sentence, such as 'later that day' and 'on the way home'

phys·i·cal /ˈfɪzɪkl/ *adjective*
1 relating to the body rather than the mind: *I need to get more physical exercise.* ⬦ compare MENTAL
2 relating to things that you can see and touch

phys·i·cist /ˈfɪzɪsɪst/ *noun*
a person who studies or works in physics

A B C D E F G H I J K L M N O P Q R S T U V W X Y Z

phys·ics /ˈfɪzɪks/ *noun*
the study of natural forces, such as heat, light, and movement

pi·a·nist /ˈpiːənɪst/ *noun*
a person who plays a piano: *Joe's a jazz pianist.*

piano

keys
pedal
playing the piano

pi·an·o /prˈænəʊ/ *noun*
a large musical instrument that you play by pressing small black and white bars

pick¹ /pɪk/ *verb*
1 to choose someone or something: *The child picked the biggest sweet. | Students have to pick three courses.*
2 to pull a flower or a fruit from a plant or tree: *She picked an apple from the tree.*
3 pick on someone to treat someone unfairly or unkindly: *He's always picking on the smaller children.*
4 pick something up to take hold of something and lift it up: *Pick up your toys and put them in the cupboard. | I picked up the phone just as it stopped ringing.* ⇨ see picture on page 207
5 pick someone up to collect someone from somewhere: *I'll pick you up at the hotel at eight o'clock.*
6 pick someone's pocket to steal something from someone's pocket

pick² /pɪk/ *noun (no plural)*
take your pick to choose something: *You can take your pick of these cakes.*

pick·et /ˈpɪkɪt/ *noun*
a person who stands outside a shop or factory to stop people entering during an argument over pay or working conditions

pick·pock·et /ˈpɪkˌpɒkɪt/ *noun*
a person who steals things from people's pockets, especially in a crowd

pic·nic /ˈpɪknɪk/ *noun*
a meal eaten outside, when you are away from home: *We had a picnic by the sea. | The whole family set out for a picnic in the countryside.* ⇨ compare BARBECUE

pic·ture¹ /ˈpɪktʃərˈ/ *noun*
1 something represented on paper as a drawing, painting, or a photograph: *She drew a picture **of** me. | Leo's picture (=photograph) was in the paper yesterday.*
2 take a picture to take a photograph of someone or something

picture² *verb (present participle* **picturing**, *past* **pictured**)
to imagine something: *I can still picture him standing there in his uniform. | Rob had pictured her **as** serious but she wasn't like that at all.*

pie /paɪ/ *noun*
a cooked dish of meat, fish, or fruit covered with PASTRY: *Mum's made an apple pie.* ⇨ compare TART

piece

a piece of cake

piece /piːs/ *noun*
a part of something that is separated or broken off from a larger thing: *He took a piece **of** the cake. | I need a piece of paper. | The plate was **in** pieces (=broken into pieces) on the floor.*

pierce /pɪəs/ *verb (present participle* **piercing**, *past* **pierced**)
to make a hole in something: *The needle pierced the material. | Jane has had her ears pierced.*

pierc·ing /ˈpɪəsɪŋ/ *adjective*
a piercing sound is loud and unpleasant: *I heard a piercing scream.*

pig /pɪg/ *noun*
1 a fat pink farm animal kept for its meat

A B C D E F G H I J K L M N O P Q R S T U V W X Y Z

2 a person who eats too much or is dirty or unpleasant

pi·geon /ˈpɪdʒən/ noun
a common grey bird with short legs that is often seen in towns

pig·let /ˈpɪglət/ noun
a young pig

pig·sty /ˈpɪgstaɪ/ noun
a place on a farm where pigs are kept

pile[1] /paɪl/ noun
1 a number of similar things put on top of each other: *There was a pile of books on the table.* ⇨ same meaning STACK
2 a large group of similar things collected together: *There was a pile of logs beside the fire.* ⇨ same meaning HEAP

pile[2] verb (present participle **piling**, past **piled**)
also **pile up** to put things in a pile: *She piled the boxes on top of each other.* | *Mum piled up the plates ready to wash.*

pil·grim /ˈpɪlgrɪm/ noun
a person who goes to pray at a holy place far away from their home

pil·grim·age /ˈpɪlgrɪmɪdʒ/ noun
a journey to a holy place far away from your home

pill /pɪl/ noun
a small hard ball of medicine that you swallow when you are not well ⇨ same meaning TABLET

pil·lar /ˈpɪlər/ noun
a strong round post used to support part of a building: *The roof of the church was supported by stone pillars.*

pil·low /ˈpɪləʊ/ noun
a cloth bag filled with soft material that you can put your head on when you are in bed ⇨ compare CUSHION

pil·low·case /ˈpɪləʊkeɪs/ noun
a cover that you put on a pillow to keep it clean

pi·lot /ˈpaɪlət/ noun
a person who flies planes ⇨ see picture on page 200

pim·ple /ˈpɪmpl/ noun
a small rough spot on your skin

pin[1] /pɪn/ noun
a small pointed piece of metal used for joining together pieces of cloth, fastening things together, etc

pin[2] verb (present participle **pinning**, past **pinned**)
to fasten or join things with a pin: *She pinned a note on the door.*

pinch[1] /pɪntʃ/ verb
1 to take something between your thumb and fingers and press it: *She pinched my arm hard, and it still hurts.*
2 informal to steal something: *He pinched an apple.*

pinch[2] noun (plural **pinches**)
1 a very small amount: *Add a pinch of salt.*
2 an act of pressing something tightly between your thumb and fingers

pine /paɪn/ noun
a tree that has thin leaves like needles

pine·ap·ple /ˈpaɪnæpl/ noun
a large yellow fruit with a hard skin and stiff leaves on top ⇨ see picture on page 199

ping-pong /ˈpɪŋ pɒŋ/ noun (no plural)
a game in which two or four players hit a small ball across a net on a table ⇨ same meaning TABLE-TENNIS

pink /pɪŋk/ adjective, noun
the colour made by mixing red and white

pint /paɪnt/ noun
a measure of liquid, equal to 0.569 litres: *There are eight pints in a gallon.*

pi·o·neer /ˌpaɪəˈnɪər/ noun
a person who goes somewhere or does something before other people: *He was one of the pioneers of space travel.*

pip /pɪp/ noun
British the small seeds in some fruits such as apples and oranges

pipe /paɪp/ noun
1 a tube for carrying water or gas: *A metal pipe carried the water away.*
2 a small tube with a round bowl at one end used for smoking TOBACCO

pi·rate /ˈpaɪərət/ noun
a person who attacks ships and steals things

pis·tol /ˈpɪstl/ noun
a small gun ⇨ same meaning REVOLVER

pit /pɪt/ noun
1 a deep hole in the ground
2 a deep hole in the ground from which people dig out coal ⇨ same meaning MINE

pitch[1] /pɪtʃ/ noun (plural **pitches**)
 1 British a part of a field on which games are played: a cricket pitch
 2 how high or low a sound is

pitch[2] verb
 to set up a tent: We pitched our tent near the river.

pit·y[1] /'pɪtɪ/ noun (no plural)
 1 the sadness that you feel when someone else is hurt, in trouble, etc: I felt great pity **for** people with nowhere to live.
 2 **a pity** a sad situation: What a pity you can't come and see us!

pity[2] verb (present participle **pitying**, past **pitied**)
 to feel sadness for someone else because they are hurt, in trouble, etc: I pity anyone who has to work in such bad conditions.

piz·za /'pi:tsə/ noun
 a round flat piece of bread covered with TOMATO, cheese, and other foods and then baked ⇨ see picture at FAST FOOD

place[1] /pleɪs/ noun
 1 a particular area, building, town, or country: This is the place where I first saw her. | He travelled to places all over the world. | Are there any good places to eat near here?
 2 a particular area, point, or position: Keep your passport in a safe place. | Paint is coming off the wall in places.
 3 the right or usual position for something: Please put the jug back in its place.
 4 someone's house or home: I'm going over to Jeff's place for dinner.
 5 **in place of something** instead of something: There's football on in place of the normal TV programmes.
 6 **take place** to happen: When will the ceremony take place? ⇨ look at HAPPEN

pirate

place[2] verb (present participle **placing**, past **placed**)
 1 to put something somewhere: She placed a book **on** the table.
 2 to put someone or something in a particular situation: Her request places me in a difficult situation.
 3 **place an order** to ask a shop, factory, etc for some goods

plain[1] /pleɪn/ adjective
 1 in one colour without a pattern on: She wore a plain green dress.
 2 easy to understand or recognize: He made it plain **that** he did not like me. | It's plain that she doesn't agree. ⇨ same meaning CLEAR
 3 ordinary or usual: I like plain food.

plain[2] noun
 a large area of flat land

plain·ly /'pleɪnlɪ/ adverb
 1 in a way that is easy to see, hear, or understand: We could hear Tom's voice plainly over the noise of the crowd.
 2 If something is plainly true, it is easy to see that it is true: It was plainly too hot to be working in the sun. ⇨ same meaning OBVIOUSLY

plait[1] /plæt/ verb
 to twist together three pieces of rope, hair, etc

plait[2] noun
 three lengths of hair that are twisted together into one piece: She wore her hair in plaits. ⇨ see picture on page 202

plan[1] /plæn/ noun
 1 something you have decided to do in the future: Have you made any plans for the weekend? | Her plan is to finish school and then travel.
 2 a drawing showing all the parts of a building, garden, machine, room, etc

plan[2] verb (present participle **planning**, past **planned**)
 to think about what you are going to do in the future and how to do it: They plan **to** build a bridge over the river. | We've been planning our holiday for months.

plane /pleɪn/ noun
 a vehicle that flies using an engine: What time does the plane land?

plan·et /'plænɪt/ noun
 one of the large objects in space like the Earth that go round the sun or a star

A B C D E F G H I J K L M N O P Q R S T U V W X Y Z

plank /plæŋk/ *noun*

a long flat thin piece of wood: *Planks of wood were lying on the ground.*

plant[1] /plɑːnt/ *noun*

something living that is not an animal, such as a tree, flower, or vegetable: *You need to water the plants.* | *She is growing tomato plants in the garden.*

plant[2] *verb*

to put plants or seeds in the ground to grow: *Spring is the best time to plant flowers.* | *Have you planted any vegetables yet?*

plan·ta·tion /plɑːnˈteɪʃn/ *noun*

a large piece of land on which tea, sugar, cotton, or rubber is grown

plas·ter[1] /ˈplɑːstəʳ/ *noun*

1 (*no plural*) a soft white substance that becomes hard when dry and is spread on walls to make them smooth

2 *British* a thin piece of sticky material that you put on your skin to protect a cut ⇨ see picture at FIRST AID

plaster[2] *verb*

to cover a wall with plaster

plas·tic /ˈplæstɪk/ *adjective, noun*

a strong substance made from chemicals and used to make containers, toys, etc: *I always give the baby a plastic bowl so she can't break it.*

plate /pleɪt/ *noun*

a flat, usually round, dish for food: *She had plain white dinner plates.* ⇨ compare BOWL

plat·form /ˈplætfɔːm/ *noun*

1 the part of a station where you get on and off trains: *The train at platform 2 is the London train.* ⇨ see picture at RAILWAY STATION

2 a raised part of a floor on which people may stand: *The head teacher gave his speech from a platform at one end of the hall.*

play[1] /pleɪ/ *verb*

1 to take part in a game or sport: *He plays football every Sunday.* | *Do you play chess?*

2 games and other activities done by children for fun: *The little girl was playing in the garden.*

3 to make sounds on a musical instrument: *She plays the drum.*

4 to act as a character in a play or film: *Who does he play in the film?*

play[2] *noun*

1 a story performed by people in a theatre, on the radio, etc: *She is in a new play about a famous singer.*

2 (*no plural*) activity done for enjoyment by children: *Children learn a lot through play.*

play·er /ˈpleɪəʳ/ *noun*

a person who plays a game or a sport: *She is a tennis player.*

play·ful /ˈpleɪfəl/ *adjective*

full of fun: *He had a playful little dog.*

play·ground /ˈpleɪɡraʊnd/ *noun*

a special piece of ground for children to play on, especially when they are at school

play·ing card /ˈpleɪ-ɪŋ ˌkɑːd/ *noun*

one of a set of pieces of stiff paper that are printed with numbers and pictures and used to play games ⇨ same meaning CARD

play·ing field /ˈpleɪ-ɪŋ ˌfiːld/ *noun*

a large area of grass where people play sports

plead /pliːd/ *verb*

1 to ask for something that you want very much: *He pleaded with her to listen to him.* ⇨ same meaning BEG

2 to say officially in a court of law if you are guilty or not: *The woman pleaded not guilty.*

pleas·ant /ˈpleznt/ *adjective*

nice or enjoyable: *We spent a pleasant day in the country.* | *Her visit was a pleasant surprise.* ⇨ opposite UNPLEASANT

pleasantly *adverb*: *The weather was pleasantly warm.*

please[1] /pliːz/

a word added to a question or an order, to make it polite: *Please bring your book to me.* | *Could I have a glass of water, please?* ⇨ compare THANK YOU

please[2] *verb* (*present participle* **pleasing**, *past* **pleased**)

to give happiness or pleasure to someone: *I'm tired of trying to please everyone.*

pleased /pliːzd/ *adjective*

happy about something

plea·sure /ˈpleʒəʳ/ *noun* (*no plural*)

the feeling of happiness or satisfaction that you get from doing something you enjoy: *She looked at the paintings with great pleasure.* | *I often read* **for** *pleasure.*

plen·ti·ful /'plentɪfəl/ *adjective*
existing in large amounts or numbers: *There was a plentiful supply of food.*

plen·ty /'plentɪ/
a lot: *We have plenty* **of** *time to catch the train.* | *She was worried there wouldn't be enough bread, but there was plenty.*

pli·ers /'plaɪəz/ *plural noun*
a tool that looks like a pair of strong scissors and is used for cutting wire or for removing nails

plod /plɒd/ *verb (present participle* **plodding**, *past* **plodded**)
to walk slowly and heavily

plot¹ /plɒt/ *noun*
1 a secret plan by a group of people to do something wrong: *There was a plot* **to** *kill the President.*
2 the story of a book, film, or play: *The film had an exciting plot.*
3 a small piece of ground

plot² *verb (present participle* **plotting**, *past* **plotted**)
to plan secretly to do something wrong: *They were plotting to kill the king.*

plough¹ /plaʊ/ *noun*
a piece of farming equipment for cutting up and turning over the earth before seeds are planted

plough² *verb*
to break and cut up the earth with a plough: *Farmers must plough the land before planting crops.*

pluck /plʌk/ *verb*
to take something quickly from someone or something: *She plucked a handkerchief* **from** *her sleeve.*

plug¹ /plʌg/   **plug**
noun
1 the object that you push into a wall to connect a piece of electrical equipment to the electricity
⇨ compare SOCKET

2 a round piece of rubber used for blocking the hole in a bath, BASIN, etc

plug² *verb (present participle* **plugging**, *past* **plugged**)
1 to block or fill a hole with something
2 **plug something in** to connect an electrical machine to the electricity: *You need to plug in the lamp.*

plum /plʌm/ *noun*
a sweet juicy red or yellow fruit with a smooth skin and one large seed ⇨ see picture on page 199

plumb·er /'plʌməʳ/ *noun*
a person whose job is to fit and repair water pipes, toilets, etc

plumb·ing /'plʌmɪŋ/ *noun (no plural)*
all the water pipes in a house or building

plump /plʌmp/ *adjective*
nicely fat: *The baby has plump little arms.* ⇨ see picture on page 202

plunge /plʌndʒ/ *verb (present participle* **plunging**, *past* **plunged**)
to fall a long way down or to push something down suddenly: *He plunged his hand into the water.*

plu·ral /'plʊərəl/ *adjective, noun*
the form of a word that shows you are talking about more than one. For example, 'dogs' is the plural of 'dog' and 'men' is the plural of 'man' ⇨ opposite SINGULAR

plus /plʌs/ *preposition*
used when one number or amount is added to another. For example, four plus two is six $(4 + 2 = 6)$: *The computer will cost £1020 plus tax.*

p.m. /piː 'em/
in the afternoon or evening: *It is 4.30 pm* ⇨ compare AM

PO Box /piː 'əʊ ˌbɒks/ *noun (plural* **PO Boxes**)
a box with a number in a post office where you can have mail sent instead of to your home

pock·et /'pɒkɪt/ *noun*
a part of a piece of clothing in which you can put things: *She took her keys out of her coat pocket*

pocket mon·ey /'pɒkɪt ˌmʌnɪ/ *noun*
money given to a child every week to spend as he or she wants

pod /pɒd/ *noun*
a long narrow part of some plants in which seeds grow

po·em /'pəʊɪm/ *noun*
a piece of writing with regular lines and

sounds expressed in powerful or beautiful language: *He wrote a poem about war.*

po·et /'pəʊɪt/ *noun*
a person who writes poems

po·et·ry /'pəʊɪtrɪ/ *noun (no plural)*
poems in general: *I was reading a book of poetry.*

point¹ /pɔɪnt/ *noun*
1 the most important idea, fact, or opinion: *Stop talking so much and get to the point! I I agreed with several of the points he made.*
2 a particular moment or time: *At the point when I left, the teacher was reading a story.*
3 an exact position or place: *The accident happened at the point where the two roads cross.*
4 *(no plural)* use or purpose: *I don't see the point of repairing a car as old as this one. I The whole point of travelling is to experience new things.*
5 the sharp end of something: *I cut my finger on the point of a nail.*
6 a sign (.) used to separate a whole number from a number that is less than one: *A quarter is the same as nought point two five per cent (0.25%).*
7 a number that you win in a game or sport: *Our team won by 15 points to 10.*
8 on the point of doing something ready to do something almost immediately: *I was on the point of phoning the police when she arrived home.*
9 point of view a belief or opinion about something: *Try to understand it from my point of view.*

point² *verb*
to show where something is with your finger stretched out: *He pointed to the building on the corner and said, "That's where I work."* ⇨ see picture on page 207

point·ed /'pɔɪntɪd/ *adjective*
having a sharp end

point·less /'pɔɪntləs/ *adjective*
with no purpose or meaning: *It was a pointless meeting.*

poi·son¹ /'pɔɪzn/ *noun*
a substance that kills or harms you if it gets into your body

poison² *verb*
to kill a person or an animal with poison: *The farmer poisoned the rats.*

poi·son·ous /'pɔɪznəs/ *adjective*
containing poison: *a poisonous plant*

poke /pəʊk/ *verb (present participle* **poking**, *past* **poked**)
to push a pointed object into someone or something: *He poked the fire with a stick.*

pok·er /'pəʊkə^r/ *noun*
a card game that people usually play for money

po·lar /'pəʊlə^r/ *adjective*
relating to the North or South Pole: *As the climate warms up the polar ice will melt.* ⇨ see picture at CLIMATE

polar bear /,pəʊlə 'beə^r/ *noun*
a large white bear that lives near the North Pole ⇨ see picture on page 195

pole /pəʊl/ *noun*
1 a long narrow piece of wood usually used to support something: *A tent is supported by tent poles.*
2 the most northern or southern end of the Earth: *the North Pole*

po·lice /pə'liːs/ *noun*
the police the group of men and women whose job is to protect people and property and to make sure that everyone obeys the law: *The police are searching for the thief. I She hoped to join the police when she left school.*

po·lice·man /pə'liːsmən/ *noun (plural* **policemen** /-mən/)
a male member of the police

police of·fi·cer /pə'liːs ˌɒfɪsə^r/ *noun*
someone who is a member of the police

police sta·tion /pə'liːs ˌsteɪʃn/ *noun*
an office or building used by the police

police·wom·an /pə'liːsˌwʊmən/ *noun (plural* **policewomen** /-ˌwɪmɪn/)
a female member of the police

pol·i·cy /'pɒləsɪ/ *noun (plural* **policies**)
a general plan agreed by a political party, a government, or a company: *Government policy is to improve education.*

polish

polishing shoes

pol·ish¹ /ˈpɒlɪʃ/ *verb*
to rub something so that it shines: *I need to polish my shoes.*

polish² *noun (no plural)*
an oily substance that helps to make things shine

po·lite /pəˈlaɪt/ *adjective*
having a kind and respectful way of behaving: *A polite child always says thank you.* ⟡ opposite IMPOLITE, RUDE

po·lit·i·cal /pəˈlɪtɪkl/ *adjective*
relating to the government or politics of a country: *The United States has two main political parties.*

pol·i·ti·cian /ˌpɒləˈtɪʃn/ *noun*
someone who works in the government, especially a Member of Parliament

pol·i·tics /ˈpɒlətɪks/ *noun (no plural)*
1 activities or opinions relating to the government of a country, state, etc: *Are you interested in politics? I I don't agree with his politics.*
2 the job of being a politician: *He wants to go into politics.*

pol·lute /pəˈluːt/ *verb (present participle* **polluting***, past* **polluted***)*
to make the air, water, or soil dirty or dangerous by adding harmful substances: *The lake was polluted by chemicals from factories.*

pol·lu·tion /pəˈluːʃn/ *noun (no plural)*
1 the process of making the air, water, or soil dirty and dangerous: *Levels of pollution are high in many rivers.*
2 a substance that makes the air, water, or soil dirty or dangerous: *The air in big cities is full of pollution.*

pond

a garden pond

pond /pɒnd/ *noun*
an area of water, smaller than a lake: *There's a duck pond in the middle of the village.* ⟡ compare PUDDLE

po·ny /ˈpəʊnɪ/ *noun (plural* **ponies***)*
a small horse

po·ny·tail /ˈpəʊnɪteɪl/ *noun*
hair tied together at the back of your head: *She wore her hair in a ponytail.*
⟡ see picture on page 202

pool /puːl/ *noun*
1 an area of water built for people to swim in: *I hate swimming in an indoor pool.*
2 a small area of liquid on a surface: *The dead man lay in a pool of blood.*
3 a small area of water, usually formed naturally: *A shallow pool had formed in the rocks.* ⟡ compare PUDDLE, POND

poor /pʊəʳ/ *adjective*
1 not having very much money: *She was too poor to buy clothes for the children.* ⟡ compare RICH, WEALTHY
2 used for showing that someone or something makes you feel sad: *The poor animal hadn't been fed. I Poor Sarah always gets the blame.*
3 not of a good standard: *Your writing is poor.*

poor·ly /ˈpʊəlɪ/ *adverb*
badly: *The work was hard and poorly paid.*

pop¹ /pɒp/ *noun*
1 *(no plural)* also **pop music** music or songs with a strong beat that many people like and dance to
2 a sudden noise like the sound of the top being pulled out of a bottle: *The balloon burst with a loud pop.*

pop² *verb (present participle* **popping***, past* **popped***)*
1 to go somewhere or put something somewhere quickly: *I'm just popping out to buy some milk. I Can you pop the letter under her door?*
2 to make a short loud sound: *Champagne corks were popping.*

pop·corn /ˈpɒpkɔːn/ *noun (no plural)*
maize that is cooked until it explodes, eaten with sugar or salt

pope /pəʊp/ *noun*
the head of the Roman Catholic Church

pop group /ˈpɒp gruːp/ *noun*
a group of people who play and sing pop music

pop·u·lar /ˈpɒpjʊləʳ/ *adjective*
liked by many people: *She is popular at*

A
B
C
D
E
F
G
H
I
J
K
L
M
N
O
P
Q
R
S
T
U
V
W
X
Y
Z

school. | *This dance is popular* **with** *young people.* ⇨ opposite UNPOPULAR

pop·u·lar·i·ty /ˌpɒpjʊˈlærəti/ *noun (no plural)*
when a lot of people like someone or something: *The band's popularity has been growing.*

pop·u·la·tion /ˌpɒpjʊˈleɪʃn/ *noun*
the number of people living in a place: *What is the population* **of** *Mexico City?*

pork /pɔːk/ *noun (no plural)*
meat from pigs

por·ridge /ˈpɒrɪdʒ/ *noun (no plural)*
a breakfast food made by cooking grain with water until it is very soft

port /pɔːt/ *noun*
an area or town where ships can arrive and leave from ⇨ compare HARBOUR

port·a·ble /ˈpɔːtəbl/ *adjective*
small, light, and easy to carry with you: *We're taking a portable television with us.*

port·hole /ˈpɔːthəʊl/ *noun*
a small round window in the side of a ship or plane

por·tion /ˈpɔːʃn/ *noun*
a part or share of something: *She only eats a small portion* **of** *her food.* | *The front portion of the rocket breaks off.*

por·trait /ˈpɔːtreɪt/ *noun*
a painting, drawing, or photograph of a person: *He painted a portrait of his daughter.*

po·si·tion /pəˈzɪʃn/ *noun*
1 the situation or condition that a person is in: *I am in a difficult position as I have just lost my job.* | *I'm not sure what I would do in your position.*
2 the way in which someone sits, stands, or lies: *That's an uncomfortable position to sleep in.*
3 a place where a person or thing is: *Our seats were in a good position to hear the music.* | *He can tell where north is by the position of the stars.*
4 a job: *He has an important position in the company.*

pos·i·tive /ˈpɒzətɪv/ *adjective*
1 confident and happy: *She has a positive attitude to life.*
2 sure that something is true: *I am positive that I gave you his address.*
⇨ same meaning CERTAIN

pos·sess /pəˈzes/ *verb*
to have or own something: *He lost everything he possessed in a fire.*

pos·ses·sion /pəˈzeʃn/ *noun*
something that you own: *She sold most of her possessions before she left.*

pos·si·bil·i·ty /ˌpɒsəˈbɪləti/ *noun (plural* **possibilities***)*
something that might happen or might be true: *They say there's a possibility* **of** *rain at the weekend.* | *There's a possibility* **that** *she will fail her history exam.*

pos·si·ble /ˈpɒsəbl/ *adjective*
able to be done, happen, or exist: *Is it possible to get to the city by train, or must I take a bus?* | *It's possible that she'll still come.* ⇨ opposite IMPOSSIBLE

pos·si·bly /ˈpɒsəbli/ *adverb*
perhaps: *"Can you come tomorrow?" "Possibly."* | *The journey will take three hours – possibly more.* ⇨ same meaning MAYBE

post¹ /pəʊst/ *noun*
1 *British* the letters and parcels that you send that are delivered to people's houses and offices (*American* **mail**): *I sent it by post.* | *Your birthday card is in the post.*
2 a thick bar of wood, metal, or stone fixed in the ground: *The fence was held up by wooden posts.*
3 an important job: *All new posts will be advertised.*

post² *verb*
British to send a letter or parcel by post

post·age /ˈpəʊstɪdʒ/ *noun (no plural)*
the amount of money that you pay to post something: *The postage for this parcel is very expensive.*

post·box /ˈpəʊstbɒks/ *noun (plural* **postboxes***)*
an official box into which you put letters if you want to send them by post ⇨ same meaning LETTER BOX

post·card /ˈpəʊstkɑːd/ *noun*
a small card, often with a picture on one side, that you send by post without an envelope

post·code /ˈpəʊstkəʊd/ *noun*
British a group of letters and numbers at the end of someone's address

post·er /ˈpəʊstər/ *noun*
a large printed notice or picture ⇨ see picture on page 197

post·grad·u·ate /ˌpəʊstˈgrædʒʊət/ noun
British a student who has done a first university degree

post·man /ˈpəʊstmən/ noun (plural **postmen** /-mən/)
British someone whose job is to collect and deliver letters and parcels

post of·fice /ˈpəʊst ˌɒfɪs/ noun
a place where you can buy STAMPS, post parcels, etc ⇨ see picture on page 201

post·pone /pəsˈpəʊn/ verb (present participle **postponing**, past **postponed**)
to change the time of an event to a later time: We postponed the match from March 5th to March 19th. ⇨ compare DELAY

pot /pɒt/ noun
1 a round container, especially one used for cooking or storing food: I've made a big pot **of** soup.
2 a container for pouring hot tea or coffee

po·ta·to /pəˈteɪtəʊ/ noun (plural **potatoes**)
a round white vegetable that grows under the ground and is cooked before eating ⇨ see picture on page 199

pot·ter·y /ˈpɒtərɪ/ noun (no plural)
1 plates, cups, and other objects made from clay
2 the activity of making objects from clay

poul·try /ˈpəʊltrɪ/ noun (no plural)
chickens and other birds kept for eggs or meat

pounce /paʊns/ verb (present participle **pouncing**, past **pounced**)
to jump on something suddenly in order to catch it: The cat pounced **on** the bird.

pound¹ /paʊnd/ noun
1 the money used in Britain and some other places: I bought a car for five hundred pounds.
2 a measure of weight equal to 16 OUNCES or 454 grams: Can I have two pounds **of** apples, please?

pound² verb
to hit something hard and often: He pounded on the door.

pour /pɔːʳ/ verb

pour

1 to make a liquid or other substance flow into or out of a container: She poured some sugar into a bowl. I He poured me a cup of tea.
⇨ see picture on page 198
2 to rain hard and steadily: It's pouring outside.

pov·er·ty /ˈpɒvətɪ/ noun (no plural)
when someone is poor: She has lived in poverty all her life.

pow·der /ˈpaʊdəʳ/ noun
a substance in the form of fine grains like dust: They washed the clothes with soap powder.

pow·er /ˈpaʊəʳ/ noun
1 (no plural) control over people or a place: He is ambitious and wants power. I She has a lot of power **over** the people in her team.
2 the right or authority to do something: The police have the power to arrest you.
3 (no plural) energy that is used to make a machine work: Disconnect the power supply before repairing the washing machine.

pow·er·ful /ˈpaʊəfəl/ adjective
very strong or having a lot of power or force: The United States is a powerful nation. I The car has a powerful engine.

pow·er·less /ˈpaʊələs/ adjective
without power or strength: I felt powerless to help her.

prac·ti·cal /ˈpræktɪkl/ adjective
1 relating to real situations and events rather than ideas: She has years of practical experience in teaching.
2 good at making decisions and dealing with problems: We've got to be practical and buy only what we can afford.
3 good at doing things with your hands: He is very practical – he can mend almost anything.

prac·ti·cal·ly /ˈpræktɪklɪ/ adverb
almost: I've practically finished – I'll come in a minute.

prac·tice /ˈpræktɪs/ noun

1 (no plural) regular activity that you do to improve your skill: You need more practice before you can play for the team.

2 something that you do in a particular way because it is usual to do it like that: In Britain, it is the practice to shake hands when you meet someone.

3 out of practice unable to do something well because you have not done it regularly enough

prac·tise /ˈpræktɪs/ verb (present participle **practising**, past **practised**)

to do something regularly so as to become better at it: You won't become a good singer if you don't practise more.

praise[1] /preɪz/ verb (present participle **praising**, past **praised**)

to say that you admire someone or something: She praised her daughter's hard work.

praise[2] noun (no plural)

things you say to praise someone or something: Her new record has received a lot of praise.

pram /præm/ noun

a small vehicle with four wheels in which a baby can lie while being pushed ⇨ compare PUSHCHAIR

prawn /prɔːn/ noun

a small sea animal that you can eat

pray /preɪ/ verb

to talk to God or a god, giving thanks or asking for something

prayer /preəʳ/ noun

1 (no plural) the act of praying

2 words that you say when you are praying

preach /priːtʃ/ verb

to give a speech about a religious subject, usually in a church

preach·er /ˈpriːtʃəʳ/ noun

a person who gives a religious speech

pre·cau·tion /prɪˈkɔːʃn/ noun

something that is done to stop something bad or dangerous from happening: He **took the** precaution of locking his door when he went out. | You should save your work regularly as a precaution **against** your computer failing.

pre·cious /ˈpreʃəs/ adjective

1 very valuable or expensive: Water is precious in the desert. | Her necklace was made of precious stones.

2 very special to you: I had precious memories of our holiday.

pre·ci·pice /ˈpresəpɪs/ noun

a very steep side of a mountain

pre·cise /prɪˈsaɪs/ adjective

exact and correct: Your instructions to the students need to be more precise. | She gave a precise description of the man.

pre·cise·ly /prɪˈsaɪslɪ/ adverb

1 exactly: I don't know precisely why she lost her job. | The show started at precisely seven o'clock.

2 a word you use to show you agree with someone: "So you think he was wrong?" "Precisely." ⇨ same meaning EXACTLY

pre·dict /prɪˈdɪkt/ verb

to say what is going to happen before it happens: The teacher predicted that we would all pass the examination and we did.

pre·dic·tion /prɪˈdɪkʃn/ noun

a statement saying what you expect to happen: Your prediction about the weather was wrong. It didn't rain at all.

pre·fer /prɪˈfɜːʳ/ verb (present participle **preferring**, past **preferred**)

to like one thing more than another: Which of these two dresses do you prefer? | I prefer swimming to cycling.

prefe·ra·ble /ˈprefrəbl/ adjective

more suitable, or better: For a holiday in August, I think France would be preferable **to** Majorca.

prefe·rence /ˈprefrəns/ noun

a liking for one thing rather than another: My preference is **for** the theatre rather than the cinema.

pre·fix /ˈpriːfɪks/ noun (plural **prefixes**)

a group of letters that can be added to the beginning of another word to change the meaning. For example, adding the prefix 'un' to the word 'happy' makes the word 'unhappy'

preg·nan·cy /ˈpregnənsɪ/ noun

the condition of having a baby developing in your body: Women should not drink much alcohol during pregnancy.

preg·nant /ˈpregnənt/ adjective
having a baby developing in your body: *She is four months pregnant.* | *She's pregnant **with** her third child.*

prej·u·dice /ˈpredʒʊdɪs/ noun
an unfair opinion that is not based on facts or reason: *He has a prejudice **against** women drivers.*

prej·u·diced /ˈpredʒʊdɪst/ adjective
having an unfair opinion about something that is not based on facts or reason: *She is prejudiced **against** foreigners.*

prep·a·ra·tion /ˌprepəˈreɪʃn/ noun
1 (no plural) the act of getting something ready: *Teachers have to do a lot of preparation before each lesson.* | *The England team have begun their preparation for next week's match.*
2 preparations arrangements for something that will happen in the future: *She's very busy with preparations **for** the wedding.*

pre·pare /prɪˈpeəʳ/ verb (present participle **preparing**, past **prepared**)
to make something ready: *I prepared the food for the party.* | *We're preparing to go on holiday.*

pre·pared /prɪˈpeəd/ adjective
1 ready to do something: *I wasn't prepared for all his questions.*
2 prepared to do something willing to do something: *Are you prepared to stay late tomorrow?*

prep·o·si·tion /ˌprepəˈzɪʃn/ noun
a word such as 'to', 'for', 'on', 'by', etc, used in front of a noun to show where, when, or how something happens. In the sentences 'She walked with her sister' and 'They went to town', 'with' and 'to' are prepositions

pre·scribe /prɪˈskraɪb/ verb (present participle **prescribing**, past **prescribed**)
to say what medicine someone should take when they are ill

pres·crip·tion /prɪˈskrɪpʃən/ noun
a special paper written by a doctor, ordering medicine for someone: *The doctor wrote me a prescription **for** pills.*

pres·ence /ˈprezns/ noun
1 the state of being present at a particular time: *Your presence is needed at the meeting.* ⇨ opposite ABSENCE

2 in the presence of someone seen or watched by someone: *The results were read out in the presence of all the parents.*

pres·ent[1] /ˈpreznt/ adjective
1 be present in a particular place at a particular time: *How many people were present?* | *There are twenty children present today.*
2 existing now: *What is your present job?*

pres·ent[2] /ˈpreznt/ noun
1 something that you give to someone, for example to celebrate something or to thank them: *He gave her a birthday present.*
2 at present at the moment of speaking: *He's on holiday at present.* | *We don't have any plans at present for closing the school.*

pre·sent[3] /prɪˈzent/ verb
to give something to someone, often as part of an official ceremony: *Who's going to present the gold cup **to** the winner?*

pre·sen·ta·tion /ˌpreznˈteɪʃn/ noun
the act of giving something to someone, often as part of an official ceremony: *The presentation of prizes starts at three o'clock.*

pres·ent·ly /ˈprezntlɪ/ adverb
soon: *The taxi will arrive presently.*

present par·ti·ci·ple /ˌpreznt ˈpɑːtɪsɪpl/ noun
the form of a verb that ends in '-ing' and is used to show continuous action, or as an adjective. In the sentence 'The child is sleeping', 'sleeping' is a present participle

present per·fect /ˌpreznt ˈpɜːfɪkt/ noun
the form of a verb made by adding the verb 'have' to the past participle of the verb. In the sentence 'I have eaten the cake', 'have eaten' is in the present perfect

present tense /ˌpreznt ˈtens/ noun
the tense of a verb that shows what is happening now

pres·er·va·tion /ˌprezəˈveɪʃn/ noun (no plural)
the action of keeping something safe and the same: *We are fighting for the preservation **of** this forest.*

A B C D E F G H I J K L M N O P Q R S T U V W X Y Z

pre·serve /prɪˈzɜːv/ verb (present participle **preserving**, past **preserved**)

to keep something from being damaged, or from going bad: You can preserve meat or fish in salt. I All the old buildings had been very well preserved.

pres·i·dent /ˈprezɪdənt/ noun

1 the official head of many countries that do not have a king or queen: The President **of** the United States is elected every four years.

2 the head of a big company or important organization

press¹ /pres/ verb

1 to push something with your finger: He pressed the doorbell. I To turn on the radio, press this button.

2 to push against something firmly: The children pressed their faces **against** the window.

press² noun (no plural)

the press all newspapers and magazines and the people working for them: Members of the press were waiting outside. I Reports of the accident appeared in the press.

pres·sure /ˈpreʃəʳ/ noun

1 the act of force or weight pressing on something: The pressure of the water turns the wheel.

2 (no plural) attempts to make someone do something by arguing with them, using influence, etc: The company has come **under** pressure to change its products.

3 conditions in your life that can cause you worry: There are a lot of pressures in his job.

pre·tend /prɪˈtend/ verb

to do something to make people believe that something is true or real, when it is not: He pretended that he was ill so that he could stay at home. I She pretended to be asleep.

pret·ty¹ /ˈprɪtɪ/ adjective (**prettier**, **prettiest**)

attractive and nice to look at: She is a very pretty child. I She was wearing a pretty pink dress. ⇨ look at BEAUTIFUL

pretty² adverb

rather, but not very: It was a pretty serious accident. I I'm pretty sure she'll say yes.

pre·vent /prɪˈvent/ verb

to stop something from happening, or stop someone from doing something: Brushing your teeth regularly helps prevent tooth decay. I He threw water on the fire to prevent it **from** spreading. I I tried to prevent her from leaving her job.

pre·ven·tion /prɪˈvenʃən/ noun (no plural)

the action of stopping something from happening: Our aim is the prevention of crime in the area.

pre·vi·ous /ˈpriːvɪəs/ adjective

happening before the present time: In my previous job, I used to travel to the city every day. I She said she had seen him the previous day.

pre·vi·ous·ly /ˈpriːvɪəslɪ/ adverb

at an earlier time: He was working in a shop. Previously, he had worked in a restaurant. I The world record was previously held by an American athlete.

prey /preɪ/ noun (no plural)

an animal that is hunted and caught by another animal

price /praɪs/ noun

the money that you must pay to buy something: House prices have gone up again. I The price of the holiday includes food and accommodation.

price·less /ˈpraɪsləs/

very valuable: He owns a priceless painting.

prick /prɪk/ verb

to make a small hole in something with a sharp object: I pricked my finger on a needle.

pride /praɪd/ noun (no plural)

the feeling of pleasure and satisfaction that you have because of something good that you have done or something nice that you own: She showed us her new home with great pride. I He **takes** great pride **in** his work.

priest /priːst/ noun

someone whose job is to lead religious ceremonies and perform religious duties

pri·ma·ry /ˈpraɪmərɪ/ adjective

main or most important: Our primary task is to provide the refugees with food and health care.

primary school /ˈpraɪmərɪ ˌskuːl/ noun

British a school for children between 5 and 11 years old

prime min·is·ter /ˌpraɪm ˈmɪnɪstəʳ/ *noun*
the leader of the government in many countries

prim·i·tive /ˈprɪmətɪv/ *adjective*
early in human history: *Primitive people lived in caves.*

prince /prɪns/ *noun*
1 the son of a king or queen
2 the ruler of a country

prin·cess /prɪnˈses/ *noun*
the daughter of a king or queen or the wife of a prince

prin·ci·pal¹ /ˈprɪnsɪpl/ *adjective*
most important: *What is your principal reason for staying here? | Her principal source of income is from teaching.*

principal² *noun*
the head of a school and some colleges

prin·ci·ple /ˈprɪnsɪpl/ *noun*
a general rule or idea that you believe is right and that you try to follow in your life: *It is a principle of mine to help people when I can. | It's against my principles to hit a child.*

print¹ /prɪnt/ *verb*
1 to put words and pictures onto paper or material by machine: *The books are printed in Hong Kong.*
2 to write something without joining the letters together: *Please print your name clearly.*

print² *noun*
1 (*no plural*) words printed on a page: *The print is too small for me to read.*
2 a mark made on a soft surface when you press something onto it: *His feet left prints in the snow.*

prin·ter /ˈprɪntəʳ/ *noun*
1 a machine connected to a computer that prints documents from the computer onto paper
2 a person or company whose job is to print books, magazines, etc ⇨ see picture on page 200

pris·on /ˈprɪzn/ *noun*
a building where criminals are kept locked up as a punishment: *He was in prison for ten years.* ⇨ same meaning JAIL

pris·on·er /ˈprɪznəʳ/ *noun*
a person who is kept in a prison ⇨ see picture at PRISON

pri·vate¹ /ˈpraɪvɪt/ *adjective*
1 only for one person or group, not for everyone: *This is private land – you can't walk across it.* ⇨ compare PUBLIC
2 private feelings, information, etc are secret or personal and not for other people to know about: *I don't talk about my private life at the office.*
3 quiet and without other people listening or seeing: *Is there a private place where we can talk?*

private² *noun*
in private without other people listening or seeing: *Can I speak to you in private?*

priv·i·lege /ˈprɪvɪlɪdʒ/ *noun*
a special right allowed to one person or only a few people: *These prisoners have the privilege of getting letters every day.*

prize /praɪz/ *noun*
something that you win in a game, race, or competition: *I won first prize in the competition.*

prob·a·ble /ˈprɒbəbl/ *adjective*
likely to happen or be true: *The probable cause of the accident was ice on the road. | It is probable that we will have to move house.*

probably *adverb*: *We will probably go to the show tomorrow.*

prob·lem /ˈprɒbləm/ *noun*
1 a difficult situation or person that you must deal with: *I have been **having** some problems **with** my car. | Unemployment is the main problem in the area.*
2 **no problem** a phrase you use to tell someone you can easily do something for them: *"Can you drive me to the airport?" "Sure, no problem."*

pro·ceed /prəˈsiːd/ *verb*
proceed to do something to do something after you have done something else: *She took out a bottle and proceeded to drink from it.*

prison

prisoner

pro·cess /'prəʊses/ noun (plural
processes)
1 a set of actions that you do in order
to get a particular result: Learning to
read is a slow process.
2 a set of changes that happen
naturally: She is studying the ageing
process in women.

pro·ces·sion /prə'seʃn/ noun
a line of people or vehicles following one
another as part of a ceremony: They
watched the procession go past.

pro·duce[1] /prə'djuːs/ verb (present
participle **producing**, past **produced**)
1 to grow or make something naturally:
The farm produces wheat. I Some
snakes produce poison.
2 to make something, especially in
large quantities: The factory produces
500 cars a week.
3 to make something happen or have a
particular effect: The drug is producing
good results in the treatment of
cancer. I He is running training courses
to produce better teachers.
4 to prepare a play or film and show it
to the public

prod·uce[2] /'prɒdjuːs/ noun (no plural)
food that is grown, especially fruit and
vegetables: The market was full of fresh
produce.

pro·duc·er /prə'djuːsər/ noun
a person who produces a play or film

prod·uct /'prɒdʌkt/ noun
something that is made or grown to be
sold: None of our products are tested
on animals.

pro·duc·tion /prə'dʌkʃən/ noun
1 (no plural) the process of making or
growing something, or the amount that
is made or grown: The company's
production has increased this year.
2 a performance of a play or film: The
film is a modern production of Romeo
and Juliet.

pro·fes·sion /prə'feʃn/ noun
a job that needs a high standard of
education and special training: Teaching
is a satisfying profession, even if it is
badly paid.

pro·fes·sion·al /prə'feʃnəl/ adjective
1 relating to a job that needs a high
standard of education and special
training: You should get some
professional advice from your doctor.

2 doing something for money, rather
than for pleasure: He is a professional
football player.

pro·fes·sor /prə'fesər/ noun
1 a teacher of the highest rank in a
British university
2 a teacher in an American college or
university

prof·it /'prɒfɪt/ noun
money that you get when you sell
something for more than you paid for it:
The fruit seller **made** a penny profit on
each orange.

prof·it·a·ble /'prɒfɪtəbl/ adjective
making a lot of profit: This business is
not very profitable.

pro·gram[1] /'prəʊgræm/ noun
a set of instructions that a computer
follows

program[2] verb (present participle
programming, past **programmed**)
to give a computer the instructions it
needs to do something

pro·gramme /'prəʊgræm/ noun
1 printed information about a play,
concert, etc
2 a show on radio or television: We
watched a programme about travelling
through the desert.

pro·gram·mer /'prəʊgræmər/ noun
someone whose job is to write
instructions to make a computer do
something

pro·gress[1] /'prəʊgres/ noun (no plural)
1 continuous improvement in
something: You have made good
progress with your English.
2 movement in a particular direction

pro·gress[2] /prə'gres/ verb
1 to go on or continue: I became very
tired as the trip progressed.
2 to improve: We progressed from
being beginners to being very good.

pro·hib·it /prə'hɪbɪt/ verb
to not allow something by law: Smoking
is prohibited in this building. ⬦ compare
BAN

proj·ect /'prɒdʒekt/ noun
1 a plan to do something: She's
running a project to help the homeless.
2 an activity in which students collect
and present information about
something in order to learn about it

prom·i·nent /'prɒmɪnənt/ *adjective*
1 large, sticking out, and easy to see: *She has a prominent nose.*
2 important and well known: *He is a prominent politician.*

prom·ise[1] /'prɒmɪs/ *verb* (*present participle* **promising**, *past* **promised**)
to say that you will definitely do something: *She promised her brother **that** she would write to him.* I *Dad's promised **to** take us to Disneyland.* I *We promised her a doll for her birthday.*

promise[2] *noun*
something you have said you will definitely do: *She **made** a promise to her son* (=promised him) *to buy him a bike.* I *He **broke** his promise and did not come to see me.*

pro·mote /prə'məʊt/ *verb* (*present participle* **promoting**, *past* **promoted**)
to give someone a higher position at work: *Our teacher has been promoted to head teacher.*

pro·mo·tion /prə'məʊʃn/ *noun*
a move to a higher position at work

prompt /prɒmpt/ *adjective*
done quickly and without delay: *She gave a prompt answer to my letter.*
promptly *adverb*: *She arrived promptly at ten.*

pro·noun /'prəʊnaʊn/ *noun*
a word like 'he', 'she', 'it', 'they', etc, that is used instead of using a noun again. For example, in the sentences 'Peter got into his car. He drove away', 'he' is used instead of repeating 'Peter'

pro·nounce /prə'naʊns/ *verb* (*present participle* **pronouncing**, *past* **pronounced**)
to make the sounds of a word: *How do you pronounce your name?*

pro·nun·ci·a·tion /prə,nʌnsɪ'eɪʃn/ *noun*
the way in which a word or sound is spoken: *There are two different pronunciations of the word 'bow'.*

proof /pruːf/ *noun* (*no plural*)
facts that show that something is true: *You need proof **of** your age to buy cigarettes.* I *Have you any proof **that** he took the money?*

pro·pel·ler /prə'pelər/ *noun*
parts that turn quickly to make a ship or plane move

prop·er /'prɒpər/ *adjective*
correct or suitable: *You aren't wearing proper clothes for this hot weather.* I *Put the book back in its proper place.*
⋄ same meaning RIGHT

prop·er·ly /'prɒpəli/ *adverb*
in a correct or suitable way: *I can't see properly without glasses.* I *Have you tidied your room properly?*

prop·er·ty /'prɒpəti/ *noun*
1 (*no plural*) something that someone owns: *Their job is to protect the property of the school.*
2 (*plural* **properties**) land or buildings: *Properties in the town are expensive.*

proph·e·cy /'prɒfəsi/ *noun* (*plural* **prophecies**)
a statement saying what will happen in the future

proph·et /'prɒfɪt/ *noun*
1 a person who tells people what is going to happen in the future
2 a person who believes that God has told them to teach or lead a special religion

pro·por·tion /prə'pɔːʃn/ *noun*
the amount of something compared to another thing: *The proportion **of** girls to boys in the school is about equal.*

pro·pos·al /prə'pəʊzl/ *noun*
1 a formal plan or suggestion: *A proposal to build a new school is being considered.*
2 the act of asking someone to marry you

pro·pose /prə'pəʊz/ *verb* (*present participle* **proposing**, *past* **proposed**)
1 to suggest something: *He proposed **that** the company should move to another factory.*
2 to ask someone to marry you: *He proposed **to** her last week, and she accepted.*

pros·per /'prɒspər/ *verb*
to do well and become rich: *His company is prospering.*

pro·sper·i·ty /prɒ'sperəti/ *noun* (*no plural*)
success and wealth·

pros·per·ous /'prɒspərəs/ *adjective*
rich and successful: *He was the son of a prosperous family.*

pro·tect /prə'tekt/ *verb*
to stop someone or something from

being harmed or damaged: *The fence is to protect the farmer's cattle.* | *The cream will protect your skin from sunburn.*

pro·tec·tion /prə'tekʃən/ *noun (no plural)*
the act of keeping a person or thing safe from harm or damage: *Her summer clothes gave her no protection against the cold.*

pro·test¹ /prə'test/ *verb*
to say strongly that you do not agree with something: *The children protested when they were punished unfairly.* | *The group is protesting against the war.*

pro·test² /'prəʊtest/ *noun*
when people complain a lot about something: *Many people joined the protest against government plans.*

Prot·es·tant /'prɒtɪstənt/ *noun*
a person belonging to a Christian church that is not Roman Catholic

proud /praʊd/ *adjective*
1 feeling pleased about your actions, family, etc because you think they are successful or good: *He is proud of his daughter's ability to speak four languages.* | *He was proud to receive the award.*
2 feeling that you are better than other people: *She is too proud to walk to school with the other children.*

prove /pruːv/ *verb (present participle* **proving**, *past* **proved**)
to show that something is definitely true: *I can prove that you were in town – James saw you there.*

prov·erb /'prɒvɜːb/ *noun*
a short well-known saying

pro·vide /prə'vaɪd/ *verb (present participle* **providing**, *past* **provided**)
to give something to someone: *We provided food for the hungry children.*

pro·vid·ed /prə'vaɪdɪd/
used to say that something will only happen if another thing happens: *I'll go to see her, provided you come too.*

prov·ince /'prɒvɪns/ *noun*
an area of a country, often with its own government for education, hospitals, etc

pro·vi·sion /prə'vɪʒn/ *noun*
(no plural) the act of giving something to people who need it

pro·voke /prə'vəʊk/ *verb (present participle* **provoking**, *past* **provoked**)
to annoy someone deliberately so that they get very angry

prowl /praʊl/ *verb*
to move round quietly, especially when hunting: *A tiger was prowling through the jungle.*

psalm /sɑːm/ *noun*
a religious song or poem

pub /pʌb/ *noun*
a building in Britain or Ireland where people can go to meet their friends and to buy and drink alcohol

pub·lic¹ /'pʌblɪk/ *adjective*
1 for everyone to use and see: *I'm going to the public library.* | *There are three public swimming pools in the town.*
2 relating to people in general: *Public opinion is now against the government.*

public² *noun (no plural)*
1 **the public** all the people in a place: *The pool is now open to the public.*
2 **in public** in a place where other people can listen and see

pub·lish /'pʌblɪʃ/ *verb*
to print and sell a book, newspaper, or magazine: *The company publishes children's books.*

pub·lish·er /'pʌblɪʃər/ *noun*
a person or company that publishes books, newspapers, or magazines

pud·ding /'pʊdɪŋ/ *noun*
British sweet food served at the end of a meal: *What's for pudding?* ⬦ same meaning DESSERT

puddle

drinking from a puddle

pud·dle /'pʌdl/ *noun*
a small amount of rain water lying on the ground ⬦ compare POOL

puff[1] /pʌf/ verb
to breathe quickly, usually after doing something tiring: *I was puffing after running so far.*

puff[2] noun
a sudden short movement of air, smoke, or wind: *A puff of wind blew the papers off the table.*

pull[1] /pʊl/ verb
1 to move something or someone towards yourself: *I managed to pull the door open.* | *Mum, Sarah's pulling my hair!* ⇨ see picture at PUSH[1]
2 to make something move along behind you: *The car was pulling a caravan behind it.*
3 pull something down to destroy a building, wall, etc: *They pulled down a lot of houses to build the new road.*

pull[2] noun
the movement you make when you pull something towards you: *He gave a pull on the rope.*

pull·o·ver /'pʊləʊvəʳ/ noun
a piece of clothing that you pull over your head and wear on the top part of your body ⇨ same meaning JUMPER

pulse /pʌls/ noun
the regular beat of your heart, especially as it can be felt on your wrist

pump[1] /pʌmp/ noun
a machine for making liquid or gas go into or out of something: *A bicycle pump puts air into the tyres.* ⇨ see picture at BICYCLE

pump[2] verb
1 to use a pump to empty or fill something with a liquid or gas: *The fire department are still pumping water out of the house.*
2 pump something up to fill a tyre, ball, etc with air

pump·kin /'pʌmpkɪn/ noun
a very large round yellow vegetable ⇨ see picture on page 199

punch[1] /pʌntʃ/ verb
1 to hit a person with your closed hand: *He punched John on the nose.*
2 to make a hole in something: *He punched a hole in the tin, and poured out the contents.*

punch[2] noun (plural **punches**)
a strong blow made with your closed hand: *He gave me a punch on the side of the head.*

punc·tu·al /'pʌŋktʃʊəl/ adjective
arriving at exactly the right time: *She is always punctual.* ⇨ compare LATE

punc·tu·ate /'pʌŋktʃʊeɪt/ verb (present participle **punctuating**, past **punctuated**)
to divide up a piece of writing into sentences, etc by using special signs like (,) (;) (.) and (?)

punc·tu·a·tion /ˌpʌŋktʃʊˈeɪʃn/ noun (no plural)
signs like (,) (;) (.) and (?) used to divide up a piece of writing into sentences, etc

punc·ture[1] /'pʌŋktʃəʳ/ noun
British a hole in something such as a tyre through which air or liquid can get out: *I need to repair the puncture before I can use my bike.*

puncture[2] verb (present participle **puncturing**, past **punctured**)
to make a small hole in something so that air or liquid gets out of it

pun·ish /'pʌnɪʃ/ verb
to make someone suffer because they have done something wrong: *Kelly was punished for telling a lie.*

pun·ish·ment /'pʌnɪʃmənt/ noun
a way in which someone is made to suffer because they have done something wrong: *Her punishment was to stay late after school.*

pu·pil /'pjuːpl/ noun
a person being taught, especially at a school

pup·pet /'pʌpɪt/ noun
a small figure of a person or animal that you can move by pulling the strings connected to it, or by putting your hand inside it

pup·py /'pʌpi/ noun (plural **puppies**)
a young dog

pur·chase[1] /'pɜːtʃɪs/ noun
1 (no plural) the act of buying something: *The school needs more money for the purchase of books.*
2 something you have bought: *Let me see all your purchases.*

purchase[2] verb (present participle **purchasing**, past **purchased**)
to buy something: *Mr Smith recently purchased a house in France.*

A B C D E F G H I J K L M N O P Q R S T U V W X Y Z

pure /pjʊəʳ/ *adjective* (**purer, purest**)
not mixed with anything and so very clean: *The water in mountain rivers is usually pure.*

pure·ly /'pjʊəlɪ/ *adverb*
only: *He did it for purely selfish reasons.* I *We met purely by chance.*

pur·ple /'pɜːpl/ *adjective, noun*
the colour made by mixing red and blue together

pur·pose /'pɜːpəs/ *noun*
1 a reason for doing something: *He went to town with the purpose of buying a new television.*
2 **on purpose** deliberately: *She broke the cup on purpose.*

pur·pose·ly /'pɜːpəslɪ/ *adverb*
deliberately: *It wasn't a mistake – you purposely opened my letter!*

purr /pɜːʳ/ *verb*
to make the soft low noise that cats make when they are happy

purse /pɜːs/ *noun*
1 *British* a small container for carrying money, used especially by women
2 *American* a bag used by women to carry money and personal things (*British* **handbag**)

pur·sue /pə'sjuː/ *verb* (*present participle* **pursuing**, *past* **pursued**)
to go after someone hoping to catch them ⇨ same meaning CHASE

pushing   pulling

push¹ /pʊʃ/ *verb*
1 to press or lean steadily so as to move someone or something: *They pushed the door open and rushed in.* I *He pushed me off the chair.*
2 to press a button to make a machine work: *Just push this button to turn the radio on.*

push² *noun*
when you push someone or something:
She gave a hard push, and the door opened.

push·chair /'pʊʃ-tʃeəʳ/ *noun*
a small folding chair on wheels in which you can push a small child ⇨ compare PRAM

put /pʊt/ *verb* (*present participle* **putting**, *past* **put**)
1 to place or move something into a particular position: *Put the books on the shelf, please.* I *Where did I put my keys?* I *I put the letter back in the envelope.*
2 **put something off** to delay something until a later date: *The meeting's been put off until next week.* I *You can't keep putting the decision off.*
3 **put something on (a)** to put clothes on your body: *She put on her coat and went out.* **(b)** to make a light or machine work by pressing a button: *Is it all right if I put the television on?*
4 **put something out** to stop a fire or cigarette from burning: *It took three hours to put the fire out.*

puz·zle¹ /'pʌzl/ *noun*
1 a person or thing that you cannot understand or explain: *It's a puzzle where all my money goes each week.*
2 a game or toy that is difficult to solve or put together: *Can you do this jigsaw puzzle?* I *She does a crossword puzzle every day.*

puzzle² *verb* (*present participle* **puzzling**, *past* **puzzled**)
to make you feel that you do not understand something: *The new machine puzzled me until Jane explained how it worked.*

py·ja·mas /pə'dʒɑːməz/ *plural noun*
a loose shirt and trousers that you wear in bed: *He was wearing a pair of pyjamas.* ⇨ see picture on page 203

pyr·a·mid /'pɪrəmɪd/ *noun*
a solid shape that is square at the base and pointed at the top ⇨ see picture at SHAPE

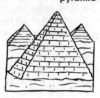

pyramid

Q, q /kjuː/
the seventeenth letter of the English alphabet

quack /kwæk/ *verb*
to make the noise that a duck usually makes

quake /kweɪk/ *verb (present participle* **quaking**, *past* **quaked**)
to shake because you are afraid: *She was quaking **with** fear.*

qual·i·fi·ca·tion /ˌkwɒlɪfɪˈkeɪʃn/ *noun*
a document that shows you have passed an examination or done special training: *You need some qualifications to find a job.*

qual·i·fied /ˈkwɒlɪfaɪd/ *adjective*
if you are qualified for something, you have the right training or skills to do it: *She is very well qualified **for** this job.*

qual·i·fy /ˈkwɒlɪfaɪ/ *verb (present participle* **qualifying**, *past* **qualified**)
to finish the training that allows you to do a particular job: *She qualified **as** a doctor last year.*

qual·i·ty /ˈkwɒlətɪ/ *noun (plural* **qualities**)
1 how good something is: *We only sell cloth of the finest quality.*
2 a good part of someone's character: *He has many good qualities – he's kind, cheerful, and very hard-working.*

quan·ti·ty /ˈkwɒntətɪ/ *noun (plural* **quantities**)
an amount: *He ate a small quantity **of** rice.*

quar·rel[1] /ˈkwɒrəl/ *noun*
an angry argument: *We had a quarrel **about** money.* ⇨ same meaning ROW

quarrel[2] *verb (present participle* **quarrelling**, *past* **quarrelled**)
to have an angry argument: *They're always quarrelling.*

quar·ry /ˈkwɒrɪ/ *noun (plural* **quarries**)
a place where stone or sand is dug out of the ground

quar·ter /ˈkwɔːtəʳ/ *noun*
1 one of four equal parts of something: *There were four of us, so we divided the cake into quarters.*

2 **quarter past 2, quarter past 3, etc** 15 minutes after 2 o'clock, 3 o'clock, etc: *I'll meet you here at quarter past two.*

3 **quarter to 4, quarter to 5, etc** 15 minutes before 4 o'clock, 5 o'clock, etc: *They should be here at quarter to five.*

quar·ter·ly /ˈkwɔːtəlɪ/ *adjective, adverb*
happening or appearing every three months: *a quarterly bank statement*

quay

quay /kiː/ *noun*
a flat area beside the sea or a river, where boats can be tied up

queen /kwiːn/ *noun*
1 the woman who rules a country, because she belongs to the family that rules it ⇨ compare KING
2 the wife of a king

quench /kwentʃ/ *verb*
quench your thirst to drink as much as you need to stop being thirsty

que·ry[1] /ˈkwɪərɪ/ *noun (plural* **queries**)
a question: *Let me know if you have any queries.*

query[2] *verb (present participle* **querying**, *past* **queried**)
to ask about something, usually because you are not sure that it is right: *If you think the price is too high, you should query it.*

ques·tion[1] /ˈkwestʃən/ *noun*
1 something you ask someone: *You haven't answered my question.*
2 a problem that people talk about and deal with: *We need to discuss the question **of** money.*

question[2] *verb*
1 to ask someone a lot of questions about something, especially a crime: *The police questioned him **about** what had happened.*
2 to think about or ask if something is real, good, or true: *I do not question his honesty.*

question mark /'kwestʃən ˌmɑːk/
noun
the sign '?', used in writing after a question

queue

queuing for the cinema

queue[1] /kjuː/ *noun*
a line of people or vehicles waiting for something: *There was a long queue outside the theatre.*

queue[2] *verb (present participle* **queuing**, *past* **queued**)
to wait in a queue: *We had to queue for ages.*

quick /kwɪk/ *adjective*
doing something or happening in a short time: *We only had time for a quick meal before going out.* I *What's the quickest way to the shops from here?* ⇨ look at SOON

qui·et[1] /'kwaɪət/ *adjective*
1 without much noise or without any noise: *The streets were quiet at night.* I *He's got a very quiet voice – sometimes it's difficult to hear him.*
2 when there is not much noise or activity, or no noise or activity: *I had a quiet day reading at home.*

quiet[2] *noun (no plural)*
when there is very little noise or activity: *Can you give your brother some peace and quiet while he does his homework?*

quilt /kwɪlt/ *noun*
a soft thick covering for a bed

quite /kwaɪt/ *adverb*
1 completely: *I quite agree.* I *That's quite ridiculous!*
2 rather, but not very much: *I was quite busy last week.* ⇨ same meaning FAIRLY
3 **not quite** not completely, but almost: *"Are you ready?" "Not quite."* I *The bananas aren't quite ripe.*

quiv·er /'kwɪvəʳ/ *verb*
to shake slightly: *He was quivering with fear.*

quiz /kwɪz/ *noun (plural* **quizzes)**
a game or competition in which people try to answer questions correctly

quo·ta /'kwəʊtə/ *noun*
an amount or limit that is expected or allowed: *There are strict quotas on imports.*

quo·ta·tion /kwəʊ'teɪʃn/ *noun*
words taken from speech or writing and repeated exactly by someone else

quote /kwəʊt/ *verb (present participle* **quoting**, *past* **quoted)**
to repeat exactly what someone said or wrote: *He was always quoting Shakespeare and other writers.* I *The President was quoted as saying that it was "a wonderful idea".*

Qur'an /kɔːˈrɑːn/ *noun*
the Qur'an the KORAN

R, r /ɑːʳ/
the eighteenth letter of the English alphabet

rab·bit /'ræbɪt/ noun
a small animal with long ears that lives in holes under the ground

race¹ /reɪs/ noun
1 a competition to see who can run, swim, walk, etc fastest: *Who won the race? | Horse races are held here every week.*
2 a group of humans different from other groups in the colour of their skin and physical appearance

race² verb (*present participle* **racing**, *past* **raced**)
to be in a race: *Paul raced John to the house. | She's racing against Mary in the 100 metres.*

ra·cial /'reɪʃl/ adjective
1 relating to the race of people that someone belongs to
2 connected with the relationships between different races of people

ra·cis·m /'reɪsɪzəm/ noun (*no plural*)
1 the idea that some races of people are not as good as others
2 the bad treatment of people of other races: *They accused the government of racism.*

ra·cist /'reɪsɪst/ noun
1 a person who believes that some races of people are not as good as others
2 a person who treats people of other races badly

rack /ræk/ noun
a frame on which things can be kept: *The bottles were stored in a rack.*

rack·et /'rækɪt/ noun
an instrument used to hit the ball in games like tennis ⇨ see picture on page 197

ra·dar /'reɪdɑːʳ/ noun (*no plural*)
a way of finding the position and speed of ships and planes by using radio waves

ra·di·a·tor /'reɪdɪeɪtəʳ/ noun
1 a metal object on a wall that has hot water going through it in order to heat a room
2 part of the system in a car that controls the temperature of the engine

radio

ra·di·o /'reɪdɪəu/ noun
1 (*plural* **radios**) a machine that receives messages or sounds sent by electrical waves, and plays them to you: *He was listening to music on the radio.*
2 (*no plural*) the sending out or receiving of sounds by electrical waves: *Ships send messages to each other by radio.*
3 (*no plural*) programmes that are broadcast for people to listen to: *I prefer television to radio.*

ra·di·us /'reɪdɪəs/ noun (*plural* **radii** /'reɪdɪaɪ/)
the distance from the centre of a circle to the edge

raft /rɑːft/ noun
large pieces of wood joined together to make a rough flat boat

rag /ræg/ noun
1 an old cloth: *He cleaned the machine with an oily rag.*
2 **rags** torn old clothes

rage /reɪdʒ/ noun
very great anger: *My father was in a rage last night.*

raid¹ /reɪd/ noun
a sudden attack: *The police arrested them after a bank raid.*

raid² verb
to attack a place: *They raided the village.*

rail /reɪl/ noun
1 a fixed metal bar: *Trains usually run on rails. | The new summer dresses are hanging from the rails.*
2 **by rail** by train

rail·ings /'reɪlɪŋz/ plural noun
a fence made of a number of metal bars: *There were railings round the park.*

rail·way /ˈreɪlweɪ/ *noun*
  1 a track for trains to run on: *They're building a new railway to the south.*
  2 the tracks, stations, organizations etc used in carrying people and goods by train: *We want more people to use the railways instead of travelling by car.*

railway line /ˈreɪlweɪ ˌlaɪn/ *noun*
a track for trains to run on: *A tree has fallen across the railway line.*

railway station

railway sta·tion /ˈreɪlweɪ ˌsteɪʃn/ *noun*
a building near a railway where trains stop and people can get on and off

rain¹ /reɪn/ *verb*
if it is raining, drops of water fall from clouds in the sky: *It rained last night.*

rain² *noun (no plural)*
drops of water falling from clouds in the sky: *There was a lot of rain last night.*

rainbow

rain·bow /ˈreɪnbəʊ/ *noun*
a large curve of different colours in the sky that you often see when there is both sun and rain

rain·coat /ˈreɪnkəʊt/ *noun*
a light coat that keeps out the rain

rain for·est /ˈreɪn ˌfɒrɪst/ *noun*
a wet area in a hot country where tall trees grow very close together: *They are working to save the Brazilian rain forest.*

rain·y /ˈreɪnɪ/ *adjective*
raining a lot: *It was cold and rainy and*

we had to stay at home. ⇨ see picture on page 194

raise /reɪz/ *verb (present participle* **raising***, past* **raised***)*
to lift something up or make something higher: *He raised his arms above his head.* | *The old-age pension should be raised immediately.* ⇨ opposite LOWER

rai·sin /ˈreɪzn/ *noun*
a small dried GRAPE

rake¹ /reɪk/ *noun*
a tool that you pull along the ground in order to make the ground level and take leaves and small stones off the surface

rake² *verb (present participle* **raking***, past* **raked***)*
to pull a rake over a piece of ground

RAM /ræm/ *noun (no plural)*
the part of a computer that keeps information that you want to use immediately

ran /ræn/
the past tense of the verb **run**

ranch /rɑːntʃ/ *noun*
a large cattle farm in the US or Canada

rang /ræŋ/
the past tense of the verb **ring**

range /reɪndʒ/ *noun*
  1 a line of mountains or hills: *the mountains of Oregon's Cascade Range*
  2 a number of different things: *You can choose from a wide range* **of** *goods.*
  3 the distance that something can reach or travel: *What is the range of your gun (=how far can you fire it)?*

rank /ræŋk/ *noun*
a group or class that is higher or lower than other groups, especially in the armed forces: *He rose to the rank of Captain.*

ran·som /ˈrænsəm/ *noun*
the money that is asked for by criminals in return for freeing a person who they are keeping as a prisoner: *They asked for a ransom of one million pounds.*

rap /ræp/ *noun (no plural)*
a type of popular music in which the words are spoken, not sung

rare /reəʳ/ *adjective (***rarer***,* **rarest***)*
not happening or seen very often: *Some birds are becoming rarer because of pollution.* ⇨ opposite COMMON

rare·ly /ˈreəlɪ/ *adverb*
not very often: *She is old and rarely*

goes out. | *He rarely leaves the office until 7 o'clock.*

ras·cal /rɑːskl/ *noun*
a badly behaved person, especially a child: *He's a naughty little rascal.*

rash[1] /ræʃ/ *adjective*
doing something too quickly, without thinking carefully first: *Don't make any rash decisions.*

rash[2] *noun*
red spots on your skin: *I got this strange rash, so I went to the doctor.*

rat /ræt/ *noun*
an animal that looks like a large mouse with a long tail

rate /reɪt/ *noun*
1 the amount of money that you are paid for a fixed amount of work: *He was paid at the rate of £14 an hour.*
2 the speed of something: *She learns at a fast rate.*

rate of ex·change /ˌreɪt əv ɪksˈtʃeɪndʒ/ *noun* (*plural* **rates of exchange**)
the value of the money of one country compared to that of another country: *"What's the rate of exchange?" "It's about $1.50 to the pound."*

ra·ther /rɑːðər/
1 slightly or to some degree: *It's rather cold today.*
2 **would rather** would prefer to have or do something: *"Shall we go and see that film?" "I'd rather stay in."*

ra·tion[1] /ˈræʃn/ *verb*
to limit the goods that someone can have: *The government had to ration petrol during the war.*

ration[2] *noun*
a limited quantity of food, petrol, etc, allowed to each person for a period, especially during a war

rat·tle[1] /ˈrætl/ *verb* (*present participle* **rattling,** *past* **rattled**)
to shake something, making a noise: *She rattled some coins in the box.*

rattle[2] *noun*
a toy that a baby shakes to make a noise

raw /rɔː/ *adjective*
not cooked: *My cat eats raw meat.*

ray /reɪ/ *noun*
a line of light: *Use the cream to protect your skin from the sun's rays.*

razors

ra·zor /ˈreɪzər/ *noun*
a sharp instrument for removing hair, especially from a man's face

razor blade /ˈreɪzə ˌbleɪd/ *noun*
a thin very sharp piece of metal that is put inside a razor

Rd
a short way of writing **Road** in an address: *17 Nelson Rd, Oxford*

're /ər/ *verb*
are: *We're late.*

reach[1] /riːtʃ/ *verb*
1 to get to a place or arrive at a place: *They reached London on Thursday.* | *She's reached the age when she can leave school.*
2 to stretch out your hand: *I reached up and took an apple from the tree.*

reach[2] *noun* (*no plural*)
1 **within reach** near enough to touch by stretching out your arm: *The dog came almost within reach, and then ran away.*
2 **out of reach** not near enough to touch by stretching out your arm: *Keep all medicines out of reach of children.*

re·act /rɪˈækt/ *verb*
to behave in a particular way because of something that has happened: *How did your mother react **to** the news?* | *She reacted by getting very angry.*

re·ac·tion /rɪˈækʃən/ *noun*
the feeling you have or the way you behave because of something that has happened: *What was his reaction when you told him?*

read /riːd/ *verb* (*present participle* **reading,** *past* **read** /red/)
1 to look at words and understand them: *She read the newspaper.* | *He read the story **to** his son.* | *He read his son a story.* | *I like reading.*
2 **read something out** to read something so that other people can hear: *Can you read out the list of names?*

A B C D E F G H I J K L M N O P Q R S T U V W X Y Z

read·er /'ri:dəʳ/ *noun*
a person who reads

read·i·ly /'redəlɪ/ *adverb*
easily: *Scottish bank notes are readily accepted in most parts of England.*

read·y /'redɪ/ *adjective*
1 prepared: *I'm not ready to go out yet; I haven't got my keys or my money.* | *He got his tools ready to start the job.* | *Is breakfast ready?* | *Is everything ready* **for** *the party?* | *These apples are nearly ready to eat.*
2 willing: *I'm always ready to help.*

real /rɪəl/ *adjective*
existing, not just imagined: *There is a real danger that the fire will spread.*

rea·li·za·tion /ˌrɪəlaɪ'zeɪʃn/ *noun* (no plural)
when you begin to understand something that you did not know before: *She suddenly came to the realization that he was guilty.*

rea·lize /'rɪəlaɪz/ *verb* (*present participle* **realizing**, *past* **realized**)
to know or understand something that you did not know before: *We suddenly realized that the fire was spreading rapidly.* | *I realized that I knew more about him than I had thought before.*

real·ly /'rɪəlɪ/ *adverb*
1 in fact or very much: *I am really worried about my work.* | *He is really nice.*
2 **Really?** used to show that you are interested in something or surprised by it: *"Have you heard – Ann's going to have a baby?" "Really?"*
3 used when you tell someone that you are annoyed with them: *Really, Jane, you are behaving badly.*

reap /ri:p/ *verb*
to cut and collect a crop: *They reaped the corn.*

rear[1] /rɪəʳ/ *adjective*
at the back: *I had a puncture in one of my rear tyres.* ⇨ opposite FRONT

rear[2] *noun*
the back part: *We sat at the rear of the bus.* ⇨ opposite FRONT

rear[3] *verb*
to care for animals or children while they grow up: *I wanted to rear a family.*

rea·son /'ri:zn/ *noun*
1 why something is done or happens: *The reason I bought one was that it was so cheap.* | *There's no reason to get up early on Sundays.*
2 (no plural) the ability to think, understand, and make decisions: *Do monkeys have the power of reason?*

rea·son·a·ble /'ri:znəbl/ *adjective*
1 fair and using good reasons: *Don't be afraid to talk to the teacher – she's very reasonable.* ⇨ opposite UNREASON-ABLE
2 a reasonable price is not too high: *I bought the house for a reasonable price.*

rea·son·a·bly /'ri:znəblɪ/ *adverb*
1 in a way that is fair and is based on good reasons: *He always behaved reasonably.*
2 not very, but enough: *It was reasonably cheap.*

re·as·sure /ˌri:ə'ʃʊəʳ/ *verb* (*present participle* **reassuring**, *past* **reassured**)
to stop someone from worrying: *His mother reassured him that everything would be all right.*

re·bel[1] /rɪ'bel/ *verb* (*present participle* **rebelling**, *past* **rebelled**)
to fight against a leader or government: *The students rebelled* **against** *the government.*

reb·el[2] /'rebl/ *noun*
a person who fights against a leader or government: *The rebels attacked at 2.30 in the morning.*

re·bel·lion /rɪ'beljən/ *noun*
an attempt to change the government by using violence: *He led an armed rebellion against the government.*

re·ceipt /rɪ'si:t/ *noun*
a piece of paper that someone gives you to show that you have paid them money: *Ask him to give you a receipt when you pay the bill.*

re·ceive /rɪ'si:v/ *verb* (*present participle* **receiving**, *past* **received**)
to get something or be given something: *Did you receive my letter?*

re·ceiv·er /rɪ'si:vəʳ/ *noun*
the part of a telephone that you hold to your ear: *Lift the receiver and dial the number.*

re·cent /'ri:snt/ *adjective*
happening a short time ago: *Please attach a recent photo to the application form.*

re·cent·ly /ˈriːsntlɪ/ adverb
not long ago: I visited Spain recently.

re·cep·tion /rɪˈsepʃən/ noun
1 (no plural) the area in a hotel or large organization that helps visitors and gives information: Leave your key at reception.
2 a large formal party: They are holding their wedding reception in a big hotel.

re·ci·pe /ˈresəpɪ/ noun
a piece of writing telling you how to cook something: The recipe tells you to use two eggs. I I followed the recipe for chocolate cake.

reck·less /ˈrekləs/ adjective
careless and dangerous: His reckless driving caused a serious accident.
◇ opposite CAREFUL

recklessly adverb: He was driving recklessly.

reck·on /ˈrekən/ verb
1 to guess because you have thought about something: I reckon he must have finished eating by now.
2 reckon something up to add up or count something: She reckoned up the money we owed her.

rec·og·ni·tion /ˌrekəgˈnɪʃn/ noun (no plural)
when you know someone or something because you have seen them before: She hoped to avoid recognition by wearing dark glasses.

rec·og·nize /ˈrekəgnaɪz/ verb (past participle **recognizing**, past **recognized**)
to know someone or something when you see them: I recognized Peter although I hadn't seen him for 10 years. I I don't recognize this word – what does it mean?

rec·om·mend /ˌrekəˈmend/ verb
to tell someone that a person or thing is good for a particular purpose: If you're going to the city, I recommend the new hotel – it's very nice. I He recommended the new hotel to me.

rec·om·men·da·tion /ˌrekəmenˈdeɪʃn/ noun
the suggestion that someone or something is good for a particular purpose: I went to the new hotel on your recommendation.

re·cord[1] /rɪˈkɔːd/ verb
1 to write about something or put it on a computer so that you can look at it later: All the information is recorded on computer.
2 to copy television programmes on a special machine called a VIDEO so that you can watch them later: I'm going to be out tonight, so I'll have to record the football.
3 to store sounds electronically so that they can be listened to later: He recorded his most popular songs in 1991.

rec·ord[2] /ˈrekɔːd/ noun
1 information that is written down and kept: I need your medical records.
2 something done better, quicker, etc than anyone else has done it: He holds the world record **for** the high jump.
3 break a record to do something better, quicker, etc than it has ever been done before: She broke the record for the 100m.
4 a round thin flat piece of plastic that stores sounds, and which you play on a special machine

re·cord·er /rɪˈkɔːdər/ noun
a simple musical instrument shaped like a tube, that you play by blowing into it

re·cord·ing /rɪˈkɔːdɪŋ/ noun
a piece of music or speech that has been recorded so that you can listen to it: I like the group's latest recording.

record play·er /ˈrekɔːd ˌpleɪər/ noun
a machine that is used to play records

re·cov·er /rɪˈkʌvər/ verb
to get well again after you have been ill: Have you recovered **from** your cold yet?

re·cov·er·y /rɪˈkʌvərɪ/ noun (no plural)
a return to good health after an illness or accident: She made a quick recovery after her accident.

rec·re·a·tion /ˌrekrɪˈeɪʃn/ noun
rest or play after you have been working: Football and watching television are the boys' main recreations. I You can't work all the time – you must have some recreation.

re·cruit[1] /rɪˈkruːt/ noun
a new member of an organization, especially of the armed forces

recruit[2] verb
to find new people to join an organization

or do a job: *They are trying to recruit new police officers.*

rec·tan·gle /'rektæŋgl/ *noun*
a flat shape with four straight sides and four equal angles, that is longer than it is wide ⇨ see picture at SHAPE ⇨ same meaning OBLONG

rec·tan·gu·lar /rek'tæŋgjʊlər/ *adjective*
having a flat shape with four straight sides and four equal angles, that is longer than it is wide: *They sat at a rectangular table.*

re·cy·cle /riː'saɪkl/ *verb (present participle* **recycling**, *past* **recycled**)
to use something again rather than throwing it away: *These bottles can be recycled.*

red /red/ *adjective, noun*
the colour of blood: *She wore a red dress. | She was dressed in red.*

re·duce /rɪ'djuːs/ *verb (present participle* **reducing**, *past* **reduced**)
to make something smaller or less: *They've reduced their prices, so it's a good time to buy. | His stay in prison was reduced to four years.*

re·duc·tion /rɪ'dʌkʃən/ *noun*
the act of making something smaller or less: *There have been some amazing price reductions.*

reed /riːd/ *noun*
a tall plant like grass, that grows in or near water

reels

a reel of film

a fishing reel　　*a reel of cotton*

reel /riːl/ *noun*
a round thing on which thread, film, etc can be wound: *a reel of cotton*

re·fer /rɪ'fɜːr/ *verb (present participle* **referring**, *past* **referred**)
1 to go to a book, map etc to get information: *Refer to a dictionary if you don't know what the word means.*
2 refer to someone or something to speak about someone or something: *He didn't refer to Jack in his letter.*

ref·er·ee /ˌrefə'riː/ *noun*
a person who is in charge of a game to make sure that the rules of the game are obeyed

ref·er·ence /'refrəns/ *noun*
1 (*no plural*) when you look at something for information: *I keep the dictionary on my desk for reference.*
2 a letter about your character and ability that is sent to someone who may give you a job: *He wrote me a really good reference.*

reference book /'refrəns ˌbʊk/ *noun*
a book that you look at to get information about a subject

re·flect /rɪ'flekt/ *verb*
1 if something such as a mirror or water reflects something, you can see that thing in the mirror or water: *She could see the mountains reflected in the lake.*
2 to think: *He reflected before answering my question.*

re·flec·tion　　　　　　**reflection**
/rɪ'flekʃən/ *noun*
1 what you see in a mirror or water: *We looked at our reflections in the lake.*
2 (*no plural*) thinking: *After a minute's reflection, he answered.*

re·form[1] /rɪ'fɔːm/ *verb*
to improve an organization or system by making changes to it: *The Government is planning to reform the law on drinking and driving.*

reform[2] *noun*
a change that improves an organization or system: *The reform of the tax system has become really necessary.*

re·fresh /rɪ'freʃ/ *verb*
to make someone less hot or tired: *Drink this – it will refresh you.*

re·freshed /rɪˈfreʃt/ adjective
less hot or tired: I felt refreshed after my bath.

re·fresh·ing /rɪˈfreʃɪŋ/ adjective
making you feel less hot or tired: a refreshing drink

re·fresh·ments /rɪˈfreʃmənts/ plural noun
food and drink that you are given at a meeting, party, sports event etc: They provided refreshments in the middle of the match.

re·fri·ge·ra·tor /rɪˈfrɪdʒəreɪtəʳ/ noun
also **fridge** a piece of electrical equipment like a cupboard, in which you keep food cold: Put the milk in the refrigerator.

ref·uge /ˈrefjuːdʒ/ noun
a safe place: The farm is their refuge from danger.

ref·u·gee /ˌrefjuːˈdʒiː/ noun
a person who has to leave their own country because they are in danger: The government is trying to convince the refugees that it is safe to go back home.

re·fus·al /rɪˈfjuːzl/ noun
when you say that you will not accept an offer or that you will not do something: Her refusal to help me made me feel angry. I I was hurt by her refusal of money and clothes.

re·fuse /rɪˈfjuːz/ verb (present participle **refusing**, past **refused**)
to say firmly that you are not willing to accept or do something: She refused to let me help.

re·gard [1] /rɪˈgɑːd/ verb
to think of someone in a particular way: We regard him **as** our cleverest student.

regard [2] noun (no plural)
care: He always says what he thinks, without regard **for** other people's feelings.

re·gard·ing /rɪˈgɑːdɪŋ/ preposition
about: I wrote you a letter regarding my daughter's school examinations. ◇ same meaning CONCERNING

re·gard·less /rɪˈgɑːdləs/ adverb
without caring: He says what he thinks regardless of other people's feelings.

re·gards /rɪˈgɑːdz/ plural noun
best wishes: Give my regards to your parents.

reg·gae /ˈregeɪ/ noun (no plural)
a type of popular music from the West Indies with a strong regular beat

re·gi·ment /ˈredʒɪmənt/ noun
a large group of soldiers who are part of an army

re·gion /ˈriːdʒən/ noun
an area: This is a farming region.

re·gis·ter [1] /ˈredʒɪstəʳ/ noun
a list, for example one that has the names of all the children in a class: The teacher has to **take** the register every morning.

register [2] verb
1 to have a name or event put on an official list: He registered the birth of his child.
2 to show something: The machine registered how fast we were going.

re·gis·tra·tion /ˌredʒɪˈstreɪʃn/ noun (no plural)
when names, facts, events etc are put on an official list

re·gret [1] /rɪˈgret/ verb (past participle **regretting**, past **regretted**)
to be sorry about something: I regret spending so much money on sweets. I I regret to say that he failed.

regret [2] noun
a feeling of being sorry: I felt deep regret that I did not visit him before he died.

reg·u·lar /ˈregjʊləʳ/ adjective
1 when something happens with the same amount of time or space between each thing or event: He is a regular visitor – he comes every Sunday.
2 ordinary or usual: Is he your regular doctor?
3 regular nouns, verbs etc follow the usual rules of grammar. For example, the verb 'walk' is regular

reg·u·lar·i·ty /ˌregjʊˈlærətɪ/ noun (no plural)
when something happens again and again after the same period of time: The building is cleaned with great regularity.

reg·u·lar·ly /ˈregjʊləlɪ/ adverb
after the same period every time: Take the medicine regularly three times a day.

reg·u·la·tion /ˌregjʊˈleɪʃn/ noun
an official rule: You have to obey the rules and regulations.

re·hears·al /rɪˈhɜːsl/ noun
a time when all the people in a

A
B
C
D
E
F
G
H
I
J
K
L
M
N
O
P
Q
R
S
T
U
V
W
X
Y
Z

performance practise it before it is shown to the public: *All the children in the play must come to the rehearsal.*

re·hearse /rɪ'hɜːs/ *verb* (*present participle* **rehearsing**, *past* **rehearsed**)
to practise something such as your speech in a play in order to make it as good as possible before it is done in public: *We need to rehearse the opening scene again.*

reign¹ /reɪn/ *verb*
to be king or queen

reign² *noun*
the time when a king or queen reigns: *It happened in the reign of George IV.*

rein /reɪn/ *noun*
a long narrow piece of leather that is fastened around a horse's head and used for controlling it: *The rider pulled on the reins, and the horse stopped.*

re·ject /rɪ'dʒekt/ *verb*
to decide that you do not want something or someone: *His application for a job in the company was rejected.*

re·joice /rɪ'dʒɔɪs/ *verb* (*present participle* **rejoicing**, *past* **rejoiced**)
to be very happy

re·late /rɪ'leɪt/ *verb* (*present participle* **relating**, *past* **related**)
1 to have a connection with something: *This film relates to what we were learning about metals last week.*
2 to tell a story: *I related my adventure to my family.*

re·lat·ed /rɪ'leɪtɪd/ *adjective*
1 of the same family: *I'm related to him – he's my uncle.*
2 connected: *The book is about electricity and related subjects.*

re·la·tion /rɪ'leɪʃn/ *noun*
a member of the same family: *Some of my relations, my mother's aunt and uncle, live in America.*

re·la·tion·ship /rɪ'leɪʃnʃɪp/ *noun*
the feelings between two people: *The teacher has a very good relationship with her students.*

rel·a·tive¹ /'relətɪv/ *noun*
a member of the same family

relative² *adjective*
compared with something of the same kind: *We compared the relative costs of travelling by train and by coach.*

rel·a·tive·ly /'relətɪvlɪ/ *adverb*
when compared with something of the same kind: *Travelling by train is relatively expensive, compared with the coach.*

relax

relaxing at work

re·lax /rɪ'læks/ *verb*
to become more calm and less worried or angry: *Don't worry about it – just try to relax.*

re·lax·a·tion /ˌriːlæk'seɪʃn/ *noun*
rest and entertainment after hard work or worry: *For relaxation, he played tennis.*

re·laxed /rɪ'lækst/ *adjective*
calm and not worried or angry: *After a long bath I began to feel more relaxed.*
⇨ opposite TENSE

re·lax·ing /rɪ'læksɪŋ/ *adjective*
making you calm and less worried: *We spent a relaxing evening listening to music.*

re·lease¹ /rɪ'liːs/ *verb* (*present participle* **releasing**, *past* **released**)
to let someone go free: *No-one is ever released from this prison. | Four hostages were released.*

release² *noun*
when someone or something is allowed to go free: *After their release, the prisoners came home.*

re·li·a·ble /rɪ'laɪəbl/ *adjective*
someone or something that is reliable can be trusted: *He is a very reliable person – if he says he will do something, he will do it.* ⇨ opposite UNRELIABLE

re·lief /rɪ'liːf/ *noun* (*no plural*)
a feeling of happiness that you have when you are no longer worried about something: *I felt great relief when I heard I had passed the exam.*

re·lieve /rɪ'liːv/ *verb* (*present participle* **relieving**, *past* **relieved**)
to make pain, a problem, a bad feeling etc less strong: *The medicine relieved his headache.*

re·lieved /rɪˈliːvd/ adjective
happy after a period of worry: *Your mother will be very relieved to hear that you are safe.*

re·li·gion /rɪˈlɪdʒən/ noun
1 (*no plural*) belief in one or more gods: *Almost every country has some form of religion.*
2 a special set of beliefs in one or more gods: *Hinduism and Buddhism are Eastern religions.*

re·li·gious /rɪˈlɪdʒəs/ adjective
1 connected with religion: *She has strong religious belief.*
2 showing a strong belief in a religion and obeying its rules: *He was a very religious man.*

re·luc·tant /rɪˈlʌktənt/ adjective
not willing: *The child was reluctant to leave her mother.*

re·ly /rɪˈlaɪ/ verb (*present participle* **relying**, *past* **relied**)
to trust in someone or something: *You can rely **on** me to help you.*

re·main /rɪˈmeɪn/ verb
to stay: *I went to the city, but my brother remained at home.* | *We remained friends for many years.*

re·main·der /rɪˈmeɪndəʳ/ noun
what is left after everyone or everything else has gone or been dealt with: *I'll go ahead with three of you, and the remainder of the group can wait here.*

re·mains /rɪˈmeɪnz/ plural noun
parts that are left: *We found the remains **of** a meal on the table.*

re·mark[1] /rɪˈmɑːk/ noun
something said: *He made a rude remark about me.*

remark[2] verb
to say something because you have just thought about it or just noticed it: *"That's where Jane lives," she remarked.*

re·mark·a·ble /rɪˈmɑːkəbl/ adjective
unusual, usually in a good way: *There is a chance England might achieve a remarkable victory.*

re·mark·a·bly /rɪˈmɑːkəblɪ/ adverb
surprisingly: *He is a remarkably lucky man.*

rem·e·dy /ˈremədɪ/ noun (*plural* **remedies**)
1 an answer to a problem: *We need a remedy for the widespread poverty in our big cities.*
2 something that gets rid of pain or illness: *He gave me a remedy **for** my stiff neck.*

re·mem·ber /rɪˈmembəʳ/ verb
to keep something or someone in your mind: *Did you remember to feed the animals?* | *I can't remember her phone number.* ⇨ opposite FORGET

re·mind /rɪˈmaɪnd/ verb
1 to make someone remember: *Remind me to write to my uncle.* | *That smell reminds me **of** the seaside.* | *Remind me about the flowers for Mary – I mustn't forget them.*
2 **remind you of someone** to be like someone else: *That man reminds me of Charlie Chaplin.*

re·mote /rɪˈməʊt/ adjective
far from towns and cities: *They have a remote farm in the hills.*

remote con·trol
/rɪˌməʊt kənˈtrəʊl/ noun
a piece of equipment that you use to control something such as a television from a distance

remote control

re·mote·ly
/rɪˈməʊtlɪ/ adverb
in any way: *He is not remotely like me.*

re·mov·al /rɪˈmuːvl/ noun
the act of taking something away from a place or moving it: *He ordered the removal of the pictures from the walls.* | *The removal of foreign soldiers has become necessary.*

removal van /rɪˈmuːvl ˌvæn/ noun
a large vehicle used to move all the things from one house to another when people go to live in a new house

re·move /rɪˈmuːv/ verb (*present participle* **removing**, *past* **removed**)
to take something away: *Will you remove your books **from** my desk?*

re·new /rɪˈnjuː/ verb
1 to arrange for something new to replace something of the same kind: *I must remember to renew the car insurance.*

2 to start something again: *The soldiers renewed their attack on the town.*

rent[1] /rent/ *noun*

money paid regularly for the use of a house, office, etc: *He pays 100 dollars a week rent.*

rent[2] *verb*

to have the use of a house or car or let someone use a house or car in return for money: *My father rents an office in the city.* | *While I was abroad I rented my house to a nice family.* ⇨ look at HIRE

re·paid /rɪˈpeɪd/

the past tense and past participle of the verb **repay**

re·pair[1] /rɪˈpeəʳ/   **repair**
verb

to fix something that is broken or damaged: *Have you repaired the chair yet?* ⇨ same meaning MEND

repairing a fence

repair[2] *noun*

something that you do to fix something that is broken or damaged: *I haven't paid for the repairs **to** my bicycle.*

re·pay /rɪˈpeɪ/ *verb* (*past* **repaid** /rɪˈpeɪd/)

to give back to someone the money that you borrowed: *I'll repay you tomorrow.*

re·peat /rɪˈpiːt/ *verb*

to say something or do something again: *Could you repeat the question?*

re·peat·ed /rɪˈpiːtɪd/ *adjective*

done again and again: *She made repeated attempts to escape.*

repeatedly *adverb*: *He shouted at me repeatedly to stop.*

rep·e·ti·tion /ˌrepɪˈtɪʃn/ *noun* (*no plural*)

when something happens again or is done again: *I don't want any repetition of this disobedience.*

re·place /rɪˈpleɪs/ *verb* (*present participle* **replacing**, *past* **replaced**)

1 to put something back in its place: *Please replace the books on the shelf exactly where you found them.*

2 to put a new or different thing in place of something: *The man who sold me the radio said he'd replace it if it didn't work.*

re·place·ment /rɪˈpleɪsmənt/ *noun*

something new or different in the place of something old or broken: *This radio doesn't work – I'm going to get a replacement.*

re·play[1] /riːˈpleɪ/ *verb*

to play a game such as a football match again because no one won it the first time

re·play[2] /ˈriːpleɪ/ *noun*

a game such as a football match that is played again because no one won it the first time: *I watched the replay between Liverpool and Arsenal.*

re·ply[1] /rɪˈplaɪ/ *verb* (*past* **replied**)

to give an answer: *"Did you forget?" I asked. "Of course not," she replied.* | *I replied that I would do it later.* | *Have they replied **to** your letter?*

reply[2] *noun* (*plural* **replies**)

an answer: *Have you had a reply **to** your letter?*

re·port[1] /rɪˈpɔːt/ *verb*

1 to tell people about something, especially in newspapers, on television, or on the radio: *The accident was reported on the radio.* | *He reported that the company had made a profit.*

2 to tell someone in authority that a crime or accident has happened: *She was stealing money and they reported her **to** the police.*

report[2] *noun*

the facts about something that has happened: *We read a report **of** the accident.* | *I saw the newspaper report.*

re·port·er /rɪˈpɔːtəʳ/ *noun*

a person who writes about the news for newspapers or magazines, or who records information about the news for television or radio

rep·re·sent /ˌreprɪˈzent/ *verb*

1 to act officially for another person or group of people: *He represented his company at the meeting.*

2 to be a sign of something: *The green signs on the map represent camp grounds.*

rep·re·sen·ta·tive /ˌreprɪˈzentətɪv/
noun

a person who acts officially for another person or group of people: *They sent a representative to the meeting.*

re·proach /rɪˈprəʊtʃ/ *verb*

to blame someone and try to make them feel sorry for what they have done: *He reproached Philip for his laziness.*

re·pro·duce /ˌriːprəˈdjuːs/ *verb (present participle* **reproducing**, *past* **reproduced**)

1 to produce young humans, animals, or plants: *Birds and fish reproduce by laying eggs.*

2 to make a copy of something: *The paintings were all reproduced in the book.*

re·pro·duc·tion /ˌriːprəˈdʌkʃən/ *noun*

1 (*no plural*) the process of producing young humans, animals, or plants: *He wrote a book on human reproduction.*

2 a copy of something: *He painted a reproduction **of** a famous picture.*

rep·tile /ˈreptaɪl/ *noun*

an animal such as a snake that lays eggs and whose blood changes temperature with the temperature around it

re·pub·lic /rɪˈpʌblɪk/ *noun*

a country whose head is a president, not a king or queen

rep·u·ta·tion /ˌrepjʊˈteɪʃn/ *noun*

the opinion that people have about someone or something: *This hotel has a good reputation.*

re·quest¹ /rɪˈkwest/ *verb*

to ask politely or formally for something: *Visitors are requested to be quiet in the hospital.* I *Please request help if you need it.*

request² *noun*

when someone politely asks for something: *She made a request **for** help.*

re·quire /rɪˈkwaɪəʳ/ *verb (present participle* **requiring**, *past* **required**)

to need something: *These plants require a lot of light.*

re·quire·ment /rɪˈkwaɪəmənt/ *noun*

something that is needed: *This shop can supply all your requirements.*

a mountain rescue

res·cue¹ /ˈreskjuː/ *verb (present participle* **rescuing**, *past* **rescued**)

to save someone from danger: *They rescued the boy from the river.*

rescue² *noun*

when someone is saved from danger: *There was a big rescue operation after a ship sank in the North Sea.*

re·search¹ /rɪˈsɜːtʃ, ˈriːsɜːtʃ/ *noun (no plural)*

careful study, especially to find out something new: *scientific research* I *medical research*

re·search² /rɪˈsɜːtʃ/ *verb*

to study something to find out new information about it

re·sem·blance /rɪˈzembləns/ *noun*

the way in which two people or things look like each other: *There is no resemblance **between** the two brothers.*

re·sem·ble /rɪˈzembl/ *verb (present participle* **resembling**, *past* **resembled**)

to look like another person or thing: *She resembles her mother in many ways.*

re·sent /rɪˈzent/ *verb*

to feel angry about something that someone has said or done to you: *He resents being treated like a child.*

re·sent·ment /rɪˈzentmənt/ *noun (no plural)*

a feeling of anger about something that someone has said or done to you: *There is a sense of deep resentment against the government.*

res·er·va·tion /ˌrezəˈveɪʃn/ *noun*

an arrangement to make sure that something is kept for your use: *Have you made a reservation at the hotel?*

re·serve¹ /rɪˈzɜːv/ *verb (present participle* **reserving**, *past* **reserved**)

to keep something for someone or arrange for something to be kept: *I have reserved a table for us at the restaurant.*

reserve² *noun*

1 an amount of something that is kept for future use: *We have large reserves of oil.* | *Water reserves are dangerously low.*

2 a place where wild animals live and are protected: *Africa has many wildlife reserves.*

res·er·voir /ˈrezəvwɑːʳ/ *noun*

a place where a lot of water is stored

res·i·dence /ˈrezɪdəns/ *noun*

1 the place where you live: *The President's official residence is in the centre of the city.*

2 (*no plural*) when someone lives in a particular place: *I am applying for residence in the United Kingdom.*

res·i·dent /ˈrezɪdənt/ *noun*

a person who lives in a place: *The residents **of** Oxford are complaining about the plan.*

res·i·den·tial /ˌrezɪˈdenʃl/ *adjective*

a residential area consists of houses, not offices or factories: *I live in a residential area outside town.*

re·sign /rɪˈzaɪn/ *verb*

1 to leave your job: *He resigned **from** the Government.*

2 resign yourself to something to accept something unpleasant calmly: *I resigned myself to a long wait.*

res·ig·na·tion /ˌrezɪgˈneɪʃn/ *noun*

1 a letter saying you are leaving your job: *I sent in my resignation last week.*

2 (*no plural*) calm acceptance of something unpleasant: *She reacted to the bad news with resignation.*

re·sist /rɪˈzɪst/ *verb*

1 to fight back against attack: *They tried to resist the enemy attack.*

2 to fight against something: *He resists any kind of change.*

3 to stop yourself doing something you would like to do: *I can't resist laughing at him.*

4 to not be changed or harmed by something: *Vitamins will help you resist disease.*

re·sist·ance /rɪˈzɪstəns/ *noun* (*no plural*)

when people fight against someone or something: *There was little resistance to the plan to build a new road.*

res·o·lu·tion /ˌrezəˈluːʃn/ *noun*

a decision to do something that you should do: *I made a resolution to work hard.*

re·solve /rɪˈzɒlv/ *verb* (*present participle* **resolving**, *past* **resolved**)

to decide: *I resolved to work hard until the examination.*

re·sort /rɪˈzɔːt/ *noun*

a town where people go on holiday: *Bournemouth is a seaside resort.* | *The forest is a tourist resort.*

re·source /rɪˈzɔːs/ *noun*

the thing or the money that a country or an organization has that it can use: *The country is rich in natural resources such as oil.*

re·spect¹ /rɪˈspekt/ *noun*

1 (*no plural*) when you admire someone and treat them well: *He has great respect **for** his parents.*

2 a way: *In some respects, he is like his father.*

respect² *verb*

to feel admiration for someone's good qualities: *All the children respected their teacher.*

re·spect·a·ble /rɪˈspektəbl/ *adjective*

with a good honest character: *He was a respectable young man.*

re·spond /rɪˈspɒnd/ *verb*

to answer: *How did she respond **to** your question?*

re·sponse /rɪˈspɒns/ *noun*

an answer: *I've had no response **to** my letter.*

re·spon·si·bil·i·ty /rɪˈspɒnsəˈbɪlətɪ/ *noun* (*plural* **responsibilities**)

something that it is your duty to do or look after: *My children are my responsibility.*

re·spon·si·ble /rɪˈpɒnsəbl/ *adjective*

taking care of someone or something, and taking the blame if anything goes wrong: *Simon is a responsible boy – we can leave him to look after the smaller children.* | *She's responsible **for** organizing the whole show.*

rest¹ /rest/ *noun*

1 a period of time when you can relax or sleep: *I had an hour's rest after work.*

2 the rest the remaining part or parts of something: *Have you seen the rest of* the children? | We'll eat the rest of the cake tomorrow.

rest[2] *verb*
1 to stop doing something and to relax for a period of time: *I rested for an hour before I went out.*
2 to put something on or against another thing: *I rested my elbows on the table.*

res·tau·rant /'restərɒnt/ *noun*
a place where you can buy and eat a meal: *We ate at the Italian restaurant.*

rest·ful /'restfəl/ *adjective*
pleasantly peaceful: *I spent a restful evening watching television.*

rest·less /'restləs/ *adjective*
not able to stop moving, for example because you are worried or bored: *The children are getting restless – we'd better find something for them to do.*

re·store /rɪ'stɔːr/ *verb (present participle* **restoring,** *past* **restored)**
1 to repair something so that it looks new: *He likes restoring old cars.*
2 to give back something that was lost or stolen: *The jewels were restored to their owners.*

re·strain /rɪ'streɪn/ *verb*
to stop or hold back something: *She couldn't restrain her tears.*

re·strict /rɪ'strɪkt/ *verb*
to limit something: *Swimming is restricted to this part of the river only – the rest is dangerous.*

re·stric·tion /rɪ'strɪkʃən/ *noun*
a limit: *There are parking restrictions in the city centre.*

re·sult[1] /rɪ'zʌlt/ *noun*
something that happens or exists because of another thing: *What was the result of your examination – did you pass or fail?*

result[2] *verb*
to happen or exist because of something: *The accident resulted in three people being killed.*

re·sume /rɪ'zjuːm/ *verb (present participle* **resuming,** *past* **resumed)**
formal to start again: *We shall resume our work in a quarter of an hour.*

re·tire /rɪ'taɪər/ *verb (present participle* **retiring,** *past* **retired)**
to stop work because of old age or

illness: *He retired from the business when he was 65.*

re·tire·ment /rɪ'taɪəmənt/ *noun*
the period of a person's life after they have stopped working because they are old: *She plans to spend her retirement travelling.*

re·treat[1] /rɪ'triːt/ *verb*
to go back or away from something or someone: *The soldiers had to retreat as the enemy advanced.*

retreat[2] *noun*
when an army moves back to avoid fighting: *The retreat is continuing, and the war is being lost.*

re·turn[1] /rɪ'tɜːn/ *verb*
1 to come or go back to a place: *He returned to his own country.*
2 to give something back: *Could you return the book I lent you?*

return[2] *noun*
1 when someone comes back or goes back to a place: *On my return from work, I saw that the door was open.*
2 a ticket for a journey to a place and back again: *Two returns to Edinburgh, please.* | *I bought a return ticket.*
▷ compare SINGLE

re·veal /rɪ'viːl/ *verb*
to say or show something that was secret or covered up before: *She revealed her fears for her son's safety.* | *The curtains opened to reveal the stage.*

re·venge /rɪ'vendʒ/ *noun (no plural)*
something bad that you do to someone who has done something bad to you: *He broke Mary's pen and in revenge she tore up his school work.*

Reve·rend /'revrənd/ *noun*
a title for a Christian priest, often written as 'Rev': *The speech was given by the Reverend Richard Jones.*

re·verse /rɪ'vɜːs/ *verb (present participle* **reversing,** *past* **reversed)**
1 to move backwards: *The driver reversed the lorry into the narrow road.*
2 to change something such as a decision or way of doing something so that it is the opposite of what it was before: *The tax rise has been reversed – we actually pay less than last year.*

re·view[1] /rɪ'vjuː/ *noun*
a written or spoken opinion of something such as a new book or film: *Her latest book got good reviews in the press.*

A
B
C
D
E
F
G
H
I
J
K
L
M
N
O
P
Q
R
S
T
U
V
W
X
Y
Z

review [2] *verb*
to give your opinion in a newspaper, on television, etc about something such as a new book or film

re·vise /rɪˈvaɪz/ *verb (present participle* **revising**, *past* **revised**)
1 to prepare for an examination by studying things again: *I've been revising all week.*
2 to look through something again and change things where needed: *He was revising what he had written.*

re·vi·sion /rɪˈvɪʒn/ *noun (no plural)*
when you study things again to prepare for an examination

re·vive /rɪˈvaɪv/ *verb (present participle* **reviving**, *past* **revived**)
to become conscious again or to make someone conscious again: *She managed to revive the woman she had saved from the river.*

re·volt [1] /rɪˈvəʊlt/ *verb*
to refuse to obey leaders or a government, and to fight against them: *The soldiers revolted **against** their officers.*

revolt [2] *noun*
when a lot of people fight against their leaders or government: *The army officers led a revolt **against** the king.*

re·volt·ing /rɪˈvəʊltɪŋ/ *adjective*
extremely unpleasant: *What a revolting smell!* ⇨ same meaning DISGUSTING

rev·o·lu·tion /ˌrevəˈluːʃn/ *noun*
a great change, especially in the government of a country: *The army officers led a revolution against the king.*

rev·o·lu·tion·ary /ˌrevəˈluːʃnrɪ/ *adjective*
1 connected with revolution: *The revolutionary army finally entered the city.*
2 completely new and different: *This is a revolutionary new treatment for cancer.*

re·volve /rɪˈvɒlv/ *verb (present participle* **revolving**, *past* **revolved**)
to go round and round: *The wheels revolved quickly.* | *The Earth revolves round the sun.*

re·volv·er /rɪˈvɒlvəʳ/ *noun*
a small gun ⇨ same meaning PISTOL

re·ward [1] /rɪˈwɔːd/ *noun*
something that is given to someone in return for doing something good, providing information etc: *The police are offering a reward **for** information about the robbery.*

reward [2] *verb*
to give a reward to someone who has done something good: *How can I reward you **for** all your help?*

rheu·ma·tis·m /ˈruːmətɪzəm/ *noun (no plural)*
an illness that makes joints and muscles painful and stiff

rhi·no /ˈraɪnəʊ/ *noun*
a rhinoceros

rhi·no·ce·ros /raɪˈnɒsərəs/ *noun (plural* **rhinoceroses**)
a large wild animal with hard skin and one or two horns on its nose, that lives in Africa and Asia ⇨ see picture on page 195

rhyme [1] /raɪm/ *noun*
1 a word that ends with the same sound as another word
2 a short poem or story, using words that rhyme

rhyme [2] *verb (present participle* **rhyming**, *past* **rhymed**)
if two words or lines of poetry rhyme, they end with the same sound: *'Weigh' rhymes **with** 'play'.*

rhyth·m /ˈrɪðəm/ *noun*
a regular repeated pattern of sounds in music: *I can't dance to music without a good rhythm.*

rib /rɪb/ *noun*
one of the narrow bones in your chest ⇨ see picture at SKELETON

rib·bon /ˈrɪbən/ *noun*
a long narrow piece of material used for tying things and making them look pretty: *She wore ribbons in her hair.*

rice /raɪs/ *noun (no plural)*
a food that consists of small white or brown grains that you boil in water: *We ate lamb with brown rice.*

rich /rɪtʃ/ *adjective*
1 having a lot of money: *He became a very rich man when he won the prize.* ⇨ opposite POOR
2 cooked with a lot of fat, sugar, or eggs: *I don't like rich food.*

rich·es /ˈrɪtʃɪz/ *plural noun*
a lot of money, or a lot of valuable things: *She gave away all her riches.*

rid /rɪd/ *adjective*
> **get rid of something** to throw away or sell something that you do not want: *He got rid of his motorbike and bought a car.*

rid·den /'rɪdn/
> the past participle of the verb **ride**

rid·dle /'rɪdl/ *noun*
> a difficult and amusing question that you must guess the answer to

ride[1] /raɪd/ *verb* (*present participle* **riding**, *past* **rode** /rəʊd/, *past participle* **ridden** /'rɪdn/)
> to travel on or in a vehicle or on an animal: *She was riding a bicycle.* | *Janet rode a beautiful black horse.* | *They rode in the back seat of the bus.*

ride[2] *noun*
> a journey on or in a vehicle or on a horse, especially for pleasure: *Can I have a ride on your bike (=bicycle)?* | *They've gone out for a ride in the car.*

rid·er /'raɪdər/ *noun*
> a person who rides, especially someone who rides a horse: *The rider was thrown off his horse.*

ridge /rɪdʒ/ *noun*
> a long narrow area of high ground, especially along the top of a mountain: *I walked along the ridge, looking down at the valleys on each side.*

ri·dic·u·lous /rɪ'dɪkjʊləs/ *adjective*
> very silly: *Don't be ridiculous – you can't play outside in the rain.*
>
> **ridiculously** *adverb*: *The examination was ridiculously easy.*

ri·fle /'raɪfəl/ *noun*
> a long gun that you hold up against your shoulder to shoot

right[1] /raɪt/ *adjective*
> **1** correct or true: *Do you know the right time?* | *I don't think it's right to let children eat too many sweets.* | *She was right to tell the police.* | *You were right about Mary – she's very nice.* | *"Is this Piccadilly Circus?" "Yes, that's right."* ⇨ opposite WRONG
> **2** on the side of the hand that most people write with: *Take the next right turn.* | *He broke his right arm.* ⇨ opposite LEFT

right[2] *noun*
> **1** (*no plural*) what is fair and good: *You must learn the difference between right and wrong.* ⇨ opposite WRONG

2 what is or should be allowed by law: *We must work for equal rights for everyone.*
> **3** the side on the same side as the hand most people write with: *The school is on the left of the road, and his house is on the right.* ⇨ opposite LEFT

right[3] *adverb*
> **1** correctly: *I did all my sums right* ⇨ opposite WRONG
> **2** towards the right side: *Turn right at the corner.* ⇨ opposite LEFT
> **3** completely or all the way: *I read right to the end of the book.*
> **4** exactly in a particular place or at a particular time: *That's our house right in front of you.* | *The show started right on time.*
> **5** **right away/right now** without any delay

right an·gle /raɪt æŋgl/ *noun*
> the shape made when two sides of a square meet at a corner: *The circle is divided into 360 degrees.* | *A right angle equals 90 degrees.*

right-hand·ed /ˌraɪt 'hændɪd/ *adjective*
> using your right hand for things such as writing ⇨ opposite LEFT-HANDED

ri·gid /'rɪdʒɪd/ *adjective*
> **1** stiff and not easy to bend: *We accept all rigid plastic containers for recycling.*
> **2** not easy to change: *Their laws are more rigid than ours.* | *He had very rigid ideas.*

rim /rɪm/ *noun*
> the outside edge of something: *There was a pattern round the rim of the plate.*

rind /raɪnd/ *noun*
> the hard outer skin of fruit, cheese, etc

ring[1] /rɪŋ/ *noun*
> **1** a circle: *The children sat in a ring.*
> **2** a circular metal band that you wear on your finger: *She wore a wedding ring.* ⇨ see picture at JEWELLERY
> **3** **give someone a ring** to telephone someone: *I'll give you a ring some time tomorrow.*

ring[2] *verb* (*past* **rang** /ræŋ/, *past participle* **rung** /rʌŋ/)
> **1** to make the sound of a bell: *He heard the telephone ringing.* | *He rang the bell but no one came to the door.*
> **2** **ring off** to end a telephone conversation: *I'd better ring off now – there's someone at the door.*

A B C D E F G H I J K L M N O P Q R S T U V W X Y Z

3 ring someone up to telephone someone: *She rang me up to say she'd be home late.* | *Has anyone rung up this evening?*

rinse /rɪns/ *verb (present participle* **rinsing,** *past* **rinsed)**
to wash the soap out of something you have washed: *I rinsed the woollen things three times.* | *Rinse your hair thoroughly.*

ri·ot[1] /'raɪət/ *noun*
when a crowd of people behave violently in a public place: *There was a riot when the workers were told they had lost their jobs.*

riot[2] *verb*
when a crowd of people riot, they behave violently in a public place: *Students were rioting in the streets.*

rip /rɪp/ *verb (present participle* **rjpping,** *past* **ripped)**
to tear: *As he climbed over the fence, he ripped his trousers on a nail.*

rip-off /'rɪp ɒf/ *noun*
something that is too expensive, so you feel that you are being cheated: *This new dress was a rip-off – it's falling apart already.*

ripe /raɪp/ *adjective*
full-grown and ready to eat: *This apple isn't ripe yet – you can't eat it.* | *Ripe bananas are delicious with grated chocolate.*

ripple

making ripples

rip·ple[1] /'rɪpl/ *noun*
a small wave on the surface of a liquid: *A gentle breeze made ripples on the lake.*

ripple[2] *verb (present participle* **rippling,** *past* **rippled)**
to move in small waves: *I sat there looking at the clear stream which rippled along.*

rise[1] /raɪz/ *verb (present participle* **rising,** *past* **rose** /rəʊz/, *past participle* **risen** /'rɪzn/)**
1 to go up: *Smoke rose from the chimney.* | *The land rises steeply from the river.*
2 to increase in number, value, etc: *Oil prices are rising all the time.*
3 to stand up: *He rose to his feet.*
4 when the sun rises, it appears in the sky

rise[2] *noun*
an increase: *There was a sudden rise in prices*

ris·en /'rɪzn/
the past participle of the verb **rise**

risk[1] /rɪsk/ *verb*
to put something in a situation where it could be lost, damaged, or harmed: *He risked his life when he saved the child from the fire.* | *You risk losing all your money.*

risk[2] *noun*
the chance that something bad may happen: *There is a risk that fire may break out again.*

ri·val /'raɪvəl/ *noun*
someone's rival is a person, team, company, etc that is trying to do better than them: *Ann's a good swimmer too – we're rivals for the swimming prize.*

ri·val·ry /'raɪvəlrɪ/ *noun (plural* **rivalries)**
when people, teams, companies, etc try to do better than each other: *There is great rivalry between the two sisters.*

riv·er /'rɪvəʳ/ *noun*
a line of water flowing across an area towards the sea: *The longest river in Africa is the Nile.* | *Let's go for a swim in the river.*

road /rəʊd/ *noun*
1 a hard wide track that people and traffic use to go from one place to another: *Where's the best place to cross the road?* | *Which road do you live in?* | *This is the road to Cambridge.*
2 by road by car, bus, etc and not on the train or by air or sea: *We're going by road.*

roam /rəʊm/ *verb*
to walk or travel with no definite purpose: *The visitors roamed around the town.*

roar[1] /rɔːʳ/ *verb*
to make a deep angry noise, like a lion

roar² *noun*
a deep angry noise such as the noise made by a lion

roast¹ /rəʊst/ *verb*
to cook food such as meat by baking it without water, or over a fire

roast² *adjective*
cooked by baking without water, or over a fire: *It's roast chicken for dinner.*

rob /rɒb/ *verb* (*present participle* **robbing**, *past* **robbed**)
to steal money or property from a person, bank, shop etc: *They planned to rob a bank.* | *They robbed her of everything she possessed.*

NOTE: Compare **rob** and **steal**. Someone **robs** a person or an organization, but **steals** things such as money: *The man pointed a gun at her and robbed her.* | *He was sent to prison for robbing a bank.* | *Someone has stolen my bag.* | *She stole the money.*

rob·ber /'rɒbəʳ/ *noun*
a person who steals something from a person, bank, shop etc: *He was a well-known bank robber.* | *He was shot by a robber who stole his motorcycle and rode off.*

rob·ber·y /'rɒbərɪ/ *noun* (*plural* **robberies**)
the crime of stealing money or property from a person, bank, shop etc: *He was charged with robbery.* | *There were eight bank robberies in the town that year.*

robe /rəʊb/ *noun*
a long loose piece of clothing that covers much of your body

ro·bot /'rəʊbɒt/ *noun*
a machine that is controlled by a computer and can do work instead of a person, for example making cars in a car factory

rock¹ /rɒk/ *noun*
1 (*no plural*) stone that forms part of the earth
2 a large piece of stone that sticks up out of the ground or the sea: *Here there is danger from falling rocks.* | *Ships were driven onto these rocks by heavy storms.*
3 (*no plural*) a type of popular modern music with a strong beat, that is played on electric instruments

rock² *verb*
to move regularly backwards and forwards or from side to side: *When I stepped onto the side of the boat it rocked.* | *A mother was rocking her baby.*

rocket

rock·et /'rɒkɪt/ *noun*
1 a machine that is forced into the air by burning gas, and is used to lift a weapon or a spaceship from the ground
2 a type of FIREWORK

rock·y /'rɒkɪ/ *adjective*
covered with rocks or made of rocks: *We climbed up the rocky path.*

rod /rɒd/ *noun*
a long thin pole or stick: *He was carrying a fishing rod.*

rode /rəʊd/
the past tense of the verb **ride**

rogue /rəʊg/ *noun*
a man or boy who behaves badly or is not honest, but who most people like: *I always knew he was a bit of a rogue.*

role /rəʊl/ *noun*
a character in a play or film: *He played the role of the old king in our school play.*

roll¹ /rəʊl/ *verb*
1 to move along by turning over and over: *The ball rolled under the table.* ⇨ see picture on page 198
2 also **roll up** to make a round shape by turning something over and over: *Roll the carpet up so that it doesn't get damaged.* | *Roll the paper – don't fold it.*
3 **roll over** to turn your body so that you are lying in a different position: *Matthew rolled over onto his stomach.*

A B C D E F G H I J K L M N O P Q R S T U V W X Y Z

roll² *noun*
1 something rolled up into a long round shape: *a roll* **of** *cloth*
2 a small round loaf of bread: *I ate a cheese roll* (=with cheese inside). ⟡ see picture at BREAD

Roll·er blade /'rəʊlə bleɪd/ *noun*
trademark
a special shoe with a single row of wheels fixed under it

Roller-blad·ing /'rəʊlə ˌbleɪdɪŋ/ *noun*
trademark (no plural)
the sport or activity of riding on Roller blades

roll·er skate /'rəʊlə skeɪt/ *noun*
a special shoe with two sets of two wheels fixed under it

roller-skat·ing /'rəʊlə ˌskeɪtɪŋ/ *noun*
(no plural)
the sport or activity of riding on roller skates: *Let's* **go** *roller-skating.*

ROM /rɒm/ *noun (no plural)*
the part of a computer that stores information that is needed for a long time

Roman Cath·o·lic /ˌrəʊmən 'kæθəlɪk/
adjective
belonging to the church whose head is the POPE

ro·mance /rəʊ'mæns/ *noun*
1 a relationship between two people who love each other: *It was a summer romance and now it's over.*
2 a story about love between two people: *I read lots of romances.*

ro·man·tic /rəʊ'mæntɪk/ *adjective*
showing or describing strong feelings of love: *I enjoy romantic stories.*

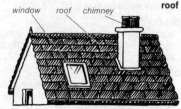
window   roof   chimney   **roof**

roof /ruːf/ *noun*
the top covering of a building, car, etc: *There's a cat on our roof.*

room /ruːm/ *noun*
1 part of the inside of a building that has its own door and walls: *The house had six rooms.*

2 (*no plural*) enough space for someone or something: *There isn't room* **for** *anyone else in the car.* | *This desk takes up a lot of room.*

root /ruːt/ *noun*
the part of a plant or tree that grows under the ground ⟡ see picture at TREE

rope /rəʊp/ *noun*
very strong thick string

rose¹ /rəʊz/
the past tense of the verb **rise**

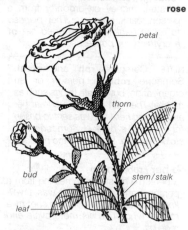
rose
petal
thorn
bud
stem/stalk
leaf

rose² *noun*
a beautiful and sweet-smelling flower

rot /rɒt/ *verb (present participle* **rotting***, past* **rotted***)*
to go bad and soft because of being old or wet: *The ripe fruit began to rot when no one came to pick it.*

ro·tate /rəʊ'teɪt/ *verb (present participle* **rotating***, past* **rotated***)*
to go round like a wheel: *The Earth rotates every 24 hours.*

ro·ta·tion /rəʊ'teɪʃn/ *noun*
a movement round and round like the movement of a wheel: *Day and night are caused by the rotation of the Earth on its axis.*

rot·ten /'rɒtn/ *adjective*
1 food, wood, etc that is rotten is in bad condition because it is old or wet: *This fish smells rotten!*
2 bad: *The way he treated her was really rotten.* | *He had a rotten cold.*

rough /rʌf/ *adjective*
1 not even or smooth: *The sea was*

rough. | *We climbed a rough mountain road.* | *I have rough skin on my feet.*

2 using too much force or violence: *He's too rough with the baby.* | *Rugby is a rough sport.*

rough·ly /'rʌflɪ/ *adverb*
1 about: *I had roughly four kilometres to go.* ⇨ same meaning APPROXIMATELY
2 not gently or carefully: *He pushed her away roughly.'*

round[1] /raʊnd/ *adjective*
like a ring or circle: *She had a little round face.*

round[2] *adverb, preposition* (also **around**)
1 with a movement like a circle: *The Earth turns round once every day.*
2 going in a circle, on all sides of something: *She wore a belt round her dress.* | *The children stood round the teacher.*
3 moving to face the opposite direction: *You're going the wrong way – you need to turn round and go back.*
4 going from one place to another: *They walked round the town for an hour.*
5 round and round going continuously in a circle: *The dog ran round and round in a circle.*

round·a·bout /'raʊndəbaʊt/ *noun*
1 a circular area where many roads meet, that you drive around until you get to the road you want: *Take the third exit from the big roundabout.*
2 a machine that turns round and round, on which children can ride for fun

route /ruːt/ *noun*
the way from one place to another: *What's the shortest route from London to Edinburgh?*

rou·tine /ruːˈtiːn/ *noun*
the usual way in which you do things: *I arrive at nine o'clock, teach until twelve thirty and then have a meal. That's my morning routine.*

row[1] /rəʊ/ *noun*
a line of people or things next to each other: *There's a row of pots on the shelf.*

row[2] /raʊ/ *noun*
an angry argument: *The two men were **having** a row.*

row[3] /rəʊ/ *verb*
to move OARS through water to make a boat move

row·ing boat /'rəʊɪŋ ˌbəʊt/ *noun*
a small boat that is moved through the water using OARS

roy·al /'rɔɪəl/ *adjective*
relating to a king or queen: *the royal family*

roy·al·ty /'rɔɪəltɪ/ *noun* (*no plural*)
members of the family of a king or queen

rub /rʌb/ *verb* (*present participle* **rubbing**, *past* **rubbed**)
1 to move something back and forward over something else: *She rubbed her shoes with a cloth to make them shine.* | *She rubbed cream into her hands.*
2 rub something out to remove something that is written down by rubbing it: *I'll have to rub it out and start again.*

rub·ber /'rʌbəʳ/ *noun*
1 (*no plural*) a soft material that is made from chemicals or the juice of a tree and is used for making things such as car tyres
2 a small piece of rubber used for getting rid of pencil marks ⇨ see picture on page 205

rubber band /ˌrʌbə ˈbænd/ *noun*
a long narrow piece of rubber in a ring shape that is used to fasten things together

rub·bish /'rʌbɪʃ/ *noun* (*no plural*)
1 things that you throw away because you do not need them: *The cupboard was full of old papers, broken toys, and other rubbish.* ⇨ compare JUNK
2 something that you think is silly, wrong, or bad: *I thought that story was rubbish.*

ru·by /'ruːbɪ/ *noun* (*plural* **rubies**)
a dark red stone often used in rings, jewellery, etc

ruck·sack /'rʌksæk/ *noun*
a large bag that you carry on your back ⇨ same meaning BACKPACK ⇨ see pictures at BAG and on page 193

rude /ruːd/ *adjective*
saying or doing unpleasant things that are not polite or kind: *It's rude to say you don't like the food.* | *Don't be so rude **to** your father.* | *She was rude **about** my old car.* ⇨ opposite POLITE

A B C D E F G H I J K L M N O P Q R S T U V W X Y Z

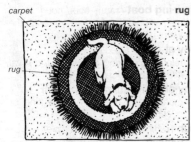

carpet   rug

rug

The dog is on the rug which is on the carpet

rug /rʌg/ *noun*
1 a piece of thick cloth or wool that you put on the floor: *The cat was sitting on a rug by the fire.* ⇨ see picture on page 204
2 a large thick cloth that you can put round you to keep you warm

rug·by /'rʌgbɪ/ *noun (no plural)*
a rough ball game played by two teams with an egg-shaped ball ⇨ see picture on page 196

rug·ged /'rʌgɪd/ *adjective*
rough and wild with many large rocks: *The country north of the river is very rugged.*

ru·in /'ruːɪn/ *verb*
to destroy something: *She poured water all over my painting, and ruined it.* | *We visited a ruined castle.*

ruin *noun*
1 a building that has been almost destroyed: *There was a ruin at the top of the hill.*
2 **ruins** the remaining parts of a destroyed building: *We saw the ruins of the church.*

rule /ruːl/ *verb (present participle ruling, past ruled)*
to have the power to control a country: *The new government rules the country firmly.* | *The country was ruled by a king.*

rule *noun*
1 an instruction that tells you what you must or must not do: *It's against the rules to pick up the ball.*
2 *(no plural)* the government or control of a country: *The country was under military rule.*

rul·er /'ruːlər/ *noun*
1 a person who controls a country
2 a piece of wood, plastic, or metal with a straight edge used for measuring and for drawing straight lines ⇨ see picture on page 205

rum /rʌm/ *noun (no plural)*
a strong alcoholic drink made from sugar

rum·ble /'rʌmbl/ *verb (present participle rumbling, past rumbled)*
to make a long low noise: *Thunder rumbled in the distance.*

ru·mour /'ruːmər/ *noun*
something that people tell each other but that may not be true: *I heard a rumour that the headmaster is leaving.*

run /rʌn/ *verb (present participle running, past ran /ræn/ past participle run)*
1 to move very quickly, moving your legs faster than when you walk: *He ran across the road.* ⇨ see picture on page 207
2 to go in a particular direction: *The road runs along the river bank.*
3 to go from one place to another at regular times: *Trains run every hour.*
4 if a machine or engine runs, it is working: *I left the engine running while I was waiting.*
5 to control a company, organization etc: *We don't have enough money to run the hospital properly.*
6 **run away** to leave a place because you are unhappy: *He ran away from home when he was thirteen.*
7 **run someone down** or **run someone over** to knock someone down with a car and hurt them: *A man was arrested for running down a policeman.*
8 **run into someone or something** to hit someone or something with a car: *I nearly ran into a lamp-post.*
9 **run off** to escape quickly from a person or place: *They took her handbag and ran off.*
10 **run out of something** to no longer have enough of something: *I've run out of petrol.*

run *noun*
1 when you run: *I always go for a run before breakfast.*
2 a journey by car or train: *We had quite a good run – it only took us 50 minutes.*
3 a point in the game of CRICKET

rung /rʌŋ/
the past participle of the verb **ring**

rung[2] *noun*
one of the bars in a ladder

run·ner /'rʌnəʳ/ *noun*
a person who runs, especially for sport or exercise

run·ning /'rʌnɪŋ/ *adjective*
running water is water that flows from a TAP: *The house has hot and cold running water.*

run·ny /'rʌnɪ/ *adjective*
something that is runny has become too liquid or contains too much liquid: *This paint is too runny to use on the ceiling.* ⇨ opposite THICK

ru·ral /'rʊərəl/ *adjective*
relating to or happening in the country, not the town: *Crops are grown in rural areas.*

rush[1] /rʌʃ/ *verb*
to hurry: *She rushed into the room to tell us the news.*

rush[2] *noun (no plural)*
a hurry: *I can't stop – I'm in a rush.*

rust[1] /rʌst/ *noun (no plural)*
a red-brown substance that forms on iron when it gets wet: *It was an old car and had a lot of rust.*

rust[2] *verb*
to become covered with rust: *If you leave your metal tools outside in the rain they will rust.*

rus·tle[1] /'rʌsl/ *verb (present participle* **rustling**, *past* **rustled**)
to make a light sound like the sound of paper being moved: *The leaves rustled in the wind.*

rustle[2] *noun (no plural)*
a light sound like the sound of paper being moved: *the rustle of leaves.*

rust·y /'rʌstɪ/ *adjective*
covered with rust: *He drove a rusty old car.*

rut /rʌt/ *noun*
a deep narrow track made by a wheel in soft ground

A
B
C
D
E
F
G
H
I
J
K
L
M
N
O
P
Q
R
S
T
U
V
W
X
Y
Z

Ss

S, s /es/

the nineteenth letter of the English alphabet

's /z, s/

1 is: *What's your name?* | *John's here.* | *She's writing a letter.*

2 has: *Polly's gone out.* | *A spider's got eight legs.*

3 used to show who is the owner of something: *Those are Tom's books* (=those books belong to Tom). | *We go round to Granny's house on Tuesdays.*

> NOTE: When there is more than one owner, write **s'**, not **'s**: *the boy's books* (=1 boy), *the boys' books* (=several boys)

sack¹ /sæk/ *noun*

1 a large bag made of thick strong material: *The lorry carried sacks **of** rice.*

2 **get the sack** *British* to be told to leave your job

sack² *verb*

British to tell someone to leave their job

sa·cred /'seɪkrɪd/ *adjective*

relating to God or religion: *A church is a sacred building.*

sac·ri·fice¹ /'sækrɪfaɪs/ *noun*

1 something that you decide not to have or do so that you can have something more important: *Her parents **made** many sacrifices so that she could study abroad.*

2 an object or animal that is offered to a god

sacrifice² *verb* (*present participle* **sacrificing**, *past* **sacrificed**)

1 to give up something important for a good purpose: *She sacrificed her job to look after her children.*

2 to offer something to a god: *They sacrificed a goat.*

sad /sæd/ *adjective* (**sadder**, **saddest**)

unhappy: *She felt very sad **that** the holiday was ending.* | *I liked my school and I was sad **to** leave.*

sad·dle /'sædl/ *noun*

1 a seat that you put on a horse's back

2 the seat on a bicycle or MOTORCYCLE ⇨ see picture at BICYCLE

sa·fa·ri /sə'fɑːri/ *noun*

a journey to look at or hunt wild animals, especially in Africa

safe¹ /seɪf/ *adjective*

1 not dangerous: *This town is very safe at night.* | *Are these toys safe for young children?*

2 not in danger: *Will you be safe travelling by yourself?*

safe² *noun*

a strong box or cupboard with a lock on it, where you keep money and important things

safe·ly /'seɪfli/ *adverb*

in a safe way: *Can we swim here safely?*

safe·ty /'seɪfti/ *noun* (*no plural*)

the state of being safe from danger or harm: *They managed to escape the fire and run to safety.* | *Some parents are worried about safety at the school.*

safety pin /'seɪfti pɪn/ *noun*

a bent metal pin with a cover over the point, used for fastening cloth ⇨ see picture at FIRST AID

sag /sæg/ *verb* (*present participle* **sagging**, *past* **sagged**)

to hang or bend down away from the usual position: *The shelf sagged in the middle.*

said /sed/

the past tense and past participle of the verb **say**

sail¹ /seɪl/ *noun*

a large cloth fastened to a boat, so that the wind will move the boat

sail

sailing on the sea

sail² *verb*

1 to travel on water in a boat or ship: *We sailed along the south coast.*

2 to control the movement of a boat or ship: *She sailed the boat without any help.*

sail·or /'seɪlər/ *noun*
a person who works on a ship, especially as a member of a navy

saint /seɪnt/ *noun*
a person who has lived a very good and religious life

sake /seɪk/ *noun*
1 for someone's sake in order to help someone or make them happy: *Please go and visit your grandmother, for my sake.* | *We moved to the countryside for Mum's sake.*
2 for goodness sake something you say when you are annoyed: *Oh, for goodness sake, hurry up!*

sal·ad /'sæləd/ *noun*
a dish of cold, usually raw, vegetables

sal·ar·y /'sæləri/ *noun* (*plural* **salaries**)
a fixed amount of money paid to someone every month for the job they do ⇨ same meaning PAY

sale /seɪl/ *noun*
1 an act of giving something to someone for money: *He got four pounds from the sale of his drawing.*
2 a time when shops sell things at lower prices: *The shoe shop is having a sale this week.*

sales·man /'seɪlzmən/ *noun* (*plural* **salesmen** /-mən/)
a man whose job is to sell things

sales·per·son /'seɪlzˌpɜːsn/ *noun*
someone whose job is to sell things

sales·wo·man /'seɪlzwʊmən/ *noun* (*plural* **saleswomen** /-wɪmɪn/)
a woman whose job is to sell things

salm·on /'sæmən/ *noun* (*plural* **salmon**)
a large river and sea fish that you can eat

salt /sɔːlt/ *noun* (*no plural*)
a white substance that is often put on food to make it taste better

salt·y /'sɔːlti/ *adjective* (**saltier**, **saltiest**)
tasting of salt or containing salt

sa·lute¹ /sə'luːt/ *verb* (*present participle* **saluting**, *past* **saluted**)
to hold your hand against the side of your head as a sign of respect to someone in the army, navy, etc: *The soldier saluted the officer.*

salute² *noun*
a sign made by holding your hand against the side of your head, done out of respect to someone in the army, navy, etc

same /seɪm/ *adjective*
the same person, place, thing, etc
(a) similar in one or more ways: *Your pen is the same as mine.* | *They all look the same to me.* ⇨ opposite DIFFERENT
(b) not changed or different: *We go to the same place every year for our holiday.* | *Kim's birthday and Roger's birthday are on the same day.*

sam·ple /'sɑːmpl/ *noun*
a small part of something that shows what the whole thing is like: *I would like to see a sample of his work.* | *I need to give a blood sample.*

sand /sænd/ *noun* (*no plural*)
very small grains of rock found next to the sea and in deserts

san·dal /'sændl/ *noun*
an open shoe that you wear in hot weather ⇨ see picture on page 203

sand·wich /'sændwɪtʃ/ *noun* (*plural* **sandwiches**)
two pieces of bread with cheese, meat, etc between them: *I made a chicken sandwich.* ⇨ see picture at FAST FOOD

sand·y /'sændi/ *adjective* (**sandier**, **sandiest**)
covered with sand: *We walked along the sandy beach.*

sane /seɪn/ *adjective*
having a healthy mind and able to think clearly and make decisions ⇨ opposite INSANE

sang /sæŋ/
the past tense of the verb **sing**

sank /sæŋk/
the past tense of the verb **sink**

sap /sæp/ *noun* (*no plural*)
the liquid inside a plant that carries food through it

sap·phire /'sæfaɪər/ *noun*
a blue stone used in jewellery

sar·cas·tic /sɑːˈkæstɪk/ *adjective*
using words in an unkind way: *He kept making sarcastic remarks.*

sar·dine /sɑːˈdiːn/ *noun*
a small fish that is eaten as food

sat /sæt/

the past tense and past participle of the verb **sit**

sat·el·lite

/'sætəlaɪt/ *noun*

satellite

an object sent into space to receive signals from one part of the world and send them to another: *The television broadcast came from America by satellite.*

sat·is·fac·tion

/ˌsætɪsˈfækʃən/ *noun* (no plural)

a feeling of pleasure: *I get great satisfaction from working with children.* | *He looked around the room with satisfaction.*

sat·is·fac·tory /ˌsætɪsˈfæktrɪ/ *adjective*

good enough: *My room is satisfactory.* | *Are the students making satisfactory progress?* ⇨ opposite UNSATISFACTORY

sat·is·fied /'sætɪsfaɪd/ *adjective*

pleased because something has happened in the way that you want: *I was satisfied **with** my exam results.* | *We want everyone to be a satisfied customer.* ⇨ opposite DISSATISFIED

sat·is·fy /'sætɪsfaɪ/ *verb* (present participle **satisfying**, past **satisfied**)

to make someone happy by giving them what they need or want: *This work does not satisfy me.*

Sat·ur·day /'sætədeɪ, -dɪ/ *noun*

the sixth day of the week after Friday and before Sunday

sauce /sɔːs/ *noun*

a liquid that you add to food to give it a particular taste: *We ate spaghetti and tomato sauce.*

sauce·pan /'sɔːspən/ *noun*

a pan with a handle for cooking things over heat ⇨ see picture at PAN

sau·cer /'sɔːsəʳ/ *noun*

a small plate that a cup stands on

saus·age /'sɒsɪdʒ/ *noun*

a mixture of meat, spices, etc cooked inside a long thin skin

sav·age /'sævɪdʒ/ *adjective*

very cruel and violent: *He owned a savage dog.*

save /seɪv/ *verb* (present participle **saving**, past **saved**)

1 to make someone or something safe from danger or harm: *I saved the animals **from** the flood.* | *Peter saved my life.*

2 also **save up** to keep money so that you can use it some other time: *How much money have you saved this month?* | *We're saving up to buy a car.*

3 to use less of something so that you do not waste it: *We'll save time if we go down this road.* | *You can save money on the ticket if you book in advance.*

4 to make a computer keep the work that you have done on it: *Have you saved the file?*

sav·ings /'seɪvɪŋz/ *plural noun*

all the money that you have saved, especially in a bank: *George used his savings to buy a bicycle.*

sa·viour /'seɪvjəʳ/ *noun*

someone or something who saves you from danger or difficulty

saw¹ /sɔː/

the past tense of the verb **see**

saw² *noun*

a tool used for cutting through wood or metal

saw³ *verb* (present participle **sawing**, past **sawed**, past participle **sawn** /sɔːn/)

to cut something using a saw: *He sawed the wood into three pieces.*

sax·o·phone /'sæksəfəʊn/ *noun*

a metal musical instrument that you blow into

say /seɪ/ *verb* (present participle **saying**, past **said** /sed/)

1 to speak words: *Dad said **that** he wanted to go to town.* | *"I'm really tired," he said.* | *Don't believe anything she says.*

2 to give information in writing, pictures, or numbers: *What does the clock say?* | *The instructions say you can clean it with soap and water.*

NOTE: Compare **say** and **tell** in these sentences: *She said something.* | *She told me something.* | *He said he was busy.* | *He told me he was busy.* **Say** never has a person as its object (to say something **to somebody**), but **tell** often has a person as its object (to tell **somebody** something).

say·ing /'seɪ-ɪŋ/ noun
a statement that people think is true or wise

scab /skæb/ noun
a hard layer of dried blood over a cut or wound

scaf·fold·ing /'skæfəldɪŋ/ noun (no plural)
a structure of metal bars fixed to a building for builders to stand on while they work on the building

scald /skɔːld/ verb
to burn yourself with steam or boiling liquid: She scalded herself with the hot milk.

scale /skeɪl/ noun
1 (no plural) the size or level of something, especially when compared to what is usual: The project is on a large scale. | The scale of the pollution was surprising.
2 scales a machine for weighing things or people: I need the scales to weigh the potatoes.
3 a set of marks on a measuring instrument: The ruler has a metric scale.
4 the relationship between the size of a map or drawing and the size of the real place: The scale of this map is one centimetre to the kilometre (=one centimetre represents one kilometre).
5 a set of musical notes going higher or lower in order
6 one of the flat hard pieces of skin that cover the body of a fish, snake, etc
⇨ see picture at FISH

scalp /skælp/ noun
the skin on the top of your head

scan·dal /'skændl/ noun
something that has happened that people think is very bad or shocking: The scandal involved several politicians.

scan·ner /'skænəʳ/ noun
a piece of computer equipment that copies a picture or words from paper onto a computer

scar[1] /skɑːʳ/ noun
a mark left on your skin by an old wound or cut

scar[2] verb (present participle **scarring**, past **scarred**)
to leave a mark on your skin: His face was badly scarred after the car accident.

scarce /skeəs/ adjective
if something is scarce, there is not enough of it: Food becomes scarce during a war. | Jobs were scarce in the region.

scarce·ly /'skeəslɪ/ adverb
almost not at all, or almost none at all: She scarcely said a word all evening.

scare[1] /skeəʳ/ verb (present participle **scaring**, past **scared**)
to make someone afraid: What was that noise? It scared me. | Spiders scare her.
⇨ same meaning FRIGHTEN

scare[2] noun
something sudden or unexpected that makes you afraid: You **gave** me **a** scare. I didn't know you were in the house.

scare·crow /'skeəkrəʊ/ noun
a figure dressed in old clothes and put in a field of crops to make birds go away

scared /skeəd/ noun
feeling afraid or nervous about something: I was scared **that** something bad would happen to her.

scarf /skɑːf/ noun (plural **scarves** /skɑːvz/)
a piece of cloth that you wear round your neck or head to keep warm or to make your clothes look more attractive

scar·let /'skɑːlət/ adjective, noun (no plural)
a very bright red colour: There were scarlet drops of blood on his hand.

scat·ter /'skætəʳ/ verb
1 to move or be made to move in different directions: The crowd scattered when it began to rain.
2 to throw or drop things over a wide area: The farmer scattered the corn in the yard for the hens.

scene /siːn/ noun
1 the things you can see in a place or in a picture: He painted a country scene with trees and a river.
2 the place where something happens: Police arrived quickly **at** the scene **of** the accident.
3 a short part of a play in which the action happens in one place: This play is divided into three acts, and each act has three scenes.

sce·ne·ry /'siːnərɪ/ noun (no plural)
1 the things that you see around you in

the country: *The scenery in the mountains is very beautiful.*

2 the painted pictures at the back of a theatre

scent /sent/ *noun*

1 a pleasant smell: *The scent of flowers filled the room.*

2 the smell left behind by an animal or person: *The dogs found the fox's scent and followed it.*

sched·ule /ˈʃedjuːl, ˈske-/ *noun*

a plan of when work is to be done: *The schedule shows that the book will take a year to finish.*

scheme¹ /skiːm/ *noun*

1 *British* a system arranged to help people: *The government is starting training schemes for young people.*

2 a plan: *He thought of a scheme to get some money.*

scheme² *verb* (*present participle* **scheming**, *past* **schemed**)

to make plans, especially ones that are not honest: *They schemed to steal money from the bank.*

schol·ar /ˈskɒləʳ/ *noun*

1 a person who knows a lot because they have studied a lot and read a lot of books

2 a clever student who has been given money so that he or she can continue to study

schol·ar·ship /ˈskɒləʃɪp/ *noun*

money given to a clever student so that he or she can continue to study: *She won a scholarship to Cambridge.*

school /skuːl/ *noun*

1 a place where children go to learn: *I'm learning to play the piano at school.* | *Mum takes us to school every morning.* | *There are several good schools in the area.*

2 (*no plural*) the time someone is at school: *What are you doing after school?* | *He started school when he was five.*

sci·ence /ˈsaɪəns/ *noun*

the study of the way things in the world are made or behave: *We have a very good teacher for science.*

science fic·tion /ˌsaɪəns ˈfɪkʃən/ *noun*

books and films about imaginary things in science such as space travel

sci·en·tif·ic /ˌsaɪənˈtɪfɪk/ *adjective*

of or about science: *He is doing a scientific study on tigers.*

sci·en·tist /ˈsaɪəntɪst/ *noun*

a person who studies or practises science

scis·sors /ˈsɪzəz/ *plural noun*

a tool for cutting paper or cloth, with two blades and holes for your thumb and finger: *If you give me **a pair of** scissors, I'll cut the string.* ⬦ see picture on page 205

scold /skəʊld/ *verb*

to tell a child in an angry way that they have done wrong: *My mother scolded me when I dropped the plates.*

scoop /skuːp/ *verb*

to pick something up with your hands, a spoon, etc: *She scooped flour out of the bag.*

scoot·er /ˈskuːtəʳ/ *noun*

1 a light small MOTORCYCLE

2 a board with two small wheels and a handle that children ride by having one foot on the board and pushing on the ground with the other one

score¹ /skɔːʳ/ *noun*

the number of points that you get in a game or competition: *What's the score?* | *The final score was four to one.*

score

Rick scored an easy goal.

score² *verb* (*present participle* **scoring**, *past* **scored**)

to win points in a game or competition: *How many goals did he score in the match?*

scorn /skɔːn/ *noun* (*no plural*)

the feeling that someone is very silly or no good: *I don't like James because he treats poor people with scorn.*

scor·pi·on /ˈskɔːpɪən/ *noun*

a small creature that stings with its tail

scout /skaʊt/ *noun*
also **boy scout, girl scout** a member of an organization that teaches young people to do good and useful things

scowl[1] /skaʊl/ *verb*
to look in an angry way at someone: *The teacher scowled at me because I was late.*

scowl[2] *noun*
an angry look on someone's face: *Brian entered the room with a scowl on his face.*

scram·ble /'skræmbl/ *verb (present participle* **scrambling**, *past* **scrambled)**
to move over something quickly but with difficulty: *The children scrambled up the hill.*

scram·bled eggs /ˌskræmbld 'egz/
eggs that have had their white and yellow parts mixed together and then cooked

scrap /skræp/ *noun*
a small piece of something: *If you've got a scrap of paper, I'll write down her phone number.*

scrape /skreɪp/ *verb (present participle* **scraping**, *past* **scraped)**
to remove something using the edge of a knife, stick, etc: *Scrape the mud off your shoes with this knife.*

scratch[1] /skrætʃ/ *verb*
1 to make a cut or mark on something using something sharp: *The stick scratched the side of the car. | The cat scratched the chair.*
2 to rub your nails lightly over a part of your body: *Try not to scratch those mosquito bites.*

scratch[2] *noun (plural* **scratches)**
a mark or small wound made by something sharp: *She has a scratch on her hand.*

scream[1] /skriːm/ *verb*
to give a loud high cry, usually because of fear or excitement: *She screamed with fear. | "Look out!" he screamed.*

scream[2] *noun*
a loud high cry of fear or excitement

screech /skriːtʃ/ *verb*
to make a loud high unpleasant noise: *The car screeched round the corner.*

screen /skriːn/ *noun*
1 the flat glass part of a television or computer
2 a large flat surface on which films are shown
3 a piece of material on a frame used for dividing one part of a room from another: *The doctor asked him to undress behind the screen.*

screw[1] /skruː/ *noun*
a small pointed piece of metal that you push and turn to fasten pieces of wood together ⇨ see picture at SCREWDRIVER

screw[2] *verb*
1 to fasten or fix something to a place with screws: *He screwed the mirror to the wall.*
2 to fasten something by turning it round and round: *Screw the lid on tightly.*

screw·driv·er /'skruːˌdraɪvə[r]/ *noun*
a tool with a long thin metal end used for turning screws

screwdriver

screw   *screwdriver*

scrib·ble /'skrɪbl/ *verb (present participle* **scribbling**, *past* **scribbled)**
to write something quickly and carelessly: *I'll scribble a note to say what time we'll come home.*

scrip·ture /'skrɪptʃə[r]/ *noun*
the holy writings of a religion

scroll /skrəʊl/ *verb*
to move information up or down a computer screen so that you can read it: *Can you scroll down to the next page?*

scroll bar /'skrəʊl bɑː[r]/ *noun*
a narrow part at the edge or bottom of a computer screen where you can use a mouse to move information up or down the screen

scrub /skrʌb/ *verb (present participle* **scrubbing**, *past* **scrubbed)**
to rub something hard to clean it, especially using a brush: *Ella was scrubbing the kitchen floor.*

sculp·tor /'skʌlptə[r]/ *noun*
an artist who makes shapes and figures from wood, stone, or metal

A B C D E F G H I J K L M N O P Q R **S** T U V W X Y Z

sculp·ture /ˈskʌlptʃər/ *noun*
1 a figure or art object made from wood, stone, or metal
2 (*no plural*) the art of making figures or art objects from wood, stone, or metal

sea /siː/ *noun*
1 the salt water that covers much of the Earth's surface: *He sat on the beach looking out at the sea.*
2 a large area of salty water: *The Mediterranean Sea*
3 **by sea** on a ship: *It's cheaper to send goods abroad by sea than by air.*

sea·food /ˈsiːfuːd/ *noun* (*no plural*)
sea creatures that you eat: *We eat a lot of seafood.*

sea·gull /ˈsiːgʌl/ *noun*
a bird that lives near the sea and eats fish and sea creatures

seal¹ /siːl/ *noun*
an animal with a thick coat that lives in or near the sea in cold areas ⇨ see picture on page 195

seal² *verb*
to close something firmly so that it cannot open by mistake: *She sealed the envelope and put a stamp on it.*

seam /siːm/ *noun*
a line where two pieces of cloth are joined together

search¹ /sɜːtʃ/ *verb*
to look carefully in a place because you want to find something: *The police searched the house.* | *I've searched everywhere for my keys.*

search² *noun* (*plural* **searches**)
an attempt to find something: *After a long search, they found the lost child.*

sea·shell /ˈsiːʃel/ *noun*
the shell of a small sea creature that you can find empty on the shore

sea·shore /ˈsiːʃɔːr/ *noun*
the land along the edge of the sea

sea·sick /ˈsiːsɪk/ *adjective*
feeling sick because of the movement of a boat on water: *He felt seasick because the sea was very rough.*

sea·side /ˈsiːsaɪd/ *noun*
the seaside a place by the sea where people go on holiday ⇨ compare COAST

sea·son /ˈsiːzn/ *noun*
1 one of the four parts of the year: *Summer is the hottest season.*
2 a special time of the year during which a sport or an activity takes place: *the football season*

seat /siːt/ *noun*
1 a place to sit, or a thing to sit on: *I could not find a seat on the bus.* | *He was sitting in the front seat of the car.*
2 **take a seat, have a seat** to sit down: *Please come in and take a seat.*

seat·belt /ˈsiːtbelt/ *noun*
a belt fixed to a seat in a car or plane that helps to protect you in an accident

sec·ond¹ /ˈsekənd/ *adjective*
2nd, after the first one: *This is the second time I have met him.* | *I came second in the race.* | *He's just scored his second goal.*

second² *noun*
a very short length of time. There are 60 seconds in one minute: *It takes about 30 seconds for the computer to start up.*

sec·ond·ary school /ˈsekəndri ˌskuːl/ *noun*
a school for children over 11 years old

second-class /ˌsekənd ˈklɑːs/ *adjective*
not the most expensive or best quality: *I'll use a second-class stamp.* | *He bought a second-class train ticket.*

se·cret¹ /ˈsiːkrɪt/ *noun*
something that has not been told to other people: *Don't tell anyone about our plan – it's a secret.* | *Can you **keep** a secret (=not tell anyone else)?*

secret² *adjective*
not known about by other people: *They had a secret plan.* | *If I tell you what happened will you **keep** it secret (=not tell anyone else)?*

sec·re·ta·ry /ˈsekrətri/ *noun* (*plural* **secretaries**)
1 someone whose job is to answer the telephone, write letters, etc in an office
2 a government official

sec·tion /ˈsekʃən/ *noun*
a part of something: *One section of the bookcase had records on it.* | *A section of the road was closed because of an accident.* | *He was reading the sports section of the newspaper.*

se·cure /sɪˈkjʊər/ *adjective*
1 locked, guarded, or protected: *Keep your money in a secure place.*
2 not likely to be lost: *He has a secure job.*

3 fixed or fastened firmly: *That shelf doesn't look very secure.*

se·cu·ri·ty /sɪˈkjʊərətɪ/ *noun* (*no plural*)
being safe and protected: *The government is responsible for the security of the country.*

see /siː/ *verb* (*present participle* **seeing**, *past* **saw** /sɔː/, *past participle* **seen** /siːn/)

1 to use your eyes to know or notice something: *It's too dark in here; I can't see anything.* | *I've lost my watch. Have you seen it?* | *I saw a man take the bag and run off.*

2 to watch something, especially on television or at the cinema: *Did you see that programme about drugs last night?* | *What film shall we go and see?* ⇨ look at (**1** and **2**) WATCH

3 to understand something: *Do you see what I mean?* | *I can't see why we have to pay so much.*

4 to meet or visit someone: *I'll see you outside the theatre.* | *You should go and see a doctor.* | *I saw Joan in the park.*

5 to discover something: *Go and see how many people have arrived.* | *I'll see if Mr Jones wants a cup of coffee while he waits.* | *I'll see what time the train leaves.*

6 **let's see** used when you are thinking about something or trying to remember something: *Let's see. How many people are coming?*

7 **I'll see, we'll see** something you say when you want to think about something before deciding: *"Can I borrow the car on Saturday?" "We'll see."*

8 **See you** a way of saying goodbye to a friend: *"Bye Bill." "See you, Terry."*

> NOTE: When you are looking at something and telling someone about it, do not say *I am seeing something*. Say *I can see it* or *I am looking at it*.

seed /siːd/ *noun*
a small grain from which a plant grows

seek /siːk/ *verb* (*present participle* **seeking**, *past* **sought** /sɔːt/)
to try to find or get something: *You should seek advice from a lawyer.*

seem /siːm/ *verb*
to appear to be: *Your sister seems very nice.* | *Henry seems a bit upset today.* | *There seems to be a problem here.*

seen /siːn/
the past participle of the verb **see**

see·saw /ˈsiːsɔː/ *noun*
a long piece of wood balanced in the middle, on which children go up and down

seize /siːz/ *verb* (*present participle* **seizing**, *past* **seized**)
to take hold of something quickly and firmly: *Ron seized the child's arms and lifted her to safety.*

sel·dom /ˈseldəm/ *adverb*
only a few times, not often: *The children are seldom ill.* ⇨ same meaning RARELY

se·lect /sɪˈlekt/ *verb*
1 to choose something or someone: *I was selected for the team.*
2 to mark something such as words on a computer screen so that you can do something with them: *Select the part that you want to copy.*

se·lec·tion /sɪˈlekʃən/ *noun*
people or things that have been chosen from a bigger group: *Here is a selection of our books.*

self /self/ *noun* (*plural* **selves** /selvz/)
the type of person you are, especially your character, abilities, etc: *Caroline has been a bit unhappy lately, but today she was her usual friendly self.*

self-con·fi·dent /self ˈkɒnfɪdənt/ *adjective*
being confident about your appearance and abilities

self·ish /ˈselfɪʃ/ *adjective*
caring only about yourself and not about other people: *Don't be so selfish with your toys!* ⇨ opposite UNSELFISH
selfishly *adverb*: *He always behaves so selfishly.*

self-serv·ice /ˌself ˈsɜːvɪs/ *adjective*
getting things for yourself instead of being served by someone: *This is a self-service restaurant.*

sell /sel/ *verb* (*present participle* **selling**, *past* **sold** /səʊld/)
1 to give something in exchange for money: *She sold her old bicycle to me.* | *What does that shop sell?* | *Do you sell milk?*
2 **sell out** to sell all of a particular thing and so have none left: *We've sold out of newspapers.*

Sel·lo·tape /'seləteɪp/ *noun*

British, *trademark* narrow thin clear material that is sticky on one side and is used for sticking things together

se·mes·ter /sɪ'mestə^r/ *noun*

American one of the periods of time in which students go to school or university (*British* **term**)

sem·i·cir·cle /'semɪ,sɜːkl/ *noun*

half a circle: *The children sat in a semi-circle with the teacher in front of them.*

sem·i·co·lon /,semɪ'kəʊlən/ *noun*

the sign (;) used in writing to separate parts of a sentence such as 'It was a long walk; I'm very tired.'

sem·i·fi·nal /,semɪ'faɪnl/ *noun*

one of two games played in a competition to decide which players or teams will be in the last part of the competition

sen·ate /'senət/ *noun*

one of the groups that make up the government in some countries

sen·at·or /'senətə^r/ *noun*

a member of a senate

send /send/ *verb* (*past* **sent** /sent/)

1 to arrange for something to go somewhere or be taken somewhere: *She sent me a present.* | *I sent Dad a birthday card yesterday.*

2 to make someone go somewhere: *Richard couldn't come so he sent his sister instead.* | *They are sending soldiers **to** the region.*

3 **send for someone** to ask someone to come to you: *Alice was very ill, so her mother sent for the doctor.*

se·nior /'siːnjə^r/ *adjective*

1 older: *She teaches a senior class.*

2 higher in position or importance: *She started as a secretary, but now she has a senior position in the company.*

⟡ opposite (**1** and **2**) JUNIOR

sen·sa·tion /sen'seɪʃn/ *noun*

1 the ability to feel, or a feeling in your body: *She felt a burning sensation on the back of her neck.*

2 (*no plural*) excitement or a lot of interest: *The new show caused a sensation.*

sense[1] /sens/ *noun*

1 (*no plural*) good understanding and the ability to think clearly and make good decisions: *I think she's got*

enough sense to ring if she's in trouble. | *Tom **had the** sense not to move the injured man.*

2 (*no plural*) a feeling about something: *I felt a strong sense **of** pride when I won the race.*

3 **make sense** to have a meaning that you can understand: *Do these instructions make sense to you?*

4 one of the five natural abilities to hear, see, taste, feel, or smell: *He has a good sense **of** smell.*

sense[2] *verb* (*present participle* **sensing**, *past* **sensed**)

to know something that is not said or shown openly: *The dog sensed **that** I was afraid.*

sen·si·ble /'sensɪbl/ *adjective*

having or showing good sense: *Tom's parents trust him because he is very sensible.* | *I think we made a sensible decision.*

sensibly *adverb*: *She sensibly decided to do her homework first.*

sen·si·tive /'sensɪtɪv/ *adjective*

able to understand how other people feel, and careful not to say or do anything that will make them unhappy: *A good teacher is sensitive to his or her students' needs.*

sent /sent/

the past tense and past participle of the verb **send**

sen·tence /'sentəns/ *noun*

a group of words that makes a statement or a question. A sentence begins with a capital letter and ends with a FULL STOP or a question mark ⟡ compare CLAUSE

sepa·rate[1] /'seprət/ *adjective*

1 not touching or connected to each other: *They have gone to separate schools.* | *We sleep in separate rooms.*

2 different: *The word has three separate meanings.*

sep·a·rate[2] /'sepəreɪt/ *verb* (*present participle* **separating**, *past* **separated**)

1 to move people or things away from each other: *Ms Barker separated the class **into** four groups.* | *Separate the egg yolk **from** the white.*

2 to keep two things divided: *A fence separated the cows **from** the pigs.*

Sep·tem·ber /sep'tembə^r/ *noun*
the ninth month of the year

se·quence /'si:kwəns/ *noun*
a series of related events or actions that have a particular result: *A sequence of events led to the murder.*

ser·geant /'sɑːdʒənt/ *noun*
an officer in the army or police force

se·ri·al /'sɪəriəl/ *noun*
a story that is told or written in parts

se·ries /'sɪəriːz/ *noun* (*plural* **series**)
a group of things that happen one after the other: *There have been a series of accidents on this road.* | *We watched a series of programmes on dance.*

se·ri·ous /'sɪəriəs/ *adjective*
1 very bad and worrying: *Her father had a serious illness.* | *The school has some serious problems.*
2 thinking carefully about what you say or do: *John is serious about becoming an actor.*
3 important and deserving people's attention: *He has written a serious article about the economy.* | *We had a serious conversation about our future.*
4 a serious person is quiet and does not often laugh: *Thomas is a serious boy.*

se·ri·ous·ly /'sɪəriəsli/ *adverb*
1 in a serious way: *She is seriously thinking of leaving her husband.* | *Brian is seriously ill.*
2 **take something seriously** to treat something as important: *The police are taking the threats seriously.* | *I was only joking – don't take everything so seriously.*

ser·mon /'sɜːmən/ *noun*
a talk given by a priest in a church

ser·vant /'sɜːvənt/ *noun*
a person who works for someone in their house

serve /sɜːv/ *verb* (*present participle* **serving**, *past* **served**)
1 to give someone food or drink as part of a meal: *Dinner will be served at eight.* | *Serve the dish with rice and a green salad.*
2 to work for an organization: *He served in the army for 15 years.*
3 to be used for a particular purpose: *The new airport will serve several large cities in the north.*
4 to help someone who wants to buy something in a shop: *Are you being served?*
5 **it serves you right** said when you think someone deserves the bad thing that has happened to them: *He's failed his exams – it serves him right for not studying.*

ser·vice /'sɜːvɪs/ *noun*
1 (*no plural*) the work that people do in a public place, especially in a restaurant or a shop: *The service in that new restaurant is very slow.*
2 (*no plural*) the work that you do for someone else: *She retired after twenty-five years of service.*
3 something useful that the public can use to help them: *There is a regular bus service into town.* | *We offer a free information service.*
4 a church ceremony: *They went to the morning service.*

ses·sion /'seʃn/ *noun*
a meeting of people for some purpose: *We had a dancing session.*

set¹ /set/ *verb* (*present participle* **setting**, *past* **set**)
1 to put something somewhere carefully: *She set the flowers on the table.*
2 to decide what something should be: *We have set a date for the wedding.*
3 if a story, film, etc is set somewhere it happens in that place or at that time: *His novel is set in seventeenth century Japan.*
4 to give work to someone: *The teacher set us a test.*
5 when the sun sets, it goes down in the sky until you cannot see it
6 **set an example** to behave well so that other people will also behave well: *Parents should set a good example to their children.*
7 **set fire to something** to make something burn
8 **set someone free** to let a prisoner go free
9 **set the table** to put plates, knives, spoons, etc on a table ready for a meal
10 **set off/set out** to start a journey: *What time shall we set off tomorrow?*

set² *noun*
1 a group of things that belong together: *She has a lovely set of plates.*
2 a television or radio: *They have three television sets in the house.*

A B C D E F G H I J K L M N O P Q R **S** T U V W X Y Z

3 the place where a film or television programme is acted and filmed

set·tle /'setl/ verb (present participle **settling**, past **settled**)
1 to decide something, especially after an argument or talk: *We finally settled who should pay for the accident.*
2 to move into a comfortable position: *He settled back and turned on the TV.*
3 to go and live in a place where you plan to stay: *My son has settled happily in France.*
4 **settle a bill** to pay a bill
5 **settle down** to become calmer and more comfortable: *It took the children a while to settle down.*
6 **settle in** to get used to a new place or job: *How are you settling in?*

set·tle·ment /'setlmənt/ noun
a formal decision or agreement at the end of an argument or talk: *After hours of talks, they finally **reached** a settlement.*

sev·en /'sevn/
the number 7

sev·en·teen /ˌsevn'tiːn/
the number 17

sev·en·teenth /ˌsevn'tiːnθ/ adjective
17th

sev·enth /'sevnθ/ adjective
7th

sev·en·ti·eth /'sevntɪ-əθ/ adjective
70th

sev·en·ty /'sevntɪ/
the number 70

sev·eral /'sevrəl/ adjective
more than a few, but not a lot: *She has several friends in the town.* | *I've been to Pam's several times.*

se·vere /sə'vɪər/ adjective
1 very bad: *He had severe injuries.* | *It was a severe winter.*
2 hard, not kind or gentle: *People who smuggle drugs get a severe punishment.*

sew /səʊ/ verb (past participle **sewn** /səʊn/)
to make or repair clothes using a needle and thread: *He sewed a button on his shirt.*

sew·ing /'səʊɪŋ/ noun (no plural)
the activity of making or repairing things using a needle and thread: *My sister is very good at sewing.*

sewing ma·chine /'səʊɪŋ məˌʃiːn/ noun
a machine on which you can sew things

sex /seks/ noun
1 (plural **sexes**) being male or female: *What sex is your cat?*
2 (no plural) the things done between a male and female to make babies

shab·by /'ʃæbɪ/ adjective
rather old and dirty: *A man in shabby clothes got on the bus.*

shade

sitting in the shade

shade¹ /ʃeɪd/ noun
1 (no plural) shelter from the sun or light: *They sat in the shade because the sun was too hot.*
2 a particular type of one colour: *I want a darker shade **of** blue.* | *The picture was painted in various shades of green.*

shade² verb (present participle **shading**, past **shaded**)
to shelter something from the sun or light: *I shaded my eyes with my hand.*

shad·ow /'ʃædəʊ/ noun
a dark shape that something makes on a surface when it is between that surface and the light: *The shadows of the trees grew longer as the afternoon went on.*

shad·y /'ʃeɪdɪ/ adjective (**shadier**, **shadiest**)
sheltered from the sun: *It's cool and shady under this tree.*

shake /ʃeɪk/ verb (present participle **shaking**, past **shook** /ʃʊk/, past participle **shaken** /'ʃeɪkən/)
1 to move quickly from side to side, up and down, etc: *The house shook as the heavy lorry went past.* | *She shook the box to see if there was any money inside.*
2 **shake hands** to take someone's

right hand in yours and move it up and down when you meet them or say goodbye: *Jim shook hands* **with** *everyone and they sat down.* ➪ see picture on page 207

3 shake your head to move your head from side to side to say 'no': *I asked if she wanted anything to eat or drink but she shook her head.*

shak·en /ˈʃeɪkən/
the past participle of **shake**

shall /ʃəl; *strong* ʃæl/ *verb*
used with **I** and **we** in questions when asking or suggesting something: *Shall we all go to the film tonight? | Shall I help you with that?*

shal·low /ˈʃæləʊ/ *adjective*
only a short distance from the bottom to the top: *The sea is shallow here. | Young children were playing at the shallow end of the swimming pool.* ➪ opposite DEEP ➪ see picture at DEEP

shame /ʃeɪm/ *noun*
1 the feeling you have when you have done something very wrong: *He felt great shame about the lies he had told.*
2 What a shame! something you say to show you think something is sad or disappointing: *"Julie won't be able to come to the cinema." "What a shame!"*

sham·poo /ʃæmˈpuː/ *noun*
a special liquid for washing your hair

shapes

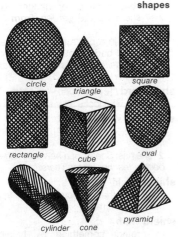

circle
triangle
square
rectangle
cube
oval
cylinder
cone
pyramid

shape¹ /ʃeɪp/ *noun*
the form of something: *What is the*

shape of a door? It is a rectangle. | You can recognize a tree by the shape of its leaves. | She made a cake **in the** shape **of** a heart.

shape² *verb (present participle* **shaping,** *past* **shaped)**
to make something into a particular form: *He shaped the clay into a pot.*

share¹ /ʃeəʳ/ *verb (present participle* **sharing,** *past* **shared)**
1 to have or use something together with someone else: *I share a flat* **with** *two other girls. | We don't have enough books for everyone, so you will have to share.*
2 also **share out** to divide something so that two or more people can have some: *We shared the cake between four of us. | We shared out the money so that all the children had some.*

share² *noun*
a part of something that has been divided: *I paid my share* **of** *the bill and left.*

shark /ʃɑːk/ *noun*
a large sea fish with very sharp teeth ➪ see picture on page 195

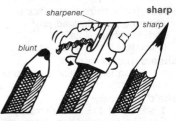

sharpener
blunt
sharp
sharp

sharp /ʃɑːp/ *adjective*
1 having an edge that can cut things easily: *I need a sharp knife. | Careful! That metal has a sharp edge.*
2 with a very small point: *You need a sharp pencil for this type of drawing.* ➪ opposite BLUNT
3 sudden and big: *There was a sharp increase in petrol prices. | Just over the hill there is a sharp bend in the road.*
4 able to see or hear things that are far away: *An eagle has sharp eyes to help it find food.*

sharp·en /ˈʃɑːpən/ *verb*
to make something sharp: *She sharpened all her pencils*

sharp·en·er /ˈʃɑːpnəʳ/ *noun*
a tool or machine that you use to make

knives or pencils sharp: *Can I borrow your pencil sharpener?* ⇨ see picture at SHARP

sharp·ly /'ʃɑːplɪ/ *adverb*
changing quickly and suddenly: *Prices have risen sharply.* | *He turned sharply and looked at me.*

shat·ter /'ʃætər/ *verb*
to break into many pieces: *The glass shattered when I dropped it.*

shave¹ /ʃeɪv/ *verb* (*present participle* **shaving**, *past* **shaved**)
to take hair from the face or body by cutting it very close: *My father shaves every day.*

shave² *noun*
when a man shaves: *He needs a shave.*

shav·er /'ʃeɪvər/ *noun*
an electric tool for removing hair from a man's face

she /ʃɪ; *strong* ʃiː/
used to talk about a female person or animal who has already been mentioned: *My sister's name is Mary and she is nine years old.* | *"I saw Suzy today." "Oh did you? How is she?"*

shear /ʃɪər/ *verb* (*present participle* **shearing**, *past* **sheared**, *past participle* **shorn** /ʃɔːn/)
to cut wool from a sheep or goat

shears /ʃɪəz/ *plural noun*
a tool like large scissors for cutting grass, plants, etc

she'd /ʃɪd; *strong* ʃiːd/
1 she would: *She'd like to meet you.* | *She'd be very upset if you were unkind to her daughter.*
2 she had: *She'd already left when we got there.* | *She made breakfast as soon as she'd dressed.*

shed¹ /ʃed/ *noun*
a small building made of wood, used for keeping things in

shed² *verb* (*present participle* **shedding**, *past* **shed**)
to let something fall off: *Some trees shed their leaves in the autumn.* | *Snakes shed their skin.*

sheep /ʃiːp/ *noun* (*plural* **sheep**)
a farm animal that is kept for meat and for the wool from its thick coat

sheer /ʃɪər/ *adjective*
1 used to emphasize what you are saying: *I won by sheer luck.* | *The people were singing for sheer joy.*
2 extremely steep: *There was a sheer drop from where we stood to the sea below us.*

sheet /ʃiːt/ *noun*
1 a flat piece of paper, metal, glass, etc: *Give me a sheet **of** paper and I'll make a list.*
2 a large piece of thin cloth that you put on a bed

shelf /ʃelf/ *noun* (*plural* **shelves** /ʃelvz/)
a board fixed to a wall or in a cupboard for putting things on: *He took a cup from the shelf.* ⇨ see picture on page 205

she'll /ʃɪl; *strong* ʃiːl/
she will: *She'll ring you tomorrow.* | *She'll be back in a minute.*

shell /ʃel/ *noun*
the hard outer covering of a nut, egg, sea creature, etc

shel·ter¹ /'ʃeltər/ *noun*
1 a covered place that protects you from bad weather or danger: *I waited for the bus in the bus shelter.*
2 (*no plural*) protection from bad weather or danger: *We **took** shelter under some trees.*

shelter² *verb*
1 to protect someone or something from bad weather or danger: *The wall sheltered the garden **from** the wind.*
2 to stay in a place that can protect you from bad weather or danger: *People sheltered in shop doorways when it started raining.*

shep·herd /'ʃepəd/ *noun*
a person who looks after sheep

she's /ʃɪz; *strong* ʃiːz/
1 she is: *She's very tall.* | *She's a good friend.*
2 she has: *She's got a new car.* | *She's been a teacher for ten years.*

shield¹ /ʃiːld/ *noun*
something that protects someone from danger or harm

shield² *verb*
to protect something by holding something over or in front of it: *He shielded his eyes **from** the sun.*

shift[1] /ʃɪft/ verb

to move something: *Can you help me shift this table?*

shift[2] noun

1 a change in the way people think about something: *There has been a shift **in** public opinion.*

2 one of the periods during the day or night when people are at work: *I'm on the night shift this week.*

shin /ʃɪn/ noun

the front part of your leg between your knee and your foot

shine /ʃaɪn/ verb (present participle **shining**, past **shone** /ʃɒn/)

1 to produce light: *The sun was shining.*

2 to look bright and smooth: *The water shone in the sunlight.*

3 to point a light towards a place or direction: *Shine the light over here so that I can see.*

shin·y /'ʃaɪni/ adjective (**shinier**, **shiniest**)

bright and smooth looking: *He wore a pair of shiny black boots.*

ship /ʃɪp/ noun

a large boat that carries things and people

shirt /ʃɜːt/ noun

a piece of clothing with buttons down the front that covers the upper part of your body and your arms ⇨ see picture on page 203

shiv·er /'ʃɪvəʳ/ verb

shiver

to shake because you are cold or afraid: *They were all shivering in the cold.*

shock[1] /ʃɒk/ noun

1 when something very bad happens that you did not expect or the feeling you have when that happens: *It was a great shock for him when his wife died.* | *He'll have a shock when he sees the bill.*

2 also **electric shock** pain caused by electricity going through you

shock[2] verb

to give someone an unpleasant surprise:

I was shocked when I heard about your accident.

shock·ing /'ʃɒkɪŋ/ adjective

very upsetting and wrong: *I read about the shocking crime in the newspaper.*

shoe /ʃuː/ noun

something made of strong material that you wear on your foot: *I need **a** new **pair of** shoes.* ⇨ compare SOCK ⇨ see pictures on pages 201 and 203

shoe·lace /'ʃuːleɪs/ noun

a string used to fasten a shoe

shone /ʃɒn/

the past tense and past participle of the verb **shine**

shook /ʃʊk/

the past tense of the verb **shake**

shoot[1] /ʃuːt/ verb (present participle **shooting**, past **shot** /ʃɒt/)

1 to kill or injure someone or something with a gun: *A police officer was shot dead and several were wounded.*

2 to fire a weapon at something or someone: *They spent the afternoon shooting at birds.*

3 to move very quickly: *He shot out of school when the bell rang.* | *The ball shot past my head.*

shoot[2] noun

a part of a plant that is just starting to grow or has just appeared above the ground

shop[1] /ʃɒp/ noun

British a building where you can buy things (American **store**)

shop[2] verb (present participle **shopping**, past **shopped**)

to go to the shops to buy things: *We often shop in Oxford Street.* | *I am shopping **for** a new television set.*

shop as·sis·tant /'ʃɒp əˌsɪstənt/ noun

a person who works in a shop

shop·ping /'ʃɒpɪŋ/ noun (no plural)

1 the activity of going to the shops to buy things: *I like shopping **for** clothes.* | *I have to **go** shopping today.*

2 the things you have just bought from the shops: *Put the shopping on the table.* | *She was carrying a bag of shopping.*

A B C D E F G H I J K L M N O P Q R S T U V W X Y Z

shore /ʃɔːʳ/ *noun*

the flat land at the edge of the sea or a large area of water: *We walked along the shore.*

short /ʃɔːt/ *adjective*

1 not a very long distance from one end to another: *It's a short distance from here to the bank.* | *He has short black hair.* | *She is wearing a short skirt.* ⇨ see picture at LONG

2 not continuing for a long time: *We have three short holidays a year instead of one long one.* | *There was a short pause and then everyone laughed.* | *She was here a short time ago.* ⇨ opposite (**1** and **2**) LONG

3 not as tall as most people: *She's the shortest girl in the class.* ⇨ opposite TALL ⇨ see picture on page 202

4 be short of something not to have enough of something: *I'm a bit short of money this week.*

short·age /ʃɔːtɪdʒ/ *noun*

when there is not enough of something: *The war led to a food shortage.* | *There was a shortage of water during the summer.*

short cut /ʃɔːt 'kʌt/ *noun*

a quicker way to go somewhere or do something: *Let's take a short cut across the park.*

short·en /ʃɔːtn/ *verb*

to make something shorter: *Can you help me shorten this skirt?* ⇨ opposite LENGTHEN

short·ly /ʃɔːtlɪ/ *adverb*

very soon: *They should be here shortly.*

shorts /ʃɔːts/ *plural noun*

trousers that stop above your knee: *I need to buy a pair of shorts for the summer.* ⇨ see picture on page 203

shot¹ /ʃɒt/

the past tense and past participle of the verb **shoot**

shot² *noun*

1 when someone fires a gun: *I heard two shots in the street.*

2 the act of hitting or kicking a ball to win a point in a game: *That was a good shot.*

should /ʃəd; *strong* ʃʊd/ *verb*

1 used to say what you think would be a good idea: *You should ring your parents to let them know you will be late.* | *We should invite Robert and Anne to the party.* | *You should see a doctor.*

2 used to say what you think will happen or what you think is true: *They should arrive soon.* | *It should be a good film.* | *She's a good cook, so there should be good food.*

shoul·der /ʃəʊldəʳ/ *noun*

the top part of your body between your neck and the top of your arm

shoulder bag /ʃəʊldə ˌbæg/ *noun*

a small bag that hangs from your shoulder

should·n't /ʃʊdnt/

should not: *You shouldn't eat so much chocolate.* | *He shouldn't work so hard.*

should've /ʃʊdəv/

should have: *You should've told me that you would be late.* | *I should've stayed at home.*

shout¹ /ʃaʊt/ *verb*

to speak in a loud voice: *He is rather far away, but if you shout he may hear you.* | *"Help!" he shouted.* | *I wish you'd stop shouting at the children.*

shout² *noun*

a loud cry or call: *I heard a shout from the next room.*

shov·el¹ /ʃʌvəl/ *noun*

a tool made of a wide piece of metal on a handle, used for moving earth, coal, etc

shovel² *verb* (*present participle* **shovelling**, *past* **shovelled**)

to move something with a shovel

show¹ /ʃəʊ/ *verb* (*past participle* **shown** /ʃəʊn/)

1 to let someone see something: *He showed me his new computer.* | *He showed the picture to his friends.*

2 to make it clear that something is true by giving facts or information: *This letter shows that she is unhappy.* | *The article shows how attitudes have changed in the past few years.*

3 if you show your feelings, other people can see how you feel because of your expression and the way you behave: *Her face showed her disappointment.*

4 to tell someone how to do something or where something is: *The teacher showed us how to use the computer.* | *Could you show me where I can leave my coat?*

5 if something shows, it is easy to see or notice: *Don't worry about that hole in your sock – it doesn't show.*

6 show off to try and get people to notice you because you want them to see how clever, rich, etc you are: *No one likes him very much because he's always showing off.*

show² *noun*
1 a performance in a theatre or on television that people watch: *This is my favourite TV show.*
2 a lot of things brought together for people to see: *Many people went to see the flower show.*

show·er /ˈʃaʊəʳ/ *noun*
1 a piece of equipment that you stand under to wash your whole body: *The phone always rings when I'm **in the** shower.*
⇨ see picture on page 204
2 when you wash your body under the shower: *He's **having** a shower.*
3 a short period of light rain: *We may have some showers today.*

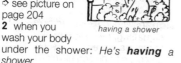
shower
having a shower

shown /ʃəʊn/
the past participle of the verb **show**

shrank /ʃræŋk/
the past tense of the verb **shrink**

shred /ʃred/ *noun*
a small piece that is cut or torn off something: *Michael tore the letter to shreds* (=into small pieces).

shrewd /ʃruːd/ *adjective*
clever, and able to act or make decisions in a way that is to your own advantage

shriek¹ /ʃriːk/ *verb*
to make a high loud sound because you are afraid, excited, angry, etc: *The crowd shrieked with delight.*

shriek² *noun*
a high loud sound made because you are afraid, excited, angry, etc: *He gave a shriek **of** horror.*

shrill /ʃrɪl/ *adjective*
a shrill sound is very high and unpleasant: *She had a shrill voice.*

shrine /ʃraɪn/ *noun*
a holy place

shrink /ʃrɪŋk/ *verb* (present participle **shrinking**, past **shrank** /ʃræŋk/, past participle **shrunk** /ʃrʌŋk/)
to get smaller: *The dress shrank when I washed it.*

shrub /ʃrʌb/ *noun*
a small bush

shrug /ʃrʌg/ *verb* (present participle **shrugging**, past **shrugged**)
to lift and drop your shoulders to show that you do not know something or do not care: *I asked her if she liked her new school but she just shrugged.*

shrunk /ʃrʌŋk/
the past participle of the verb **shrink**

shud·der /ˈʃʌdəʳ/ *verb*
to shake because you are afraid, cold, or have had an unpleasant shock: *The thought of going back there again made him shudder.*

shut /ʃʌt/ *verb* (present participle **shutting**, past **shut**)
1 to move something so that it is not open: *Please will you shut the door?* | *He shut his eyes and went to sleep.*
2 *British* if a shop, bank, or other public place shuts, it stops being open to the public: *The shops shut at 5.30.* ⇨ same meaning (**1** and **2**) CLOSE
3 Shut up! a rude way of telling someone to stop talking

shut·tle /ˈʃʌtl/ *noun*
1 a plane, train, or bus that makes regular short journeys between places
2 a vehicle that can fly into space and return to Earth more than once

shy /ʃaɪ/ *adjective* (**shier**, **shiest**)
nervous or afraid to be with other people: *The child was shy and hid behind his mother.*

sick /sɪk/ *adjective*
1 ill: *My father's sick – he's got to stay in bed.*
2 be sick to bring food up from your stomach and out of your mouth: *She was sick on the bus.*
3 feel sick to feel that you might soon start bringing up food from your stomach and out of your mouth: *I felt sick when the ship started to move.*
4 be off sick not to be at work because you are ill: *John's off sick this week.*
5 be sick of something to be annoyed and bored about something

that has been happening for a long time: *I'm sick of all this arguing.*

6 make someone sick to make someone feel angry: *People like you make me sick!*

side /saɪd/ *noun*
1 one of the two parts that something is divided into: *The part of the brain that controls language is in the left side of the brain.* | *They live on the other side of town.*
2 the part of something that is not the top, bottom, back, or front: *He went round to the side of the house.* | *The chair had arms at the sides.*
3 one of the flat surfaces of something: *Write on both sides of the paper.* | *A cube has six sides.*
4 the part of your body from your shoulder to the top of your leg: *I have a pain in my side.*
5 one of two people, teams, countries, etc in a game, competition, argument, or war: *Which side do you want to win?*
6 by the side of something next to something: *She lives by the side of a big lake.*
7 side by side next to each other: *We sat side by side in the car.*

side·walk /ˈsaɪdwɔːk/ *noun*
American a path or hard surface at the side of a road for people to walk on (*British* **pavement**)

side·ways /ˈsaɪdweɪz/ *adverb*
1 towards one side: *He stepped sideways to let me pass.*
2 turned so that the side is at the front: *We turned the table sideways.*

sigh¹ /saɪ/ *verb*
to breathe deeply once, because you are tired, sad, bored, etc: *She stared out of the window and sighed.*

sigh² *noun*
a deep breath out that you make when you are tired, sad, bored, etc: *He gave a sigh of relief.*

sight /saɪt/ *noun*
1 (*no plural*) the ability to see: *She lost her sight because of an illness.*
2 a thing that you see: *The fire was a frightening sight.*
3 catch sight of something to see something suddenly: *She caught sight of him as she was passing a restaurant.*
4 the sights the places that are interesting to visit in a city, country, etc

sight·see·ing /ˈsaɪtˌsiːɪŋ/ *noun* (*no plural*)
visiting interesting places when you are on holiday: *Shall we go sightseeing today?*

sign¹ /saɪn/ *noun*
1 a set of words or shapes in a public place that gives information or instructions: *He ignored the 'No Smoking' sign.* | *Just follow the road signs.*
2 an event, fact, etc that shows that something exists or is starting to happen: *There were signs that someone had been there earlier.* | *Being very tired can be a sign of illness.*

sign² *verb*
to write your name, for example at the end of a letter

sig·nal¹ /ˈsɪgnəl/ *noun*
a sound, action, or movement that tells you to do something: *Don't start until I give the signal.*

signal² *verb* (*present participle* **signalling**, *past* **signalled**)
to make a movement or sound that tells someone to do something

sig·na·ture /ˈsɪgnətʃər/ *noun*
a person's name written in their own particular way, especially on a letter, cheque, etc ⇨ compare AUTOGRAPH

sig·nif·i·cance /sɪgˈnɪfɪkəns/ *noun* (*no plural*)
the importance of something: *What is the significance of this speech?*

sig·nif·i·cant /sɪgˈnɪfɪkənt/ *adjective*
noticeable and important: *There has been a significant increase in crime.*

sign·post /ˈsaɪnpəʊst/ *noun*
a road sign that shows people which way to go and tells them how far it is to a place

si·lence /ˈsaɪləns/ *noun* (*no plural*)
when there is no sound: *They worked in silence.*

si·lent /ˈsaɪlənt/ *adjective*
not saying anything or not making any sound: *Simon was silent for a moment.*
silently *adverb*: *The children worked silently.*

silk /sɪlk/ *noun* (*no plural*)
a soft cloth made from smooth threads

sil·ly /ˈsɪli/ *adjective* (**sillier, silliest**)
not serious or reasonable: *Don't be*

silly – that insect can't hurt you. | What a silly question!

sil·ver /'sɪlvə^r/ *noun (no plural)*
1 a soft shiny grey-white metal used for jewellery
2 the colour of this metal

sim·i·lar /'sɪmɪlə^r/ *adjective*
almost the same but not exactly the same: *Our dresses are similar. | His interests are similar **to** mine.*

sim·i·lar·i·ty /ˌsɪmɪ'lærətɪ/ *noun (plural* **similarities***)*
when people or things are similar: *Can you see any similarities **between** the two brothers?* ⇨ opposite DIFFERENCE

sim·ple /'sɪmpl/ *adjective (***simpler***, ***simplest***)*
1 easy to understand: *The questions were all quite simple.* ⇨ opposite DIFFICULT
2 not having a lot of decoration: *The food was simple but tasted wonderful.*

sim·pli·fy /'sɪmplɪfaɪ/ *verb (present participle* **simplifying***, past* **simplified***)*
to make something easier to understand or do: *The story has been simplified so that children can read it.*

sim·ply /'sɪmplɪ/ *adverb*
1 just or only: *I simply wanted to help. | Some students lose marks simply because they don't read the questions properly.*
2 in a simple way: *Let me explain it simply.*

sin /sɪn/ *noun*
something that a religion says is wrong

since /sɪns/ *adverb, preposition*
between a time in the past and now: *She has been ill since Christmas. | He has lived in London since 1990. | It has been a long time since I wrote to her. | He came to school last week, but I haven't seen him since. | We have been friends **ever** since we were children* (=from when we were children until now). ⇨ look at AGO

sin·cere /sɪn'sɪə^r/ *adjective*
honest and really meaning what you say: *Do you think he was being sincere?*

sin·cere·ly /sɪn'sɪəlɪ/ *adverb*
1 in a sincere way: *I sincerely hope that you succeed.*
2 **Yours sincerely** something you write at the end of a formal letter before you sign your name ⇨ look at YOURS

sing /sɪŋ/ *verb (present participle* **singing***, past* **sang** /sæŋ/*, past participle* **sung** /sʌŋ/*)*
to make musical sounds with your voice: *She sang a song. | I can hear the birds singing.*

sing·er /'sɪŋə^r/ *noun*
a person who sings: *She is a pop singer.*

sin·gle [1] /'sɪŋgl/ *adjective*
1 only one: *She didn't say a single word. | We lost the game by a single point.*
2 not married: *Terry is 34 and he's still single.*
3 for one person only: *a single bed* ⇨ compare DOUBLE
4 *British* a single ticket is for a trip from one place to another but not back ⇨ compare RETURN
5 **in single file** in a line, one person behind the other: *Walk in single file, please.*

single [2] *noun*
British a ticket for a trip from one place to another but not back: *Can I have a single to Liverpool please?* ⇨ compare RETURN

sin·gu·lar /'sɪŋgjʊlə^r/ *noun*
the singular the form of a word for only one person or thing. For example, 'dog' is the singular of 'dogs' ⇨ opposite PLURAL

sink [1] /sɪŋk/ *noun*
a large container into which water flows, used for washing clothes or dishes ⇨ see picture on page 204

floating   sink

sinking

sink [2] *verb (present participle* **sinking***, past* **sank** /sæŋk/*, past participle* **sunk** /sʌŋk/*)*
1 if a ship or object sinks, it moves down below the surface of the water towards the bottom: *The ship is sinking. | He watched his keys sink to the bottom of the river.* ⇨ compare FLOAT

A
B
C
D
E
F
G
H
I
J
K
L
M
N
O
P
Q
R
S
T
U
V
W
X
Y
Z

2 to make something go down below the surface of the water towards the bottom: *An iceberg sank the Titanic.*

sip[1] /sɪp/ *verb* (*present participle* **sipping**, *past* **sipped**)
to drink something by taking very small amounts in your mouth: *She sipped the hot tea.*

sip[2] *noun*
a very small amount of a drink that you sip: *I had a sip of his beer.*

sir /sɜːʳ/ *noun*
1 a polite way of speaking or writing to a man you do not know: *Can I help you, Sir?* | *I began my letter "Dear Sir".*
⇨ compare MADAM ⇨ look at YOURS
2 the title of a KNIGHT: *Sir Edward Heath*
⇨ compare LADY

si·ren /ˈsaɪərən/ *noun*
something that makes a loud warning sound, used on police cars, AMBULANCES, etc

sis·ter /ˈsɪstəʳ/ *noun*
1 a girl who has the same parents as you: *My sister is much taller than I am.* | *We are sisters.* | *Have you any brothers or sisters?* ⇨ compare BROTHER
2 a NUN

sister-in-law /ˈsɪstər ɪn lɔː/ *noun*
(*plural* **sisters-in-law**)
1 the sister of your wife or husband
2 the wife of your brother

sit /sɪt/ *verb* (*present participle* **sitting**, *past* **sat** /sæt/)
1 to rest your body on something such as a chair: *Come and sit here.* | *He was sitting on a chair in front of the fire.*
⇨ see picture on page 207
2 sit down to rest your body on something such as a chair after you have been standing up: *Would you like to sit down?*
3 sit up to move your body up, after you have been lying down, so that your weight is on your bottom: *I sat up in bed when I heard the noise.*

site /saɪt/ *noun*
1 the place where something happened: *We visited the site of the battle.*
2 a place where a building is, was, or will be: *The site of the new hotel is by the sea.* | *No one is allowed on the building site unless they are wearing a hard hat.*

sit·ting room /ˈsɪtɪŋ ruːm/ *noun*
British the room in a house where people sit to rest, watch television, etc

sit·u·at·ed /ˈsɪtʃʊeɪtɪd/ *adjective*
be situated somewhere to be in a particular place: *The hotel is situated next to the airport.*

sit·u·a·tion /ˌsɪtʃʊˈeɪʃn/ *noun*
the things that are happening at a particular time and place: *I'd better explain the situation to the head teacher.* | *She's in a very difficult situation.* | *There will be no pay increases because of the company's financial situation.*

six /sɪks/
the number 6

six·teen /sɪkˈstiːn/
the number 16

six·teenth /sɪkˈstiːnθ/ *adjective*
16th

sixth /sɪksθ/ *adjective, noun*
1 6th
2 one of six equal parts

sixth form /ˈsɪksθ fɔːm/ *noun*
the classes of school students between 16 and 18 years old in Britain

six·ti·eth /ˈsɪkstɪ-əθ/ *adjective*
60th

six·ty /ˈsɪkstɪ/
the number 60

size /saɪz/ *noun*
how big or small something or someone is: *His room is the same size as mine.* | *She makes cakes in different shapes and sizes.* | *These shoes are size 5.*

skate[1] /skeɪt/ *verb* (*present participle* **skating**, *past* **skated**)
to move smoothly over ice or over the ground wearing skates: *She skated over the ice towards us.*

skate[2] *noun*
a special shoe with wheels or a blade fixed under it: *roller skates* | *ice skates*

skate·board /ˈskeɪtbɔːd/ *noun*
a short board with wheels under it that you stand on and ride along the ground for fun

skat·ing /ˈskeɪtɪŋ/ *noun* (*no plural*)
the activity or sport of moving or dancing over ice or over the ground wearing special shoes

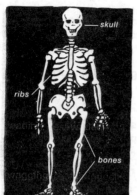

skeleton

skull

ribs

bones

skel·e·ton /ˈskelɪtən/ *noun*
the bones of a whole animal or person

sketch¹ /sketʃ/ *noun (plural* **sketches**)
a quick drawing that does not have a lot of detail: *She made a sketch of a bird.*

sketch² *verb*
to draw a picture quickly and without a lot of detail

ski¹ /skiː/ *noun*
one of a pair of long narrow pieces of wood or plastic that you wear on your feet to travel on snow

ski² *verb (present participle* **skiing**, *past* **skied**)
to move over snow wearing skis: *I'm learning to ski.*

skid /skɪd/ *verb (present participle* **skidding**, *past* **skidded**)
if a vehicle skids, it slides suddenly sideways on a wet surface: *The car skidded on a pool of oil and ran into the fence.*

ski·ing /ˈskiːɪŋ/ *noun (no plural)*
the activity of moving over snow with skis on your feet: *Do you like skiing? | We're **going** skiing this winter.* ⇨ see picture on page 196

skil·ful /ˈskɪlfəl/ *adjective*
good at doing something well: *He's a skilful driver.*
  skilfully *adverb*: *She answered the question skilfully.*

skill /skɪl/ *noun*
an ability to do something well, especially because you have practised it: *Everyone should have some basic computer skills. | As a footballer he shows great skill.*

skilled /skɪld/ *adjective*
having the knowledge or training to do a particular thing well: *The job needs skilled workers.*

skin /skɪn/ *noun*
the outer covering of a person, animal, vegetable, or fruit: *You can make shoes from the skins of animals. | a banana skin | She has pale skin. | I put sun cream (=cream that protects you from the hot sun) on my skin.*

skin·ny /ˈskɪnɪ/ *adjective (* **skinnier**, **skinniest**)
a skinny person is very thin ⇨ compare SLIM ⇨ see picture on page 202

skip /skɪp/ *verb (present participle* **skipping**, *past* **skipped**)
1 to move forwards with quick jumps from one foot to the other: *The two girls were skipping down the street.*
2 to jump up and down over a rope that you move over your head and under your feet

skirt /skɜːt/ *noun*
a piece of woman's clothing that hangs down from her waist and covers part of her legs ⇨ see picture on page 203

skull /skʌl/ *noun*
the bones that form your head ⇨ see picture at SKELETON

sky /skaɪ/ *noun (plural* **skies**)
the space above the Earth where the sun, moon, and stars are: *The sky was blue.*

skyscrapers

sky·scrap·er /ˈskaɪˌskreɪpəʳ/ *noun*
a very tall modern building in a city

slab /slæb/ *noun*
a large flat block of something hard: *a concrete slab*

slack /slæk/ *adjective*
1 loose: *Keep the rope slack until I say "pull".* ⇨ opposite TIGHT

A B C D E F G H I J K L M N O P Q R **S** T U V W X Y Z

2 not busy: *Things are very slack at work.*

slam /slæm/ *verb (present participle* **slamming**, *past* **slammed**)
to shut a door or window with a loud noise: *He slammed the door angrily.*

slang /slæŋ/ *noun (no plural)*
informal language with its own set of words, expressions, and meanings

slant¹ /slɑːnt/ *verb*
to lean or slope to one side

slant² *noun*
a sloping position or angle: *The house is on a slant.*

slap¹ /slæp/ *verb (present participle* **slapping**, *past* **slapped**)
to hit someone or something with the flat inside part of the hand ⟡ compare PUNCH

slap² *noun*
a hit made with the flat inside part of the hand: *She gave him a slap across the face.*

slaugh·ter¹ /'slɔːtər/ *verb*
1 to kill an animal for its meat
2 to kill large numbers of people in a violent way: *Over 500 men, women, and children were slaughtered.*

slaughter² *noun (no plural)*
1 the killing of animals for food
2 the killing of large numbers of people in a violent way

slave¹ /sleɪv/ *noun*
a person who is owned by another person and is not free

slave² *verb*
to work very hard: *I spent all day slaving in the kitchen.*

sla·ve·ry /'sleɪvəri/ *noun (no plural)*
when people are kept as slaves: *Britain ended slavery in 1833.*

sledge /sledʒ/ *noun*
a vehicle used for sliding over snow with two long narrow pieces of wood or metal fixed under it

sleep¹ /sliːp/ *verb (past* **slept** /slept/)
to rest with your eyes closed and your mind unconscious, the way people do in their beds at night: *I didn't sleep very well last night.* | *Will you be OK sleeping on the floor?* | *The baby's sleeping.*

sleep² *noun*
1 *(no plural)* when you are sleeping:

I need to get some sleep. | *We didn't get much sleep last night.*
2 go to sleep to begin to sleep: *She went to sleep as soon as she closed her eyes.*

sleep·ing bag /'sliːpɪŋ ˌbæg/ *noun*
a large bag that you sleep in to keep warm, usually when you are sleeping outdoors ⟡ see picture on page 193

sleep·less /'sliːpləs/ *adjective*
a sleepless night a night when you cannot sleep, for example because you are worried

sleep·y /'sliːpɪ/ *adjective* (**sleepier**, **sleepiest**)
wanting to sleep: *I felt sleepy all day.* ⟡ same meaning TIRED

sleet /sliːt/ *noun (no plural)*
a mixture of rain and snow

sleeve /sliːv/ *noun*
the part of a piece of clothing that covers your arm: *He wore a shirt with short sleeves.*

slen·der /'slendər/ *adjective*
thin in an attractive way: *She has a slender figure.* ⟡ same meaning SLIM

slept /slept/
the past tense and past participle of the verb **sleep**

slice¹ /slaɪs/ *noun*
a flat piece of bread, meat, etc cut from a larger piece: *She cut a thin slice of cheese.*

slice² *verb (present participle* **slicing**, *past* **sliced**)
also **slice up** to cut something into thin flat pieces: *I sliced the bread.* ⟡ see picture on page 198

slide

sliding on ice

slide¹ /slaɪd/ *verb (present participle* **sliding**, *past* **slid** /slɪd/)
to move smoothly over a surface: *The children were sliding on the ice.*

slide[2] *noun*

1 a tall structure with a slope for children to slide down

2 a small piece of film in a frame that you shine light through to show a picture

slight /slaɪt/ *adjective*

small and not very important or noticeable: *I have a slight headache.* | *There will be a slight delay.*

slight·ly /'slaɪtlɪ/ *adverb*

by a small amount: *She's slightly older than me.* | *I'm slightly worried about the cost.*

slim[1] /slɪm/ *adjective*

thin in an attractive way: *He's tall and slim.* ⇨ same meaning SLENDER ⇨ see picture on page 202

slim[2] *verb (present participle **slimming**, past **slimmed**)*

to try to become thinner by eating less food

sling /slɪŋ/ *noun*

a piece of cloth passed round your neck to support your arm when it is injured: *She had her arm in a sling for weeks.*

slip[1] /slɪp/ *verb (present participle **slipping**, past **slipped**)*

1 to slide on a smooth surface by accident: *He slipped on the ice and fell.*

2 to go somewhere quickly and quietly: *He slipped out of the room when nobody was looking.* | *She slipped into the car and drove off.*

3 to put something somewhere quickly and without people noticing: *He slipped the money into his pocket.*

4 to slide out of the correct position or out of your hand: *The knife slipped and cut her finger.*

5 **slip up** to make a mistake: *The school slipped up and didn't send the letter.*

slip[2] *noun*

1 a small piece of paper: *I have a slip of paper with her phone number on it.*

2 British a small mistake

slip·per /'slɪpər/ *noun*

a soft shoe that you wear inside your home

slip·per·y /'slɪpərɪ/ *adjective*

smooth or wet and difficult to hold or walk on: *Be careful – the floor is slippery.*

slit[1] /slɪt/ *noun*

a long narrow cut in something: *Light was shining through a slit in the door.*

slit[2] *verb (present participle **slitting**, past **slit**)*

to make a long narrow cut in something: *I slit open the letter with a knife.*

slo·gan /'sləʊgən/ *noun*

a short phrase that people will remember, used in advertisements and in politics

slope[1] /sləʊp/ *noun*

a surface that is higher at one end than the other: *He ran up the slope to the top of the hill.*

slope[2] *verb (present participle **sloping**, past **sloped**)*

if a surface slopes, it is higher at one end than the other: *The hill slopes down to the town.*

slop·py /'slɒpɪ/ *adjective (**sloppier**, **sloppiest**)*

1 not careful or tidy enough: *He did a sloppy piece of work.*

2 sloppy clothes are large, loose, and not tidy: *She was wearing a sloppy T-shirt and jeans.*

slot /slɒt/ *noun*

a long narrow hole in something: *Put the coins in this slot.*

slot ma·chine /'slɒt məˌʃiːn/ *noun*

a machine that you put coins into to try and win more money

slow[1] /sləʊ/ *adjective*

1 not moving or happening quickly: *She's always slow getting ready in the morning.* | *The bus goes at a slow speed.*

2 a clock or watch that is slow shows a time that is earlier than the correct time: *My watch is five minutes slow.* ⇨ opposite FAST

slow[2] *verb*

slow down to go less fast than before: *Slow down – you're driving too fast.* | *Could you slow down? I can't keep up with you.* ⇨ opposite SPEED UP

slow·ly /'sləʊlɪ/ *adverb*

at a slow speed: *He writes very slowly.* | *The clouds moved slowly across the sky.* ⇨ opposite FAST

slug /slʌg/ *noun*

a soft creature without bones or legs that lives on land and eats plants

A
B
C
D
E
F
G
H
I
J
K
L
M
N
O
P
Q
R
S
T
U
V
W
X
Y
Z

slum /slʌm/ noun
an area in a city where the houses are in bad condition and where poor people live

slump /slʌmp/ verb
to sit or fall with your body bent, as if you were unconscious

smack /smæk/ verb
to hit a child with your open hand to punish him or her

small /smɔːl/ adjective
1 not large in size or amount: *He has a small farm.* | *This bag is too small.* | *Katherine's smaller than I am.* ⇨ opposite BIG, LARGE
2 not important or serious: *You made a few small mistakes but the rest was fine.*
3 a small child is young: *Mary has three small children.*

smart /smɑːt/ adjective
1 clever: *The smartest kids go to university.*
2 British dressed in attractive or tidy clothes: *My sister always looks smart.*

smash /smæʃ/ verb
to break into small pieces, or to make something do this: *She dropped the plate and it smashed.* | *The crowd smashed the windows of the shop.*

smear[1] /smɪər/ verb
to leave a sticky, dirty, or oily mark on something: *The child's face was smeared with chocolate.*

smear[2] noun
a sticky, dirty, or oily mark on something: *He had a smear of grease on his hands.*

smell[1] /smel/ noun
something that you can notice or discover through your nose: *I like the smell of fresh bread.* | *What is that horrible smell?*

smell[2] verb (past **smelt** /smelt/)
1 to have a particular smell: *The flowers smell nice.* | *This fish smells bad.* | *It smells of cigarettes in here.*
2 to have an unpleasant smell: *Something in the refrigerator smells.*
3 to notice or recognize the smell of something: *He smelt the flowers.* | *I can smell gas.*

smell·y /'smelɪ/ adjective (**smellier**, **smelliest**)
having an unpleasant smell: *He has smelly feet.*

smelt /smelt/
the past tense and past participle of the verb **smell**

smile[1] /smaɪl/ verb (present participle **smiling**, past **smiled**)
to turn up the corners of your mouth to show that you are happy or pleased: *The baby's smiling.* | *Keith smiled at me.*

smile[2] noun
the expression you have when you smile: *He had a big smile on his face.*

smoke[1] /sməʊk/ noun (no plural)
the white or black gas that is caused by something burning: *There was a lot of black smoke from the burning building.*

smoke[2] verb (present participle **smoking**, past **smoked**)
1 to use cigarettes or a pipe: *Do you smoke?* | *He smokes ten cigarettes a day.*
2 to make smoke: *The fire's still smoking.*

smok·er /'sməʊkər/ noun
a person who uses cigarettes or a pipe: *This part of the restaurant is for smokers.*

smok·ing /'sməʊkɪŋ/ noun (no plural)
the use of cigarettes or a pipe: *Smoking is not allowed in school.*

smok·y /'sməʊkɪ/ adjective (**smokier**, **smokiest**)
full of smoke: *We sat in a smoky room.*

smooth /smuːð/ adjective
1 having an even surface: *Her skin is very smooth.* | *Glass has a smooth surface.* ⇨ opposite ROUGH
2 a substance that is smooth has no big pieces in it: *Beat the eggs and flour until they are smooth.*
3 without problems or difficulties: *We had a smooth journey all the way.*

smooth·ly /'smuːðlɪ/ adverb
well and without problems or difficulties: *Everything went smoothly at work.*

smoth·er /'smʌðər/ verb
1 to stop someone from breathing by putting something on their face
2 to cover something completely: *The cake was smothered in chocolate.*

smoul·der /'sməʊldər/ verb
to burn slowly without a flame

smudge /smʌdʒ/ verb (present participle **smudging**, past **smudged**)
if a substance such as ink or paint smudges or is smudged, it becomes unclear because someone has rubbed it: Look, you've smudged my drawing. | Your lipstick is smudged.

smug·gle /'smʌgl/ verb (present participle **smuggling**, past **smuggled**)
to take something secretly and illegally from one country into another country: They were caught smuggling drugs into the country.

smug·gler /'smʌglə^r/ noun
a person who brings illegal things secretly into a country

snack /snæk/ noun
a small quick meal

snag /snæg/ noun
a small difficulty or problem

snail /sneɪl/ noun
a soft creature without bones or legs, but with a round shell on its back, that eats plants

snake /sneɪk/ noun
a very long thin animal without legs that slides across the ground ⇨ see picture on page 195

snap[1] /snæp/ verb (present participle **snapping**, past **snapped**)
1 to break with a short loud noise: The branch snapped under his foot. ⇨ see picture at BEND
2 to suddenly speak to someone in an angry way: I'm sorry I snapped **at** you.
3 if a dog snaps at someone, it tries to bite them

snap[2] noun
1 a short loud sound of something breaking: I heard a snap and the tree fell over.
2 a photograph: She showed me her holiday snaps.

snarl /snɑːl/ verb
1 if an animal snarls, it makes an angry noise with the mouth open and teeth showing: The two dogs snarled at each other, and then started fighting.
2 to say something in an angry violent way

snatch /snætʃ/ verb
to take hold of something quickly and roughly: She snatched the book **from** my hands. ⇨ same meaning GRAB

sneak /sniːk/ verb
to go quietly because you do not want people to see or hear you: The children sneaked out of school and went to the park.

sneer /snɪə^r/ verb
to smile in an unpleasant way to show that you have no respect for someone or something: She sneered at the mention of his name.

sneeze /sniːz/ verb (present participle **sneezing**, past **sneezed**)
to suddenly push air out of your nose and mouth, making a noise, for example when you have a cold ⇨ compare COUGH

sniff /snɪf/ verb
to take air into your nose with short noisy breaths to clear your nose or to smell something: Stop sniffing – use a handkerchief! | The dog sniffed the bone.

snob /snɒb/ noun
a person who admires people who are from rich and important families and does not respect people who are not

snoo·ker /'snuːkə^r/ noun (no plural)
a game played on a table with a green top in which people try to push balls into holes using long sticks ⇨ see picture on page 196

snooze[1] /snuːz/ verb (present participle **snoozing**, past **snoozed**)
to have a short light sleep: She was snoozing in her armchair. ⇨ same meaning DOZE

snooze[2] noun (no plural)
a short light sleep: I've just had a snooze.

snore /snɔː^r/ verb (present participle **snoring**, past **snored**)
to make a loud noise each time you breathe when you are asleep

snow[1] /snəʊ/ noun (no plural)
soft white pieces of frozen water that fall from the sky and cover the ground when it is cold

snow[2] verb
if it snows, snow falls from the sky: It's snowing! | It snowed throughout the night.

snow·ball /'snəʊbɔːl/ noun
a small ball of snow that children make and throw at each other for fun

snow·board·ing /'snəʊbɔːdɪŋ/ *noun*
(*no plural*)
a sport in which you travel on snow with
your feet on a wide board

snow·flake /'snəʊfleɪk/ *noun*
a soft white piece of frozen water that
falls from the sky ⇨ see picture at
SNOWMAN

snow·man
/'snəʊmæn/ *noun*
(*plural* **snowmen**
/-men/)
a figure like a
round man made
out of snow

snowman

snowflake

snow·y /'snəʊi/
adjective (**snowier,**
snowiest)
if it is snowy, the
ground is covered
with snow or
snow is falling: *The snowy weather will
continue.* ⇨ see picture on page 194

so¹ /səʊ/ *adverb*
1 used to emphasize what you are
saying: *I was so tired that I fell asleep
on the bus.* | *The party was so boring.* |
You have been so nice to me!
2 also: *Ann was there, and so was
Mary.* | *If you're going to have another
drink then so will I.* | *Frank loves dogs
and so does his wife.*
3 used when you are giving a short
answer to a question: *"Will I need my
coat?" "I don't think so."* | *"Is dinner
ready?" "I hope so."*
4 used to show agreement: *"Look, it's
raining!" "So it is!"*
5 or so used when you are not giving
the exact number or amount: *The
journey takes an hour or so.* | *She left a
week ago or so.*
6 and so on used after a list to say
that there are other things that you have
not mentioned: *She does the cooking,
cleaning, and so on.*

so²
1 for this reason: *I promised to send
him a letter, so I'll write it now.* | *I was
very hungry, so I ate the cake.*
2 in order to do something or make
something happen: *We got up early so
that we could go for a swim.* | *I put your
keys in the drawer so they wouldn't get
lost.*

soak /səʊk/ *verb*
1 to leave something in a liquid: *She
soaked the dishes **in** hot water.*
2 to make something very wet: *The
rain soaked us.*

soak·ing /'səʊkɪŋ/ *adjective*
also **soaking wet** very wet: *My clothes
are soaking wet.*

soap /səʊp/ *noun*
a substance that cleans things when it
is put with water: *She washed her
hands with soap.*

soap ope·ra /'səʊp ,ɒprə/ *noun*
a story that continues on television or
radio about the lives and problems of a
group of imaginary people

soap pow·der /'səʊp ,paʊdər/ *noun*
(*no plural*)
a powder that you put in water for
washing clothes

soar /sɔːr/ *verb*
1 to rise or become very high: *The
temperature soared to 32 degrees.*
2 to fly high in the air: *Birds soared
above the hills.*

sob /sɒb/ *verb* (*present participle*
sobbing, *past* **sobbed**)
to cry, making a lot of short noises: *She
was sobbing, with tears running down
her cheeks.*

so·ber /'səʊbər/ *adjective*
if someone is sober, they have not
drunk too much alcohol ⇨ opposite
DRUNK

soc·cer /'sɒkər/ *noun* (*no plural*)
football

so·cia·ble /'səʊʃəbl/ *adjective*
enjoying the company of other people:
She's a very sociable person.

so·cial /'səʊʃl/ *adjective*
1 relating to people and the way they
live together: *Social problems such as
crime are not easy to solve.* | *People
from different social backgrounds all
enjoy the game.*
2 relating to things you do with other
people when you are not working: *He
has a lot of friends and a good social
life.*

so·cial·ize /'səʊʃəlaɪz/ *verb* (*present
participle* **socializing**, *past*
socialized)
to spend time with other people in a
friendly way

A B C D E F G H I J K L M N O P Q R S T U V W X Y Z

social se·cu·ri·ty /ˌsəʊʃl sɪˈkjʊərətɪ/
noun (no plural)
money paid by the government to people who are very poor, not working, ill, etc

so·ci·e·ty /səˈsaɪətɪ/ noun
1 (no plural) people who live together and share the same laws and ways of doing things: Society makes laws to protect people.
2 (plural **societies**) an organization with members who have the same interests: a music society

sock /sɒk/ noun
a soft piece of clothing you wear on your foot and the bottom part of your leg ➪ compare SHOE ➪ see picture on page 203

sock·et /ˈsɒkɪt/ noun
a place in the wall where you connect a piece of equipment to the electricity ➪ compare PLUG

sofa /ˈsəʊfə/ noun
a long soft chair for two or more people to sit on: We were sitting on the sofa in front of the television. ➪ see picture on page 204

soft /sɒft/ adjective
1 not hard or firm but easy to press: There were soft cushions on the chair. I Her feet sank into the soft ground. ➪ opposite HARD
2 feeling smooth and pleasant: The baby has soft skin. ➪ opposite ROUGH
3 soft sounds are quiet: There was soft music in the background. I She has a soft voice.
4 soft colours or lights are not bright: Soft lighting is more romantic.

soft drink /ˈsɒft drɪŋk/ noun
a drink with no alcohol in it: Have you got any soft drinks?

soft·en /ˈsɒfən/ verb
to become softer or make something become softer: This cream will soften your skin.

soft·ly /ˈsɒftlɪ/ adverb
quietly: She spoke softly so that the baby did not wake

soft·ware /ˈsɒftweəʳ/ noun (no plural)
the programs that you put into a computer: Which software can I use with this computer?

sog·gy /ˈsɒgɪ/ adjective
wet and soft: The ground was very soggy.

soil /sɔɪl/ noun (no plural)
the earth in which plants grow

so·lar /ˈsəʊləʳ/ adjective
of or using the sun: The building is heated using solar energy.

solar sys·tem /ˈsəʊlə ˌsɪstəm/ noun
the sun and all the planets that go around it

sold /səʊld/
the past tense and past participle of the verb **sell**

sol·dier /ˈsəʊldʒəʳ/ noun
a person in the army

sole /səʊl/ noun
the bottom of your foot or shoe

sol·emn /ˈsɒləm/ adjective
very serious: Solemn music was played at the funeral.

so·lic·i·tor /səˈlɪsɪtəʳ/ noun
a type of LAWYER in Britain

solid

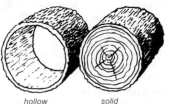

hollow   solid

sol·id¹ /ˈsɒlɪd/ adjective
1 hard and firm with no holes: Gold is solid, but when you heat it, it becomes liquid. I We had to dig through solid rock.
2 made of one material all the way through: This table is solid wood.

solid² noun
a substance that is hard, not a liquid or gas: Water changes from a liquid to a solid when it freezes.

so·lu·tion /səˈluːʃn/ noun
the answer to a problem or question: No one has found a solution **to** the problem.

solve /sɒlv/ verb (present participle **solving**, past **solved**)
to find the answer to a problem: He thinks money will solve all his problems. I Police have been unable to solve the crime (=discover who did it).

some /səm; strong sʌm/
1 an amount or number of some-thing: She had a big piece of cake

A B C D E F G H I J K L M N O P Q R S T U V W X Y Z

and she gave me some. | Would you like some sweets? | We invited all our friends but only some **of** them came. | Would you like some more coffee? ⇨ look at ANY

NOTE: Use **some** when you do not need to say exactly how much of something there is: I went out and bought some new clothes and a pair of shoes.

2 used when speaking about people or things without saying exactly which ones: Some girls are dancing, others are talking.

some·bod·y /'sʌmbədɪ/
1 used to mention a person without saying who the person is: There is somebody knocking at the door. | I know somebody who lives near you.
2 somebody else a different person: I thought it was Gary but it was somebody else. ⇨ same meaning SOMEONE ⇨ look at ANYBODY

some·how /'sʌmhaʊ/ adverb
in some way that is not known: We haven't got enough money, but we'll get it somehow.

some·one /'sʌmwʌn/
1 used to mention a person without saying who the person is: Someone is waiting to see you. | Will someone please explain what is happening?
2 someone else a different person: "Does Mike still live there?" "No, someone else lives there now." ⇨ same meaning SOMEBODY ⇨ look at ANYBODY

som·er·sault /'sʌməsɔːlt/ noun
a movement when you turn your body so that your feet go over your head and then touch the ground

some·thing /'sʌmθɪŋ/
used to mention something without saying its name or what it is: I want to tell you something. | She bought something to eat. | She said something about it, but I can't remember what it was. ⇨ look at ANYTHING

some·time /'sʌmtaɪm/ adverb
at some time in the past or the future: I hope I'll see you again sometime.

some·times /'sʌmtaɪmz/ adverb
at some times but not always: Sometimes I help my mother in the

house. | We sometimes go to the cinema, but not very often.

some·where /'sʌmweəʳ/ adverb
1 in, to, or at a place: At last he found somewhere to park the car. | She's looking for somewhere to live.
2 somewhere else in a different place: Go and play somewhere else – I'm working.

son /sʌn/ noun
someone's male child: I have a son and a daughter.

NOTE: The word **son** is used when you are talking about a male child. The word **daughter** is used when you are talking about a female child. Compare the questions: Do you have any sons? (=do you have any male children), Do you have any daughters? (=do you have any female children), and Do you have any children? (=do you have any sons or daughters?)

song /sɒŋ/ noun
a piece of music with words that are sung: Turn up the radio – that's my favourite song.

son-in-law /'sʌn ɪn lɔː/ noun (plural **sons-in-law**)
the husband of your daughter

soon /suːn/ adverb
1 in a short time: Dinner will be ready soon. | Come and see me soon. | He arrived soon after 8 o'clock.

NOTE: Compare these sentences. I must go to bed **soon** (=in a short time from now), I must go to bed **early** (=before the usual time). Compare also **soon** and **quickly**: Do it soon (=do it in a short time from now), Do it quickly (=do it fast).

2 as soon as immediately after something has happened: I phoned as soon as I heard the news. | She came as soon as she had finished work.
3 as soon as possible as quickly as possible: I'll get the car repaired as soon as possible.
4 sooner or later used to say that something will definitely happen but you

are not sure when: *He will find out the truth sooner or later.*

5 too soon too early: *It's too soon to know the results of the test.*

soot /sʊt/ *noun (no plural)*
the black powder left by smoke

soothe /suːð/ *verb (present participle* **soothing**, *past* **soothed**)
1 to make someone calm when they are angry or afraid: *She did her best to soothe the anxious parents.*
2 to make something less painful: *The medicine will soothe your sore throat.*

sore[1] /sɔːʳ/ *adjective*
painful because you are ill or injured: *I've got a sore foot.*

sore[2] *noun*
a painful place on your skin especially one caused by an illness

sor·ry /'sɒri/ *adjective* (**sorrier**, **sorriest**)
1 sorry, I'm sorry used when you feel ashamed or unhappy about something you have done: *I'm sorry, I didn't mean to be rude.* I *Sorry about all the mess.*
2 disappointed about something: *Dad's still sorry that he never learnt to play the piano.*
3 feel sorry for someone to feel sad for someone who has problems: *I couldn't help feeling sorry for her.*

sort[1] /sɔːt/ *noun*
a type of person or thing: *"What sort of flowers do you like best?" "Roses, I think." I He's playing some sort of computer game. I My favourite sort of ice cream is chocolate.*

sort[2] *verb*
1 to put things in the right order or arrange them in groups: *The post office sorts letters according to which town they are going to.*
2 sort something out to organize something that is untidy or in the wrong order: *Can you sort out this room? It's a mess.*

sought /sɔːt/
the past tense and past participle of the verb **seek**

soul /səʊl/ *noun*
the part of a person that contains their deepest thoughts and feelings, which many people believe continues after death

sound[1] /saʊnd/ *noun*
something you hear: *I could hear the sound of voices from the next room. I There was the sound of breaking glass.*

sound[2] *verb*
1 to seem: *That sounds **like** a good idea. I It sounds as if you like your new job.*
2 to show a particular quality or feeling in your voice: *You sound upset. Are you OK?*
3 to make a sound: *When the bell sounds you must come in.*

sound[3] *adjective*
1 practical and based on good reasons: *I think you have made a sound decision.*
2 healthy or strong: *I've repaired the roof and it's quite sound now.*

sound[4] *adverb*
sound asleep completely asleep: *The baby is sound asleep.*

sound·ly /'saʊndli/ *adverb*
sleep soundly to sleep well without waking up

soup /suːp/ *noun*
a liquid food made from meat, fish, or vegetables: *Here's a bowl of chicken soup.*

sour /saʊəʳ/ *adjective*
1 having a strong taste like a LEMON or VINEGAR
2 milk that is sour is not fresh and has a bad smell

source /sɔːs/ *noun*
where something comes from: *They get money from various sources. I That book is a good source **of** information.*

south[1] /saʊθ/ *noun*
the direction that is on the right when you look at the sun at the start of the morning: *London is in the south of England. I He lives on the south side of the city*

south[2] *adjective, adverb*
in or towards the south: *The south side of the building gets a lot of sun. I The birds fly south in winter.*

south·east /ˌsaʊθˈiːst/ *noun (no plural)*
the direction that is between south and east: *The wind is coming from the southeast.*

south·ern /'sʌðən/ *adjective*
in or from the south part of an area, country, etc: *We are going on holiday to southern Italy.*

south pole /ˌsaʊθ ˈpəʊl/ *noun*
the place that is the furthest south in the world, where it is very cold

south·west /ˌsaʊθˈwest/ *noun (no plural)*
the direction that is between south and west: *Bristol is a city in the southwest of England*

sou·ve·nir /ˌsuːvəˈnɪəʳ/ *noun*
something that you buy or keep to help you remember a place or an event: *We brought back some holiday souvenirs.*

sow /səʊ/ *verb (past participle **sown** /səʊn/)*
to put seeds in the ground so that they will grow into plants: *We sow beans in the spring.*

space /speɪs/ *noun*
1 an empty area that can be used for something: *There isn't enough space for any more furniture.* | *We've kept you a space* (=a place to sit) *at our table.* | *Can you see any parking spaces?*
2 (*no plural*) the empty area that surrounds the sun, the Earth, etc: *Astronauts are trained to travel in space.*

space·ship /ˈspeɪsʃɪp/ *noun*
a vehicle that can carry people through space: *They travelled to the moon in a spaceship.*

space shut·tle /ˈspeɪs ˌʃʌtl/ *noun*
a vehicle that can fly into space, return to the Earth again, and then be used the same way again

spade /speɪd/ *noun*
a tool that you use for making holes in the earth or turning the earth over before growing plants

spa·ghet·ti /spəˈɡeti/ *noun (no plural)*
a kind of Italian food made from flour and water, that looks like long thin pieces of string

span [1] /spæn/ *noun*
the length of time in which something continues: *Most children have a short attention span.*

span [2] *verb (present participle **spanning**, past **spanned**)*
to include all of a period of time: *Her singing career spanned the 1990s.*

span·iel /ˈspænjəl/ *noun*
a type of dog with long hair and long soft ears

spank /spæŋk/ *verb*
to hit a child on the bottom with an open hand, as a punishment ⋄ same meaning SMACK

span·ner /ˈspænəʳ/ *noun*
British a tool that you use for turning NUTS to make them tight or loose

spare [1] /speəʳ/ *adjective*
1 a spare key, tyre, room, etc is one that you do not usually use, but which you have for the times when you need it: *If you have a spare bed, may I stay tonight?*
2 something that is spare is not being used and is available for another person to use: *Are there any spare seats?*
3 **spare time** time when you are not working or busy: *He paints pictures in his spare time.*

spare [2] *verb (present participle **sparing**, past **spared**)*
to let someone have or use something: *Can you spare me some money?*

spark /spɑːk/ *noun*
a very small piece of burning material that jumps from a fire

spar·kle /ˈspɑːkl/ *verb (present participle **sparkling**, past **sparkled**)*
to shine with bright points of light: *The diamond sparkled in the light.* | *Her eyes sparkled.*

spar·row /ˈspærəʊ/ *noun*
a small brown bird that is very common in many parts of the world

spat /spæt/
the past tense and past participle of the verb **spit**

speak /spiːk/ *verb (present participle **speaking**, past **spoke** /spəʊk/, past participle **spoken** /ˈspəʊkən/)*
1 to say something: *Children learn to speak when they are very small.* | *Can I speak **to** you about something?* | *Have you spoken to Michael **about** this?*
2 to be able to talk in a particular language: *She speaks English and German.*
3 **speak up** to say something more loudly: *Can you speak up, please – I can't hear you.*

speak·er /ˈspiːkəʳ/ *noun*
1 a person who is talking to a large group of people about something: *Politicians were among the speakers at the meeting.*

2 the part of a radio, CD PLAYER, etc where the sound comes out

spear /spɪəʳ/ *noun*
a long thin weapon with a pointed end that is thrown at a person or an animal

spe·cial /'speʃl/ *adjective*
1 better or more important than ordinary things, events, or people: *This is a special day in the history of our country.* | *She wants to go somewhere special on her birthday.*
2 intended for a particular person, group, or thing: *He goes to a special school for deaf children.*

spe·cial·ist /'speʃəlɪst/ *noun*
a person who knows a lot about a particular thing: *Dr Carlton is a heart specialist.*

spe·cial·ize /'speʃəlaɪz/ *verb* (*present participle* **specializing**, *past* **specialized**)
to study or know about one particular thing: *She specializes in children's illnesses.*

spe·cial·ly /'speʃli/ *adverb*
1 for one purpose: *I came here specially to meet you.*
2 more than usual: *He is not specially clever, but he works hard.*

spe·cies /'spiːʃiːz/ *noun* (*plural* **species**)
a group of plants or animals of the same type: *I saw a rare species of bird while on holiday.*

spe·cif·ic /spə'sɪfɪk/ *adjective*
1 a particular type of person or thing: *There are three specific types of treatment.*
2 clear and exact: *Can you be specific about the reasons for this decision?*

spe·cif·ic·al·ly /spə'sɪfɪkli/ *adverb*
1 for a particular type of person or thing: *The film is specifically for children.*
2 clearly and exactly: *I specifically told you not to do that.*

spe·ci·men /'spesɪmən/ *noun*
a small amount of something that is used as an example of what the whole thing is like: *The doctor took a specimen of blood from Andrew's arm.*

speck /spek/ *noun*
a very small piece of something: *I had a speck of dust in my eye.*

spec·tac·u·lar /spek'tækjələʳ/ *adjective*
very impressive or exciting: *There's a spectacular view of the mountains.*

spec·ta·tor /spek'teɪtəʳ/ *noun*
someone who watches a game, event, etc

sped /sped/
the past tense and past participle of the verb **speed**

speech /spiːtʃ/ *noun*
1 (*plural* **speeches**) a talk given to a group of people: *The President **gave** a speech.*
2 (*no plural*) the ability to speak, or the way someone speaks: *Speech is learnt in the first years of life.*

speed¹ /spiːd/ *noun*
how fast something moves: *The car was travelling at a speed of 70 miles an hour.* | *Police are advising motorists to reduce speed.*

speed² *verb* (*past* **speeded** *or* **sped** /sped/)
1 to move or happen quickly: *The car sped off into the distance.* | *The holidays sped by* (=passed very quickly).
2 **speed up** to go faster: *Your work is too slow – you must speed up.*
⇨ opposite SLOW DOWN

speed lim·it /'spiːd ˌlɪmɪt/ *noun*
a law that says how fast you can travel: *He was stopped by police for breaking the speed limit.*

spell¹ /spel/ *verb* (*past* **spelled** *or* **spelt** /spelt/)
to write the letters of a word correctly: *How do you spell 'embarrassed'?*

spell² *noun*
a set of magic words used to make something happen

spell·ing /'spelɪŋ/ *noun*
1 (*no plural*) the ability to spell words correctly: *Her spelling has improved.*
2 (*no plural*) the correct way of writing a word: *The American spelling is different from the British one.*

spend /spend/ *verb* (*past* **spent** /spent/)
1 to use your money to buy or pay for something: *How much money do you spend each week?* | *She spent £150 on clothes.*
2 to use time doing something: *I spent an hour reading.*

A B C D E F G H I J K L M N O P Q R **S** T U V W X Y Z

sphere /sfɪəʳ/ *noun*
a solid round shape like a ball

spice /spaɪs/ *noun*
a seed, root, or other part of a plant used to give food a special taste: *Pepper is a spice.*

spic·y /'spaɪsɪ/ *adjective* (**spicier, spiciest**)
spicy food contains a lot of spices: *The fish was served with a spicy sauce.*

spi·der /'spaɪdəʳ/ *noun*
a creature with eight legs, that uses threads from its body to catch insects

spider
web

spied /spaɪd/
the past tense and past participle of the verb **spy**

spike /spaɪk/ *noun*
a thin sharp piece of metal: *The fence has spikes on top.*

spill /spɪl/ *verb* (*past* **spilled** *or* **spilt** /spɪlt/)
if a liquid spills or you spill it, it goes over the edge of a container: *I spilt coffee **on** my shirt.*

spin /spɪn/ *verb* (*present participle* **spinning**, *past* **spun** /spʌn/)
1 to turn round very fast: *The wheels were spinning round.*
2 to make thread by twisting cotton, wool, etc

spin·ach /'spɪnɪdʒ/ *noun* (*no plural*)
a vegetable with big dark green leaves

spine /spaɪn/ *noun*
the long row of bones in your back ⇨ same meaning BACKBONE

spi·ral /'spaɪrəl/
a shape that goes round and round as it goes up

spire /spaɪəʳ/ *noun*
a tall part of a church with a point at the top ⇨ same meaning STEEPLE

spir·it /'spɪrɪt/ *noun*
1 a person's mind, including their opinions, thoughts, and feelings: *I'm 85 but I still feel young in spirit.*
2 **spirits** strong alcoholic drink such as RUM or WHISKY

3 a living thing without a physical body such as a GHOST or ANGEL: *the spirits of the dead*

spir·i·tu·al /'spɪrɪtʃʊəl/ *adjective*
relating to the spirit and not the body or mind

spit /spɪt/ *verb* (*present participle* **spitting**, *past* **spat** /spæt/)
to force a small amount of liquid or food out of your mouth: *He spat on the floor.* | *The child spat out her food.*

spite /spaɪt/ *noun* (*no plural*)
1 **in spite of** although something else happens or is true: *We went out in spite of the rain.* | *In spite of being the youngest, she was the cleverest child in the class.*
2 the feeling of wanting to hurt or annoy another person: *She refused to see him out of spite.*

spite·ful /'spaɪtfəl/ *adjective*
unkind and intended to upset someone: *She made a spiteful remark.*

splash¹ /splæʃ/ *noun* (*plural* **splashes**)
the sound made by something falling into a liquid: *She jumped into the river with a splash.*

splash

splashing water

splash² *verb*
to move or hit water and make someone or something wet: *The children splashed about in the pool.* | *He splashed some water on his face.*

splen·did /'splendɪd/ *adjective*
extremely good or impressive: *You've done a splendid job.*

splin·ter /'splɪntəʳ/ *noun*
a thin sharp piece of wood or metal: *I have got a splinter in my finger.*

split¹ /splɪt/ *verb* (*present participle* **splitting**, *past* **split**)
1 to tear or break something,

especially from one end to the other: *We split the wood into long thin pieces.* | *My trousers split when I sat down.*

2 also **split up** to divide something into parts, groups, etc: *We split the work* **between** *us.*

split [2] *noun*
a long straight hole in something: *There is a split* **in** *her skirt.*

spoil /spɔɪl/ *verb (past* **spoiled** *or* **spoilt** /spɔɪlt/)
1 to damage something good so that it is less useful or enjoyable: *The new road has spoilt the countryside.* | *His actions spoiled our evening.*
2 to let a child have or do whatever they want, with the result that they behave badly: *You must not spoil your children.*

spoilt [1] /spɔɪlt/
the past tense and past participle of the verb **spoil**

spoilt [2] *adjective*
a spoilt child has been allowed to have or do whatever they want and, as a result, behaves badly: *Jean is a spoilt child.*

spoke [1] /spəʊk/
the past tense of the verb **speak**

spoke [2] *noun*
one of the bars joining the outer ring of a wheel to the centre ⇨ see picture at BICYCLE

spok·en /ˈspəʊkən/
the past participle of the verb **speak**

sponge /spʌndʒ/ *noun*
a piece of a soft substance full of holes, used for washing your body

spool /spuːl/ *noun*
an object like a small wheel that you wind thread, wire, etc round

spoon /spuːn/ *noun*
an instrument with a handle that has a round end, used for eating liquid foods, mixing things in cooking, etc: *You eat soup with a spoon.* ⇨ see picture at CUTLERY

spoon·ful /ˈspuːnfʊl/ *noun (plural* **spoonsful** *or* **spoonfuls**)
the amount a spoon holds: *You must take three spoonfuls* **of** *medicine.* | *Add a spoonful of cream to the soup before serving it.*

sport /spɔːt/ *noun*
a game or competition that you play by using your body, such as tennis or football: *What is your favourite sport?* | *He's good at sport.*

sports car /ˈspɔːts kɑːr/ *noun*
a fast car, usually for two people, often with a roof that opens

spot [1] /spɒt/ *noun*
1 a small area that is different from the rest of a surface: *It was a white dog with black spots.* | *There were spots* **of** *paint on the floor.*
2 a place: *It's a very pretty spot.*
3 *British* a small red mark on someone's skin: *Most teenagers get spots.*

spot [2] *verb (present participle* **spotting**, *past* **spotted**)
to see or notice someone or something: *I spotted you at the party.*

spot·less /ˈspɒtləs/ *adjective*
completely clean: *The kitchen was spotless.*

spot·ted /ˈspɒtɪd/ *adjective*
covered with small circles of colour ⇨ see picture at PATTERN

spout /spaʊt/ *noun*
the long thin part of a container through which liquid is poured

sprain /spreɪn/ *verb*
to damage a part of your body by turning it suddenly: *He sprained his ankle when he fell.*

sprang /spræŋ/
the past tense of the verb **spring**

spray [1] /spreɪ/ *verb*
to make liquid come out of something in very small drops: *She sprayed some perfume* **on** *her wrist.* | *He sprayed the flowers* **with** *water.*

spray [2] *noun*
liquid in a special container that forces the liquid out in very small drops: *Can I borrow your hair spray?*

spread /spred/ *verb (past* **spread**)
1 also **spread out** to open something so that it covers a wide area: *Spread the map out on the table.* | *The bird spread its wings.*
2 to affect a larger area or more people: *The illness spread through the town.* | *Rain will spread throughout the area tonight.*

3 to make something known to a lot of people: *The news of her death spread quickly.*

4 to cover something thinly: *She spread the bread with butter.* | *Spread the cream over the top of the cake.* ⇨ see picture on page 198

spring¹ /sprɪŋ/ *noun*
1 the season between winter and summer when plants start to grow again: *The show opens in the spring.* | *I love spring flowers.* ⇨ see picture on page 194
2 a place where water comes up from the ground
3 a twisted piece of metal wire that will return to its normal shape after it has been pressed

spring² *verb* (*past* **sprang** /spræŋ/, *past participle* **sprung** /sprʌŋ/)
to jump suddenly: *Elsie sprang **out** of bed and rushed to the window.*

sprin·kle /ˈsprɪŋkl/ *verb* (*present participle* **sprinkling**, *past* **sprinkled**)
to let small drops or pieces fall on the surface of something: *She sprinkled sugar on the cake.* ⇨ see picture on page 198

sprout¹ /spraʊt/ *verb*
to start to grow: *The seeds are beginning to sprout.*

sprout² *noun*
a small round, green vegetable made of leaves pressed tightly together ⇨ see picture on page 199

sprung /sprʌŋ/
the past participle of the verb **spring**

spun /spʌn/
the past tense and past participle of the verb **spin**

spy¹ /spaɪ/ *noun* (*plural* **spies**)
a person whose job is to watch people secretly in order to discover facts or information about them

spy² *verb* (*past* **spied**)
to watch people secretly in order to discover facts or information about them: *She's been spying **on** her neighbours.*

squab·ble¹ /ˈskwɒbl/ *verb* (*present participle* **squabbling**, *past* **squabbled**)
to argue about things that are not important: *The children were squab-*

bling **about** who had won the game of football.

squabble² *noun*
an argument about something that is not important

square¹ /skweəʳ/ *noun*
1 a shape with four straight sides of equal length ⇨ see picture at SHAPE
2 an open place in a town with buildings all around it

square² *adjective*
something that is square has four straight sides of equal length: *The room had square windows.*

squash¹ /skwɒʃ/ *verb*
to press something flat, usually damaging it: *The fruit at the bottom of the box had been squashed.*

squash² *noun* (*no plural*)
1 a game played by two people who hit a small rubber ball against the four walls of a court: *I'm playing squash at lunch time.*
2 British a drink that tastes like fruit: *Can I have a glass of orange squash?*

squeak¹ /skwiːk/ *verb*
to make a very high sound: *Mice squeak.* | *My chair is squeaking.*

squeak² *noun*
a very high sound: *She gave a squeak of alarm.*

squeal¹ /skwiːl/ *verb*
to make a loud high cry or sound: *Pigs squeal.*

squeal² *noun*
a loud high cry: *The baby gave a squeal of pain.*

squeeze /skwiːz/ *verb* (*present participle* **squeezing**, *past* **squeezed**)
to press something firmly, especially with your hand: *He squeezed an orange to get the juice out.* | *She squeezed Jo's arm and smiled at him.* ⇨ see picture on page 198

squid /skwɪd/ *noun*
a sea creature with a long soft body and ten arms

squir·rel /ˈskwɪrəl/ *noun*
a small brown or grey animal with a thick tail that lives in trees and eats nuts ⇨ see picture on page 195

St
1 a short way of writing the word **Saint**
2 a short way of writing the word **Street**

stab /stæb/ verb (present participle **stabbing**, past **stabbed**)
to push a sharp object into someone or something using force: *He stabbed her with a knife.*

sta·ble[1] /'steɪbl/ noun
a building in which a horse lives

stable[2] adjective
firm, and not likely to move or change: *Is that ladder stable? | They have a stable marriage.*

stack[1] /stæk/ noun
a large tidy pile of things: *There was a stack of books by the door.*

stack[2] verb
to put things into a tidy pile: *Will you stack the dirty plates?*

sta·di·um /'steɪdɪəm/ noun
a large outdoor sports field with seats all round it: *a football stadium*

staff /stɑːf/ noun (no plural)
a group of people working together for the same organization: *The meeting was for the staff of the school. | The staff in our London office deal with European orders.*

stage /steɪdʒ/ noun
1 a time or state in a long process: *When a book has been written, the next stage is printing it. | The disease is still in its early stages.*
2 the part of a theatre where the actors stand and perform

stag·ger /'stægər/ verb
to walk as if you are going to fall: *The wounded man staggered down the street.*

stain[1] /steɪn/ verb
to make a mark on something that is difficult to remove: *The coffee stained his shirt.*

stain[2] noun
a mark on something that is difficult to remove: *How do you get wine stains out of a tablecloth?*

stair·case /'steəkeɪs/ noun
a set of steps inside a building: *Jane was standing at the top of the staircase.*

stairs /steəz/ plural noun
a set of steps that go from one level of a building to another: *He ran up the stairs. | There was a mirror at the top of the stairs.* ⇨ see picture on page 204

stale /steɪl/ adjective
tasting old and dry and no longer fresh: *stale bread*

stalk /stɔːk/ noun
the tall main part of a plant ⇨ see picture at ROSE

stall /stɔːl/ noun
a small open shop outdoors: *He runs a fruit and vegetable stall.*

stam·mer /'stæmər/ verb
to speak with difficulty repeating the first sound of a word: *"Th-th-thank you," he stammered.* ⇨ same meaning STUTTER

stamp[1] /stæmp/ noun
1 a small piece of special paper that you stick on a letter or parcel to show how much you have paid to send it ⇨ see picture at ENVELOPE
2 a mark made by an instrument that is pressed onto ink and then pressed onto paper: *The official put a stamp in my passport.*

stamp[2] verb
1 to walk with noisy heavy steps or to bring your foot down hard on something: *Tony stamped upstairs. | He stamped on the insect.*
2 to print an official mark on a document by pressing a small block covered with ink onto it: *She stamped the date at the top of the letter.*

stand[1] /stænd/ verb (past **stood** /stʊd/)
1 to be upright on your legs and feet: *I had to stand all the way home in the bus. | Hundreds of people stood watching.*
2 also **stand up** to move so that you are on your feet: *All the children stood up. | Please stand when it is your turn to read.*
3 to be in a particular place: *The house stands at the top of the hill.*
4 **can't stand someone or something** to hate someone or something: *I can't stand getting up early. | Dave can't stand dogs.*
5 **stand back, stand aside** to stand further away from something: *She stood back to let me pass.*
6 to not change but remain the same: *My offer to lend you the money still stands.*
7 **stand by (a)** to do nothing while something unpleasant is happening:

How can you stand by while he's hitting her? **(b)** to be ready to help if someone needs you: *Doctors are standing by to treat any injured people.*

8 stand for something to be a short form of a word or phrase: *UN stands for the 'United Nations'.*

9 stand up for someone or something to say that someone or something is good or right: *He should have stood up for me.* | *He always stands up for his wife.*

stand² *noun*
a place where people can stand or sit to watch sports

stan·dard¹ /'stændəd/ *noun*
1 a level of quality or skill that is considered acceptable: *There is a high standard of service at the restaurant.* | *This work is not up to the necessary standard.*
2 the idea of what is normal, when you are comparing something: *By European standards this is a low salary.*

standard² *adjective*
usual or normal: *It's standard practice to check luggage at airports.* | *He is paid the standard salary for the job.*

stank /stæŋk/
the past tense of the verb **stink**

star¹ /stɑːʳ/ *noun*
1 a small point of light that can be seen in the sky at night
2 a famous actor, singer, sportsperson, etc: *She always wanted to be a film star.*
3 a shape with five or six points

star² *verb* (*present participle* **starring**, *past* **starred**)
to act as the most important person in a film or show: *We were watching an old film starring Charlie Chaplin.*

stare /steəʳ/ *verb* (*present participle* **staring**, *past* **stared**)
to look steadily at something for a long time: *He stared at the word trying to remember what it meant.*

start¹ /stɑːt/ *verb*
to begin: *The children started singing.* | *It's starting to rain.* | *The race starts in ten minutes.* ⇨ opposite FINISH, STOP

start² *noun*
the beginning of an activity, event, or situation: *It was a close race from start to finish.* | *I don't want to miss the start of the film.* ⇨ opposite END, FINISH

star·tle /'stɑːtl/ *verb* (*present participle* **startling**, *past* **startled**)
to surprise someone or give them a shock: *You startled me when you shouted.*

starv·a·tion /stɑː'veɪʃn/ *noun* (*no plural*)
when someone becomes ill or dies because they do not have enough to eat

starve /stɑːv/ *verb* (*present participle* **starving**, *past* **starved**)
to die of hunger

starv·ing /'stɑːvɪŋ/ *adjective*
1 dying of hunger: *There were starving children among the refugees.*
2 very hungry: *I'm starving – is dinner ready yet?*

state¹ /steɪt/ *noun*
1 the condition that someone or something is in: *This book is in a very bad state.* | *The driver was still in a state of shock.*
2 also **State** one of the parts that some countries are divided into, which each have their own government: *Mississippi is one of the 50 states in the United States of America.*
3 (*no plural*) the government of a country: *In Britain the health service is run by the state.*

state² *verb* (*present participle* **stating**, *past* **stated**)
to say something in a formal way or on a formal occasion: *He stated that he had never seen the woman before.*

state·ment /'steɪtmənt/ *noun*
something that is said in a formal way or on a formal occasion: *The man made a statement to the police.*

sta·tion /'steɪʃn/ *noun*
1 a place where buses or trains stop: *Where is the railway station?* | *I'll meet you at the bus station.*
2 a building for some special work: *Police officers work at a police station.*

sta·tion·a·ry /'steɪʃənrɪ/ *adjective*
not moving: *The car was stationary when the accident happened.*

sta·tion·er·y /'steɪʃənrɪ/ *noun* (*no plural*)
paper, pens, pencils, and other things used for writing

stat·ue /'stætʃuː/ *noun*
a figure of a person, animal, etc made of stone, metal, or wood

stay /steɪ/ verb

1 to continue to be in a particular place, state, job etc: *Stay in your classroom until it is time to go home.* | *Can you stay here and look after my bags for me?* | *She decided to stay in her present job.*

2 to live somewhere as a guest for a short time: *They're staying at a hotel.*

stead·i·ly /'stedɪlɪ/ adverb

at a speed or level that does not change very much: *We drove steadily at 30 miles an hour.*

stead·y /'stedɪ/ adjective, adverb

(**steadier**, **steadiest**)

1 firmly in one place and not moving: *Hold the chair steady while I stand on it.*

2 staying at the same level, speed, etc over a period of time: *We were travelling at a steady speed.*

steak /steɪk/ noun

a thick flat piece of meat or fish

steal /stiːl/ verb (past **stole** /stəʊl/, past participle **stolen** /'stəʊlən/)

to take something that does not belong to you, without asking for it: *Who stole my money?* | *Someone has stolen my passport.* ⇨ look at ROB

steam[1] /stiːm/ noun (no plural)

the gas that water becomes when it boils: *There was steam coming from the kettle.*

steam

steam[2] verb

1 to cook something by putting it in steam: *Steam the vegetables for five minutes.*

2 to produce steam

steel /stiːl/ noun (no plural)

a strong hard metal made of specially treated iron, used to make knives, machines, etc

steep /stiːp/ adjective

having a slope that is high and difficult to go up: *We had to climb a steep hill.*

steeply adverb: *The road goes up very steeply here.*

stee·ple /'stiːpl/ noun

a tall part of a church with a point at the top ⇨ same meaning SPIRE

steer /stɪəʳ/ verb

to move a vehicle in a particular direction: *He steered the ship carefully between the rocks.*

steer·ing wheel /'stɪərɪŋ ˌwiːl/ noun

the wheel that you turn to make a car move to the left or right

stem /stem/ noun

the central part of a plant from which the leaves or flowers grow ⇨ see picture at ROSE

step[1] /step/ verb (present participle **stepping**, past **stepped**)

to move one foot up and put it down in front of the other: *He stepped over the dog.*

step[2] noun

1 one movement forwards or backwards with your foot: *He took a step towards the door.*

2 the sound made when you take a step: *I heard steps outside.*

3 one part of a set of stairs: *There are two steps up onto the bus.*

4 one action in a series that you do to get a particular result: *The first step when an accident happens is to call for help.*

step·fa·ther /'stepfɑːðəʳ/ noun

a man who marries your mother but is not your father

step·moth·er /'stepmʌðəʳ/ noun

a woman who marries your father but is not your mother

ster·ling /'stɜːlɪŋ/ noun (no plural)

the type of money used in Britain

ster·e·o /'sterɪəʊ/ noun

a machine for playing music on records, CDs, etc that produces music from SPEAKERS

stern /stɜːn/ adjective

severe and unfriendly: *We had a stern teacher.*

stew[1] /stjuː/ noun

meat or fish and vegetables, cooked slowly together in liquid

stew[2] verb

to cook food slowly in liquid

stew·ard /'stjuːəd/ noun

someone whose job is to look after you on a boat or plane

A B C D E F G H I J K L M N O P Q R S T U V W X Y Z

stew·ard·ess /ˈstjuːədes/ *noun*

a woman whose job is to look after you on a boat or plane

stick [1] /stɪk/ *verb* (*past* **stuck** /stʌk/)

1 to join one thing to another, using a substance such as GLUE: *I stuck a stamp on the envelope.*

2 to put something somewhere: *Just stick your coat on that chair.*

3 to push a pointed object into something: *The nurse stuck a needle into my arm.*

4 if something sticks, it becomes fixed in one position: *The car is stuck in the mud.*

5 stick something out to make something come out from inside: *She stuck her hand out of the car and took the ticket.*

stick [2] *noun*

1 a long thin piece of wood

2 a thin piece of wood or metal used for a particular purpose: *Grannie has to walk with a stick now.*

stick·y /ˈstɪkɪ/
adjective
(**stickier,
stickiest**)
covered with or
containing
something that
fixes itself to
anything it
touches: *My
hands are sticky. I
Try one of these
sticky sweets.*

sticky

stiff /stɪf/ *adjective*

not able to move or bend easily: *The cards were made of stiff paper.*

still [1] /stɪl/ *adverb*

1 continuing to happen or continuing to do something: *My father still remembers his first day at school. I Andy was still asleep. I Do you still play tennis?*

2 continuing to be possible: *We could still catch the bus if we hurry.*

3 in spite of something: *It was raining, but she still went out.*

still [2] *adjective*

not moving: *Keep still while I comb your hair. I The sea was calm and still.* ⇨ see picture at FIZZY

sting [1] /stɪŋ/ *verb* (*past* **stung** /stʌŋ/)

if an insect, animal, or plant stings you it hurts you by putting poison into your skin: *The bee stung her leg.*

sting [2] *noun*

a pain or wound caused by a sting ⇨ see picture at WASP

stink [1] /stɪŋk/ *verb* (*past* **stank** /stæŋk/, *past participle* **stunk** /stʌŋk/)

to have a very unpleasant smell

stink [2] *noun*

a very unpleasant smell

stir /stɜːʳ/ *verb* (*present participle* **stirring**, *past* **stirred**)

1 to mix a liquid or food by moving a spoon around in it: *He put sugar in his tea and stirred it.*

2 to move slightly: *The leaves stirred in the wind.*

stitch [1] /stɪtʃ/ *noun* (*plural* **stitches**)

1 one of the small lines of thread that join cloth: *The dress was sewn with small stitches.*

2 a small circle of wool round a needle in KNITTING

stitch [2] *verb*

to use a needle and thread to join or decorate cloth

stock [1] /stɒk/ *noun*

1 a store of goods in a shop: *We have a large stock of tinned fruit.*

2 **in stock** ready for sale in a shop: *I'm sorry, we've only got black boots in stock.*

3 **out of stock** not there in the shop or ready for sale: *Their old CD is out of stock.*

stock [2] *verb*

to have something for sale in a shop: *They do not stock flowers, only fruit and vegetables.*

stock·ing /ˈstɒkɪŋ/ *noun*

a thin piece of clothing that covers a woman's leg and foot ⇨ compare TIGHTS

stole /stəʊl/

the past tense of the verb **steal**

sto·len /ˈstəʊlən/

the past participle of the verb **steal**

stom·ach /ˈstʌmək/ *noun*

the part of your body where food goes when you swallow it

stomach ache /ˈstʌmək eɪk/ noun
a pain in your stomach: I've got a stomach ache.

stone /stəʊn/ noun
1 a small piece of rock: The boys threw stones into the lake.
2 (no plural) rock: The walls are made of stone.
3 (plural **stone** or **stones**) a measurement of weight used in Britain that is equal to 14 pounds or 6.35 kilograms
4 British a large hard single seed in the centre of a fruit
5 a valuable piece of rock, used in jewellery

stood /stʊd/
the past tense and past participle of the verb **stand**

stool /stuːl/ noun
a chair without a back or sides ⇨ see picture at CHAIR

stoop /stuːp/ verb
to bend your body over forwards and down: He had to stoop to get through the doorway.

stop¹ /stɒp/ verb (present participle **stopping**, past **stopped**)
1 to end an activity, event, movement, etc: The baby has stopped crying. | The rain has stopped. | Lena's trying to stop smoking.
2 to not allow something to happen or continue: They stopped me going out of the door. | You must stop Joe **from** telling them about it.
3 to wait or not continue during an activity, journey, etc: We need to stop to get some petrol.

stop² noun
1 a place where a bus or train stops: We waited at the bus stop.
2 **come to a stop** stop moving: The taxi came to a stop outside his house.

store¹ /stɔːr/ verb (present participle **storing**, past **stored**)
to put something away and keep it there until you need it: I stored all the potatoes from the garden. | My old clothes are stored in those boxes.

store² noun
1 American a building where you can buy things (British **shop**)
2 an amount of something to be used later: Granny always had a special store **of** chocolate for us.

sto·rey /ˈstɔːri/ noun
one level in a building: Our house has three storeys.

storm /stɔːm/ noun
a time of bad weather when there is a lot of wind and rain

storm·y /ˈstɔːmi/ adjective (**stormier**, **stormiest**)
very rainy and windy: The stormy weather will continue ⇨ see picture on page 194

sto·ry /ˈstɔːri/ noun (plural **stories**)
a description of a set of events that can be real or imaginary: Please **read** us a story! | She **told** us a story **about** magic.

straight¹ /streɪt/ adjective
1 not bending or curved: Can you draw a straight line? | My sister has straight hair. ⇨ see picture on page 202
2 level or upright and not leaning: The picture is not straight – you must move the left side up.
3 honest and direct: I wish you'd give me a straight answer.

straight² adverb
1 in a line that does not bend: The car went straight down the road. | The keys are on the table straight in front of you.
2 immediately and directly, without any delay: He went straight to his friend to ask for help.
3 **straight away** now: I must see you straight away.
4 **straight on** in the same direction: Go straight on until you get to the crossroads.

straight·en /ˈstreɪtn/ verb
to make something straight, or to become straight: She straightened the picture on the wall.

strain /streɪn/ verb
1 to damage a part of your body by using it wrongly or too much: I strained my back when I lifted the box.
2 to do something with great effort: She had to strain her ears to hear me.
3 to take the lumps out of a food or liquid by putting it through a sieve (=kitchen tool with small holes in it)

strait /streɪt/ noun
a narrow piece of water that joins two larger areas of water

strand /strænd/ *noun*
a long thin piece of thread, hair, wire, etc: *She pushed a loose strand* **of** *hair behind her ear.*

strand·ed /'strændɪd/ *adjective*
in a difficult place or state with no help: *I was stranded in a foreign country with no money.*

strange /streɪndʒ/ *adjective*
not ordinary or not known: *I heard a strange noise from the next room.* | *I had a strange dream last night.* | *I was in a strange city trying to find a hotel.*

strang·er /'streɪndʒəʳ/ *noun*
a person you do not know

strange·ly /'streɪndʒlɪ/ *adverb*
in an unusual or surprising way: *She was looking at me very strangely.*

stran·gle /'stræŋgl/ *verb* (*present participle* **strangling**, *past* **strangled**)
to kill someone by pressing round their throat

strap[1] /stræp/ *noun*
a narrow piece of leather, plastic, cloth, etc used for fastening something or carrying something

strap[2] *verb* (*present participle* **strapping**, *past* **strapped**)
to fasten something with a strap: *He strapped the bag onto his bicycle.*

straw /strɔː/ *noun*
1 (*no plural*) dry stems of wheat or similar plants, used for animals to sleep on or for making things such as baskets
2 a thin tube for drinking through: *He drank the milk through a straw.*

straw·ber·ry /'strɔːbərɪ/ *noun* (*plural* **strawberries**)
a small soft red fruit ⇨ see picture on page 199

stray[1] /streɪ/ *adjective*
a stray animal is lost and has no home: *He found a stray dog.*

stray[2] *verb*
to move away from a safe place although not intending to: *She strayed* **from** *the road and got lost.*

streak /striːk/ *noun*
a long thin line: *There was a streak of paint on the wall.*

stream /striːm/ *noun*
1 a small river ⇨ see picture on page 193

2 a long line of people or vehicles: *A steady stream* **of** *traffic came through the village.*

street /striːt/ *noun*
a road in a town: *Across the street from the school is the library.* | *Robert lives in Bridge Street.*

street light /'striːt laɪt/ *noun*
a light on a long pole that stands next to a street

strength /streŋθ/ *noun* (*no plural*)
1 the ability to move or lift heavy things: *I haven't the strength to lift this box.* | *He pushed the door with all his strength.*
2 the power of an organization, country, or relationship, etc: *He talked about the strength of the US economy.*

strength·en /'streŋθən/ *verb*
to make someone or something stronger: *Exercise will strengthen your arms.*

stress[1] /stres/ *noun*
1 (*no plural*) the feeling of being worried and tense because of difficulties in your life: *The stress of working for examinations made him ill.*
2 **be under stress** be in a situation that causes stress: *Dad's been under a lot of stress at work.*
3 (*plural* **stresses**) special force that you use when you say a word or part of a word. In the word 'chemistry' the stress is on the first part of the word

stress[2] *verb*
1 to give special attention or importance to a fact, idea, etc: *I must stress that we haven't much time.*
2 to say a word or part of a word with more force. You should stress the second part of the word 'machine'

stretch /stretʃ/ *verb*
1 to become larger or longer by pulling, or make something do this: *She stretched the rope between the two poles.* | *Rubber stretches easily.*
2 to make your arms, legs, and body straight: *He stretched his legs in front of him.* ⇨ see picture on page 207
3 to spread over or cover a large area: *The forest stretched for miles.*

stretch·er /'stretʃəʳ/ *noun*
a frame on which a person who is ill or wounded can be carried

strict /strɪkt/ *adjective*
making sure that rules are obeyed: *They are very strict with their children.*

strict·ly /'strɪktlɪ/ *adverb*
1 in a way that must be obeyed: *Smoking is strictly against the rules in this building.*
2 exactly and correctly: *What he says is not strictly true.*

strike[1] /straɪk/ *verb* (*present participle* **striking**, *past* **struck** /strʌk/)
1 to hit someone or something: *The car struck a tree.* | *He was struck on the head by a falling rock.*
2 if something strikes you, it gives you a particular feeling or idea: *It suddenly struck me **that** she was lying.* | *He strikes me **as** being a very clever man.*
3 to stop working, usually because you want more money or better conditions
4 if a clock strikes, it makes a sound to show what time it is: *The clock struck three.*

strike[2] *noun*
1 a time when people do not work because they want more money or better conditions: *There is a strike at the factory.*
2 on strike refusing to work: *The workers are on strike.*

string /strɪŋ/ *noun*
1 (*no plural*) thin rope used for fastening things: *The parcel was tied with string.*
2 a thin piece of wire used in a musical instrument such as a VIOLIN

strip[1] /strɪp/ *noun*
a long narrow piece of something: *I tore off a strip **of** paper.*

strip[2] *verb* (*present participle* **stripping**, *past* **stripped**)
1 to pull off an outer covering: *He stripped the paper off the wall.*
2 also **strip off** to take off your clothes: *John stripped and got into the shower.*

stripe /straɪp/ *noun*
a long thin line of colour: *A tiger has dark stripes.*

striped /straɪpt/ *adjective*
having long thin lines of colour: *He wore a striped shirt.* ⇨ see picture at PATTERN

strode /strəʊd/
the past tense of the verb **stride**

stroke[1] /strəʊk/ *noun*
1 a sudden illness in your brain: *She couldn't walk very well after her stroke.*
2 a movement of your arms when you are swimming: *With a few strong strokes he reached the child.*
3 a soft gentle movement of your hand across something: *Give the cat a stroke.*
4 a stroke of luck something lucky that happens to you: *By a stroke of luck we got the last hotel room.*

stroke[2] *verb* (*present participle* **stroking**, *past* **stroked**)
to move your hand over something gently: *He stroked the baby's head.*

stroll[1] /strəʊl/ *verb*
to walk slowly: *We strolled through the park.*

stroll[2] *noun*
a slow walk for pleasure: *Let's go for a stroll.*

strong /strɒŋ/ *adjective*
1 having power or force: *He is a strong man.* | *She is a strong swimmer.* ⇨ opposite WEAK
2 not easy to break or damage: *I need a strong rope.* | *Use very strong glass that won't break.*
3 having a lot of power or influence: *Is he a strong leader?* | *She has a strong personality.*
4 strong feelings, ideas, etc are very important to you: *His religious beliefs are strong.* | *It is a subject that causes strong emotions in people.*
5 a strong smell or taste is easy to notice: *This cheese has a strong flavour.* | *There was a strong smell of gas.*

strong·ly /'strɒŋlɪ/ *adverb*
1 if you believe something strongly, you think it is important
2 tasting or smelling of something very noticeable: *The house smells strongly of fish.*

struck /strʌk/
the past tense and past participle of the verb **strike**

struc·ture /'strʌktʃər/ *noun*
1 something that has been built: *The new hospital will be a very tall structure.* | *He is an engineer who designs structures like bridges.*
2 the way in which something is arranged: *The structure **of** the company will not change.* | *Scientists are learning more about the structure of the brain.*

A B C D E F G H I J K L M N O P Q R S T U V W X Y Z

strug·gle[1] /ˈstrʌgl/ *verb* (*present participle* **struggling**, *past* **struggled**)

1 to try to do something that is very difficult: *He was struggling* **to** *learn English.*

2 to fight: *She struggled with the man and screamed for help.*

struggle[2] *noun*

a fight: *The men were involved in a struggle.*

stub·born /ˈstʌbən/ *adjective*

not willing to change your ideas easily: *She won't do what I ask – she's very stubborn.* ⟡ same meaning OBSTINATE

stubbornly *adverb*: *She stubbornly refused to answer me.*

stuck /stʌk/

the past tense and past participle of the verb **stick**

stu·dent /ˈstjuːdnt/ *noun*

a person who studies at a school or university: *He is a medical student.*

studio

a television studio

stu·di·o /ˈstjuːdɪəʊ/ *noun*

1 a room or building where films or radio or television shows are made: *I'll show you the TV studio where I work.*

2 a room for working in, especially at painting or photography

stud·y[1] /ˈstʌdɪ/ *verb* (*past* **studied**)

1 to learn about something: *I am studying art.* | *She is studying for an exam.*

2 to look at something carefully: *Before we go we'll have to study the map.*

study[2] *noun* (*plural* **studies**)

1 a piece of work that someone does to find out about something: *He is doing a study* **of** *how much time people watch television.*

2 **studies** subjects that people study: *He will finish his studies next year.*

3 a room for working in

stuff[1] /stʌf/ *noun* (*no plural*)

any substance or material: *There's some white stuff on this plate.* | *What's this stuff on the floor?* | *The dress was made of some silky stuff.*

stuff[2] *verb*

1 to fill something with a substance: *The pillow was stuffed* **with** *feathers.*

2 to push something into something else quickly and untidily: *She stuffed the letter into her pocket.*

stuff·y /ˈstʌfɪ/ *adjective* (**stuffier**, **stuffiest**)

with no clean air: *This room seems stuffy – open a window.*

stum·ble /ˈstʌmbl/ *verb* (*present participle* **stumbling**, *past* **stumbled**)

to nearly fall when you are walking: *She stumbled over the cat in the dark.*

stump /stʌmp/ *noun*

part of something that is left when the rest of it is cut off: *He sat on a tree stump.*

stung /stʌŋ/

the past tense and past participle of the verb **sting**

stunk /stʌŋk/

the past participle of the verb **stink**

stu·pid /ˈstjuːpɪd/ *adjective*

not clever or reasonable: *How could you be so stupid?* | *I made a stupid mistake.*

stupidly *adverb*: *I stupidly forgot my purse and had to go back for it.*

stu·pid·i·ty /stjuːˈpɪdətɪ/ *noun* (*no plural*)

behaviour that is not clever or reasonable

stur·dy /ˈstɜːdɪ/ *adjective* (**sturdier**, **sturdiest**)

strong and not likely to break: *The child had sturdy legs.*

stut·ter /ˈstʌtəʳ/ *verb*

to speak with difficulty, repeating the first sound of a word or phrase: *"I c-c-can't help it," she stuttered.* ⟡ same meaning STAMMER

sty /staɪ/ *noun* (*plural* **sties**)

a place where pigs live

style /staɪl/ *noun*

1 a way of doing something: *I like his style* **of** *writing.*

2 the way of dressing that everyone likes at a particular time: *Styles from the 1970s are coming back in fashion.*

sub·ject /ˈsʌbdʒɪkt/ *noun*
1 something that you study: *English is one of our school subjects.*
2 something that you talk or write about: *She has written several books on the subject.* | *Please don't **change the** subject* (=talk about something else).
3 a person who belongs to a country: *She is a British subject.*
4 a word that usually comes before the verb in a sentence and shows who is doing the action of the verb. In the sentence 'Jane bought the bread', 'Jane' is the subject ⇨ compare OBJECT

sub·mar·ine /ˌsʌbməˈriːn/ *noun*
a ship that can travel under the water ⇨ see picture on page 206

sub·stance /ˈsʌbstəns/ *noun*
something you can touch like a liquid, a solid, or a powder: *Salt is a substance we use in cooking.*

sub·tract /səbˈtrækt/ *verb*
to take one number away from another: *If you subtract 3 from 5 you get 2.* ⇨ compare ADD

sub·trac·tion /səbˈtrækʃən/ *noun*
the process of subtracting one number from another ⇨ compare ADDITION

sub·urb /ˈsʌbɜːb/ *noun*
an area away from the centre of a city: *He lives in a suburb of London.*

suc·ceed /səkˈsiːd/ *verb*
to do what you have tried to do: *If you try hard, you'll succeed.* | *He succeeded in passing his driving test.* ⇨ opposite FAIL

suc·cess /səkˈses/ *noun*
1 (*no plural*) when you achieve what you have been trying to do: *Her success is due to hard work.* | *Have you had any success in finding her?*
2 (*plural* **successes**) someone or something that succeeds or that people like: *Her party was a great success.* ⇨ opposite (**1** and **2**) FAILURE

suc·cess·ful /səkˈsesfəl/ *adjective*
having succeeded: *He is a successful actor.* ⇨ opposite UNSUCCESSFUL

such /sʌtʃ/
1 like the person or thing you have just mentioned: *You were fighting and such*

behaviour is not allowed at school. | *What would you do in such a situation?*
2 **such as** for example: *I like sports such as tennis.*
3 used to make what you say stronger: *It's such a lovely day.* | *He's such an idiot.*

suck /sʌk/ *verb*
to pull liquid into your mouth with your lips: *The baby was sucking milk from its mother.*

sud·den /ˈsʌdn/ *adjective*
1 done or happening quickly or without being expected: *Her illness was very sudden.*
2 **all of a sudden** quickly and with no warning: *All of a sudden the lights went out.*

sud·den·ly /ˈsʌdnli/ *adverb*
quickly and unexpectedly: *I suddenly remembered that it was Jim's birthday.*

sue /sjuː/ *verb* (*present participle* **suing**, *past* **sued**)
to start a legal process to get money from someone who has harmed you

suede /sweɪd/ *noun* (*no plural*)
a material with a slightly rough surface, made from animal skin

suf·fer /ˈsʌfər/ *verb*
to be in pain or trouble: *She was suffering from a headache.*

suf·fer·ing /ˈsʌfərɪŋ/ *noun*
great pain or trouble that you experience: *There was a lot of suffering during the war.*

suf·fi·cient /səˈfɪʃnt/ *adjective*
enough: *This amount of food is sufficient to feed four people.*

suf·fix /ˈsʌfɪks/ *noun* (*plural* **suffixes**)
letters that you add to the end of a word to make a new word. For example, you add the suffix 'ness' to 'kind' to make the word 'kindness' ⇨ compare PREFIX

sug·ar /ˈʃʊɡər/ *noun* (*no plural*)
a substance made from some plants, used to make food sweet

sug·gest /səˈdʒest/ *verb*
to tell someone your idea about what should be done: *I suggested that it would be quicker to travel by train.*

sug·ges·tion /səˈdʒestʃən/ *noun*
an idea or plan that someone suggests: *Can I **make** a suggestion?*

suit [1] /suːt/ verb
1 to be right or acceptable for someone: *It's a small house, but it suits our needs.* | *It's difficult to find a date that suits everyone.*
2 to make someone look attractive: *That dress suits you.* ⟡ compare FIT

suit [2] noun
a set of clothes made from the same material, including a short coat with trousers or skirt: *I bought a dark brown suit.*

suit·able /ˈsuːtəbl/ adjective
right or acceptable for a particular set of conditions or purpose: *This toy is not suitable for young children.* | *We are hoping to find a suitable school.* ⟡ opposite UNSUITABLE

suit·case /ˈsuːtkeɪs/ noun
a case for carrying clothes etc, when you travel ⟡ compare BRIEFCASE ⟡ see picture at UNPACK

sulk /sʌlk/ verb
to feel angry for a time, and often not talk: *When we told her she couldn't come with us, she went and sulked in her room.*

sum /sʌm/ noun
1 a simple calculation using numbers: *Children learn to do sums at school.*
2 an amount of money: *I've had to spend a large sum of money on my car.*

sum·mer /ˈsʌmər/ noun
the season between spring and autumn, when it is warmest: *Are you going on holiday this summer?* ⟡ compare WINTER ⟡ see picture on page 194

sum·mit /ˈsʌmɪt/ noun
the top of a mountain

sum·mon /ˈsʌmən/ verb
to order someone to come to a place: *They were summoned to the head teacher's office.*

sun /sʌn/ noun
1 the large ball of fire in the sky that gives light and heat ⟡ compare MOON
2 (no plural) the light and heat from the sun: *Sit in the sun and get warm.*

sun·bathe /ˈsʌnbeɪð/ verb (present participle **sunbathing**, past **sunbathed**)
to lie in the sun to make your body brown

sun·burn /ˈsʌnbɜːn/ noun (no plural)
when the sun has burned your skin ⟡ compare SUNTAN

Sun·day /ˈsʌndeɪ, -di/ noun
the seventh day of the week after Saturday and before Monday

sung /sʌŋ/
the past participle of the verb **sing**

sun·glass·es /ˈsʌnglɑːsɪz/ plural noun
glasses with dark glass in them that you wear when it is very sunny or bright

sunk /sʌŋk/
the past participle of the verb **sink**

sun·light /ˈsʌnlaɪt/ noun (no plural)
natural light from the sun: *He walked out into the bright sunlight.*

sun·ny /ˈsʌni/ adjective (**sunnier**, **sunniest**)
full of bright light from the sun: *The day was bright and sunny.* ⟡ see picture on page 194

sun·rise /ˈsʌnraɪz/ noun
the time in the morning when the sun first appears and day begins

sun·set /ˈsʌnset/ noun
the time in the evening when the sun disappears and night begins

sun·shine /ˈsʌnʃaɪn/ noun (no plural)
light and heat from the sun: *The children played in the sunshine.*

sun·tan /ˈsʌntæn/ noun
also **tan** skin that has turned brown from being in the sun: *She's got a great suntan.* ⟡ compare SUNBURN

su·perb /sjuːˈpɜːb/ adjective
very good: *The food here is superb.* ⟡ same meaning EXCELLENT

su·pe·ri·or /suːˈpɪəriər/ adjective
better than other things: *She was superior to other candidates for the job.*

su·per·la·tive /suːˈpɜːlətɪv/ noun
a word or a form of a word that shows that something is the best, worst, biggest, smallest, etc of its kind. The superlative of 'fast' is 'fastest' ⟡ compare COMPARATIVE

su·per·mar·ket /ˈsuːpəmɑːkɪt/ noun
a big shop selling food and other things for your home ⟡ see picture on page 201

su·per·son·ic /ˌsuːpəˈsɒnɪk/ adjective
faster than the speed of sound: *a supersonic plane*

su·per·sti·tion /ˌsuːpəˈstɪʃn/ *noun*
a belief that some things are lucky and some things are not: *It is only a superstition that the number 13 is unlucky.*

su·per·vise /ˈsuːpəvaɪz/ *verb* (*present participle* **supervising**, *past* **supervised**)
to watch people to make sure that they do the right things when they work or that they behave correctly: *All the exams are supervised by the teachers.*

su·per·vi·sion /ˌsuːpəˈvɪʒn/ *noun* (*no plural*)
watching over people to make sure that they do the right things when they work: *We worked under the teacher's supervision.*

sup·per /ˈsʌpəʳ/ *noun*
an evening meal ⇨ compare DINNER

sup·ply[1] /səˈplaɪ/ *noun*
1 (*plural* **supplies**) an amount of something that you keep so that you can use some when it is needed: *We keep a large supply of food in the house.* | *He was given a month's supply of medicine by the doctor.*
2 supplies (*plural noun*) things that you need: *We cannot get supplies to the village because of the snow.* | *We need to buy supplies for a camping trip.*

supply[2] *verb* (*past* **supplied**)
to give or sell something that someone needs: *The company supplies paper to the printers.* | *We supply schools with books.*

sup·port[1] /səˈpɔːt/ *verb*
1 to hold or keep something up: *These posts support the roof.* | *I held on to the railings to support myself.*
2 to help someone or something: *My family supported me when I decided to become an actor.*
3 to want a team, group, etc to succeed: *Which football team do you support?*

support[2] *noun*
1 (*no plural*) friendly help that you give to someone: *Thank you for your support.* | *Teachers like it when they have the support of the parents.*
2 something that holds something else up: *There are two large wooden supports that hold up the roof.*

sup·pose[1] /səˈpəʊz/ *verb* (*present participle* **supposing**, *past* **supposed**)
to think that something is probably true or that something will probably happen: *I suppose he's gone home.* | *He'll come with us, I suppose.*

suppose[2]
also **supposing** used to ask what might happen: *Suppose Mum found out? She'd go crazy!*

sup·posed /səˈpəʊzd/
be supposed (a) to be expected or intended to happen, especially when it does not: *There's supposed to be a bus at half past four.* | *I thought this was supposed to be a holiday.* **(b)** to do something because of a rule: *You're not supposed to smoke in here.*

su·preme /suːˈpriːm/ *adjective*
highest, best, or most important: *The most important law court in the United States is the Supreme Court.*

sure /ʃʊəʳ/ *adjective*
1 very confident or definite: *I am sure that I put the money in the bank.* | *I'm not sure how many people are coming to the party.*
2 make sure (a) to check that something is true or that something has been done: *I'll just make sure the car's locked.* | *He phoned to make sure that we got home safely.* **(b)** to arrange that something will definitely happen: *Make sure you get here before 3 o'clock.*

sure·ly /ˈʃʊəlɪ/ *adverb*
1 used to show that you are surprised at something: *Surely you're not leaving yet?*
2 used when you think something must be true: *There must surely be some explanation.*

surf[1] /sɜːf/ *noun* (*no plural*)
white waves when they come onto land

surf[2] *verb*
to ride on a special narrow board over waves as they come in to the land

sur·face /ˈsɜːfɪs/ *noun*
the outside or top part of something: *Don't scratch the surface of the table.* | *Men have walked on the surface of the moon.*

surf·board /ˈsɜːfbɔːd/ *noun*
a special narrow piece of wood or plastic that people lie or stand on when travelling over big waves as they come in to the land

surf

surfing

surf·ing /'sɜːfɪŋ/ *noun (no plural)*
the sport of riding on a surfboard over waves as they come in to the land ⇨ see picture on page 196

sur·geon /'sɜːdʒən/ *noun*
a doctor who cuts into people's bodies to repair parts inside them

sur·ge·ry /'sɜːdʒəri/ *noun*
1 (*no plural*) the cutting open of a part of someone's body to repair parts inside them ⇨ compare OPERATION
2 (*plural* **surgeries**) a place where you can go to see a doctor or DENTIST

sur·name /'sɜːneɪm/ *noun*
your family name ⇨ compare FIRST NAME

sur·prise¹ /sə'praɪz/ *noun*
1 something that is not expected: *Don't tell him about the present – it's a surprise. | What a surprise to see you here!*
2 (*no plural*) the feeling that you have when something unexpected happens: *I looked at him in surprise.*
3 take someone by surprise to happen unexpectedly: *When he offered me the job it took me completely by surprise.*

surprise² *verb (present participle* **surprising**, *past* **surprised**)
to do something that someone does not expect: *His anger surprised me.*

sur·ren·der /sə'rendəʳ/ *verb*
to stop fighting because you know that you cannot win: *They were determined never to surrender.*

sur·round /sə'raʊnd/ *verb*
to be or go all round something: *The fence surrounds the school. | Jill sat on the floor surrounded by boxes.*

sur·round·ings /sə'raʊndɪŋz/ *plural noun*
the area around something: *The house is in beautiful surroundings.*

sur·viv·al /sə'vaɪvəl/ *noun (no plural)*
continuing to live after a difficult or dangerous time: *We had little hope of survival.*

sur·vive /sə'vaɪv/ *verb (present participle* **surviving**, *past* **survived**)
to continue to live after a dangerous or difficult time: *The man was very ill, but he survived.*

sus·pect¹ /sə'spekt/ *verb*
1 to think that something is true, although you do not know: *He seems poor, but I suspect **that** he has quite a lot of money.*
2 to think that someone may be guilty of a crime: *He's suspected of murder.*

sus·pect² /'sʌspekt/ *noun*
a person who you think has done something wrong: *Police have taken the suspect to the police station.*

sus·pend /sə'spend/ *verb*
1 to hang something from something else: *The lamp was suspended **from** the ceiling.*
2 to delay or stop something: *We suspended the building work during the rain.*

sus·pense /sə'spens/ *noun (no plural)*
a feeling of not knowing what is going to happen next: *Don't keep us **in** suspense. Tell us what happened!*

sus·pi·cion /sə'spɪʃn/ *noun*
1 a feeling that something may be true: *She had a suspicion that Steve might be right.*
2 a feeling that something may be wrong: *I have a suspicion that he's not telling the truth.*

sus·pi·cious /sə'spɪʃəs/ *adjective*
1 not willing to trust someone or something: *I am suspicious **of** her ideas.*
2 making you feel that something is wrong: *His behaviour was very suspicious.*

swal·low¹ /'swɒləʊ/ *verb*
to take food or drink down your throat and into your stomach: *She swallowed some milk.*

swallow[2] *noun*
a small bird with a tail divided into two parts

swam /swæm/
the past tense of the verb **swim**

swamp /swɒmp/ *noun*
land that is always soft and very wet

swan /swɒn/ *noun*
a large white water bird with a long curved neck

swap /swɒp/ *verb (present participle* **swapping**, *past* **swapped**)
to exchange something you have for something that someone else has: *Can I swap seats with you?*

sway /sweɪ/ *verb*
to move slowly from side to side: *The trees swayed in the wind.*

swear /sweər/ *verb (present participle* **swearing**, *past* **swore** /swɔːr/, *past participle* **sworn** /swɔːn/)
1 to use very bad words: *He was so angry that he swore at his mother.*
2 to promise something: *I swear I won't tell anyone your secret.*

sweat[1] /swet/ *noun (no plural)*
water that comes out of your skin when you are hot or afraid: *Sweat poured down his face as he ran.*

sweat[2] *verb*
to produce water through your skin because you are hot or afraid: *She was sweating as she reached the top of the hill.*

sweat·er /swetər/ *noun*
a piece of clothing, usually made of wool, that covers the top part of your body ⇨ same meaning JUMPER

sweat·shirt /swetʃɜːt/ *noun*
a soft thick shirt with no buttons down the front

sweep /swiːp/ *verb (present participle* **sweeping**, *past* **swept** /swept/)
1 to clean the dirt from something using a brush: *I swept the floor.* ⇨ same meaning BRUSH
2 to move quickly: *The crowd swept through the gates.*

sweet[1] /swiːt/ *adjective*
1 containing or tasting of sugar: *I don't like sweet coffee.*
2 kind, gentle, and friendly: *What a sweet smile she has!*

sweet[2] *noun*
1 *British* a small piece of sweet food made of sugar or chocolate (*American* **candy**): *Eating too many sweets is bad for your teeth.*
2 sweet food served at the end of a meal ⇨ same meaning PUDDING, DESSERT

sweet·corn /swiːtkɔːn/ *noun (no plural)*
the yellow seeds of a tall plant, eaten as food

sweet·heart /swiːthɑːt/ *noun*
someone that you love: *Hello, sweetheart. Did you have a nice day?*

swell /swel/ *verb (present participle* **swelling**, *past* **swelled**, *past participle* **swollen** /swəʊlən/)
to become larger: *A bee stung my hand and it is swelling up.* | *After the rain, the river swelled.*

swell·ing /swelɪŋ/ *noun*
a place on your body that has become larger than usual: *I have pain and swelling in my knee.*

swept /swept/
the past tense and past participle of the verb **sweep**

swerve /swɜːv/ *verb (present participle* **swerving**, *past* **swerved**)
to move suddenly to one side when you are moving quickly: *The car swerved to avoid the dog.*

swift /swɪft/ *adjective*
fast: *She is a swift runner.*

swim[1] /swɪm/ *verb (present participle* **swimming**, *past* **swam** /swæm/, *past participle* **swum** /swʌm/)
to move through water by using your legs and arms: *He swam across the river.* | *She swims in the pool every day.* ⇨ see picture on page 196

swim[2] *noun*
an act or time of swimming: *Shall we **go for a** swim?*

swimm·er /swɪmər/ *noun*
someone who swims: *Gina is a good swimmer.*

swim·ming /swɪmɪŋ/ *noun (no plural)*
the act of moving through the water using your arms and legs: *I'm going to have swimming lessons.*

swimming pool /swɪmɪŋ puːl/ *noun*
also **pool** an area of water built for people to swim in

A B C D E F G H I J K L M N O P Q R **S** T U V W X Y Z

swim·suit /'swɪmsuːt/ *noun*
a piece of clothing that a girl or woman wears for swimming

swing¹ /swɪŋ/ *verb (present participle* **swinging**, *past* **swung** /swʌŋ/)
to move freely from a fixed point: *The boy swung on the rope tied to a tree.* | *The door was swinging in the wind.*

swing

swing² *noun*
a seat hanging from a frame or tree, for children to play on

switch¹ /swɪtʃ/ *noun (plural* **switches**)
the part that you press on a machine, light, etc so that it starts or stops working

switch² *verb*
1 to change: *I used to cook on an electric cooker, but I've switched to gas.*
2 switch something off to make something stop working by pushing a switch: *Could you switch the television off?*
3 switch something on to make something start working by pushing a switch: *Could you switch on the light?*

swol·len /'swəʊlən/
the past participle of the verb **swell**

swoop /swuːp/ *verb*
to fly down very quickly: *The bird swooped down to catch a fish.*

sword /sɔːd/ *noun*
a sharp pointed weapon like a long knife that you hold in your hand and fight with

swore /swɔːr/
the past tense of the verb **swear**

sworn /swɔːn/
the past participle of the verb **swear**

swum /swʌm/
the past participle of the verb **swim**

swung /swʌŋ/
the past tense and past participle of the verb **swing**

syl·la·ble /'sɪləbl/ *noun*
a part of a word that contains one vowel sound. For example, there are two syllables in 'window', 'win' and 'dow'

sym·bol /'sɪmbl/ *noun*
a sign that means or shows something else: *The symbol for a church on a map is usually a cross.* | *'O' is the symbol for 'oxygen'.*

sym·pa·thet·ic /ˌsɪmpə'θetɪk/ *adjective*
kind and understanding about someone else's unhappiness: *When I told her why I was worried, she was very sympathetic.* | *I have a sympathetic doctor.*
⇨ opposite UNSYMPATHETIC

sym·pa·thy /'sɪmpəθɪ/ *noun (plural* **sympathies**)
a feeling of understanding and support for someone's hurt or unhappiness: *I have been a prisoner, so I have a lot of sympathy with other people in prison.* | *I have no sympathy for Joan. It's her own fault.*

symp·tom /'sɪmptəm/ *noun*
a sign of something, especially an illness: *Fever is a symptom of many illnesses.*

syn·a·gogue /'sɪnəgɒg/ *noun*
a building where Jewish people go for religious services

syn·o·nym /'sɪnənɪm/ *noun*
a word that has the same meaning as another word. 'Shut' and 'close' are synonyms

sy·ringe /sə'rɪndʒ/ *noun*
an instrument with a needle at one end for giving people medicine through their skin ⇨ see picture at NEEDLE

syr·up /'sɪrəp/ *noun (no plural)*
a thick liquid made by boiling sugar in water or fruit juice

sys·tem /'sɪstəm/ *noun*
a group of things or ideas working together in one arrangement: *We have a large system of railways.* | *What system of government do you have in your country?*

T, t /tiː/

the twentieth letter of the English alphabet

ta·ble /ˈteɪbl/ *noun*

a piece of furniture with a flat top supported by legs: *The family was sitting at the kitchen table.*

ta·ble·cloth /ˈteɪblklɒθ/ *noun*

a cloth that you put over a table

ta·ble·spoon /ˈteɪblspuːn/ *noun*

a large spoon that you use for serving food

tab·let /ˈtæblɪt/ *noun*

a small hard ball of medicine that you swallow when you are not well ⇨ same meaning PILL

table tennis

playing table tennis

table ten·nis /ˈteɪbl ˌtenɪs/ *noun (no plural)*

a game in which two or four players hit a small ball over a net across a table: *Let's have a game of table tennis.* ⇨ same meaning PING-PONG

tab·loid /ˈtæblɔɪd/ *noun*

a newspaper that has small pages, short simple articles, and usually not much serious news: *Don't believe everything you read in the tabloids.*

tack·le /ˈtækl/ *verb (present participle* **tackling**, *past* **tackled***)*

1 to begin work on something: *I must tackle that report this evening.*

2 to try to take the ball away from someone in a game such as football: *He tackled the other player and kicked the ball across the field.*

tact /tækt/ *noun (no plural)*

the ability to do or say things without making people feel unhappy or angry

tact·ful /ˈtæktfəl/ *adjective*

careful not to say or do things that hurt or offend people: *She's very upset, so try to be as tactful as possible.* ⇨ opposite TACTLESS

tact·less /ˈtæktləs/ *adjective*

not careful about hurting or offending people: *His tactless remarks upset her very much.* ⇨ opposite TACTFUL

tag /tæg/ *noun*

a small piece of paper or material fixed to something to give information about it: *Look for a name tag on the coat to see who it belongs to.* | *a price tag*

tail /teɪl/ *noun*

the part of an animal that sticks out at the end of its back: *The dog was happy to see her and wagged its tail.*

tai·lor /ˈteɪlər/ *noun*

a person who makes clothes for people

take /teɪk/ *verb (present participle* **taking**, *past* **took** /tʊk/, *past participle* **taken** /ˈteɪkən/)

1 to get hold of something: *The mother took her child by the hand.* | *Shall I take your coat?*

2 to carry something to another place: *Can you take this shopping home for me, please?*

3 to go with someone to another place: *I'll take you to the station.*

4 to remove something from a place or to steal it: *Who has taken my chocolate from the fridge?* | *The thief took all the jewellery.*

5 to swallow medicine: *I've taken some medicine for my cough.*

6 to travel in a vehicle: *We took a taxi.*

7 to need a particular amount of time: *The journey to London takes three hours.*

8 take after someone to look or behave like an older member of your family: *He takes after his father.*

9 take care of someone to look after someone: *Who will take care of me when I am old?*

10 take it for granted that... to believe something without having any doubts about it: *I took it for granted that I would be invited to my brother's wedding.*

11 take off when a plane takes off, it

leaves the ground ⇨ opposite LAND ⇨ see picture at LAND

12 take something off to remove a piece of clothing: *He took his coat off.*

13 take place to happen: *The accident took place on Saturday night.* ⇨ look at HAPPEN

14 take a seat something you say when you are inviting someone to sit down

take·a·way /'teɪkəweɪ/ *noun*

1 a cooked meal that you buy to eat at home or outside: *We had a takeaway for our supper last night.*

2 a place that sells cooked meals for you to eat somewhere else: *Let's go to the Chinese takeaway.*

tak·en /'teɪkən/

the past participle of the verb **take**

tale /teɪl/ *noun*

a story: *He told us a long and complicated tale.*

tal·ent /'tælənt/ *noun*

the ability to do a particular thing very well: *My sister has a talent **for** singing.*

tal·ent·ed /'tæləntɪd/ *adjective*

able to do a particular thing very well: *He was a talented actor.*

talk¹ /tɔːk/ *verb*

to say things to someone: *They were talking **about** the weather.* | *Their baby is just learning to talk.*

talk² *noun*

1 a conversation: *We had a long talk.*

2 an informal speech: *The singer came to our school to give a talk on music.*

talk·a·tive /'tɔːkətɪv/ *adjective*

someone who is talkative likes to talk a lot

tall /tɔːl/ *adjective*

1 higher than other people or other things: *James is taller than Paul, but Richard is the tallest.* | *The office was in a tall building.* ⇨ see picture on page 202

2 used for talking about someone's height: *He is 1 metre 80 centimetres tall.* | *How tall are you?*

tame¹ /teɪm/ *adjective*

a tame animal is trained to live with people: *He had a tame monkey.* ⇨ opposite WILD

tame² *verb* (*present participle* **taming**, *past* **tamed**)

to train a wild animal to live with people: *Monkeys are easily tamed and one soon learns to love them.*

tan /tæn/ *noun*

also **suntan** the brown colour of your skin after you have been out in the hot sun: *She got a tan on holiday.*

tan·ge·rine /ˌtændʒə'riːn/ *noun*

a fruit like a small sweet orange

tan·gle /'tæŋgl/ *noun*

a knotted mass of string, hair, or thread: *The string was in a tangle.*

tan·gled /'tæŋgld/ *adjective*

twisted into knots: *Her hair was all tangled.*

tank /tæŋk/ *noun*

1 a container to hold liquids or gas: *The petrol tank in our car is empty.*

2 a heavy vehicle with guns on it

tank·er /'tæŋkər/ *noun*

a ship or road vehicle that carries large amounts of oil or other liquids: *an oil tanker*

tap¹ /tæp/ *verb* (*present participle* **tapping**, *past* **tapped**)

to hit something lightly: *Lucy's mother tapped on her bedroom door to see if she was awake.*

tap² *noun*

something that you turn on or off in order to control the flow of water from a pipe: *I turned the tap on to wash my face.*

tap danc·ing /'tæp ˌdɑːnsɪŋ/ *noun* (no plural)

a type of dancing in which dancers wear special shoes to make a sound when they move their feet to the music

tape¹ /teɪp/ *noun*

1 a long thin band of plastic inside a small case, on which you can record sound or pictures: *Which tape (=of music) shall we listen to next?*

2 a long thin band of cloth or paper

tape² *verb* (*present participle* **taping**, *past* **taped**)

1 to record music, a film, etc: *Shall we tape the film and watch it tomorrow?*

2 to fasten something with tape that sticks: *She closed the box and taped it.*

tape mea·sure /'teɪp ˌmeʒəʳ/ *noun*
a narrow band of cloth or plastic used for measuring things

tape re·cord·er /'teɪp rɪˌkɔːdəʳ/ *noun*
a machine that records and plays music and other sounds

tar /tɑːʳ/ *noun (no plural)*
a thick black substance that is used in making roads

tar·get /'tɑːgɪt/ *noun*
something that you try to hit, for example with a gun: *I hit the target with my first shot.*

tar·mac /'tɑːmæk/ *noun (no plural)*
a mixture of TAR and very small stones, used to make the surface of roads

tart /tɑːt/ *noun*
a small PIE without a top, usually with fruit in it: *Her jam tarts are excellent.* ⇨ compare PIE

tar·tan /'tɑːtn/ *noun*
a cloth with a special pattern of squares on it

task /tɑːsk/ *noun*
a piece of work that someone has to do: *Washing the dishes is a task I do not enjoy.* ⇨ same meaning JOB

taste¹ /teɪst/ *noun*
1 the special sense by which we know one food from another: *My sense of taste isn't very good; I have a cold.*
2 the feeling that a particular food gives you when it is in your mouth: *Chocolate has a sweet taste.*
3 someone's particular choice: *She has good taste **in** clothes.*

taste² *verb (present participle* **tasting**, *past* **tasted**)
1 to try food or drink by taking a small amount into your mouth: *Can I taste your drink?*
2 to have a particular feeling in your mouth: *This wine tastes sweet.*

tast·y /'teɪstɪ/ *adjective*
having a very nice taste: *It was a tasty meal.*

tat·too¹ /tæ'tuː/ *verb*
to draw a picture or write words on

tattoo

someone's skin using a needle and ink

tattoo² *noun*
a picture or words that are put on someone's skin using a needle and ink

taught /tɔːt/
the past tense and past participle of the verb **teach**

tax¹ /tæks/ *noun (plural* **taxes**)
money that must be paid to the government from the money that you earn or when you buy something: *Taxes on alcohol and cigarettes have gone up again.*

tax² *verb*
to make people pay an amount of money to the government: *Alcohol is heavily taxed.*

tax·i /'tæksɪ/ *noun*
a car with a driver who you pay to take you somewhere: *I'll take a taxi to the station.* ⇨ see pictures on pages 200 and 206

tea /tiː/ *noun*
1 (*no plural*) a hot drink made by pouring boiling water onto special dry leaves: *I'll make a pot of tea.*
2 a cup of tea: *Two teas, please.*
3 *British* an evening meal: *What are we having for tea tonight?*
4 a small meal in the afternoon when people eat bread and cakes and drink tea

teach /tiːtʃ/ *verb (past* **taught** /tɔːt/)
1 to give people lessons in a particular subject, especially in a school: *Ms Jones teaches history.*
2 to show someone how to do something: *Who taught you to ride a bicycle?* ⇨ look at KNOW

teach·er /'tiːtʃəʳ/ *noun*
a person who gives lessons, especially in a school

team /tiːm/ *noun*
1 a group of people who play games against other groups: *I'm trying to get into the football team.*
2 a group of people who work together on something: *There is a strong research team working on the project.*

tea·pot /'tiːpɒt/ *noun*
a container used for making and serving tea

tear¹ /tɪəʳ/ *noun*
1 a drop of water from your eye: *Tears were rolling down her cheeks.*

tattoo

team

a football team

2 in tears crying: *She was in tears all morning.*

tear² /teəʳ/ *noun*
a hole in a piece of paper, cloth etc: *He had a tear in his trousers.*

tear³ /teəʳ/ *verb (past* **tore** /tɔːʳ/, *past participle* **torn** /tɔːn/)
1 to make a hole in something: *He tore his trousers.* I *She tore the piece of paper in half.*
2 to pull something roughly from a place: *You can tear a page out of my notebook.*
3 tear something up to destroy something made of paper by pulling it into small pieces: *She tore up the letter.*

tease /tiːz/ *verb (present participle* **teasing**, *past* **teased**)
to make fun of a person, either in play or unkindly: *You must not tease your little sister.*

tea·spoon /'tiːspuːn/ *noun*
a small spoon used to measure small amounts of food or to mix sugar or milk in tea, coffee, etc

tech·ni·cal /'teknɪkl/ *adjective*
relating to the practical skills, knowledge, etc used in science and industry: *There have been a lot of technical advances in this field.*

tech·ni·cian /tek'nɪʃn/ *noun*
a person who has special knowledge about particular machines or instruments: *Anne is training to be a technician.*

tech·nique /tek'niːk/ *noun*
a special skill or way of doing something: *new teaching techniques*

tech·nol·o·gy /tek'nɒlədʒɪ/ *noun (no plural)*
knowledge about science, and about the making of machines, instruments, etc: *Modern technology has made many jobs easier.*

ted·dy bear /'tedɪ beəʳ/ *noun*
a soft toy that looks like a bear

te·di·ous /'tiːdɪəs/ *adjective*
long and boring: *It was a long and tedious story.* ⇨ same meaning BORING

teen·ag·er /'tiːneɪdʒəʳ/ *noun*
a person who is between 13 and 19 years old ⇨ same meaning ADOLESCENT

teeth /tiːθ/
the plural of **tooth** ⇨ see picture at HEAD

tel·e·phone¹ /'telɪfəʊn/ *noun*
also **phone** a piece of equipment that you use to speak to someone who is in another place: *Can I use your telephone, please?* I *Will you answer the telephone?* ⇨ see picture on page 204

telephone² *verb (present participle* **telephoning**, *past* **telephoned**)
also **phone** to speak to someone by telephone: *I telephoned the office but there was no reply.* I *I telephoned the restaurant and spoke to the manager.*

telephone box /'telɪfəʊn ˌbɒks/ *noun (plural* **telephone boxes**)
a small shelter in the street where there is a public telephone

telephone num·ber /'telɪfəʊn ˌnʌmbəʳ/ *noun*
the number that you ring when you want to talk to someone on the telephone: *Do you have John's telephone number?*

tele·scope /'telɪskəʊp/ *noun*
an instrument you look through that makes things that are far away seem larger or nearer

telescope

tel·e·text /'telɪtekst/ *noun (no plural)*
a system for providing written information on television

tele·vi·sion /'telɪvɪʒn/
1 a thing shaped like a box with a screen that you use to watch programmes: *Turn the television on.* ⇨ see picture on page 197

2 (*no plural*) the programmes that you can watch on a television: *They were watching television.*
3 on television shown on the television: *What's on television tonight?*

tel·e·work·er /'telɪˌwɜːkəʳ/ *noun*
someone who works from home using a computer and email

tell /tel/ *verb* (*past* **told** /təʊld/)
1 to speak to someone or give them some information: *Tell me what happened.*
2 to give someone advice or instructions: *I told him to see a doctor about his chest pains.* I *Dad told me to be home by ten.*
3 tell someone off to speak angrily to someone because they have done something wrong: *My mother told me off for swearing.*
4 tell tales to say something that is not true about someone else, especially to cause them trouble: *Charlie is always telling tales about Susie.*
5 I told you so something you say to someone who did not believe what you said earlier, but must now accept it

tel·ly /'telɪ/ *noun* (*plural* **tellies**)
a television

tem·per /'tempəʳ/ *noun*
1 the way you feel, especially when you are angry: *He was in a bad temper all day.*
2 lose your temper to become angry suddenly

tem·pera·ture /'temprətʃəʳ/ *noun*
1 the amount of heat or cold: *Water boils at a temperature of 100 degrees.*
2 have a temperature to have a higher body temperature than usual, especially because you are ill: *I took his temperature in the night, and it was very high.*

tem·ple /'templ/ *noun*
1 a building where people in some religions go to pray, sing, etc
2 the part of your head above and in front of your ears

tem·po·ra·ril·y /'tempərərəlɪ, 'tempərəlɪ/ *adverb*
for a short time only: *The shop is temporarily closed.*

tem·po·ra·ry /'tempərərɪ, 'tempərɪ/ *adjective*
existing or happening for a short time

only: *I'm getting a temporary job in the summer.* ⇨ compare PERMANENT

tempt /tempt/ *verb*
1 to try to make someone do something wrong: *He was tempted by the money he could make through a life of crime.*
2 to make someone want to do something: *Can I tempt you to eat some more of this cake?*

ten /ten/
the number 10

ten·ant /'tenənt/ *noun*
a person who pays money to use a house or land

tend /tend/ *verb*
tend to to be likely to do a particular thing: *I tend to get tired in the evening.*

ten·den·cy /'tendənsɪ/ *noun* (*plural* **tendencies**)
something that happens regularly: *She has a tendency to shout when she gets angry.*

ten·der /'tendəʳ/ *adjective*
1 soft, and easy to eat: *The meat was very tender.* ⇨ opposite TOUGH
2 kind and gentle: *She had a tender expression on her face.*

ten·nis /'tenɪs/ *noun* (*no plural*)
a game played by two or four people in which you hit a ball over a net: *Let's have a game of tennis.* ⇨ see picture on page 196

tense¹ /tens/ *adjective*
1 nervous and worried: *The players were tense at the start of the game.*
2 muscles that are tense feel tight and stiff: *His neck muscles were very tense.* ⇨ opposite (**1** and **2**) RELAXED

tense² *noun*
the form of a verb that shows when the action of the verb happens. 'I look' and 'I am looking' are present tenses; 'I looked', 'I was looking', and 'I have looked' are past tenses; 'I will look' and 'I am going to look' are future tenses

tent /tent/ *noun*
a shelter made of thick cloth spread over poles: *It was difficult to put up the tent while it was raining heavily.* ⇨ see picture on page 193

tenth /tenθ/ *adjective, noun*
1 10th
2 one of ten equal parts

A B C D E F G H I J K L M N O P Q R S T U V W X Y Z

term /tɜːm/ *noun*
1 a fixed length of time: *He was made captain of the football team for a term of one year.*
2 a part of the school year: *The summer term starts soon.*

ter·mi·nal /'tɜːmɪnl/ *noun*
a place where buses, planes, etc begin or end their journey

terms /tɜːmz/ *plural noun*
the things that you must agree to do or accept

ter·race /'terɪs/ *noun*
1 a level area cut from the side of a hill: *The grapes are grown on terraces stretching down the hillside.*
2 a flat area outside a house where you can sit
3 a row of houses joined together

ter·raced house /ˌterɪst 'haʊs/ *noun*
a house that is part of a row of houses all joined together

ter·ri·ble /'terəbl/ *adjective*
very bad or unpleasant: *Your writing is terrible.* I *The food in the hotel was terrible.*

ter·ri·bly /'terəbli/ *adverb*
1 very: *We're terribly sorry.*
2 very badly: *She behaved terribly.*

ter·ri·fic /tə'rɪfɪk/ *adjective*
very good or enjoyable: *We had a terrific holiday.*

ter·ri·fy /'terɪfaɪ/ *verb* (present participle **terrifying**, past **terrified**)
to frighten someone a lot: *I was terrified by the storm.*

ter·ri·tory /'terɪtri/ *noun* (plural **territories**)
1 land that a particular country controls: *This island is British territory.*
2 an area that one person or animal thinks is their own: *Some wild animals will not allow other animals to enter their territory.*

ter·ror /'terər/ *noun* (no plural)
great fear: *She screamed in terror.*

ter·ror·ist /'terərɪst/ *noun*
a person who uses violence to try to force a government to do something

test¹ /test/ *verb*
1 to use or check something to see if it works properly, is safe, etc: *Before he bought the car, he drove it to test it.*
2 to ask someone questions to see if they know the answers: *The teacher tested the children on their homework.*

test² *noun*
an examination: *I passed my driving test today.* I *There's a history test on Monday.*

test tube /'test tjuːb/ *noun*
a small thin glass container used in scientific tests

text /tekst/ *noun*
the writing in a book, magazine etc, not the pictures

tex·ture /'tekstʃər/ *noun*
the way that a surface, material, food etc feels when you touch it or taste it: *The fats in chocolate are what give it its smooth texture.*

text·book /'tekstbʊk/ *noun*
a book with facts about a particular subject that is used by students: *Can I borrow your history textbook?* ⇨ see picture on page 205

than /ðən; *strong* ðæn/
used when you are comparing things: *My brother is older than me.* I *Mary sings better than anyone else in the class.*

thank /θæŋk/ *verb*
1 to tell someone that you are pleased or grateful: *I thanked her for the present she sent me.*
2 **Thank you, Thanks** something you say to someone to show you are pleased or grateful: *Thank you for the present.* I *"Do you want another piece of cake?" "No, thank you."*

thank·ful /'θæŋkfəl/ *adjective*
grateful: *I was thankful that the exams were over.*

thanks /θæŋks/ *plural noun*
1 the things you say to show you are grateful: *I wrote a letter of thanks.*
2 **thanks to** because of: *Thanks to Peter, we won the game.* I *We've missed the train, thanks to you.*

that /ðət; *strong* ðæt/
1 (plural **those** /ðəʊz/) used to talk about someone or something that is a distance away from you: *They don't live in this house; they live in that one over there.*
2 (plural **those**) used to mean the one mentioned already or that is already known about: *Did you bring that photograph?* I *We played football and after that we went home.*

3 used instead of **who** or **which**: *He's the man that sold me the bicycle.*

4 used to join two parts of a sentence: *I think that it will rain tomorrow.*

5 so: *Please slow down – I can't walk that fast!*

6 That's it something you say when you have finished something

thatched /θætʃt/ *adjective*
used to describe a roof that is made of dry grass: *I live in a thatched cottage.*

thaw /θɔː/ *verb*
to become soft or liquid, after having been frozen: *The ice started to thaw.*

the /ðə, ðɪ; *strong* ðiː/
1 a word used before another, when it is clear who or what is meant: *There's a boy outside; it's the boy from the house across the road.*

2 used in front of the names of seas, rivers, deserts, etc: *the Mediterranean Sea*

3 used to talk about a class or group of people or things: *The rich* (=rich people) *should help the poor* (=poor people).

4 used when telling the date: *Tuesday the fifth of May*

theatre

acting in the theatre

thea·tre /ˈθɪətəʳ/ *noun*
a building in which people can go and see plays being acted: *We went to the theatre to see 'Macbeth'.*

theft /θeft/ *noun*
1 (*no plural*) the crime of stealing: *He was put in prison for theft.*

2 when someone steals something: *When she discovered the theft* **of** *her bag she went to the police.*

their /ðeəʳ/
belonging to them: *The children carried their bags to school.*

theirs /ðeəz/
something belonging to them: *They*
looked at our pictures, but they didn't show us theirs.*

them /ðəm; *strong* ðem/
the people or things that have already been mentioned: *We gave them some food.* | *We gave the presents to them.* | *I can't find my shoes; have you seen them?*

theme /θiːm/ *noun*
the main subject or idea in a book, film etc: *The theme of the film is love between two young people.*

them·selves /ðəmˈselvz/
1 the same people, animals, or things as the sentence is about: *The travellers washed themselves in the river.* | *They bought themselves a new car.*

2 used to give **they** a stronger meaning: *They decorated the house themselves.* | *The doctors themselves admit that the treatment does not always work.*

3 by themselves without help from anyone else: *The children did the drawing by themselves.*

4 by themselves alone: *They spent the afternoon by themselves.*

then /ðen/ *adverb*
1 at a particular time in the past or future: *She lived in a village then, but now she lives in a town.*

2 after something has happened: *We watched a film and then went for a meal.*

3 if that is true: *"I have lost my ticket." "Then you must pay again."*

theo·ry /ˈθɪərɪ/ *noun* (*plural* **theories**)
an idea that tries to explain something: *Darwin's theory of evolution*

there[1] /ðeəʳ/ *adverb*
in or near that place: *Don't sit there by the door; come and sit here.* | *Look at that man over there.* | *"Have you been to that new restaurant?" "Yes, we went there last night."*

there[2]
there is used to show that someone or something exists or that something happens: *There is a letter for you.* | *There was a policeman outside the house yesterday.* | *Is there anything I can do to help?*

there·fore /ˈðeəfɔːʳ/ *adverb*
for that reason: *He has broken his leg and therefore cannot walk.*

A
B
C
D
E
F
G
H
I
J
K
L
M
N
O
P
Q
R
S
T
U
V
W
X
Y
Z

ther·mom·e·ter /θəˈmɒmɪtəʳ/ noun
an instrument that measures the temperature of the air, your body, etc: *The doctor put a thermometer in my mouth to see if I had a high temperature.*

these /ðiːz/
the nearer ones: *I don't like these sweets; those are better.*

they /ðeɪ/
the people, animals, or things that have already been mentioned: *My friends are playing football and they want us to play too.*

they'd /ðeɪd/
1 they had: *They'd already left the house.*
2 they would: *They said they'd help.*

they'll /ðeɪl/
they will: *They'll probably arrive tomorrow.*

they're /ðeəʳ, ðeɪəʳ/
they are: *They're playing football.*

they've /ðeɪv/
they have: *They've gone shopping.*

thick /θɪk/ adjective
1 having a large distance between one side and the other: *The house has thick walls.*
2 growing very close together with not much space in between: *He had thick black hair.* ⇨ opposite (**1** and **2**) THIN
3 difficult to see through: *The smoke in the room was very thick. | Thick clouds hid the sun.*
4 a liquid that is thick does not flow easily: *This soup is too thick.* ⇨ opposite RUNNY
5 not clever: *Her brother's really thick.*

thief /θiːf/ noun (plural **thieves** /θiːvz/)
a person who steals: *The thief was sent to prison.* ⇨ compare ROBBER

thigh /θaɪ/ noun
the part of your leg above your knee

thin /θɪn/ adjective
1 having a small distance between one side and the other: *This string is too thin; I need a thicker piece. | He was wearing a thin summer jacket.* ⇨ opposite THICK
2 not having much fat on your body: *You should eat more; you're too thin.* ⇨ opposite FAT

3 a liquid that is thin flows very easily: *This soup is very thin.*

thing /θɪŋ/ noun
1 an object: *What is that thing you are carrying?*
2 an act or event: *That was a silly thing to do.*
3 things your belongings: *They packed all their things for the journey.*

think /θɪŋk/ verb (past **thought** /θɔːt/)
1 to use your mind to decide or remember something or to solve a problem: *Think carefully before you decide. | What are you thinking about?*
2 to have an opinion or to believe something: *What do you think of my singing? | "Do you think it will rain tomorrow?" "Yes, I think so." | "Is Emma coming to the party?" "I don't think so."*

thin·ly /ˈθɪnli/ adverb
without using or having much: *Spread the butter thinly.*

third /θɜːd/ noun, adjective
1 3rd
2 one of three equal parts: *Divide the cake into thirds.*

thirst /θɜːst/ noun (no plural)
the feeling of wanting or needing to drink something: *These children are suffering from thirst.* ⇨ compare HUNGER

thirst·y /ˈθɜːsti/ adjective
wanting or needing to drink something: *Can I have some water? I'm really thirsty.* ⇨ compare HUNGRY

thir·teen /θɜːˈtiːn/
the number 13

thir·teenth /θɜːˈtiːnθ/ adjective, noun
13th

thir·ti·eth /ˈθɜːtɪ-əθ/ adjective, noun
30th

thir·ty /ˈθɜːti/
the number 30

this /ðɪs/
1 (plural **these** /ðiːz/) used to talk about someone or something that is near to you: *This is my bowl; that bowl is yours. | Look – he gave me this ring.*
2 near to the present time: *Shall we go out this afternoon, or wait till tomorrow?*

thorn /θɔːn/ noun
a sharp or pointed part of a plant ⇨ see picture at ROSE

thor·ough /ˈθʌrə/ adjective
complete and careful: *The police made a thorough search of the house.*

thoroughly adverb: *He always does his work thoroughly.*

those /ðəʊz/
the ones further away: *I don't like these sweets; those are better.*

though /ðəʊ/
1 although: *Though he was poor, he was happy.*
2 **as though** as if: *She looked as though she had been crying.*

thought¹ /θɔːt/
the past tense and past participle of the verb **think**.

thought² noun
1 (*no plural*) when you think about something: *After much thought he decided not to buy the car.*
2 an idea or opinion that you have in your mind: *She's a quiet girl and doesn't share her thoughts.*

thou·sand /ˈθaʊznd/
the number 1,000: *a thousand years ago* | *thousands of miles away*

thou·sandth /ˈθaʊzndθ/ adjective, noun
1,000th

thread¹ /θred/ noun
a long single piece of cotton used for making, joining, or decorating cloth: *Mend it with a needle and thread.*

thread² verb
to put a thread through something: *I can't thread this needle.*

threat /θret/ noun
when you tell someone that you will hurt them or cause problems for them if they do not do what you want: *Threats were made against his life.*

threat·en /ˈθretn/ verb
to tell someone that you will hurt them or cause problems for them if they do not do what you want: *The thieves threatened to shoot him if he did not give them all his money.*

three /θriː/
the number 3

three-quar·ters /θriː ˈkwɔːtəz/ plural noun, adverb
three out of four equal parts of something: *The box was three-quarters full.*

threv /θruː/
the past tense of the verb **throw**

thrill¹ /θrɪl/ verb
to make someone very excited or pleased: *The traveller thrilled us with his stories.*

thrill² noun
a strong feeling of excitement or pleasure

throat /θrəʊt/ noun
1 the part at the back of your mouth, where you swallow: *He couldn't speak because he had a sore throat.*
2 the front part of your neck

throne /θrəʊn/ noun
a special chair on which a king or queen sits during special ceremonies

through /θruː/ preposition
1 from one side or end of something to the other: *The nail went through the wood.* | *We walked through the market to the car park.* | *She looked through the book until she found the page she wanted.* ⟿ see picture on page 208
2 by way of: *The thief got in through the window.*

through·out /θruːˈaʊt/ preposition
1 in every part of a place: *He is famous throughout the world.*
2 from the beginning to the end of something: *It rained throughout the night.*

throw

throwing a cricket ball

throw¹ /θrəʊ/ verb (present participle **throwing**, past **threw** /θruː/, past participle **thrown** /θrəʊn/)
1 to make something fly through the air by letting it go from your hand with a quick movement of your arm: *He threw the ball to me, and I caught it.* ⟿ see picture on page 207
2 **throw something away** to get rid of something you do not want ⟿ see picture on page 207

3 throw something out to get rid of something you do not want

4 throw someone out to force someone to leave a place: *He was thrown out of the restaurant because he was drunk.*

throw² *noun*
when you throw something such as a ball

thrown /θrəʊn/
the past participle of the verb **throw**

thrust /θrʌst/ *verb (past* **thrust***)*
to push suddenly and hard: *We thrust our way through the crowd.*

thud /θʌd/ *noun*
a sound made when something heavy and soft falls: *He fell out of the tree and landed on the ground with a thud.*

thug /θʌg/ *noun*
a violent person

thumb /θʌm/ *noun*
the short thick finger on your hand that is separate from your other fingers ⇨ see picture at HAND

thump /θʌmp/ *verb*
to hit someone or something hard with your hand tightly closed

thun·der /ˈθʌndəʳ/ *noun (no plural)*
the loud sound heard in the sky during a storm

thun·der·storm /ˈθʌndəstɔːm/ *noun*
a storm with heavy rain, thunder, and LIGHTNING

Thurs·day /ˈθɜːzdeɪ, -dɪ/ *noun*
the fourth day of the week after Wednesday and before Friday

tick¹ /tɪk/ *noun*
1 the sound made by a watch or clock
2 a mark ✔ that shows that something is correct or has been done: *All the correct answers had ticks beside them.*

tick² *verb*
1 to make the sound that a clock makes
2 to make a mark ✔ to show that something is correct or has been done: *My teacher ticked all the correct answers.*

tick·et /ˈtɪkɪt/ *noun*
a small piece of paper or card that shows you have paid to do something such as travel on a bus or plane or watch a film at the cinema: *a bus ticket*

tick·le /ˈtɪkl/ *verb (present participle* **tickling***, past* **tickled***)*
to touch a person lightly and make them laugh: *I tickled her under her arms.*

tide /taɪd/ *noun*
the rise and fall of the sea that happens twice every day: *We sailed the boat out at high tide.*

ti·dy¹ /ˈtaɪdɪ/ *adjective*
in good order, with things neatly arranged: *She kept her room very tidy.*
⇨ opposite UNTIDY

ti·dy² *verb (past* **tidied***)*
to make something tidy: *Tidy your room, please.*

tie

to tie   a tie

tie¹ /taɪ/ *noun*
a narrow band of cloth worn around the neck, especially by a man ⇨ see picture on page 203

tie² *verb (present participle* **tying***, past* **tied***)*
1 to fasten something with string or rope: *She tied the dog to the lamppost.*
2 tie something up to fasten something with string or rope: *Tie the parcel up with some string.*

ti·ger /ˈtaɪgəʳ/ *noun*
a large wild cat that has yellow fur with black bands

tight /taɪt/ *adjective*
1 pulled or drawn closely together: *She tied a very tight knot.* ⇨ opposite SLACK
2 fitting part of your body closely: *These shoes are too tight.* ⇨ opposite LOOSE

tight·en /ˈtaɪtn/ *verb*
to make or become tight: *I need to tighten this screw; it's very loose.*
⇨ opposite LOOSEN

tight·ly /ˈtaɪtlɪ/ *adverb*
firmly: *Tie the string tightly.*

tights /taɪts/
a very tight piece of clothing, made of thin material, that women wear to cover

their feet, legs and the lower part of their body: *a pair of tights*

tile /taɪl/ *noun*

a flat piece of baked clay used for covering roofs, floors, or walls: *The bathroom walls were covered in white tiles.*

till [1] /tɪl/ *noun*

a container or drawer for money in a shop

till [2]

until: *Let's wait till tomorrow.*

tilt /tɪlt/ *verb*

to move or cause something to move by lifting one end

tim·ber /'tɪmbə[r]/ *noun (no plural)*

wood prepared for building or trees to be used for building

time [1] /taɪm/ *noun*

1 (*no plural*) minutes, hours, days, weeks, months, years: *How do you spend your time at home?*

2 (*no plural*) a number of minutes, hours, etc: *It takes a long time to learn a new language.*

3 a particular occasion: *We'll go by car next time.*

4 a particular minute or hour of the day: *What time is it?*

5 times used to show how often something happens: *I go swimming three times a week.* | *How many times have you seen that film?*

6 times used when you compare things to say how much bigger, smaller, etc one thing is than another: *This school is three times bigger than my old one.*

7 times MULTIPLIED by: *Five times four is twenty.*

8 about time used to say that something should be done now: *It's about time you got a job.*

9 all the time continuously: *It rained all the time on holiday.*

10 at a time in one group or together: *She can only have two visitors at a time.*

11 at times sometimes: *I hated my job at times.*

12 for the time being for now or for a short while: *You can live with us for the time being.*

13 from time to time sometimes, but not very often: *We go to the theatre from time to time.*

14 have a good time to enjoy yourself: *Have a good time at the cinema.* | *Did you have a good time last night?*

15 just in time at the last possible moment: *The police arrived just in time to prevent the robbery.*

16 on time at the right time, neither early nor late: *The train arrived on time.*

17 take your time to use all the time you need to do something: *There's no hurry – take your time.*

18 tell the time to read a clock or watch correctly: *She can't tell the time yet; she's only two!*

time [2] *verb (present participle* **timing**, *past* **timed**)

to measure how long it takes to do something: *We timed the journey to London – it took three hours.*

time·ta·ble /'taɪmˌteɪbl/ *noun*

a list of times and dates when things will happen: *a train timetable* | *a school timetable*

tin /tɪn/ *noun*

1 (*no plural*) a soft white metal

2 a container made of this metal: *a tin of beans* ⇨ same meaning CAN

tin·kle /'tɪŋkl/ *verb (present participle* **tinkling**, *past* **tinkled**)

to make a sound like small bells: *The glasses tinkled as he carried them.*

tinned /tɪnd/ *adjective*

sold in a tin: *Have some tinned plums.*

tin o·pen·er /'tɪn ˌəʊpnə[r]/ *noun*

a tool for opening tins of food

ti·ny /'taɪnɪ/ *adjective*

very small: *He set off alone in his tiny boat.* | *He only had a tiny sum of money to live on.*

tip [1] /tɪp/ *verb (present participle* **tipping**, *past* **tipped**)

1 to lean or cause to lean at an angle: *I tipped the table and the glasses fell off it.*

2 to give a small amount of money to a waiter, a taxi-driver, etc: *I always tip generously.*

3 to turn over or cause something to turn over: *I tipped the box over and the chocolates fell out.*

tip [2] *noun*

1 the narrow or pointed end of something: *the tip of a finger*

2 a small amount of money given to someone who has done something for you: *Shall we leave the waiter a tip?*

3 a useful piece of advice: *Have you got any tips on making cakes?*

tip·toe¹ /'tɪptəʊ/ *verb (present participle* **tiptoeing**, *past* **tiptoed**)

to walk on your toes, especially when you are trying not to make any noise: *I tiptoed past the sleeping child.*

tiptoe² *noun*

on tiptoe walking on your toes, especially when you are trying not to make any noise: *Let's walk on tiptoe so they don't hear us.*

tire /taɪəʳ/ *verb (present participle* **tiring**, *past* **tired**)

to make someone feel that they need rest: *Even short journeys tire me.*

tired /taɪəd/ *adjective*

1 needing rest or sleep: *I felt tired after work.*

2 be tired of something to lose interest in something because you have done it many times before: *She was tired of cooking for her family.*

3 be tired out to be very tired: *It had been a long hard day, and they were all tired out.*

tis·sue /'tɪʃuː/ *noun*

a thin soft piece of paper used for cleaning your nose

ti·tle /'taɪtl/ *noun*

1 the name of a story, a book, a film, etc: *What's the title of his latest novel?*

2 a word such as Mr, Mrs, or Dr (=Doctor) that is used in front of a person's name

to /tə, tʊ; *strong* tuː/

1 in the direction of: *He ran to the door.* | *He sent a letter to his parents.* | *We are driving to town.*

2 as far as: *When we got to the river, we sat down.*

3 until: *She works from two o'clock to ten o'clock.*

4 used to show how many minutes there are until the next hour: *It's ten to nine.*

5 used to show why you do something: *She worked hard to earn some money.*

6 used with a verb to show the INFINITIVE: *I want to go.* | *She tried to stop.*

toad /təʊd/ *noun*

an animal like a large FROG with short legs

toast /təʊst/ *noun (no plural)*

bread that has been heated until it is brown: *I had toast for breakfast.* ⇨ see picture at TOASTER

toast·er /'təʊstəʳ/ **toaster**
noun

an electric machine that is used for making toast ⇨ see picture on page 204

toast

to·bac·co /tə'bækəʊ/ *noun (no plural)*

the dried leaves of a plant used for smoking in pipes and cigarettes

to·day /tə'deɪ/ *noun, adverb*

1 this day: *It's Monday today.*

2 modern times: *Many people use computers today.*

tod·dler /'tɒdləʳ/ *noun*

a young child who has just learned to walk

toe /təʊ/ *noun*

one of the five parts on the end of your foot ⇨ see picture at FOOT

toe·nail /'təʊneɪl/ *noun*

the nail on a toe ⇨ see picture at FOOT

tof·fee /'tɒfiː/ *noun*

a hard brown sweet

to·geth·er /tə'geðəʳ/ *adverb*

1 with each other, or in a group: *The children played together in the street.* | *I stuck the two pieces of paper together.*

2 at the same time: *The two letters arrived together.*

toi·let /'tɔɪlɪt/ *noun*

1 a large bowl that you sit on to get rid of waste substances from your body ⇨ see picture on page 204

2 a room with this in it: *Where is the toilet, please?* ⇨ same meaning (**1** and **2**) LAVATORY

toilet pa·per /'tɔɪlɪt ˌpeɪpəʳ/ *noun*

thin soft paper that you use for cleaning yourself after you have used the toilet

toilet roll /'tɔɪlɪt ˌrəʊl/ *noun*

toilet paper that is wound round a small tube

to·ken /'təʊkən/ *noun*

a sign: *We shook hands as a token of our friendship.*

told /təʊld/
the past tense and past participle of the verb **tell**

to·ma·to /təˈmɑːtəʊ/ noun (plural **tomatoes**)
a red juicy fruit that you eat raw or cooked: *A kilo of tomatoes, please.* ➪ see picture on page 199

tomb /tuːm/ noun
a hole in the ground in which a dead person is put

tomb·stone /ˈtuːmstəʊn/ noun
a piece of stone put over a tomb, often with the name of the dead person on it

to·mor·row /təˈmɒrəʊ/
the day after this day: *It's too late to do it now; let's do it tomorrow.* ➪ compare YESTERDAY

ton /tʌn/ noun
1 a measure of weight equal to 2,240 pounds
2 also **tonne** a measure of weight equal to 1,000 kilos

tone /təʊn/ noun
the sound of a voice or a musical instrument, etc: *Her voice has a pleasant tone.*

tongs /tɒŋz/ plural noun
an instrument made of two narrow pieces of metal joined at one end, used for picking things up: *He picked up the hot metal with a pair of tongs.* ➪ compare TWEEZERS

tongue /tʌŋ/ noun
1 the part inside your mouth that you use for tasting and speaking
2 **hold your tongue** not to speak: *I wanted to tell the teacher she was stupid but I held my tongue.*

to·night /təˈnaɪt/ adverb
the evening or night at the end of today: *We are going to a party tonight.*

tonne /tʌn/ noun
a measure of weight equal to 1,000 kilos

too /tuː/ adverb
1 also: *I like bananas, but I like oranges too.*
2 more than is needed or wanted: *He drives too fast. I She talks too much.*

took /tʊk/
the past tense of the verb **take**

tool /tuːl/ noun
an instrument that helps you to do special jobs such as building or repairing

something: *Get the hammer – it's in the tool box.*

tooth /tuːθ/ noun (plural **teeth** /tiːθ/)
1 one of the white things in your mouth that you use for biting food: *You should brush your teeth after every meal.*
2 something that is shaped like this, for example each of the sharp parts on a COMB

tooth·ache /ˈtuːθeɪk/ noun (no plural)
a pain in a tooth: *I've had toothache all day.*

tooth·brush /ˈtuːθbrʌʃ/ noun
a small brush for cleaning your teeth ➪ see picture at BRUSH

tooth·paste /ˈtuːθpeɪst/ noun (no plural)
a substance used for cleaning your teeth

top¹ /tɒp/ noun
1 the highest part of something: *He climbed to the top **of** the hill.*
2 the lid or cover of something: *He raised the top of the box.*
3 a piece of clothing that you wear on the top part of your body: *I need a top to wear with these trousers.*

top² adjective
1 highest: *Put it in the top drawer.*
2 **be top of the class** to have the highest marks in the class

top·ic /ˈtɒpɪk/ noun
a subject that you talk or write about: *Their wedding was the main topic of conversation.*

top·ple /ˈtɒpl/ verb (present participle **toppling**, past **toppled**)
to fall over: *The pile of books toppled onto the floor.*

torch /tɔːtʃ/ noun (plural **torches**)
an electric light that you can carry around with you: *He used a torch to see into the dark cupboard.* ➪ see picture at LAMP

tore /tɔːʳ/
the past tense of the verb **tear**

torn /tɔːn/
the past participle of the verb **tear**

tor·na·do /tɔːˈneɪdəʊ/ noun (plural **tornadoes** or **tornados**)
a storm with a strong circular wind

tor·pe·do /tɔːˈpiːdəʊ/ noun (plural **torpedoes**)
a weapon that is fired through the water from a ship to destroy another ship

tor·rent /'tɒrənt/ *noun*
a fast flow of water: *The river was a torrent after the storm.*

tor·ren·tial /tə'renʃəl/ *adjective*
torrential rain falls quickly and in large amounts: *We had some torrential rain last night.*

tor·toise /'tɔːtəs/ *noun*
a land animal that has a body covered by a round hard shell and moves very slowly

tor·ture[1] /'tɔːtʃəʳ/ *verb (present participle* **torturing***, past* **tortured***)*
to cause great pain to someone deliberately, for example to get information from them: *The leaders of the attack were tortured in prison.*

torture[2] *noun*
when someone is tortured, especially so that they give you information

toss /tɒs/ *verb*
1 to throw, especially in a careless way: *They tossed the ball to each other.*
2 to move about or up and down: *The horse tossed its head in the air.*

to·tal[1] /'təʊtl/ *noun*
everything added together: *Add up these numbers and tell me the total.*

total[2] *adjective*
complete: *There was total silence.*

to·tal·ly /'təʊtl-ɪ/ *adverb*
completely: *I totally agree.*

touch[1] /tʌtʃ/ *verb*
1 to put your hand or finger on something: *Don't touch that pot; it's very hot.*
2 if two things are touching, there is no space in between them: *The branches of the tree touched the water.*

touch[2] *noun*
1 (*plural* **touches**) when you put your hand or finger on something: *I felt the touch of his hand.*
2 (*no plural*) the sense that you use in order to feel things, especially by putting your hand on something
3 **get in touch** to write to someone or telephone them: *I must get in touch* **with** *my old schoolfriends to see what they are doing now.*
4 **keep in touch** to speak or write to someone regularly: *Do you still keep in touch* **with** *John?*

tough /tʌf/ *adjective*
1 strong and brave: *People think I'm tough, but really I'm easily frightened.*
2 hard, and not easy to bite: *This meat is tough.*
3 difficult: *The exam was tough.*

tour[1] /tʊəʳ/ *noun*
1 a journey during which several places are visited: *They have gone on a tour* **of** *Europe.*
2 a trip through a place in order to see the things in it: *We went on a quick tour* **of** *the museum.*

tour[2] *verb*
to visit many different parts of a country or an area: *We toured France during the summer holidays.*

tour·is·m /'tʊərɪzəm/ *noun (no plural)*
when people travel to a place for pleasure on their holidays: *The town depends on tourism for most of its income.*

tour·ist /'tʊərɪst/ *noun*
a person who travels for pleasure: *Stratford-on-Avon is always full of tourists.*

tourist of·fice /'tʊərɪst ˌɒfɪs/ *noun*
a place where tourists can go to get information

tour·na·ment /'tʊənəmənt/ *noun*
a sports competition: *a tennis tournament*

tow /təʊ/ *verb*
to pull a vehicle along: *We towed the car to the garage.*

to·wards /tə'wɔːdz/ *preposition*
1 in the direction of: *She walked towards the door.* | *He stood with his back towards us.* ⇨ see picture on page 208
2 near a time or place: *Towards evening, the weather became cooler.*

tow·el /'taʊəl/ *noun*
a piece of cloth used for drying things

tow·er /'taʊəʳ/ *noun*
a tall narrow building or part of a building such as a church: *We visited the Eiffel Tower.*

tower

bell

town /taʊn/ *noun*
a place with many houses and other buildings where people live and work: *We lived in a little town on the south coast.* ⇨ compare CITY

town hall /ˌtaʊn ˈhɔːl/ *noun*
a building used by the government of an area or for public meetings

tox·ic /ˈtɒksɪk/ *adjective*
containing dangerous substances: *The children live within four miles of a toxic waste site.*

toy /tɔɪ/ *noun*
a thing for children to play with: *Her favourite toy was an old teddy bear.* ⇨ see picture on page 201

trace[1] /treɪs/ *noun*
a mark or sign that shows that someone or something has been in a place: *They searched the building but did not find any trace of the burglar.*

trace[2] *verb* (*present participle* **tracing**, *past* **traced**)
1 to copy a picture, plan, etc by drawing on a thin piece of paper put over it
2 to try to find someone or something that has disappeared by looking carefully for them: *They traced the killer to a house in the city.*

track[1] /træk/ *noun*
1 a rough path: *We walked along a narrow track through the woods*
2 a set of marks on the ground left by an animal, person, or vehicle: *We followed the tyre tracks across a muddy field.*
3 a special path for races

track[2] *verb*
to follow a person or animal by looking for signs of where they have been

track·suit /ˈtræksuːt/ *noun*
a warm loose suit that you wear for sport or when you want to feel comfortable ⇨ see picture on page 203

trac·tor /ˈtræktəʳ/ *noun*
a strong vehicle with large wheels, used for pulling farm equipment ⇨ see picture on page 206

trade[1] /treɪd/ *noun*
1 (*no plural*) the buying and selling of goods, especially between one country and another: *We are trying to encourage British trade with China.*

2 a kind of business: *He worked in the hotel trade.*
3 a job that needs special teaching: *She's a dressmaker by trade.*

trade[2] *verb* (*present participle* **trading**, *past* **traded**)
to buy and sell goods, especially between one country and another: *We trade **with** other countries.*

trad·er /ˈtreɪdəʳ/ *noun*
a person who buys and sells goods

trades·man /ˈtreɪdzmən/ *noun* (*plural* **tradesmen** /-mən/)
a person who buys and sells goods, especially a person who runs a shop

tra·di·tion /trəˈdɪʃn/ *noun*
a custom, belief, or way of doing things that has existed for a long time: *The family has a long tradition of wine-making.*

tra·di·tion·al /trəˈdɪʃnəl/ *adjective*
used to describe something that has been done in the same way for a long time: *We spent a traditional family Christmas.*

traf·fic /ˈtræfɪk/ *noun* (*no plural*)
the movement of cars and people in the streets, or of ships or planes: *The city streets are full of traffic.*

traffic jam /ˈtræfɪk ˌdʒæm/ *noun*
a long line of vehicles that cannot move forward, or that move very slowly: *I got stuck in a traffic jam on my way home from work*

traffic lights /ˈtræfɪk ˌlaɪts/ *plural noun*
a set of coloured lights where two roads meet, that tell cars when to stop: *Turn right at the second set of traffic lights.*

traffic war·den /ˈtræfɪk ˌwɔːdn/ *noun*
an official whose job is to check that cars are parked where they are allowed to park

tra·ge·dy /ˈtrædʒədɪ/ *noun* (*plural* **tragedies**)
1 when something very sad happens: *Her son's death was a tragedy.*
2 a serious play with a sad ending ⇨ compare (1 and 2) COMEDY

tra·gic /ˈtrædʒɪk/ *adjective*
very sad: *Her death was a tragic accident.*

tragically /-klɪ/ *adverb*: *He was killed tragically in an accident.*

A B C D E F G H I J K L M N O P Q R S **T** U V W X Y Z

trail /treɪl/ *noun*
1 a set of marks on the ground that show where someone or something has been: *He left a trail of blood from the wound in his leg.*
2 a path across rough country

trail·er /'treɪlər/ *noun*
a vehicle that can be pulled behind a car

train¹ /treɪn/ *noun*
1 a vehicle that travels along a railway ⇨ see picture on page 206
2 **by train** on a train: *We went to the seaside by train.*

train² *verb*
1 to teach yourself or someone else how to do something, for example a job: *She is training to become a nurse.*
2 to prepare for a sports event by exercising: *I am training for the race.*

train·er /'treɪnər/ *noun*
a person who teaches you a sport or helps you to exercise

train·ers /'treɪnəz/ *plural noun*
soft shoes that are like sports shoes but which people wear every day: *a new pair of trainers* ⇨ see picture on page 203

train·ing /'treɪnɪŋ/ *noun (no plural)*
activities in which you learn how to do a particular job or play a sport

trai·tor /'treɪtər/ *noun*
a person who helps a country that is fighting his or her own country: *The traitor was sent to prison.*

tramp /træmp/ *noun*
a person with no home or job who moves from place to place

tram·ple /'træmpl/ *verb (present participle* **trampling**, *past* **trampled**)
to walk heavily on something: *He trampled on my flowers when he was getting his football.*

trans·fer¹ /træns'fɜːr/ *verb*
to move people or things from one place to another: *His employer transferred him to another office.*

trans·fer² /'trænsfɜːr/ *noun*
when someone or something is transferred: *Can I have a transfer to a new office?*

trans·form /træns'fɔːm/ *verb*
to change something or someone completely, especially in a way that improves them: *She transformed the room by painting it.*

tran·sis·tor /træn'zɪstər/ *noun*
also **transistor radio** /træn,zɪstə 'reɪdɪəʊ/) a small radio

tran·si·tive /'trænzətɪv/ *noun, adjective*
a transitive verb has an object. In the sentence 'I gave the book to Jane', 'gave' is a transitive verb ⇨ compare INTRANSITIVE

trans·late /træns'leɪt/ *verb (present participle* **translating**, *past* **translated**)
to change speech or writing from one language into another: *He translated the speech **from** Spanish **into** English.*

trans·la·tion /træns'leɪʃn/ *noun*
1 something that has been translated: *I read 'Crime and Punishment' in an English translation.*
2 (*no plural*) when you translate something into a different language

trans·par·ent /træns'spærənt/ *adjective*
clear and able to be seen through: *The table was made of transparent plastic.*

trans·port¹ /træn'spɔːt/ *verb*
to carry goods or people from one place to another in a vehicle: *The goods were transported by train.*

trans·port² /'trænspɔːt/ *noun (no plural)*
1 a kind of vehicle, or a system of buses, trains, etc that you use for going from one place to another: *The car's broken down – we'll have to use public transport.*
2 when people, goods, etc are moved from one place to another: *The transport of live animals is often very cruel.*

trap¹ /træp/ *noun*   trap
1 an instrument for catching an animal: *We had to use mousetraps.*
2 a plan to catch a person: *The police set a trap **for** the thieves.*

a mousetrap

trap² *verb (present participle* **trapping**, *past* **trapped**)
1 to catch a person or an animal in a trap: *The police trapped the thieves.*
2 **be trapped** to be unable to escape from a dangerous place or unpleasant

situation: *She was trapped in the burning house.*

trav·el /'trævəl/ *verb (present participle* **travelling**, *past* **travelled**)
1 to make a journey from one place to another: *We spent the summer travelling round Europe.*
2 to move from one place or person to another: *At what speed is he travelling?* | *News travels fast in this town.*

travel a·gen·cy /'trævəl ,eɪdʒənsɪ/ *noun (plural* **travel agencies**)
a business that arranges people's journeys and holidays

travel a·gent /'trævəl ,eɪdʒənt/ *noun*
a person who owns or works in a travel agency

trav·el·ler /'trævələʳ/ *noun*
a person who is on a journey

traveller's cheque /'trævələz ,tʃek/ *noun*
a special cheque that can be exchanged for the money of another country

trawl·er /'trɔːləʳ/ *noun*
a large fishing boat

tray /treɪ/ *noun*
a flat piece of plastic, wood, etc on which you carry plates and food

tread /tred/ *verb (past* **trod** /trɒd/, *past participle* **trodden** /'trɒdn/)
1 to put your foot on something: *I trod on his foot by accident.*
2 **tread water** to remain upright in deep water by moving your legs

trea·son /'triːzn/ *noun (no plural)*
the crime of doing something that could cause great harm to your country or government

trea·sure /'treʒəʳ/ *noun (no plural)*

treasure

an amount of gold, jewellery, or other valuable objects, especially one that has been hidden: *They found the treasure buried under a tree.*

treat¹ /triːt/ *noun*
something special that gives you pleasure: *Her birthday treat was a visit to the theatre.*

treat² *verb*
1 to behave towards someone in a particular way: *He treats his children very badly.*
2 to handle something in a particular way: *Glass must be treated carefully.*
3 to do something to make someone better when they are ill or injured: *Doctors cannot treat this illness.*
4 to give someone something special: *I'm going to treat myself* **to** *a new coat.*

treat·ment /'triːtmənt/ *noun*
1 something that is done to make you better when you are ill or injured: *They have found a new treatment for cancer.*
2 (*no plural*) the way you behave towards someone: *His treatment of those animals is cruel.*

treat·y /'triːtɪ/ *noun (plural* **treaties**)
an agreement between two or more countries: *They signed a peace treaty.*

tree

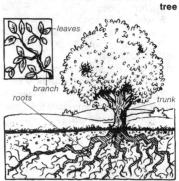

leaves
branch
roots
trunk

tree /triː/ *noun*
a large plant with branches, leaves, and a thick TRUNK

trem·ble /'trembl/ *verb (present participle* **trembling**, *past* **trembled**)
to shake because you are very afraid or very angry: *Anna trembled with fear.*

tre·men·dous /trə'mendəs/ *adjective*
1 very large or very great in amount: *He did a tremendous amount of damage to the house.*
2 very good or impressive: *We went to a tremendous party.*

tre·men·dous·ly /trə'mendəslɪ/ *adverb*
very: *My maths homework was tremendously difficult.*

trench /trentʃ/ *noun (plural* **trenches**)
a long narrow hole dug in the earth

A
B
C
D
E
F
G
H
I
J
K
L
M
N
O
P
Q
R
S
T
U
V
W
X
Y
Z

trend /trend/ *noun*
the way a situation is generally developing or changing: *Tourist numbers are lower this year, a trend which is worrying the tourism industry.*

trend·y /'trendɪ/ *adjective*
modern and popular: *We ate in a trendy Italian restaurant.*

tres·pass /'trespəs/ *verb*
to go onto someone else's land without permission: *The farmer said we were trespassing.*

tres·pass·er /'trespəsəʳ/ *noun*
a person who goes onto someone else's land without permission

tri·al /'traɪəl/ *noun*
1 the process of deciding in a court of law if someone is guilty of a crime: *The murder trial lasted a month.*
2 **on trial** in court while people decide if you are guilty of a crime: *She was on trial for murder.*
3 when someone or something is tested to find out how good they are: *The new drug is going through thorough trials.*

tri·an·gle /'traɪæŋgl/ *noun*
a flat shape with three straight sides and three angles ⟡ see picture at SHAPE

tri·an·gu·lar /traɪ'æŋgjʊləʳ/ *adjective*
shaped like a triangle

trib·al /'traɪbl/ *adjective*
belonging to a tribe: *They played interesting tribal music.*

tribe /traɪb/ *noun*
a group of people who have the same race, language, customs, etc

trib·u·ta·ry /'trɪbjʊtərɪ/ *noun* (*plural* **tributaries**)
a small stream or river that joins a larger river

trib·ute /'trɪbjuːt/ *noun*
something that you say or do to show how much you admire or respect someone: *The doctor **paid** tribute **to** the nurses by praising their work.*

trick¹ /trɪk/ *noun*
1 something that you do in order to deceive someone: *The phone call was a trick to get him out of the office.*
2 when someone does something that seems like magic in order to entertain people: *Do you know any good card tricks?*

3 **play a trick on someone** to do something to deceive or surprise someone, especially to make other people laugh: *The children played a trick on their teacher.*

trick² *verb*
to deceive or cheat someone: *He tricked me into giving him the money.*

trick·le¹ /'trɪkl/ *verb* (*present participle* **trickling**, *past* **trickled**)
when liquid trickles somewhere, it flows slowly in drops or in a thin stream: *Blood trickled from the wound.*

trickle² *noun*
when a small amount of a liquid flows somewhere

trick·y /'trɪkɪ/ *adjective*
difficult to do or to deal with: *I had this really tricky maths problem to solve.*

tri·cy·cle /'traɪsɪkl/ *noun*
a bicycle with three wheels

tried /traɪd/
the past tense and past participle of the verb **try**

trig·ger /'trɪgəʳ/ *noun*
the part of a gun that you pull with your finger to fire it: *He pointed the gun and pulled the trigger.*

trim /trɪm/ *verb* (*present participle* **trimming**, *past* **trimmed**)
to make something tidy by cutting a small amount off it: *She trimmed his hair.*

trip¹ /trɪp/ *noun*
a short journey: *We made a trip into town.*

trip² *verb* (*present participle* **tripping**, *past* **tripped**)
to hit your foot against something while you are walking or running so that you fall or nearly fall: *Be careful! Don't trip over that box.*

tri·umph /'traɪʌmf/ *noun*
when someone is successful in an important activity, game, or fight: *It was a great triumph when our team won the race.*

triv·i·al /'trɪvɪəl/ *adjective*
not important or serious: *He told me all the trivial details of his daily life.*

trod /trɒd/
the past tense of the verb **tread**

trod·den /'trɒdn/
the past participle of the verb **tread**

trol·ley /'trɒlɪ/ noun (plural **trolleys**)
a metal container on wheels used for carrying bags, for example when shopping or at an airport

troops /truːps/ plural noun
soldiers

tro·phy /'trəʊfɪ/ noun (plural **trophies**)
a prize for winning a game or race, especially a silver cup

trop·i·cal /'trɒpɪkl/ adjective
1 in or from the hottest parts of the world: He keeps tropical fish.
2 very hot: The weather is so hot it's almost tropical. ⟡ see picture at CLIMATE

trop·ics /'trɒpɪks/ plural noun
the tropics the hottest parts of the world

trot /trɒt/ verb (present participle **trotting**, past **trotted**)
to walk or run with quick short steps: The horse trotted along the road. | The little girl trotted behind her father.

troub·le[1] /'trʌbl/ noun
1 (no plural) difficulty: Did you have any trouble finding the restaurant?
2 (no plural) to cause someone worry, sadness, or pain: He hasn't got a job; that's the trouble.
3 be in trouble to have a difficult problem, usually because you have done something wrong: He's in trouble **with** the police.
4 get into trouble to get yourself into a difficult situation, for example because you have done something wrong: He's always getting into trouble at school.
5 get someone into trouble to get someone else into a difficult situation: He broke the window, then he tried to get me into trouble about it.
6 no trouble used to say that you are very willing to do something because it is not a problem for you: I'll drive you to the station; it's no trouble.
7 troubles problems: Tell me all your troubles.

trouble[2] verb (present participle **troubling**, past **troubled**)
1 to cause someone unhappiness, anxiety, or pain: Her child's bad behaviour troubled her.
2 to ask someone to do something for you when it is difficult for them: I'm sorry to trouble you but could you help me with this letter?

trough /trɒf/ noun
a long narrow container that is used to hold food or water for animals

trou·sers /'traʊzəz/
a piece of clothing that covers the lower part of your body, with a separate part covering each leg: She was wearing a pair of black trousers. ⟡ see picture on page 203

trow·el /'traʊəl/ noun
a small garden tool used for digging small holes, taking plants out of the ground, etc

tru·ant /'truːənt/ noun
1 a child who stays away from school without a good reason
2 play truant to stay away from school without a good reason: The teacher punished David for playing truant.

truck /trʌk/ noun   **truck**
1 a large vehicle for carrying heavy goods on the road: My father drives a truck. ⟡ same meaning LORRY
2 an open container used on a railway for carrying heavy goods

true /truː/ adjective
1 correct or real: Is it true that you are rich? | It's a true story.
2 come true if dreams or wishes come true, they really happen: His dreams of success came true.

tru·ly /'truːlɪ/ adverb
really: I am truly grateful for all your help.

trum·pet /'trʌmpɪt/ noun
a musical instrument made of BRASS that you play by blowing through it

trun·cheon /'trʌnʃən/ noun
a short thick stick used by the police as a weapon

trunk /trʌŋk/ noun
1 the thick main stem of a tree ⟡ see picture at TREE
2 the main part of your body, not including your head, arms, or legs
3 a large box that you carry clothes, books, etc in when you travel
4 the long nose of an ELEPHANT
5 trunks (plural noun) a piece of

A B C D E F G H I J K L M N O P Q R S T U V W X Y Z

clothing that men wear for swimming: *He was wearing a pair of black trunks.*

trust¹ /trʌst/ *verb*

1 to believe that someone is honest or good: *Don't trust him – he never tells the truth.*

2 to be sure that someone will do something: *Can I trust you to do this work well?*

trust² *noun (no plural)*

the belief that someone is good or honest: *Don't put your trust in that man; he may trick you.*

trust·wor·thy /ˈtrʌstwɜːðɪ/ *adjective*

a trustworthy person can be trusted: *Let Paul look after the money; he's trustworthy.*

truth /truːθ/ *noun (no plural)*

the true facts about something: *You should always tell the truth.* ⇨ compare LIE

truth·ful /ˈtruːθfəl/ *adjective*

1 a truthful person is honest and does not tell lies: *Paul is very truthful.*

2 correct: *The account of the accident was truthful.*

try¹ /traɪ/ *verb (present participle **trying**, past **tried**)*

1 to attempt to do something: *He tried to climb the tree, but he could not.* | *Please try not to be late.*

2 to test something to see if you like it: *Have you tried this chocolate?*

3 try something on to put on a piece of clothing to see if it fits you

try² *noun (plural **tries**)*

an attempt: *If you can't open the box, let me have a try.*

T-shirt /ˈtiː ʃɜːt/ *noun*

a shirt, usually made of cotton, with a round neck and short SLEEVES ⇨ see picture on page 203

tub /tʌb/ *noun*

a round container for holding things: *I bought a tub of strawberry ice-cream.*

tube /tjuːb/ *noun*

1 a hollow pipe made of metal, plastic, glass, or rubber

2 a soft narrow container: *I bought a new tube of toothpaste.* ⇨ see picture at CONTAINER

3 the Tube the London Underground railway

tuck /tʌk/ *verb*

1 to push the end of a shirt, sheet, etc under something so that it looks tidy: *Tuck your shirt into your trousers.*

2 tuck someone in to make someone comfortable in bed by pulling the covers over them: *He asked his mum to come and tuck him in.*

Tues·day /ˈtjuːzdeɪ, -dɪ/ *noun*

the second day of the week after Monday and before Wednesday

tuft /tʌft/ *noun*

a short thick group of hairs, grass, etc growing together: *She sat down on a tuft of grass.*

tug¹ /tʌɡ/ *verb (present participle **tugging**, past **tugged**)*

to pull hard: *The child tugged at my hand to make me go with her.*

tug² *noun*

1 a sudden strong pull

2 a small powerful boat used for pulling large ships

tum·ble /ˈtʌmbl/ *verb (present participle **tumbling**, past **tumbled**)*

to fall suddenly: *She tumbled down the stairs.*

tum·bler /ˈtʌmblər/ *noun*

a glass for drinking out of, that has a flat bottom and straight sides

tum·my /ˈtʌmɪ/ *noun (plural **tummies**)*

your stomach: *I've got a tummy ache.*

tune¹ /tjuːn/ *noun*

a number of musical notes put together to make a pleasant sound: *That song has a happy tune.* ⇨ compare SONG

tune² *verb (present participle **tuning**, past **tuned**)*

to make changes to a musical instrument so that it plays the right musical notes: *A man came to tune the piano.*

tun·nel¹ /ˈtʌnl/ *noun*

a long hole that has been dug through a hill, under a river etc for cars or trains to go through: *We travelled through the Channel Tunnel.*

tunnel² *verb (present participle **tunnelling**, past **tunnelled**)*

to dig a long hole through a hill, under a river etc, for cars or trains to go through

tur·ban /'tɜːbən/ noun
a long piece of cloth that you wind tightly round your head to cover it

tur·key /'tɜːkɪ/ noun
a bird that is similar to a chicken but larger, or the meat from this bird

turn

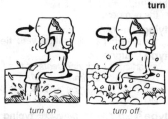

turn on   turn off

turn¹ /tɜːn/ verb
1 to go round and round, or make something go round and round: *The wheels were turning.* | *Turn the wheel to the right.*
2 to change direction, or make something change direction: *She turned left at the end of the road.* | *He turned the box upside down.*
3 to move so that your body is facing a different way: *She turned round to look behind her.* | *He turned and waved.*
4 turn a corner to go round a corner
5 turn something down to reduce something such as the sound from a radio or the heat from an electric fire: *Turn the television down; it's too loud.*
6 turn something down to say no to an offer: *He turned down the job.*
7 turn something into something to change something into something else: *She turned her bedroom into an office.*
8 turn something off to make something stop working: *Turn the radio off.*

tunnel

9 turn something on to make something start working: *Turn the heating on.*
10 turn something out to make a light stop shining: *She turned out the light.*
11 turn over to move so that you are lying in a different position: *He turned over and went to sleep.*
12 turn up to arrive at a place: *He turned up with his brother.*

turn² noun
1 a turning movement: *Give the wheel another turn.*
2 a change of direction: *The car made a left turn at the traffic lights.*
3 the time when you can or should do something, after or before the other people who are also doing it: *It's my turn to play.*
4 take it in turns to do something one person after the other: *We took it in turns to drive.*

turn·ing /'tɜːnɪŋ/ noun
a road that connects with the one you are on: *Take the second turning on the right.*

tur·tle /'tɜːtl/ noun
an animal that has four legs, a hard round shell over its back, and lives mainly in the sea ⇨ see picture on page 195

tusk /tʌsk/ noun
one of the two long pointed teeth that grow outside the mouths of animals such as ELEPHANTS

tu·tor¹ /'tjuːtəʳ/ noun
a person who teaches one student or a small group of students: *Her tutor teaches her at home.*

tutor² verb
to teach someone: *He tutored me **in** English.*

TV /ˌtiː ˈviː/ noun
1 a television: *Turn on the TV.*
2 (*no plural*) the programmes that you can watch on a television: *We're watching TV tonight.*
3 on TV shown on the television: *There's a good film on TV tonight.*

twee·zers /'twiːzəz/ plural noun
a small instrument made of two narrow pieces of metal joined at one end, used for picking up very small objects: *I used a pair of tweezers to take the splinter out of my finger.* ⇨ compare TONGS

A B C D E F G H I J K L M N O P Q R S T U V W X Y Z

twelfth/twelfθ/ *noun, adjective*
12th

twelve/twelv/
the number 12

twen·ti·eth/'twentɪ-əθ/ *noun, adjective*
20th

twen·ty/'twentɪ/
the number 20

twice/twaɪs/ *adverb*
two times: *You've asked me that question twice.*

twig/twɪg/ *noun*
a very thin branch that grows on a larger branch of a tree

twin/twɪn/ *noun*
one of two children who are born to the same mother at the same time: *I have a twin sister.*

twin·kle/'twɪŋkl/ *verb (present participle* **twinkling**, *past* **twinkled**)
if a star or light twinkles, it shines and changes very quickly from being bright to dark: *The stars twinkled in the sky.*

twist[1]/twɪst/ *verb*
  1 to wind things together or around something else: *She twisted her hair round her fingers.*
  2 to turn something round: *Twist the lid to open it.*
  3 to turn in different directions: *The path twisted up the hill.*

twist[2] *noun*
  1 a shape made by twisting something such as rope or hair: *Decorate the cake with twists of lemon peel.*
  2 a movement that turns something round: *He gave the lid a twist to open the tin.*
  3 a bend: *The road was full of twists and turns.*

twitch[1]/twɪtʃ/ *verb*
to move suddenly and quickly without control: *Her fingers twitched nervously.*

twitch[2] *noun*
a sudden movement of a muscle that you cannot control

two/tuː/
the number 2

tying/'taɪ-ɪŋ/
the present participle of the verb **tie**

type[1]/taɪp/ *noun*
a particular kind: *Accidents of this type happen all the time.* | *I realized I was doing the wrong type of work.* ⇨ look at KIND[1]

type[2] *verb (present participle* **typing** *past* **typed**)
to write something using a computer or typewriter: *to type a letter*

type·writ·er/'taɪp,raɪtər/ *noun*
a machine that you use to print letters, numbers, etc onto paper, which you work by pressing buttons with the letters and numbers written on them

typ·i·cal/'tɪpɪkl/ *adjective*
the same as other people or things belonging to a particular group or kind: *He's a typical little boy who enjoys being naughty.*

typ·ist/'taɪpɪst/ *noun*
a person whose job is to type

ty·rant/'taɪərənt/ *noun*
a person with a lot of power who uses it in a cruel or unfair way: *Her father was a real tyrant.*

tyre/taɪər/ *noun*
a round piece of rubber filled with air, that fits around the wheel of a car, bicycle etc: *I need to pump up my bicycle tyres.* ⇨ see picture at BICYCLE

A B C D E F G H I J K L M N O P Q R S T U V W X Y Z

U u

U, u /juː/
the twenty-first letter of the English alphabet

ug·ly /ˈʌɡlɪ/ *adjective* (**uglier**, **ugliest**)
unpleasant to look at: *an ugly building*

ul·cer /ˈʌlsər/ *noun*
a painful area inside your body or on your skin that may bleed or produce unpleasant liquid: *I've got a mouth ulcer.*

um·brel·la /ʌmˈbrelə/ *noun*
a round piece of plastic or cloth on a frame that you hold over yourself when it is raining

arguing with the umpire

um·pire /ˈʌmpaɪər/ *noun*
the person who decides about the points won in a game

UN /juː ˈen/ *noun*
the UN the UNITED NATIONS

un·a·ble /ʌnˈeɪbl/ *adjective*
unable to do something if you are unable to do something, you cannot do it, for example because you do not have enough power, skill, time, or money: *She was unable to attend the meeting because she was ill.*
⇨ opposite ABLE

u·nan·i·mous /juˈnænɪməs/ *adjective*
agreed by everyone: *a unanimous decision*

un·armed /ʌnˈɑːmd/ *adjective*
not carrying a gun or other weapon

un·at·tract·ive /ˌʌnəˈtræktɪv/ *adjective*
not beautiful or attractive: *an unattractive industrial area of the city*

un·bear·a·ble /ʌnˈbeərəbl/ *adjective*
if something is unbearable, it is very unpleasant and you do not want to experience it: *The noise was unbearable and we hurried out of the room.*

un·be·liev·a·ble /ˌʌnbɪˈliːvəbl/ *adjective*
very surprising or difficult to believe: *It was unbelievable how quickly she did it.*
unbelievably *adverb*: *These shirts are unbelievably cheap.*

un·cer·tain /ʌnˈsɜːtn/ *adjective*
not sure or definite: *He was uncertain what to do.* | *Our holiday plans are still uncertain.*

un·cle /ˈʌŋkl/ *noun*
the brother of one of your parents, or the husband of the sister of one of your parents: *Hallo, Uncle John.* ⇨ compare AUNT

un·com·fort·a·ble /ʌnˈkʌmftəbl/ *adjective*
1 not pleasant to sit on, lie on, or wear: *This bed is really uncomfortable.* | *These trousers are a bit uncomfortable.*
2 embarrassed or worried: *She felt a bit uncomfortable standing next to him.*
⇨ opposite COMFORTABLE

un·com·mon /ʌnˈkɒmən/ *adjective*
unusual: *an illness that is uncommon among children* ⇨ same meaning RARE
⇨ opposite COMMON

un·con·scious /ʌnˈkɒnʃəs/ *adjective*
if you are unconscious, you are in a state similar to sleep, because you are ill or have been injured: *She was unconscious for several minutes after she fell.* ⇨ opposite CONSCIOUS

un·con·trol·la·ble /ˌʌnkənˈtrəʊləbl/ *adjective*
impossible to control or stop: *uncontrollable laughter*

un·cooked /ʌnˈkʊkt/ *adjective*
uncooked food has not been cooked ⇨ same meaning RAW

un·cov·er /ʌnˈkʌvər/ *verb*
1 to take something from on top of something else: *I think we're ready to eat – let's uncover the food.*
2 to find out about something, especially a crime: *Fortunately the police uncovered the plan.*

un·der /ˈʌndər/ *adjective, adverb*
1 below something: *She was sitting*

under the tree. | *Go under the bridge and then turn right.* ⇨ see picture on page 208

2 less than a particular price, amount, or age: *I can't remember the exact price, but it was under five pounds.* | *There is no charge for children under three years old.*

un·der·go /ˌʌndəˈgəʊ/ *verb (present participle* **undergoing**, *past* **underwent** /ˌʌndəˈwent/, *past participle* **undergone** /ˌʌndəˈgɒn/)
to experience something that is unpleasant: *He underwent five operations on his foot.*

un·der·grad·u·ate /ˌʌndəˈgrædjuət/ *noun*
someone who is studying for a DEGREE

un·der·ground¹ /ˌʌndəˈgraʊnd/ *adjective, adverb*
under the ground: *an underground passage* | *They're putting the telephone lines underground.*

un·der·ground² /ˈʌndəgraʊnd/ *noun*
a railway system under the ground, especially the system in London: *We went there by underground.*

un·der·growth /ˈʌndəgrəʊθ/ *noun (no plural)*
plants that cover the ground between trees: *They pushed their way through the undergrowth.*

un·der·line /ˌʌndəˈlaɪn/ *verb (present participle* **underlining**, *past* **underlined**)
to put a line under a word or words: *I've underlined the bit which I think is wrong.*

un·der·neath /ˌʌndəˈniːθ/ *preposition, adverb*
under or below: *She sat underneath the tree out of the sun.* | *They looked down from the bridge at the water underneath.*

un·der·stand /ˌʌndəˈstænd/ *verb (present participle* **understanding**, *past* **understood**)
1 to know the meaning of words or ideas: *I don't understand this word here.* | *She doesn't understand English.*
2 to know why something is happening: *People don't understand what's happening in their own country.*

3 to know what someone feels or thinks: *She said her parents didn't understand her.*

NOTE: Do not use **understand** in the present continuous tense. Do **not** say "I am understanding something", say "I understand": *I don't understand the joke.* | *I understand all of the questions except one.*

un·der·stand·ing¹ /ˌʌndəˈstændɪŋ/ *noun (no plural)*
knowledge of something, especially the meaning of words or ideas: *His understanding of English is very good.*

understanding² *adjective*
kind and willing to listen: *I told her why I was worried and she was very understanding.*

un·der·stood /ˌʌndəˈstʊd/
the past tense and past participle of the verb **understand**

un·der·take /ˌʌndəˈteɪk/ *verb (present participle* **undertaking**, *past* **undertook** /-ˈtʊk/, *past participle* **undertaken** /-ˈteɪkən/)
undertake to do something *formal* to promise or agree to do something: *She undertook to pay the money back before July.*

underwater

swimming underwater

un·der·wa·ter /ˈʌndəˌwɔːtər/ *adjective*
used or done below the surface of the water: *an underwater camera* | *He's really good at swimming underwater.*

un·der·way /ˌʌndəˈweɪ/ *adjective*
if an activity is underway, it has started. If it gets underway, it starts

un·der·wear /ˈʌndəweər/ *noun (no plural)*
clothes that you wear next to your body, under other clothes

un·der·went /ˌʌndəˈwent/
the past tense of the verb **undergo**

un·did /ʌnˈdɪd/
the past tense of the verb **undo**

un·do /ʌnˈduː/ verb (present participle
undoing, past **undid** /ʌnˈdɪd/, past
participle **undone** /ʌnˈdʌn/)
to untie or unfasten something: He
undid the string round the parcel. I Can
you undo my necklace for me?

un·done /ʌnˈdʌn/ adjective
if something is undone, it has not been
fastened: Your skirt's undone.

un·doubt·ed·ly /ʌnˈdaʊtɪdlɪ/ adverb
without doubt: He is undoubtedly the
best man for the job.

un·dress /ʌnˈdres/ verb
1 to take your clothes off: You can
undress in here.
2 to take someone's clothes off: She
undressed the baby.
3 **get undressed** to take your clothes
off: I got undressed and went to bed.

un·eas·i·ly /ʌnˈiːzɪlɪ/ adverb
in a way that shows that you are slightly
worried or afraid: He looked at me
uneasily.

un·ea·sy /ʌnˈiːzɪ/ adjective
slightly worried or afraid: I had an
uneasy feeling that someone was
watching me.

un·em·ployed /ˌʌnɪmˈplɔɪd/ adjective
someone who is unemployed does not
have a job for which they are paid: He
was unemployed for two months after
leaving college.

un·em·ploy·ment /ˌʌnɪmˈplɔɪment/
noun (no plural)
when people do not have jobs for which
they are paid: Unemployment here has
been high since the factory closed.

un·e·ven /ʌnˈiːvn/ adjective
not level or flat: The road's very uneven
here. ⇨ opposite EVEN

un·ex·pect·ed /ˌʌnɪkˈspektɪd/ adjective
not what you expected: an unexpected
visitor

un·fair /ʌnˈfeəʳ/ adjective
not treating people equally: I think it's
very unfair to let him go and not me.
unfairly adverb: He's been very unfairly
treated. ⇨ opposite FAIR

un·fash·ion·a·ble /ʌnˈfæʃnəbl/
adjective
not popular at the present time: I'm not
wearing that horrible shirt – it's so
unfashionable! ⇨ opposite FASHIONABLE

un·fas·ten /ʌnˈfɑːsn/ verb
to move something such as a button or
piece of string, so that it stops holding
something together: James unfastened
his coat.

un·fin·ished /ʌnˈfɪnɪʃt/ adjective
not finished: You can do any unfinished
work after lunch.

un·fit /ʌnˈfɪt/ adjective
1 not healthy because you have not
been taking enough exercise
2 unsuitable or not good enough for
something: They said the meat was
unfit **for** humans. I The committee
decided he was unfit **to be** captain.
⇨ opposite FIT

un·fold /ʌnˈfəʊld/ verb
to open out something from a folded
position: She took the letter out of the
envelope and unfolded it carefully.

un·for·tu·nate /ʌnˈfɔːtʃənət/ adjective
unlucky: He's been very unfortunate.
⇨ opposite FORTUNATE

un·for·tu·nate·ly /ʌnˈfɔːtʃənətlɪ/ adverb
used to say that you are sorry or
disappointed about something:
Unfortunately, I can't come to the party.
⇨ opposite FORTUNATELY

un·friend·ly /ʌnˈfrendlɪ/ adjective
not pleasant or kind: He always seems
rather unfriendly. ⇨ opposite FRIENDLY

un·grate·ful /ʌnˈɡreɪtfəl/ adjective
if you are ungrateful, you do not feel that
you want to thank someone, although
they have done something kind for you:
Don't think I'm ungrateful, but I can't
accept your offer. ⇨ opposite GRATEFUL

un·hap·pi·ly /ʌnˈhæpɪlɪ/ adverb
in an unhappy way: "I can't," she said
unhappily.

un·hap·py /ʌnˈhæpɪ/ adjective
1 not happy: He's obviously not
happy. I an unhappy marriage
2 feeling worried or not sure: She was
unhappy **about** the children going out
alone. ⇨ opposite HAPPY

un·health·y /ʌnˈhelθɪ/ adjective
1 not in good health: He looks thin and
unhealthy.

A B C D E F G H I J K L M N O P Q R S T U V W X Y Z

2 making you unhealthy: *It's very unhealthy to eat so much fat.* ⇨ opposite HEALTHY

un·help·ful /ʌn'helpfəl/ *adjective*
not helpful: *Thank you – you've been very helpful.*

u·ni·form /'juːnɪfɔːm/ *noun*
clothes worn for a special job or for school: *British policemen wear dark blue uniforms.*

un·im·por·tant /ˌʌnɪm'pɔːtnt/ *adjective*
not important: *All these small details are quite unimportant.*

un·in·hab·it·ed /ˌʌnɪn'hæbɪtɪd/ *adjective*
if a place is uninhabited, no one lives there: *an uninhabited island*

u·nion /'juːnjən/ *noun*
1 a group of workers who have joined together to protect their pay and working conditions
2 (*no plural*) when two or more people, groups, or countries are joined together: *the union of East and West Germany*

u·nique /juː'niːk/ *adjective*
if something is unique, it is the only one of its type: *a unique chance to see inside the palace* | *Each plate is painted by hand, and therefore unique.*

u·nit /'juːnɪt/ *noun*
1 one complete thing or set: *This lesson is divided into four units – speaking practice, writing practice, new words, and a word game.*
2 an amount or quantity used as a standard of measurement: *The pound is the unit of money in Britain.*

u·nite /juː'naɪt/ *verb* (*present participle* **uniting**, *past* **united**)
to join together: *The threat of attack united the government and its opponents.*

U·nit·ed Na·tions /juːˌnaɪtɪd 'neɪʃnz/ *noun*
the United Nations an organization of countries that tries to solve the world's problems

u·ni·ver·sal /ˌjuːnɪ'vɜːsl/ *adjective*
affecting everyone in the world or in a particular group: *There was almost universal agreement.*

u·ni·verse /'juːnɪvɜːs/ *noun*
all of the stars and PLANETS in space

u·ni·ver·si·ty /ˌjuːnɪ'vɜːsətɪ/ *noun* (*plural* **universities**)
a place where you study a subject at a high level, usually so that you can get a DEGREE: *He's still at university.* | *Which university is she going to?*

un·kind /ʌn'kaɪnd/ *adjective*
rather cruel: *I don't know why he's always so unkind* **to** *me.* ⇨ opposite KIND

un·known /ʌn'nəʊn/ *adjective*
1 not known: *The cause of the disease is unknown.*
2 not famous: *an unknown writer*

un·lead·ed /ʌn'ledɪd/ *adjective*
unleaded FUEL causes less damage to the environment, because it does not contain any LEAD

un·less /ən'les/
1 used to say that something will happen if something else does not happen: *You'll be late unless you leave right now.*
2 not... unless, never... unless used to say that something happens only if another thing happens: *The baby never cries unless it's hungry.*

un·like /ʌn'laɪk/ *preposition*
different from another person or thing: *She's quite unlike her mother.*

un·like·ly /ʌn'laɪklɪ/ *adjective*
something that is unlikely is probably not going to happen: *I think they're unlikely* **to** *come now – it's getting late.* ⇨ opposite LIKELY

un·load /ʌn'ləʊd/ *verb*
to take goods off a vehicle: *Two men unloaded the lorry.* ⇨ opposite LOAD

un·lock /ʌn'lɒk/ *verb*
to open something with a key: *She unlocked the door and went in.* ⇨ opposite LOCK

un·luck·y /ʌn'lʌkɪ/ *adjective*
bringing or having bad luck: *Some people think that 13 is an unlucky number.* | *We were unlucky with the weather.* ⇨ opposite LUCKY

un·mar·ried /ʌn'mærɪd/ *adjective*
not married: *an unmarried man*

un·mis·tak·a·ble /ˌʌnmɪ'steɪkəbl/ *adjective*
easy to recognize: *the unmistakable smell of gas*

un·nat·u·ral /ʌnˈnætʃərəl/ *adjective*
not what is usual, expected, or normal:
It's unnatural for a child to be so quiet.

un·ne·ces·sa·ry /ʌnˈnesəsəri/ *adjective*
not needed: *They've made a lot of unnecessary changes – people were happy before.* ⇨ opposite NECESSARY

unpack

unpacking a suitcase

un·pack /ʌnˈpæk/ *verb*
to take things out of a case or box: *I'm just going to unpack my case.* | *He unpacked and had a bath.* ⇨ opposite PACK

un·pleas·ant /ʌnˈpleznt/ *adjective*
not nice: *There's no need to be so unpleasant.* | *There's rather an unpleasant smell in here.* ⇨ opposite PLEASANT

un·pop·u·lar /ʌnˈpɒpjʊləʳ/ *adjective*
not liked by many people: *His policies were very unpopular.* ⇨ opposite POPULAR

un·rea·son·a·ble /ʌnˈriːznəbl/ *adjective*
not fair or reasonable: *He's being completely unreasonable – he's asking for something that's impossible.* ⇨ opposite REASONABLE

un·re·li·a·ble /ʌnrɪˈlaɪəbl/ *adjective*
if someone or something is unreliable, you cannot depend on them to do what you want: *I wouldn't ask him to help – he's very unreliable.* | *My car's getting a bit unreliable.* ⇨ opposite RELIABLE

un·ru·ly /ʌnˈruːli/ *adjective*
behaving in an uncontrolled way: *unruly children*

un·safe /ʌnˈseɪf/ *adjective*
dangerous: *Keep off the bridge – it's unsafe.* ⇨ opposite SAFE

un·sat·is·fac·tory /ʌnsætɪsˈfæktri/ *adjective*
not good enough: *Their explanation was entirely unsatisfactory.* ⇨ opposite SATISFACTORY

un·self·ish /ʌnˈselfɪʃ/ *adjective*
someone who is unselfish thinks about

other people's needs, not their own needs: *She's a very sweet girl – completely unselfish and very loving.* ⇨ opposite SELFISH

un·stead·i·ly /ʌnˈstedɪli/ *adverb*
in an unsteady way: *The old woman rose unsteadily to her feet.*

un·stead·y /ʌnˈstedi/ *adjective*
shaking or moving in an uncontrolled way: *That chair's rather unsteady – be careful.*

un·suc·cess·ful /ʌnsəkˈsesfəl/ *adjective*
not achieving what you wanted: *After several unsuccessful attempts to start the car, we gave up and phoned for help.* ⇨ opposite SUCCESSFUL

un·suit·a·ble /ʌnˈsuːtəbl/ *adjective*
not good for a particular purpose or person: *It's a good movie, but unsuitable for young children.* ⇨ opposite SUITABLE

un·sym·pa·thet·ic /ʌnsɪmpəˈθetɪk/ *adjective*
not kind or understanding about someone else's unhappiness ⇨ opposite SYMPATHETIC

un·ti·dy /ʌnˈtaɪdi/ *adjective* (**untidier**, **untidiest**)
not tidy: *Her room was so untidy – there were clothes all over the floor.* ⇨ opposite TIDY

un·tie /ʌnˈtaɪ/ *verb* (*present participle* **untying**, *past* **untied**)
to unfasten something that has been tied: *She untied the parcel and looked inside.*

un·til /ənˈtɪl/
up to a particular time: *The shop's open until 5 o'clock.* | *Let's wait until Dad gets home.* | *I couldn't swim until I was seven.*

un·true /ʌnˈtruː/ *adjective*
not true: *That's completely untrue, and you know it!*

un·used /ʌnˈjuːzd/ *adjective*
something that is unused has not been used: *They said we could return any unused bottles to the shop.*

un·u·su·al /ʌnˈjuːʒʊəl/ *adjective*
not usual or ordinary: *It's unusual to have so much rain.* | *an unusual hat*

un·well /ʌnˈwel/ *adjective*
ill: *He's been unwell since Sunday.*

A
B
C
D
E
F
G
H
I
J
K
L
M
N
O
P
Q
R
S
T
U
V
W
X
Y
Z

un·wil·ling /ʌnˈwɪlɪŋ/ *adjective*
not willing: *He seemed unwilling to come with us.*

un·wind /ʌnˈwaɪnd/ *verb* (*past* **unwound** /ʌnˈwaʊnd/)
1 to stop being busy or worried and start to become calm: *I'm hoping he'll be able to unwind when we go on holiday.*
2 to undo something that has been wound: *She unwound some wool from the ball.*

un·wise /ʌnˈwaɪz/ *adjective*
not reasonable or wise: *It would be very unwise to let him go alone.*

un·wound /ʌnˈwaʊnd/
the past tense and past participle of the verb **unwind**

un·wrap /ʌnˈræp/ *verb* (*present participle* **unwrapping**, *past* **unwrapped**)
to take the covering off a parcel: *Are you going to unwrap your present?* ⇨ opposite WRAP

up¹ /ʌp/ *adjective, adverb, preposition*
1 to or in a higher position: *She climbed up the tree.* | *The village is high up in the hills.* ⇨ opposite DOWN ⇨ see picture on page 208
2 into an upright position: *Stand up for a minute.* | *He turned his collar up.*
3 out of bed: *Are you up yet?* | *Come on, get up!*
4 used to say that something increases in amount or strength: *Can you turn the music up?* | *Sales are up this year.* ⇨ opposite DOWN
5 further along a road or line: *They live just up the road.* | *Can you move up a bit and make room for Peter to sit down?*
6 come up to someone, go up to someone, run up to someone, etc to walk, run, etc towards someone until you are next to them: *He came up to me and asked my name.*
7 eat something up, finish something up, etc to eat, finish, etc something completely, so that there is no more left: *Eat up your potatoes.* | *Someone's finished up the milk.*
8 up to as much as a particular amount: *He can earn up to £45,000 a year.* | *The room can hold up to 200 people.*
9 up to, up until until: *It hasn't been a problem up to now.* | *She lived at home right up until she got married.*

10 be up to something (a) to be secretly busy doing something bad: *I think he's up to something.* **(b)** to be strong enough or good enough to do something: *Are you up to a walk along the beach?* | *They don't think he's up to the job.*
11 What's up? used to ask what is upsetting someone

up² *verb* (*present participle* **upping**, *past* **upped**)
to increase an amount or level: *They've just upped her pay.*

up·date /ʌpˈdeɪt/ *verb*
to change something so that it includes things that are recent or new: *We need to update our files.*

up·grade /ʌpˈɡreɪd/ *verb*
to change something so that it is better: *We've just upgraded our PC.*

uphill

walking uphill

up·hill /ʌpˈhɪl/ *adverb*
going towards the top of a hill: *They were walking uphill, and she was getting tired.* ⇨ opposite DOWNHILL

up·on /əˈpɒn/ *preposition*
on: *The village stands upon a hill.*

up·per /ˈʌpəʳ/ *adjective*
the upper part of something is the higher part of it: *the upper part of the body*

upper case /ˌʌpə ˈkeɪs/ *noun*
letters written in their large form, for example A, B, D, G, R etc ⇨ compare LOWER CASE

up·right /ˈʌpraɪt/ *adjective*
with the top part facing up: *Keep the bottle upright.*

up·set¹ /ʌpˈset/ *adjective*
feeling unhappy or worried about something: *She was upset because he wouldn't talk to her.*

upset² verb (present participle **upsetting**, past **upset**)
1 to knock something over: *I upset my drink all over the table.*
2 to make someone unhappy or worried: *It upset me when you said I was lazy.* | *He upset me when he laughed at my idea.*
3 to spoil something that was planned: *The weather upset our plan to have the meal outside.*

up·side down /ˌʌpsaɪd 'daʊn/ adjective, adverb
with the top facing down and the bottom facing up: *I think you've put that picture upside down.*

upside down

The picture is upside down.

up·stairs /ˌʌp'steəz/ adjective, adverb
on or towards an upper floor in a building: *We could hear a party in the flat upstairs.* | *"Where's Jane?" "Upstairs."* | *The children watched from an upstairs window.* ⇨ opposite DOWNSTAIRS ⇨ see picture at DOWNSTAIRS

up-to-date /ˌʌp tə 'deɪt/ adjective
modern or recent: *They've got the most up-to-date equipment.* | *Is our information up-to-date?*

up·wards /'ʌpwədz/ adverb
also **upward** going, looking, or facing up: *The plane moved gently upward.* | *I looked upwards towards his window.*
upward adjective: *He made an upward movement with his hand.* ⇨ opposite DOWNWARDS

ur·ban /'ɜːbən/ adjective
relating to towns or cities: *Most people live in urban areas.* ⇨ compare RURAL

urge¹ /ɜːdʒ/ verb (present participle **urging**, past **urged**)
to try very hard to persuade someone to do something: *He urged her to rest.*

urge² noun
a strong wish: *She suddenly had an urge to go back to New York.*

ur·gent /'ɜːdʒənt/ adjective
very important and needing to be done without delay: *She said she had an urgent message for you.*
urgently adverb: *I need to speak to him urgently.*

us /əs; strong ʌs/
the person who is speaking and some other person or people: *The teacher told us to be quiet.* | *"Where did you get that book from?" "Granny gave it to us."*

use¹ /juːz/ verb (present participle **using**, past **used**)
1 to do something with something, for a particular purpose: *Do you know how to use the printer?* | *What do you use this thing **for**?*
2 use something up to use something until it has all gone: *We've used all the toothpaste up.*

use² /juːs/ noun
1 a purpose for which something is used: *This piece of equipment has many uses.*
2 the fact that something is used, or the way that it is used: *the use of animals in experiments*
3 (no plural) the fact that you can use something: *I've got the use of her car while she's away.*
4 be no use to be useless: *It's no use asking her – she doesn't know.*

used /juːzd/ adjective
a used car or piece of clothing has had an owner already: *Are you looking for a new or used car?*

used to¹ /'juːst tuː/ adjective
if you are used to something, you have done it or seen it many times before and so it does not surprise you or worry you: *He's used to driving in heavy traffic.* | *You'll soon get used to his bad temper.*

used to² verb
if something used to happen, it happened regularly or often in the past, but it does not happen now: *He used to play football every Saturday when he was young.* | *My father never used to smoke, but he does now.*

NOTE: The negative of **used to** is **didn't use to** or **didn't used to**: *I didn't use to like fish.* The question form of **used to** is **did you/he/she use to ...?**: *Did you use to go there often?*

use·ful /'juːsfəl/ adjective
helpful, or with a good purpose: *This information will be very useful.* | *That's a useful knife.*

use·less /'juːsləs/ adjective
with no good purpose: *These scissors are useless – the handle's broken!* | *It's useless trying to persuade her – she's already decided.*

us·er /'juːzəʳ/ noun
a person who uses something: *This affects all road users, not just car drivers.*

user-friend·ly /ˌjuːzə 'frendlɪ/ adjective
easy to use or understand: *a user-friendly guide to computing*

u·su·al /'juːʒʊəl/ adjective
1 done or happening most often, or as expected: *We had lunch at our usual table by the window.*
2 **as usual** in the way that something most often happens: *He was late, as usual.*

u·su·al·ly /'juːʒʊəlɪ/ adverb
generally: *He usually behaves very well; I don't know why he was so naughty today.*

u·ten·sil /juːˈtensl/ noun
a tool or object used when preparing food or cooking: *cooking utensils*

ut·most /'ʌtməʊst/ adjective, noun
1 **the utmost care, the utmost importance, etc** the greatest care, the greatest importance, etc: *We have taken the utmost care to ensure their safety.*
2 **do your utmost** to make the greatest possible effort: *They did their utmost to prevent the disease spreading.*

ut·ter[1] /'ʌtəʳ/ verb
if someone utters something, they make a sound or say something: *He looked at me without uttering a word.*

utter[2] adjective
complete: *What he is doing is utter stupidity!*

utterly adverb: *That's utterly ridiculous!*

V, v /viː/
the twenty-second letter of the English alphabet

v. /viː, ˈvɜːsəs/
a short way of writing and saying the word **versus**: *the England v. Australia cricket match*

va·can·cy /ˈveɪkənsɪ/ noun (plural **vacancies**)
1 a room in a hotel or guest house that is not being used: *There was a sign outside saying 'No Vacancies'.*
2 a job that is available for someone to start doing: *There is a vacancy **for** a driver.*

va·cant /ˈveɪkənt/ adjective
1 if a seat, room, or house is vacant, it is not being used or lived in: *We looked all over town for a vacant room.* | *The toilet is vacant now.*
2 a vacant job is available for someone to start doing.

va·ca·tion /vəˈkeɪʃn/ noun
a holiday from school or university: *She worked in France during the summer vacation.*

vac·cin·ate /ˈvæksɪneɪt/ verb (present participle **vaccinating**, past **vaccinated**)
to put a substance into a person's or animal's body as a protection against an illness: *Have you been vaccinated against German measles?*

vac·cin·a·tion /ˌvæksɪˈneɪʃn/ noun
when a substance is put into a person's or animal's body as a protection against an illness

vac·uum¹ /ˈvækʊm/ noun
a space with no air in it

vacuum² verb
to clean a floor with a VACUUM CLEANER: *Have you vacuumed the sitting-room yet?*

vacuum cleaner

vacuum clean·er /ˈvækjʊm ˌkliːnəʳ/ noun
a machine that cleans the floor by sucking up dirt

vacuum flask /ˈvækjʊm ˌflɑːsk/ noun
also **flask** a container used to keep drinks either hot or cold

vague /veɪg/ adjective
not clear in your mind: *I have only a vague idea where the house is.*
vaguely adverb: *I know vaguely where the house is.*

vain /veɪn/ adjective
too proud of yourself, especially of what you look like: *She's very vain – she's always looking at herself in the mirror.*

val·id /ˈvælɪd/ adjective
a valid ticket, document, etc can be used legally and is officially acceptable: *If you want to travel abroad, you need a valid passport.*

valley

val·ley /ˈvælɪ/ noun
the low land lying between two lines of hills or mountains, often with a river running through it

val·u·a·ble /ˈvæljʊəbl/ adjective
1 worth a lot of money: *He gave her a valuable diamond ring.*
2 very useful: *Your help has been very valuable.*

val·ue¹ /ˈvæljuː/ noun
the amount that something is worth: *What is the value of your house?* | *The thieves took some jewellery of great value.* | *Your help has been of great value.*

value² verb (present participle **valuing**, past **valued**)
1 to think that something is worth a lot: *I value your advice.*
2 to say how much something is worth: *He valued the ring **at** £100.*

valve /vælv/ noun
part of a pipe that opens and shuts in order to control the flow of liquid, air, or gas passing through it: *I need a new valve for my bicycle tyre.*

A B C D E F G H I J K L M N O P Q R S T U V W X Y Z

van /væn/ noun
a road vehicle like a big car, used for carrying goods

van·dal /'vændl/ noun
a person who deliberately damages or destroys things, especially public property: *All the seat covers on the train had been torn by vandals.*

van·dal·ism /'vændəlɪzəm/ noun (no plural)
the crime of deliberately damaging or destroying things, especially public property

van·dal·ize /'vændəlaɪz/ verb (present participle **vandalizing**, past **vandalized**)
to deliberately damage or destroy public property: *All the public telephones round here have been vandalized.*

va·nil·la /və'nɪlə/ noun (no plural)
a substance with a slightly sweet taste, added to ICE-CREAM and other foods: *Get some vanilla ice cream when you go shopping.*

van·ish /'vænɪʃ/ verb
to disappear suddenly: *I thought it would rain, but the clouds have vanished and it's a fine day.* | *They have been searching the streets of Glasgow for their son since he vanished six weeks ago.*

van·i·ty /'vænəti/ noun (no plural)
when someone is too proud of their appearance, abilities etc

va·pour /'veɪpər/ noun (no plural)
a lot of small drops of liquid in the air, for example in the form of clouds or steam: *water vapour*

va·ri·e·ty /və'raɪəti/ noun
1 (no plural) different things: *You need variety in your life.*
2 **a variety of** a group containing different types of the same thing: *These shirts come in a variety of colours.*
3 (plural **varieties**) a type that is different from others in the same group: *There are many different varieties **of** bananas.*
4 (no plural) theatre or television entertainment that includes singing, dancing, jokes, and acts of skill: *We went to a brilliant variety show last night.*

var·i·ous /'veəriəs/ adjective
many different: *There are various colours to choose from; which do you like best?*

var·nish[1] /'vɑːnɪʃ/ noun (plural **varnishes**)
a liquid that is put onto wood to protect it and to give it a hard shining surface

varnish[2] verb
to put a special liquid on wood to protect it and give it a hard shining surface

var·y /'veəri/ verb (present participle **varying**, past **varied**)
to change: *Prices vary from shop to shop.* | *His moods vary a lot.*

vase /vɑːz/ noun
a container for putting cut flowers in

vast /vɑːst/ adjective
very big: *There is a vast difference between temperatures in the north and in the south.* | *A vast majority of people watch television every evening.* ⇨ same meaning HUGE, ENORMOUS

've /v, əv/
have: *I've got a letter for you.* | *We've finished.*

veal /viːl/ noun (no plural)
meat from a very young cow

vege·ta·ble /'vedʒtəbl/ noun
a plant such as a CARROT, CABBAGE or potato, that is grown in order to be eaten: *They sell fruit and vegetables.* ⇨ see picture on page 199

ve·ge·tar·i·an /,vedʒɪ'teəriən/ noun
a person who does not eat meat or fish, usually because they believe that it is wrong to kill animals for food
vegetarian adjective: *She only eats vegetarian food.*

ve·hi·cle /'viːəkl/ noun
something such as a bicycle, car, or bus, that carries people or goods

veil /veɪl/ noun
a covering for a woman's head and face: *The bride wore a white veil.*

vein /veɪn/ noun
one of the tubes in your body that carry blood to your heart

Vel·cro /'velkrəʊ/ noun
trademark a material used for fastening shoes, clothes etc, made from two special pieces of cloth that stick to each other

vel·vet /'velvɪt/ noun (no plural)
a type of cloth with a soft surface: *I bought some velvet curtains for the sitting room.*

ven·ti·late /'ventɪleɪt/ verb (present
participle **ventilating**, past **ventilated**)
to allow fresh air into a room or building

ve·ran·dah /və'rændə/ noun
an open area that is built onto a house,
with a roof and floor but no outside wall:
Let's take our drinks and sit out on the
verandah.

verb /vɜːb/ noun
a word that tells you that someone does
something or that something happens
or exists, for example, 'go', 'eat',
'finish', and 'be'

ver·dict /'vɜːdɪkt/ noun
a decision made by a law court: What's
the verdict? Is he guilty or not guilty?

verse /vɜːs/ noun
1 (no plural) writing in the form of a
poem, often so the words at the ends of
the lines sound similar: He's just
published a book of verse.
2 a set of lines that forms one part of a
poem or song: She sang the first verse
of the famous song.

ver·sion /'vɜːʃn/ noun
someone's description of what
happened: I have heard two different
versions **of** the story.

ver·sus /'vɜːsəs/ preposition
against a person or team in a sports
match: Are you going to watch the
football match? It's England versus
Germany.

ver·ti·cal /'vɜːtɪkl/ adjective
standing or pointing straight up: Her
shirt had grey and green vertical stripes.
⇨ compare HORIZONTAL

ve·ry /'veri/ adverb
1 used to make another word stronger:
It's very hot in this room. | I'm very well,
thank you. | The robbery was very
carefully planned.
2 **not very** used to make another word
weak. For example, if you say that
someone is 'not very big', you mean
that they are rather small: They didn't
stay very long (=they only stayed a short
time).

vest /vest/ noun
a piece of clothing that you wear next to
your skin and under other clothes on
the upper part of your body ⇨ see
picture on page 203

vet /vet/ noun
a doctor for animals: We had to take our
cat to the vet. ⇨ see picture on page 200

vi·a /'vaɪə/ preposition
travelling through a place when you are
going to another place: I went from
London to Birmingham via Oxford.

vi·brate /vaɪ'breɪt/ verb (present
participle **vibrating**, past **vibrated**)
to shake with small fast movements:
The music was so loud, the whole
house was vibrating.

vi·bra·tion /vaɪ'breɪʃn/ noun
a continuous small shaking movement:
I could feel the vibration of the building
as the train went by.

vic·ar /'vɪkər/ noun
a Christian priest who looks after one
church ⇨ compare BISHOP

vice /vaɪs/ noun
a bad part of someone's character:
Smoking is my only vice.

vice-pres·i·dent /,vaɪs 'prezɪdənt/
noun
the person who is next in rank to the
president of a country: We had a visit
from the American Vice-President.

vi·cin·i·ty /vɪ'sɪnəti/ noun (no plural)
the area around a place: The car was
found in the vicinity **of** (=near) the
school.

vi·cious /'vɪʃəs/ adjective
wanting to hurt people: He gave the
dog a vicious blow with his stick.

vic·tim /'vɪktɪm/ noun
someone who has been hurt or killed by
someone or something: She was the
victim **of** a road accident.

vic·to·ri·ous /vɪk'tɔːriəs/ adjective
successful in a fight or sports match:
We cheered the victorious team.

vic·to·ry /'vɪktəri/ noun (plural **victories**)
when a player or team wins a war, fight,
election, sports match, etc: The party is
hoping for victory in the next election.
⇨ opposite DEFEAT

vid·e·o[1] /'vɪdiəʊ/ noun
1 also **video cassette, videotape** a
TAPE of a film, television programme, or
real event, or a TAPE that you can use for
recording films, programmes, etc: Can I
have a video for my birthday? | Where's
the video of the wedding? | We've got
the football match **on** video.

2 also **video recorder** a machine used for playing and recording videos: *Set the video to go on at eight o'clock.*

video² *verb (present participle* **videoing,** *past* **videoed)**
also **videotape** to record a film, a television programme, or a real event on a special TAPE that you can play back later on your television: *I haven't got time to watch the film tonight, but I'm going to video it.*

video cas·sette /ˌvɪdɪəʊ kəˈset/ *noun*
a TAPE of a film, television programme, or real event ⇨ see picture on page 197

video game /ˈvɪdɪəʊ ˌgeɪm/ *noun*
a game in which you move pictures on a screen by pressing electronic controls

video re·cord·er /ˈvɪdɪəʊ rɪˌkɔːdəʳ/ *noun*
also **video** a machine that you use to record television programmes and play them back later. You can also use it to play videos that you have bought or hired ⇨ see picture on page 197

video shop /ˈvɪdɪəʊ ˌʃɒp/ *noun*
a shop where you can pay to borrow videos

vide·o·tape¹ /ˈvɪdɪəʊteɪp/ *noun*
a long narrow band of material in a plastic container, on which films, television programmes, or real events can be recorded

videotape² *verb (present participle* **videotaping,** *past* **videotaped)**
also **video** to record a film, a television programme, or a real event on a special TAPE that you can play back later on your television

view /vjuː/ *noun*
1 the ability to see something from a particular place: *The factory spoilt my view of the mountain.*
2 the things that you can see from a particular place: *The view from the top of the hill was lovely.*
3 an opinion: *In my view, he should never have been allowed out of prison.*

view·er /ˈvjuːəʳ/ *noun*
a person who watches television: *The programme is watched by millions of viewers.*

vig·or·ous /ˈvɪɡərəs/ *adjective*
very active or strong: *He's ninety, but he's as vigorous as someone much younger.*

vil·la /ˈvɪlə/ *noun*
a house with a garden in a country area or by the sea, used especially for holidays: *We rented a villa in the south of France.*

vil·lage /ˈvɪlɪdʒ/ *noun*
a small place in the country where people live, smaller than a town

vil·lag·er /ˈvɪlɪdʒəʳ/ *noun*
a person who lives in a village

vil·lain /ˈvɪlən/ *noun*
1 a bad character in a play or film
2 a criminal: *The villains got away with thousands of pounds in cash.*

vine /vaɪn/ *noun*
a climbing plant, especially one that produces the fruit from which wine is made

vin·e·gar /ˈvɪnɪɡəʳ/ *noun (no plural)*
a very sour liquid used in preparing food

vine·yard /ˈvɪnjɑːd/ *noun*
a piece of land where vines are grown for producing wine

vi·o·lence /ˈvaɪələns/ *noun (no plural)*
1 when people use force to attack other people and try to hurt or kill them: *There is a lot of violence on television these days.*
2 when something happens suddenly with a lot of force: *I ran into the nearest building to escape the violence of the storm.*

vi·o·lent /ˈvaɪələnt/ *adjective*
1 attacking other people and trying to hurt or kill them: *He was a violent man who often hit his wife.*
2 happening with a lot of force: *There was a violent storm last night.*

vi·o·let¹ /ˈvaɪələt/ *noun*
1 a small flower with a sweet smell
2 the colour of the violet, which is a mixture of blue and red

violet² *adjective*
having a colour that is a mixture of blue and red

vi·o·lin /ˌvaɪəˈlɪn/ *noun*
a musical instrument that you play by pulling a special stick across the strings, while holding it under your chin: *I'm learning the violin at school.* ⇨ see picture at VIOLINIST

vi·o·lin·ist violinist
/ˌvaɪəˈlɪnɪst/ noun
a person who
plays the violin

VIP /ˌviː aɪ ˈpiː/
noun
a very important
person; someone
who is famous or
powerful and
receives special
treatment

playing the violin

vir·tu·al re·al·i·ty
/ˌvɜːtʃuəl riːˈæləti/ noun (no plural)
when a computer makes you feel that
you are in a real situation by showing
you pictures and producing sounds that
seem to surround you

vir·tue /ˈvɜːtjuː/ noun
a good quality in someone's character:
Honesty is a virtue. | Susan has many
virtues.

vi·rus /ˈvaɪərəs/ noun
a very small living thing that causes
illnesses, or an illness caused by this: I
caught a virus and had to stay away
from school.

vi·sa /ˈviːzə/ noun
an official mark that is put on your
PASSPORT, that allows you to enter or
leave another country: Do Americans
need a visa to visit Britain?

vis·i·ble /ˈvɪzəbl/ adjective
able to be seen: The smoke from the fire
was visible from the road. ⇨ opposite
INVISIBLE

vi·sion /ˈvɪʒn/ noun
1 (no plural) the ability to see: She has
good vision.
2 an idea or picture in your mind about
what might happen in the future: He
had a vision of himself as a rich
businessman.

vis·it¹ /ˈvɪzɪt/ verb
to go and see a person or place: We
visited our friends in town.

visit² noun
when you visit a person or place: We
had a visit from your teacher. | She paid
us a visit. | I paid a visit **to** the doctor.

vis·it·or /ˈvɪzɪtər/ noun
someone who visits a person or place:
London has millions of visitors every
year.

vi·su·al aid /ˌvɪʒuəl ˈeɪd/ noun
something such as a picture or film that
is used to help people learn

vi·tal /ˈvaɪtl/ adjective
extremely important or necessary: She
gave the court a vital piece of
information.

vit·a·min /ˈvɪtəmɪn, ˈvaɪ-/ noun
a substance found in food that is
important for good health: Oranges
contain vitamin C.

viv·id /ˈvɪvɪd/ adjective
1 bright or strong in colour: She had
vivid red hair.
2 producing clear pictures in your
mind: He gave a vivid description of the
accident.

vo·cab·u·la·ry /vəˈkæbjʊləri/ noun
(plural **vocabularies**)
1 (no plural) words: After we'd done
the grammar exercise we learnt some
new vocabulary.
2 all the words you know in a
language: He has a very large
vocabulary (=he knows a lot of words).

voice /vɔɪs/ noun
the sound that you make when you
speak or sing: We could hear the
children's voices in the garden. | She
spoke in a loud voice.

voice mail /ˈvɔɪs meɪl/ noun (no plural)
a system that records telephone calls
so that you can listen to them later: If
I'm not there, leave a message on my
voice mail.

volcano

lava

vol·ca·no /vɒlˈkeɪnəʊ/ noun (plural
volcanoes)
a mountain that sometimes explodes
and makes smoke and hot melted rock
come out of the top

vol·ley·ball /ˈvɒlibɔːl/ noun (no plural)
a game in which two teams hit a ball to
each other across a net with their hands
and try not to let it touch the ground

A B C D E F G H I J K L M N O P Q R S T U V W X Y Z

volt /vəʊlt/ *noun*
a measure of electricity

vol·ume /'vɒljʊm/ *noun*
1 (*no plural*) the amount of space that an object contains or that a substance fills: *What is the volume of this box?*
2 the amount of sound that is produced by a television, radio etc: *She turned down the volume on the radio.*
3 a book, especially one of a set: *We bought a twenty-volume encyclopedia.*

vol·un·ta·ri·ly /'vɒləntərəlɪ, -trəlɪ/ *adverb*
something that is done voluntarily is done because you want to do it, not because someone says you must do it

vol·un·tary /'vɒləntrɪ/ *adjective*
working without being paid, especially to help people: *She's a voluntary worker at the hospital.*

vol·un·teer[1] /ˌvɒlən'tɪər/ *noun*
a person who offers to do something without being told that they must do it: *We want some volunteers to deliver the food to the old people.*

volunteer[2] *verb*
to offer to do something without being told that you must do it: *We all volunteered to deliver the food to the old people.*

vom·it /'vɒmɪt/ *verb*
if you vomit, food comes up from your stomach and comes out through your mouth: *I think I must have eaten bad meat, because I was vomiting all night.*

vote[1] /vəʊt/ *verb* (*present participle* **voting**, *past* **voted**)
to show which person you want to choose for an official position, which plan you support, etc by, for example, secretly making a mark on a piece of paper or by putting up your hand in a meeting: *70 per cent of the people voted **for** independence.* | *Parliament voted **to** increase taxes.*

vote[2] *noun*
when you show that you support a particular person, party, plan, etc by, for example, secretly making a mark on a piece of paper or putting up your hand in a meeting: *There were seven votes **for** the plan and three votes **against** it.*

vow·el /'vaʊəl/ *noun*
the sounds shown by the letters **a, e, i, o,** and **u** ⇨ compare CONSONANT

voy·age /'vɔɪ-ɪdʒ/ *noun*
a long journey by sea or in space

vul·gar /'vʌlgər/ *adjective*
behaving in a way that is not polite, especially by talking in a rude way

W, w /'dʌblju:/
the twenty-third letter of the English alphabet

wade /weɪd/ verb (present participle **wading**, past **waded**)
to walk through water: We had to wade **across** the river.

wag /wæg/ verb (present participle **wagging**, past **wagged**)
if a dog wags its tail, it shakes it from side to side

wag·es /'weɪdʒɪz/ noun
the money that you get for the work that you do: I can't buy anything until I get my wages.

wag·on /'wægən/ noun
1 a vehicle that is pulled by a horse
2 British an open container with four wheels that is pulled by a train ⟹ same meaning TRUCK

wail /weɪl/ verb
to cry with a long loud sound, because you are sad or in pain: The child was wailing unhappily.

waist /weɪst/ noun
the narrow part around the middle of your body: Ann wore a belt around her waist.

waist·coat /'weɪskəʊt/ noun
a piece of clothing that you wear on the upper part of your body over a shirt. It has buttons down the front and does not cover your arms

wait¹ /weɪt/ verb
to stay somewhere until someone comes or until something happens: Could you wait here **until** I come back? | I was waiting **for** the bus.

wait² noun
a time of doing nothing until something happens: We had a long wait **for** the train.

wait·er /'weɪtər/ noun
a man who brings food to people in a restaurant

wait·ing room /'weɪtɪŋ ruːm/ noun
a room for people who are waiting, for example to see a doctor or to get on a train

wait·ress /'weɪtrəs/ noun (plural **waitresses**)
a woman who brings food to people in a restaurant

wake /weɪk/ verb (present participle **waking**, past **woke** /wəʊk/, American or **waked**, past participle **woken** /'wəʊkən/, American or **waked**)
1 also **wake up** to stop sleeping: I woke up very early this morning.
2 also **wake someone up** to make someone stop sleeping: Be quiet, or you'll wake the baby. | Can you wake me up at 8 o'clock?

walk¹ /wɔːk/ verb
to move forward by putting one foot in front of the other: We usually walk **to** school. ⟹ see picture on page 207

walk² noun
a journey on foot: Shall we **go for a walk** this afternoon? | It's a long walk into town.

walk·man /'wɔːkmən/ noun
trademark a small machine for playing music, that you carry with you ⟹ see picture on page 197

wall /wɔːl/ noun
1 an upright structure made of stone or brick, that surrounds an area or separates it from another area: There was a wall around the park.
2 one of the sides of a building or room: We've painted all the walls white.

wal·let /'wɒlɪt/ noun
a small flat case for your money

wallet

wall·pa·per /'wɔːlpeɪpər/ noun (no plural)
paper that is used to cover the walls of a room

wal·nut /'wɔːlnʌt/ noun
a large light brown nut

wan·der /'wɒndər/ verb
to walk slowly around or across a place without a purpose: The children wandered **about** in the woods. | Don't wander **off**.

want¹ /wɒnt/ verb
1 to wish to have something or do something: What do you want **for** your

A B C D E F G H I J K L M N O P Q R S T U V W X Y Z

birthday? | *The kids want to go to the park.*

2 to need something: *We want a smaller hammer for the next part of the job.* | *This cloth wants washing.*

3 used for suggesting what someone should do: *You want to leave early to avoid the traffic.*

want² *noun (no plural)*
a situation in which people need something such as food or money: *a life of want*

war /wɔːʳ/ *noun*
1 a time of fighting between countries: *The two countries were at war for two years.* | *The country is preparing to go to war.* ⇨ compare BATTLE
2 **declare war** to start a war: *They've declared war on three neighbouring states.*

ward /wɔːd/ *noun*
a room in a hospital

war·den /'wɔːdn/ *noun*
a person who looks after a large building or a public area

war·drobe /'wɔːdrəʊb/ *noun*
a cupboard in which you hang your clothes ⇨ see picture on page 204

ware·house /'weəhaʊs/ *noun (plural* **warehouses** /-haʊzɪz/)
a large building for storing goods

war·fare /'wɔːfeəʳ/ *noun (no plural)*
the fighting that happens in a war

warm¹ /wɔːm/ *adjective*
1 not cold but not very hot: *warm water*
2 able to keep you warm: *warm clothes*
3 friendly: *a warm welcome*

warm² *verb*
1 also **warm someone or something up** to make someone or something warm: *Here, drink this – it'll soon warm you up.*
2 **warm up (a)** to do gentle exercises before doing some sport: *He swam a few lengths of the pool to warm up.* **(b)** to become warmer: *I've put the heating on so it should warm up fairly quickly now.*

warm·ly /'wɔːmlɪ/ *adverb*
1 in a way that will stop you from feeling cold: *You need to dress warmly.*
2 in a friendly way: *She greeted them warmly.*

warmth /wɔːmθ/ *noun (no plural)*
1 a feeling of being warm: *the warmth of the fire*
2 friendliness: *the warmth of her welcome*

warn /wɔːn/ *verb*
to tell someone about a possible problem or danger: *She warned me that it could be dangerous.*

warn·ing /'wɔːnɪŋ/ *noun*
something that tells someone about a possible problem or danger: *What can we do if people ignore our warnings?*

war·rant /'wɒrənt/ *noun*
a paper saying that someone may do something: *The police must have a warrant to search a house.*

was /wəz; *strong* wɒz/ *verb*
the past tense of the verb **be**, used with 'I', 'he', 'she', and 'it': *I was angry.*

wash¹ /wɒʃ/ *verb*
1 to make something clean with soap and water: *Have you washed your hands?*
2 **get washed** to clean yourself with soap and water
3 to flow over or against something: *The waves washed against the shore.*
4 **wash up (a)** British to clean the dishes, knives, forks, etc after a meal: *Whose turn is it to wash up?* **(b)** American to clean your hands: *Go wash up before dinner.*

wash² *noun*
1 **have a wash** to wash yourself, especially your hands and face: *She had a quick wash.*
2 **give someone or something a wash** to wash someone or something: *Could you give the car a wash?*
3 *(no plural)* American clothes that need to be washed or that have just been washed

wash·ba·sin /'wɒʃbeɪsn/ *noun*
a large bowl fixed to a wall for washing your hands and face ⇨ see picture on page 204

wash·ing /'wɒʃɪŋ/ *noun (no plural)*
British clothes that need to be washed or that have just been washed

washing ma·chine /'wɒʃɪŋ məˌʃiːn/ *noun*
a machine for washing clothes ⇨ see picture on page 204

was·n't /ˈwɒznt/

was not: *I wasn't at school yesterday.*

wasp /wɒsp/ *noun*

a yellow and
black insect
that stings

waste¹ /weɪst/
*verb (present
participle*
wasting, *past*
wasted)

to use something
wrongly or use too much of something:
Don't waste your money. | *Let's stop
wasting time.*

waste² *noun (no plural)*

1 a wrong or bad use of something: *The
meeting was a complete waste of time.*
2 unwanted materials or substances
that are left after something has been
used or produced: *household waste* |
industrial waste

watch¹ /wɒtʃ/ *noun (plural* **watches**)

1 a small clock that you wear on your
wrist
2 **keep watch** to look out for danger:
*He offered to keep watch while the
others slept.*
3 **keep a close watch on something**
to keep looking at something carefully:
Police kept a close watch on the house.

NOTE: Compare **watch**, **see**, and **look
at**. **See** is the general word for what
you do with your eyes: *I can't see – it's
too dark.* | *We saw them standing
outside the station.* If you **look at**
something, you move your eyes
towards it because you want to see it:
Look at me! | *They were looking at some
pictures.* If you **watch** something, you
pay attention to it for a long time: *We
watched a film on television.* | *He goes
to watch the football every Saturday.*
When you are talking about something
you will watch in the future or
something you have watched in the
past, you can use the verb **see**: *Did
you see that programme about wild
birds at the weekend?* | *I'd like to go
and see a film this evening.*

---

watch² *verb*

1 to look at something and pay

attention to it: *Watch, and I'll show you
how to do it.* | *They're watching
television in the other room.*
2 to look after someone or something:
Will you watch the baby for me?
3 to be careful: *Watch what you're
doing with that knife!*
4 **watch out** to be careful to avoid
something dangerous or unpleasant:
*You have to watch out **for** fast traffic
along here.* | *Watch out – you nearly
spilled your coffee all over me!*

wa·ter¹ /ˈwɔːtəʳ/ *noun (no plural)*

the liquid in rivers, lakes, and seas

water² *verb*

to put water onto land or plants

wa·ter·fall
/ˈwɔːtəfɔːl/ *noun*
a place where
water falls over
rocks from a
high place to a
lower place
⇨ see picture
on page 193

wa·ter·proof
/ˈwɔːtəpruːf/
adjective
waterproof

waterfall

clothing does not allow water to go
through it: *waterproof trousers*

watt /wɒt/ *noun*

a measure of electrical power: *a 60 watt
bulb*

wave¹ /weɪv/ *noun*

1 one of the raised lines of water on the
surface of the sea, that rise and fall
2 a movement of your hand from side
to side: *She gave a wave as she left the
house.*

wave² *verb (present participle* **waving**,
past **waved**)

1 to hold your arm up in the air and
move your hand from side to side: *We
waved goodbye to them.* ⇨ see picture
on page 207
2 to move from side to side or up and
down, or to make something do this:
The branches waved in the wind.

wax /wæks/ *noun (no plural)*

a substance used to make CANDLES, to
make a surface shine, or to remove hair

way /weɪ/ *noun*

1 direction: *Look both ways before you
cross the road.*

2 the road or path that will take you to a particular place: *Excuse me, is this the way to the station?*

3 distance: *It's quite a way to school.* ⇨ look at FAR

4 the way that you do something is how you do it: *There are many different ways of cooking potatoes. | Look at the way he's dressed!*

5 **be in a bad way** to be feeling very ill or upset

6 **by the way** a phrase you use when you want to talk about something different from what you have just been talking about: *"Do you want some coffee?" "Yes, please. By the way, did you phone Elaine?"*

7 **give way (a)** to break because of too much weight or pressure: *The branch gave way and she fell.* **(b)** to let another vehicle go along the road before moving your vehicle

8 **in the way** in a position that stops you from going somewhere: *You won't get through – there's a lorry in the way.*

9 **out of the way** not in a position that stops you going somewhere: *Could you get that chair out of the way?*

10 **no way** a phrase used for saying that you will definitely not do something: *"Can I go out, Mum?" "No way – you've got loads of homework to do!" | There's no way I'm going to agree to what he wants.*

11 **on the way** while going somewhere: *We'll stop and have lunch on the way.*

12 **the right way round** facing in the right direction: *Is this skirt on the right way round?*

13 **the wrong way round** not facing in the right direction: *You've got your T-shirt on the wrong way round.*

WC /ˌdʌblju: 'si:/ *noun*
a TOILET

we /wɪ; *strong* wi:/
the person who is speaking and some other person or people: *Shall we have lunch soon?*

weak /wi:k/ *adjective*
1 if you are weak, your body is not strong: *She was weak after her illness.*
2 a weak person does not have a strong character: *He was too weak and always let her do what she wanted.*

3 something that is weak cannot support a lot of weight: *a weak bridge*
4 a weak liquid has a lot of water in it: *a cup of weak tea* ⇨ opposite STRONG

weak·en /'wi:kən/ *verb*
to become less strong, or to make something less strong: *Her heart had been weakened by the disease.*

weak·ness /'wi:knəs/ *noun* (*plural* **weaknesses**)
1 a fault: *Spending too much money on clothes is her main weakness.*
2 (*no plural*) when you have no strength in your body

wealth /welθ/ *noun* (*no plural*)
a large amount of money and things that you own: *The country's wealth comes from its oil. | Charles inherited his father's wealth.*

wealth·y /'welθɪ/ *adjective* (**wealthier**, **wealthiest**)
someone who is wealthy has a lot of money: *She comes from a wealthy family.* ⇨ same meaning RICH ⇨ opposite POOR

weap·on /'wepən/ *noun*
something that you use to fight with, for example a gun or knife

wear /weəʳ/ *verb* (*past* **wore** /wɔ: ʳ/, *past participle* **worn** /wɔ:n/)
1 to have clothes or jewellery on your body: *She was wearing a really pretty dress.*
2 to weaken or damage something because of continual use: *You've worn a hole in your sock.*
3 **wear well** to remain in good condition: *This dress has worn really well – I've had it for years.*
4 **wear off** if a feeling wears off, it stops slowly: *The pain was wearing off.*
5 **wear something out** to damage something or make it weak because of continuous use: *I need some new trainers – I've worn my last pair out.*
6 **wear someone out** to make someone feel extremely tired: *You kids are wearing me out!*

wear·i·ly /'wɪərɪlɪ/ *adverb*
in a tired way: *"I can't help you any more," she said wearily.*

wear·y /'wɪərɪ/ *adjective* (**wearier**, **weariest**)
tired: *I felt weary after work.*

weath·er /'weðə^r/ noun (no plural)
the state of the wind, rain, sunshine, etc: *I don't like cold weather.* I *The weather was lovely all week.*

weave /wiːv/ verb (present participle **weaving**, past **wove** /wəʊv/, past participle **woven** /'wəʊvn/)
to make something such as cloth or a basket, by passing pieces of thread, grass, etc under and over other pieces of thread, grass, etc

web /web/ noun
1 a net of thin threads made by a SPIDER ⇨ see picture at SPIDER
2 the Web the WORLD WIDE WEB

web·cam /'webkæm/ noun
a camera that films something and then sends the images immediately from your computer to other computers

web·site /'websaɪt/ noun
a place you can visit on the INTERNET, to get information about a particular person, company, or subject: *The club has a very good website.*

we'd /wɪd; *strong* wiːd/
1 we would: *We'd like you to stay.*
2 we had: *We'd already eaten.*

wed·ding /'wedɪŋ/ noun
the ceremony in which a man and a woman get married: *I'm going to my brother's wedding tomorrow.* ⇨ compare MARRIAGE

Wednes·day /'wenzdeɪ, -dɪ/ noun
the third day of the week after Tuesday and before Thursday

weed¹ /wiːd/ noun
a plant that grows where you do not want it

weed² verb
to remove weeds from the ground: *I spent the afternoon weeding the garden.*

week /wiːk/ noun
a period of seven days, especially from Monday to Sunday: *I play tennis twice a week.* I *Will you come and see us next week?*

week·day /'wiːkdeɪ/ noun
any day except Saturday and Sunday

week·end /wiːk'end/ noun
Saturday and Sunday: *I don't work at the weekend.*

week·ly /'wiːklɪ/ adjective, adverb
happening or appearing once a week: *a weekly meeting* I *The magazine is published weekly.*

weep /wiːp/ verb (past **wept** /wept/)
to cry: *She wept when she heard the news.*

weigh

weigh /weɪ/ verb
1 to measure how heavy something is: *He weighed the fish.*
2 to have a particular weight: *He weighs about 70 kg.*

weight /weɪt/ noun (no plural)
how heavy someone or something is, or the fact that they are heavy: *The baby's weight was four kilos.* I *The weight of the books made it hard for her to run.*

weird /wɪəd/ adjective
strange: *weird clothes* ⇨ same meaning ODD

wel·come¹ /'welkəm/ adjective
1 if someone is welcome, people are pleased that they have come: *You're always welcome here.*
2 if something is welcome, people are pleased to see, hear, or have it: *That's welcome news.* I *A cup of tea would be very welcome.*
3 make someone welcome to behave in a friendly way towards someone when they arrive

welcome² verb (present participle **welcoming**, past **welcomed**)
1 to give someone a friendly greeting: *My aunt welcomed me warmly.*
2 to show that you are pleased about something that has been said or done: *They welcomed the change in the rules.*

welcome³ noun
a greeting when someone arrives: *We were given a warm welcome.*

wel·fare /'welfeə^r/ noun (no plural)
having the things you need to be

comfortable, healthy, or happy: *I'm only interested in your welfare.*

we'll /wɪl; *strong* wiːl/
we will: *We'll see Jane tomorrow.*

well [1] /wel/ *adjective*
in good health: *"How are you?" "Very well, thank you." | I don't feel very well.*

well [2] *adverb*
1 in a good way: *Mary can read very well.*
2 well done a phrase used to show that you have done something in a good way: *Well done! You read that beautifully.*
3 completely or thoroughly: *Wash your hands well before you eat.*
4 as well also: *Can you bring me a pencil – and a rubber as well?*
5 as well as and also: *I'm learning French as well as German.*

well [3]
a word you often say when you start speaking: *"Where are you going on holiday?" "Well, we may go to France."*

well [4] *noun*
a deep hole in the ground from which water or oil is taken

well-known /ˌwel ˈnəʊn/ *adjective*
known by many people: *a well-known writer*

well-off /ˌwel ˈɒf/ *adjective*
someone who is well-off has a lot of money ⇨ same meaning RICH

went /went/
the past tense of the verb **go**

wept /wept/
the past tense and past participle of the verb **weep**

we're /wɪəʳ; *strong* wiːəʳ/
we are: *We're in the same class.*

were /wəʳ; *strong* wɜːʳ/ *verb*
the past tense of the verb **be**, used with 'you', 'we', and 'they': *They were very happy.*

weren't /wɜːnt/
were not: *You weren't here yesterday, were you?*

west /west/ *noun, adjective, adverb*
the direction in which the sun goes down: *We travelled west for two days. | a village towards the west of the island*

west·ern /ˈwestən/ *adjective*
in or from the west: *Western areas will have some rain tomorrow.*

west·wards /ˈwestwədz/ *adverb*
towards the west: *We travelled westwards.*

wet [1] /wet/ (**wetter**, **wettest**)
1 covered with or containing liquid: *My hair's still wet. | Look out – that paint's wet.*
2 with a lot of rain: *a wet day* ⇨ opposite DRY

wet [2] *verb* (*present participle* **wetting**, *past* **wet** American or **wetted**)
to make something wet: *You've wet my skirt!* ⇨ opposite DRY

we've /wɪv; *strong* wiːv/
we have: *We've missed the train!*

whale /weɪl/ *noun*
a large animal like a fish, that lives in the sea

whale

wharf /wɔːf/ *noun* (*plural* **wharfs** or **wharves** /wɔːvz/)
a place built on the edge of water where you can take things on and off a ship

what /wɒt/
1 used when asking questions about something: *What's your name? | What did you say? | What time is it? | What colour shall I get?*
2 the thing that someone has done or will do: *She told me what he said. | Show me what you bought. | What we'll do is leave them a note.*
3 used to show surprise or other strong feelings: *What a silly thing to do!*
4 what about? used to make a suggestion: *"Where shall we go?" "What about the park?"*
5 what for? why: *What are you telling me for?*
6 what's this for, what's that for? used to ask what use something has

what·ev·er /wɒtˈevəʳ/
1 anything at all: *You can do whatever you want.*
2 used to say that nothing will change a situation: *Whatever he says I won't change my mind. | Whatever happens, I'm not leaving.*

3 used to show that you do not mind what happens: *"Do you want me to invite him or not?" "Whatever."*

wheat /wiːt/ *noun (no plural)*
a crop that is grown for its grains, which are made into flour

wheel /wiːl/ *noun*
one of the round things on a vehicle that turns around so that the vehicle can move ⇨ see picture at BICYCLE

wheel·bar·row /'wiːlbærəʊ/ *noun*
a container with a wheel at the front and two handles at the back

wheel·chair /'wiːltʃeər/ *noun*
a chair with big wheels that is used by people who cannot walk ⇨ see picture at CHAIR

when /wen/
1 at what time: *When will the bus come?*
2 at a particular time: *I lived in this village when I was a boy.*

when·ev·er /wen'evər/
1 every time that a particular thing happens: *Please come to see me whenever you like.* I *Whenever I see him, I speak to him.*
2 used in questions instead of 'when', to show that you are surprised: *Whenever did you have time to do all that work?*

where /weər/
at, to, or from a particular place: *Where's that train going?* I *Do you know where Jane is?*

wher·ev·er /weər'evər/
1 at or to any place: *I'll drive you wherever you want to go.*
2 used instead of 'where', to show that you are surprised or angry: *You're late – wherever have you been?*

wheth·er /'weðər/
if: *I don't know whether he'll come or not.* I *She can't decide whether to go or not.*

which /wɪtʃ/
1 used to ask about a person or thing, when there is a choice: *Which of you is taller?* I *Which shoes shall I wear?* I *Which one do you want?*
2 used to give more information about something: *We went to Ely, which is a town near Cambridge.* I *Did you see the letter which came today?*

while[1] /waɪl/
during the time that something is happening: *I met her while I was at school.* I *While the child played, her mother worked.*

while[2] *noun*
a while a length of time: *After a while she fell asleep.* I *We've been here quite a while.*

whim·per[1] /'wɪmpər/ *verb*
to make small weak cries of fear or pain: *The dog whimpered in the corner.*

whimper[2] *noun*
the sound made by someone or something that is whimpering: *The dog gave a whimper.*

whine[1] /waɪn/ *verb (present participle* **whining**, *past* **whined**)
1 to make a high sad sound: *The dog whined at the door.*
2 to complain a lot in an annoying voice: *Will you stop whining!*

whine[2] *noun*
a long high sound: *the whine of an aircraft engine*

whinge /wɪndʒ/ *verb (past* **whinged**)
to complain about things in an annoying way: *I wish you'd stop whingeing!*

whip[1] /wɪp/ *noun*
a long piece of leather or rope fastened to a handle, used for hitting animals or people

whip[2] *verb (present participle* **whipping**, *past* **whipped**)
1 to hit a person or an animal with a whip: *He was whipping the horse to make it run faster.*
2 to move eggs or CREAM around very fast in a bowl with a fork, etc: *whipped cream* ⇨ see picture on page 198

whirl /wɜːl/ *verb*
to move around very fast, or to make something do this: *The wind whirled the leaves into the air.*

whis·ker /'wɪskər/ *noun*
one of the long stiff hairs that grow near the mouth of a dog, cat, rat, etc

whis·ky /'wɪskɪ/ *noun (no plural)*
a strong alcoholic drink made in Scotland

whis·per[1] /'wɪspər/ *noun*
the way that you speak when you are whispering: *She spoke in a whisper.*

A B C D E F G H I J K L M N O P Q R S T U V W X Y Z

whisper[2] *verb*

to speak very quietly, so that it is difficult for people to hear you: *What are you two whispering about?*

whis·tle[1] /'wɪsl/ *noun*

1 an instrument that makes a high sound when you blow through it: *The teacher blew a whistle to start the race.*

2 a thin high sound made by putting your lips together and blowing through them: *He gave a whistle, and the dog ran up to him.*

whistle[2] *verb* (*present participle* **whistling**, *past* **whistled**)

1 to make a high sound by putting your lips together and blowing through them: *He whistled to his dog.*

2 to make music by whistling: *He was whistling a tune she'd heard before.*

white[1] /waɪt/ *adjective*

1 something that is white is the colour of the paper in this book: *She was wearing a white dress.*

2 someone who is white belongs to a race of people with light-coloured skin

3 white tea or coffee has milk in it

white[2] *noun*

1 (*no plural*) the colour of the paper in this book: *She was dressed in white.*

2 someone who belongs to a race of people with light-coloured skin

3 the white of an egg is the part that is not yellow or orange ⇨ see picture at EGG

who /huː/

1 used in questions to ask about a person or people: *Who gave you that book?* | *Who are those people?*

2 used to give more information about a person or people: *That's the man who lives in our old house.* | *I've discussed it with my sister, who's a teacher.*

who'd /huːd/

1 who had: *She asked who'd seen the film.*

2 who would: *He wanted to know who'd be helping.*

who·ev·er /huː'evər/

1 used to say that it is not important who someone is: *Whoever those people are, I don't want to see them.*

2 used in questions instead of 'who', to show that you are surprised or angry: *Whoever told you that silly story?*

whole[1] /həʊl/ *adjective*

all of something: *They told me the whole story.*

whole[2] *noun* (*no plural*)

1 the complete amount or thing: *Two halves make a whole.*

2 **the whole of** all of something: *It was raining the whole of the day.*

3 **on the whole** in general: *On the whole, I agree with you.*

who'll /huːl/

who will: *Who'll be there tomorrow?*

whol·ly /'həʊl-lɪ/ *adverb*

completely: *This is wholly unacceptable.*

whom /huːm/

formal a form of **who**, used as the object of a verb or after a word such as 'of', 'from', or 'with': *Whom did you see?* | *The club has fifty members, most of whom are men.*

who's /huːz/

1 who is: *Who's coming to the party?*

2 who has: *Who's eaten my apple?*

whose /huːz/

used to ask or tell who something belongs to: *Whose coat is that?* | *This is the woman whose little boy was ill.*

why /waɪ/

1 used to ask or talk about a reason: *Why is she crying?* | *I don't know why she's upset.* | *No one knows why.*

2 **why don't you?, why not?** used to make a suggestion: *Why don't you have a rest?* | *Why not phone her?*

wick·ed /'wɪkɪd/ *adjective*

very bad or immoral: *a wicked person*

wide[1] /waɪd/ *adjective* (**wider**, **widest**)

1 something that is wide measures a lot from one side to the other: *a wide road* ⇨ opposite NARROW ⇨ see picture at NARROW

2 used for saying how much something measures from one side to the other: *The table's about a metre wide.*

3 used for saying that something involves a large number of things or people: *We offer a wide range of activities.*

wide[2] *adverb*

fully: *The door was wide open.* | *At six o'clock he was wide awake.*

wide·ly /ˈwaɪdli/ *adverb*
1 happening in a lot of different places or done by a lot of different people: *Her books have been widely read.*
2 a lot: *Prices vary widely.*

wid·en /ˈwaɪdn/ *verb*
to make something wider, or to become wider: *They're going to widen the road.*

wid·ow /ˈwɪdəʊ/ *noun*
a woman whose husband is dead

wid·ow·er /ˈwɪdəʊəʳ/ *noun*
a man whose wife is dead

width /wɪdθ/ *noun*
how wide something is from one side to the other, or the fact that it is wide: *What's the width of the table?*

wife /waɪf/ *noun* (*plural* **wives** /waɪvz/)
the woman who a man is married to
⇨ compare HUSBAND

wig /wɪg/ *noun*
a covering for your head, that is intended to look like your own hair: *I think she's wearing a wig.*

wild /waɪld/ *adjective*
1 living in a natural state, rather than being kept or grown by humans: *The woods are full of wild flowers.* I *wild animals*
2 violent or excited: *She had a wild look in her eyes.*
3 **go wild** to become very excited: *The children went wild **with** delight.*

will¹ /wɪl/ *verb*
1 used with other verbs to show that something is going to happen: *It will probably rain tomorrow.* I *She says she will be coming to the party.*
2 used when asking someone to do something: *Will you help me with this?*

will² *noun*
1 (*no plural*) power in your mind to do what you want: *He no longer has the will to live.*
2 a piece of paper that says who will have a person's belongings after he or she is dead: *The man left the farm to his son in his will.*

will·ing /ˈwɪlɪŋ/ *adjective*
if you are willing to do something, you will do it happily or will agree to do it: *I wonder if they'd be willing to help?*
willingly *adverb*: *Many people would willingly pay more for better quality.*

win¹ /wɪn/ *verb* (*present participle* **winning**, *past* **won** /wʌn/)
1 to be best or first in a competition, race, or fight: *Who won the race?*
2 to be given something because you have done well in a race or competition: *He won first prize in the competition.*

win² *noun*
a success in a competition, race, or fight: *They've had several wins this season.*

wind¹ /waɪnd/ *verb* (*past* **wound** /waʊnd/)
1 to twist something around something else: *She wound the rope **around** her arm.*
2 to bend and turn: *The path wound **along** the side of the river.*
3 **wind someone up** *informal* to annoy or upset someone: *She really knows how to wind me up!*

wind² /wɪnd/ *noun*
air that moves quickly: *The wind blew the leaves off the trees.*

wind·mill /ˈwɪndmɪl/ *noun*
a tall building with large sails that are turned around by the wind

windmill

win·dow /ˈwɪndəʊ/ *noun*
an opening in the wall of a building, that lets air or light come in: *Could you shut the window?*

window-sill /ˈwɪndəʊsɪl/ *noun*
a flat shelf below a window

wind·screen /ˈwɪndskriːn/ *noun*
the piece of glass across the front of a car

wind·y /ˈwɪndi/ *adjective* (**windier**, **windiest**)
if it is windy, there is a lot of wind ⇨ see picture on page 194

wine /waɪn/ *noun* (*no plural*)
an alcoholic drink made from GRAPES

wing /wɪŋ/ *noun*
the part of its body that a bird or insect uses to fly ⇨ see picture at EAGLE
2 the parts on either side of a plane that look like a bird's wings

A B C D E F G H I J K L M N O P Q R S T U V W X Y Z

wink¹ /wɪŋk/ *verb*
to look at someone and deliberately close and open one eye quickly: *He winked **at** me.*

wink² *noun*
when you wink at someone

win·ner /'wɪnər/ *noun*
the person who wins a competition, race, or fight

win·ter /'wɪntər/ *noun*
the season when it is cold, or not as hot as in summer ⇨ compare SUMMER ⇨ see picture on page 194

wipe¹ /waɪp/   **wipe**
verb (*present participle* **wiping**, *past* **wiped**)
to make something dry or clean using a cloth: *Will you wipe the table? | She wiped the marks **off** the table.*

wiping a mirror

wipe² *noun*
1 when you wipe something with a cloth: *She gave her face a wipe.*
2 wipes are small pieces of wet paper or cloth that you can buy and use for cleaning your face, hands, etc

wire /waɪər/ *noun*
1 (*no plural*) thin metal thread: *a wire fence*
2 a piece of thin metal used for carrying electricity from one place to another

wis·dom /'wɪzdəm/ *noun* (*no plural*)
good sense and judgement: *a man of great wisdom*

wise /waɪz/ *adjective* (**wiser**, **wisest**)
a wise person is able to understand things and make the right decision: *a wise old man*
wisely *adverb*: *He nodded wisely.*

wish¹ /wɪʃ/ *verb*
1 to want something that is unlikely to happen: *I wish I was rich.*
2 *formal* to want to do something: *I wish to make a complaint.*
3 wish someone luck, wish someone success, etc to say that you hope someone has good luck, success, etc: *We wish you success in your new job.*

wish² *noun* (*plural* **wishes**)
1 something that you hope for or want: *It was my mother's wish that I should go.*
2 have no wish to do something to not want to do something: *I've no wish ever to see him again.*
3 make a wish to think about something that you want, and hope that you will have it or do it
4 Best wishes a friendly way of ending a letter to someone who is not a close friend

wit /wɪt/ *noun* (*no plural*)
the ability to talk in a clever and amusing way

witch /wɪtʃ/ *noun* (*plural* **witches**)
a woman who is believed to have magic powers

with /wɪð/ *preposition*
1 in the company of someone: *She comes to school with her sister.*
2 using something: *He opened the door with his key. | Simon filled the bucket with water.*
3 used for saying that someone or something has something: *Who's that little girl with blonde hair? | a white dress with red spots*
4 because of something: *They smiled with pleasure.*
5 used when saying what other people or things are involved: *She's always fighting with her brothers. | Mix the flour with some milk.*
6 showing a particular way of behaving: *He fought with great courage.*

with·draw /wɪð'drɔ:/ *verb* (*past* **withdrew** /wɪð'dru:/, *past participle* **withdrawn** /wɪð'drɔ:n/)
1 to take something away: *She withdrew all her money from the bank.*
2 to say you will no longer be part of an activity: *They've withdrawn **from** the talks. | We've withdrawn our team from the competition.*
3 to leave a place, or to order someone to do this: *The soldiers withdrew.*

with·er /'wɪðər/ *verb*
to become dry and die: *The plants had all withered in the sun.*

with·in /wɪð'ɪn/ *adverb, preposition*
1 in less than a particular period of time: *Within six months he was speaking English.*

2 inside a place: *Within these old walls there was once a town.*

with·out /wɪðˈaʊt/ *adverb, preposition*
1 not having something: *You can't see the film without a ticket.*
2 not doing something: *He left without saying goodbye.*
3 **do without** to manage to do something although you do not have what you need: *We'll just have to do without.*

wit·ness[1] /ˈwɪtnəs/ *noun* (*plural* **witnesses**)
a person who sees something happen: *She was a witness at the accident.*

witness[2] *verb*
to see something happen: *Did you witness the accident?*

wit·ty /ˈwɪti/ *adjective* (**wittier**, **wittiest**)
clever and amusing: *She's the wittiest person I ever met.*

wives /waɪvz/
the plural of the word **wife**

wiz·ard /ˈwɪzəd/ *noun*
a man who is believed to have magic powers

wob·ble /ˈwɒbl/ *verb* (*present participle* **wobbling**, *past* **wobbled**)
to move unsteadily, or to make something do this: *The table's wobbling.* I *Will you stop wobbling your chair!*

woke /wəʊk/
the past tense of the verb **wake**

wok·en /ˈwəʊkən/
the past participle of the verb **wake**

wom·an /ˈwʊmən/ *noun* (*plural* **women** /ˈwɪmɪn/)
a fully grown female human ⇨ compare MAN

womb /wuːm/ *noun*
the part inside a woman's body where a baby grows

won /wʌn/
the past tense and past participle of the verb **win**

won·der[1] /ˈwʌndər/ *verb*
1 to think about something and try to guess why it happens, or what will happen: *I wonder **why** James is always late for school.* I *I wonder **if** they'll come.*
2 to be surprised by something: *We all wondered **at** his rudeness.*

wonder[2] *noun*
1 (*no plural*) a feeling of surprise and admiration: *They were filled with wonder when they saw the paintings.*
2 **no wonder** it is no surprise: *No wonder he's not hungry – he's been eating sweets all day.*
3 someone or something that makes you feel great admiration: *the wonders of technology*

won·der·ful /ˈwʌndəfəl/ *adjective*
extremely good or extremely enjoyable: *That's wonderful news!*

won't /wəʊnt/
will not: *We won't be late home.*

wood /wʊd/ *noun*
1 (*no plural*) the material that trees are made of
2 a small forest: *He was lost in the wood.* ⇨ see picture on page 193

wood·en /ˈwʊdn/ *adjective*
made of wood: *wooden furniture*

wool /wʊl/ *noun* (*no plural*)
1 (*no plural*) the soft thick hair of sheep
2 the thread or material made from the hair of sheep: *The dress was made of wool.*

wool·len /ˈwʊlən/ *adjective*
made of wool: *a woollen dress*

word /wɜːd/ *noun*
1 a group of letters, that together make something we can understand: *What's the French word for 'mouse'?* I *How do you pronounce this word?*
2 (*no plural*) a promise: *I give you my word that I will return.*
3 **give the word** to tell someone to start doing something: *When I give the word you may start.*
4 **have a word with someone** to talk to someone about something: *Peter, could I have a word with you after class?*
5 **in other words** a phrase you use before you repeat the same thing using different words
6 **in your own words** not repeating what someone else has said: *Tell me what happened in your own words.*
7 **take someone's word for it** to believe what someone says about something
8 **word for word** using exactly the same words: *They printed the speech word for word.*

A
B
C
D
E
F
G
H
I
J
K
L
M
N
O
P
Q
R
S
T
U
V
W
X
Y
Z

wore /wɔːʳ/
the past tense of the verb **wear**

work[1] /wɜːk/ verb
1 to be busy doing an activity: *I've been working in the garden all afternoon.*
2 to do a job that you get paid for: *He works in a factory.*
3 to move or go properly: *Does this light work?*
4 to succeed: *I don't think this plan of yours is going to work.*
5 to make something move or go properly: *How do you work the CD player?*
6 **work someone hard** to make someone work hard
7 **work out (a)** to be successful or end well: *The marriage didn't work out.* **(b)** to do physical exercises so that you will be fit
8 **work something out** to find an answer to something: *She likes working out sums in her head.*

NOTE: Compare **work** and **job**. **Job** is a noun that has a plural (=jobs). **Work** has the same meaning but has no plural: *He's trying to find **a** job.* | *He's trying to find **some** work.* **Work** can also be used as a general word when you are talking about several different jobs. If you say "I've got a lot of work to do", it could mean either that you have one big job to do, or lots of different jobs.

work[2] noun (no plural)
1 an activity that keeps you busy and is usually not for pleasure: *Dad's doing some work on the car.*
2 a job or business from which you earn money: *What line of work are you in?*
3 the place where you go to do a job that you get paid for: *Mum's gone **to** work.* | *Peter's still **at** work.*
4 what you produce while doing your job: *He sells his work in the market.*
5 **in work** if you are in work, you have a job that you get paid for: *The number of people in work has risen.*
6 **out of work** if you are out of work, you do not have a job although you would like one: *I've been out of work for 6 months.*

7 **get to work, set to work** to start doing something: *They set to work on the garden.*
8 **works** (plural noun) a factory: *the steel works*

work·er /ˈwɜːkəʳ/ noun
a person who does a particular job: *office workers*

work·man /ˈwɜːkmən/ noun (plural **workmen** /-mən/)
a man who works with his hands, for example building or repairing things

work·sheet /ˈwɜːkʃiːt/ noun
a piece of paper with exercises or activities for students on it

world /wɜːld/ noun
1 the planet we live on: *This car is used all over the world.*
2 everyone: *I don't want the whole world to see us.*
3 a particular area of activity or work: *the world of television*
4 **think the world of someone** to admire or love someone very much

World Wide Web /ˌwɜːld waɪd ˈweb/ noun
the World Wide Web the system that connects computers around the world, so that people can use the INTERNET

worm /wɜːm/ noun
a very small creature with a long body and no legs, that lives in the ground

worm

worn /wɔːn/
the past participle of the verb **wear**

worn out /ˌwɔːn ˈaʊt/ adjective
1 extremely tired: *I'm worn out – I'm off to bed.*
2 no longer in good condition, because of being used a lot: *These shoes are worn out – look at the soles.*

wor·ried /ˈwʌrɪd/ adjective
unhappy and afraid: *He seems worried **about** something.* | *She had a worried look on her face.*

wor·ry[1] /ˈwʌri/ verb (present participle **worrying**, past **worried**)
to feel unhappy and afraid about something, or to make someone feel like this: *My parents worry **about** me if*

I come home late. I *The news of the fighting worried us.*

worry[2] *noun*

1 (*no plural*) a feeling of fear and of not being sure about something: *The worry showed on her face.*

2 (*plural* **worries**) a problem that makes you worry: *My father has a lot of worries.*

worse /wɜːs/ *adjective, adverb*

1 not as good as something else that is bad: *My writing is untidy, but yours is worse!* I *The weather's worse* **than** *last year.*

2 more ill: *She's worse today.*

3 more badly: *You're behaving worse than your brother*

4 worse off if you are worse off, you have less money or fewer advantages than before, or than other people: *We're worse off since Mary stopped working.*

wor·ship[1] /'wɜːʃɪp/ *verb* (*present participle* **worshipping**, *past* **worshipped**)

1 to pray to and show great respect to God

2 to love and admire someone very much: *She really worshipped him.*

worship[2] *noun* (*no plural*)
the activity of worshipping God

worst /wɜːst/ *adjective, adverb*

1 the worst most bad: *Your spelling is the worst I've seen.*

2 most badly: *They were all very bad but he behaved worst of all.*

worth[1] /wɜːθ/ *preposition*

1 be worth £50, be worth $100, etc to have a value of £50, $100, etc: *The house is worth about £100,000.*

2 be worth doing if something is worth doing, you will not waste your time if you do it: *That film is really worth seeing.* I *It's not worth trying to talk to him – he won't listen.*

worth[2] *noun* (*no plural*)

1 value: *The thieves took £1000 worth of clothing.* I *She feels she has no worth.*

2 a week's worth, a day's worth, etc an amount that will last a week, a day, etc: *We've got several hours' worth of work left.*

worth·less /'wɜːθləs/ *adjective*
without any use or value: *The paintings are worthless.*

worth·while /ˌwɜːθ'waɪl/ *adjective*
if something is worthwhile, it is good to spend time, effort, or money on it: *It was a very worthwhile meeting.*

wor·thy /'wɜːði/ *adjective* (**worthier**, **worthiest**)
deserving respect, attention, or admiration: *He is worthy* **of** *our praise.*

would /wəd; *strong* wʊd/ *verb*

1 the word for 'will' in the past tense: *They said they would play football on Saturday.*

2 used when you are talking about what could happen, if another thing happened: *Dad would be very angry* **if** *he knew.* I *I'd be delighted if you came.*

3 would you? used to ask someone something in a polite way: *Would you pass me the salt, please?* I *Would you mind if Jamie came too?*

would·n't /'wʊdnt/
would not: *I knew she wouldn't come.*

would've /'wʊdəv/
would have: *I would've come if I'd had time.*

wound[1] /waʊnd/
the past tense and past participle of the verb **wind**

wound[2] /wuːnd/ *verb*
to hurt someone, especially by cutting or damaging their skin: *Was he badly wounded?*

wound[3] /wuːnd/ *noun*
a part of your body that has been cut or damaged

wove /wəʊv/
the past tense of the verb **weave**

wov·en /'wəʊvn/
the past participle of the verb **weave**

wrap /ræp/ *verb* (*present participle* **wrapping**, *past* **wrapped**)
also **wrap something up** to put something such as cloth or paper around someone or something: *She wrapped the baby in a blanket.* I *Shall we wrap up the presents?* ⬦ opposite UNWRAP

wreath /riːθ/ *noun*
a ring of flowers and leaves that is put on a door or on a COFFIN

wreck[1] /rek/ *noun*
a vehicle or building that has been destroyed or very badly damaged

A B C D E F G H I J K L M N O P Q R S T U V W X Y Z

wreck² *verb*
to destroy something or damage something very badly: *You've wrecked our model!*

wreck·age /'rekɪdʒ/ *noun (no plural)*
the broken parts of a vehicle or building: *the wreckage of the plane*

wrench /rentʃ/ *verb*
to pull or turn something suddenly, with a lot of force: *He wrenched the door open.*

wres·tle /'resl/ *verb (present participle* **wrestling**, *past* **wrestled**)
to fight a person and try to throw them to the ground

wres·tler /'reslər/ *noun*
a person who wrestles as a sport

wrest·ling /'reslɪŋ/ *noun (no plural)*
a sport in which people fight and try to throw each other to the ground

wrig·gle /'rɪgl/ *verb (present participle* **wriggling**, *past* **wriggled**)
to twist from side to side: *Will you stop wriggling so I can put this T-shirt over your head!*

wring /rɪŋ/ *verb (past* **wrung** /rʌŋ/)
also **wring something out** to remove the water from clothing by twisting it: *Have you wrung your swimming costume out?*

wrin·kle /'rɪŋkl/ *noun*
1 a line or fold in cloth
2 a line in someone's skin ⇨ see picture on page 202

wrist /rɪst/ *noun*
the part of your body where your hand is joined to your arm ⇨ see picture at HAND

write /raɪt/ *verb (present participle* **writing**, *past* **wrote** /rəʊt/, *past participle* **written** /'rɪtn/)
1 to make letters or words on paper, or on a computer: *He can already read and write.*

2 to write a letter and send it to someone: *He writes to me every day.*
3 to write something such as a book or play: *She's written several books.*

writ·er /'raɪtər/ *noun*
a person who writes books

writ·ing /'raɪtɪŋ/ *noun (no plural)*
1 the activity of writing: *I enjoy writing.*
2 the way or style in which someone writes: *What beautiful writing!*

writ·ten /'rɪtn/
the past participle of the verb **write**

wrong¹ /rɒŋ/ *adjective*
1 morally bad: *Telling lies is wrong.*
2 not correct: *I got the wrong answer.*
3 not suitable: *This is the wrong time to visit her.* ⇨ opposite RIGHT

wrong² *adverb*
1 incorrectly: *You've spelt that word wrong.* ⇨ opposite RIGHT
2 **get something wrong** to make a mistake or not get the correct answer: *I only got one of my sums wrong.*
3 **go wrong (a)** to stop working properly: *The television's gone wrong.* **(b)** to not succeed in the way that you hoped: *I wonder what went wrong.*

wrong³ *noun (no plural)*
something that is bad or immoral: *Small children do not know right from wrong.* ⇨ opposite RIGHT

wrong·ly /'rɒŋli/ *adverb*
because of a mistake or wrong belief: *He was wrongly accused of stealing.*

wrote /rəʊt/
the past tense of the verb **write**

wrung /rʌŋ/
the past tense and past participle of the verb **wring**

www /,dʌblju: ,dʌblju: 'dʌblju:/
used at the start of INTERNET addresses

X, x /eks/

the twenty-fourth letter of the English alphabet

Xe·rox /'zɪərɒks/ noun

a copy of a piece of paper that is made by using a special machine

X·mas /'krɪsməs, 'eksməs/ noun (no plural)

a way of writing CHRISTMAS

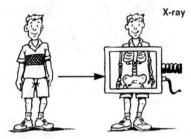

X-ray

X-ray /'eks reɪ/ noun

a photograph of the inside of your body, taken with a special light that cannot normally be seen: *The X-ray showed that the boy's leg was broken.*

A
B
C
D
E
F
G
H
I
J
K
L
M
N
O
P
Q
R
S
T
U
V
W
X
Y
Z

Yy

Y, y /waɪ/

the twenty-fifth letter of the English alphabet

yacht /jɒt/ *noun*

yacht

1 a boat with sails used for racing or sailing for pleasure

2 a large motor-boat or sailing boat ⬦ see picture on page 206

yard /jɑːd/ *noun*

1 a piece of ground next to a building with a wall or fence round it: *We were playing in the school yard.*

2 a measure of length, the same as three feet or nearly a metre: *I bought five yards of material.*

yawn¹ /jɔːn/ *verb*

to open your mouth wide and breathe deeply because you are tired or do not find something interesting: *I felt so sleepy I couldn't stop yawning.*

yawn² *noun*

when someone yawns: *She gave a huge yawn, looking very bored.*

yd

a short way of writing the word **yard** when giving measurements

yeah /jeə/

informal yes

year /jɪəʳ/ *noun*

a measure of time equal to 365 days: *She is seven years old.* | *It happened in the year 1267.*

year·ly /ˈjɪəlɪ/ *adjective, adverb*

happening every year or once a year: *The meeting is held twice yearly.*

yeast /jiːst/ *noun (no plural)*

a substance that is used for making bread rise and for producing alcohol in beer, wine, etc

yell /jel/ *verb*

yell

to shout or cry very loudly

yel·low /ˈjeləʊ/

adjective, noun

the colour of the sun, or the middle part of an egg: *I picked some yellow flowers.* | *She was dressed in yellow.*

yes /jes/ *adverb*

a word you use to answer a question, to say that you want something, that something is true or that you agree with something: *"Can you read this?" "Yes, I can."* | *"You look tired." "Yes, I didn't sleep much last night."*

yes·ter·day /ˈjestədeɪ, -dɪ/ *noun*

the day before today: *It was very hot yesterday.* ⬦ compare TOMORROW

yet /jet/ *adverb*

1 used in questions to ask if something you are expecting to happen has already happened: *Has he come yet?*

2 not yet used when you are saying that something you are expecting to happen has not happened until now, but you think it will happen soon: *He hasn't come yet.* | *"Are they there?" "No, not yet."*

> NOTE: Use **yet** in questions and in negative sentences: *Have you finished yet?* | *I'm not ready yet.* In other types of sentences, use **already**: *I have already finished.*

yield /jiːld/ *verb*

1 to accept that someone else has won, or give someone else control: *The government yielded to public demands for lower taxes.* | *The politicians yielded power to the army.*

2 to produce fruit, vegetables, etc: *The trees yielded a large crop of fruit.*

yo /jəʊ/

informal used to say hello to someone or to get their attention

yob /jɒb/ *noun*

a young man who is rude and often violent: *A gang of yobs damaged all the seats in the train.*

yo·ga /ˈjəʊɡə/ *noun* (*no plural*)
a system of exercises that helps you to relax your body and mind

yog·hurt /ˈjɒɡət/ *noun* (*no plural*)
a food made with milk that has been treated in a special way to make it thick and sour

yolk /jəʊk/ *noun*
the yellow part inside an egg
⇨ compare WHITE ⇨ see picture at EGG

you /juː/
1 the person or people that someone is speaking or writing to: *You can swim fast.* | *Shall I get you a drink, John?*
2 people in general: *It's not good for you to eat too much meat.* | *You can't believe everything that politicians say.*

you'd /juːd/
1 you had: *I called at your house but you'd already left.*
2 you would: *If you brushed your hair, you'd look tidier.*

you'll /juːl/
you will: *You'll get it tomorrow.*

young[1] /jʌŋ/ *adjective*
someone who is young has not lived for a long time: *He was speaking to a young child.* | *She was a nice young woman.* ⇨ opposite OLD

young[2] *noun* (*no plural*)
young people or animals: *Animals protect their young.*

your /jəʳ; *strong* jɔːʳ/
belonging to you: *Put your books on your desks.*

you're /jəʳ; *strong* jɔːʳ/
you are: *You're late again!*

yours /jɔːz/
1 something belonging to you: *Are all these pencils yours?*
2 **Yours faithfully,** words used at the end of a formal or business letter that begins **Dear Sir** or **Dear Madam**

3 **Yours sincerely,** words used at the end of a formal or business letter that begins **Dear Mrs Smith, Dear Mr Jones**, etc

your·self /jɔːˈself/ (*plural* **yourselves** /jɔːˈselvz/
1 the person that someone is speaking or writing to: *Look at yourself in the mirror.* | *You can't lift that by yourself* (=without help). | *Why are you playing by yourself* (=alone) ?
2 used to make the word **you** have a stronger meaning: *You told me the story yourself.*

youth /juːθ/ *noun*
1 (*no plural*) the time when a person is young: *In his youth he was a soldier.*
2 (*plural* **youths** /juːðz/) a young man: *Some youths broke into the shop last night.*
3 (*no plural*) young people: *The youth of this country have fought hard for greater freedom.*

youth club /ˈjuːθ klʌb/ *noun*
a place where young people can meet and enjoy themselves

youth hos·tel /ˈjuːθ ˌhɒstl/ *noun*
a building in which people on holiday can stay without spending a lot of money

you've /jəv; *strong* juːv/
you have: *You've forgotten your coat.*

yuck /jʌk/
informal used to say that you think something is unpleasant: *Yuck! This stuff tastes disgusting!*

yuck·y /ˈjʌki/ *adjective*
informal something that is yucky looks or tastes unpleasant

yum·my /ˈjʌmi/ *adjective*
informal food or drink that is yummy tastes very good: *We ate some yummy chocolate cake.*

A B C D E F G H I J K L M N O P Q R S T U V W X Y Z

Zz

Z, z /zed/

the twenty-sixth letter of the English alphabet

zap·per /'zæpə^r/ *noun*

informal a thing you point at the television to change the programme, make it louder, etc

ze·bra /'zebrə, 'zi:brə/ *noun*

an African wild animal like a horse that has black or dark brown and white lines all over its body ⇨ see picture on page 195

zebra cross·ing

/,zebrə 'krɒsɪŋ, ,zi:brə-/ *noun*

a place with black and white lines where people can cross a road safely in Britain

zebra crossing

ze·ro /'zɪərəʊ/ *noun* (*plural* **zeros** or **zeroes**)

the number 0 ⇨ same meaning NOUGHT

zig·zag /'zɪgzæg/ *noun*

a pattern like a long line of Zs all joined together ⇨ see picture at PATTERN

zilch /zɪltʃ/ *noun* (*no plural*)

informal nothing: *We've been questioning him for hours, but he's told us zilch.*

zil·lion /'zɪljən/ *noun*

an extremely large number or amount

zinc /zɪŋk/ *noun*

a blue white metal

zip¹ /zɪp/ *noun*

a thing that you use for fastening clothes, bags, etc, which consists of two lines of small pieces of metal or plastic and a sliding piece that pulls them together ⇨ see picture at FASTENER

zip² *verb* (*present participle* **zipping**, *past* **zipped**)

to fasten something with a zip: *She zipped up her dress.*

zoo

zoo /zu:/ *noun*

a place where a lot of different animals are kept so that people can look at them or study them

Irregular Verbs

Here are a few simple rules to help you find the correct ending for different verbs.

A

Verbs that end in a consonant and a silent 'e', eg *like, hope, create, advise, amuse*

1 In the present tense you add 's' to the 'he', 'she', or 'it' forms:

She **likes** cheese

He **loves** her

2 In the past tense you add 'd' to all forms:

She **created** a terrible noise

They **liked** the film

He **hoped** to win a prize

3 In the continuous tenses you take away the 'e' and add 'ing':

She's **hoping** to pass the exam

I was just **admiring** your new car

B

Verbs that end in 'y' (NOT verbs that end in -ay, -oy, -uy, -ey)

1 In the present and past tenses you change 'y' into 'ie':

cry   –   The baby **cries** a lot
            She **cried** all night

worry –   It **worries** me
            He **worried** his mother

2 In the continuous tenses you do not change the 'y'. You add 'ing' to the 'y':

fly   –   She's **flying** a kite

dry   –   She's **drying** her hair

hurry –   He's **hurrying** to work

C

Verbs that double the consonant

1 If a verb has one syllable and ends in a single vowel and a consonant, eg *hit, clap, plan, pin*, the consonant is usually doubled:

clap   –   She **clapped** her hands

plan   –   I'm **planning** to go home tomorrow

2 If a verb has more than one syllable, but ends in a single vowel and a consonant, and has the stress on the last syllable, the consonant is usually doubled:

begin –   I'm **beginning** to understand

upset –   She's always **upsetting** me

3 If a verb has more than one syllable and the stress is not on the last syllable, the last consonant is not usually doubled:

offer –   She **offered** me some tea

open   –   He **opened** the door

4 If the last vowel sound of a verb is written with two letters, you do not double the final consonant:

heat   –   I'm **heating** the soup

book   –   He **booked** a taxi

5 If a verb ends with a vowel and final 'l' or 'p', you usually double the 'l' or 'p', even if the final syllable is not stressed:

travel –   They **travelled** the world

channel –   They **channelled** the water towards the field

Table of Irregular Verbs

verb	present participle	past tense	past participle
arise	arising	arose	arisen
be	being	was	been
bear	bearing	bore	borne
beat	beating	beat	beaten
become	becoming	became	become
begin	beginning	began	begun
bend	bending	bent	bent
bet	betting	betted *or* bet	betted *or* bet
bind	binding	bound	bound
bite	biting	bit	bitten
bleed	bleeding	bled	bled
bless	blessing	blessed *or* blest	blessed *or* blest
blow	blowing	blew	blown
break	breaking	broke	broken
breed	breeding	bred	bred
bring	bringing	brought	brought
broadcast	broadcasting	broadcast	broadcast
build	building	built	built
burn	burning	burned *or* burnt	burned *or* burnt
buy	buying	bought	bought
catch	catching	caught	caught
choose	choosing	chose	chosen
cling	clinging	clung	clung
come	coming	came	come
cost	costing	cost	cost
creep	creeping	crept	crept
cut	cutting	cut	cut
deal	dealing	dealt	dealt
die	dying	died	died
dig	digging	dug	dug
do	doing	did	done
draw	drawing	drew	drawn
dream	dreaming	dreamed *or* dreamt	dreamed *or* dreamt

verb	present participle	past tense	past participle
drink	drinking	drank	drunk
drive	driving	drove	driven
eat	eating	ate	eaten
fall	falling	fell	fallen
feed	feeding	fed	fed
feel	feeling	felt	felt
fight	fighting	fought	fought
find	finding	found	found
fly	flying	flew	flown
forbid	forbidding	forbade	forbidden
forget	forgetting	forgot	forgotten
freeze	freezing	froze	frozen
get	getting	got	got
give	giving	gave	given
go	going	went	gone
grind	grinding	ground	ground
grow	growing	grew	grown
hang	hanging	hung *or* hanged	hung *or* hanged
have	having	had	had
hear	hearing	heard	heard
hide	hiding	hid	hidden
hit	hitting	hit	hit
hold	holding	held	held
hurt	hurting	hurt	hurt
keep	keeping	kept	kept
kneel	kneeling	knelt	knelt
know	knowing	knew	known
lay	laying	laid	laid
lead	leading	led	led
lean	leaning	leaned *or* leant	leaned *or* lent
leap	leaping	leaped *or* leapt	leaped *or* leapt
learn	learning	learned *or* learnt	learned *or* learnt
leave	leaving	left	left
lend	lending	lent	lent
let	letting	let	let

verb	present participle	past tense	past participle
lie[1]	lying	lay	lain
lie[2]	lying	lied	lied
lose	losing	lost	lost
make	making	made	made
mean	meaning	meant	meant
meet	meeting	met	met
mistake	mistaking	mistook	mistaken
mow	mowing	mowed	mowed *or* mown
outgrow	outgrowing	outgrew	outgrown
overhear	overhearing	overheard	overheard
oversleep	oversleeping	overslept	overslept
overtake	overtaking	overtook	overtaken
panic	panicking	panicked	panicked
pay	paying	paid	paid
picnic	picnicking	picnicked	picnicked
put	putting	put	put
quit	quitting	quit	quit
read	reading	read	read
repay	repaying	repaid	repaid
ride	riding	rode	ridden
ring	ringing	rang	rung
rise	rising	rose	risen
run	running	ran	run
saw	sawing	sawed	sawn
say	saying	said	said
see	seeing	saw	seen
seek	seeking	sought	sought
sell	selling	sold	sold
send	sending	sent	sent
set	setting	set	set
sew	sewing	sewed	sewn
shake	shaking	shook	shaken
shear	shearing	sheared	shorn
shed	shedding	shed	shed
shine	shining	shone	shone

verb	present participle	past tense	past participle
shoot	shooting	shot	shot
show	showing	showed	shown
shrink	shrinking	shrank	shrunk
shut	shutting	shut	shut
sing	singing	sang	sung
sink	sinking	sank	sunk
sit	sitting	sat	sat
sleep	sleeping	slept	slept
slide	sliding	slid	slid
sling	slinging	slung	slung
slit	slitting	slit	slit
smell	smelling	smelt	smelt
sow	sowing	sowed	sown
speak	speaking	spoke	spoken
speed	speeding	speeded *or* sped	speeded *or* sped
spell	spelling	spelled *or* spelt	spelled *or* spelt
spend	spending	spent	spent
spill	spilling	spilled *or* spilt	spilled *or* spilt
spin	spinning	spun	spun
spit	spitting	spat	spat
split	splitting	split	split
spoil	spoiling	spoilt	spoilt
spring	springing	sprang	sprung
stand	standing	stood	stood
steal	stealing	stole	stolen
stick	sticking	stuck	stuck
sting	stinging	stung	stung
stink	stinking	stank	stunk
stride	striding	strode	stridden
strike	striking	struck	struck
swear	swearing	swore	sworn
sweep	sweeping	swept	swept
swell	swelling	swelled	swollen
swim	swimming	swam	swum
swing	swinging	swung	swung

verb	present participle	past tense	past participle
take	taking	took	taken
teach	teaching	taught	taught
tear	tearing	tore	torn
tell	telling	told	told
think	thinking	thought	thought
throw	throwing	threw	thrown
thrust	thrusting	thrust	thrust
tie	tying	tied	tied
tread	treading	trod	trodden
undergo	undergoing	underwent	undergone
understand	understanding	understood	understood
undertake	undertaking	undertook	undertaken
undo	undoing	undid	undone
unwind	unwinding	unwound	unwound
upset	upsetting	upset	upset
wake	waking	waked *or* woke	woken
wear	wearing	wore	worn
weave	weaving	wove	woven
weep	weeping	wept	wept
wet	wetting	wet *or* wetted	wet *or* wetted
win	winning	won	won
wind	winding	wound	wound
withdraw	withdrawing	withdrew	withdrawn
wring	wringing	wrung	wrung
write	writing	wrote	written